Ragging It

Ragging It

Getting Ragtime Into History
(and some history into ragtime) ©

H. Loring White

iUniverse, Inc.
New York Lincoln Shanghai

Ragging It
Getting Ragtime Into History (and some history into ragtime) ©

Copyright © 2005 by H. Loring White

All rights reserved. No part of this book may be used or reproduced by any means, graphic, electronic, or mechanical, including photocopying, recording, taping or by any information storage retrieval system without the written permission of the publisher except in the case of brief quotations embodied in critical articles and reviews.

iUniverse books may be ordered through booksellers or by contacting:

iUniverse
2021 Pine Lake Road, Suite 100
Lincoln, NE 68512
www.iuniverse.com
1-800-Authors (1-800-288-4677)

ISBN-13: 978-0-595-34042-2 (pbk)
ISBN-13: 978-0-595-78831-6 (ebk)
ISBN-10: 0-595-34042-3 (pbk)
ISBN-10: 0-595-78831-9 (ebk)

Printed in the United States of America

To the

Collectors

Performers

Composers

and

Scholars

who made the Ragtime Revival.

> You have to understand the background; you can't pretend
> It has nothing to do with ragtime.
>
> Eubie Blake [1]

---

[1]. Terry Waldo, *This Is Ragtime*, viii.

Contents

Contents by Topic xiii

Prelude: Getting Ragtime into History (and some history into Ragtime) 1

Part I. The Transformation of the Nineties 5

1. Getting to the Nineties (I) 7
   1.1 Blind Boone and Our Lost Music 7
   1.2 Pop Goes the Culture 11
   1.3 The Art of Rag (I): Beginnings 15
   1.4 Introducing TR 20

2. Getting To The Nineties (II) 25
   2.1 Reign of Terror 25
   2.2 Rails 30
   2.3 There's No Business Like Race Business (I): Minstrelsy 37
   2.4 The Social Evil! 43

3. The Music Business: Puttin' On the Hits 48

4. TR: Reforming the Civil Service and the Police 54

5. Fathers of Vaudeville (I) 60

6. White Cities and Midways 66

7. 1896 71

8. Judge Lynch 78

9. Fathers of Vaudeville (II) 87

10. TR and the Splendid Little War 91

11. There's No Business Like Race Business (II):
    Cakewalks and Coonsongs 98

12. Wilmington Coup 106

13. The Business of the Social Evil 115

14. The Art of Rag (II): Sedalia 120

    14.1 "Queen City of the Prairies" 120

    14.2 Texas Interlude: A Ragtime Stunt 125

    14.3 The Maple Leaf Rag 129

Part II. Living the Ragtime Life, 1900-1904 135

15. TR: The New Presidency 137

16. Progressives (I): The March King 149

17. Mindset 153

18. Vaudeville: Headliners (I) 166

19. The Art of Rag (III): St. Louis 176

20. Progressives (II): The Unexpected Miracle 188

21. Boley or Self-Segregation 194

22. Ragging It in the White House 204

23. Varieties of the Social Evil 220

Part III. The Ragtime Nation, 1905-1910 (and a Little Beyond) 231

24. "Take Me Out to Lakeside" 233

25. Progressives (III): "A Man, A Plan, A Canal, Panama!" 247

26. There's No Business Like Race Business (III): From Coontown to Jungletown 260

27. "The Brownsville Affray" 275

28. Progressives (IV): SRP 294

29. The Art of Rag (IV): New York (I) 303

30. The Art of Rag (V): Indianapolis Excursion and the Ragtime Women 312

31. The Art of Rag (VI): New York (II) 319

32. TR: Regulation, Reform, Conservation 330

33. Vaudeville: Headliners (II) 342

34. Progressives (V): Peary and Henson 353

35. The Art of Rag (VII): Ragtime and the Social Evil 361

Acknowledgements 379

Bibliography 381

Index of Names and Titles..393

Contents by Topic

This book can be read either in chapter order, or, because of its episodic structure, each chapter containing an independent narrative, the reader is free to go into a particular topic without taking up other topics. The book aims at being comprehensive of the period in a cumulative, chronological sequence, but it is an assemblage of discrete segments, each chapter presenting aspects of topics. These are listed below:

Music: Ch's 1.1, 1.3, 2.3, 3, 6, 11, 14, 16, 18, 19, 22, 24, 26, 29, 30, 31, 35

Vaudeville and Entertainment: Ch's 2.3, 5, 6, 9, 11, 14.2, 16, 18, 22, 24, 26, 31, 33

Politics: Ch's 1.4, 2.1, 4, 6, 7, 10, 15, 21, 22, 25, 27, 28, 32

Ideas and Culture: Ch's 1.2, 2.2, 2.3, 2.4, 3, 6, 17, 20, 24, 25, 27, 28, 32, 34

African Americans: Ch's 1.1, 1.3, 2.1, 2.3, 8, 11, 12, 21, 26, 27, 34

Prostitution and Disease: Ch's 2.4, 5, 13, 23, 35

Transportation and Technology: Ch's 2.2, 6, 20, 24, 25, 28, 34

Prelude: Getting Ragtime into History (and some history into Ragtime)

One day in 1975, I listened to pianist Joshua Rifkin's recordings (Nonesuch: H-71248 and H-71264) of the Rags of Scott Joplin for the first time. Initial pleasure in hearing these compositions, oddly labeled as "rags," gave way to questions. Why hadn't I heard this American music before? Where did it come from? From the dates of composition, covering two decades, 1899 to about 1918, I located it in the "Progressive Era," the period preceding World War I. Standard histories of this dynamic reform period inform readers of politics, economics, ideas, technology, urbanization, demographics, manners, plus particular concerns of the period such as immigration, prohibition and journalism. But little or nothing came up about ragtime, and very little more about popular culture and entertainment. The more I learned about ragtime, the more troubled I became. Certainly, a "veil of obscurity" has hidden it from view. Why? Vast numbers of folks heard it at home, on vaudeville stages, in cabarets, dance halls, amusement parks, and in places where sex was sold. Ragtime permeated the culture as a "craze"; Tin Pan Alley commodified it. Then, with amazing abruptness, jazz seemingly displaced it, and ragtime vanished in a few years.

Jazz since then has come and gone in a variety of modes and styles, hot and cool, with and without the blues, reborn each decade or so. All of its phases are remembered and cherished by fans and aficionados. Why do we recall so much about jazz and so little of ragtime? True, ragtime was a longer time ago. It was poorly and sparsely recorded because the early technology was crude. Still, when I inventoried my awareness of the music of the period, I recalled Sousa, George M. Cohan, Victor Herbert, Edward McDowell, Charles Ives, and such European imports as waltzes and operettas. Plus some pop songs: "Ragtime Cowboy Joe" (my grandmother sang it), "Bill Bailey" (sung at parties), and the perennial "Alexander's Ragtime Band" of Irving Berlin. Ask any barroom piano stylist for "ragtime" and you usually get this one.

I did not know when I saw the film *The Sting* (1973) a few years before, that I was hearing Joplin's *The Entertainer* or *Solace*. *The Sting* told a delicious tale of scamming during the 1930's—also (like the Twenties) known by its music, the age of "Swing." Many years before that, when I delighted in a circus tune, Karl L. King's *Broadway One-Step* (1919), no one told me this was ragtime either. How did I live through forty years as a music lover without knowing about instrumental ragtime? I get a little morose wondering why the purveyors of both high culture (chiefly things European) and entertainment (chiefly things American) have neglected ragtime. Looking into this, I discovered that when some music historians raise the subject, they portray ragtime as an incomplete stage in jazz development, a half-way house on the road to syncopation, and a source of snappy tunes for jazzmen to tap into for improvisations. I also learned that a "ragtime revival" got underway about 50 years ago when Rudi Blesh and Harriet Janis wrote *They All Played Ragtime* (1950). Just before that, Wally Rose and some other California musicians began inserting a few rags into their gigs between sets. With positive feedback, these latterday ragtimers searched out surviving sources, and they located an aging barber in Venice, California, named Sanford Brunson Campbell. From 1898 until 1908, when he married and took on respectability, "Brun" Campbell had been an itinerant "perfessor" or pianist in turn-of-the-century saloons and honky-tonks. These ragtime revivers sat him at a piano and captured everything he played on their recording machines. The hunt for old sheet music and other old piano players was in high gear by the Fifties, and this "revival" spread underground across the nation.

Until it surfaced in the early Seventies in a film soundtrack and on a few disks, ragtime existed only for the fortunate few it had somehow reached. Then came a few years of pop recognition of the Joplin rags, after which, by the Eighties, ragtime had resubmerged. Currently it is almost as esoteric as medieval motets, once again the exclusive cultural property of the small audiences that love and care about it. Occasionally, piano teachers let their pupils do a rag or two to conclude or encore a recital. Which is meagre recognition! By 1940, over 3000 rags had seen publication, many, many comparable in quality to those of Joplin. No European country neglects its native composers: they know Sibelius in Finland; Dvorak, Smetana, and Janacek in the Czech Republic; Enesco in Romania; Lehar and Bartok in Hungary; Schubert and the Strausses in Austria; Elgar, Gilbert & Sullivan, and Williams in Britain, Tchaikowsky and the "Five" in Russia, and Debussy and "Les Six" in France. We have finally come to respect Louis Armstrong and many others of our great jazzmen, but our equally great ragtimers remain in some limbo of forgotten history.

Thanks to the Ragtime Revival, which unearthed many old recordings and much sheet music, plus more human survivals, including Eubie Blake and Charley Thompson, the music has been restored to us. Ragtime scholarship flourishes, and has so far produced at least half a shelf of volumes to set beside *They All Played Ragtime*. There are six or ten festivals of rag held annually, and many jazz festivals feature a "ragtime corner." The Scott Joplin Foundation of Sedalia, Missouri, carries on the chief festival (first weekend in June) and retails everything ragtime in its "Ragtime Store." Thus the music itself is no longer "lost" (a few, like the late Bob Darch, who had carried it on between and after the World Wars never believed it was); however ragtime still lacks historical presence. From the late 1890's until after WWI, it flowed as the mainstream of pop. Ragtime was the first musical style of the urban-popular category, everywhere recognized, whether liked or disliked, and so typical that foreigners called it "American music." Rags and ragtime songs were peppy and syncopated, upbeat and inviting, music for enjoyment, for fun. For these new urbanites, some off the farm, others off the boat from Europe, ragtime gave off a new attitude: celebrating, sociable, guilt-free, humorous, delighting in the moment. It stamped <u>legitimate</u> on the "pursuit of happiness"; it implied that there had to be more to life than unremitting hard labor, continuous pregnancy, unchanging poverty, and subservience to the well-off.

Not only was ragtime present and permeating the culture, but it was having effects, helping people to "lighten up," an outcome which may deserve more attention from historians of the period. The Irving Berlin song stated "Everybody's Doing It!" And just what was "It"? Whatever people thought it was or wanted it to be. Other than obvious risque meanings, "it" also meant personal freedom or individualism, seeing your own life as having significance and uniqueness. Which implied democracy: one life matters as much as any other. This outlook propagated in cities where tens of thousands were jammed into squalid neighborhoods. Such feelings of personal worth and a belief in a better future relieved overcrowding and set up a barricade against desperation and despair.

We can't simply claim that ragtime alone caused this collective upbeatness. Industry, technology, population, knowledge and understanding, new opportunities, a more egalitarian society, improved standards of living: the "times" result from the convergence of a set of conditions. What ragtime did was to interact with culture and the conditions of human life. It reenforced the outlook and attitudes of society, and it reflected them back into the culture. Synergistically ragtime's effects went beyond individuals to somehow touch or impinge upon other spheres of culture and society. Ragtime reflects the dynamism of the Progressive Era, a period when many enlisted in reform movements (trust-busting, pure food, conservation, an end to social evils, Prohibition), all of which were based optimistically upon beliefs that present evils could be eradicated. The presidents of the time, Roosevelt, Taft, and Wilson, each a man of learning and ideals, led campaigns to end abuses and improve the quality of life. Metaphorically these leaders, like surfers, rode near the crest of a wave. They didn't churn it up themselves. A collective desire for remedies and hopes for better times did that. But many things motivated this collective will, and ragtime played an interactive role. Just as jazz colored the moods and stimulated the 1920's, so did ragtime act upon its era.

Ragtime's presence permeated and gave momentum to the popular culture of vaudeville, sports, music, dancehalls, cabarets, and cinema. Ragtime was the music of a society that traveled faster (rails, steamships, automobiles), read more (daily newspapers, magazines, books), bought more (department stores, ready-to-wear clothes, packaged foods), and played more (see above). Excluded from this progressive loop were African Americans. For them, a more accurate period label would be "Repressive Era." Just out of slavery, they struggled against exploitation, oppression, and terror (lynching and many abuses), but they too would find a new direction. After 1910, they rallied to form a new militant organization, the National Association for the Advancement of Colored People (NAACP). This was a rejection of the passive accommodation of previous leadership for a fighting strategy to counter the prevailing poverty and terrorism. At the same time, they were the primary source of the new music of ragtime and were developing both the blues and jazz.

Ragtime is unique because of its "first's": it was the first popular syncopated music and the first music of the masses. It was a dynamic music for a progressive time. It was heard when the Wright Brothers flew ("Come, Josephine, In My Flying Machine"); when Ford brought out the Model-T for the masses ("Get Out and Get Under"); when explorers took it to the North Pole (a player piano on Peary's ship *Roosevelt*); when Americans were "making the dirt fly" down on the Panama Canal ("Panama Rag"); when the Rough Riders fought in Cuba ("A Hot Time In the Old Town Tonight"); and when the doughboys marched to the Western Front in 1917 ("Over There"). Its movement and rhythm animated the period. What everybody was doing was "Ragging It!"

Part I

The Transformation of the Nineties

1. Getting to the Nineties (I)

1.1 Blind Boone and Our Lost Music

Blind Boone (1864-1927) was no minstrel man. Most black entertainers before 1900, in order to survive, sang and danced in shows that ridiculed their race. Regardless, minstrel show jobs were plums for those lucky enough to find work in them: a chance to perform, regular meals, attractive clothes, changes of scene, and some applause to offset the abuses endured by all African Americans. Minstrel shows (Chapter 2.3) were colorful, displayed happy faces, and sent patrons home in friendly moods. Also less fortunate was the itinerant black piano player or "perfessor," who played for the less benevolent habitues of drinking places and the resorts where men sought women. Dependent upon tips for playing requests demanded by drunks, roughnecks, and whores, the perfessor led a life that was lonely with frequent exposure to violence.

Boone enjoyed a far better life, achieving most of the material parts of the "American Dream": an upscale income, a good marriage, and a fine home. Few African Americans gained so much during those times (ca. 1890-1920). But Boone's beginnings were surely less than fortunate. He received his surname from his mother Rachel, a runaway slave who had served the Missouri Boone family (Daniel's direct descendants), and who had become a cook for Company I, Seventh Regiment, Missouri Militia, at its encampment (Miami, Missouri) on the Missouri River, where he was born during March or May of 1864.[1] His father's name is another datum lost in the guerilla warfare that destructively raged over that bloodied state. The determining event in Boone's life came early, when he was six months old, in the condition of an illness believed to be potentially fatal (what sudden fever isn't in a baby?) and called "brain fever" by the ignorant medical practitioners of that time. The doctor-surgeon removed the baby's eyeballs in the belief that they were the location or cause of the illness and sewed his eyelids shut. Then, instead of dying from the trauma, this robust infant lived, growing up with the double handicap of blindness and blackness.[2]

Boone was fortunate in both his mother and his talent. A capable cook never starved, and during the post-Civil War years Rachel Boone found work as a domestic for the prosperous families of Warrensburg, Missouri. Things improved when she married Harrison Hendrix when the child was eight. It was only a one-room cabin on a small farm outside Warrensburg, but it meant a more secure home. By then blind "Willie" was revealing his musical talents. He could imitate birdsong and played the tin fife at picnics and elsewhere in public.[3] He certainly made a strong impression on local folk, because in 1873 the community raised funds to enroll him in the St.Louis School for the Blind (which taught music in braille). A friendly crowd gathered to cheer the nine-year-old blind, black boy off on the train, but at the school the promise of music wasn't kept. The school ordained that a black boy—he was only one of six in the school—should learn a simple, practical skill, and during the second term, he was consigned to the humble vocation of broom-making. Boone hated this, and during free time, he sat listening to white students practice the piano. Enoch Donley a senior befriended Boone and gave him the lessons withheld by the school. Then came an audition for a teacher and the grant of music instruction. By year's end he had achieved such proficiency that after one hearing, he could perform a composition. Now the superintendent showed off the boy's amazing capabilities at parties in his home.

It all went wrong again in the second year when a new, and more racially prejudiced, faculty took over. They put him back to making brooms and chair bottoms. He soon rebelled by sneaking out at night and vanishing for two or three days at a time. These truancies took him to the dives of the St.Louis tenderloin where he listened to and undoubtedly played the music popular in such places after the Civil War. He faced expulsion after a series of these escapes, but fortuitously a group of prominent people and politicians arrived to evaluate the institution. In this exigency, the new superintendent cannily presented his "star pupil" to these notables, whose highly enthusiastic response provided a timely reenforcement (on both sides). Boone basked in the praise, but his promise of reform didn't last. He kept up his aberrational behavior for a year and a half, a blind boy exiting the premises with practiced stealth, lured toward the sounds of music that he found irresistible. Caught by irate school authorities, promises of reform were extracted, again promises broken, pleadings, threats of expulsion, another escape, a final stern confrontation, and the disgrace of the return to Warrensburg.[4]

Fearful of facing family and town after expulsion, Boone remained in St.Louis playing when they'd let him in joints along Franklin Avenue and Morgan Street. After several days of street life and hunger, a railroad conductor heard him, saw his plight, fed him, and sent him home on the train. Warrensburg failed to note his disgrace and welcomed him back. Boone's luck equaled his talent. A local school employed him to play as the students marched to and from classes.[5] He was regularly called upon to play for fairs, picnics, and other public occasions, plus gigs away from home, as word of mouth got around about the eyeless young darky musician with the fabulous ability. This uniqueness got him into difficulty when, at a fair, he accepted the offer of a man named Cromwell to travel with him and play in the streets for tips. Soon Cromwell, on a losing streak in poker, bet Boone and lost him. The winner forced Boone to continue working for him, and it took the intervention of Hendrix his stepfather to rescue him from this bondage of little food and harsh treatment. But Boone kept on with this itinerancy, teaming up with others to play across Missouri.[6]

In 1879 at age fifteen, he was hired to perform at a Christmas music festival in Columbia where he met John Lange, a prosperous (though black) local contractor. Much impressed, Lange subsequently offered friendship and to manage him as a touring attraction. But first, with the encouragement of Lange and others, Boone undertook further musical studies (in that university town) and learned a classical repertoire. Then came the formation of the "Blind Boone Concert Company," a group consisting of Lange the manager, its star, plus a female singer, a banjoist, and a violinist. With occasional changes of personnel, the company toured for almost fifty years, until just before his death in 1927 (Lange died earlier in 1916). They began humbly, hauling a piano in a wagon, dragging along the dirt roads of small-town mid-America. They soon graduated to trains and cities, reaching beyond the Mid-West to other regions and Canada.[7] Where there was segregation, Boone played two concerts. Hotels turned them away, and black folk accommodated them. Once in Kansas, an old black woman refused Boone's payment for the room and board. He learned of a $350 mortgage on her home and paid it off.[8]

By 1885 the Blind Boone Concert Company toured a ten-month season with receipts averaging $200 a performance. In larger places they sometimes took in $600. During their peak years, Boone's income rose to $17,000. In 1888 he married Lange's sister Eugenia and eventually purchased a sizeable two-story brick home in Columbia (later used as a funeral home and now intended to become a museum of Booneiana). Besides the classics, he played his own works. These included songs of several varieties: folk songs, spirituals, plantation songs (a la Stephen Foster), and even coon songs (Chapter 11). For these he accompanied the female singer of the company. His instrumental pieces included variations, transcriptions, and fantasies on traditional tunes like "Dixie," "Our Boys Will Shine Tonight," "Swanee River," or "Home, Sweet Home." He also performed his own medleys of ragtime (below) and impressionistic pieces of his own composition, such as imitations (trains, banjo, birdsong, music box, etc.), camp meetings, and dances. His most popular work was "Marshfield Tornado," a description of the cyclone that hit Marshfield, Missouri, in April 1880, killing 105. Boone composed it immediately after Lange read him the newspaper account of the disaster. He played it at every concert for the next 35 years to satisfy the perpetual demand.[9]

Audiences loved the piece, probably in part because of the enthusiasm of his attack. Unfazed by handicaps, Boone was self-propelled, buoyant, almost bulletproof. At five he organized seven older boys into a spasm band (kazoo, harmonicas, tin horn, drum) to play for pennies. In this band he performed as a "teacup artist," using a teacup to vary the sounds of his harmonica. Frustrated in St.Louis, he rebelled: "But they wouldn't let me play the piano all the time—they made me make brooms—so I ran off." Out on tour, he often arrived at a concert leading up to a dozen children—whose names he would recite—as his guests, thus exasperating a management averse to involuntary donations. Later in an interview, he explained his attitude:

> Blindness has not affected my disposition. It has never made me at outs with the world…. I have shown that no matter how a person is afflicted, there is something he can do worthwhile…. I regard my blindness as a blessing for had I not been blind I would not have given the inspiration to the world that I have.[10]

Another idiosyncrasy was to conclude his performances with ragtime selections. After the sonata movements, operatic transcriptions, concerto arrangements, and his typical impressionistic pieces, Boone would shift around to the audience and announce that he was "…putting the cookies on the lower shelf so that everyone can get at them," and beat out the popular tunes, coon songs, and the ragtime he loved. The chief evidence that connects Boone to the popular ragtime of the era—other than published songs in Negro dialect (i.e., coon songs), such as "Georgia Melon" or "When I Meet 'Dat Coon Tonight"—are the ten piano rolls that he cut for the QRS company in 1912. These rolls were the earliest recordings of folk music by a black musician, and the most important of them were

Blind Boone's Southern Rag Medley #1:
 Strains from the Alleys

Blind Boone's Southern Rag Medley #2:
 Strains from the Flat Branch

These compositions are, as "Medley" indicates, little suites, each a series of folk strains.[11] But lacking syncopation, they are not true ragtime. Boone's biographer Jack A. Batterson states that, "Boone's particular style in ragtime also set him apart from other ragtimers. He began performing ragtime <u>before it became an established form in the 1890s</u>, and he seems to have <u>improvised</u> ragging as part of his concerts" (underlining added).[12] Thus the medleys seem to be something older, their loose timing only suggestive of syncopation, perhaps an archaic form of ragtime. Which brings us back to St.Louis in the mid-1870s: What compelled a culturally deprived blind boy of twelve to risk his unique and only opportunity for an education by venturing out into a dangerous nightworld? What musical fix did his soul require that the European classics couldn't fulfill? Do these medleys preserve some of the sounds heard in the alleys of post-Civil War St.Louis? They offer a few tantalizing glimpses into the sources of ragtime.

Notes: Chapter 1.1

1. Jack A. Batterson, *Blind Boone: Missouri's Ragtime Pioneer*, 21-22, indicates some uncertainty about Boone's birthdate. His mother had gained her freedom by fleeing to Union lines.
2. *Ibid.*, 23-24. It is impossible to determine the illness, but the author quotes a recent theory that Boone was born with *opthalmia neonatorum*, a result of gonorrhea (since 1884, curable with silver nitrate drops), and that this infection, after developing for six months, could have spread from eyes already scarred and blind.
3. *Ibid.*, 24-29.
4. *Ibid.*, 29-31.
5. *Ibid.*, 32.
6. *Ibid.*, 32-34.
7. *Ibid.*, chapters 3 and 4 for the touring years; for the quotation, 55.
8. *Ibid.*, 49.
9. *Ibid.*, 44-45; see list of works, 101-105.
10. *Ibid.*, 24, 27, 32 for quotations.
11. Tunes in Medley #1: "Make Me a Pallet on the Floor," "I Got a Chicken on My Back," "Oh, No, Babe," "I Certainly Does Love 'Dat Yellow Man," and "Dat Nigger Got Lucky At Last." Medley #2: "Carrie's Gone to Kansas City," "I'm Alabama Bound," "So They Say," and "Oh, Honey, Ain't You Sorry?" "I'm Alabama Bound" is the oldest known blues strain. The "alleys" may refer to St.Louis, certainly to cities; "Flat Branch" is both a neighborhood and a stream in Columbia, MO.
12. Batterson, 86.

1.2　Pop Goes the Culture

Ragtime filled the soundtrack of the new Twentieth Century. It set a tone and it altered style. Its songs and instrumentals were the main music of the emerging popular culture. Popular culture came about because of the cultural needs of the new urban-industrial society—the first in human history. Urban because the concentration of very large numbers of people in huge cities created mass markets; and industrial because this economy in employing these human masses produced wealth enough for them to purchase, along with the essentials for life, the products of mass culture. This critical mass of spenders demanded diversions and amusements, and pop was the sum of the products of the industries that arose in response to these demands.

Before pop, in rural times amusements were an exception to life, not daily events. Amusements, not being mass-produced, had to be crafted. Speeches, sermons, dramatic and musical performances occurred only in "live" presentations, and for that reason, diversions and amusements were always singular, out of the ordinary—and probably much cherished and long remembered. The nostalgia for country life forgets its downside, its boredom and isolation. Farmers "went to town" only to get what the farm didn't produce, rarely for amusement such as an annual fair or a duty such as voting. When he troubled to go to town, after collecting and harnessing the horses, dressing appropriately, and taking the time to drive over the rough, dusty—or muddy—roads, he arrived in another familiar location where he saw the same people as on his last visit. The local "general" store offered few extras and comforts, and the farmer lacked the ready cash to buy many of these. When he married, he usually took whatever female was locally available, and subsequently they endured each other's company and their mutual offspring. An Indian attack or alert may have been a welcome relief from the sameness of things, and the occasional religious revivals must have been vital outlets for dammed up emotions.

Then began what Frederick Lewis Allen called "The Big Change."[1]

Allen depicted a change from a subsistence to a consumption standard, from rural isolation to urban and suburban living, and from cultural scarcity to cultural abundance. The acceleration phase of the Big Change gave to the Twentieth Century a jump start, but the patterns had been emerging during the four preceding decades. Before the 19th Century, most mass movements had been religious, large crowds of humanity joining fervently together in public confessions of faith. Such massive outbreaks of religious emotions are labeled "awakenings," and they seem to occur every fourth generation, or about every 85 to 90 years. (Most recently, in case you missed it, there was a significant increase in emotional and fundamentalist religion during the 1960's and '70's.)[2]

Independence, followed by the democratization of our republic that was completed during the 1820's through the 1840's (universal manhood suffrage plus free public schooling) drew the masses of common folk into political activity. The defeat of the oligarchic John Quincy Adams by that self-styled man of the people Andrew Jackson in 1828 signaled this democratic change. In 1840, a blue-blooded descendant of an old Virginia family, William Henry Harrison, the hero of Indian wars (Tippecanoe, Indiana, 1811) promoted his presidential campaign using the humble symbols of the log cabin and jug of hard cider. These suggestions of lowly origins and the poor man's drink, images with great mass appeal, certainly contributed to Harrison's victory. Another instance of pop politics was the Lincoln-Douglas debates of 1858, when a contest for the Senate consisted of a series of open meetings throughout Illinois to debate the slavery question. Lincoln "lost" the Senate, but after the quality of his firm stand percolated through the collective national conscience, he gained the presidency within two years. The following Civil War or War of the Rebellion has been characterized as "irrepressible," a way of saying that the national leadership, those at the top, lacked the power to prevent it. This terrible war—over 600,000 killed and more than 1,000,000 casualties—was caused by the hardened collective wills of the antagonistic North and South, a pop war resulting from pop politics.

After this war of the people came a culture of the people. This pop culture developed in increments, one or two elements per decade. First came sport, big-time athletics with fandom, commencing with baseball. Originally "base ball" or "town ball," it had arrived in some form from Britain during the 18th Century. By 1860 baseball was played on a diamond with bases 90 feet apart and runners being tagged "out." Amherst and Williams played the first college game in 1851, and a National Association of Base Ball Players was formed in 1858. After the war amateur clubs soon gave way to professional clubs (as of 1867, no African Americans allowed), the first pro club being the Cincinnati Red Stockings (1869). In 1876 came the National League of Professional Baseball Clubs, an association of team owners rather than players. The rival American Association of Baseball Clubs appeared four years later, setting up the major leagues by 1880.[3]

About this same time, football became a college sport at the Ivy League schools (where some blacks were admitted and allowed to participate). Boxing also drew large crowds during these years, and it became regularized with the adoption of the "Queensbury" rules from 1869: three-minute rounds, ten second counts, and gloves. Blacks, who had boxed as slaves, were allowed into the sport at first, but the South rejected interracial boxing. They continued to fight in northern cities, but were never allowed to contend in heavyweight bouts, and white promoters often made them lose.[4] Then came basketball, invented at the Springfield, MA, YMCA in 1891 (as everyone knows from sports trivia questions) by one James Naismith, a Canadian. It caught on fast (among both sexes) and crowds were attending games by 1894. Pro games commenced in 1896, and the National Basketball League (NBL) followed quickly in 1898. Finally pro sports entered fully into the "big-time" in 1903, when big league baseball teams met in the first "World's Series," Boston defeating Pittsburgh.

Big-time sport soon had a rival in big-time entertainment. This came from "variety," the generic term that designates a series of "acts" or performances by different kinds of entertainers, such as singers, dancers, comedians, jugglers, acrobats, etc. When the minstrel show materialized during the 1830's, its outer two parts framed an "olio" or series of variety acts. After the Civil War a former circus performer and showman named Tony Pastor opened New York City's first "decent" variety theatre (Chapter 5). His bills were clean, unlike those of the infamous concert-saloon—where the females onstage and the serving girls below stage attracted all-male audiences. Pastor conceived the idea of clean, wholesome family entertainment; he simply realized the potential for greater ticket sales by luring in the family. By the mid-1880's other entrepreneurs followed Pastor's example, giving birth to what became known as vaudeville.

With the 1890's came the next major pop phenomenon, popular music, the demand for it stimulated by the needs of vaudeville performers for new material. In 1886 three brothers named Witmark, not even out of their teens, incorporated a music publishing enterprise in New York under their father's name (M. Witmark & Sons). Taking advantage of the surprising marriage of a beautiful lass of twenty-one (Frances Folsom) to the heavy, portly, and middle-aged President, they published a song entitled "President Grover Cleveland's Wedding March." Thus commenced the first of the "Tin Pan Alley" publishers (Chapter 3).[5] By the early 1890's there was a constellation of pop song publishers, constantly jostling one another, hoping to produce the next song to grab the public's fancy, the next "hit." The first major hit, in 1892, was Charles K. Harris's "After the Ball," a teary ballad which was the sales leader for several years (throughout the 1890's depression), eventually selling millions of copies. Then came the eruption of ragtime, the musical craze that grew until 1912, and then receded until jazz eclipsed it after 1917.

From 1912 ragtime generated the next pop sensation, the ballroom "dance craze." Now collectively labeled the ragtime dances, the majority of these lively steps were given such animal names as the Bunny Hug, Turkey Trot, Grizzly Bear, and Fox Trot. Coming after the two-step and the cakewalk, they shocked genteel America because couples danced alone and actually held one another, rather closely in some dances. This was a much freer expression, so free that many women went to afternoon "Tea Dances"—unescorted. The ragtime dance was causing a severe reaction, viewed by many as a threat to social stability, when, in 1913 a brilliant married couple defused the situation by their wholesome example. They became popular because of their grace, dignity, and seemingly endless creativity. Slender, elegant Vernon Castle and wife Irene glided across the pop scene and dealt a decisive blow to genteel, Victorian conventions. Cleancut, respectable, and decent, they reversed the slide of ballroom dancing into infamy and gained it a general (if somewhat grudging) acceptance. They were married, much in love, and the creators of a new lifestyle that was glamorous, suburban, and upper middle class. They were showbiz, but far above the sleaze aura that had previously tarnished performers. Now husbands, coming off commuter trains, could expect the occasional romantic evening of dinner and dancing or attending local parties where they rolled back the carpets.

Or they might take in a "picture show" (movie) instead. By the late teens of the ragtime era, feature films, having succeeded the earlier one- and two-reelers, had become the next element of pop. The "stars" were out, and storefront nickelodeons were being replaced by cinema palaces (many were converted vaudeville houses). To get to parties, stage shows, and films, these commuting suburbanites rolled out their newest and grandest acquisition, an automobile. By the period's end the middle classes and the more prosperous tradespeople had become freed from the restraints of society's arbiters and public transportation. Pop had brought about a totally new society. The common, ordinary people were up, no longer in subordination to their "betters," the ruling classes that had controlled life since the start of civilization five or six thousand years ago. You could wear whatever you wanted—a crown if you wished—go wherever you wanted, buy anything you could afford; your future did not depend upon whether you could find a "place" with some superior, in a servile capacity. The only nonlegal restraint was economic: you had to pony up the cash.

Notes: Chapter 1.2

1. Frederick Lewis Allen, *The Big Change: America Transforms Itself, 1900-1950*.
2. See William Strauss and Neil Howe, *Generations: The History of America's Future, 1584-2069*, 92-96, 299-316.
3. Arthur R. Ashe, Jr., *A Hard Road to Glory: A History of the African-American Athlete, 1610 to the Present*, I, 68-70.
4. *Ibid.*, 21-25, 90-93.
5. David A. Jasen, *Tin Pan Alley: The Composers, the Songs, the Performers*, 6-7.

1.3   The Art of Rag (I): Beginnings

>And a pervasive figure, a ubiquitous character in the show business landscape, the ragtime pianist, a new black man playing a new black music for America.[1]

Ragtime materialized as a popular style of music following two major outcomes in our history. These were Emancipation and the extension of rails to all parts of the country. The musical elements of ragtime pre-existed, but it required freedom and movement to bring about the creative synthesis. Simply put, African and European musical components melded to produce a new music. Emancipation solved the moral problem of slavery, but having achieved that goal, too few abolitionists looked beyond it to consider the consequences. In 1865 about 5,000,000 unskilled, inexperienced people of all ages became citizens. Their emancipators failed to develop policies and programs adequate to the difficult challenge of enabling the "Freedmen," as the former slaves were labeled, to fulfill the rights and responsibilities of citizenship. These needs included work skills; an understanding of the basics of money and the economy; enough knowledge of public issues to vote rationally; literacy; and even domestic skills such as sewing, infant care, home medicine, and maintenance of a home.[2]

This unreadiness to look after themselves, combined with the poverty, post-war devastation, and the resulting repression (see Chapter 2.1), left the Freedpeople with few choices. Most seem to have sunk into peonage, unable to rise above agricultural servitude, as sharecroppers, tenant farmers, or laborers. A minority found small wages in the towns, again as laborers or in domestic service. Only a few of the talented and fortunate escaped southern locales—at times actually escaped, because white vigilantes forcibly returned them when plantation labor was in short supply. For travelers and wanderers it was necessary to avoid notice by moving at night and avoiding towns. If seen, a stranger with a black face could expect capture and either a forced return to where he came from, or criminal charges and a harsh sentence at labor. The best chance for escape was along a rail line through the open door of a moving boxcar.[3]

Some of the hardier types possessing survival skills trailed along to the West to enlist in the Indian-fighting army. The 24th and 25th Infantry Regiments and the 9th and 10th Cavalry Regiments enlisted African Americans exclusively, though officered by whites. These regiments did good service on the frontier and established a proud tradition, securing a respected place in the historical memory. Others found something better in northern cities: slightly higher pay, much less abuse, and freedom from constant terror. A few improved themselves with schooling and applied their skills in business and professions to form the tiny nucleus of a future middle class. Also among the more fortunate were the entertainers, chiefly musicians, most of whom went into variety entertainment, at first in newly formed companies of black minstrels (see Chapter 2.3). Before the Civil War most local entertainment in the plantation South had been performed by slaves, who, showing aptitude, were permitted to learn from others, usually on the piano, fiddle, or banjo, and to play for dances and other events. These experienced performers soon found their ways into the itinerant life of the musical theatre, in and out of cities and towns, anywhere that people would line up to buy tickets for a show.

The best musical job turned out to be piano playing. None of the hazards of a touring company, such as getting stranded without money, either because too few tickets were sold or because the manager vanished with the receipts, or being attacked by vicious whites, or having no place to eat or sleep because there were no "colored" accommodations or restaurants. And piano playing paid more because the work was in saloons and in the places where sex was sold: music halls, dancehalls, concert-saloons, cheap hotels, and the better whorehouses. Out "on the town," in vice districts, men spent money freely, and a steady trickle of this easy cash flowed toward the "perfessor" as tips for playing, either lively or with feeling, depending upon the patron's mood. Seeing this, many fiddlers and banjo pickers rapidly converted to the piano. Before the war pianos had been scarce and expensive. Like pipe organs and harpsichords, pianos were individually built and affordable only for the wealthy. This changed abruptly after the war because the new steel-making technology resulted in more and better instruments. The new steel frames could take a much greater string pressure, producing a louder, richer, and hence more dynamic sound. Factories, not workshops, turned them out in such large numbers that the price fell to the means of the middle class, resulting in the appearance of the new upright models nearly everywhere, in churches, lodgehalls, theatres, good restaurants, the homes of aspiring people, and in the better drinking establishments and resorts of "ill repute." This multiplied the need for people to play on the instrument, a demand quickly met by black perfessors, a class of men also increasing, and willing to give up any home and family life for the itinerant life along the rail lines.[4]

Much has been written—and will continue to be—about the sources and the sequence of the development of the art of rag. Evidence is scarce and fragmentary. The sources lie back in the time of slavery, the folk period of a preliterate people. Although whites have passed on a few memories of this period, the surviving musical examples, which come chiefly from post-emancipation decades, give mainly hints and suggestions of the earlier musical practices of a people in bondage. However from such fragments, we can extrapolate backward to at least a hypothetical understanding of ragtime's origins in religious singing, work songs, and the European music of plantations. African Americans encountered and modified Christian hymns, marches, and European dances and songs. Slave owners forbade drums, but slaves clapped their hands, divided texts into call-and-response, combined regular and off-beats, and created a stringed instrument out of available materials that was close enough to African originals to retain the name "banjo." [5]

Out of all this musical activity, the most familiar product is the "spiritual," first performed for white audiences by the Fiske Jubilee Singers in the early 1870's. Funding for newly founded black institutions such as Fiske College in Nashville, Hampton Institute in Virginia, and Howard University in Washington, D.C., was raised by traveling choirs. White audiences much appreciated the dignified and serious renditions of African-American religious songs. What they didn't hear, and certainly would not have approved, was the instrumental music that blacks were creating along the rail routes in places that respectable whites chose to avoid and ignore.[6] Here flourished a livelier music, from the adept fingers of piano players, that owes much to earlier banjo pickers. Ragtime clearly existed before the first piano rags were written. It was the style of banjo virtuosi and string bands, minstrel shows and buck dancers. It was a folk style, a black mode that grew through the nineteenth century.[7] A number of banjo pieces sound much like ragtime.[8] The popular name for this raggy style of performing song, dance, and march tunes was "jig piano," a term later displaced by "rag-time." [9] For the white folks who first heard it, syncopation put an odd crimp in the ears; it was irregular, off-balance, loose. They called it "raggéd time," then, simply, "rag-time."

Probably most of these piano "ticklers" were self-taught, but a few of those whose names and styles were remembered were conservatory-trained. But whatever their backgrounds, all of them were relegated to underground itinerant circuits because African Americans were never allowed to perform as "art" musicians, being considered incapable of learning or understanding "serious" music. A few exceptions like Blind Boone and another called Blind Tom did reach the concert halls, but they were marketed as novelties and freaks. Thanks to the boyhood recollections of Eubie Blake, who lived long enough to find respect and a biographer, we know about "Old Man" "Metronome" French who played ragtime on a banjo: "'He was really old then; it must have been before 1890. He went way back, before the Civil War.'" [10] Eubie also listened to "Old" Jesse Pickett whose *Dream Rag*, which he liked to play, could be the oldest known strain of the music.[11] He also recalled "Big Head" Wilbur, "Jack the Bear" Wilson, "Big Jimmy" Green, William Turk, Sammy Ewell, "Slew Foot" Nelson, and Willy "Egg Head" Sewall. "Shout" Blake (no relation) and "One-Leg Willy" Joseph were classically trained. Except for the fragment of Pickett's *Dream*, nothing survives from the works of these legendary perfessors.[12]

A younger contemporary of this group who did break out of obscurity was Scott Joplin (1868-1917). Joplin, who traveled the same ragtime routes, but whose music survived, put some of the main final touches to the "coming together" of ragtime form and style. His life and background, until the point (in 1897) when ragtime found the critical mass of listeners that caused publication, resembled that of his fellow perfessors. His parents, Giles and Florence Givens Joplin, according to the 1870 Census, worked on a cotton plantation in northeast Texas, near the present day town of Linden, owned by one William Cave. They were one of five black families that included Florence's parents, Milton and Susan Givens, and families named Crow, Shepherd, and Smith.[13] Joplin's date of birth is unknown, but the censuses of 1870 and 1880 indicate 1868 as the year; however, they fail to reveal whether the Joplins lived on the Cave plantation at that time. Nor do we know whether they were sharecroppers, tenants, or hired help. Scott was the second child, his older brother Monroe seven, which suggests that Giles and Florence had lived as a family at least since the outbreak of the Civil War. Giles, born ca. 1842, had come as a slave from North Carolina to Texas, but was freed prior to the war. Florence, born ca. 1841, had come from Kentucky with her parents who were free. Both were musical, Giles a competent fiddler who had played the waltz, polka, schottische, quadrille, and reel at plantation dances, and Florence played the banjo and sang.[14]

Whatever their farming arrangement, shares, rent, or wages, the Joplins in 1870 existed at the low end of the socio-economic spectrum, a state of poverty aptly characterized by the clichè "grinding." But within five years of Scott's birth, the Joplins reached a higher living standard that lifted them out of near destitution. Post-war rail expansion reached northeast Texas with the meeting in 1874 of the Texas and Pacific (T&P) with the Missouri Pacific("MoPac"), connecting St.Louis and Dallas. At their meeting place, exactly on Texas-Arkansas border, just above Louisiana, towns were platted in December-January 1873-1874, both named Texarkana because of the tri-state location. This joint route of the two railroads was crossed a few years later by both the Kansas City Southern Lines and the St.Louis Southwestern Railway Lines ("Cotton Belt Route"), making Texarkana a prosperous, growing railway center. Giles had the luck to be hired as a laborer on the T&P, getting not only a higher income—between $1.00 and $1.25 per day, probably three times his farm earnings—but also securing a life in town for his family. Town life meant opportunities to improve and social life, qualities of existence lacking in rural isolation. Florence added still more to the family income doing housework for the well-to-do, and Monroe found a job as a porter.[15]

Giles apparently passed on his violin skills to Scott and younger brothers Robert and William, but Scott, accompanying his mother on her rounds to clean and launder, took an early interest in the pianos he saw set in positions of honor in genteel parlors. So palpable were his desire and natural ability that one family, the W.G. Cooks, allowed Scott to practice while his mother worked. In the early 1880's Giles decamped with his railroad wages to take up with another woman, throwing the support burden on Florence. Somehow, despite this fall into a more precarious condition, she managed to buy an old, much-used piano for Scott. When he was eleven, a music teacher from Germany accepted him as a free pupil. Julius Weiss, born 1840 or 1841, graduated from a university in Saxony and probably arrived in the U.S. during the 1860's, in order to avoid military service (a common cause of German emigration at that time). During the late 1870's Robert W. Rodgers, a businessman and a founder of Texarkana, engaged Weiss to tutor his children in mathematics, science, and music, and allowed him to give music lessons to other children. With Weiss's help and encouragement Scott became a competent musician and gained some significant exposure to the art music of Europe. Soon Scott was playing for the community and winning recognition for his fine performances and services. Weiss left Texarkana in 1884 when Rodgers died, but he and Scott carried on a lifelong correspondence, and during Weiss's last years Scott sent him sums of money.[16]

After 1882, his fourteenth year, Scott became an itinerant professional musician, going off on ever wider circuits, of which few records survive. When home, he earned money from guitar and mandolin lessons, and played a role in the musical life of the flourishing little city (population 4000 by the early 1880's) that stayed in the local memory. He started touring as a singer in the Texas Medley Quartet, which probably included his brother Robert. Robert went on to become a star in vaudeville as a musician and dancer. Scott also began his career as a perfessor, playing first in dancehalls. Probably his first trips covered the Red River valley region, where he could not have missed the universal poverty and terror suffered by his race. He certainly learned something of the violence of the robed nightriders and the lynchings common in northeast Texas and the Red River area. As he ranged farther over Texas, Arkansas, and the Mississippi Valley, he heard more of the music of the people: Civil War and Forty-niner songs, work and religious songs of his people, dances and marches, folk and popular, just about all of the elements of the American musical heritage. He also performed in minstrel shows, one of which brought him back home in the summer of 1891. This is one of the very few glimpses we catch of him during these anonymous years of wandering.[17]

Notes: Chapter 1.3

1. William J. Schafer and Johannes Riedel, *The Art of Ragtime: Form and Meaning of an Original Black American Art*, 20.
2. Lorenzo J. Greene, Gary R. Kremer, and Antonio F. Holland, *Missouri's Black Heritage,* 88-100.
3. *Ibid.*, 104-105.
4. Eileen Southern, *The Music of Black Americans: A History*, 313; Terry Waldo, *This Is Ragtime*, 7-9, for itinerancy; Craig H. Roell, *The Piano in America, 1890-1940*, 31-32, for the development and spread of the piano.
5. Burton W. Peretti, *The Creation of Jazz: Music, Race, and Culture in Urban America*, 14-15; Waldo, 7-9.
6. Roell, 33; John Edward Hasse, "The Creation and Dissemination of Indianapolis Ragtime, 1897-1930," 80.
7. Schafer & Riedel, 12.
8. James Lincoln Collier, *The Rise of Selfishness in America*, 88, mentions Daniel D. Emmett's *Pea Patch Jig* as probably derived from an old plantation tune. Schafer and Riedel, 176-186, analyze this banjo style to show that it is an early folk variety of ragtime.
9. Russell Sanjek, *American Popular Music and Its Business: The First Four Hundred Years*, 290-291; Southern, 313.
10. Al Rose, *Eubie Blake*, 150-151.
11. *Idem.*
12. *Ibid.*, 20, 150; Southern, 327-328.
13. Edward A. Berlin, *King of Ragtime: Scott Joplin and his Era*, 4-5; Susan Curtis, *Dancing to a Black Man's Tune: A Life of Scott Joplin*, 28-29.
14. Berlin, *King*, 6; Curtis, 33.
15. Berlin, *King*, 5-6; Curtis, 34-36.
16. Berlin, *King*, 6-7; Curtis, 36-38; Rudi Blesh and Harriet Janis, *They All Played Ragtime*, 37.
17. *Ibid.*, 38; Berlin, *King*, 7-8, 9-10; Curtis, 38-39.

1.4   Introducing TR

Every historical period has its typicals, individuals who embody some essence, whose qualities of character/personality evoke the associative feelings of our mind's-eye view of that time. Often this exemplary function reduces to a simple label: Periclean, Augustan, Elizabethan, Napoleonic. The ragtime-progressive years are also called The Era of Theodore Roosevelt. His personal qualities and actions thus "stamp" or "mark" this time in our history. He possessed dynamic traits and wide-ranging interests. His inputs influenced most areas of the nation's life and culture: party politics, foreign and military affairs, labor and the economy, social problems, intellectual concerns, the arts, natural history and conservation, and even such arcane things as the coinage and phonetic spelling. Discussions of public issues and policies were incomplete without his views; people always asked, "What does Teddy think?" They sensed that he expressed the nation's earnest desires and its optimism and good spirits.

The first Roosevelt reached the Netherlands colonial town of New Amsterdam in 1649. Most Roosevelts preferred business to agriculture, but by Independence, there was a landed or "Hudson River Branch" as well as the "Manhattan" or "Knickerbocker Branch." From the former descended Franklin Delano Roosevelt (32nd President), and from the latter came both Theodore Roosevelt (26th President) and his niece Eleanor, who married her distant cousin Franklin. The Manhattan Roosevelts grew prosperous in hardware, real estate, and investments. The best of them were givers rather than takers, serving the public when called to do so. Theodore's chief role models were his father and uncles active in politics and philanthropy. Uncle Robert B. Roosevelt (1825-1905) held public offices (Congress, an ambassadorship), fought the Tammany Hall corruption of Boss Tweed, helped oversee the construction of the Brooklyn Bridge, and was an early conservationist. As New York's Commissioner of Fish and Game, he worked 20 years to clean up lakes and streams and restock them with fish. He passed along this legacy of environmental concern to his nephew whose 1905 inauguration he lived long enough to attend.[1]

The strongest influence on the formation of the character of Theodore Roosevelt certainly was his father and namesake Theodore Roosevelt, Sr (1831-1878). TR Senior may have been the century's greatest philanthropist, known to family members as "Greatheart" after the character in *Pilgrims Progress* who carried the burdens of others.[2] He was known and loved throughout his city; he greatly loved and nurtured his family.[3] His love of children extended to the homeless, the hungry, and the abused. He was an organizer of the Children's Aid Society which sent out the fabled "orphan trains" that ran from 1869 to 1924. Over the time, these trains carried 100,000 homeless children from New York streets to new homes on Western farms. For the many boys who subsisted selling newspapers, he set up the Newsboys Lodging House where a warm, safe room cost five cents. He visited his newsboys every Sunday night after having taught a Sunday school class for poor children in the morning.[4]

Theodore the elder's other benefactions included founding an orthopedic hospital (later called the Roosevelt Hospital) and co-founding both the American Museum of Natural History and the Metropolitan Museum of Art. During the Civil War he looked after the great needs of the soldiers. When Johnny marched off to war, he left inadequate or no provision for dependents. Theodore Senior conceived the idea of a pay allotment, a withheld portion of pay to be sent home. He moved to Washington, got a bill introduced, lobbied it through Congress (at the same time becoming a close friend of the Lincolns), and then served on the Allotment Commission. As a Commissioner, he traveled extensively, enduring bad roads and weather, to sell this unheard-of and untried idea to troops whose comforts were meager. He also served on the Sanitary Commission (the predecessor of the Red Cross) and raised funds to decently equip the first African-American regiment of the Union forces. Later he organized the Protective War Claims Commission to procure the rightful back pay for families of deceased and crippled soldiers. After the War he set up the Soldiers Employment Bureau to find jobs for the disabled.[5]

But the greatest achievement of this remarkable man may have been his careful nurture of his chronically ill, asthmatic son. Instead of overprotection, he encouraged young Theodore to develop both body and mind in home gymnasium and library. He took the family (wife Martha, children Anna, Theodore, Elliot, Corinne) on foreign travels (two yearlong trips to Europe), outdoor excursions, and encouraged each child to pursue interests and hobbies. He drew out the children at the dinner table in discussions and recitations. Contemporaries regarded the Roosevelts as singular for making their children the center of family attention, a very unVictorian folkway. When young Theodore matriculated at Harvard in 1876, he had never attended any school, but he spoke French and German, had been tutored in Classics, was an accomplished biologist and taxidermist, and well read in history and literature. He could ride and care for a horse and name most birds by their songs.[6]

As he packed for Harvard the son never forgot the father's parting words on priorities: "Take care of your morals first, your health second, and finally your studies." [7] Theodore set the course of his life by this Victorian admonition. At Harvard he attracted attention in that time of gentlemanly indifference to academics by actually studying and raising serious questions in class. He became a natural speed-reader who consumed one or two books daily throughout his life. Still trying to overcome asthma and the sickly tendencies of childhood, he gave part of each day to intense physical activity. He walked everywhere, never boarding the horsecars, and when he rode, it was on the horse that he fed and groomed himself. He always pushed beyond the limits of previous exertions, pursuing what he called the "Strenuous Life," probably overcompensating for the puniness of childhood and youth, and thereby creating a regime that he championed all of his life. Despite poor vision he boxed on the college team, enduring much punishment. Although he developed a formidable intellect, physical activity stayed a notch higher in the priorities inherited from his father.[8]

Both love and death seasoned him at Harvard. During his sophomore year, his adored father died from a painful cancer of stomach and intestines (February 1878); he was eulogized by the *New York Herald* as "Eyes To the Blind, Feet To the Lame, and Good To All." 2000 people crowded in to his funeral in a Fifth-Avenue church.[9] This terrible blow was softened by the total surrender of his affections to Alice Hathaway Lee, blonde daughter of a Boston banker whose cheerful, outgoing disposition had earned the nickname "Sunshine." At 17 this sheltered girl had backed away from the enthusiastic advances of the awkward, nearsighted, immature youth who came at her so forcefully. But two years of persistence (Theodore told fellow students that he was going to marry her) overcame rejection, and they were joined on his birthday (27 October 1880) four months after graduation. Their European honeymoon elicited only a single sentence in his diary: "Our intense happiness is too sacred to be written about."[10]

After moving in with his widowed mother (6 West 57th Street), Theodore sought a vocation. At Harvard he had decided not to pursue his favorite subject biology because he desired more than the genteel poverty and obscurity of a professorship. Instead he looked into history, law, and politics. During 1881-1882 he upgraded his senior paper on naval activity during the War of 1812 and then published *The Naval War of 1812* (1883), a book so well received by critics that it qualified him as an expert in naval affairs (still definitive and still in print!). This established a vocation in history.[11] At the same time he attended law lectures at Columbia University (walking miles uptown and back) and "read law" in the office of his Uncle Robert. But if history suited him, the law did not; law seemed always too bogged down in details and too pedestrian for him. Forsaking the gentility of courts and law offices, he chose instead the very ungenteel practice of politics. He not only joined the Republican Party (like others of his class), but he also attended district meetings in the party's "hall" over a saloon and often dropped by to converse with fellow members. Family friends soon counseled that he should remain above such gritty involvement, but Theodore found that he actually enjoyed being a politician. So in such a declassé environment as a district party meeting room, a career began. Within a year, thanks to a local factional fight, he found himself a candidate for the legislature, and subsequently won, going on to serve three terms.[12]

To the veteran pols of the New York State Assembly in Albany, this bumptious young man of privilege with fancy clothes and Harvard accent came across as a naive buffoon, someone to be toyed with, humiliated, and sent back to his elevated but useless place in the social scheme. Instead he managed to unify and lead the scattered Republicans from smaller upstate communities (later known as "Roosevelt Republicans") who shared the same idealistic urge to end business-caused graft and corruption and bring about reforms. Together they exposed the bribery of judges and other officials, defeated bills granting special privileges to corporations, worked for humane labor legislation (unfortunately overturned in the courts), and, more important, cooperated with Democratic Governor Grover Cleveland to achieve civil service reform for the state of New York. These three years in the Assembly (1882-1884) provided a practical political education and led to a change in philosophy, from an inherited conservative belief that the alliance of business and politics (if cleaned up) should rule the republic, to an understanding that these interests were inherently too selfish to place the good of the public first. By degrees what he experienced drove him to conclude that government should intervene to regulate economic enterprise in the public interest.[13]

It all fell apart in 1884. On February 14, he was summoned home from Albany to find his mother dying from typhoid, and his beloved Alice, after giving birth to their daughter, also dying, from kidney failure (nephritis or Bright's Disease). After enduring this double whammy, Theodore dragged himself through the Assembly term, and then abandoned the life he had known. The previous summer, while hunting down one of the final buffalo in Dakota Territory, on impulse, after seeing the rapid increases in the cattle markets, he had bought a ranch. Now, full of his grief, he fled West to the distraction of producing cattle. Curiously he stopped over in Chicago as a delegate to the Republican National Convention, where he joined former Harvard professor and mentor Congressman Henry Cabot Lodge in unsuccessfully opposing the nomination of the notoriously corrupt James G. Blaine for President. On the national stage for the first time, he made a favorable impression and followed this up by swallowing his distaste and campaigning for Blaine that fall. This set a pattern. Ranching became his chief occupation, but after every two-month stay in Dakota—where he did most of the writing of a stream of books, some on history, others on his ranching experiences—he usually returned to New York. Porters on the Northern Pacific came to know him very well on his frequent runs between Chicago and Medora, Dakota Territory. Over a three-year period he spent only about twelve months in the West.[14]

Those scattered months on that ruggedly individualistic, somewhat lawless frontier did cure his grief. But his sojourn was more than a detour to bury some pain on the prairie. Besides the anecdotes of cowboying, the ranch life forged the Theodore Roosevelt figure known to the public later on. He exerted himself to the utmost on the spring and fall round-ups, orgies of activity—daylong rides followed by the drudgeries of roping, branding, and loading for shipment. Here was the truly Strenuous Life, and it produced a hard, strong body full of health and well being. The sickly child faded into memory.

The frontier ranch milieu was democratic. In that line of work one hoped for acceptance as an equal. The landowner paid the cowhands and took the income (if any), but labor was scarce, and skilled cowmen soon quit any boss they disliked. Out on the open range, the relatively few humans had to cooperate to protect and keep herds intact. Outlaws, predators, and bad weather regularly took a toll of the herds. Theodore came to know ordinary people for the first time as equals, as he met the challenge to come up to their standards. He may have read Tolstoy and crafted his prose in their proximity, but these activities did not impinge on them. It mattered more that his rope lassoed the cow, and that his bullet killed the wolf.

First stereotyped as a tenderfoot, Theodore achieved respect and acceptance because of his integrity, courage, intelligence, and sense of humor. Respect increased the day he stopped a cowboy from branding a stray off someone else's part of the range and fired him abruptly. His point: "A man who will steal for me will steal from me."[15] His courage showed the night he encountered the drunken cowboy in Mingusville (named after Minnie and Gus its founders). As he came into the "hotel" for some warm coffee, a drunk waving two handguns, who had already holed the clock, came at him, demanding, "Four eyes is going to treat." Theodore played along, forcing a laugh as he took a seat. As the man stood over him, cursing him and repeating the demand, Theodore came up fast with both fists, knocking the man down as his guns discharged—harmlessly through the ceiling.[16] When he called upon his fellow stockmen to organize against rustling, violence, and inadequate range laws, Theodore found himself elected the first chairman of the Little Missouri Stockmen's Association. His two years of leadership ended a crime wave.[17] Occasionally laughter seasoned the admiration. Once at a round-up, he ordered one of his men to move faster, shouting, "Hasten forward quickly there!" The story spread rapidly, and in the saloons, thirsty cowhands commanded bartenders to "hasten forward quickly" whenever service on refills was slow.[18]

Disaster ended this three-year venture on the cattle frontier. By 1886 supply had surged so far ahead of demand that the market price had fallen to a fraction of the costs of breeding and raising cattle. This loss became permanent during the terrible winter of 1886-87 when most of these devalued cattle froze and starved to death. This fiasco carried off a large part of Theodore's inheritance (a $20,000 loss after the properties were sold ten years later), but this Badlands experience turned into the pay-off that kept on paying. What he gained was a constituency. They never forgot him, and his legend spread as he emerged from obscurity. The West considered him one of its own; they followed him into battle in 1898 and proudly gave him their votes after that. A doctor who treated him after a long ordeal of chasing and capturing some thieves gave an early expression of this regard:

> He impressed me and he puzzled me, and…I told my wife that I had met the most peculiar and at the same time the most wonderful man I had ever come to know. I could see that he was a man of brilliant ability and I could not understand why he was out there on the frontier.[19]

Notes: Chapter 1.4

1. Allen Churchill, *The Roosevelts: American Aristocrats*, 117-118.
2. *Theodore Roosevelt: Autobiography*, 18.
3. Corinne Roosevelt Robinson, *My Brother, Theodore Roosevelt*, 106; Churchill, 125; TR, *Auto.*, 14; David McCullough, *Mornings on Horseback*, 143.
4. TR, *Auto.*, 10; McCullough, 28-29; Churchill, 118-121.
5. McCullough, 50-61; C. Robinson, 20-21; Churchill, 126-127.
6. *Ibid.*, 129-133; McCullough, 82-112; William Henry Harbaugh, *Power and Responsibility: The Life and Times of Theodore Roosevelt*, 17.
7. Edmund Morris, *The Rise of Theodore Roosevelt*, 97.
8. McCullough, 210-214; Churchill, 137-140; TR, *Auto*, 30.
9. Churchill, 140-141; C. Robinson, 105; McCullough, 182-183, 185.
10. Churchill, 157-160; Howard Teichmann, *Alice: The Life and Times of Alice Roosevelt*, 8-11; Harbaugh, 24.
11. *Idem.*, Churchill, 161-162.
12. TR, *Auto.*, 57-58; Churchill, 162-166; McCullough, 251-252.
13. Churchill, 162-168; Mark Sullivan, *Our Times*, II, 215-218, 226-235, 381-391; TR, *Auto.*, 81-83, 84-93; McCullough, 259; Harbaugh, 33-35.
14. Churchill, 169-170; McCullough, 67, 284-285, 337-341; Harbaugh, 53; Teichmann, 112.
15. McCullough, 329.
16. Peter Collier, with David Horowitz, *The Roosevelts: An American Saga*, 67; Harbaugh, 54; McCullough, 329.
17. Harbaugh, 56-57.
18. Noel F. Busch, *TR: The Story of Theodore Roosevelt and His Influence on Our Times*, 64-65.
19. McCullough, 341, 348; Harbaugh, 57-66. The ordeal involved building a raft and a run down the Little Missouri River to retrieve a stolen boat and capture and convey the thieves to justice; it took about 12 days.

2. Getting To The Nineties (II)

2.1 Reign of Terror

W.C.Handy (1873-1958) recalls a frightening experience in *Father of the Blues*:

> One day in a Texas town I began to think that my turn was next. While playing a cornet solo in the public square during the noon concert, I suddenly turned around to discover a rifle pointed at my eye. I ignored the threat, playing as if nothing was happening. A few moments later, the drums rumbling as we began the march back to the theatre, a gang of cowboys appeared and began roping our walking gents with their lassos. A swarm of rowdy boys joined in the fun and threw rocks down the bell of the big bass horn. They pelted our drums so vigorously the noise sounded like the rat-tat-tat of a machine-gun. I was furious and stoutly refused to play a note during the parade. We marched faster than usual, but we kept our ranks. Later Mahara complimented me warmly for keeping the parade in formation and refusing to play.[1]

Here a quick-witted response, literally thinking on his feet, prevented bloodshed and injury or death. Nowhere at the turn of the century could an African American let go of his caution. Common civil rights, especially that of doing one's work in public, could be, and sometimes were, denied. In the South a white could ridicule, curse at, or strike any black without fear of arrest or reprisal. In the North where segregation was not on statute books, restaurants refused service and hotels were always full. Drunken whites routinely attacked lone blacks they saw on the streets. This was a casual brutality. Blacks were perceived as grotesques, living caricatures, animate creatures of two dimensions, surfaces without backing. H.L.Mencken recalls the ludicrous stereotypes prevalent during his 1880's Baltimore childhood: "We boys believed in all the traditional Southern lore about them—for example that the bite of one with blue gums was poisonous, that those of very light skin were treacherous and dangerous, that their passion for watermelon was at least as powerful as a cats for catnip, and that no conceivable blow on the head could crack their skulls, whereas a light tap on the shins would disable them." [2]

Compared with northern areas, where this dehumanization happened occasionally, in the South it became a constant. There terror evolved into a system. Emancipation brought African Americans a freedom that remained theoretical. No change occurred in the attitudes of whites, who believed Negroes to be an inferior species, unable to govern themselves. During the hated era of Reconstruction (1867-1877) following the Civil War, white attitudes hardened a great deal more (if that were possible). Under the humiliation of "Radical" Reconstruction's harsh military rule, temporarily disfranchised ex-Confederates, trying to scratch a subsistence from devastated lands, burned with hatred over the loss of political control. They tasted gall at the spectacle of local and state governments in the hands of a coalition of "carpetbaggers" (believed to be northern opportunists and con men—who arrived with possessions in cheap luggage fabricated from carpeting), "scalawags" (the same, with southern accents), and the former slaves said to be manipulated as puppets in elective offices. All compounded by the dire poverty that descended on everyone except the hated forces of occupation and the civilian "trash" that parasitically fed on the universal destitution. By 1878, with Reconstruction over, and the southern states readmitted, the ex-Confederates resumed their birthright of control over inferiors. Self-labeled as the

"Redeemers," they acted during the two following decades to consolidate their power by setting up a system of repression, a system that not only cancelled emancipation but which also manipulated poor whites by pandering to race fears and race hatreds.

The terror that came down on black folk was a race system consisting of four parts:

1. Disfranchisement
2. Economic subordination
3. Segregation
4. Violence

Whites believed that Emancipation had given black people false and dangerous ideas of equality, and that such illusions had to be replaced by a humble submissiveness. This would demand constant reenforcement. Such was the view of southern whites who saw themselves as "tolerant" and "moderate." There were many to the right who took a more radical stance: the race problem required nothing less than removal, either through emigration or genocide. Their great fear exuded an implacable hatred that rejected all restraints, legal or moral. Henry J. Hearsey, ex-Confederate Major, founder-editor of the *New Orleans States* (1880), constantly ranted against Negroes. He once used "nigger" twenty-eight times in one editorial and regularly hinted at a drastic solution to the race problem. During the troubled summer of 1900, he produced an editorial entitled, "The Negro Problem and Its Final Solution," which recommended "extermination." He predicted race war, a war to the death, because northern agitators (he felt) were stirring up demands for equality. Only an unconditional surrender, very soon, could ward off this ultimate catastrophe. Hearsey was not some rural editor whose verbal poisons stirred up a small group of backcountry farmers. His doomsaying voice spoke for the leading afternoon daily of the South's only large city: "Then the Negro problem of Louisiana at least will be solved—and that by extermination." [3]

Whence the persecution and hostility? Certainly throughout history, and before history, there has always been a servile class, whether slave or free, workers brought in to do the dirty jobs rejected by the dominant class. Always this dispensation erodes as inferiors strive upward and earn their way to equality. As the process moves on, a new set of inferiors, captive or volunteer, replaces its predecessors. If the movement is gradual, there is no great sense of fear or threat. The older class always resents the strivers coming up the ladder, but fresh money and intermarriage soon wipe away most stains, whether social or pigmentary. We adapt.

However, when the losers in a bitterly fought war, a war fought in part to settle the question of the condition of the inferior class, a condition believed essential to the viability of the economy, when these losers return in anguish at the outcome, to homes and economies devastated by that war, they will apply every remaining resource to hold back change that threatens. It was too much for the former rebels to confront their former bondsmen suddenly made free. It was unthinkable that a people who had been regarded for over two centuries as mere property, of subhuman intelligence, that suddenly, without any allowance for a period of transition or even some material compensation for the loss, that such creatures could be declared by the victors to be the equals, in law and rights of citizenship, of anyone else. Obviously the only possible reaction to their world, ravaged and turned upside down, was denial, a rejection of equality as a perverse and destructive notion, a vicious idea put on them by demon Yankees.[4]

This was a crisis, and it was doubled (if not redoubled) by the dire economic conditions. The South, which had always lagged economically and in which poverty had always been the norm, in April of 1865 was near to starvation, its rudimentary and incomplete pre-war infrastructure destroyed: railroads, docks, ships, financial institutions, professional people, and slave labor, all reduced, damaged, or lost. Subsequently, because most knew how to farm, the food crisis was averted, but poverty remained universal. Progress toward a much-hoped-for "New South" inched along only in miniscule increments. A very small wealthy class arose to grab the meagre profits that accrued out of the much heralded, but overstated, New South, but these few lawyers, merchants, agri-businessmen, railroad investors, lumbermen, speculators, and their parasites (politicians) clutched most of the pieces of this skimpy pie. The poor whites and blacks had to gnaw on leftovers, more gristly than nourishing. For the poor white the crisis was perpetual: a diet of starches and inadequate protein, nothing fresh beyond fall; shabby housing; worn clothing with few changes; a scarcity of cash; chewing tobacco, occasional candy, and homemade whiskey the only luxuries; long days of drudgery; a lonely, boring rural isolation for most; church and summer revivals the sole amusements (excepting the hunting and fishing that furnished some protein); an anemic schooling during winter months that achieved only a basic literacy; and no hope of getting out of such a life.[5]

Usually lethargic—such lives were not vigorous—these people were easily stirred to rage against their black neighbors, neighbors who generally had less to eat than they did. Whose clothes were more ragged than worn. Whose cabins had newsprint pasted on the walls to cover the gaps in the unfinished boards. Who never got out of debt to the man on whose land they sharecropped. Who got even less schooling than whites—when they got any. Whose only consolation and opportunity for expression came to them in the sanctuary of their churches. Who could anticipate gratuitous abuse and violence whenever they ventured out into the towns and onto the roads. Who never received justice from the white authorities, which refused to indict any white for a crime against a black, and in whose courts any black could expect a guilty verdict—and a sentence to a work gang to labor arduously on the white man's railroads, timber claims, and quarries and mines.

The money class maintained its power through exploitation and division. Whenever poor whites grew restive, as they did during the Greenbacker agitation of the 1880's and the Populist clamor of the 1890's, the wealthy sent their politician/henchmen out to the stump to rant against black folk. It always worked, the threats that "northern agitators" were pushing the "uppity niggers" who wanted to take the white man's jobs and farms, and that the shiftless, lazy, vicious bad niggers were on the increase, out there, lurking, intending to rob and burn and rape. Unless someone "taught them a lesson," soon, no one's womenfolk would be safe. This was the raw nerve, the running sore of the South. Race poisoned life, keeping one group terrorized and the other group paralyzed by fear and hatred.[6]

One day in Mississippi, his band hired to provide martial music for a gubernatorial campaigner, W.C.Handy and his fellow black bandsmen listened to the following sentiments and views about the potential of their race:

> Ladies and Gentlemen:
>
> I come before you as a candidate for the governorship of the grand old state of Mississippi. And I pledge you my sacred word of honor that if you elect me governor, I shall not spend one dollar for nigger education. Now I want to tell you why I will not spend one dollar of the state's money for nigger education; education unfits the nigger.

Let me prove it to you conclusively. I am right. When this great country of ours was torn by strife, and we followed the fortunes of the Confederacy, we left behind our mothers, our daughters, our sweethearts and our wives; and we left them behind with our niggers, and they guarded them like so many faithful watch-dogs. Now what kind of nigger did we leave them with? It was the uneducated nigger. Suppose we again had to go to war, would you trust them with the nigger of today? (A chorus of no's came in answer.) That's why I wouldn't spend one dollar for nigger education.

Handy adds that when the oration concluded, they struck up *Dixie* and afterwards were able to laugh about it. But he further mentions that when he first heard such poisonous words as a schoolboy in Florence, Alabama, he went home and "…buried my head in a pillow and wept…." [7]

Notes: Chapter 2.1

1. W[illiam] C[hristopher] Handy, *Father of the Blues: An Autobiography*, 43-44.
2. H[enry] L[ouis] Mencken, *The Days of H.L. Mencken*, I, 137.
3. William Ivy Hair, *Carnival of Fury: Robert Charles and the New Orleans Race Riot of 1900*, 91.
4. W.J. Cash, *The Mind of the South*, 115-120, 125, 137-141, presents a full consideration of southern violent tendencies, including the rape fears of southern whites.
5. *Ibid.*, 22-27, for diet and social conditions of poor whites, 132-133, for political situation, 150-156, 160-161, for economics.
6. Ray Stannard Baker, *Following the Color Line: An Account of Negro Citizenship in the American Democracy*, 260-263; Benjamin Quarles, *The Negro in the Making of America*, 134-137, 150-151.
7. Handy, 80-81.

2.2 Rails

Ragtime like everything else traveled by rail. Cities and towns were islands in a green, rural sea. However most of the connecting lines on the map were not water routes followed by ships; they were corridors of railroad tracks. Rails took the fear out of travel by making arrival a certainty. Before rails mail traveled slowly, in small volume, and often never arrived. Rails brought about cheap, high volume mail service. Besides joining cities and towns, rails actually created them because people could live wherever rails went. Without rails there would have been no small-town America, just isolated rural areas growing divergent in customs and speech, and hostile to outsiders. If water transportation (steamboats) had not been followed by rails, there likely would have been three regions: two coasts and a north-south riverine segment, joined in loose federation and liable to break up in disputes. In fact this occurred once, during the 1860's, just before the completion of the rail network.[1]

Between 1865 and 1917 the American States became both more united and populous. Population tripled, from 35,000,000 to 103,400,000, and railroads increased seven times, from 35,000 miles in 1865 to 254,000 in 1917.[2] Every day small towns received freight, mail, metropolitan newspapers, and an infusion of new people; nonresidents come to visit, sell things, or relocate. The same trains then carried away other people, plus mail and freight for other cities and towns. Thus the town had become an extension of the city, and small-town life along the rail corridors became culturally almost equal to city life. Each town's "depot" became the hub of local activities. Prior to the Civil War, people went to the general store or post office, which often shared the same location, to catch up on the news or meet friends. Now people directed their steps to the railroad station, usually located on "Depot Street" or "Railroad Avenue," to transact business, find out what news was coming over the telegraph wire, send and receive telegrams, greet travelers or business associates, or leave town on a business or pleasure trip. Families regularly boarded trains to pay visits to relatives in towns nearby, one or two stops up or down the line. An "inland" town, one lacking a close railroad connection, was deemed insignificant and futureless. Even if they had no particular business at the station, people often dropped by to chat or watch trains pass through, to glimpse people eating in dining cars or enjoying drinks in the club car or "smoker." [3]

Railroads caused the cities as we know them, with "downtown" in the center, concentrically surrounded by varied belts of commerce, manufacturing, and residences. The primary reason for the dominant role of railroads in the process of urbanization lies in the effects of steam power, which are such that steam concentrates. The steam engine, in both manufacturing and transportation, caused the concentration of industries near the terminals of the central cities. These were the destinations of the coal-carrying trains, and industries tended to locate economically at the points where coal could be delivered by trains. Labor needed to reside near available jobs. This centralizing trend began to reverse just after 1900 because the new electric street railways (trolleys) and, a bit later, the automobile, led people out to the suburbs. However cities maintained steady growth by annexing such suburbs, which were, after all, new belts or circles. Eventually, as we have witnessed later on, decline and decentralization would hit the central cities as internal combustion and jet engines replaced steam as the chief transporters of people and goods. Even the railroads forsook steam. Thus while steam concentrates, electricity and internal combustion disperse.[4]

But railroads dominated the 1900 scene. They would grow another 60,000 miles, from then until 1916. Besides creating the cities, railroads generated the second wave of the Industrial Revolution (the first wave had been mainly textiles, coal, and iron) because they needed rails, rolling stock, and mining machinery. All of these generated further demands for tools, machine tools and other manufacturing equipment, steel and other metals, more mining, and factory construction. Without the industrializing thrust provided by railroading, there would never have been the succeeding electrical, chemical, automotive, or airframe industries. In addition to the needs of railroads, the services of railroads also drove the industrializing impulse. Railroads lowered the cost of freight enough to permit the shipment of bulky, low-value items, the raw materials, like coal, grain, and ore that kept cities alive and productive.[5] Steamboats may have started the revolution in transportation, but they could reach only waterway locations. Without rails, Minnesota and Michigan iron ore could reach Chicago, Milwaukee, Detroit, Toledo, and Cleveland, but not Pittsburgh or other locations near coal, and sufficient quantities of coal could not have reached the lake cities.

Railroads also revolutionized time. Time had always been local, based upon the sun. With people making longer rail journeys after the Civil War, the old ways of reckoning time put travelers and railroads into a snarl of time differentials. Railroads first standardized their own times, setting each station's clock to conform with printed timetables. They could now announce their own arrivals and departures, but this failed to resolve confusion because each railroad's clocks proclaimed a different time. Passengers changing railroads never knew if they would make a connection. For example Buffalo had three different times and Pittsburgh six. Travelers had to reset watches every time they came into a station or boarded another train. From Maine to California required 20 changes of time. Standard time had been suggested as early as 1870, but this met universal opposition, as no community wanted to surrender its sovereignty over time. Finally in 1883 the railroads in concert set all objections aside and adopted a standard time based upon the 75th, 90th, 105th, and 120th meridians on which were located, approximately and respectively, Philadelphia, Memphis, Denver, and Fresno. The time zone lines were set midway between the meridian cities. Many opposed and resented this highhanded, unilateral act of the all-powerful railroads, contending that they ran their lives on "God's time—not Vanderbilt's!" A demonstrative minister in Tennessee took out his watch in the pulpit and destroyed it with a hammer, which apparently failed to convince either God or the arrogant railroads of the error. One either accepted the new time dispensation or missed the train.[6]

The "Golden Age of Railroad Travel" coincides with the Ragtime Years, from the mid-1890's to the mid-teens. As rail mileage reached the maximum in 1916, costs went down, from 2.17 cents per passenger mile in 1890, to 1.93 cents in 1909.[7] Of more importance to the traveler, railroads had finally achieved a high standard of safety and comfort. Previously, danger and discomfort had been the lot of all who boarded the cars. Accidents regularly resulted from the failure of couplings, flaws in rails, poor brakes, and inadequate signals at grade crossings. By the 1890's these problems had been solved by automatic couplers (no longer costing brakemen their fingers), steel rails, electric signals, and air brakes.[8] Before the 1890's, baggage went unchecked and mishandled; schedules were erratic—only in part because time wasn't standard. Earlier, smoke had poured in through open windows and the combined stenches of tobacco, whiskey, and unwashed bodies permeated closed cars; seats were hard and lacked headrests.[9]

However by the mid-1890's, with the new safety features and the improved models of George Pullman's sleeping, dining, and parlor cars, railroads at last provided an acceptable level of comfort. Nor were the costs excessive. Until 1917, when the U.S. Government assumed wartime control of the railroads, the Interstate Commerce Commission (ICC) allowed only a modest extra charge for Pullman fares, which did not permit increases to cover rising costs, in effect forcing the railroad companies to subsidize first-class travel.[10] A series of new first-class trains, introduced from the mid-1890's, combined comfort with faster speeds. These gave luxury and pampered service. Porters and stewards kept busy bringing food and drinks, collecting outgoing mail and telegrams, answering calls for morning coffee and magazines, shining shoes, and carrying luggage. A few luxury trains had barber and beauty shops. These servants, porters, waiters, and chefs, were mature black men, very senior employees, proud of their positions on crack trains.

First-class cars featured polished metal, wood paneling, fine upholstery and carpeting, brass fittings, electric fans, indirect lighting, and mahogany tables and chairs. Such trains presented food service specialties of the regions they served—at well-below-cost prices: grouse and salmon on the Northern Pacific, antelope steak on the Union Pacific, Maine lobster and fish on New England lines, terrapin stew on the Baltimore and Ohio, and succulent sirloins on the Chicago, Northwestern. A dining car crew of thirteen included chefs, stewards, waiters, and busboys.[11] First class trains huffing into a station or roaring through a grade crossing filled the attention span with a burst of glamor. Stepping up from the porter's stool to the stairs, the passenger entered an extended arm of the big city. Etiquette books of the time suggested the clothes to wear, cosmetics to use, how to direct a porter, how to obtain proper seating in a diner.[12]

On June 15, 1902, the New York Central introduced the *Twentieth-Century Limited*, the first deluxe all-Pullman train. Actually two trains, one departing New York and the other out of Chicago, on a rapid run of 20 hours over the "Water Level Route," following the Hudson River system to Buffalo and then the Great Lakes lowlands to Chicago. It cost extra but the glamor commenced with walking down the platform on a plush red carpet six feet wide and 120 feet long. There were no daycoaches for the hoi polloi, and initially just five cars: one for buffet-baggage, a parlor-club car, two Pullmans, and a Pullman-observation car. The buffet-dining car was furnished in "Santiago mahogany," and the linens, flatware, and crockery displayed the train's logo in a custom design. Soon its popularity required more cars, and such additional services as a library, barber, beautician, and large "drawing rooms" with bath-shower. There were also maid and valet services, manicures, and stock market reports and telephones available at major stops and terminals. When late in arrival, passengers received a dollar for every hour behind schedule, and the superb meals, served with courtesy and assiduousness in the diner, cost only one dollar, which foreign travelers considered amazing. Within months the competing Pennsylvania Railroad retaliated with the equally luxurious *Broadway Limited,* creating a rivalry that kept prices down and services up.[13]

Similar standards of luxury soon characterized western trains out of Chicago and St.Louis and north-south trains out of New York and Chicago. The first was the *Overland Limited* from Chicago to San Francisco, jointly operated by the Union Pacific and Southern Pacific lines. Others include the *Sunset Limited*, Southern Pacific, the Los Angeles-New Orleans special, which ran the long way across Texas, over 900 miles in one state; the *City of Portland*, Union Pacific, out of Chicago to the Northwest; and the *Empire Builder*, Great Northern, Chicago to Seattle via the Twin Cities. Often these luxury trains pulled the private cars of the very rich, each custom built and usually ostentatious. People enjoyed reading descriptions of them in magazines—an early example of celebrity puffery. Readers reveled in such details as those of the Busch family, the St.Louis beer barons, whose car had beer piped into every room, fixtures of gold and silver, marble washbasins, and stained glass windows. These cars were the first true "mobile homes," yachts on rails. For the moderately wealthy, deluxe cars could be rented for single trips. Millionaires could also rent five-car trains to transport more people than could be transported in a single car. Hunting groups often rented cars for outings in remote areas that lacked luxury hotels. Hunters' cars came especially fitted with gun racks, ammunition closets, and cold storage cabinets for game. All such cars had wine racks, buffered to prevent breakage on rough roadbeds. Politicians rented rolling stock for campaigns, and showbiz stars like Nora Bayes lived in them on long theatrical tours.[14]

If indeed there actually have been any "good old days," they occurred while on board the crack trains of this period. Trains carried 98% of intercity travelers and 77% of the freight traffic. The value of railroad enterprises rose from 2.5 billion dollars of capitalizations in 1865, to 21 billion in 1917. The number of employees went from 163,000 in 1865 to 1,701,000 in 1917.[15] People took pride in railroad employment. "He's a railroad man" meant that a person earned "good money" at a "steady job," and that connection to such a great enterprise stamped one with sound traits of character and reliability. Railroad men were perceived as steady and as solid as the "turnip" pocket watches they frequently consulted. Most Americans lived within a short buggy or taxi ride from a depot where trains regularly stopped or could be stopped with a flag. No other form of public, long distance transportation has ever been as convenient. Air travel, with its time-consuming drives to and from airports, its traffic snarls caused by weather that would not hold back a train, and its tiresome waits between flights—not downtown where there were things to see and do, but in noisy, crowded, uncomfortable terminals with very bad, overpriced food—has never achieved the standards of comfort and convenience found on good trains. No first-class seat on a jet plane equals a first-class rail experience such as the Rock Island line concisely boasted of in an advertisement: "…every desire is gratified and every moment a pleasure." [16]

RAGTIME ALMANAC 17

First Class Trains	RR	ROUTE
Twentieth Century Limited	N Y C	N Y - Chicago
Broadway Limited	P R R	N Y - Chicago
Orange Blossom Special	S A L	N Y - Miami
Panama Limited	I C	Chicago - New Orleans.
Empire Builder	G N	Chicago - Seattle
City of Portland	U P	Chicago - Portland
City of San Francisco	U P & S P	Chicago - S F
Overland Limited	U P & S P	Chicago - S F
Golden State Limited	R I & S P	Chicago - Los Angeles
Sunset Limited	S P	Los Angeles - N O
North Coast Limited	N P	Chicago - Seattle

Growth of Railroads, 1865-1919

Year	Mileage
1865	35,000
1870	53,000
1880	93,000
1890	164,000
1900	193,000
1910	240,000
1916	254,000

Train Safety

Year	Billions of Pass. Miles	No. Persons Killed	Fatalities Per Billions Pass Miles
1890	11.8	286	24.2
1900	16.0	249	15.5
1910	32.3	324	10.0
1920	47.4	229	4.8

Railroad Passenger Travel

Year	Passengers (Millions)	Pass. Cars In Service	Miles Per Passenger	Per Revenue Mile in Cents
1890	492	26,820	24.0	2.167
1900	577	34,713	27.7	2.003
1910	972	47,179	33.2	1.938
1920	1.270	56,102	37.3	2.755

Notes: Chapter 2.2

1. Albro Martin, *Railroads Triumphant: The Growth, Rejection, and Rebirth of a Vital American Force*, 81-96.
2. John F. Stover, *The Life and Decline of the American Railroad*, 62.
3. John R. Stilgoe, *Metropolitan Corridor: Railroads and the American Scene*, 193.
4. George Will, in the *Arizona Republic*, May 16, 1991.
5. Martin, 81, 119, 195-196; Stover, 62.
6. *Ibid.*, 68-70.
7. Martin, 122.
8. Stover, 70-72, 77.
9. Otto Bettmann, *The Good Old Days—They Were Terrible*, 176-177.
10. Martin, 87.
11. Stilgoe, 54-55; Stover, 77.
12. Stilgoe, 66, 70.
13. Stover, 122-123; Stilgoe, 59-60.
14. *Ibid.*, 62-63, 66.
15. Stover, 93, 98.
16. Stilgoe, 66; Martin, 93.
17. Sources: Stover, 62, for growth; Stilgoe, 93, for safety, 124, for passenger travel.

2.3 There's No Business Like Race Business (I): Minstrelsy

The white may have educated the black; but that education has been returned in a dozen subtle ways. We taught him things; he taught us feelings. We gave him knowledge; he has helped to give us passion, which is not the meaner of the gifts. From the first, the white has been under some psychological compulsion to mimic the Negro, at first in ridicule and superiority, then in understanding and sympathy. The Negro, at almost every step, has participated in the meaning of our popular song.[1]

Despite the fact that slave art—and the art of the descendants of slaves—has left a major imprint on American culture, it does not appear that white Americans regard themselves, in any degree, as Africans culturally, a matter seldom discussed even in specialized studies of slavery. Few scholars, white or black, have so much as touched on this subject.[2]

RAGTIME ALMANAC[3]

African Contributions to American Culture

1. Proverbs, aphorisms, folktales, words
2. Artistic influences of African masks and sculptures
3. The effects of figure caricature on cartoons
4. Plants: okra, coffee, chocolate, sorghum, blackeyed peas
5. Gumbos, fish stews, deep fat frying
6. Cowboying and cattle herding
7. Elements of religious worship: possessional trances, speaking in tongues, ritual dancing, drumming, snake handling
8. Southern hospitality and formal courtesy
9. The rights of women to own property and to engage in trade
10. Contributions to types of American music: ragtime, blues, jazz, soul, reggae, bluegrass, rock
11. The banjo

African Americans, unlike their fellow immigrants, came involuntarily. Their legal status, from first arrival in 1619 to proclaimed emancipation in 1863, was that of "chattel," i.e., tangible movable or immovable property other than real estate. Unfortunately their new free status did not transform previously animate properties into recognized human beings. By emancipation time, African Americans, having been denied a human existence, had come to occupy a virtual existence, analogous to cyberspatial reality, as stereotypes. Perceived as subhuman beings, of inferior mentality, and unmoral, they were allowed no relationships with whites except master and servant.

This unequal situation underlies the universal fascination for whites of black life. Like good dogs they obeyed their masters with happy faces, and they loved to frisk and sing and laugh. Like livestock they were expected to reproduce, so whites seldom imposed any regulations (other than some degree of public order) on slave quarters after dark. After all, the reality was merely virtual, just stereotypes carrying on their simple unhuman lives. But tension built up between the actual and the virtual. It took little imagination to grasp that the slave, the one in bondage, had more freedom in his intimate, personal life. He expressed feelings and acted upon physical urges. He lived free from most cares, inhibitions, and the opinions of neighbors. One curious result of this intense white fascination with negritude was that white entertainers started "blacking up" and acting out on the stage their fantasies of the virtual existences of African Americans.

Sources indicate that by the late 1700's, performers were doing comic imitations of black folk.[4] By the mid-19 C, this activity had evolved into minstrelsy, a full evening's entertainment of songs, dances, and jokes presented by blacked-up whites. From the 1840's to 1900, the minstrel show was the favorite theatrical entertainment in the U.S. It constituted America's first artistic contribution to the stage, and it parallels the English music hall as the harbinger and premier manifestation of pop culture.

The most famous of the earlier "Ethiopian Delineators" (a common hoopla name for blackface performers) was Thomas Dartmouth Rice (1808-1860). Rice, an itinerant player from New York City, joined a stock company in Louisville, Kentucky, in 1828. At that time blackface entertainment, songs, dances, comic sketches, was interpolated between the acts of plays, something marginal, an intermezzo to brighten a serious mood. One day in a livery stable, Rice watched a rheumatic old black man shuffle through a funny little song and dance: "Weel about and turn about and do just so; ebery time I weel about, I jump Jim Crow." "Daddy" Rice (as he came to be known) soon presented his Jim Crow imitation on the Louisville stage where the song, his grotesque costume of rags and patches, and odd shuffling step and jump brought big applause. Everywhere audiences loved the Jim Crow number, and by 1836 when Rice took it to London, it had become a universal sensation.[5]

Following the Jim Crow character, the amusing black bumpkin or rustic, Rice's contemporary, George Washington Dixon (1808-1861), in his "Long Tail Blue" song gave us the urban, strutting Negro dandy in a swallow-tailed coat.[6] Thus were established what entertainment historian Ian Whitcomb calls "the two basic characters" of "stage Sambos" created by whites. Jim Crow, lazy and laid back, a figure of content on the old plantation, and Zip Coon, type A, overdressed, just as lazy, but a con artist floating along on luck and wits.[7]

After a decade, these solo turns gave way to the first group performance in New York in February 1843. There were four of them, the "Virginia Minstrels," just enough for the basic instrumental combo of violin, banjo, bone castanets ("Bones"), and tambourine ("Tambo"). The fiddler was Daniel Decatur Emmett (1815-1904), who not only shares credit with Edwin P. Christy (1815-1862) for originating this "Ethiopian Business," but went on to greater fame as the composer of "Dixie" (1859).[8]

Reflecting contemporary attitudes and show business practices, the form kept evolving but retained its basic elements. The perpetual scene was the southern plantation where a handsome, kindly master presided over a congregation of smiling black faces. The day's work is past, all hands have donned Sunday clothes, there is yet time to frolic a bit. The curtain rises on the performers seated in a row with the master figure, sometimes called "the Conversationalist," usually "Mr. Interlocutor," seated center, standing out in his formal wear and lone white face. "Tambo" and "Bones" sit at opposite ends of the line and do one-liners and little comic dialogs with the man in the center and each other. The quickness of wit of these "end men" paces the show and keeps the audience attentive—and friendly.

The minstrel show developed three parts: ensemble, "olio," and finale. At the outset the group performs together, singing in chorus with Bones vs. Tambo interludes. Part two, the olio, was a series of variety acts, allowing the principals to do their specialties (a source of the later vaudeville), after which the company returned for some kind of finale. Over time these varied; some were farces that poked fun at contemporary subjects, while presenting some interpolated songs. Other finales consisted of song-and-dance movements. The "walk-around" brought out the group to sing, play, and move in elaborate figures around the playing area. Emmett's "Dixie" was one of about thirty-five walk-around pieces that he composed during a long career. Its program title was "Plantation Song and Dance," and the chorus came in after the soloist with "Look Away! Look Away! Dixie Land." [9]

Surpassing Emmett as a composer of minstrel tunes, Stephen Collins Foster (1826-1864) never blacked up himself, precluded by his genteel background. Early on, he became friends with Daddy Rice (ca. 1845) and sold him a couple of songs ("Long Ago Day" and "This Rose Will Remind You").[10] He reached fame with "Oh! Susannah" in 1847, a song hummed and strummed and sung from the Atlantic tidewater to trail's end on the Pacific, which appeared in at least 20 editions by 1851. That year he produced his biggest seller "Old Folks At Home" ("Way Down Upon the Swanee River"), which sold 40,000 copies in 12 months. People never wearied of hearing these and others: "Camptown Races," "My Old Kentucky Home, Good Night," and "Old Black Joe"—in minstrel shows. People recognized Foster as the leading composer of American songs and have continued to enjoy them. Critics have also praised him, one (Gilbert Chase) commending a convergence of popular (folk) and cultivated (art) strains, and another (Wilfrid Mellers) points out that he transformed sadness into a nostalgia for happier times back home, that in an uncanny way, he felt and used the Negro's melancholy to touch the same emotions in white audiences.[11]

Certainly minstrelsy did more than entertain; for 75 years people preferred it over other entertainment. For many the light-hearted scene of happy days on the old plantation recalled their own "good, old days" on the farm before accepting wage slavery in town and city (some irony here). Besides nostalgia, another strong appeal of minstrelsy lay in its humor, which was essentially caricature. The sadness did not evoke the slave conditions of poverty, drudgery, brutality, and monotony. Slavery onstage was a happy situation, portraying a benevolent master who protected his slaves from a world too complex and harsh for their inferior capacities. Such harmless, stupid, and innocent creatures both amused and soothed the uncertainties of the audience.[12]

There appear to be several facets to minstrelsy's appeal: (1) The depictions of African-American inferiority reassured white males of their identity and sense of superiority. Most were urban workers, some uprooted from European homelands, and others native born but of rural origins. Recently arrived, both groups carried a burden of socio-economic and cultural anxieties. The crude stereotypes of Uncle Toms, Aunt Jemimas, and Jim Crows calmed their fears. (2) Most urban whites seldom encountered blacks as individuals. Blacks functioned as furniture in the background, performing menial tasks and passing from their daily drudgeries to homes on unknown streets. Even if the races shared a workplace, there were differences in job status. This separation-in-proximity resulted in compulsive curiosity and a fascination with physical features: color, noses, lips, width of mouth, hair, speech sounds, body types, and the parts hidden under clothing.

(3) The physical appeal reenforced the emotional appeal of stereotypes that were freer and less inhibited. As the songs revealed, black folk never resisted temptation—to fight, steal, eat, drink, laugh, or love—and they never knew guilt. Caught in the tension between their inhibitions and the imagined stereotypes, minstrelsy hinted at fuller satisfaction of hidden appetites. (4) If a blackface minstrel passed a joke about a prominent person, he didn't have to fear violence or a duel or a lawsuit. The offended party usually preferred to avoid further exposure. Thus minstrels served the century as jesters. (5) Slavery was a perpetual reproach to a proud democracy. In its benevolent portrayal of slavery, minstrelsy soothed the collective conscience, reenforced the stereotypes, and colored abolitionism fanatical.[13]

In the disruption of the War's end, talented African Americans headed north to attempt a living from entertaining. In April 1865 Charles B. Hicks, a fair-complexioned black man, led the flow by enlisting a dozen ex-slaves into the company of "The Original Georgia Minstrels." Northern audiences packed the theatres, full of curiosity to see the astonishing sight of unblacked black men. From then minstrelsy of both races dominated the stage until the turn of the century, and companies grew in both numbers and size. From about a dozen members, black companies more than doubled in size during the 1870's, with the larger ones reaching a hundred or more by the '90's. Increasingly the casts included women and skilled instrumentalists.[14]

Since hotels and restaurants excluded them, and as yet few existed to serve their race, these minstrel troupes ate and slept in their rented railroad cars. To get safely over the distance from tracks to theatre (a serious matter down south), the companies marched in full costume behind their wind band, which joined the orchestra for the performance. This parade, fronted by the company's gaudy banner, attracted the townsfolk to a free spectacle to raise interest in the following show. The good will thus generated brought in full houses and usually (though not always) preserved the company from violence or malicious mischief. Safety also required blacking up, as audiences expected to look up at black faces, definitely not at faces which could "pass" for white, i.e., resembled their own. Even up north, threats of boycott and violence forced black companies to maintain the convention of burnt cork.[15]

There was no escape from minstrel stereotypes: Sambo, Tambo, Bones, Jim Crow, and Zip Coon, all were perceived by whites as contemptible and/or pathetic. Though in their eagerness to succeed and survive, they infused a trite form with new vitality, the African-American thrust into minstrelsy also increased its decadence. While the choirs of the new black colleges created the exaltation of the "Negro Spiritual"[16], the overly familiar and threadbare antics of the minstrel stage lacked the vitality and richness of both the spirituals and the ragtime to come. African-American critic Alain Locke labeled the period "an age of slap-stick caricature," and while admitting the subsequent influence of minstrel tunes on popular song, he dubbed minstrels "pseudo-Negroes." He further demonstrated that the real peasant humor and the more authentic music of Afro-America emerged on other stages and in other media. Most minstrel songs were forgotten, the humor came from stereotypes, and the nostalgia for plantation life was phony. Like the other chief American entertainment, ca. 1870-1900, the circus, minstrelsy became gaudy and cheap.[17]

James Bland (1854-1911), unlike most black minstrelmen, didn't have a slave or peasant background. Born in New York City, he grew up in black middle class Washington, DC, where his father worked for the government as an examiner in the Patent Office. Bland attended Howard University where he studied music, but he abandoned both genteel background and higher education to enter minstrelsy to play the banjo and sing his own songs. In 1881 he toured England with Haverly's Colored Minstrels and made a startling discovery: The English admired him! They didn't merely applaud his turns in the show; they liked him as an individual performer. He was more than an anonymous grin in a wave of darkies. No violence or humiliation to fear. No problems or inconveniences in locating a bed or a meal. He remained twenty years, touring Britain and the Continent where he also achieved popularity in Germany. Europe loved Bland's songs and compared him favorably with Stephen Foster and John Philip Sousa. This is not surprising, as he composed over 700 songs, both sentimental ballads and jubilee-style spirituals. His best songs reveal a worthy successor to Foster, and a few have been popular for over a century: "Carry Me Back to Old Virginny," "Oh, Dem Golden Slippers," and "In the Evening By the Moonlight." Unfortunately he eventually felt the expatriate's anguish. Britain had treated him well, even tolerated his alcoholic lapses onstage, but by degrees over two decades, the British lost interest in him and in his music. Pop had arrived by then, bringing the indigenous songs of the music hall and the imports from America of the crude coonsong and exciting ragtime. When Bland recrossed the Atlantic in 1901, he found himself a has-been. His comebacks, including a musical, *The Sporting Girl*, failed. His songs lived on, but he was forgotten. He died "penniless" in Philadelphia in 1911. When the state of Virginia adopted "Carry Me Back To Old Virginny" in 1940 as its state song, no one recalled either Bland or his race.[18]

The violence and abuse that Bland escaped perpetually dogged black performers. Any show of spirit or resistance to white bullying could rapidly escalate. In 1902, shortly after arriving in New Madrid, Missouri, a player with the Georgia Minstrels, Louis Wright, and a fellow company member, on their way to the Opera House, were pelted with volleys of hard snowballs. The two begged for mercy, which only produced another volley of the slush-made snowballs. Wright, who tried to keep his dignity and avoid his Sambo role offstage, lost his temper and cursed the whites. These then passed the word that "a nigger had dared curse a white man." [19] Right after the curtain went down that evening, the males in the audience exited the front and collected at the stage entrance. At this point confusion took over; someone fired a shot, and someone else took a graze across the scalp. The mob accused the minstrels who claimed to be unarmed, and they were arrested and held in a dank jail. The next day, Sunday, each was taken across to the courthouse and questioned singly before an ad hoc "body of law-abiding citizens," and threatened with lynching if no one confessed. All professed ignorance of the shooting, and no guns were found. At midnight Wright was taken out again with the excuse of further testimony, but instead of a courtroom, Wright was immediately hanged "in front of a colored family's door." At 10:00 AM Monday, the mob cut him down, removed his finger rings, and placed his body in a box addressed to his mother at 3221 State Street, Chicago. Louis Wright, 22, played the trombone in the band. His accusers claimed to have seen the handle of a revolver in his pocket during the snowballing incident. "Several" other members of the company were shot and seriously wounded.[20]

Bluesman W. C. Handy, conductor for Mehara's Minstrels, relates several violent episodes (one cited in Chapter 5). Even their private railroad car in motion offered no safe haven:

> Orange was the Texas town we dreaded most. Whenever it became known to the home town mob that our show was routed their way, they would sit up all night waiting for the train to pass. Their conception of wild he-man fun was to riddle our car with bullets as it sped through the town. Our strategy was to extinguish the lights and lie quietly on the floor. Fortunately none of our company ever got killed during these assaults.[21]

The Mehara Minstrels' Pullman car had a hidden compartment under the floor where both food and guns were cached for emergencies, and where anyone in danger could be hidden. Handy himself hid from a Murfreesboro, Tennessee, sheriff because he had intercepted a blow aimed at a company member. In Tyler, Texas, smallpox broke out among the company, and the railcar was pushed onto a siding. During a siege of several days, the hidden provisions and arms enabled them to survive. They also kept off the mob by staging concerts and variety outside. They managed to get the victims off to hospitals and safety disguised as females, but the unfortunate publicity over the outbreak curtailed the tour.[22]

Minstrelsy flourished into the 1890's, but the rise of pop forced it to adapt. Nostalgia for the old plantation gave way to a greater variety of entertainment. The olio or variety segment expanded to include jugglers, acrobats, magicians, and other specialty acts. This and the third part of the show, consisting of a one-act comedy or an elaborately costumed cakewalk, offered to black performers a whole new range of opportunities. By 1900 vaudeville and the musical stage had freed African-American entertainers from the bondage of minstrelsy. It trained some great performers such as Ernest Hogan, Bert Williams, George Walker, Sam Lucas, W. C. Handy, Ma Rainey, and Bessie Smith, but it was poorly paid, gritty, degrading, comfortless, and sometimes dangerous.[23]

Notes: Chapter 2.3

1. Isaac Goldberg, *Tin Pan Alley*, 31.
2. Sterling Stuckey, "Slavery and the Freeing of American History Instruction," *Perspectives*, Vol. 33, No.4 (April, 1995): 13.
3. Craig Lockard, "Integrating African History Into the World History Course: Some Transgressional Patterns," *World History Bulletin*, Vol. X, No. 29 (Fall/Winter 1993-1994): 21; John Edward Philips, "The African Heritage of White America," in *Africanisms in American Culture*, 228-233.
4. Henry T. Sampson, *The Ghost Walks: A Chronological History of Blacks in Show Business*, 1; Thomas W. Morgan and William Barlow, *From Cakewalks to Concert Halls: An Illustrated History of African American Popular Music from 1895 to 1930*, 13.
5. Douglas Gilbert, *Lost Chords: The Diverting Story of American Popular Songs*, 17-18, for lyrics; Gilbert Chase, *America's Music from the Pilgrims to the Present*, 233-234; James Lincoln Collier, *The Rise of Selfishness in America*, 76; Morgan & Barlow, 13; Ian Whitcomb, *Irving Berlin and Ragtime America*, 86-87 note.
6. Chase, 233.
7. Whitcomb, *Berlin*, 86-87.
8. Chase, 232; Sampson, 2.
9. Chase, 239-243; Goldberg, 41-42; Sampson, 2-3.
10. Chase, 249-252.
11. *Ibid.*, 252-262; Wilfrid Mellers, *Music in a New Found Land: Themes and Developments in the History of American Music*, 346; Whitcomb, *Berlin*, 47-51.
12. Mellers, 246.
13. Hamilton Holt, Ed., *The Life Stories of Undistinguished Americans*, 14-17; Whitcomb, *Berlin*, 84-85, 100.
14. Sampson, 4-5, 38; Whitcomb, *Berlin*, 87, 92-93; Morgan & Barlow, 15.
15. W.C. Handy, *Father of the Blues: An Autobiography*, 43-44; Sampson, 4; Morgan & Barlow, 15-16.
16. Begun in 1871 by the Fiske Jubilee Singers.
17. Alain Leroy Locke, *The Negro and his Music*, 52-56; Burton W. Peretti, *The Creation of Jazz: Music, Race, and Culture in Urban America*, 14-15.
18. Chase, 330-331; Whitcomb, *Berlin*, 96-97.
19. Sampson, 247.
20. *Ibid.*, 246-248; Handy, 43. Handy corroborates this account which was written by a member of the company and appeared in the *Indianapolis Freeman* (March 15, 1902), but he adds that Wright did have a gun and shot in fear. Handy was not a witness.
21. *Ibid.*, 44.
22. *Ibid.*, 45-51.
23. Sampson, 38-39; Handy, 32-33. Sam Lucas was the first black male to play a major role in a film; Ma Rainey and Bessie Smith went on to legendary fame as blues singers.

2.4 The Social Evil!

> The streets were covered with men. Police were always in sight, never less than two together, which guaranteed the safety of all concerned. Lights of all color were glittering and glaring. Music was pouring into the streets from every house. Women were standing in the doorways, singing or chanting some kind of blues—some were happy, some very sad, some with the desire to end it all by poison, some planning a big outing, a dance or some other kind of enjoyment. Some were real ladies, in spite of their downfall, and some were habitual drunkards and some were dope fiends....
>
> Jelly Roll Morton[1]

The pre-W W I prostitution scene has become a legend. Towns were "wide open" to seekers of pleasure. The buyer was restricted only by the money in his pocket. Ten or twenty dollars bought the best of this nocturnal life: a young and beautiful woman in a clean and commodious feather bed. This was the "sporting life," just walk in on an instant all-night party. The friendly, talkative "Madam" escorted the customer into the parlor, called for good champagne, told the "Perfessor" to start playing lively songs and rags, and then lined up the girls, stylishly gowned, who each cooed her delight at hearing the client's name. After the welcoming came the pleasure of getting to know the chosen lady of the evening, a little champagne and conversation at one end of the sofa or in an intimate corner of one of the parlors. Their friendly basis established, the couple now exited up the stairs to an elegant boudoir, perhaps one with a mirrored ceiling. Following this interlude of life's supreme pleasure (across which we must draw a decorous veil), it was back to the party. More champagne, cordial chats with other goodfellows, likely a few songs around the piano, perhaps some requested numbers. For the free-spending sport the party lasted until dawn, the music, drink, and sex good to the last. So what if the tab ran to fifty or sixty dollars instead of the intended fifteen or twenty? Think of the happy and satisfying memories!

Embellished thusly, this recollected aura of glamour fades to ridicule. The truth is that the sporting life was on the wane when ragtime came along. House of prostitution, whorehouse, parlor house, house of assignation, cathouse, roadhouse, bagnio, brothel, bordello, nocturnal resort, call house, tenement (in context), "disorderly" hotel, house of horizontal refreshment—a clump of synonyms always points to something socially significant. Prostitutes also pursued their "profession" in drinking establishments: the saloon, concert-saloon, dancehall, cabaret, music hall, deadfalls (cheap wine and beer places), barrelhouses (if they were customers), cellar places (such as a rathskeller), and "blind pigs" or semi-secret unlicensed places.

By 1890 such facilities, which solicited male patronage with female companionship as a come-on, had become centrally concentrated in U.S. cities usually adjacent to the downtown sections. Such areas that featured vice and alcohol were generally called "Red Light Districts." There was never any legal sanction for these areas—public opinion violently opposed any kind of legalization, including regulation. However these "districts" did in fact materialize in the central city, as much for reasons of control as for the convenience of patrons. In a single location the whole smorgasbord of sin presented itself to customers, deliverymen with liquor, linens, and food, and to the police to maintain order and hold down crime. For all having business in the district, including also various collectors of bills and graft, it was extremely convenient to locate vice resorts near to hotels, theatres, and banks. The origin of the term hasn't been fixed, but one story points back to the coming of the railroads to Kansas City. There brakemen, coming off the trains with their red signal lamps, would hang them outside the houses when they entered. This indicated to the dispatcher where to find a brakeman when his train was about to pull out.[2] Subsequently Madams posted red lights to inform customers that they were open and ready for business. The most famous districts had names: Five Points, the Bowery, and the Tenderloin in New York; Chicago, the Levee and the Midway; New Orleans, Storyville; San Francisco, the infamous Barbary coast, Chinatown, and the uptown Tenderloin; Baltimore, the Block; Boston, the Hub; Denver, the Market Street Line; Kansas City, Petticoat Lane; St.Louis, Chestnut Valley. One source states that 72 cities had such districts.[3]

Every society has known some form of prostitution, definable by payment for sexual activity. If it occurs out-of-doors, it is called streetwalking. In or out, it is frequently termed "hooking," after the women who serviced the troops of General Hooker, military commander of the District of Columbia during the Civil War, who received the label of "Hookers." This form of the social evil persists in all cities; it would require a policeman on every block, out to the final suburb, to eradicate it—even temporarily. By the mid-19th Century the "house" or brothel had become the principal venue in sex-selling. Historians believe it to be a social outcome of the Industrial Revolution's second wave, a time when heavy industry appeared and hired chiefly men. This concentrated hordes of young males in the fast-growing cities. Released from the restraints of farm life and small towns, lacking the companionship and support of families and churches, and lonely after long, boring days of work, these youths were desperate for both recreation and companionship. No one had thought to make provision for such needs. There were yet no YMCA's, no public libraries, no church "youth groups," no associations for athletics or hobbies, and hardly any associations for meeting "respectable" women. Clean, family-oriented vaudeville didn't become universal until the late 1880's.

Most nights, a man just fell into bed after eating, knowing he had to be at the factory gate when the last whistle summoned at dawn. Saturday night promised a longer sleep on the Sabbath, a dull day of church-going when the sight of families together brought a sad reminder of exile from a happier past. The only amelioration in this drab existence, the only variety available to the working man in that epoch before paid vacations—and instant gratifications—was a "Saturday Night." As the old song tells us:

> On a Saturday night,
> Dear old Saturday night,
> When your pockets are filled with coin,
> Everybody is asked to join;
> On a Saturday night,
> Dear old Saturday night;
> The next day is Sunday,
> But still on a Monday,
> We dream of our Saturday night.[4]

Which meant chiefly going out with a mate or two, or alone, to a place where drink was sold, where lights were brighter, people more open and friendly, music playing, crowds on the pavement, and to imbibe the drinks that put some feeling into all this. Pleasure begets expectations, stimulated by the abundance of females in the district. If there was a little money in the pocket, there was a woman after it, in the saloon, the dancehall, or the fifty-cent or dollar "parlor house." He might wake up on Sunday with a sore head and some guilt about the sinning and lost cash, but that is all the city offered.[5]

Thus the brothel flourished as the 19th-century center of the sporting male subculture. Here was a new freedom of available sex with no traditional restraints. Sex was open and affordable. In the cheaper places ($.50) men just lined up, some on benches sliding along by degrees, standees waiting for the next space on a bench, until their turn came. No pretence of conversation, no picking and choosing, they accepted the next available woman in her kimono, followed her to a room to return in 8-12 minutes. Sex was almost a public act in such places, in the heyday of the brothel.[6]

The inmates who catered to these sports were equally a product of the Industrial Revolution. This "second wave" denied women the better jobs in factories, mines, and railroads. The young, single women who migrated to the cities along with the men had to accept work in textile mills, shops, and stores, and as domestics. They received much lower wages, seldom enough to cover rent, food, and clothing. Their lot was exploitation. Twenty cents a day left little when a room cost a dollar a week. Usually economics alone did not drive women into prostitution (see Chapter 23 for reasons), but temptation was great when the earnings were five times what a maid or shop girl received.[7]

Alas the stakes were far more dire than poverty. That single step into sex outside marriage was fatal, the death of "respectability." Any girl who simply "gave in" to some man wore the scarlet letter for the remainder of her miserable, short, and nasty life. No circumstances were deemed mitigating; prostitutes and "ruined" women both received the label of whore. There were two sound reasons for the chastity imperative: pregnancy and disease. People knew little about contraception or where to obtain it, and sexually transmitted diseases were incurable. The Victorian view was absolute: a woman was either pure or depraved. Pure women were believed to possess little or no sexuality. The other kind of woman craved it. Which left men unsure, ambivalent. A wife who enjoyed sexual relations with her husband probably desired to have other men too. Such was thus <u>whorish</u> behavior. Men and women shared bedrooms chiefly for procreation. A woman who behaved lasciviously might not turn out to be a fit mother. Every well-reared bride learned all this from her mother: sex was for having children and not for enjoyment. Husbands desired no other kind of wives.[8]

But men had to have it. The male sex drive was strong and passionate. What was a man with an asexual wife to do? He couldn't force her to accept all of his animal demands and emotions. His only "solution" was to unload all his pent-up desires onto prostitutes. Some well-to-do men "kept" mistresses, even had second families, dividing their time between two households. One heard of this among railroad men and traveling salesmen. But whether they lived bigamously or resorted to the occasional whore, the man was caught in an uncomfortable moral dilemma. Such consortings denied God's commandment, which could be punished by the coming of a dreaded disease. Pasteur's concept of a "germ theory" of disease was not yet well assimilated, and most believed that any sickness manifested the "judgment of God." The highminded man perceived danger in his sex drive and believed he had to control it. For him the solution was to devote his energies to business, attend to the precepts and observances of his religion, and simply keep his thoughts clean. But many lacked the strength—or low sex drive—to focus constantly on virtuous things. So the troubled male never found his way out of the woods on this question. If his wife pleased him she likely was a "bad" woman; if she was "good," possessed of little or no sexual urges (or hid them), he could only suffer, try to ignore the problem, or else sin, thereby bringing both body and soul into peril.

This conflicted state of affairs resulted in a kind of toleration. Victorians looked the other way and did not criminalize prostitution. They condemned it in public, but in private saw necessity and tacitly tolerated it. Besides, prostitution furnished much of the income of police, landlords, procurers, madams, doctors, politicians, druggists, and liquor dealers. Also the powers that governed associated prostitution with the lower classes, immigrants, and nonwhites, elements that did not threaten the lives and neighborhoods of the higher classes. In addition it was a prop to the patriarchal control of the male. The only safe place for a woman lay behind the walls of masculine protection. If she rebelled and ventured outside on her own, she would fall into a pit of degradation among depraved and evil creatures. The unsatisfied male could always find solace for his sexual dilemma in the power he held over his women.[9]

However as the new century approached, women increasingly questioned their condition of vulnerability and dependence. They began to want things: education, more personal freedom, control over money and property, the vote, occupations. They didn't demand the orgasm—probably few even knew about it—but they wanted the men to change their behaviors, to spend leisure time at home and away from saloons and brothels. In the 1870's they had determinedly fought off attempts to regulate the social evil, demanding that it be eradicated. This controversy ran on for decades. Men sullenly resisted, attacking feminist reformers as wrongfully rebellious against male authority and as unfeminine. The women were divided by their causes of feminism, temperance, and social purity, but they learned in time to cooperate and join forces. And their forces increased with each success. They managed to stop all but one attempt to regulate prostitution (in New Orleans). County by county and state by state, they brought in prohibition. They even got the vote in a few places, starting in Wyoming Territory in 1869. They won the right to control property in most places. By the 1890's reformers could see enough progress to be certain that all their goals would be achieved within a few decades. As ragtime swept the country in the late 1890's, the forces of moral purity understood that the new century would witness the final victory over organized prostitution. The reforming Progressives would declare Victorian toleration of the social evil unacceptable.[10]

Notes: Chapter 2.4

1. Al Rose, *Storyville, New Orleans*, 114.
2. Ruth Rosen, *The Lost Sisterhood: Prostitution in America, 1900-1918*, 105.
3. Howard B. Woolston, *Prostitution in the United States Prior to the Entrance of the United States into the World War*, 119-120.
4. Source of song unknown to author.
5. Rose, *Storyville*, 161.
6. Timothy J. Gilfoyle, *City of Eros: Prostitution and the Commercialization of Sex, 1790-1920*, 163-165.
7. Rosen, 3; Herbert Asbury, *The Barbary Coast: An Informal History of the San Francisco Underworld*, 310-311.
8. Gilfoyle, 181.
9. Rosen, 4-7.
10. Ibid., 7-13.

3. The Music Business: Puttin' On the Hits

RAGTIME ALMANAC

Increases In Music Copyrights [1]

1880 5628
1885 6808
1890 9132
1895 18,563
1902 19,706
1905 24,595
1910 24,345
1915 21,406
1920 29,151

Coming along after baseball in the 1870's and vaudeville in the 1880's, popular music rose like the sun over the 1890's. A century later, it fills the globe with a rainbow of varieties. Thus far no machine or computer has fabricated a song—a possibility if "artificial intelligence" becomes a reality. But from the outset, during the late 1880's and 1890's, popular songs and dances were developed and marketed as products. Such music was "manufactured" by a publishing process and distributed, like produce or textiles, through wholesalers or jobbers to retailers. Producers competed strenuously to demonstrate their products, and retailers went after customers with cutthroat tactics. By 1907 a New York department store had gone to the extreme of offering sheet music for one cent a copy, dumping 20,000 copies in a single hour. [2]

Demand caused this. Having heard it first in vaudeville houses and on other stages, the new urban populations craved for more and converged on all locations of presentation. Besides theatres and places that pushed drinks, there were soon eating places featuring entertainment and dancing (cabarets), dance palaces, the silent movie storefront places called "nickelodeons," mechanical instruments with coin slots. For the more affluent classes, there was home entertainment. Though of poor audio quality, many enjoyed the phonograph, which best reproduced the percussive sounds of brass and banjos. (Not until the 1920's would records achieve audio quality that outsold sheet music.) The favored home instrument was the versatile piano, long a principal item of conspicuous consumption in Victorian homes where genteelly reared daughters cultivated modest musical skills, to entertain the family as well as to attract suitors. From 1870 on, the percentage growth of piano production exceeded population growth by five or six times. This peaked in 1909 with 364,545 pianos produced by 295 separate manufacturers, amounting to sales of $58,500,000.[3]

The sunshine of pop brightened the new world of entertainment during 1890-1895 when the number of music copyrights issued by the patent office doubled, from 9132 in 1890 to 18,563 in 1895. (See Almanac table above.) Before this, music publishing had been decentralized and local. Without a distribution system, most sheet music had been produced in nearby cities, or else music store proprietors published local compositions using the closest job printers with music-publishing capability. During the 1880's some publishers, seeking to expand distribution, placed copies of songs with salesmen of other products as a side venture. Some of these musically inclined drummers seemed to have glimpsed the future and soon left off their gloves and utensils to specialize in music. A few of these then composed and published their own songs, and the successful ones became the group of publishers in the New York cluster known as "Tin Pan Alley." These included the Witmark brothers, Joseph Stern, F. A. Mills, T. B. Harms, Maurice Shapiro, and Harry Von Tilzer.[4]

The exemplar of these entrepreneurial folk was Charles K. Harris (1867-1930). Working as a bellhop and banjo player in the area of the southern shore of Lake Michigan, Harris began composing in his teens. Upset by a tiny royalty check (85 cents from the Witmarks), at age 18 in 1885, he opened a small office in Milwaukee after inducing two friends to back him with a $1000 investment. The sign out front proclaimed:

> Charles K. Harris
> Banjoist and Song Writer
> Songs Written to Order

Rent and overhead took $10.00 a month, but the first year ended with a $3000 profit. Harris learned a few major lessons early and thereafter seldom deviated. These were to push the song hard by advertising and by getting performers to plug it; then make the appeal to women because they bought the music; finally tell a story which easily captures feminine attention and emotions. This meant love ballads, tears, and heavy sentiment.

These formulas paid off with "After the Ball" in 1892. In the story a young man, after leaving his date for a moment, returns to find her in the arms of another. Stalking angrily away without a confrontation, he never sees her again. Years later, he accidentally discovers that the other man was a long-lost brother. The chorus, following each verse, expresses the residual sadness:

> After the ball is over
> After the break of morn,
> After the dancers' leaving,
> After the stars are gone.
> Many a heart is aching
> If you could read them all;
> Many the hopes that have vanished
> After the ball.

This was Tin Pan Alley's first major hit. Harris placed it in vaudeville with the star May Irwin and got it interpolated into the very popular Broadway touring show *A Trip to Chinatown*. John Philip Sousa admired it enough to program it for his daily concerts on the Midway at the Chicago Fair. During 1893-94 it set a sales record, eventually, over twenty years, selling 10,000,000 copies! It transformed Harris from small-time producer to a wealthy major publisher, bringing in $25,000 per month during the mid-1890's. He was king of the Alley for this first pop decade, and while he inflexibly stuck to his formulas and rejected the ragtime and syncopation that replaced them, he continued to prosper in the business. Other hits included the teary "Hello, Central, Give

Me Heaven," about the little girl who tries to phone her dead mother. Success also came with nostalgia songs, such as "Better Than Gold, Or Three Wishes," "'Mid the Green Fields of Virginia," and "Just Behind the Times." If Harris' times grew a bit thinner after 1900, he turned out a couple of major hits as late as 1909: "I Wonder Who's Kissing Her Now" and "Heaven Will Protect the Working Girl"—a humorous number![5]

Harris, as shown, pursued music as a business using processes of composition, promotion, and sales. By the mid-1890's these aggressive new men of the music business were concentrating at the center of New York's entertainment district. They moved into the low-rent areas of old brownstones once inhabited by the well-to-do who had forsaken them for more fashionable locations uptown. Tin Pan Alley, following northward-shifting locales of theatres, restaurants, bars, brothels, and hotels, never settled down in one place. From the Bowery after the Civil War, it reached 14th Street near Union Square during the 1880's, moved up to 28th Street between Sixth Avenue and Broadway in the 1890's, and began shifting again after 1903 up into the low Forties. But the name itself transcended Manhattan; it applied to all publishers of hits distributed nationally.

Metaphorically publishers were the hunters and show people the big game. Promotion aimed for performances on all musical stages. Performers, particularly vaudeville big-timers, were aggressively persuaded—even physically dragged, it has been affirmed—to visit a publisher's "professional department" to hear songs demonstrated by the firm's composers and "pluggers" of potential hits. Vaudevillians toured the provinces and insured the wide diffusion necessary to foment national demand for a tune. The relationship soon became symbiotic; the "house" composers tailored their products to the needs of headliners. Nothing hit-or-miss in this process: songs were intended to showcase the talents of particular "artists" (and publishers rejected compositions considered unsuitable or too difficult). If nothing satisfied the visiting artist, the man at the piano stood ready to whip up a new one to specifications, often on the spot if juices were flowing. Introducing a song brought both payola and publicity. Payola could be cigars, drinks, dinners, jewelry, and even cold cash. Publicity resulted in advertising and feature stories, and it put the performer's name and picture on the cover. Cover art, one of the new things under the sun of pop, conferred upon the artist an aura that was major glamour. For the buyer this was irresistible, a link in the imagination to a celebrity, someone already known in the big-time or to be experienced on future bills. Many famous graphic artists executed these song fronts, including such comic strippers and caricaturists as Rudolph Dirks, Bud Fisher, George McManus, and Al Hirschfeld.

Outside publishers' studios, song pluggers worked long days. All retailers employed them (music stores, five-and-dimes, departments of major stores) to demonstrate any tune plucked from the racks by a customer. It cost nothing to hear a piece marked from 20 to 50 cents to find out if it was enjoyable and playable. Elsewhere pluggers worked excursion boats and any large gatherings like picnics, ballgames, carnivals, amusement parks, even political rallies (a regular occurrence in that oratory-oriented time), wherever "chorus slips," sheets with words, could be passed out for communal singing. At night song pluggers turned up in restaurants, beer joints, theatres at intermission, brothels on occasion, and anywhere crowds collected and there was a piano or an orchestra willing to oblige for a little payola. If the song was already featured on a bill, the plugger, by prearrangement, would rise in the spotlight, and sing several verses to teach the song.[6]

Closely neighbored along 28th Street, the publishers subdivided their spacious old brownstones into cubicles, each with a secondhand, untuned piano, and somewhat larger studios and rehearsal rooms. With the windows raised in warm weather, the street filled up with the cacophony of dozens of pianos, vocalizing singers, a few blaring horns, tap-dancing feet. This leaves no uncertainty as to the source of "Tin Pan Alley," but historians of the Street cherish an oft-told anecdote, of variant tellings, which certainly is true in part. However it seems probable that such an aptly descriptive tag occurred independently to many imaginative souls.

One of the first inhabitants of this famous street and one of its greatest "characters" was Monroe H. Rosenfeld (1862-1918), songwriter and journalist. Like Charles K. Harris, "Rosie" broke into the business with songs of sentiment and tears. He produced his share of hits, including "Johnny, Get Your Gun," "With All Her Faults I Love Her Still," and "Take Back Your Gold." Rosie was a raffish type, a bohemian sqanderer who frittered his advances on poker, horses, and women, an avoider of landladies who never seemed to have a permanent address. Living on his wits, he sometimes tried to market music he'd heard recently—to as many publishers as would allow him in the door. His publisher Edward Marks referred to him as a "melodic kleptomaniac." When his back hit the wall, he resorted to the rubber check. He limped, and a story tells that on one occasion, as he attempted to foist a bad check on a bank, he fell two storeys from a window backing away from the police. He also hired others to flesh out his musical ideas with notes and lyrics, calling the practice "subcontracting."

The time eventually arrived when Rosie ran out of salable tunes and other people's money. But an old friend, an editor at the *New York Herald*, rescued him with a commission to produce a series on the pop industry along 28th Street. Out of this came the famous anecdote of his interview with composer-publisher Harry Von Tilzer (1872-1946). Harry—he was born Gumm, but took his mother's maiden name of Tilzer, then tarted it up with the "Von"—ran away from his Indiana home, played first for a circus, then in a vaudeville band. He reached New York in 1891, succeeded as a songwriter in 1898 with "My Old New Hampshire Home," and became a partner of Shapiro, Bernstein. His biggest hits include "A Bird in a Gilded Cage"(1900) and "Wait Till the Sun Shines, Nellie"(1905). He also composed rags (*Cubanola Glide* {1909}, *Jamaica Jinger* {1912}), coon songs ("Rufus Rastus Johnson Brown"), plus such major sellers as "Down Where the Wurzburger Flows"(1902), which recalled a popular brand of beer and not a waterway, and that perennial favorite of quartets and bathroom singers: "I Want a Girl Just Like the Girl That Married Dear Old Dad."

In the interview one of them (depending upon the version) indicated the crescendo of noise flowing into the street. Rosie in his article credited himself with the observation that this musical noise resembled kitchen clatter. In another version Von Tilzer felt pity for the shabby state his friend had fallen into and, to help him a little, graciously offered "Tin Pan Alley" gratis. In return he asked for the credit, but Rosie, true to his tendency to piggyback on the inspiration of others, passed off this smart phrase as his own.[7]

Between 1900 and 1910, about 100 songs sold over 1,000,000 copies to a national population of 90,000,000. Since 600,000 constituted a hit, 1,000,000 or more was a "big hit." Before Tin Pan Alley, sheet music often cost a dollar. Subsequently the volume increases of the mid-1890's and the sudden eruption of new publishers drove the price down to forty cents. By 1900 it had fallen to twenty-five cents, and eventually to a mere ten cents. As noted above, there could also be "sales"—not for clearance of old stock but to weaken competitors—where case lots of sheet music were dumped for a single cent.[8]

Such was pop, the result of the new urban society's cultural needs. Demand became insatiable because of the growth of the new entertainment media:

Vaudeville

Musical stage
  1.Operetta
  2.Revue
  3.Burlesque

Silent Films

Mechanical music
  1.Player piano
  2.Phonograph
  3.Juke box

Home piano and organ

    These added up to a whole new realm of entertainment, a variety and a profusion never before available to so many people. The rural milieu, which knew chiefly church music and country dancing, was vanishing rapidly. The elite retained their "high" culture of opera, the "legitimate" stage, art music, literature, and visual arts, but pop now competed, democratically, for the patronage and attention of all. Those who claimed to be genteel and who stigmatized pop with such epithets as "common," "low," or "trivial," were often dissemblers and hypocrites who, right after their moral sermonettes, would sneak off to vaudeville matinees or even burlesque shows. And who could resist an infectious tune like "In the Good Old Summertime," "By the Light of the Silvery Moon," or "Put On Your Old Gray Bonnet"? [9]

Notes: Chapter 3

1. John Edward Hasse, "The Creation and Dissemination of Indianapolis Ragtime," 214.
2. David A. Jasen, *Tin Pan Alley: The Composers, the Songs, the Performers*, xx.
3. Craig Roell, *The Piano in America, 1890-1940*, 32.
4. Jasen, TPA, xvi-xvii.
5. Ronald L. Davis, *A History of Music in American Life*, II, 175-178; Russell Sanjek, *American Popular Music and its Business: The First Hundred Years*, II, 321-322; Ian Whitcomb, *Irving Berlin and Ragtime America*, 55-60; Gilbert Chase, *America's Music,* 337-338.
6. Davis, II, 178-181; Jasen, TPA, xv-xxiv, 1-7; Chase, 335-339.
7. Davis, II, 181; Whitcomb, *Berlin*, 60-63; Chase, 338-339; Jasen, TPA, xv.
8. Whitcomb, *Berlin*, 40-41; Jasen, TPA, xx.
9. Hasse, "Creation," 214-215; Roell, 31-32.

4. TR: Reforming the Civil Service and the Police

In 1886 TR rode away from the ranching fiasco and reset himself on tracks that ran toward political destinations. First came his party's call to run for mayor of New York City. This was a three-way race against popular Democrat Abraham Hewitt and the United Labor Party's Henry George, well known author of the reformist work *Progress and Poverty* (1879) (which advocated the panacea of a "single tax" on land). The situation for the Republicans was hopeless, and a reluctant Theodore took on this sacrificial chore chiefly out of party loyalty. Although he ran actively and spoke as often as possible, he came in a poor third, 8000 votes behind third-party George, and 30,000 votes behind Hewitt. George's fiery speeches had drawn large crowds, and many Republicans, fearful of Socialist and radical politics, deserted their man to back the able and respected Hewitt. At 28, and the youngest man ever to run for the office, Theodore had to endure ridicule as well as defeat. But it had provided useful practical experience, and he came out of it with a very good party standing.[1]

Political duties behind him, the next item on the agenda was remarriage. The following month (December 1886), a steamship took Theodore to England where he married his lifelong friend Edith Kermit Carow. Three years younger, Edith had been younger sister Corinne's playmate, regularly at the Roosevelt home, almost a family member. The Carows like the Roosevelts had been in commerce and shipping, but their business had declined after the easier money of the Civil War years. Financial failure combined with the alcohol problem of Edith's father had culminated in a troubled and broken home. Eventually Edith's mother and sister Emily decided that their dwindled dollars would stretch further on the Italian Riviera, but Edith chose to go it alone in her own country, rather than put up with a complaining mother, an unhappy sister, and fewer economic and marital prospects in a foreign country.

Edith it seems had grown up loving Theodore (always the center of Roosevelt attention). Until Alice Lee overwhelmed him, he had kept company with Edith on Harvard vacations and often written to her. The wedding of October 27, 1880, had apparently blighted the future for nineteen-year-old Edith, who seemed to face a sad and lonely life of semi-charity as governess or tutor. Females of the genteel class had few occupational choices, but if Alice Lee Roosevelt had lived, very possibly Edith might have done much better, becoming headmistress of a finishing school or a successful writer. Throughout her life, she was not only respected but looked up to with awe for her intelligence, acquired knowledge, ability to manage, sensitivity, and strength of personality.

At Alice's death, TR had pledged himself not to remarry (his fundamental flaw was saying never) He turned baby Alice over to his mature sister Anna ("Bamie" usually, but her niece Eleanor Roosevelt called her "Auntie Bye") and resided with them on his frequent hiatuses from the West. Edith, as a continuing friend of the Roosevelt sisters, visited frequently, but saw their brother seldom or never. Apparently he had asked that Edith not be present when he was there, and Edith, extremely sensitive, required only a few hints to comply with this (temporary) rejection. For the next two years Theodore nursed his grief and loyalty to Alice's memory behind the screen of the proprieties of grief. Then came the day when he happened into the house and accidentally (?) encountered Edith. Abruptly the moratorium on the relationship ended, and they came rapidly to an understanding, not having to go through the leisurely stages of Victorian courtship. Although comfortable, the relationship turned out to be as emotional as it was companionable. She ultimately bore him five children (and miscarried several times afterwards in the White House). Years later, stating his views of an ideal marriage in a letter to a friend, TR was certainly drawing on his own experience:

> I think that the love of the really happy husband and wife—not purged of passion, but with passion heated to a white heat of intensity and purity and tenderness and consideration, and with many another feeling added thereto—is the loftiest and most ennobling influence that comes into the life of any man or woman, even loftier and more ennobling than wise and tender love for children…[2]

During 1887-1888, following their return from England, TR occupied himself writing and starting a life with Edith in his newly completed home on Sagamore Hill at Oyster Bay on the North Shore of Long Island, New York. Many assumed that defeat in the mayoral contest had brought an early end to his political aspirations. One publication, *Puck,* bestowed a rather mean political epitaph:

> Bright visions float before your eyes of what the Party can and may do for you. We wish you a gradual and gentle awakening. We fear the Party cannot do much for you. You are not the timber of which presidents are made. [3]

Not heeding this derisive stab, he went out to campaign vigorously for Benjamin Harrison in the election of 1888. Then he waited to see if indeed the party would do something for him. Thanks to mentor, now Senator, Henry Cabot Lodge and other friends, Harrison found a spot for him as one of the Commissioners of the recently created (1883) Civil Service.

The Roosevelt who assumed his first national post in May 1889 was 30, married a second time, father of a first son, Theodore, Jr. b. 1887, a daughter Alice, age five, from his first marriage, and a second son, Kermit, born just before taking office. Theodore was no longer the effete-appearing, foppish political dilettante perceived until recently by the press (see above quotation). He had become tough, vigorous, and combative; the old image of the "silk stocking" politician was speedily forgotten. [4]

TR was well qualified for the job secured through party influence and presidential patronage. Back in the New York Assembly he had combined his anti-machine faction of "Roosevelt Republicans" with Governor Grover Cleveland's anti-Tammany Democrats to put through reform legislation to create a state Civil Service Commission. [5] Subsequently President Cleveland (1885-89) had extended the Federal civil service rolls. (Established by the Pendleton Act of 1883 in response to the 1881 assassination of President James Garfield by a disappointed job seeker.) Commissioner Roosevelt now saw himself as continuing the work of the previous president, colleague in reform, and fellow New Yorker. The system continued to be puny with most jobs still subject to the spoils approach. Although Cleveland had defied traditional political powers and added 7000 positions to the classified list, Harrison felt tremendous pressure to carry on with the spoils system. At the outset he yielded to the politicos and turned out the Democratic appointees of his predecessor. Thus TR came into office with virtually no leverage for his perceived mission of fattening the classified list at the expense of the spoils of office used as currency to pay political debts. Harrison's chief spoilsman, Postmaster General John Wanamaker (the department store magnate), quickly filled 30,000 Third Class Postmasterships with loyal Republicans.

Wanamaker's dominant position as chief contributor to Harrison's campaign, party leader, and dispenser of patronage forced TR to lie low and bide his time until the corruption waxed great enough to supply the weapons to attack so powerful a figure. The next year (1890) a diligent TR uncovered irregularities in Civil Service appointments, including fraudulent examinations and corruption on Post Office appointments, which led him to demand that Wanamaker dismiss certain appointees. An outright refusal produced a major clash, exposures of scandals, a demand for a Congressional investigation, and plenty of headlines. This first national exposure placed Roosevelt at the center of a storm hurling thunderbolts of righteousness at a corrupt system. The Democratically controlled House of Representatives was very pleased to investigate and allow its hearings to become a platform for the maverick Civil Service Commissioner. An aroused public condemned the spoils system, ironically turning TR's victory into a major blow to his chief's (Harrison's) reelection. Some years later, Harrison gave this sour, but not altogether unfair, comment on TR's performance: "The only trouble I ever had with managing him was that…he wanted to put an end to all the evil in the world between sunrise and sunset." [6]

TR proved too popular for Harrison to fire, and subsequently Cleveland, back in 1893 for term two, chose to retain the reforming Commissioner despite the party difference. This enabled him to serve six years, enough time for significant achievements, not the least of which was the increased importance and stature of the Civil Service Commission. Second the classified list more than doubled with the transfer of 26,000 more jobs out of patronage. Third TR reformed the appointment process by improving civil service examinations, making the questions pertain to the job.

Besides a minor place in the history books as a major reformer of government service, Theodore Roosevelt gained familiarity with national government and an acquaintance with the inhabitants of the capital city. He and Edith became friends of the leaders of Washington culture and society, including the historian Henry Adams, his father's old Civil War friend John Hay, the British author Rudyard Kipling, members of the diplomatic services, plus such future leaders and colleagues as William Howard Taft, Solicitor General under Harrison and his own ultimate successor. He came out of the civil service experience with a national reputation. If regular, conservative Republicans retained a dubious view of him, the reform-minded ones sensed a dynamic leader for the future. [7]

However, by 1895 it was time to leave a Democratic administration that had failed to alleviate the catastrophic mid-1890's Depression that had inflicted poverty and hunger on too much of the population. Time to return to political roots and Republican fold and prepare a role in the 1896 election. Thus he was very receptive to a call to head the Police Commission of the recently elected reform administration of his native New York City. Having voted out the corrupt Democrats of Tammany, the City, now on the high side of its political cycle, had elected a "clean slate" of "honest" officials. This was only an intermission during which a few idealists would fail to change the corrupt system of ward politics, favors, bribes, insider information, and cheating on contracts. These reformers failed because in its way, the dirty system did what no clean system could at that time: It filled the real needs of people, doling out charity, jobs, and emergency aid to loyal voters. This was the only "support system," and the providers were the ward leaders who, in effect, recycled some of the public money back to the public. The public voted where they survived.

As President of the Police Commission of NYC, TR knew what he intended to do: enforce the laws and reform the police. He tore into the job with a force and vigor that surprised the city, not only felons and crooked cops, but also his three well meaning but more cautious colleagues on the Commission. Instead of bureaucratically ducking the press (the usual practice of those in office), his door was continually open to newsmen. He told them what he was trying to do and invited suggestions and comments—something seldom or never done. He let them follow him around on supervisory runs. [8] He suddenly appeared at known trouble spots to check on law enforcement. He often did this late at night in high crime areas. He fired men he caught derelict in duty or taking bribes, but he also visited his men to talk and learn their problems. This was a continuing investigation to uncover the problems and requirements of the department and to learn what was happening in the streets and in the vice resorts. When he found a hardworking officer getting the job done, he promoted him. [9]

But if the NYPD remembered TR for strenuous supervision and lasting reforms, his fellow New Yorkers mostly perceived his tenure as bogged down in an angry controversy that defied resolution: enforcement of the closing laws on drinking places. Refusing all compromises or exceptions, he staked out the absolutist position on all law enforcement. Police integrity drove him out on nightly forays to arrest violators. Eventually persistence succeeded in forcing licensed bars and saloons to close on time, although this success drove all of the late-night business into clandestine (illegal) after-hours places, including houses of ill repute. And these charged much higher prices.

Beyond this very partial victory stood a wall resistant to all battering: Sunday drinking customs. Although state law prohibited the sale of alcohol on Sunday, people universally ignored it, believing that having a drink on their one day off from work was a right. Legislators understood this perfectly and wanted to repeal such an intolerable regulation, but they feared the wrath of the churches at a time when Prohibition sentiment was on the upswing. However, unlike the Upstate areas, the City was not a WASP-ruled community where a dominant minority could force its group will on an immigrant population. Most New Yorkers belonged to European subcultures which exhibited no puritanical or anti-alcohol attitudes. The reverse was true; these ethnic groups relished their wines, beers, and spirits and were quick to resent anything that restrained or limited their folkways. Particularly the German-Americans, New York's second largest ethnic community (760,000),[10] long established, hard working, and respected, who socialized each weekend in their beergardens. Sunday after church was the time to relax, eat, drink, and dance the waltz or two-step to an ompah band. Entire families filled the tables wholesomely enjoying themselves.

Then came this wild man Roosevelt padlocking the doors on Sunday, taking away the families' pleasures. Just before the 1895 elections, this swelling discontent boiled over when angry Germans staged a parade and protest rally. In such a spirit they invited the Commissioner of Police to be on the reviewing stand and see for himself how decent people felt about his interference. To everyone's surprise he did show up, taking his place and watching quietly as grim marchers strode by carrying signs and banners inscribed "Roosevelt's Russian Rule," "Roosevelt's Razzle Dazzle Reform Racket," and "Send the Police Czar to Russia." Word soon reached paraders that the object of their antagonism was up on the stand, and they craned their necks as they went by. Near the end, one short-sighted protestor shouted, "Wo ist der Roosevelt?" and a grinning TR leaned out, thumped his chest, and shouted back, "Hier bin ich!" Which caused a huge laugh and a friendly conclusion of the affair. [11]

This was only comic relief, and 80% of the German vote switched to the Democrats.[12] Then the legislature compounded the disaster in an attempt to ameliorate the problem. Lacking the guts to defy prohibitionist sentiment with a simple repeal, the Assembly passed a new law (Raines Law) excepting hotels, which could now serve liquor with food on the Sabbath. This sloppily drawn measure permitted every bar and saloon with an upstairs or backroom space to put a "hotel" sign out front. Prostitutes quickly took over these facilities, and the nightly turnover, which could run thirty minutes a trick, put a rich windfall into the saloon owner's pockets.

For TR this scandal of the "Raines Law hotels" amounted to another major setback, which, combined with the election defeat, turned much of the NY Republican Party against him. It fixed his image in the eyes of the bosses as a "loose cannon," and a threat to their dominion. Ironically TR had done his duty against his own convictions: he was anti-prohibition and fully believed that government could not and should not prevent people from drinking.[13]

A greater irony, apparent only afterwards, was that this "failure" gave his career a major boost. Newspapers outside New York (including the *London Times*) portrayed him as a heroic reformer, establishing his national reputation for honesty and strength. His being always open and friendly to journalists brought him the big pay-off of a public relations bonanza, the image of a crusading police commissioner. Quick to grasp this point, TR developed a public relations sense decades before such terms and concepts as "image" were conceived by the political schlockmeisters.

If he failed to deter New Yorkers from illicit behaviors, he did achieve substantive police reforms. They were glad to see him go in 1897 when he became Assistant Secretary of the Navy, but most city residents admitted that he had been impressive. The *New York Times* editorialized: "The service he has rendered to the city is second to that of none, and…it is in our judgment unequaled."[14] He had demonstrated that an unpopular law could be enforced. His enforcement of the election laws had given New York its only honest election in memory. He had ended the sale of police jobs and promotions (a captaincy could cost $10,000) and dismissed a flood of corrupt officers. Police ties with the underworld were broken. He replaced corrupt practices with civil service reform, creating an examining board to pass on police appointments and requiring both written examinations and probationary periods. Once appointed, a recruit had to undergo training. Between 1895 and 1897 TR added 1600 men to the force who were taller, younger, and smarter. He also put patrolmen on bicycles and added telephone communications.[15]

Streets had become more orderly, crime and vice rates decreased, policemen learned courteous speech, and calls for help received a rapid response. TR also achieved condemnation and closure of about a hundred of the worst slum buildings that he had seen on nightly patrols. Such technical efficiency, along with the end of bribery and political influence, made the force a national model, imitated in Europe as well as the U.S.[16]

Notes: Chapter 4

1. William Henry Harbaugh, *Power and Responsibility: The Life and times of Theodore Roosevelt*, 70-71; David McCullough, *Mornings on Horseback*, 359-361; Allen Churchill, *The Roosevelts*, 184.
2. Quoted in Noel F. Busch, *The Story of Theodore Roosevelt and His Influence on Our Times*, 213.
3. Henry F. Pringle, *Theodore Roosevelt: A Biography*, .
4. Frank Sullivan, *Our Times*, II, 226-235.
5. Harbaugh, 35.
6. Busch, 89.
7. Pringle, 84-91; Harbaugh, 77-83; Busch, 88-93.
8. Lincoln Steffens, *The Autobiography of Lincoln Steffens*, 255-291, for first hand accounts.
9. Corinne Robinson, *My Brother, Theodore Roosevelt*, 159.
10. Edmund Morris, *The Rise of Theodore Roosevelt*, 502.
11. *Ibid.*, 509; Busch, 9; Robinson, 158; Pringle, 102.
12. E. Morris, 513.
13. Harbaugh, 86-88; Pringle, 98-102; E. Morris, 497.
14. *Ibid.*, 561.
15. *Ibid.*, 561-562; Pringle, 105-106; Harbaugh, 90-92; Busch, 111; Willard B. Gatewood, Jr., *Theodore Roosevelt and the Art of Controversy: Episodes of the White House Years*, 9.
16. E. Morris, 561-562.

5. Fathers of Vaudeville (I)

Big-time entertainment made its entrance following big-time athletics. What the new and expanding cities lacked was family entertainment. The concert-saloons—there were already 75 to 80 of them in NYC by 1872—were underworld hang-outs, not only an affront to all-important respectability, but dangerous locations where criminals, whores, and pimps stalked the cash of diversion-seeking family men.[1] The circus wheeled into town only occasionally, and many respectable people avoided it because of the sleaze factor: tawdry sideshows, acrobats in tights, mangy animals, and petty rip-offs. Most of the populace lacked access to or couldn't afford theatre and opera. Baseball's appeal was seasonal and masculine. Village socializing, barn raisings, and rural festivals had become memories of lost country life.

The concert-saloon was both a cabaret and a dancehall, punctuating dancing with interludes of entertainment. Waiter girls, called "beer jerkers," served food and alcoholic drinks to the male customers at the small tables around the dance floor. Large establishments employed over 100 of these girls. They received no salary except for a 10% commission on drinks and tips, which probably added up to $15 to $30 per week. During breaks or off-hours, they could augment their earnings with prostitution. These waiter girls vied with performer girls as the concert-saloon's chief attraction: the men came for the women. Besides dances that showed off legs, girls in the tightest of tights would pose in tableaux called "living model" "art poses." Such voyeuristic feasts were passed off as esthetic, but the intentions were lascivious, the amusement and arousal of men. With beer only 5 cents a glass and amiable females within arm's reach, these places gave good value.

But they could be as dangerous as they were bawdy and rowdy. There were always a few fights with broken furniture and flying missiles. In the rougher and tackier places, actual fights rather than girly prancing were the standard entertainment. For that 5-cent beer, you could enjoy boxing and wrestling, very rough, gouging matches with few rules. A few lowdown places even offered butting matches that concluded with the sickening sound of a fracture. On other nights, men liked to match their fighting dogs or fighting cocks, and in some of the very worst places, rat fights went on.[2]

In these disorderly houses with their vicious employees and customers, the "perfessor" furnished most of the music (a fiddler often helped out for the dancing), trying to please a rude clientele for tips and drinks. The French called this milieu the *demimonde*, the half-world. A whole world it isn't. In this half-or night-world of late 19th-century America, the scenes were squalid and the outcomes sordid: degradation, disease, violations, and death. Below the concert-saloons were the barrel houses. In barrel houses, customers sat at long tables opposite a row of racked barrels. To fill an earthenware mug cost a nickel. The barrels contained adulterated alcoholic liquids labeled "Brandy," "Whiskey," and "Wine." Anyone who didn't refill frequently was ejected. When a drunk sagged into unconsciousness, he was dragged out to an alley where waiting thieves took not only any unspent coins but his clothing as well. They split the meager takings with the proprietor.[3]

The barrel house offered no music, just foul drinks and a bad end to a day—or a life. Nearby were "druggists" whose small shops sold quick fixes of morphine and other types of opium including the smokable kind, plus the ever popular cocaine, known then also as "coke." This was all legal, as were the drinks, the most expensive of which contained a mixture of wine and cocaine.[4] Toward morning, bodies were scattered through the alleys, most sleeping off the effects of these intoxicants and depressants, the odd one dead from either an overdose or a stab wound.

It was Tony Pastor who separated sin from entertainment. Antonio Pastor (1834-1908), son of an American mother and a Spanish theatre musician, began at age eight singing in minstrel shows on Commodore Vanderbilt's steamboats and in shows at P.T.Barnum's "Museum." He graduated to circuses, working up from clown to minor acrobat, to equestrian, and ultimately to ringmaster. When the Civil War started, he commenced a four-year stint as singer and song leader at 444 Broadway in NYC, then called the American Concert Hall, later Mitchell's Olympic Theatre and Fellow's Opera House.[5]

Pastor conducted sing-alongs of popular and sentimental pieces, plus topical songs which usually consisted of new lyrics set to familiar tunes. He added to his income by publishing such lyrics in songster pamphlets. The majority of these songs were humorous and racy, many of them war songs. The male audiences also enjoyed singing about women, work, and disliked minority groups, especially immigrants and blacks. Songs about blacks were usually in dialect and ridiculed the race using stereotypes. A popular example in the guise of a war song was "The Contraband's Adventures," which told of a slave freed by the Union Army who was taken to an abolition meeting but was too dimwitted to comprehend the uplifting sentiments preached. The song concludes with the (racist) viewpoint that passed for folk wisdom at the time:

> …de nigger will be nigger
> Till de day of jubilee
> For he neber was intended for a white man.
> Den just skedaddle home—leave de colored man alone;
> For you're only makin' trouble for de nation;
> You may fight and you may fuss,
> But you will neber make tings right
> Until you all agree
> For to let de nigger be
> For you'll neber neber neber wash him white! [6]

When the war ended, Pastor opened a variety theatre at 201 Bowery, a tough district where entertainment was a come-on for liquor and sex. The problem was that a theatre in a vice district offered about the same ambience and competed for the same sporting male clientele as any of the too numerous music halls and concert-saloons. After a few years of ineffectual struggle against such competition, he tried a new direction using his mentor Barnum as a model. Barnum's earlier "Museum," where Pastor had sung in the 1840's, had attempted to pull in families (hence "museum") with clean bills of variety and no booze or prostitutes to offend. The museum idea had begun in Philadelphia during the 1780's when Charles Wilson Peale, the famous painter, set up a collection of specimens that included a menagerie and collections of minerals, insects, animal skeletons, seashells, plus freaks and oddities such as a five-legged cow. Peale also offered occasional lectures, art exhibits, and musicales. Decades later (in 1841), Phineas T. Barnum bought the American Museum in New York and presented variety entertainment as well as the usual museum-type exhibits. Although this approach to the idea of entertaining families met with some success, its career was cut short by a fire (1865) that destroyed the exhibits which had taken decades to assemble.

Like Barnum, Pastor was more concerned with profits than morals: families buy more than a single ticket. However this initial effort of cleaning up the acts failed because the theater's bar remained open and because ladies of the night lurked nearby.[7] By 1873 Pastor had removed the bar, and ladies properly accompanied received free admission every Friday night. He also put on special matinees for women and children. Still he wasn't filling enough seats. This led to his most creative strategy: the giveaway. Door prizes generated the appeal that pulled the housewives into variety theatre. Tony went at it inventively: Ticket stubs would be drawn one week for sacks of potatoes, the next for hams, subsequently for barrels of flour, even sewing machines. On other nights door prizes were handed to the first twenty-five women coming in. He offered successively flowers, candy, dress patterns, and dishes, but the most popular lure was silk dresses.[8]

After a decade on the Bowery, the increase in vice made a move to a cleaner neighborhood imperative. New York women of 1875 had become frightened by stories of "mashers," men who walked up to respectable women on the streets and tried to lure them into saloons. Once inside, it was believed, decent women were drugged, seduced, and shanghaied to brothels. Worse, others were carried onto ships and transported to the white slave marts of Latin America. These villains were felt to be lurking on all busy streets, but more so in vice areas. This commenced the "White Slavery" hysteria that troubled urban women for the next 40 years.[9] *Tony Pastor's Theatre* moved north, following the rapid growth of Manhattan, to 585-587 Broadway, from 1875 to 1881, then to a final location within the Tammany Building (Democratic Party Headquarters) at Fourteenth Street and Third Avenue. This lay in the heart of the theatre district known as the Rialto, which also contained the better stores.[10]

In his theatres vaudeville took shape. A small man, Tony all but lived in his theatre, always ready to audition new talent, always interested in his performers, always kind. He remained more of a showman than an entrepreneur, unlike the businessmen who soon dominated variety. His satisfactions came from launching the careers of vaudeville's early "headliners": Pat Rooney, Emma Carus, Flora and May Irwin, Nat Goodwin, Eddie Foy, and Lillian Russell. With a headliner—the name on the marquee out front—on each week's bill, Tony was father to the "Big-Time," also known as the "two-a-day" (matinee and evening shows), and he always preferred the simpler "variety" to the more pretentious "vaudeville." Each night after closing, he prayed at the shrine he kept backstage.[11]

Enter now the big-time big-timers: Benjamin Franklin Keith (1846-1914) and Edward Francis Albee (1857-1930). These New Englanders, Keith from New Hampshire and Albee from Maine, started out, like Pastor, as circus men, but unlike him, never performers. Keith had been a small-time circus con man selling phony "blood testers." These were small glass bowls that tapered to a closed spout at the top, the bottom filled with water dyed red. When the "mark" clasped the bottom in his palm, the reddish fluid rose—proof of high blood pressure. Used daily, no need to see a doctor. They cost him a dime and sold for a dollar. In 1883 Keith moved up to the theatre, opening Keith's Museum in Boston, a Barnum imitation. The first major exhibit was "Baby Alice," a premature two-week-old black baby billed as so tiny that she fitted comfortably into a milk bottle. Rapid growth led to her replacement by a string of similar oddities, including unusual birds and animals. There was even a "dancing chicken" act, whereby small chicks were made to "dance" by applying heat to the metal floor of their cage.[12]

It was Albee who led Keith off this back road of tawdry failure onto the main road of the Big-Time. Like Keith he had run off with the circus, and he too became an able practitioner of circus ethics. He was the fast talker in the ticket booth. For ten cents extra, no waiting in line. Coins vanished in his palm. The real money came from short-changing, a trick so ancient that it probably originated at the time of the invention of paper money in China. Fold the bills in half in the palm and count each bill twice. When on occasion the angry mark came flying back out of the tent with a yelp that he'd been cheated, Albee was always ready: with a sigh of annoyance he would point to some change on the counter and say he'd been waiting for the customer to come back for it.[13]

That year (1883) the *Mikado* enjoyed a popular run in Boston, inspiring these newly met collaborators to mount an abbreviated version. Out front Keith harangued, "Why pay $1.50, when you can see it in our theatre for 25 cents?" Suddenly the tiny museum (35x18) filled up for several performances a day. With the money rolling in, they sent a second company out on the road. It was obviously time to move, and they took over the ruined Bijou Theatre. Keith did the renovation carpentry while his missus cleaned it all out. Next she opened the "New York Hotel," a boarding house for actors, enabling her to recoup some of the money her husband paid the "artists" (all vaudevillians were referred to as "artists"). The Bijou became the initial unit of the fabled "Keith-Albee" circuit, which grew during the 1890's into the top chain in the big-time, the summit which all artists hoped one day to reach. Although they actually opened rather "small-time" with a continuous bill running 11:00 AM to 9:00 PM, they were soon presenting two-a-day with big-timers out of Pastor's in NYC, with prices rising from ten cents to a quarter.

Unlike Pastor, sleaze was OK when it sold tickets. Despite signs posted backstage forbidding whatever might be deemed "suggestive" and "sacreligious," K-A tolerated off-color comedy sketches, risqué song lyrics, and even staged the notorious "living statue" acts popular in concert saloons. Also called "living female paintings" and "tableaux vivants," they featured one or more "model artists" in tights or see-through draperies assuming stationary poses to illustrate classical or Biblical stories such as "Venus Rising from the Sea," the "Greek Slave," or "Susannah in the Bath." Slow changes in position, sometimes on revolving stages, made the views more revealing. The pretense of serious art fooled no one in the fully male audiences. No fuss was ever made about the posted moral standards unless there were complaints. Expansion followed, to Providence in 1888, Philadelphia in 1889, and Keith's Union Square opened to New York in 1893.[14]

During these final decades of the 19th Century, the entertainment revolution, paralleling—and interacting with—the industrial and demographic (rural to urban) revolutions achieved a rapid conquest. What James Lincoln Collier labels "The New Business of Show Business," and the "organized entertainment industry" seized the attention of America. "In 1880 there was no recorded sound, no moving pictures, no football, no basketball, no vaudeville, no ragtime, jazz, or blues, no Tin Pan Alley. By the first decade of the 20th Century all were in place and were—or about to be—matters of intense national concern." "Revolution" may have become a cliché, often too easily and casually applied, but 150 years ago, most humans lived without experiencing professional entertainment. Today people put in more hours being entertained than they do working or socializing. Those who entertain receive the highest honors and the greatest amounts of money. Some accuse us of worshipping them. Collectively they are called "celebrities." [15]

Notes: Chapter 5

1. Robert W. Snyder, *The Voice of the City: Vaudeville and Popular Culture in New York*, 10.
2. Herbert Asbury, *The French Quarter*, 236-237.
3. *Ibid.*, 234-236.
4. William Ivy Hair, *Carnival of Fury: Robert Charles and the New Orleans Race Riot of 1900*, 76-77.
5. Russell Sanjek, *America's Popular Music and Its Business: The First Four Hundred Years*, II, 306; Sophie Tucker, *Some of These Days: The Autobiography of Sophie Tucker*, 46; Snyder, 13; Charles and Louise Samuels, *Once Upon a Stage: The Merry World of Vaudeville*, 17.
6. Quoted in Snyder, 14.
7. *Ibid.*, 5-7; Tucker, 46; James Lincoln Collier, *The Rise of Selfishness in America*, 75-76.
8. Samuels, 19-20; Sanjek, II, 309; Tucker, 46; Snyder, 18-20.
9. Samuels, 19.
10. Snyder, 17-21; Sanjek, II, 309-313.
11. Samuels, 19-20; Tucker, 48; Sanjek, II, 309, Snyder, 18-20.
12. Samuels, 35-36.
13. *Ibid.*, 36-37.
14. *Ibid.*, 38-40; Snyder, 26-35; Timothy J. Gilfoyle, City of Eros: Prostitution and the Commercialization of Sex, 1790-1920, 127.
15. Collier, 74-75, 103.

(Ch. 6)

RAGTIME ALMANAC

U. S. Fairs and Expositions, 1876-1916

1. Centennial Exposition, Philadelphia 1876
2. World's Industrial and Cotton Exposition, New Orleans 1885
3. World's Columbian Exposition, Chicago 1893
4. Cotton States and International Exposition, Atlanta 1895
5. Tennessee Centennial Exposition, Nashville 1897
6. Trans-Mississippi and International Exposition, Omaha 1898
7. Pan-American Exposition Buffalo 1901
8. South Carolina Interstate and West Indian Exposition, Charleston, 1901-02
9. Louisiana Purchase Exposition, St.Louis 1904
10. Lewis and Clark Centennial and American Pacific Exposition, Portland, 1905
11. Alaska-Yukon-Pacific Exposition, Seattle 1909
12. Panama-Pacific International Exposition, San Francisco 1915
13. Panama-California Exposition, San Diego 1915-16

6. WHITE CITIES AND MIDWAYS

Expositions are timekeepers of Progress. (President William McKinley, speaking in September 1901 at the Pan-American Exposition, Buffalo, just before his assassination.)

Cities have learned to market themselves like commodities. Such attractions as "bowl" games, World Series, Olympiads, centennials, various "festivals," celebrity honorings, hero homecomings, and other celebrations have become municipal events. Seeking to attract new enterprises and increased tourism, cities preen themselves on the national stage. These outpourings of civic hopes and pride commenced over a century ago with the "world's fair" movement. Such displays of industrial and cultural "progress" were an obvious and natural result of the new urban and industrial culture. Caught in the spell cast by rapid growth and change, the newly industrialized nations (Britain, France, Germany, the U.S.) invited the world to come, see, and admire, their superior achievements.

The movement began with the Crystal Palace Exhibition of 1851 in London, but took 25 years to reach the U.S. because the sectional controversy, Civil War, and Reconstruction had absorbed most of the nation's attention and resources. However by 1873, the growing collective desire to heal the nation's wounds combined with awareness of the approaching national anniversary to spur efforts to create an international celebration of the Centennial. That year Congress authorized a Centennial Commission, and President Grant designated Philadelphia as the site. The Commission studied Europe's previous world's fairs and planned on a grand scale. When the Centennial Exposition opened on May 10, 1876, there were 194 buildings erected on the 236 acres of Fairmont Park. All together there were 30,000 exhibitors from 38 states and 50 nations. Exhibits were arranged in seven categories:

1. Mining and metallurgy
2. Manufactured products
3. Machinery
4. Science and education
5. Agriculture
6. Horticulture
7. Fine arts

Although patriotism, union, and peace—intended to foster national reunification—were the designated themes, manufactured goods and machinery, the evidences of material progress, drew the largest crowds. Steam power triumphant, a tamed giant, dominated the exposition. At the center of Machinery Hall ensconced on a platform fifty-six feet in diameter labored the Corliss double-cylinder steam engine providing power for all of the other machines in the hall—about 8000 of them! The forty-four inch diameter cylinders absorbed the pistons' ten-foot strokes. They powered a flywheel thirty feet in diameter weighing fifty-six tons. Steam was produced by twenty boilers outside the building. Visitors were transfixed by the smooth, efficient movement of this gigantic engine. Five months of the fair brought 8,000,000 to gaze at this mightiest creation of humankind.[1]

But fairgoers desired more than education and national pride. A day of thrusting pistons, turning wheels, patriotic displays, architectural aspirations, and visualized ideals deposited a rigid glaze over the most studious and earnest eyes. Recovery called for some nightlife, family fun, and entertainment. Unfortunately the Centennial Commission had failed to foresee such mundane needs. For married couples and families seeking relief from long hours of unalloyed uplift, a pre-bedtime stroll brought a rather flat end to the day. Whereas for single males, entertainment beckoned just outside exposition gates: saloons, freak shows, dioramas, music-hall shows, variety theatres, concert-saloons, and brothels. Showmen, liquor sellers, performers, and whores flocked to the fair, posing a considerable affront to respectable people passing in and out. So conspicuous were these enterprises that exposition authorities forced city officials to condemn and burn many of the shacky structures.[2]

Sixty years earlier wolves had howled along Lake Michigan's shore where the gleaming White City of 1893 mirrored the pride of surrounding Chicago in hosting the World's Columbian Exposition, which commemorated—a year late—the epochal Columbian "discovery" of 400 years before. Chicago offered the "new and improved" model of a world's fair. In its purity and exalted aspect the White City stood for high culture without compromise, but the planners moderated this effect with a new section where fairgoers might discard the mask of highmindedness and stroll among exhibits intended to entertain: the mile-long Midway Plaisance. President Cleveland opened the fair by turning an electric switch that awakened the dynamos of the central generating station. For the first time people thrilled to the nocturnal charm of a lighted city—which foreshadowed the future role of electric power. Besides illumination, the humming dynamos powered the elevated railroad that ran along the exposition's perimeter. Even the launches on the lagoons operated on electricity rather than the customary steam.[3] Sixteen years after Philadelphia, Chicago attracted over three times the visitors, 27,000,000, which was a third of the population. They found idealism and uplift in the core structures housing the exhibits, the alabaster buildings that gleamed along the lagoons and Lake Michigan. This "White City" presented a model to correct the architectural chaos of cities, an aspiration for unity and harmony, a Dream City perceived as Venice reborn.[4] Led by the sculptor Augustus Saint-Gaudens (1848-1907), the exposition's architects, all trained in the beaux-arts tradition of Paris, built in the classical, Renaissance style of imperial France. This presented a significant novelty for the U.S. which lacked a national style. The special quality of the White City then lay as much in its embodiment of uniformity as in its stated classicism. Rising from these Old World foundations, its appealing qualities, besides monumentality and grandeur, were symmetry, harmony, and futurity.[5]

But intensity too soon falls away to monotony. The eye wanders off from triumphal arches and colonnades, columns and statues. At Chicago the buildings erected by foreign nations and the states offered a variety of styles, and on the Midway, 600 feet wide and stretching a mile, fairgoers encountered buildings that were merely functional. Here they found official (respectable) entertainment. Planners had recognized the need for diversions, but had been hesitant and uncertain over content. These arbiters of genteel taste: men of wealth, social leaders, managers of enterprises, architects, artists, and academics, feared spoiling their exhibits of high and elite culture with attractions that were tawdry, tacky, and in poor taste. Uncertain about the emerging popular culture and how to showcase mere entertainment, they hired (for $50,000) one of its new impresarios, twenty-one-year-old Sol Bloom of San Francisco, to oversee and arrange the amusements of the Midway. Sol Bloom (who, following a long career in business, music publishing, and politics, would, as Chair of the House of Representatives Foreign Relations Committee, help write the United Nations Charter in 1945) visited the Paris International Exposition in 1889 and had learned that concessionaire fees had contributed $700,000 toward the cost of constructing and operating the fair. He had also been impressed by the ethnic exhibits: the Algerian Village, the Bedouin acrobats, and the Egyptian *danse du ventre* or belly dance. Subsequently he brought the belly dance to Chicago, where Americans labeled it the "hootchy-kootchy," and it went on to become the ultimate lure on most midways and sideshows. However, contrary to most reminiscences of the Columbian Exposition, Bloom did <u>not</u> bring over the famous dancer "Little Egypt." But he did hire on the spot in Paris, with the intention of touring the U.S., the

Algerian Village. The Algerians, living on-site in their own dwellings, performing daily tasks, and presenting exhibitions of their skills to fairgoers, turned out to be one of the hits in Chicago.[6] (Bloom does remember seeing Little Egypt emerge from a pie at a stag dinner at the Waldorf-Astoria a few years later.)

Along with such exhibits, the Chicago Midway Plaisance was crammed with restaurants, shops, souvenir sellers, theatres, and rides. Its role in the history of popular culture was to provide the generic name of "midway" and the model for amusements at circuses, carnivals, and amusement parks. As the democratic, urban model for public recreation, the midway has pursued a life of its own, popping up everywhere, as entertainment overcame the stricter mores of Victorian life.[7] Symbolizing this triumph of entertainment was the great rotating wheel devised by George W. G. Ferris that most fairgoers found irresistible. Its diameter was 300 feet and its capacity was 1440 passengers! [8] There were genteel commentators who deplored all of this frivolity, condemning the Midway for offering shallow pleasures, instant gratification, and crude stimulation. They went largely ignored. Preferring fun and fireworks, people rejected entertainment intended to elevate their tastes. They avoided the symphony concerts led by the great Theodore Thomas, who reacted by resigning. They rejected the borrowed musical culture of Europe in favor of the new pop music on the Midway.[9]

Although no ragtime performances have yet been documented at or near the World's Columbian Exposition, hearsay indicates that substantial numbers of whites heard the music there for the first time. This first hearing brought ragtime into the mainstream of pop. Whites returned home demanding more of this heady, intoxicating music. This increased demand put more performers to work, which prompted a further demand for fresh music. Also a growing number of listeners wanted sheet music for home entertainment. Thereupon music stores and departments asked jobbers and publishers to supply this need. Many retailers met the demand themselves by publishing local composers, and music publishers responded just as quickly with the output of their staff composers and other urban ragmen (and women). The process from first hearing to publication took five years from 1893 to 1897.[10]

Hearsay also places Scott Joplin at the exposition. He may have performed as a pianist, but sources indicate that he formed and led a small band in the city's "District" in which he played cornet. He met many ragtimers, including Otis Saunders of Springfield, Missouri, who became a friend and companion. Pianists from all over the central U.S. converged on the site, and Scott must have heard and met many. He probably met "Plunk" Henry, who, like "Old Man" French (Chapter 1.3), had played a syncopated proto-ragtime on the banjo. Another new acquaintance was Johnny Seymour, later known for the saloon he ran in Chicago's District. Also there, Jesse Pickett played his *Dream Rag*, the only ragtime strain known from that pre-publication time.[11]

Offering escape from things banal and familiar, the exotic, new ragtime caught on instantly. In the Midway setting, away from honky-tonks and sporting houses, it was non-threatening and easy to enjoy.[12] Sources mention one example in Chicago of a show possessing ragtime elements. This was the *Creole Show* on tour from New York. Organized in 1890 by white impresario Sam T. Jack, the Creole Show was the first black show to break with the minstrel tradition. It featured some of the best minstrel and ragtime performers of the period including Bob Cole, here working as both comedian and stage manager, who would go on to compose hit ragtime songs ("Under the Bamboo Tree") and create the first all-black musical play (*A Trip to Coontown*, 1897; Chapter 26). The Creole Show presented the first female chorus line, with a mistress of ceremonies who introduced the acts and skits. Another sensation of the show proved to be the cakewalk dance, which in a few years would bring on the first dance craze of the ragtime era, with contests and exhibitions. Going beyond spiritual singing and minstrel shows, the *Creole Show* opened new stages for African-American performers.[13]

Yet another Chicago Midway attraction was the Dahomean Village whose inhabitants entertained all day with drumming and chants. The ethnic villages fascinated fairgoers; they were prominently displayed on the midways of all subsequent fairs. Classed as "ethnological exhibits," these human assemblages of the darker races set down among white strangers afforded a leisurely examination of the outlandish elements that comprised the Other (i.e., the foreign). At Chicago and the expositions following, the same group of social scientists from the Smithsonian Institution and universities arranged the ethnic displays. Besides the ever popular Africans, fairgoers saw groups of Native Americans, particularly such western tribes as Apache, Navajo, Sioux, and northwestern tribes. Like the Native Americans, the Filipinos, whose islands we acquired in 1898 and whom we overcame in the Philippine Insurrection of 1899-1901, were another conquered people who piqued curiosity. Other peoples exhibited on whom we had exerted our imperial muscle included the Eskimos, Chinese, and Japanese.[14]

These ethnic sideshows served ideological purposes: the validation of nationalism and racism. The elite powers of wealth and academe staged these exhibitions to reenforce their control over the lesser classes. Seeing the exotic villages of dark-skinned peoples with their simpler economics and technologies instilled the Darwinian lesson that white peoples, through further evolution, had achieved a decisive superiority. After experiencing the high achievements of steam power, electricity, and architecture, the contrast with simpler societies led to inevitable conclusions about the nation's greatness, racial superiority, and imperial strength. Imbibing such intended perceptions, middle and lower-class whites tended to forget their conflicts with the overclass that dominated the nation. Seduced by their masters, they became more accepting of the political and economic repression of African Americans, Native Americans, and Asian Americans.[15] Robert W. Rydell, the historian of these fairs, also points out that the government supported these purposes: Congress appropriated funds for all of the expositions. To sum up: these fairs, presented by the upper class, conveyed certain ideas and notions:

1. Progress
2. Evolution—the process that caused progress
3. Cultural superiority—Europe and the U.S. portrayed as the most evolved
4. Cultural inferiority—Middle Eastern, East Indian, East Asian, and African, shown in descending order
5. National pride
6. Respect for the financial-industrial elite

These lessons were sweetened by the new urban pleasures of the midways. They were planned adjuncts. From 1904 at St.Louis, midways became incorporated within the main exposition grounds. As integral parts of the fairs, the entertainments of popular culture became legitimized. Bluestockings and other genteelists might frown on ragtime, jazz, vaudeville, and the cinema, but with the sanctions from powers on high, complaints sounded querulous and irrelevant. Another point is that the expositions were staged by interlocking groups. These managers and academics consisted of close colleagues, many from the Smithsonian, who shared the same views and purposes and passed them on to juniors, who replicated their intentions. Fair historian Rydell concludes:

> Far from simply reflecting American culture, the expositions were intended to shape that culture.[16]

Notes: Chapter 6

1. Howard Mumford Jones, *The Age of Energy: Varieties of American Experience, 1865-1915*, 139-142; Robert W. Rydell, "World's Fairs," 1168-1170.
2. Robert W. Rydell, *All the World's a Fair: Visions of Empire at American International Expositions, 1876-1916*, 236.
3. Peter J. Ling, *America and the Automobile: Technology, Reform, and Social Change,* 99; William L. Shirer, *Twentieth-Century Journey: A Memoir of a Life and Times, 1904-1930*, 95.
4. John F. Kasson, *Amusing the Million: Coney Island at the Turn of the Century*, 18; Ling, 113.
5. Jones, 254; Kasson, 18.
6. Sol Bloom, *The Autobiography of Sol Bloom,* 107; *Rydell,* All the World's a Fair, 62-63.
7. Kasson, 21-27.
8. Bloom, 138.
9. James Gilbert, *Perfect Cities: Chicago's Utopias of 1893*, 128; Ling, 121; Susan Curtis, *Dancing to a Black Man's Tune: A Life of Scott Joplin*, 49-50.
10. *Ibid.*, 48-49, 61.
11. Edward A. Berlin, *King of Ragtime: Scott Joplin and His Era*, 12; Curtis, 5-46; Rudi Blesh and Harriet Janis, *They All Played Ragtime*, 18, 41, 152.
12. Curtis, 60-62.
13. Thomas L. Morgan and William Barlow, *From Cakewalks to Concert Halls: An Illustrated History of African American Popular Music from 1895 to 1930*, 37; Thomas L Riis, *Just Before Jazz: Black Musical Theatre in New York, 1890-1915*, 26; Tom Fletcher, *One Hundred Years of the Negro in Show Business*, 103. Fletcher states that the cakewalk had earlier been performed at Philadelphia in 1876.
14. Rydell, *All the World's A Fair,* 62-63, 199; Blesh and Janis, 149.
15. Rydell, *All the World's A Fair, 235-237;* Rydell, "World's Fairs, 1169.
16. Rydell, *All the World's A Fair,* 237.

7. 1896

In political history 1896 stands out, like 1828, 1860, and 1932, years when deep conflicts and strong emotions rose to the surface in electoral contests. This election climaxed a twenty-five-year battle over the nation's money supply, a struggle that divided East from West, rural from urban, and poor from rich. There was a chronic shortage of cash because the supply lagged behind the growths of enterprise and population. From 1865 to 1890 the rate of increase in the annual production of gold had either remained flat or had actually declined, resulting in scarcity.[1] Fewer dollars in circulation per capita meant higher prices for the consumer and greater economic power for financiers and manufacturers, since they tended to accumulate a disproportionate share of the dwindling currency. Farmers suffered the most because the packers and middle men who purchased their commodities could offer low prices based upon the high cost of money, and the bankers who held the farm mortgages could charge high interest rates for the same reason. Even more galling than these predations were the extortions of the railroads, which monopolized transportation so as to extract the rest of the farmer's scarce dollars, even on short hauls.

For decades advocates for the indebted and the impoverished had demanded a more abundant currency, based upon cheaper silver instead of gold. Farmers were the majority (these demographics would not change until after 1920), and their problems of high consumer prices, high interest rates, high transportation costs, low commodity prices, drought, isolation, and poverty gripped the nation. They had formed the Populist Party during the 1880's to fight for their interests (General James B. Weaver of Iowa their standard bearer), but its third-party protest effect tainted their program with the label of radicalism. Conservatives, both Republicans and "Gold" Democrats, held on to the two major parties, keeping the discontented "Silver" Democrats and Populists divided and impotent.

Discontent multiplied after the election of the conservative Gold Democrat Grover Cleveland to a second term in 1892. From 1893 the nation fell into its worst depression, doubly aggravated in the western farm states by a prolonged drought. The pulverized soil of the recently plowed high plains (the Dakotas, Nebraska, Kansas, Oklahoma, Texas, Colorado, Montana) rose in clouds before the winds to cause the first "Dustbowl," forerunner to the better remembered catastrophe of the 1930's. By 1896 the unemployed of the cities and towns and the dispossessed and impoverished of the countryside clamored for some relief. They were not going to settle for platform nonsense promising "better days." They dreamed of cures and solutions and were extremely vulnerable to panacea salesmen. By this time the panacea, silver, had become popular, with a large number of people presold on it. What the unhappy masses lacked was a leader, a standard bearer, who could retail their panacea to enough of the unconvinced to carry an election. It seemed simple enough, just find a leader, but the Democrats' deep division over silver apparently precluded the unity imperative for major party leadership. The July 10, 1896, *New York World*, a Democratic paper, commenting on the Democratic National Convention, just getting underway in Chicago, stated:

> The Silverites will be invincible if united and harmonious; but they have neither machine nor boss. The opportunity is here; the man is lacking.[2]

Conventional expectations turned out to be dead wrong, for by day's end a young (36) ex-congressman from Nebraska had convinced the excited delegates that he, William Jennings Bryan, was their candidate. It was a wild day. First Senator Benjamin R. Tillman of South Carolina, known as "Pitchfork Ben" for his 1894 election promise to stick his pitchfork into Cleveland's "old ribs," angrily attacked the pro-gold, pro-Wall Street policies of his hated enemy. Then Senator David B. Hill of New York tried to convince the noisy and increasingly restive delegates that both he and his conservative principle of a combined gold and silver standard—already rejected in the ratified platform—were the only logical and correct choices for the convention to make. After a forceful rejection of Hill's foolish attempt to turn the convention around, the task of closing this dissonant debate was handed to the former congressman from Nebraska, because of his notorious advocacy for "the free and unlimited coinage of silver," rather than because party chiefs considered him a front runner for the nomination. When he stepped up to the podium, "the man" was still "lacking."[3]

This churned up a rare, charged moment in U.S. history, when a speech overwhelmed its hearers with the power of revelation. In an era that cherished oratory, Bryan, whatever people thought of his political ideas (or the lack thereof), had no close rivals. From his school days, public speaking had become his metier, pursued as "elocution" in school, as debate in college, and as a lecturer on the Chautauqua circuit the rest of his life. Although he "read" law after college, he soon gave up its practice for politics. He was only thirty when he stood for Congress in Nebraska (1890) as a Democrat, winning a sensational victory in a Republican district, undoubtedly owing much to his talent on the rostrum. In Congress (1891-1895) he joined the Silverites, making this his sole issue. In 1895 he left Congress to edit the *Omaha World Herald* but expended most of his time and energy speaking on the silver issue, polishing the elements of the basic speech that he delivered on July 10, 1896, in Chicago.[4]

The 20,000 vociferous, sweating Democrats had worked themselves up into pandemonium, but when Bryan stepped up to the rostrum, the uproar abruptly trailed off into a silence of anticipation. His strong voice, precise delivery, the flow and ebb of swelling emotions, the march of his sentences toward the expectations of his audience boiled up a supreme moment of communication, a rare fullness of interaction. It was as much theatre as dialog between speaker and audience. Years later, people recalled this experience as an incredible "high." From the arresting phrase of its peroration, it was soon named the "Cross of Gold" speech.

Bryan opened with a plea for "the cause of humanity," a reference to the Silverite demand to coin silver in a ratio to gold of sixteen-to-one. He then stated that "this has been a contest over principle." Next came a passionate assertion that this demand was the will of the nation, followed by a note of regret about the conflict. Now, on a rising series of parallels and contrasts (the man who engages in small business or who sells his labor to an employer is also a businessman), he demolished the claim that a coinage based upon silver would seriously injure business (exactly the opposing thesis), because "We come to speak for this broader class of business men." Letting this concept sink in, he moved to an arousal of sentiment in praise of the pioneers of the West "who rear their children close to nature's heart...." Having established the righteousness of both cause and constituents, he went on to defy the moneyed exploiters of them and to attack their man McKinley, warning of the coming wrath of the people. Finally after rejecting the Republican laissez-faire belief that the prosperity of the rich "will leak on those below," he drew his socio-economic line between rural victims and urban predators:

> You come to tell us that the great cities are in favor of the gold standard. We reply that the great cities rest upon our broad and fertile prairies. Burn down your cities and leave our farms, and your cities will spring up again as if by magic. But destroy our farms and the grass will grow in the streets of every city in the country.

Letting this heady assertion take hold, Bryan expounded further on the rights and wrongs, urging defiance. Then came the few but tremendously inspiring lines that drove his audience to its feet in a roar of unity:

> Having behind us the producing masses of this nation and the world, supported by the commercial interests, the laboring interests, and the toilers everywhere, we will answer their demand for a gold standard by saying to them: You shall not press down upon the brow of labor this crown of thorns, you shall not crucify mankind upon a cross of gold. [5]

A century later, knowing that the rest of WJB's life was a thirty-year anti-climax, we call this moment political showbiz. Contemporaries, whether from hope or fear, believed it a prelude to greater things. Three leaders stood out above all others in Progressive-Ragtime America: Theodore Roosevelt, Woodrow Wilson, and William Jennings Bryan. Bryan was a constant presence in the nation's awareness, and his party nominated him three times: 1896, 1900, and 1908. He spoke up for the people against the wrongs and sufferings caused by the new industrial order. He did it with great and sincere compassion, and he never failed his farm and small town constituents who loved and deeply believed in him. His great voice was always at their service. For the country people, sadly subsisting in the loneliness and squalor of their paltry farms out on the distant quarter sections, WJB was the Moses to lead them out of bondage to bankers, railroads, and town merchants.

The election of 1896—which he lost—left behind it his legend, a heroic image fixed in the minds of his rural folk. He was often fanatical, ran for office too frequently, ate too much, and was not a careful student or clear thinker. But he never betrayed his people, particularly in 1915 when he resigned as Wilson's Secretary of State because he believed that Wilson's get-tough policies against Germany (because of unrestricted submarine warfare in the Atlantic) threatened the peace desired by Americans and might force the U.S. into war (which eventually happened). Like his beloved people, Bryan was a devout Christian who believed in the literal truth of the Bible (inerrancy). Each night he knelt to pray before getting into bed.[6]

II

For Theodore Roosevelt the coming election generated both hope and anxiety. He intended to participate in his party's campaign and hoped for something better to come out of it. By this time he was, as New York Police Commissioner, weary of the ceaseless municipal struggles to enforce unpopular laws and feared his career had reached a dead end. But after the quickening in Chicago, the campaign drew him in like iron to a magnet. In fact the Republicans very much needed a vigorous campaigner like TR. Prior to Chicago their St.Louis convention had nominated the Ohio politician William McKinley, a bland undynamic (though far from weak) soul who refused to travel for votes. The day following his "Cross of Gold" speech, Bryan had been nominated by the Democrats, which abruptly wiped out complacency at Republican headquarters. Marcus Alonzo Hanna, the industrialist from Cleveland who managed McKinley and now chaired the Republican Party, cancelled his summer vacation plans to organize a complex campaign to assure the election of his non-campaigning candidate. Tidings from west of the Appalachians were alarming: predictions of class war, communism, the doom of capitalism, even anarchy. Hanna passed the word for all of the cash and power speakers he could get.[7]

The only sure states for McKinley were New England, New York, New Jersey, Pennsylvania, and his native Ohio, whereas Bryan had strong support throughout the South, Mid-West, and West, because both Democratic and Populist Silverites had united behind him (the Populists had also nominated Bryan). Following some voluntary speeches in behalf of McKinley in New York, TR, accompanied by his close friend and mentor

Senator Henry Cabot Lodge of Massachusetts, like other Republican supporters, called on McKinley at his home in Canton, Ohio. The sedentary McKinley was carrying on his "front porch" campaign. (Probably the chief reason for this came from the physical problems of wife Ida McKinley, a chronic epileptic whose sole caregiver was her husband. Her "fits" came frequently and unpredictably. She also exhibited great emotional dependence upon her husband, seldom allowing him out of eye or earshot.) The railroads, also much in fear of a Bryan victory, cooperated with cheap excursion rates, and parties of loyalists stepped off numerous trains each day. After detraining, they marched up Market Street, passing under a large plaster arch displaying the candidate's picture, drummed and serenaded along by a brass band until they reached the front lawn of the McKinley residence. Then, on schedule, occurred a modest ceremony: Each spokesman read a preapproved speech of support followed by McKinley's words of welcome and handshakes on the porch steps. After he had performed this ritual gesture of loyalty, Hanna changed TR's initial campaign assignment (for Maryland and West Virginia) and put him right on Bryan's trail in the difficult states of Illinois, Michigan, and Minnesota.[8]

The unstationary Bryan carried out one of the great itinerant campaigns, traveling 18,000 miles through 27 states (he avoided most McKinley territory). The epic quality of all this is suggested by the epithets or names people hung on him: "Boy Orator of the Platte," "Bryan the Brave," "The Great Commoner," "The Peerless One," and "Magnet of the Platte."[9] No one has evoked this campaign better than the poet Vachel Lindsay in "Bryan, Bryan, Bryan, Bryan." Lindsay, recalling that "It was eighteen ninety-six/and Altgeld ruled in Springfield, Illinois," describes the excitement and colors of Bryan's day in that city. Bryan was

> The one American poet who could sing outdoors,
>> He brought in tides of wonder, of unprecedented splendor
>> Wild roses from the plains, that made hearts tender,
>> All the funny circus silks
>> Of politics unfurled…

To an impressionable youth, he was

>> Prairie avenger, mountain lion,
>> Bryan, Bryan, Bryan, Bryan,
>> Gigantic troubadour speaking like a siege gun,
>> Smashing Plymouth Rock with his boulders
>>   from the West,
>> And just a hundred miles behind, tornadoes piled across the sky,
>
>> Blotting out sun and moon,
>> A sign on high.[10]

But the East held firm against rhetorical boulders and tornadoes. In the Mid-West the sometime cowboy and New York Police Commissioner demonstrated that he too could shoot words and hit bullseyes. One of TR's verbal trick shots was to hold up two odd-sized loaves of bread, pointing out that the bigger one cost eight cents on a gold basis, and the smaller one nine cents on a silver basis. Audiences happily devoured such oversimplifications. He scored his greatest success in the Chicago Coliseum (backed up on the platform by Robert Todd Lincoln), where Bryan had been triumphally nominated, when he compared Populists and

Silverites to the leaders of the French Terror, asserting that Bryan's silver program would benefit one class by stealing the wealth of another. It was a solemn warning, complete with Marx and Anarchists (much feared at that time), but people thoroughly enjoyed such fearsome stuff because of the beaming fervor and obvious relish the speaker radiated, the sheer fun of it all. Applause shook the rafters, and the *Chicago Tribune* printed all 7000 words of it the following morning.[11]

The campaign was skillfully, brilliantly orchestrated by party chairman-campaign manager Hanna (around a nearly passive central figure) who "fried the fat" out of worried capitalists and dogged the Democrats with forceful rebuttors. The Gold Democrats stampeded over to the Republican side to guarantee victory. They were needed; Bryan actually received more popular votes than had any other candidate in previous elections: 6,502,925. But McKinley topped that with 7,102,246, winning 271 Electoral Votes to 176. Another recollection comes from the solidly industrial Northeast where bosses produced a solid Republican tally by leading their workers to the polls warning that a Bryan victory could cost their jobs.

The 1896 conflict was epochal: the last great agrarian protest, the last farm depression when rural voters were the majority. Bryan failed to carry the very states of the upper Mid-West where Theodore Roosevelt had campaigned against him (Michigan, Illinois, Minnesota, plus Iowa, Indiana, Wisconsin, and North Dakota). Clearly many pulled back from taking their stand on the single silver plank of the Great Commoner's platform; it was simply too anemic a program. And, as TR and others warned, "free silver" would have weakened U.S. currency, driving the nation into financial isolation and delaying the prosperity that soon followed. TR—and the majority of intellectuals and economists—never took WJB seriously (other than as a political and economic threat). He derided Bryan and the Silverites, saying that they were "as regards the essentials of government, in hearty sympathy with their remote skin-clad ancestors who lived in caves and fought one another with stone-headed axes and ate the mammoth wooly rhinoceros." [12]

This was typical of the editorial derision in Republican papers that year. But there was more to McKinley's triumph than verbal one-upmanship and excessive campaign funds. Prosperity <u>was</u> finally starting to return to the farms that fall. Crops had been bountiful, but instead of a rich harvest driving down the prices, foreign demand (the result of major crop failure in India) leveled the surplus and raised prices. Plus the bottom dropped out of silver (again India buying grain instead of silver), rendering it too cheap on which to base a currency.[13] Even more influential in causing the economic turnaround were increases in gold production. Bryan had risen on the gold shortage, a twenty-five-year trend (1865-1890). But in the year of Bryan's election to Congress (1890), major annual increases had commenced, and by 1897 had nearly doubled, from $118,848,700 to $236,073,700. All thanks to new discoveries and new technologies, the 1890's were a gold decade. Major new discoveries were made in South Africa, Australia, Canada, and Alaska. By 1908, the year of Bryan's final presidential race, gold production would total $442,837,000. Besides these discoveries, production had been boosted by the cyanide process, a method that extracted more gold from a given amount of ore. This abundance of the yellow metal made silver irrelevant, and by 1900 debtors were getting clear on a rising tide of prosperity.[14]

In supporting McKinley, Theodore Roosevelt did not (like Bryan) speak out for "the producing masses of this nation." However he was developing an agenda of his own closer to Bryan's humane idealism than to McKinley's commitment to the welfare of corporations. TR's police work had led him into the squalid ghettoes where he felt the impact of the realities of poverty (malnutrition, diseases, filth, crowding, noise, smells, high infant and child mortality, degradation) depicted in his friend journalist Jacob Riis's book *How the Other Half*

Lives (1890). He knew that the wealthy owned these ugly blocks, and he personally rejected the constitutional argument against laws designed to obtain better conditions: the right of a citizen to do whatever he wished with his private property. He recalled, in his 1913 *Autobiography*, the mindset maturing within him by the mid-1890's: "I dimly realized that an even greater fight must be waged to improve economic conditions, and to secure social and industrial justice…." [15] He never said so—he gave Bryan no respect—but perhaps this inner focus on reform gained reenforcement from Bryan's strong advocacy for the victims of the economic system.

Notes: Chapter 7

1. Mark Sullivan, *Our Times*, I, 296-298.
2. *Ibid.*, 112-113.
3. Thomas A. Bailey, Ed., *The American Spirit*, II, 581-583; Sullivan, *OT*, 110-114.
4. *Ibid.*, 114-125.
5. *Ibid.*, 127-131; Bailey, 583-586.
6. William Henry Harbaugh, *Power and Responsibility: The Life and Times of Theodore Roosevelt*, 136-137; Henry F. Pringle, *Theodore Roosevelt: A Biography*, 111-112; Henry L. Mencken, *The Days of H. L. Mencken*, II, 281-285.
7. Edmund Morris, *The Rise of Theodore Roosevelt*, 545-547.
8. *Ibid.*, 551-552; Sullivan, *OT*, 291-295.
9. *Ibid.*, 293.
10. In Oscar Williams, Ed., *A Little Treasury of American Poetry*, 331, 333.
11. E. Morris, 552-553.
12. Sullivan, *OT*, I, 292.
13. *Ibid.*, 295.
14. *Ibid.*, 295-301.
15. Theodore Roosevelt, *An Autobiography*, 162-164, 206-207.

8. Judge Lynch

As racial subordination was reimposed in the long process of "redeeming" the South, racial boundaries had to be drawn in new ways. A taboo on sexual contact between black men and white women became central to that boundary. Southern whites stripped away voting rights and other public attributes of equal citizenship. Racial subordination also was continually recreated in the routine actions of the everyday world. In that world, racial etiquette and violence served to mark a new color line.[1]

RAGTIME ALMANAC

LYNCHINGS IN THE U. S., 1889-1918 [2]

1889 175	1904 86
1890 91	1905 65
1891 194	1906 68
1892 226	1907 62
1893 153	1908 100
1894 182	1909 89
1895 178	1910 90
1896 125	1911 71
1897 162	1912 64
1898 127	1913 48
1899 109	1914 54
1900 101	1915 96
1901 135	1916 58
1902 94	1917 50
1903 104	1918 67

NAACP: SOME BRIEF ACCOUNTS OF LYNCHINGS

Texas 1897

Robert Henson Hilliard, a Negro, for a murder to which he confessed and for alleged rape, was burned to death by a mob at Tyler, Texas. Hilliard confessed the murder but stated that he killed his victim because he had unwittingly frightened her and feared that he would be killed.

A report of the crime and its punishment was written by an eye-witness and printed by a local publishing house. It ended as follows:

"Note: Hilliard's power of endurance was the most wonderful thing on record. His lower limbs burned off before he became unconscious and his body looked to be burning to the hollow. Was it decreed by an avenging God as well as by an avenging people that his mortal sufferings be prolonged beyond the ordinary endurance of mortals?

"We have sixteen large views under powerful magnifying lenses now on exhibition. These views are true to life and show the Negro's attack, the scuffle, the murder, the body as found, etc. With eight views of the trial and burning. For place of exhibit see street bills. Don't fail to see this."

Breckenridge-Scruggs Co.

No indictments were found against any of the mob's members.

Louisiana 1899

A peculiarly horrible affair occurred two days ago at Lindsay, near Jackson, La. Mitchell Curry, hearing that someone was in his cornfield, took two Negroes and went to drive away the intruder. There had been an attempted assault on a white woman by a Negro, Val Bages, and by some unexplained course of reasoning, Mitchell Curry, on seeing a large Negro in the field, became convinced that the man was the criminal.

The fellow took fright, was followed, and finally climbed a magnolia tree. The tree was surrounded and the Negro ordered to remain where he was while one of the pursuers was sent for rope to hang him. Presently, however, the man deliberately slid down out of the tree, and halfway down he was shot to death. On examination of the body the man's clothing marked No. 43, was found to be that worn at the State Insane Asylum in the neighboring town of Jackson. On investigation it was learned that the insane occupant had escaped a few days before and the helpless fellow, wandering at large, had suffered death for a crime he had not committed.

Special despatch to New York Tribune, July 27, 1899.

South Carolina 1906

For attempting to enter a house and frightening a child who was alone in it, Willie Spain, a young Negro at St. George, S. C., was taken from jail and hung to a tree. The mob then shot five hundred bullets into his body.

New York Tribune, August 24, 1906.

Georgia 1911

T. W. Walker, a colored man of Washington, Ga., killed C. S. Hollinshead, a wealthy planter of the same place. It was stated that there was no apparent cause for the crime, but a Northern colored paper published the charge that Walker killed Hollinshead for attacking his wife and an Atlanta paper reprinted it. A crowd of white men tried to lynch Walker, who had been sentenced to death, but were so drunk that he succeeded in escaping. He was caught and resentenced to instant execution. Before he could be taken from the court room, a brother of Hollinshead shot and severely wounded him. He was then taken out and hanged, the court announcing that the brother would not be prosecuted. The only arrest made in connection with the affair was that of the Negro editor who published the charge against Hollinshead.

The Crisis, January, 1912.

West Virginia 1912

In Bluefield, W. Va., September 4, 1912, Robert Johnson was lynched for attempted rape. When he was accused he gave an alibi and proved every statement that he made. He was taken before the girl who had been attacked and she failed to identify him. She had previously described very minutely the clothes her assailant wore. When she failed to identify Johnson in the clothes he had, the Bluefield police dressed him to fit the description and again took him before her. This time she screamed on seeing him, "That's the man." Her father had also failed to identify him but now he declared himself positive that he recognized Johnson as the guilty man. Thereupon Johnson was dragged out by a mob, protesting his innocence, and after being severely abused, was hung to a telegraph pole. Later his innocence was conclusively established.

"The Lynching of Robert Johnson," James Oppenheim in *The Independent*, October 10, 1912.

Oklahoma 1914

Marie Scott of Wagner County, a seventeen-year-old Negro girl, was lynched by a mob of white men because her brother killed one of two white men who had assaulted her. She was alone in the house when the men entered, but her screams brought her brother to the rescue. In the fight that ensued one of the white men was killed. The next day the mob came to lynch her brother, but as he had escaped, lynched the girl instead. No one has ever been indicted for this crime.

The Crisis, June 1914. [3]

We may have forgotten ragtime and progressive reform, but we are probably aware that these years witnessed plenty of lynching. Both anecdotes and statistics fill books on the reign of terror, from then till now. This heavy load of material fully supports the point made by an African-American leader during the 1960's that "Violence is as American as apple pie."

"Lynch Law" means law determined and carried out by a mob, usually ending with an execution. The word apparently looks back to both James Lynch, a 15th-century Mayor of Galway, Ireland, and Col. Charles Lynch (1736-1796), a Virginia magistrate, both achievers of notoriety for practicing summary justice. The American Lynch punished Tories and felons during the unsettled period of the American Revolution. Later the lawless conditions of the 19th-century frontier drove people to act in vigilance committees to bring criminal elements under control. Highwaymen, rustlers, crooked gamblers, and bullies would be "terminated with extreme prejudice" whenever they threatened a community still beyond the boundary of due process.

To restore control over their former slaves, southern whites resorted to the vigilante tradition after the Civil War and Reconstruction. First came the terrorists of the hooded Ku Klux Klan, dramatic apparitions in torchlight, applying arson, the whip, and the noose to discourage aspirations to equality. After a few years these Klansmen, most of them ex-Confederates, could retire from the terror scene, having shown the poor white elements how to proceed as ad hoc lynch mobs. These mobs gathered to deal with offenses, real and imagined, serious and trivial, that the mob believed to be a threat to the control and power of white over black. From the first statistics (1882), until "Freedom Riders" Schwerner, Chaney, and Goodman were murdered in the swamps near Philadelphia, Mississippi, in 1964, 3446 African-American men and women were executed by angry mobs. This is contrasted with 1297 non-African American victims, most lynched in states bordering the South, and in western states. Most of those lynched in the West were Indians and Spanish speakers. [4]

An insightful contemporary account of the race problem was Ray Stannard Baker's *Following the Colour Line* (1908). Baker, one of the chief "muckrakers" or investigative reform journalists of the period, spent several years, 1904-1908, interviewing and observing on-site, both North and South, asking the reporter's questions: who, when, where, why, and how much? Thus, analyzing the 56 lynchings of 1907: 49 black men, 3 black women, 4 white men, he tabulated the specific offenses for which the offenders were put to death:

> For being father of boy who jostled white women......................1
> For being victor over white man in fight...................….......1
> Attempted murder...…...………5
> Murder of wife...…...1
> Murder of husband and wife............................…..............1
> Murder of wife and stepson..........................…................1
> Murder of mistress....................................…..................1
> Manslaughter..…....10
> Accessory to murder..1
> Rape...8
> Attempted rape..11
> Raping own stepdaughter...................….............1
> For being wife and son of a raper.....................….......2
> Protecting fugitive from posse..................................1
> Talking to white girls over telephone........................1
> Expressing sympathy for mob's victim...............……3
> Three-dollar debt...…....2
> Stealing seventy-five cents....................…..............1
> Insulting white man..............................…………....1
> Store burglary..…….3 [5]

Baker concentrated on a few locations, seeking answers from an in-depth investigation: Statesboro, Georgia, and Bulloch County; Huntsville, Alabama, and Madison County; Springfield, Ohio, and Clark County; and Danville, Illinois, and Vermilion County. First he examined the Negro populations, which comprised 40% of Bulloch County, Georgia, located in the "Black Belt," an interstate area where blacks made up almost half or more of the population. Madison County, Alabama, lying north of the Black Belt, contained fewer African Americans. In Springfield, Ohio, population 41,000, blacks amounted to 6000 or one-seventh of the city population, and in Danville, Illinois, "a growing Negro population" had raised social tensions. In each case Baker found two quite different populations: the "self-respecting resident Negro," having steady employment and an established place in the community, and a "class, who float from town to town, doing rough work, having no permanent place of abode, not known to the white population generally." [6]

Next he found that the "floating, worthless Negro caused most of the trouble." [7] Poverty, illiteracy, domestic deprivation, and homelessness made them vulnerable to wrong choices. Another universal malignance Baker uncovered was "the extraordinary prevalence in all these lynching counties, North as well as South, of crimes of violence." [8] All four areas exhibited high homicide rates. Bulloch County had 32 homicide cases in a five-year period. Madison County during the same five years saw 33 homicide cases tried in the courts, plus 8 indictments which never went to trial. Springfield had 10 homicides in two years, and Danville averaged a homicide every 60 days. [9]

Another characteristic in common was that one victim was never enough. The sight of a mutilated body increased a mob's frenzy and desire for more victims: "All the stored-up racial animosity came seething to the surface; all the personal grudges and spite." A rampaging mob usually attacked and battered or shot every black person unlucky enough to be visible. Often a "get even" motive caused certain members of a mob to call for the death of a particular person, but more often it was only a general hatred that drove a mob of poor white folk to commit unspeakable atrocities, a collective fury that blamed all of their misery on a people whose misery was greater. [10] An "intelligent farmer" told Baker: "Life is cheap in Madison County. If you have a grudge against a man, kill him; don't wound him. If you wound him, you'll likely be sent up; if you kill him you can go free. They often punish more severely for carrying concealed weapons or even for chicken stealing in Madison County than they do for murder." [11] Few were indicted for murdering blacks, none convicted. Nor were many convicted even for the murder of whites. African Americans seldom survived to go to trial. Grand juries usually attributed violent death to "unknown causes." Trial juries regularly returned verdicts of not guilty. [12]

Before the Civil War the South had pumped itself up to a vociferous advocacy of slavery: Slavery was ordained by God because inferior Negroes required the control and guidance of superior whites. Whites denied shame and guilt over slavery, claiming instead to be proud and positive in carrying on the "peculiar institution." This same aggressive-defensive attitude transferred to lynching after the War. The Negro had to be kept "in his place" beneath white society, for the same reason, racial inferiority. Hence lynching, the only effective way to teach a lesson to subhumans, became justice, dire and extreme perhaps, but justified because nothing less would work. Lacking wealth, they couldn't be sued or fined. Their labor supported the South, so the threat of job loss was hollow. The real threats lay on the other side: the black might reject his mean socio-material lot and depart for a better life up North—or, driven beyond endurance, he might turn violent; if he did, he would not only rob and murder, he would certainly overthrow the ultimate taboo: the rape of white women. This was the white man's nightmare. Everyone believed that the Negro lacked the higher faculty of conscience to control the powerful sexual appetite that raged within like a wild animal. Nature drove him to rape. These beliefs loomed absolute, beyond all debate, in the mentality of the South. Murder was the common offense that brought on the mob, and rape never exceeded one-quarter of the lynching offenses, but a Negro out of control who killed, robbed, or even acted with insolence toward whites, such a Negro would rape an unprotected woman. Lynching became imperative whenever a Negro threw over discipline. When Baker, the ignorant outsider, posed the (to him) logical and rational question of why the rape crime couldn't be left up to the law and constituted authority, he was told: "It is too great an ordeal for the self-respecting white woman to go into court and accuse the Negro ravisher and withstand a *public* (italics added) cross-examination. It is intolerable. No woman will do it. And, besides, the courts are uncertain. Lynching is the only remedy." [13]

A recent study (1995) agrees with Baker's findings of ninety years ago and observes further that whites controlled race relations through a code of etiquette. This was "a relatively consistent set of rules [that] governed face-to-face behavior in meetings between blacks and whites." [14] A black man had to remove his hat to speak to a white person and to touch his hat when passing whites. Whites kept theirs on. Whites had to be addressed as Boss, Mister, Missus, Miss, Mam, and Sir. Blacks, like medieval serfs, could only be addressed by first names and never called mister. A black could never enter or depart a white person's house by the front door. Physical contact was the ultimate breach of etiquette because blacks were perceived as unclean. Here etiquette rose to ritual, the avoidance of impurity. Pollution came from physical contact, such as a handshake, wearing, or even touching, clothing worn by a black. This was extended to drinking fountains, rest rooms, and eating places, though it is curious that there was contamination in dining together but not in consuming food prepared by a black person. When a white perceived a violation of this social code, violence became mandatory for restoring correct relations and for proper expiation of the misdeed. And the final retribution, for the breaking of the ultimate taboo, for going over the farthest boundary, carried the violator beyond all rights and claims of civilized treatment and consideration. [15]

This demanded not only a punishment that fitted the crime but an expiation that would purge away the contamination and restore purity. Thus lynchings had become "highly ritualized punishments." Whites had a duty to attend and demonstrate solidarity and a correct attitude. Any lurking pity for a victim transgressed what the community stood for. Sometimes the lynchee was paraded, dragged, or driven, noose already fitted, through the squalid lanes of "niggertown"—a "lesson" for all potential wrongdoers skulking therein—then perhaps through the downtown to collect more spectators. From there they proceeded to the crime scene to reenforce convictions of rectitude, and then on to the scene of execution, if the crime scene was not to be the execution scene.

The mob craved a slow death by torture, plus, for the worst crimes, the injuring, killing, or raping of a white woman, only fire could satisfy the revenge lust. Chained to a log on the ground or suspended from a branch, a victim received fire in his lower extremities first, and the game was to keep him in an agonized consciousness, as the flames progressively consumed him up the torso. Then, before death or unconsciousness took over, the victim was hung quickly, and as the charred flesh twisted, the watchers, women as well as men, emptied their guns into the corpse—sometimes wounding or killing fellow spectators in the shooting frenzy. The concluding stage of the lynching ritual was the collection of souvenirs. The mob eagerly coveted pieces of the rope, links of chain, remnants of clothing, and parts of the body, particularly fingers, the nose, lips, a piece of wooly scalp, and slices of internal organs. Often castration commenced the rites of torture, but if the genitalia survived intact, they were highly prized. All of these artifacts became "sacred objects, talismans that could bring good luck to the owners." [16]

Lynching peaked in the 1890's, years that saw a hundred or more of these atrocities. Decline set in after 1900 when the number fell consistently below 100, although it held steady at 50 or more during the Teens. We have yet to discover all of the reasons for this change. Was there a growth of compassion and a resultant willingness to let "the law take its course"? Did the increased prosperity of the Progressive Era somehow lower interracial stress? Did the increasing migration northward cause whites to regard blacks as too valuable to waste on mere object lessons? Certainly more African Americans migrated from country to city, where they were more likely to be arrested, detained in safety, tried in a courtroom, and have a sentence carried out, than to be handed over to a vengeful throng of poor whites. Thus more blacks were "legally" killed for crimes white juries found them guilty of perpetrating.

At that time counties and cities carried out capital sentences, states not yet having a monopoly on the death penalty. Henry Louis Mencken(1880-1956) as a police reporter in Baltimore regularly witnessed hangings by city and county authorities. All murderers and rapists were capitally punished, quickly executed after speedy trials. He comments that "…the majority of culprits hanged below the Mason and Dixon Line were of that great race [Negroes]." [17] On July 28, 1899, the eighteen-year-old rookie journalist witnessed the hanging of four blacks in the yard of the Baltimore City Jail. A large assembly of journalists attended, most drinking copiously. After being harangued by "relays of colored evangelists," each prisoner was hung. Mencken further comments that the sheriff, who sprang the trap himself, was also drunk, and that afterward he was "…assisted out of the jail yard by his deputies, and departed at once for Atlantic City, where he dug in for a week of nightmare." [18]

Another possible reason for the drop in lynching figures could be that many went unrecorded. Some locations were so isolated and underpopulated that their doings went unnoticed by the nearest country editor. In other cases such editors may have omitted such news, because violence might scare away much desired investors—all cotton-producing areas wanted textile mills—and also to fend off any investigations by outsiders. Outback communities lacked all recreational facilities (theatres, athletic fields, local teams, dance places, and even saloons—blue laws and churches were as responsible for this as demographics). Rural boredom lay as heavily as the dust from off the plowed fields. Groups of youths, whether or not liquored-up from someone's jug of illegal moonshine, often seized some unfortunate, passing Negro in order to "have some fun." Initially they may have meant only to scare a "darkie," making mock threats to lynch a male or gang rape a female. Running and resisting spiced up the game. But then too often came the point where too fierce a resistance, defiant words and blows returned, or a female gone into hysterical scratching and biting, turned cruel humor into anger, and a scene of horror followed. Some of the perpetrators may have felt guilt—they usually knew the victim—but to public opinion it was only a "nigger." The body in the grass or hanging from a limb provided a timely warning to any black folk likely to forget their "place." And if the woman survived, she had only gotten what they all wanted anyway. [19]

Except for these almost furtive lynchings, the practice flourished very publically out in the open. Since lynching's primary purpose was educational, "to teach them a lesson," it had community sanction. Negroes were like animals that become dangerous if let off the leash, animals with short memories which needed constant retraining. Such folk wisdom had to be instilled early, so men brought their families to witness these events, far too solemn to be considered family entertainment, but sanctioned domestic activity nevertheless. How else would children come to grasp the seriousness of the race problem? One of the more elaborate lynchings took place in Newman, Georgia, on April 23, 1899. Here one Sam Hose (or Holt), merely on suspicion of rape and murder, was slowly tortured, then burned alive before a large crowd that included family groups. Special trains had run out of Atlanta so that out-of-community people could take in this event. Afterward the semi-incinerated body, pulled from the fire, was cut open, the heart and liver extracted, then sliced into pieces, and passed around as souvenirs. One enthusiast even carried a slice back to Atlanta to present to the Governor. [20]

W. C. Handy, who experienced much of the African-American ordeal during his career in music, recalled a particularly gruesome and bizarre scene in Memphis:

> One morning while passing the square on Beale Street that now bears my name, I noticed a crowd of Negroes gathered around a skull. The day before that skull had belonged to a pleasant easy-going fellow named Tom Smith. Now it was severed from his body. The eyes had been burned out with red-hot irons. A rural mob, not satisfied with burning his body, had brought the skull back to town and tossed it into a crowd of Negroes to humiliate and intimidate them. [21]

THE LYNCHING

His spirit in smoke ascended to high heaven.
His father, by the cruelest way of pain,
Had bidden him to his bosom once again;
That awful sin remained still unforgiven.
All night a bright and solitary star
(Perchance the one that ever guided him
Yet gave him up at last to fate's wild whim)
Hung pitifully over the swinging char.
Day dawned, and soon the mixed crowds came to view

The ghastly body swaying in the sun.
The women thronged to look, but never a one
Showed sorrow in her eyes of steely blue;
And little lads, lynchers that were to be,
Danced round the dreadful thing in fiendish glee.
                              Claude McKay

from **THE BIRD AND THE TREE**

Blackbird, blackbird in the cage,
There's something wrong tonight.
    Far off the sheriff's footfall dies,
    The minutes crawl like last years flies
    Between the bars, and like an age
    The hours are long tonight.
The sky is like a heavy lid
    Out here beyond the door tonight.
    What's that? A mutter down the street.
What's that? The sound of yells and feet.
For what you didn't do or did
You'll pay the score tonight.
No use to reek with reddened sweat,
No use to whimper and to sweat.
    They've got the rope; they've got the guns,
They've got the courage and the guns;
An' that's the reason why tonight
No use to ask them anymore.
They'll fire the answer through the door—You're out to die tonight.
There where the lonely cross-road lies,
There is no Place to make replies;
But silence, inch by inch, is there,
And the right limb for a lynch is there;
And a lean daw waits for both your eyes,
Blackbird.
                              Ridgely Torrence

Notes: Chapter 8

1. J. William Harris, "Etiquette, Lynching, and Racial Boundaries in Southern History: A Mississippi Example," 390.
2. National Association for the Advancement of Colored People, *Thirty years of Lynching in the United States.*
3. *Ibid.*, 12-23.
4. Robert L Zangrando, "Lynching," 684-686; Zangrando, *The NAACP Campaign Against Lynching, 1909-1950,* 3; J. C. Furnas, *The Americans,* 848-850.
5. Ray Stannard Baker, *Following the Colour Line: An Account of Negro Citizenship in the American Democracy,* 176-177.
6. *Ibid.*, 177-178, 191-193, 201-202, 210-211.
7. *Ibid.*, 178.
8. *Ibid.*, 183.
9. *Idem.* and *Ibid.*, 193, 205, 211.
10. *Ibid.*, 187-188, 207-208.
11. *Ibid.*, 194.
12. *Idem.* and *Ibid.*, 197-198, 204-205, 208-209; Zangrando, "Lynching," 686.
13. Baker, 198-199.
14. Harris, 391.
15. *Ibid.*, 390-393.
13. *Ibid.*, 393-394; Baker, 185-187, 195-207; James Weldon Johnson, *Along This Way,* 361; Zangrando, "Lynching," 685-686.
14. Henry Louis Mencken, *The Days of H.L. Mencken,* III, 57-59.
15. Mencken, *Days,* II, 25-27.
16. Zangrando, "Lynching," 685; NAACP, 4.
17. William Ivy Hair, *Carnival of Fury: Robert Charles and the New Orleans Race Riot of 1900,* 107; NAACP, 12-13.
18. W. C. Handy, *Father of the Blues,* 178.

9. Fathers of Vaudeville (II)

In 1900 Keith-Albee joined five other theatre chains in forming what performers called the "Syndicate." Also known as the United Booking Office (or UBO), this combination (which certainly was, in anti-trust terms, "in restraint of trade") became the controlling instrument of the big business of vaudeville. Ten years later, the Syndicate's UBO booked all the acts for 700 theatres nationwide. The UBO hired all artists; planned the weekly bills for every house on the various circuits; handed the artists their season itineraries; and set all salaries. Everything was prearranged. No bargaining permitted. Refuse a billing, disobey a procedure or a theatre manager, and you were blacklisted. Anyone involved in organizing or unionizing the artists was blacklisted. The UBO determined who worked and who didn't. For these employment services, it deducted 5% off everyone's top. Even theatre owners had to accept whatever set of acts that opened the weekly show every Monday. [1] (The UBO's absolute hold was finally broken in 1916 when the Shubert Brothers successfully challenged it.)

Vaudeville dominated showbiz for the half-century before the cinema replaced it (1880-1930). Within, vaudeville was a subculture of outsiders. It served as a socio-economic ladder for those outside the pale of the native born and the middle class. Its expanding ranks filled rapidly with talents from immigrant and working-class backgrounds, especially Irish, Jews, and (a relative few) African Americans. Collectively these representatives of submerged ethnicities and classes did much to undermine Victorian manners and moral attitudes. Where Victorian ways were formal and deliberate, genteel and austere, variety entertainment was exuberant, funny, irreverent, and sensual. Eager to imbibe a new freedom from restraints, people lined up at box offices and left their proper selves outside. Vaudeville was boomed as wholesome entertainment fit for families, which it mostly was. But on most bills something racy or suggestive of the risqué usually turned up: clever song lyrics, double entendres, bits of dialogs, revealing costumes, wicked dance gyrations, or a facial leer. Audiences loved dancers in tights; they sniggered at "coon songs" about black folk whose wenching, thieving, fighting, and crude humor broke all the politeness rules; they roared at the suggestive jokes in comic sketches—as long as performers kept to the right side of the fine line of what was considered decent. Profanity, even "hell" or "damn," was over the line. The trick was to verbalize the unsayable so cleverly and archly that audiences were forced to laugh. [2]

As long as they heard no complaints, theater owners gladly—and hypocritically—bent the rules of good taste and morality. Full figured women in tights made it to the vaudeville stage from the concert-saloon. Besides the "classical statue" poses, they now danced. One bill offered "The World of Dancers," featuring "prehistoric barbarians," "the flesh pots of Egypt," and a finale in which "dancers of the ages past become acquainted with syncopation." There was "La Napierkowska," a "pantomimist and dancer," who, according to the *Billboard* reviewer:

> …is some dancer…. There isn't a portion of her body that she can not make wriggle at will, and there is very little of it that isn't constantly wriggling during the time which she spends on the stage in her offering *The Captive*. She is supposed—so the story program runs—to have been stung by a bee and the gyrations that follow are consequent of the pain she feels. It must be some pain for such wriggling has never been seen on a high-grade vaudeville stage.

And there was Annette Kellerman the famous swimmer. Kellerman packaged her exhibition as a musical show with elaborate costumes, but the in the finale she came on in bathing tights and performed fancy dives into a tank onstage. A reviewer classified the preceding musical spectacles as "merely a time filler." [3]

Wife jokes were typical comic fare, such as Bert Williams' famous sally: "If you have two wives, that's bigamy. If you have many wives, that's polygamy. If you have one wife, that's monotony." [4] Another celebrated quip carried the notion a little further by implication: "I sent my wife to the Thousand Islands for a vacation—a week on each island." [5] This is more bluntly put in two of Irving Berlin's song titles: "My Wife's Gone to the Country (Hurray! Hurray!)," and "I Love My Wife But Oh, You Kid!" This jokey mode of playing on sex enlivened many other song titles: "Mary took Her Calves to the Dairy Show"(1908), "This Is No Place for a Minister's Son"(1909), and "If You Talk in Your Sleep, Don't Mention My Name"(1910) (Chapter 18). [6] Another comic trick was to perform suggestive material in dialect in coon songs and comic sketches. Most humor in vaudeville was in fact ethnic, and since blacks and foreigners were viewed as having low—or no—moral standards, audiences could feel superior as they laughed. Here is a famous example from the sketch "The Art of Flirtation":

> Straight: Ven you flirt, you meet a pretty woman in a shady spot.
> Comedian: Oh, you met a shady woman in a pretty spot?
> Straight: Not a shady woman. A pretty woman in a shady spot! [7]

This verbal loosening tended to erode the formality and restraints of the common language. What was heard in the hall was taken out to the streets. Young ladies came to be called "chickens" and "flappers." Flippancy took over with common rejoinders like: "You said something!" "You said it!" "You said a mouthful!" [8] Climaxing this onslaught against Victorian folkways was Eva Tanguay (Chapter 18), the most explosive solo act in vaudeville. When Eva cavorted in her (almost) demented manner around the stage, belting out her signature song, "I Don't Care," audiences caught her immoral message. There may have been a general disapproval, but her high voltage obliterated it, momentarily at least. What vaudeville poured out into the pop mainstream helped to create a freer, more open, if more morally ambiguous, America. [9]

Another father of vaudeville was Fred F. Proctor (b. 1852), the chief rival of B.F. Keith and E.F. Albee. From Maine like Albee, Proctor rose from department store errand boy to variety juggler to theatre owner. By the late 1870's he was proprietor of a New England chain offering "small-time," which presented either three-a-day or continuous shows. His chain expanded in the 1880's starting in Albany (1880), and by the 1890's, he had four NYC theatres. These charged 10-20-30 cents, the price rising as the day advanced. Running from 11:00 to 11:00, his NY theatres advertised: "After breakfast go to Proctor's/After Proctor's go to bed." He proudly labeled himself the "pioneer" of continuous vaudeville, thereby causing B.F. Keith much heartburn. Later (1929) the sale of his eleven major theatres to Joseph P. Kennedy's RKO movie corporation for about $18,000,000 climaxed his great success. When he died in 1914, B.F. Keith was worth only $10,000,000. [10]

However the biggest of the small-timers, the creator of a chain that was truly transcontinental, was Marcus Loew, the future film magnate. Coming after the "pioneers" and "fathers" of the medium, he gloried in the title of "the Henry Ford of Show Business." Ensconced in the nation's small-town "opera houses," his chain paid the least for talent that was either just starting or finishing careers, and thereby sold the most tickets for the lowest prices. Further economies were achieved by staging local beauty contests and amateur nights, awarding prizes that cost a fraction of the cheapest talent. Showbiz went no lower than this, when rejected talent was ignominiously jerked offstage by "the hook." Amateur night audiences loved being loud and nasty, their boo's backed up by rotten veggies, followed by derisive shouts and laughter as the expected hook encountered and pulled its hapless victim into the wings. The MC would determine the winner by holding a $5 bill over the head of each amateur who had successfully completed his routine, the winner getting the cash. [11]

The wages of small-time began at $20/week and could reach $90. Big-time, the goal of all small-timers, meant a mammoth increase into the hundreds, with headliners often receiving thousands. But a small-timer earning $3000 a year lived far above a factory worker making $1300 or a domestic getting $600. Vaudeville stardom was—like big-time sports today—an escape from the streets. Maggie Cline, Eva Tanguay, Eddie Cantor, Sophie Tucker, all progressed from poverty through small-time to big-time. However touring was an ordeal of loneliness and hard conditions. Every week meant another town with terrible food and bad accommodations. Hotels were too few and poor, and many boardinghouses posted the sign: "No dogs or actors allowed." [12] Shows closed Saturday night, and artists had to be packed and ready to board the next train out. After an exhausting Sunday on jolting trains, came another suspicious town with a shabby room and a lumpy mattress. At Monday matinees, the local managers checked for offending material. Their instructions to delete were inserted into blue envelopes and sent backstage (hence "blue" meaning off-color). Such acts of censorship did not cause any temperamental responses. To disobey such commands meant immediate discharge, the blacklist, and loss of livelihood. In these small cities and towns of the heartland, where they encountered a universal dislike of Jews, Catholics, and African Americans, artists felt like outcasts. [13]

Each week the UBO sent out a typical bill to each theatre. Nine acts usually constituted the bill for two-a-day houses on big-time circuits. First came the "dumb" act, something unspectacular, dancers or animals, to fill the time while the audience entered and settled down. Singers—plural—always filled the second spot. A bill had to be assembled carefully, so as not to peak too soon. Now came the time for the third act to get a grip on the audience, a comedy sketch which served to draw out responses and laughter. Number four further heightened interest by bringing on the first "name" performer, a soloist who sang, played, danced, or any combination thereof. Five brought on another "name" act that cranked up the audience one more notch and sent them out buzzing during intermission. Then it was the tough job of six to recapture the audience and raise expectations further. Seven had to be even stronger, building to the climax, which was number eight, the "headliner," the star everyone came to see. Then, after the last encore, the final bow, as attention fell off the peak, it was the indifferent task of nine to close the show, again perhaps with animals doing tricks or a pyramid of acrobats or some juggling, something to relax the departing audience. [14]

Vaudeville's big take-off synchronized with the turn of the century. NYC had 10 major variety theatres in 1896; this had tripled by 1910 to 31. Chicago had 22 houses that year. By1913 there were 2973 regularly booked theatres nationwide, and 1200 variety companies on tour. The *New York Times* estimated that the public was spending 25 to 30 million dollars on entertainment. By 1917 Keith-Albee's UBO was booking over 7900 acts (and getting 5% of each). Altogether it has been estimated that from 1875 to 1925, 25,000 artists worked about 4000 theatres, from big-time down to the smallest small-time, including split-weeks and "one-night stands" in lodge halls and converted barns. [15] The cheapest vaudeville in New York's neighborhood houses ("nabes") presented six acts for five cents. The biggest and costliest attractions, the actress Sarah Bernhardt and the singer Harry Lauder, were European imports. After much dickering, Lauder finally came over in 1908 to do his Scottish schtick ("Roamin' in the Gloamin'" and "I Luv a Lassie") for $2500 a week. He was getting $4000 by 1913 and traveled in his own railroad car. Sarah Bernhardt, 73 years old, minus a leg, speaking only in French, broke all road records in 1911. For her most popular role, *Camille*, she received $23,000 for one week's work at Keith's Palace. [16]

Notes: Chapter 9

1. Robert W. Snyder, *The Voice of the City: Vaudeville and Popular Culture in New York*, 35; Russell Sanjek, *American Popular Music and Its Business: The First Four Hundred Years* II, 324.
2. Snyder, 43, 142-145, Abel Green and Joe Laurie, Jr., *Show Biz: From Vaude to Video*, 46.
3. Snyder, 142-145.
4. Charles and Louise Samuels, *Once Upon a Stage: The Merry World of Vaudeville*, 188.
5. Green and Laurie, 5.
6. *Ibid.*, 101.
7. Snyder, 146-147.
8. Green and Laurie, 167.
9. Samuels, 54-57.
10. *Ibid.*, 41-44; Green and Laurie, 154, for Keith.
11. Snyder, 96-100.
12. Samuels, 14.
13. Snyder, 47-57; Samuels, 5.
14. Snyder, 66-67.
15. *Ibid.*, 68-69; Samuels, 4-5, 221, 248.
16. Green and Laurie, 29-31, 46, 69-70, 157.

10. TR and the Splendid Little War

The Planning Stage

What a difference a century makes in attitudes. We look back on nine decades of hostilities, interrupted occasionally by peace. Back then, many (not everyone) still viewed going to war as a coming-of-age thing. A highly regarded novel of the time, *The Red Badge of Courage* (1895), by Stephen Crane, portrays a youth who panics and runs away from his first Civil War battle, wanders behind the lines through a dark night of his soul to a dawn of self-understanding, and returns calmly to his unit capable of enduring the war's terrors and carnage. Crane knew that "war is hell," but he did not think of rejecting it like Frederick Henry in Ernest Hemingway's *A Farewell to Arms* (1928) a generation later. (Henry, an ambulance driver on the Italo-Austrian front during WWI, while downing a couple of cool, dry martinis in a resort hotel, decides to decamp for the Swiss Alps along with his pregnant lover, a nurse.)

The Civil War, which killed about 620,000 during four years in the bloodiest and grittiest battles of the century, failed to inoculate Americans against war. By 1895, the old soldiers who knew better were either dead or unlistened to, as the nation became excited over the rebellion of the Cubans against Spain. Terrible things happen in a rebellion: mass incarcerations, torture, exposure, hunger, epidemics, rape, loss and destruction of property, both casual and deliberate cruelties, and wrongful deaths. But such events usually arouse only local interests—and the interests of business and governments. Until we hear about them, until the popular media broadcast the messy details. The mass circulation newspaper had hit the streets by the early 1890's, and there were endless columns to fill. It was a monster with an insatiable appetite for "news"—daily novelties and dramas. The "barons" of the "yellow press," especially William Randolph Hearst and Joseph Pulitzer, sent reporters to Cuba with instructions to telegraph fresh daily stories to maintain and increase daily circulation. In effect they pushed the button that started the perpetual conveyor belt of the news process. (Today it is merely "new and improved.") The Cuban rebellion soon got a boost from this news process. As the rebels became aware of their mass audience in the great Anglo republic to the north, the struggle intensified and events came about oftener and sooner. This in turn aroused U.S. "public opinion". Thus not only did pressures on Spain and the rebels escalate (as we now say), but a sympathetic pressure, a kind of huge false pregnancy, arose in the U.S. By 1897 there was talk of intervention.

One old soldier who did not want to intervene was the new president William McKinley (1843-1901) who had run the full gamut of the Civil War going from private to major (old friends and wife Ida usually referred to him as "the Major"). No fire-eater, he was a gentle, careful, and laidback Victorian gentleman. One historian called him "a kindly soul in a spineless body" [1], but another perceived an amiability that "masked his strength of character and capacity to deal with Congress and dominate his advisers." [2] McKinley wasn't inept; he was just alone on the belligerency question. Plus, globally, he was up against imperialism, a potent national motive just peaking in the 1890's. In the "developed" nations of Europe, North America, and Japan, there was a mass lust for new territories (colonies). The slightest victory in an overseas skirmish brought out patriotic mobs to cheer. People gloated over the appearance of their country's color in yet another square on the world map. The lonely Major was about to be caught in the undertow of vicarious excitement. McKinley's innate pacifism recoiled from the intense vibes of Theodore Roosevelt who applied influence and pressure for appointment as Assistant Secretary of the Navy. As the author of *The Naval War of 1812* (1882), TR was respected in Navy circles. The book had been adopted as a textbook at the recently founded Naval War College, and every Navy ship carried a copy. The English had found it so fair to their side that they had requested its author to write the War of 1812 section for their multi-volume *History of the Royal Navy*. TR had since done his homework, staying current with naval affairs and corresponding with leading officers and authorities, like Alfred Thayer Mahan, author of that bible of global strategy, *The Influence of Sea Power Upon History (1660-1783)* (1890).

TR had the credentials and expertise, plus the determination to create a strong navy. The problem was that too much of this showed. McKinley wanted government to serve business while keeping the necessary peace. Sensing the volatility in the times, he felt uncertain about inviting into his cabinet an aggressive advocate for a first-class fleet. Such tendencies could not only push the nation willy-nilly into war, but push up the taxes to pay for it, thereby leaching away the profits of business.

But Roosevelt had presented a bill for campaign services rendered. He had done a lot of the heavy lifting out on the speaking platforms of the Midwest where Bryan's defeat had been accomplished (Chapter 7). The sedentary, homebound candidate had not needed to exert himself past his front porch in Canton, Ohio. As a politician McKinley well understood that the *quid pro quo* principle applied to all political transactions: people do things for you because they expect you to do something for them. Unlike charity, the reward of politics is not the simple satisfaction of giving. When TR's friends backed his recommendation to the number-two spot in the Navy, McKinley knew that a refusal would lead to future political damage. Still the prospect of Roosevelt's hands on the levers of military power made him uneasy, and he fretted to TR's mentor Senator Henry Cabot Lodge: "I hope he has no preconceived plans which he would wish to drive through the moment he got in." [3]

McKinley had been in Congress when Civil Service Commissioner Roosevelt, a bureaucrat of the third rank, had attacked Postmaster General Wanamaker, the Republican patronage boss, over corrupt practices in appointments (a little over five years earlier). And there had been the recent Sunday-closing battle in New York that pitted Police Commissioner Roosevelt against the entire state. Despite these quite accurate misgivings, the President, after some weeks of sighing over the potential difficulties, gave in to the political flow and acceded to the appointment. TR on his side promised to be good and to support his new chief, Secretary of the Navy John D. Long, ex-Governor of Massachusetts. Long was an older man, easy-going, relaxed, who did not want to rock boats, political or naval. He was an amiable, fatherly type and a hypochondriac who reacted to pressures by going to see his doctor. TR came in stroking his likeable superior, but they looked in different directions rather than at each other. Soon the new Assistant Secretary became deeply involved in naval complexities: inspecting facilities and ships, planning new construction, developing global strategy, planning a Cuban campaign, addressing naval officers about his concerns, and getting his choices selected for the more important commands. All of which troubled and mystified the Secretary who had entered office knowing little of naval affairs. Long praised the industry of his turbulent assistant while trying to impose some fatherly restraints, which failed utterly. With his rather vague and uncertain grasp of technicalities, Long usually learned about changes—the significance of which he was unable to grasp—only after the fact.

For about a year TR had a marvelous time running the Navy, bringing it up to strength for the coming war against Spain that he believed inevitable. McKinley's political apprehensions were soon aroused by the vigor and industry apparent over at Navy, and he invited Roosevelt (who was batching it while Edith concerted the move from NYC to DC) to the Executive Mansion on several occasions for dinner and for company on carriage rides.

Incapable of reticence, the youthful Assistant Secretary gave the President more than an earful: He (TR) was certain about a war with Spain, and when it came, he planned to resign, join the army, and go to Cuba—regardless of any objections by his wife or his mentor Senator Lodge. On the last occasion, whetted by the President's open-eyed interest, he reeled off a strategic plan developed at the Navy Department outlining operations in the coming war. Here in the late spring of 1897, a new president—whose heart and mind sought the avoidance of war—almost a year before the public clamored for it—learned that the main fleet, running out of Key West, would blockade Cuba within 48 hours. Then the army would invade for a quick victory. At the same time, the Asiatic Squadron would steam to the Philippines and attack the Spanish fleet based there. There is no record of the effect of these disclosures upon McKinley, which prophesied the events that produced victory a year later. [4]

Meanwhile, ignoring the provocations of the horror tales telegraphed to the press by correspondents in Cuba, McKinley bided his time and held a peaceful stance. Secretary Long adhered to the official peace policy by not giving in to his number two's insistence that the North Atlantic Fleet be based in Key West and put on alert status. However the Cuban conflict worsened in January 1898, causing the President to dispatch the second-rate battleship *Maine* to Havana, hoping that the concern manifested in a show of force would influence the combatants toward moderation. Then on February 15, the *Maine* blew up and sank, losing 266 lives. The picture of the tops of her masts marking the site of the catastrophe became the symbol that hit the universal patriotic nerve. The U.S. erupted in flag burnings and riots. The President urged calm and ordered an investigation, but the momentum of war sentiment was not restrained. McKinley protested in vain: "I have been through one war. I have seen the dead piled up, and I do not want to see another." [5]

On February 25, Secretary Long, worn down by the crisis and the series of emergency meetings, took the afternoon off to consult his physician. Roosevelt seized this opportunity to send out battle orders to the U.S. fleets. Ships were sent to new stations; ammunition orders went out to suppliers; coal was ordered; ship owners were notified that certain vessels were to be purchased to serve as auxiliary cruisers; members of Congress were asked to sponsor legislation authorizing enlistments; guns were ordered; officers were reassigned. Quite a full afternoon's work! The most important order went to Commodore George Dewey in Hong Kong. Months earlier, TR had promoted Dewey to command of the Asiatic Squadron—over the heads of officers more senior—because of a reputation for aggressive tactics, a presumption that he would fight hard. The telegram ordered:

> Keep full of coal. In the event declaration of war Spain, your duty will be to see that the Spanish Squadron will not leave the Asiatic coast and then offensive operations in the Philippine Islands.[6]

This unauthorized activity may have been ahead of the game, but it accurately reflected the national will. The daily media outflow of violence and atrocities had stimulated bellicose appetites, and the *Maine* catastrophe triggered a mass feeding frenzy. Virtually no one believed the explosion to be accidental; all universally assumed this to be yet another chapter in the "black legend" of Spanish cruelty in the New World. (No definite conclusion has ever been reached on the *Maine* explosion, but the weight of informed opinion points to spontaneous combustion in a forward coal locker.) [7] A very unhappy President McKinley, dragged along in the wake of public demands, took us into war against Spain on April 20, 1898. [8]

Theodore Roosevelt gladly exchanged his desk job for a commission on May 5.

A Star Turn in Cuba

It turned out to be a ragtime war: short, snappy, upbeat. (It was Secretary of State John Hay who called it the "splendid little war.") It engendered a national mood so buoyant that the "Gay Nineties" have been more recollected than the decade's years of depression. Coming out of it a hero, TR projected qualities of gusto, optimism, power, and the joy of life. The troops sailed off to Cuba singing the new ragtime songs, one of which, "A Hot Time in the Old Town Tonight," became TR's theme and campaign song. [9]

Except for three years in the New York National Guard (1882-1884, promoted captain in 1883), Theodore lacked military experience. In April he and Captain Leonard Wood decided to raise an elite cavalry regiment of volunteers. Wood (1860-1927) is a curious figure, both a soldier—Indian Wars and frontier service, including the Geronimo campaign in Arizona—and an M D—he was McKinley's official physician. On their frequent long walks around the nation's capital, the two had become close friends and fellow schemers. TR looked up to Wood's professional background, and when McKinley graciously offered the colonelcy of the First Voluntary Cavalry Regiment, TR declined it in Wood's favor, accepting the number two rank of Lt. Colonel instead. The First V. C. Regiment was elite because only experienced horsemen were enlisted. The press jumped heavily on the concept and glamorized it, calling the troops "Rough Riders." There were about 23,000 applications, resulting in a careful selection of polo players and cowboys, who represented all levels of society and all sections of the nation. Elite certainly, but also very democratic. [10]

Just before leaving Navy for the training camp in San Antonio, Texas, TR ordered a dozen pairs of spectacles and some smokeless powder. Wood organized the few weeks of training, but TR dominated by leading this unlikely combination of university graduates and reformed western badmen in field exercises. They became his—and remained so until he died. Throughout the next twenty years, they would write, sometimes from jail, and would come to see him for help and advice. He even gave them government jobs when he could (probably his only corrupt acts in office). They turned up in his political campaigns. They received the hospitality of the White House. It was a remarkable bonding. [11]

The regiment entrained for Tampa after three enjoyable May weeks in Texas, were embarked on June 7, and, after an inept delay, sailed for Cuba on June 13. The expeditionary force invaded near Santiago at the island's eastern end. They were victorious within a few weeks, but a rough time was had by the Rough Riders and all. The shipping was inadequate, and some of the troops, including half of the RR's, and a large amount of supplies, had to be left on the docks in Tampa. The commanding general William Shafter was physically disabled; he was so obese as to be unable to walk or ride any distance. He had to be carted around on a door. Without adequate food, clothing (the army issue was woolen), medicine, or supplies, a green army came ashore in unfamiliar tropics. The few brief and furious battles killed 379 soldiers, while over 5000 died from tropical and other diseases. [12]

The press focused on the glamorous, but horseless (no space for livestock on the ships), half-regiment of Rough Riders. After holding up well in their first battle at Las Guasimas on June 24, they attained glory on July 1 in the skirmish and charge up a well defended hill, not San Juan, which was nearby, but Kettle Hill, named for the large iron caldron, used to reduce cane juice to sugar, which sat at the top. Roosevelt started the charge on his pony Little Texas, but the Spanish bullets were so profuse that he dismounted halfway up and led on foot. After taking Kettle Hill, they fired at San Juan Hill in support of the Regulars' advance there. Then they attacked farther ahead, victorious when the remaining enemy soldiers retreated at day's end. Although he had been point man in a wild battle, Theodore came through with only a grazed elbow. Bob Ferguson, a family friend, described him in action in a letter to Theodore's younger sister Corinne:

> Theodore moved about in the midst of shrapnel explosions like Shadrach, Meschach, & Sons in the midst of the fiery furnace, unharmed by vicious Mauser balls or by the buzzing exploding bullets of the irregulars. Theodore preferred to stand up or walk about snuffling the fragrant air of combat. I really believe firmly now that they cannot kill him. [13]

It became a legend, but it was real—and very deadly. Of 490 Rough Riders, 86 were killed or wounded, 40 fell down from the heat, and 6 were missing. In 133 days of service, one in three died from bullets or disease, the highest casualty rate for any unit in the force. Previously Colonel Wood had moved up to Brigadier General to replace an ailing colleague, and Theodore had led the regiment into the decisive battle as its Colonel. [14]

But there is more than legend. The glory part may be grandstanding by a legend-seeking politician—the political instinct never sleeps—but TR was savior as well as leader. Conditions in Cuba soon went to the bad. As soon as landed, the troops became victims of inept planning, unscouted and difficult terrain, and the lack of adequate shelter in an oppressive climate. Theodore described it precisely in a letter to Edith:

> I have been sleeping on the ground in the macintosh, and so drenched with sweat that I haven't been dry a minute day or night…. My bag has never turned up, like most of our baggage…I have nothing with me, no soap, toothbrush, razor, brandy, medicine chest, socks, or underclothes… For four days I never took off my clothes…and we had no chance to boil the water we drank…. The morning after the fight we buried our dead in a great big trench, reading the solemn burial services over them and all the regiment joined in singing "Rock of Ages." The vultures were wheeling overhead by hundreds. They plucked out the eyes and tore the faces and the wounds of the dead Spaniards before we got to them, and even one of our men who lay in the open. The wounded lay in the path, a ghastly group; but there were no supplies for them…The woods are full of land crabs…when things grew quiet they slowly gathered in gruesome rings around the fallen. [15]

He was constantly scrounging for his men, even buying food and supplies with his own money. He was seen emerging from the jungle lugging a heavy sack filled with rolled oats, rice, condensed milk, dried fruit, and other delicacies for the sick and wounded who couldn't eat the cruder army rations. The novelist Stephen Crane watched this activity and recorded it for Pulitzer's *New York World*: "He tried to feed them. He helped build latrines. He cursed the quartermasters and the "dogs" on the transports, to get quinine and grub for them. Let him be a politician if he likes. He was a gentleman down there." [16]

The surrender came on July 17 as many troops sickened and more of them died. There were no orders to reembark. Feeling powerless, the regular army officers turned to their famous civilian colleague for help. The cabal offered silent support to a letter from Colonel Roosevelt to General Shafter (who was in on it too), strongly criticizing the failures of the War Department to support the troops and to get them out of Cuba. Which was then leaked to the press and caused a furor stateside (as hoped). This hard-ball tactic and breach of military etiquette outraged the President and Secretary of War Russell Alger. Again Roosevelt angered party regulars by apparently and gratuitously turning on the political friends who had appointed him. But fearing a public relations donnybrook, Alger and his subordinates sent ships racing to Santiago, Cuba, and the earlier return saved many men from yellow fever, malaria, and dysentery. Alger got his revenge by withholding the Congressional Medal of Honor. [17] (What Theodore was denied in 1898, his son Brigadier General Theodore Roosevelt, Jr earned in Normandy in 1944, leading a division on D-Day.)

So the time in Cuba didn't turn out to be quite a ragtime. Like most wars, it was an exercise in survival. But somehow throughout Theodore carried on blithely as well as bravely. It shows in the bond with his men. If he'd been too grim about it, they wouldn't have kept coming back. He made it fun too. They loved him for it. He was the exemplar, what we now call a "role model," of good spirits. It was this ragtime aura that provided an essential boost to the career of the future Ragtime President.

Notes: Chapter 10

1. Samuel Eliot Morison, *The Oxford History of the American People*, 799.
2. Ari Hoogenboom, "McKinley, William," 714.
3. Nathan Miller, *Theodore Roosevelt: A Life*, 246-247, 129-130; Henry F. Pringle, *Theodore Roosevelt: A Biography*, 45.
4. N. Miller, 260-261; Sylvia Jukes Morris, *Edith Kermit Roosevelt: Portrait of a First Lady*, 166; Corinne Robinson, *My Brother, Theodore Roosevelt*, 160-161.
5. N. Miller, 266.
6. *Ibid.*, 267.
7. *Ibid.*, 266n.
8. *Ibid.*, 266-267; Pringle, 116, 123-125; William Henry Harbaugh, *Power and Responsibility: The Life and Times of Theodore Roosevelt*, 93, 95, 97-100.
9. N. Miller, 186.
10. Pringle, 45, 127-129; Robinson, 165; Harbaugh, 105-106.
11. Pringle, 130-139.
12. Morton Keller, "Spanish-American War," 1015-1016; Pringle, 127, 131-135.
13. Robinson, 174.
14. N. Miller, 278-279; S.J. Morris, 180-181; Pringle, 186-187; Robinson, 174-175.
15. S.J. Morris, 179-180.
16. *Ibid.*, 182-183.
17. Harbaugh, 108; S.J. Morris, 182-183; Pringle, 137.

11. There's No Business Like Race Business (II): Cakewalks and Coonsongs

> All coons look alike to me,
> I've got another beau you see.
> And he's just as good to me
> As you, nig, ever tried to be.
> He spends his money free;
> I know we can't agree.
> So I don't like you no how-
> All coons look alike to me.
>
> Ernest Hogan (1896)

There has been a craze for Negro songs and dances. This craze, judging from the size and quality of the audiences that Negro performers are attracting, has not even reached its zenith. I realize that there is a decided demand for Negro acts, and so long as they prove acceptable to audiences I cater to, I shall endeavor to supply them (the manager of Koster and Bial's Music Hall, NYC, in 1898). [1]

RAGTIME ALMANAC

Coonsong Hits

My Gal Is a High Born Lady (Early 1890's) Barney Fagan
You've Been a Good Old Wagon,
     But You Done Broke Down (1894) Ben Harney
The Bully Song (1895) Charles Travathan
All Coons Look Alike To Me (1896) Ernest Hogan
My Coal Black Lady (1896) W. T. Jefferson Mr. Johnson, Turn Me Loose (1896) Ben Harney
Coon, Coon, Coon (1898) Gene Jefferson & Leo Friedman
Cakewalk in the Sky (1899) Ben Harney

Cakewalk Hits

Rastus On Parade (1895) Kerry Mills
At a Georgia Camp Meeting (1897) Kerry Mills
Mississippi Rag (1897) W. H. Krell
Eli Green's Cakewalk (1898) Sadie Koninski
Smokey Mokes (1899) Abe Holzmann Ragtime Skedaddle (1899) George Rosey
Whistling Rufus (1899) Kerry Mills
Bunch O' Blackberries(1900) Abe Holzmann
Creole Belles (1900) J. Bodewalt Lampe
A Coon Band Contest (1900) Arthur Pryor
Hunky Dory (1901) Abe Holzmann

By the 1890's African Americans, emancipated for 25 years, wanted to appear onstage as themselves, not as Sambo stereotypes. Outside minstrelsy and spirituals, very few had reached the stage, and those exceptions, usually cripples like Blind Boone or females like the Hyer Sisters, performed mainly art music, which appealed to a relative few. A curious example of the former was the pianist Blind Tom. Thomas Green Bethune (1849-1908), born to slavery on a Georgia plantation, seems to have been what today is termed an "idiot savant." He could play every composition that he had ever heard, including his own works, and he amazed audiences with stupendous improvisations on suggested themes. The Bethune family exhibited him as early as 1858 to supplement plantation income. After emancipation the Bethunes retained this musical asset, sending Blind Tom out on national and some European tours until 1904, whenever they needed more income. (The Hyer Sisters, Anna and Emma, performed opera arias and sentimental songs after the Civil War.) [2]

During the 1890's African Americans gained new opportunities on the vaudeville and musical stages, but audiences forced them to transfer the old stereotypes to these new venues. In vaudeville, where, because of the hostility of white artists, no more than one "colored" act could appear on a program, blacks were still expected to black up, sing coon songs in southern dialect, wear outlandish costumes, and conclude the act with a "darkey" dance, clog, or cakewalk. In fairness, it must be added that all stage humor of that period was ethnic. Comedians came on as Irish, Hebrew, German, Scandinavian, blackface, hayseed, and city slicker, and were thus characterized in the program. All was stereotypical: tough Irishmen, stupid Germans, clever Jews, etc. But equal treatment for ethnics stopped at the color line: whites could appear in any ethnic guise including blackface, but blacks could play only caricatures of their presumed bad traits. [3]

James Weldon Johnson (1871-1938), poet and lyricist of ragtime songs, says that coonsongs "were concerned with jamborees of various sorts and the play of razors, with the gastronomical delights of chicken, pork chops and watermelon, and with the experiences of red-hot 'mammas' and their never too faithful 'papas.'" [4] Johnson's distinguished career included song lyrics, poetry, fiction, autobiography, diplomacy—U.S. Consul in Venezuela and Nicaragua—and Field Secretary of the NAACP. The coonsong was a relic of minstrelsy in that it came burdened with the old, hated freight of minstrel stereotypes, but its appeal lay in its new, raggy music. Minstrels had long sung of coons; ragtime added syncopation. [5]

It all came together during 1895-96, as the exciting new ragtime percolated along the rail routes into the city sin districts. Three people appear to be the chief instigators: Ernest Hogan, Ben Harney, and May Irwin. May Irwin created the first coonsong hit in 1895 with "The Bully Song." This number shot the zaftig Irwin to fame as a "coon shouter." It was interpolated into *The Widow Jones*, a musical play created for her. She had struggled her way up from the seamier kind of variety to the respectability of Broadway, but had made her mark belting out loud comic numbers. "The Bully Song," about a rivalry between two black badmen that was settled with razors, apparently came out of "Babe Connor's Castle," the famous St.Louis parlor house (see Chapter 35). May scored big with a cleaned-up version, and it became her signature piece, always requested at her appearances. [6] The song that set off the craze—about 600 coonsongs appeared from 1895 to 1900—was "All Coons Look Alike To Me." Like "The Bully Song," "All Coons" can claim bordello origins. African-American showman Ernest Hogan had come upon it in a Chicago location where it was sung as "All Pimps Look Alike To Me." Hogan added new words (epigraph above) and gave it some cakewalk syncopation. It sold 1,000,000 copies. Hogan may have enjoyed the prestige that a hit song brought, but for the rest of his life, he felt shame and a sense of race betrayal. (Perhaps his misery was increased by that year's major Supreme Court decision Plessey vs. Ferguson which legalized segregation: proof to most whites of black inferiority.) In asserting sameness, the song's title reenforced this impression by denying individuality: only an expert could tell them apart. The unhappy reality was that audiences paid to hear coonsongs. Self-billed as the "Unbleached American," he was one of the few African-American headliners in vaudeville's big-time:

> A real coon, one Ernest Hogan, who calls himself an unbleached American, received the lion's share of the attentions of the large audience at Keith's yesterday, in the excellent program. His clever way of rendering coon songs created a wild furor. Hogan had about the hardest place in the bill to fill, too, and that he did so satisfactorily was the more to his credit. *Boston*, MA, *Globe*, April 15, 1902 [7]

Hogan received the highest pay of all black vaudeville artists of that period, starred in musicals, achieved international fame, but lived a haunted figure, more focused on potential violence than upon his very real success. [8]

Fellow black showman Tom Fletcher credits Hogan with putting ragtime syncopation into the coonsong: "[He] was the first to put on paper the kind of rhythm that was being played by non-reading musicians." Further "…the fact remains that the combination of the word and the new rhythm created a big sensation and gave show business of that era a badly needed shot in the arm." [9] Hogan himself made no such claim of innovation, but one who did was Ben Harney. Benjamin Robertson Harney (1871-1938) injects some confusion into the ragtime story. He played so authentically that some ragtime historians think he could have been a Negro. [10] From Kentucky, he left military school at 17 to become an itinerant performer, and a few years later married fellow Kentuckian Jessie Boyce. Harney combined an affinity for black music and culture along with the talent for delighting white audiences with such (then) unknown material. From 1889 until April 1896, Ben and Jessie hit the road as entertainers. Details are few, but in the early 1890's Ben created and staged an "all-colored" musical show of the minstrel type, *The South Before the War*, for which he composed and played the music. At the Chicago Fair (1893), Ben met and formed a team with Strap Hill, an African American. This must have been one of the few examples of racial integration in the show business of that time. [11]

They formed a vaudeville act, with Ben billing himself as the "Originator" or "Inventor" of ragtime, which reached the stage of Keith's Union Square Theatre in NYC in April 1896. Coming on in evening dress but incongruously wearing a straw hat, Ben proclaimed that he was Ben Harney from Louisville and that he was here to perform "in ragtime!" Then he proceeded to the piano, where he ripped into a familiar tune, transforming it with syncopation. While playing, he did his "stick dance," tapping with the cane in his left hand against the tapping of his feet under the piano. After which, he would pretend to start a new tune, when a black man out in the audience began to yell out a song, but in language incomprehensible. This was Strap Hill, and after a round of this confusing patter, Harney tore into the song and belted it out in gravelly tones, talking and singing both, moving in rhythm to the accompaniment of the pit band, telling a story to ragtime syncopation. Then Strap, now onstage, put on an exaggerated imitation of Harney's step, strutting while leaning alternately back and forth. This was just a touch of cakewalk, after which Ben reappeared, and the two did the step in tandem with Strap behind playing shadow. Then Jessie came on, blacked-up, and the three sang the finale, two-stepping off at the end. [12]

This breakthrough appearance made Ben a headliner on the top Keith, Orpheum, and Williams vaudeville circuits. During the next three years his dozen raggy songs, along with the performances of May Irwin and Ernest Hogan, fixed in the public awareness the sense of ragtime that predominated. Ben's major hits "Mr. Johnson, Turn Me Loose" and "You've Been A Good Old Wagon, But You Done Broke Down" were coonsongs, but their actual folk quality moderated the offensive stereotypical aspects. Beside his picture, the sheet music cover proclaimed:

> You've Been A Good Old Wagon But You Done Broke Down—Written Composed, and Introduced By Ben Harney, Original Introducer to the Stage of the Now Popular 'Rag Time' in Ethiopian Songs. [13]

Ben Harney's role in ragtime history was catalytic. As a wayward teenager, his amazing ear had registered the authentic qualities in the songs and banjo tunes of incipient ragtime. As an unblacked-up white man, having a strong stage presence and an appealing talent, he could put over the music with more humor than caricature. Both "Mr. Johnson" and "You've Been A Good Old Wagon" present tales of hard luck and harsh treatment. In the latter a black man is arbitrarily arrested on a street corner, jailed, then chained and put "on board a Frankfort train." As the train passes each station on the route, he imagines his woman telling him a final farewell. The Mr. Johnson of the former song is a mean policeman who raids a crap game and collars the singer, who unhappily pleads:

> Oh, Mister Johnson, turn me loose;
> Got no money, but a good excuse.
> Oh, Mister Johnson, I'll be good.
> Oh, Mister Johnson, turn me loose,
> Don' take me to the calaboose.
> Oh, Mister Johnson, I'll be good.

Ben Harney brought ragtime out of the honky-tonk backrooms where he found it—he was not its "inventor" but its propagator—onto the main stage of white America. [14]

So the public's first impression of ragtime was songs—and dances. Like the coonsong, the cakewalk came out of minstrelsy, which (as noted earlier) derived from hi-jinx down on the old plantation. Presumably on rather benign plantations where field hands and house slaves were allowed a role in celebrations. When white folks weren't looking, the "servants" put on comic imitations of their lordly ways. The cakewalk mimicked the dancing in the big house, the stately, decorous figures of the quadrille transformed to an arch and exaggerated strut, bobbing back and forth. The masters noticed and appreciated this comedy. To encourage the fun on appropriate occasions, a large decorated cake was donated for the prize to the best dancers. (Leading to: This "takes the cake.") So commenced "walkin' for dat cake" or, in the verbiage of the interlocutor: "a peregrination for the pastry." Absorbed into minstrelsy, the cakewalk, a grand march with syncopation increasingly added, became the concluding "walk-around" segment of most shows. [15]

These jaunty cakewalks suddenly took off during the mid-1890's to become an early pop "craze," something audiences couldn't get enough of, both as spectators and as participants. After watching, people couldn't resist trying it at home. Most traveling shows featured it. Soon contests took place, with whites so caught up in the spirit that many put on the burnt cork. Minstrelsy had gone off the stage into the audience. Each couple developed their own routine with spots left open for improvisations. Contest prizes ran as high as $250, with each couple's friends on hand to cheer. At intervals judges stopped the music to eliminate the lesser and the marginal, until the winners remained to capture the trophy or cash. [16]

Along with coonsongs, cakewalks impressed on the public first notions of the new musical sensation called ragtime. This march-like dance, less syncopated than the rags that appeared on music counters a year or so later, helped to launch Tin Pan Alley into the big-time with a succession of "hits." (See Almanac above) The leading composers of these hit tunes were "Kerry" Mills (1869-1948), b. Frederick Allen Mills, who gave up a professorship of violin at the University of Michigan to publish music; Abe Holzmann (1874-1939), also a classically trained Alleyman; and J. Bodewalt Lampe (1869-1929), a Danish-born classical musician. Cakewalks achieved great popularity in band arrangements, and John Philip Sousa (1854-1932), the towering figure of band history, spread the music everywhere, including Europe. His exciting successes on tours owed much to the cakewalks of Holzmann and Mills. (A spin-off in France was *Golliwog's Cakewalk* that Debussy composed for his *Children's Corner Suite*.) Following the cakewalk craze, bands continued to program them. In a complex band arrangement, these slightly syncopated marches sounded very well. They remain in the band tradition. [17]

The cakewalk became a headliner on vaudeville stages because of the duo billed as "Two Real Coons," Bert Williams (1874-1922) and George Walker (1873-1910). They had come together in a chance meeting on the street in San Francisco in 1893, each seeking a niche in show business above the massed caricature of minstrelsy. Egbert Austin Williams came from New Providence Island, Bahamas, the son of a rum exporter and the nephew of an Anglican clergyman. About seven-eighths of his ancestors were white; he had experienced little if any racism as a child. The family relocated to Riverside, California, in 1885 where Bert's father became a conductor on the Southern Pacific. Bert went from high school to Stanford, but soon relocated to nearby San Francisco, becoming a minstrel and variety performer. The rough-and-tumble of the Barbary Coast joints seasoned him, as did touring the small port and lumber towns along the West Coast. Unfriendly receptions by white audiences forced him to turn coon, which he hated. Until his death, thirty years later, the coon role exacerbated a spiritual wound which never healed. Offstage he was tall, dignified, and literate; onstage he became Jim Crow: kinky wig, blackface, shabby clothes, oversized shoes, shuffling gait, and poorly spoken. Walker, a policeman's son from Lawrence, Kansas, having a dark skin, accepted coonery with less conflict. Taking it all the way, he polished his stage persona, becoming a sharp, masterful song-and-dance man and a top black entertainer. When the two met, George had just walked away from the medicine show which had brought him across the country. [18]

They contrasted effectively, Jim Crow and Zip Coon, the clod and the slicker. At first Williams played the straight to Walker's comic role. They tried minstrel shows, medicine shows, and small-time variety. Working their way east, a white mob in El Paso, Texas, stripped off their dressy, actors' clothes and forced them into burlap sacking. Humiliated, they fled this show, which was headed into the South, and never took an engagement below the Mason-Dixon Line. Again, in Chicago, they flopped, finding audiences cold to a restrained Bert strumming along for George's comic songs. They worked up a fresh act, "Two Real Coons," in which George's role of the dandy or "swell," the carefree sport, was fine-tuned toward arrogance, verging on the preposterous. Bert emphasized the opposite, raggedy, slow, shambling, the foil for the city sport. The extreme contrast helped, but the applause remained modest. Then, experimenting with new bits of stage business, Bert started to get some big laughs. His full stage personality blossomed, and his incredible gift for comedy materialized. The act shifted center to his stage personality, the slow-witted confused, unlucky black man, who is either broke, too late, or outsmarted. In 1896 someone spotted them in Indiana and gave them a New York offer to appear in *The Gold Bug*, a musical farce that was mostly variety acts. It opened September 14 but closed after a week, a failure for the composer, newcomer Victor Herbert, despite some excellent music and appealing performances. But this was 1896; cakewalks and coonsongs were "packing them in"; New York soon was cheering lustily for "Two Real Coons." [19]

From there Williams and Walker moved to Koster and Bial's Music Hall to create a vaudeville sensation. The act played for six months, sending them to vaudeville stardom as the top African-American entertainers. They opened with coon songs that established their stereotypes and ended with contrasting cakewalks. An account by the critic of the leading black newspaper, the *Indianapolis Freeman*, still conveys, across the gap of a century, the sense of a thrilling performance:

> …One pair held the floor at a time, and the men's manners are in strong contrast. One chap [Williams] is clownish, though his grotesque paces are elaborate, practiced, and exactly timed, while the other [Walker] is all airiness. It is a revelation to most observers to see so much of jauntiness in one human being…. Pointed shoes, tight trousers, red and white striped shirt front, and shining silk hat…and there is a smile that for size and convincingness is unequaled. Away up on stage he and his partner meet and curtsey, she with the utmost grace, he with exaggerated courtliness. Then down they trip, his elbow squared…and with a mincing gait that would be ridiculous were it not absolute in its harmony with the general scheme of airiness. With every step his body sways from side to side and the outstretched elbows see-saw but the woman clings to his arm…till the footlights are reached.

In the concluding verbal snapshot:

> …The other chap's rig is rusty, and his joints work jerkily, but he has his own ideas about high stepping and carries them out in a walk that starts like his companion's but ends at the other side of the stage. Then the first fellow takes both women, one on each arm, and, leaving the other one grimacing, vengefully, starts on a second tour of grace. Even then he [Williams] walks across the front of the stage with that huge smile wide open, and goes off, leaving the impression that he'd had a pretty good time himself. [20]

The act grew until seven more cakewalking couples had been added, performing a prelude to the entry of the principals. From the excitement generated during the long run at Koster and Bial's, came the national cakewalk "craze" to match the parallel one in coonsongs. Thus ragtime became identified as the new syncopation in song and dance—a year or two before reaching publication in its more syncopated form, the instrumental rag. Score another hit for 1896, that volatile year of depression anxieties, foreclosed farmers, a growing concern over the power of trusts, the "free silver" controversy, and the high political drama of McKinley and the plutocratic establishment vs. Bryan and Populism. Although three of the four ragtime principals of 1896 were African Americans—Hogan, Williams, and Walker—once into the mainstream, it became the property of all. Europeans, hearing Sousa's band arrangements of cakewalks, recognized "American" music. But this triumphant arrival of the music in the new democracy of pop culture occurred in a racial context: a subject race just out of bondage in a hostile society. To survive, black show folk had to perform minstrelsy and coonery. Except for freaks like the blind men Boone and Tom, they experienced the same segregation in culture as in public accomodations and transportation. They were denied venues for the serious and the "legitimate"; the Metropolitan Opera was as forbidden as the Waldorf-Astoria.

After 1905 the coonsong receded from the marketplace, followed by the less vicious ragtime song. Songs like "Bill Bailey, Won't You Please Come Home" (1902) left out "coon" and "nigger," but they perpetuated the stereotype. Whites apparently perceived little more than the confirmation of their prejudices—with or without the offensive words, the songs accurately depicted African-American inferiority. But in the black press, unknown to whites, this complacent—and insidious—mindset evoked anguish and condemnation. Bob Cole, who created the first all-black musical *A Trip To Coontown* in 1898, by 1905 was protesting the term. In 1907 the *Freeman's* critic Sylvester Russell flatly stated: "…a lot of harm has already been done [by] 'All Coons Look Alike To Me,' 'Coon, Coon, Coon,' and 'Nigger, Nigger, Never Die.'" An anonymous but knowledgable contributor to the *Freeman* in 1909 laid out the history and case against coonsongs: "As much as to say the Negro has now changed his name: He is no longer human, but a 'coon.'" Tracing the history of "unbleached" Ernest Hogan and the "Two Real Coons," the writer states that "[they] were not old enough then to know the harm they had brought on the whole race." Very acutely, he points out that stage coonery wasn't innocent fun, that it immediately entered social usage: "The people, especially the children, are educated that a black man is a 'coon.'" He concludes: "Abraham Lincoln once wrote a harsh letter to a man and after considering how the man might feel over it he threw the letter into the stove. Every composer who writes a song with the word 'coon' in it should do the same." [21]

> Coon! Coon! Coon!
> I wish my color would fade;
> Coon! Coon! Coon!
> I'd like to be a different shade.
> Gene Jefferson and Leo Friedman (1900)

Negro

> I am a Negro;
> Black as the night is black,
> Black like the depths of my Africa.
>
> I've been a slave:
> Caesar told me to keep his door-steps clean.
> I brushed the boots of Washington.
>
> I've been a worker:
> Under my hand the pyramids rose.
> I made mortar for the Woolworth Building.
>
> I've been a singer:
> All the way from Africa to Georgia
> I carried my sorrow songs.
> I made ragtime.
>
> Langston Hughes (1926)

Notes: Chapter 11

1. Henry T. Sampson, *The Ghost Walks: A Chronological History of Blacks in Show Business, 1865-1910*, 162.
2. Burton W. Peretti, *The Creation of Jazz: Music, Race, and Culture in Urban America*, 15; Sampson, 16-17 for the Hyer Sisters.
3. David Nasaw, *Going Out: The Rise and Fall of Public Amusements*, 51-53, 57-59; Rudi Blesh and Harriet Janis, *They All Played Ragtime*, 92-93.
4. James Weldon Johnson, *Along This Way: The Autobiography of James Weldon Johnson*, 152-153.
5. Tom Fletcher, *One Hundred Years of the Negro in Show Business*, 135-137; Alain Leroy Locke, *The Negro and His Music*, 59; Blesh and Janis, 85-88.
6. Ian Whitcomb, *Irving Berlin and Ragtime America*, 111-112; Gerald Bordman, *The American Musical Theatre: A Chronicle*, 138-139.
8. 7. Sampson, 96-97, for a sample program; Mark Sullivan, *Our Times*, IV, 242, for another description.
9. Johnson, *Along This Way*, 85-87; Fletcher, 103-108.
Blesh and Sampson, 250.
10. Thomas L. Riis, *Just Before Jazz: Black Musical Theatre in New York, 1890-1915*, 37-39; Sampson, 249-251; Whitcomb, *Berlin*, 119-122; Fletcher, 135-139.
11. *Idem.*
12. Blesh and Janis, 10; David Jasen and Trebor Tichenor, *Rags and Ragtime: A Musical History*, 12-13.
13. Blesh and Janis, 212-213.
14. *Ibid.*, 211-213; Whitcomb, *Berlin,* 112-114.
15. *Ibid.*, 118-119.
16. Douglas Gilbert, *Lost Chords: The Diverting Story of American Popular Songs*, 239-241; Blesh and Janis, 211-213.
17. *Ibid.* 96-97; Edward A. Berlin, *Ragtime: A Musical and Cultural History*, 104-105; Janis, 74, 96-100; Gilbert, *Lost Chords*, 245-246; William J. Schafer and Johannes Riedel, *The Art of Ragtime: Form and Meaning of an Original Black American Art*, 29, 30-31,112-115; Edward A. Berlin, *King of Ragtime: Scott Joplin and his Era*, 34-35; David A. Jasen, *Tin Pan Alley: The Composers, the Songs, the Performers*, 18-19.
18. Ann Charters, *Nobody: The Story of Bert Williams*, 8-24. David A. Jasen and Gene Jones, *Spreadin' Rhythm Around: Black Popular Songwriters, 1880-1930*, 42, presumably from more recent research, indicate that Williams was born at Nassau, New Providence, Bahamas (same year), where his father was a hotel waiter, that he worked as a laborer in Riverside, CA, and that young Bert abandoned high school around 1890 to join a medicine show, leaving that for minstrelsy a year later, where he met George Walker.
19. *Ibid.*, 24-30; Bordman, 146.
20. *Sampson, 125.*
21. *Ibid.*, 403, for the comment on cultural segregation, 349-350 for Bob Cole, 407-408 for Sylvester Russell, 446-449 for the anonymous writer.

12. Wilmington Coup

> Since we met in these walls we have taken a city. That is much. But it is more because it is our city that we have taken…not by investment and siege, not by shot and shell, but as thoroughly, as completely as if captured in battle.
> Wilmington clergyman on the Sunday afterwards (11-13-98) [1]

Racism in the United States based itself on the universal belief in African-American inferiority. Not just race haters, but also those who appreciated black culture and sympathized with the plight of a subject race accepted the truism. At best, African Americans were innocents turned loose in a world too complex to grasp; at worst, they were animals, amoral, appetites without souls, responsive only to doses of fear regularly administered. This mindset ran deep in the folklore. Fathers worried about their children's potential would warn: "You don't have to be black to be a nigger." The reverse of this unfortunately was denied: you did have to be white to be a white man. Wilmington, N.C., in 1898 shows what happened when a significant number of blacks exercised their civil and economic rights.

Wilmington in 1898 with 20,000 population was the largest city and metropolis of a largely rural state. Blacks outnumbered whites 11,300 to 8700 in this coastal Black Belt city, where, thirty years after the Civil War, poverty and unemployment ran high with country people moving in to escape rural destitution. But compared with other southern communities, African Americans had improved their economic lot, owning businesses, serving in the professions, working as craftsmen, doing most of the service jobs (as elsewhere)—and—serving in public offices, some as elected officials. There were even black policemen. Black businessman Thomas H. Miller, real estate agent, auctioneer, the only listed pawnbroker, and owner of many city lots, was one of the richest men in town. Many whites owed him money. Wilmington had a black newspaper, the *Daily Record*, a rarity in the South. In 1897 President McKinley appointed black John Campbell Dancy to be Collector of Customs for the port. At an annual salary of $4000, this exceeded the Governor's by $1000. Complaints by poor whites about preference being given to blacks in hiring had some factual base. There seems to have been a consensus among employers that blacks worked harder and with more efficiency than poor whites come to town from failed farms.

Wilmington conditions owed much to the political turmoil of the 1890's. The Populist revolt had been strong enough in North Carolina to oust the Democratic Party from its monolithic hold. Everywhere poor farmers, black and white, had rejected their Democratic leaders, who had always claimed to know what was best for them, and joined the agrarian-led Populist Party, which had achieved electoral victory by joining with the Republicans (heretofore discredited as Carpetbaggers) on a combination ticket designated as the "Fusion" Party. The Fusionists had taken over in Wilmington in 1894, throwing out an enraged body of Democrats, whose hatred of "black rule" promised future political destabilization. Taking over the state legislature, the Fusionists passed a new election law, weakening the hold of the legislature in favor of local power, thereby giving voters, including African Americans, more control over elected officials. In 1896 Fusion power had elected Republican Daniel L. Russell Governor. In the 1897 General Assembly of North Carolina, there were in the House 54 Republican Fusionists and 24 Democrats, in the Senate 25 Populists, 18 Republicans, and only 7 Democrats. Facing a hopeless situation, Democrats ground their teeth seeing about 1000 blacks given public employment. In the 1897 municipal election in Wilmington (3-25-97), seven Fusionists and three Democrats were elected to the Board of Aldermen, including three blacks. The majority elected Dr. Silas Wright, a respected physician, as Mayor. The three Democrats, persuaded by party leaders, decided not to serve. This calculated intransigence was the opening move by Democrats intent on restoring control. The second move was the refusal of the previous Board to vacate City Hall. Which led to a challenge in the local Superior Court in which a Democratic judge ruled the new election law invalid, leaving the first Board still in power. Not until September did the State Supreme Court reverse the lower court, permitting the Wright administration to take over.

The frustrated Democrats now began plotting to overthrow a legal government. Little is known of early meetings, but by 1898 a secret group, the Nine, had set up a network in each of the five city wards, block lieutenants reporting to a ward captain—all very military, as many leaders held commissions in the National Guard and Reserve units. Two of the Nine acted as liasons with the network elements, but the Nine remained a secret body, telling no one of their existence. The conspirators plotted an insurrection for November 9, 1898, the day after the election for state offices. From this point, the Nine had to build public support. Very simply, as the Democrats always had done, and would continue to do until the Civil Rights actions of the 1960's, they proceeded to build up the fires of hatred in the hearts of the discontented mass of poor whites. Playing off blacks against whites was the political formula that distracted the South for the century following the Civil War, enabling a few to extract wealth from a meager economy. Rumors and propaganda circulated that the Fusionist, and black, government was corrupt and too incompetent to deal with the wave of crime that had followed the Fusion victories. Aspersions were cast upon Governor Russell, his Fusion-Republican legislature, also upon Mayor Wright, who, however respected he was as a medical man, had arrived during Reconstruction—and thus could be labeled a "Carpetbagger," an outsider come to enrich himself. Some of the strongest attacks fell on the Populist Chief of Police John R. Melton as unqualified, and his black and white police force as weak and incapable of maintaining security. Perhaps the most hated Republican was G.Z. French, holding a low profile office as Deputy Sheriff, but clearly in charge of county law enforcement, and the most influential Republican locally. The claim was made that the courts no longer convicted blacks, and the white lawyers refused all criminal cases, leaving that field to the city's four black lawyers.

On the state level, a white supremacy campaign reenforced the Wilmington Democrats. State Democratic Party Chairman Furnifold M. Simmons countered the threat of Fusion rule by stirring up the issue of white supremacy vs. black rule. Simmons recruited Josephus Daniels, Editor of the *Raleigh News and Observer* (and later Secretary of the Navy in Wilson's World War I cabinet), to be the militant voice of the campaign. From the November 20, 1897, meeting of the Democratic Executive Committee came a call for statewide unity in the struggle to restore "Anglo-Saxon rule and honest government," and to "redeem" the state from the evils of black Fusion control. Daniels and other editors and politicians offered Wilmington and New Hanover County as the horrible example of what Fusion had caused. They claimed that 93 Negroes held city/county jobs, giving them jurisdiction over whites, as magistrates, policemen, and sanitary inspectors. The *Wilmington Messenger*, like other local papers, stoked the fires of indignation.

The Democratic press supported the formation of "White Government Union" clubs, urging all concerned whites to join and reporting fully the inflammatory anti-black speeches given. This movement spread all over the coastal Black Belt of North Carolina. In Wilmington the several WGU Clubs were amalgamated into the "White Government Union" controlled by the local executive committee of the Democrats. The *Messenger* exhorted every white man to join. Club members threatened non-members to join or leave the city. There was much agitation against employers who hired blacks, willing to work for less, forcing whites to accept "Negro wages." Starting in

August 1898, the Democrats staged large anti-black rallies. The largest ones were led by Charles B. Aycock (who would be elected Governor in 1900), who railed on the platform against "Russellism, Fusionism, and Black Domination," all of this repeated by the press and paid for by businessmen. In October the Wilmington Chamber of Commerce attacked the city administration in a resolution claiming incompetence and the failure to protect citizens, especially women, from black criminals, and that such conditions had injured commerce.

At the next mass meeting of October 7, business and professional men called for preference to be given to whites in hiring (giving in to pressure from the White Government Union). A new claim escalating the angry mood was that black leaders were conspiring to import large numbers of their own to "colonize" the area and thus drive out whites. This rumor not only ricocheted around the state but also received attention in the national press, strengthening its illusion of reality. It gave weight to the preposterous conclusion that black folk intended to set up their own commonwealth in North Carolina. This new fear cancelled all factional disputes among whites bringing the unity needed by the Nine to execute their (actual) conspiracy. Fusionists tried to disprove these big lies, but the state's major papers—all owned by Democrats—ignored their rebuttals and printed only Democratic propaganda.

However, ironically, and tragically, it was a black utterance, soon notorious as the "Manly Editorial," that stimulated the greatest degree of indignation among whites, convincing all but the very few skeptical and humane that the commonwealth was in disorder and in need of purging. Manly was Alex Manly (1866-1944), editor of the black *Record*. Manly and his siblings were the children of Charles Manly, North Carolina's Governor from 1849-51, and a slave woman. The Manlys, with their light skin and caucasian features, could have "passed" for white elsewhere—which some of them did later. Alex and two brothers had founded the *Record*, which, because it was an anomaly, reached black subscribers statewide. It attracted plenty of white advertising and had begun to flourish. Manly championed the cause of African Americans and fought for the black community's share of civic improvements. Such boldness soon earned him the animosity of race-haters, especially for his stated view that few black men threatened or wished to rape white women.

In August 1898, a prominent woman in Georgia spoke publicly and passionately about the dangers to white women from black rapists. Obviously fed up and frustrated, to a point where he lost the greatest survival skill of all, discretion, Manly attacked the myths of black sexuality and lynching as the only effective restraint. Manly asserted in an editorial that: 1) The argument for lynching was unchristian in setting one class above another; 2) Blacks lived by and obeyed the same moral standards as whites; 3) The rape crime was seldom committed; 4) White editors blamed all blacks for the crimes of very few. The above points were generally left out of the inflammatory responses, which focused on Manly's other points: 5) Poor whites failed to adequately protect their women; 6) Poor white women carried on illicit sexual relations with black men, about as often as white men did with black women; 7) In these situations, the black man was lynched and the white man went free; 8) A large number of the lynchees were the light-skinned sons of white fathers; 9) Whites should teach their youth to leave black women alone:

> .... Teach your men purity. Let virtue be something more than an excuse for them to intimidate and torture a helpless people. Tell your men that it is no worse for a black man to be intimate with a white woman than for a white man to be intimate with a colored woman.... You set yourselves down as a lot of carping hypocrites; in fact you cry aloud for the virtue of your women while you

seek to destroy the morality of ours. Don't think ever that your women will remain pure while you are debauching ours. You sow the seed—the harvest will come in due time.

Whether courageous or foolish, this blunt revelation, quite likely unique (below the Mason-Dixon Line) during the century of terror, elicited only dire hostility. Manly was told to apologize, leave town, and to desist from publishing. All white papers erupted with fury and cries for vengeance. The editorial was characterized as an unforgivable attack on white women. Blacks cringed in fear, warning Manly to recant and close down the paper. Very few dared to agree. Manly might have been quickly lynched if the Nine hadn't sent out word to keep calm and wait for the time when things would be taken care of. However the Manly matter kept boiling away, as a sure-fire issue to stir up white supremacy meetings. In October, papers in Wilmington and elsewhere reprinted the "Manly Editorial" with inflammatory comments; over 100,000 copies were reprinted and handed out.

Also in October, the terror progressed from the verbal to the physical. Consisting mainly of unemployed poor whites (who deeply resented local hiring preferences), and officered by merchants, bankers, and landowners, the Redshirts (the name borrowed from a similar group in South Carolina) appeared, riding to rallies and staging impromptu parades wherever African Americans worked and lived. Armed with their shotguns and Winchesters, uniformed in red shirts and boots, they rode out to terrorize. En masse with their leaders, they conveyed an image of power at parades and demonstrations, but away from their respectable leadership, they broke up into small gangs to carry out minor acts of violence and theft throughout the county. Each week, the Redshirts made sudden appearances on city streets and back roads, their principal message a warning to blacks not to show up at the polls on election day, November 8.

Citing this unrest, Wilmington Democrats demanded that the Fusion Party offer no candidates, that an election contest would bring on a race war. The determined Fusionists struck back, setting a rally for October 24 and announcing that Governor Russell and Senators Pritchard and Butler would be on the platform to speak on behalf of the local Republican-Populist Fusion slate. This galvanized the Democrats to send a committee to Raleigh to warn these leaders that their coming would set off a racial explosion, while at the same time they scheduled a counter-rally the same night. The Governor and Senators quickly caved in and cancelled their Wilmington appearance, but the Democrats held their meeting in the Opera House with Redshirts conspicuously present. Here they unleashed a new force, the fiery Alfred Waddell, ex-congressman and Confederate colonel, embittered by penury and obscurity, outcomes of the Lost Cause of the War Between the States. With oratorical power, Waddell spelled out a stark choice in the coming election: government by one race or another. He loaded the blame for the coming race battle on white Republican leaders who had incited Negroes to rise above their place, citing Governor Russell as chief instigator. He concluded: "…we will never surrender to a ragged raffle of Negroes, even if we have to choke the Cape Fear River with [black] carcasses."

Two days later (Oct. 26), Governor Russell tried once more to support his fellow Wilmingtonians and fend off white supremacist-Democratic violence. But all he could do was to issue a feeble Proclamation "to preserve the peace" and stop the vigilantism of the Redshirts, against which Wilmington's small police force was helpless. Which led the *Wilmington Messenger* on October 29 to find a sinister provocation: the Governor intended to bring in Federal troops to control the election. Again the paper yelped about probable race war and vowed defiance. Whatever the Fusionists tried, their fanatical opposition twisted into menace, the secret Nine adroitly orchestrating its violent scenario. On October 28, the Democrats staged another monster rally, at Goldsboro, of 8000 white supremacists. A series of speakers raised the heat on black rule, preparing the audience for Alfred

Waddell's consuming outpouring. This was another stemwinder, spouting the big lie of black insults, threats, and crimes against white women, and a frank promise to drive out the white and black Fusion Republicans. A series of local rallies followed all over the coastal Black Belt, keeping up the fever pitch, including the November 2 parade and rally in Wilmington. Here the Redshirts were augmented by the "Rough Riders," veterans of that year's war with Spain. Again on the 5th, Waddell, who had achieved a rapid celebrity, boomed his outrage against the Manly Editorial from the Opera House platform.

After this came daily rallies with free food and liquor supplied (willingly or not) by saloonkeepers. Battening on this heady, and filling, ambience, mobs of poor whites demanded to lynch the infamous Manly and the Negro-loving G. Z. French, Deputy Sheriff and Republican leader. Again, discreet emissaries of the Nine circulated among Redshirts and Rough Riders counseling patience and coolness. As for Manly, realizing what his unguarded outburst had led to, he decamped. Abruptly he closed down his *Record*, and, aided by friends who knew the password, slipped by a Redshirt patrol seeking him. The exact date is unknown.

By November 8, 1898, election day, Wilmington had, literally, been transformed into an armed camp. Every white man walked around with a gun, probably made possible by the affluent citizens' subscriptions to a fund that, according to a source, amounted to $30,000. Each block Lieutenant supplied a roster of armed men to his ward Captain, who awaited marching orders from a central command. Redshirt patrols guarded all roads in and out. Also part of the plot, unofficially, were the Army and Navy Reserve units. The National Guard unit, the Wilmington Light Infantry, furnished an automatic weapon, a Gatling Gun, and the crew to operate it. No gunsmith or arms dealer would sell to African Americans. On election eve, forewarned whites sent their families out of town on full trains. Then a hush fell on city and state. Governor Russell in Raleigh, aware of assassination threats, moved now with a bodyguard. His attempt to ban liquor and guns had been ignored. Alfred Waddell in his final pre-election speech told whites to kill any black trying to vote. Although quiet, the patrolling Redshirts kept up the level of fear, frightening most blacks from the polls. Governor Russell boarded a train intending to cast his ballot in Wilmington, but a mob along the route came on board to seize him, presumably to lynch, frightening him back to Raleigh concealed ignominiously in a boxcar. After the polls closed, armed whites ran off black poll workers and completed the count. The Democrats made an easy sweep reaching a majority of 6000 votes; this constituted an 11,000 vote gain in two years, the Republicans having come out 5000 ahead in the previous election of 1896.

November 9 began quietly, but the *Wilmington Messenger* carried an ominous notice: "Attention White Men," telling all white men to assemble at 10:00 AM at the courthouse. The Nine, having taken the election, now moved to destroy all opposition. With about 1000 jamming the courtroom and corridors, the Chair called up chief orator Alfred Waddell and handed him the "Wilmington Declaration of Independence" to read. This document opened with the observation that the framers of the original Declaration had not foreseen a takeover by an inferior race, and that it was necessary therefore to declare that never again would Wilmington or New Hanover County be ruled by men of African origin. After this prelude came a set of resolutions: that whites were rightfully in control because they owned over 90% of the property and paid the same amount of taxes; that Fusion rule had to end because of the stagnation of business; that it was in the best interests of the city henceforth to prefer whites over blacks in all hiring; that the *Daily Record* must cease publication and Manly its editor be banished (by now Manly had reached safety in Asbury Park, New Jersey); that the Mayor and Board of Aldermen should be expelled (they had not been up for reelection) because of "…incapacity to give the city a decent government and maintain law and order." Next a Committee of 25 was selected (by spokesmen of the Nine) to carry out these resolutions.

After considering its mission at a 3:30 meeting, the committee of 25 summoned 32 of the prominent blacks to come before them at 6:00 PM. With Waddell presiding, the Resolutions were handed out as an ultimatum demanding a reply of obedience at 7:30 the next morning. Frightened, uncertain of how to respond, this unorganized group of individuals drafted a faltering note that they took no responsibility for the Manly Editorial, but that they would ask the city administration to resign. One of them, a lawyer, was deputed to deliver the message, but he was too afraid to do so. A black man caught going into a white neighborhood risked violence and possibly loss of life. Too fearful to go to the door, he dropped it into a mailbox and fled. At 8:00 AM, November 10, whites assembled at the armory of the Wilmington Light Infantry to hear the reply. Having received none, the mob headed toward the black Second Ward known as "Brooklyn." As they moved up Market the principal street, more joined until there were about 2000 armed marchers. The National Guard officers, unwilling to participate officially, held back, and the mob marched behind their spokesman Waddell.

Before heading to Brooklyn, these irregulars destroyed Manly's press (which he did not own, having bought it from the *Messenger* on installments). Manly had run his paper out of Ruth Hall, an African-American assembly hall on South Seventh Street. After sledge-hammering the press, the mob torched this black community center and crossed town to Brooklyn. Blacks reacted in panic and ran, lacking guns and leadership—which put the lie to the claim that they planned to attack. All that day, mobs, Redshirts and Rough Riders, Army and Naval Reserves, and the National Guard rushed to wherever rumors indicated that blacks were shooting back. Any black running from them was shot down by volleys. One humane witness characterized the actions in her diary:

> Some blood was drawn by a colored man it is claimed, for I suppose a few armed colored men hearing the uproar, had appeared on the scene, and then the carnage began. It is pitiful to hear the accounts of reliable eye-witnesses to the harrowing scenes. We are just shooting to see the niggers run! they cried as the black men began to fall in every direction.
>
> (Jane Murphy Cronly)

This was the situation just two hours later (11:00 AM). By then the horror-stricken black community had taken to the roads or fled into the woods. Most had run hastily without food or blankets facing exposure to the chill November nights. Martial Law was proclaimed in Wilmington, and the various military units now took station at all intersections and on every block. Next a committee designated by the Nine summoned Mayor Wright and any aldermen still in the city and forced them to resign. Then ten Democrats were sworn in to fill the vacated offices, and Alfred Waddell, mob leader and figurehead of the Nine, accepted the votes of the new Board of Aldermen to become Mayor. With the appointment of a new Chief of Police, the race riot ended. A revolutionary movement had overthrown an elected government in a *coup d'etat* in the United States.

After the coup, the Nine furnished Colonel Taylor the military commander with a list of names for banishment, which had been drawn up well in advance. The manhunt proceeded immediately with the police driving a wagon accompanied by a mounted detachment of the Wilmington Light Infantry. Prominent black and white Fusionists were rounded up and jailed overnight. These included ex-Chief of Police Melton; Thomas Miller, black landowner, money lender, and pawnbroker, one of the wealthiest Wilmingtonians; U.S. Commissioner Robert Bunting, exiled because his wife was black; and G.Z. French, carpetbagger, Fusionist leader, and principal Deputy Sheriff, much hated by poor whites. Mayor Wright had escaped just ahead of these searchers. The crowd at the jail demanded to lynch these men, but a military guard of 60 protected them all night. The next morning, the six foremost black men were placed in a guarded special car on a train going out-of-state. At Two PM six whites were pushed onto another northbound train. As they were boarding, the mob broke through the soldiers, grabbed French, and dragged him to the nearest tree. He was already choking on the noose when three white leaders threatened to hang the lynchers. During the heavy-breathing silence of confrontation, the rope fell slack, and French ran in terror for his life, climbing aboard the train as it left the station.

Some mopping up remained. Democrats fired all black employees, opening all city and county jobs to whites. Given the shortage of jobs in a meager southern economy—before the Civil War, Wilmington had been a major producer of naval stores, masts and pitch from its long leaf pines, not needed for the iron ships of the postwar period—political leaders had to appease the poor whites with such gestures. Blacks, like whites, drifting in from failed farms, had been preferred, because they were more docile and worked much harder. White resentment of such practices had fueled the rage that drove the coup. Whites followed their leaders as much in the hope of employment as in hatred of the race that had held most of the menial jobs. Businessmen too soon yielded to pressure and replaced black employees with less efficient whites. Many now jobless blacks simply went away, going to northern cities and points west, in advance of the migration that would swell by World War I. This included the rest of the middle class blacks, lawyers and merchants, given twelve hours to leave. Some had to abandon homes and property, which subsequently ended up in the hands of whites when these properties were "sold for taxes." In 1890 Blacks had outnumbered whites in Wilmington by 2593; by 1900 whites had become the majority.

In the new and emergent mass media, the Wilmington event played large on the front pages. President McKinley huddled with his cabinet. The nation gave close attention. But nothing happened. No messages reached Washington from North Carolina. Governor Russell, undoubtedly afraid, kept silent. Although Secretary of War Russell Alger publicly characterized the Wilmington situation as "a disgrace to the state and to the country," President McKinley made no comment. Public figures had acted criminally, traitorously, but the Feds did not intervene to restore legitimate government to the City of Wilmington and New Hanover County. Civil rights groups and the African-American press clamored for action, but officially nothing was wrong in the Tar Heel State. Even Booker T. Washington, the acknowledged spokesman for black America, failed to respond (a protest might have weakened white support for his Accomodationist strategy). All the mass meetings, angry resolutions, and indignant letters disappeared into a black hole of indifference.

Alex Manly, whose notorious editorial had enraged the South and excited curiosity in the North, did manage, with a friend's help, to get in to see the President. The scene opened politely, but when McKinley grasped that the well-favored person across from his desk wasn't white, he terminated the interview and ordered him out of the Executive Mansion. After which, Manly sensibly turned away from the tragedy. He went to Philadelphia, where he passed over into the white race to become a painting contractor.

What should have been done? Federal intervention might have spilled blood everywhere that southern hotheads rose to lynch and rape and riot. Would Reservists and National Guardsmen have obeyed commands to fire on their neighbors? Where would it all have led? No one knew. No one wanted to find out.

from **The Fledgling Bard and The Poetry Society**

We hail thee, land of liberty,
Star of our hope and destiny
Where long we've been and long must be
In freedom's fabled place.
We bless thee, land, in love's sweet name
Whereto as slaves our fathers came,
Where still we struggle lashed and lame,
As exiles torn from grace.
The Scotchman tunes his pipe and drum,
Old Ireland's Harp is never dumb,
We make our rag-time banjo hum
To Uncle Sam's swift pace.
We follow where his footsteps lead,
We copy him in word and deed,
 E'en though his low and vicious creed
Our morals would debase.
With him we hail the stripes and stars,
Stripes that stand for color bars,
The stars that burn and leave their scars
On our black bleeding race.

George Reginald Margetson

RAGTIME ALMANAC

Race Riots 1865-1925

Memphis, TN 1866
New Orleans, LA 1866
Colfax, LA 1873
Coushatta, LA 1874
Hamburg, SC 1876
Danville, VA 1883
Wilmington, NC 1898
Phoenix, SC 1898

New Orleans, LA 1900
New York, NY 1900
Springfield, OH 1904
Atlanta, GA 1906
Greenburg, IN 1906
Springfield, IL 1908
E. St.Louis, IL 1917
Houston, TX 1917

20 Race Riots of the "Red Summer" of 1919, including:

Chicago, IL
Charleston, SC
Omaha, NE
Tulsa, OK 1921

Washington, DC
Longview, TX
Elaine, AR

Notes: Chapter 12

1. H. Leon Prather, *We Have Taken A City*, is the main source for this chapter.

13. The Business of the Social Evil

> There was profit in selling girls to houses, profit in selling their services, profit in selling clothes to them, and profit in selling liquor.
>
> Hartford Vice Commission [1]

TR on the Social Evil:

> My experience is that there should be no toleration of any "tenderloin" or "red light" district, and that, above all, there should be the most relentless war on commercialized vice. The men who profit and make their living by the depravity and the awful misery of other human beings stand far below any ordinary criminals, and no measures taken against them can be too severe. [2]

During the 19th C prostitution followed the same track as other enterprises: from cottage industry to big business. From a home operated by its occupant and two or three other resident females, the bordello grew into a "house" owned by a landlord or several shareholders and operated by a supervising "madam" and ten or more inmates. This larger scale of activity generated a variety of economic activities and large amounts of cash. By this time men had taken control of prostitution away from women. Someone estimated that the traffic in women was a fifteen-million-dollar business in Chicago. In Storyville, New Orleans, the weekly gross was believed to be $1,000,000, with the annual profit running close to Chicago's. This cash produced a political dimension. The beneficiaries of the sex trade protected it with powerful opposition to all efforts to enforce the law against it and to all attempts to take away their control of it. [3]

Profits from vice flowed upward to the real estate interests, the landlords. Vice was an easy-money machine to these people. It required only a bare bones investment in land, with a suitable building, minimal fixtures and furniture, and a very little occasional maintenance. The pay-off would be at least three times the usual rent from substandard housing (also viewed as a good investment), and there never were any collection problems. Depending upon the size and extent of the establishment, a whorehouse landlord pocketed from $1000 to $5000 each month. This proved irresistible to both old and new money types. [4] In New York City where vice resorts, numbering in the hundreds, were located everywhere, an underground market in shares emerged. Fractional interests, usually halves and quarters in brothels, were regularly sold and resold by landlords. Values were based upon proven grosses. Any fluctuation affected share value. This speculation allowed landlords to earn more than the rental income. A successful landlord of these houses earned from $15,000 to $60,000 annually, where an upper-level white-collar executive took home $2000 per year, a middle manager received $1000/year, and industrial workers earned $300 to $500/year. [5]

The next dip out of the money pot was taken by police and politicians. They grabbed their shares because no tenderloin could function without their support. Politicians worked to keep anti-prostitution laws off the statute books, and the police did not enforce any such laws that politicians failed to defeat. The other vital police function was control. Police carefully observed and thwarted criminal elements, and they quickly put down any disturbance of the peace by angry customers or rowdy types. Any threat to cash flow was not tolerated. Policing tenderloins called for the best men on the force, and the assignments were coveted. Which recalls the famous story of the New York Police Captain, who, upon hearing that he was to command the entertainment district, announced that he would now regularly be consuming tenderloin, which subsequently became generic, a synonym for vice district. The precinct captain's job was to receive the "fines" sent in by each house and distribute appropriate shares up and down: city councilmen, office of the chief of police, supervisors, and patrolmen. Collections were formulaic: $1 for each house girl and 25 cents for each crib girl, or so much weekly per house or crib, $5 to $10 for a crib, $20 to $30 for a house. In Storyville, New Orleans, the money was left outside on the stoops on designated nights. Strollers saw a stack of coins by the doorstep of each resort. Knowing the destination of the cash, no one dared touch it. It was as secure as a bank. Soon the beat cop ambled by, scooping each pile of dollars into his bag, which his captain would receive in the morning. [6]

Police put their finest resources and personnel into sin districts for very good reason: Robberies and assaults on citizens, especially the prominent, shined the publicity spotlight on the district, which not only embarrassed both the police and citizens, but likely meant demotions and loss of jobs for incompetence. [7] Evidence of police corruption surfaces in a 1912 study of New York City. In a seven-month period, police records show a mere 542 complaints against prostitution in 112 locations, but the investigation revealed prostitution being carried on in 429 parlor houses, plus thousands of other sites: saloons, concert-saloons, hotels, "disorderly" hotels (those lacking actual guests), tenements, assignation houses, and other places. Clearly major pay-offs were ongoing. [8] Although the public strongly opposed the regulation of vice—in the belief that regulation meant legalization— the police always instituted a de facto regulation: they issued their own "rules" to insure control. Such rules forbade: underage activity, whether buying or selling (always a bombshell when exposed); improper (scanty or revealing) attire in public; unescorted women entering brothels; streetwalking—being unregulated, this activity existed outside organized graft; soliciting from the doors or windows of buildings; swinging doors on houses; signs, lights (other than discreet reds), or outside pictures; and the forcible detention of women inside. [9]

The fine-tuning in these controls points to a dominant priority: the avoidance of public scrutiny. The El Paso, Texas, "Reservation," an area of cribs (rented rooms fronting on the street), posted rules extremely precise and fussy. Women were instructed to sit back from doors and windows and never to cross their legs. They were forbidden to embrace men on the street or to try to pull men into their cribs. They were permitted to cross streets only at intersections, never in the middle of a block. They were never to yell or use vulgar language. Public arguments were forbidden. They could not accept drunken men as customers. Patrolmen could not mingle with prostitutes or favor a side in a quarrel: "They must be disinterested at all times." [10]

Wholesalers and retailers of liquor had just as vital a stake as the vendors and protectors of illegal sex. The Chicago Vice Commission in 1911 estimated that liquor sales in houses amounted to more than $7,000,000 per year, and that this equaled one-half of the gross of sex transactions. [11] Liquor lubricated the vice system, from the sport in the house who coughed up an extortionate $5 for a split of champagne out of dread of being called a piker or a cheapskate, to the poor Saturday-night beer drinker in the rough corner saloon paying several times what his neighborhood bar charged. The vice system was rigged to assure a copious flow of liquor in all the resorts where women waited for men. Such women paid men no attention until they ordered. Every overpriced, watered, and adulterated drink brought a small commission, something to show for a hard night's work when the "tricks" didn't turn. Drinking places lay along the reveler's route, broadcasting their lights, music, and noise, beckoning him in for a drink or two before he got around to the evening's ultimate activity. This explains why San Francisco could support over 3000 liquor licenses along with another 2000 unlicensed "blind pigs." Saloon keepers in debt to breweries and wholesalers were required to keep a string of girls on the premises to stimulate consumption and attract more customers. [12]

Recently archaeologists in Washington, DC, dug up further evidence of liquor's role in the economics of prostitution. In a redevelopment area south of Pennsylvania Avenue, diggers unearthed part of the old tenderloin dating from the original "hookers" of the Civil War period to its closure in 1914. A contemporary newspaper source from the mid-1890's listed 109 brothels and 50 saloons in this district and pointed out that President Grover Cleveland could see it all from his bedroom window. What investigators found were such imperishables as perfume bottles, gaudy buttons, costume jewelry, and garter hooks. The major find was a cellar full of whiskey and beer bottles, including such popular brands as Pabst, Milwaukee, Schlitz, and John Fitzmorris Old Berwick Rye. [13]

All of the above points to the prostitute's situation at the <u>bottom</u> of the money chain. Earnings varied, from $30 to $50/week for lowly crib girls and streetwalkers, to $70 to $90/week for inmates of the cheaper and cheapest houses charging a dollar or only fifty cents, and on to upwards of $200/week for those inhabiting the better $5 and $10 parlor houses. It went higher in the few $20 houses, which took only known and recommended clients, often by appointment only. And there were the "stars," women reputed for either beauty or unusual expertise, who developed a considerable following and could take in $300/week or more. [14] Compare this with working-class women who typically earned $10/week or less. [15] In 1915 an economist reported that only 23% of working women earned at least $8/week, considered the necessary wage for subsistence, and that about one-half of working women earned less. [16] Such exploitation produced a large pool of candidates, an entire class of women desperate enough to enter an occupation that ultimately paid off in social stigmata and sickness.

However, the whore's tragedy consisted of more than social exile and incurable disease. Her flight from one kind of exploitation landed her in the midst of a set of voracious claimants to her increased disposable income. It was expenses that shriveled the wages of sin. The first cut, half the fee, belonged to the house, going to the landlord and the protecting "authorities," i. e., police and politicians, with a lesser share going to the madam as her wages. The prostitute actually received the other half, but she owed the madam weekly rent on her room, something like 25% of her half (1/8 of the total), plus $1.50/day for meals. [17]

She was forced to pay these inflated and extortionate expenses because she inhabited the demi-monde or night world. Police "rules" effectively banned her from daily life, nullifying her civil rights. However much they might have desired her trade, downtown merchants could not serve a "scarlet woman." No "respectable" woman would knowingly mingle with such creatures in department stores, shops, and restaurants. Restricted to their districts, prostitutes could deal only with salesmen, grocers, druggists, liquor dealers, "doctors," and other merchants who perceived cheating whores to be their right and privilege. This was all very beneficial to madams: Besides room and board, they took cuts of all sales and services occurring on their premises, both from whatever they sold to their women, as food items, liquor, drugs, and notions, and from whatever outside people brought in. Salesmen appeared frequently to offer clothing: coats, dresses, suits, kimonos, chemises, hosiery, hats, shoes, gloves, feathers, and underwear. Others presented notions: perfume, combs, hairpins, lotions, and other grooming items, plus jewelry. If local "rules" commanded it, the girls had to pay the doctor or quack who appeared weekly, gave no true examination, and signed a health certificate. Those without the knack for beautifying themselves took yet another hit from beauticians who tended hair and nails, essential services when income depends upon personal appearance.

Thus a whore's lot: rejection, abuse, disease, and exploitation. Their parasites impoverished them to the point of indebtedness. They paid a very high price for some small comforts. The final parasite, who fed very well from their failing bodies, was the pimp. Practices varied for house girls; many preferred the control of the madam, but others either chose or were too weak to fend off masculine domination. Many women were procured by pimps. They went after poor girls, lonely and desperate for some good thing in their lives, promising something like marriage or a job. Then the quick seduction, the brutal strokes that terrorized the girl, and her delivery to the waiting madam. Afterward the procurer became the pimp, appearing before dawn, taking the girl's earnings, leaving her a pittance, and moving on to his next girl. [18]

Notes: Chapter 13

1. Quoted in Ruth Rosen, *The Lost Sisterhood: Prostitution in America, 1900-1918,* 77-78.
2. *Autobiography*, 202-203.
3. *Ibid.*, 6, 42, 72; Al Rose, *Storyville, New Orleans: An Authentic Illustrated Account of the Notorious Red-Light District*, 29-30; Herbert Asbury, *The French Quarter*, 256.
4. Timothy J. Gilfoyle, *City of Eros: Prostitution and the Commercialization of Sex, 1790-1920*, 53; Rosen, 76; Asbury, FQ, 256.
5. Gilfoyle, 267; George J. Kneeland, *Commercialized Prostitution in New York City*, 128-133; Rosen, 77.
6. Asbury, FQ, 258-259; Herbert Asbury, *The Barbary Coast: An Informal History of the San Francisco Underworld*, 245; Otto Bettmann, *The Good Old Days—They Were Terrible,* 99; Kneeland, 128-133; Rosen, 5, 74.
7. *Ibid.*, 75.
8. Kneeland, *379.*
9. Rosen, 10, 79.
10. Howard B. Woolston, *Prostitution in the United States: Prior to the Entry of the United States into the World War*, 336-337.
11. *Ibid.*, 99-100.
12. Asbury, BC, 123-126; Rosen, 31, 77.
13. Associated Press, "Underbelly of a City: Dig reveals vice," *Arizona Republic*, September, 14, 1989.
14. Woolston, 65; Asbury, BC, 242-243.
15. Kneeland, 125-128; Rosen, 147-148; Gilfoyle, 61.
16. Quoted in Mark Thomas Connelly, *The Response to Prostitution in the Progressive Era*, 31.
17. Kneeland, 96, 125-128; Rosen, 76.
18. *Ibid.,* 75-76, 108-110, 129-131; Kneeland, 4, 9-10; Asbury, BC, 244; Woolston, 86; Rose, *Storyville*, 164-165.

14. The Art of Rag (II): Sedalia

14.1 "Queen City of the Prairies"

> St.Louis, Sedalia, and Kansas City were the three most important cities of ragtime's beginning. Sedalia was the "hub" of the ragtime wheel, and the most important.
>
> Brun Campbell [1]

Evidence indicates that Scott Joplin moved from St. Louis to Sedalia in 1894. With his reticent nature and black man's discretion, he put down few clear tracks for us to follow. Around age 16, in 1884 or 1885, he had gone into the itinerant life with his vocal quartet (which may have included brother Robert), probably starting on local circuits then ranging farther, going beyond the Red River Valley, until he found a base in St.Louis ca. 1890. In St.Louis Joplin found a milieu of African-American entertainers and musicians. He found his closest friends there in the Turpin family. "Honest John" Turpin owned and operated the Silver Dollar Saloon at 425 S 12th Street in the tenderloin; here Turpin and sons Tom and Charley provided a gathering place for performers.

The principal sightings of Joplin during this time were his return in 1891 to Texarkana to perform with the "Texarkana Minstrels" (Chapter 1.3), and his performing off the Midway (in his own band) at the fair in Chicago during the summer of 1893 (Chapter 6). After this he surfaces in Sedalia, rooming with the Marshalls at 135 West Henry, where he became role model, teacher, and close friend to young (13) Arthur Marshall, later his chief follower and protegé. Just a train ride away from St.Louis, Joplin was in and out on his tours with the new quartet he had formed (probably in late 1894). This new "Texas Medley Quartette" was a double quartet or octet that included brothers Robert and Will. [2]

Curiously Sedalia, both in its founding and in the kind of community it became, shows forth the qualities of its founder. Today we would label General George Rapin Smith (1804-1879) a developer, but Sedalia owes much more to his vision and humanity. Smith reached Pettis County, Missouri, from Kentucky, with family and portables, including slaves, in 1833. Although a southerner and slave owner, he had been reared and educated to be an opponent of slavery; he later freed his slaves and founded Sedalia as a free community. His town went on to become a place where African Americans were never terrorized (though facing the usual discrimination). Smith's vision perceived that future prosperity would come from over rails rather than along rivers. Missouri, as queen of the water routes, saw her great expectations fall apart in the 1850's when Chicago emerged as the rail hub. St.Louis, at the meeting of our two greatest rivers, had dreamed of becoming the new nation's capital. Not until 1874, when the great Eads Bridge finally spanned the river, could trains cross the Mississippi at St.Louis.

Smith in the 1850's bought up tracts of land where the "Pacific Railroad" would come through Pettis County. The future Missouri Pacific Railroad (MOPAC) had been creeping west from St.Louis since 1851.

Smith had platted a town and obtained a depot by 1858, calling the location "Sedville" after his younger daughter Sarah, nicknamed "Sed." A few months before the first train steamed in (January 1861), he renamed it, more euphoniously, "Sedalia"; it was soon known as "Queen City of the Prairies," and later (1895) became the site of the Missouri State Fair. During the Civil War its forward position on the rail line gave the new town a jump start as a military post. This Union presence provided the wartime blessing of security in a state of divided sympathies. Although Missouri had chosen the Union, guerilla clashes ripped the state; more than 1000 battles and skirmishes over the four years killed 27,000 civilians (exceeded only in Virginia and Tennessee). Thus Sedalia grew up unscarred by the slavery controversy, without any of the bloody ground sites that mark the maps of western Missouri and eastern Kansas. [3]

Instead the Queen City prospered as a new railroad town, open and welcoming to any coming in with positive and constructive intentions. In 1872 the Missouri, Kansas, and Texas Railroad (MKT or Katy) crossed the MOPAC and put up repair shops east of town. Both railroads used the town as a division point for changing train crews. These activities produced hundreds of jobs, and the population grew rapidly, from about 4500 in 1870, to 9561 in 1880, to 14,068 in 1890. By then it was the state's fifth largest city (after St. Louis, Kansas City, St. Joseph, and Springfield), with twenty churches (two for blacks), thirteen schools (one segregated), numerous secret and benevolent societies ("lodges"), several baseball teams, two bands, an orchestra, a theatre (Wood's Opera House at Lamine and 2nd), four music stores, nine banks, five newspapers, and thirty-five saloons. It was the center of business between Jefferson City (the state capital) and Kansas City. It went right on bustling after dark. Main Street, running parallel to the east-west railroad tracks, contained most of the saloons, pool halls, dance halls, gambling places, and brothels. Ohio Street bisected this central area, running south through the main business district, and north, across the tracks, through "Lincolnville," the black section. Other than "Main Street" the vice district lacked a name, although occasionally, after a rough night, editors referred to it as "Battle Row." The constant drunkenness, open prostitution, and occasional violence hovered like a bad smell over the center of the small city. But it brought in business, which soon leached away the force of any would-be decency crusaders. [4]

Other than a friendly and musical town, Sedalia offered Scott Joplin a superb location. Both of its railroads, MOPAC and Katy, connected St.Louis to Kansas City, and from those hubs trains ran in all directions. Both of these railroads, the Missouri Pacific via the Mississippi Valley, and the Missouri-Kansas-Texas going inland down the plains of Oklahoma, reached the cities on the Gulf of Mexico. No itineraries of the Texas Medley Quartette are extant, but the publication of two songs, in Syracuse, NY, in 1895, his first published compositions, hints at times traveled and distances covered. [5] Joplin also traveled alone as a "perfessor," a ubiquitous black man who tended piano in the lowlife locations of city and country. In his travels he probably absorbed the elements of the developing ragtime style. In the cultural half-light of honky-tonks, tent shows, waterfront dives, and tenderloin spots, flourished a semi-outcast subculture. In some of these places the races dared to mingle (called "black and tans"), and white and black musicians exchanged techniques and styles. Sex and music often brought the races together, usually in furtive provinces off the map of the day world. [6]

While working out his ragtime role, Joplin also took up his role and relationship in Sedalia's music/entertainment milieu. These were the final years of "live" sound when music could be heard only in performance (exceptions such as music boxes and other machines, e.g., coin operated instruments, account for very little of time spent listening). Edison and others were developing technologies of sound reproduction, but the quality would remain poor for the next two decades. Sheet music outsold records until the Twenties. So gigs were plentiful, and Joplin kept busy playing for dances and balls; cakewalk contests; in private clubs like the Black 400 Club or the Maple Leaf Club; in theatre orchestras at Woods Opera House or Smiths Opera House, playing for minstrel shows, operettas, and concerts; accompanying vocal groups; and at private parties. He also played second cornet in the Queen City Cornet Band. This was a 12-piece brass ensemble, the pride of the black community. This band performed at parades, celebrations, political rallies, other public occasions, and at its own concerts. Although its members had to stick to their day jobs, the Queen City Cornet (later "Concert") Band achieved musical eminence statewide, winning contests and carrying what became the Sedalia style of ragtime to Kansas City, St.Louis, and even Des Moines on one occasion.

Joplin enlisted about half of the bandsmen into a dance band that played for local dances, both black and white. Undoubtedly he preferred the more wholesome environment of dances, shows, and public occasions, but the full-time musician couldn't live on part-time employments. And parades, rallies, and celebrations usually paid off only in food and beverages. To get by Joplin had to descend to Sedalia's Main-Street underworld. Much of the male population held jobs on or near Main Street, and enticements lay on each block reaching out for their wages: saloons, pool halls, gambling rooms, honky-tonks, dance halls, and bordellos. Besides locals, these places served visitors and transients, including railroad men "laying over" on their round trips, commercial travelers ("drummers"), cattle drovers who shipped from there, wholesale grocers, and the annual State Fair crowd. Sedalia was well known for this "district," smaller, more compact than those of bigger cities. Many itinerant folk no doubt preferred its small-town friendly, more open ambience, with its police force more easily able to spot pickpockets and alley robbers. Madams paid the perfessor $1.50/night, the usual gig price, and the proverbial "big spenders" "out on the town" handed over 50 cent and dollar tips, which totaled out $7.00 on a slow night and $10 to $15 on a good night. For an African American these high wages caused no loss of respectability or status. Most black folk lived daily hand-to-mouth beneath a lowering threat of destitution. Whorehouse and honky-tonk employment piped much needed money into their communities directly out of white men's wallets. [7]

Besides good money and good friends, Sedalia offered the recently opened George R. Smith College for Negroes (January 1894). George R. Smith, who had held his part of Missouri for the Union and freed his own slaves, put a legacy into his will for African Americans. His daughters Martha Smith and Sarah Cotton ("Sed") subsequently donated 24 acres east of the town's Lincolnville section to the Methodist Church, which erected a four-story brick and stone building. Because few blacks made it into secondary school (nor did most whites), the college offered preparatory education. Thus it functioned as a high school as well as a college; its major programs were probably teacher education (or "normal training") to supply teachers for the segregated schools of the time, and industrial trades, such as carpentry, plumbing, and metal trades courses for railroad men (though whites probably held most of the skilled jobs). A relative few others would have taken liberal arts programs, and some would have taken commercial subjects such as typewriting and shorthand. Because the college and its records burned in 1925, we know little of Joplin's connection to it other than that he seems to have enrolled in 1896 or 1897. As an older student of 28 or 29, regularly employed, he probably was not taking a degree program, but a part-timer, taking some courses in music, or, perhaps, to round out a sketchy background, something in history or literature. Attending with him was friend and protegè Arthur Marshall. The college was important as a cultural center for the black community, and it offered one of the few roads out of poverty for the race held down on the bottom level. [8]

RAGTIME ALMANAC

A BAKER'S DOZEN OF THE FIRST WORKS OF INSTRUMENTAL RAGTIME—PUBLISHED IN 1897

City	Title	Composer	Publisher
Chicago:	Mississippi Rag	William H. Krell	S. Brainard's Sons
	Louisiana Rag	Theodore H. Northrup	Thompson Music
	Night on the Levee	T. H. Northrup	Sol Bloom
	Plantation Echoes: Rag Two-Step	T. H. Northrup	Sol Bloom
Cincinnati:	A Bundle of Rags	Robert S. Roberts	Philip Kussel
	Pride of Bucktown	R. S. Roberts	Philip Kussel
Kansas City:	The Coon's Frolic	George Southwell	George Southwell
New Orleans:	Roustabout Rag	Paul Sarabresole	Gruenewald
New York:	At A Georgia Campmeeting	Kerry Mills	F. A. Mills
	Forest & Stream: Polka or Two-Step	William H. Tyers	F. A. Mills
	Rag Medley	Max Hoffmann	M. Witmark & Sons
Philadelphia:	Shifty Shuffles	Eva Note Flennara	Welch & Wilsky
St. Louis:	Harlem Rag	Tom Turpin	Robert DeYong & Co. (9)

Notes: Chapter 14.1

1. Quoted in John Edward Hasse, Ed., *Ragtime: Its History, Composers, and Music*, 150.
2. Edward A. Berlin, *King of Ragtime: Scott Joplin and his Era*, 8, states that there is "no convincing evidence" for Joplin's early travels. He also presents evidence that Joplin had spent his teen years in Sedalia, living with a (supposed) relative and attending school (8-9). Joplin's only certainties are his music.
3. Paul C. Nagel, *Missouri: A Bicentennial History*, 12-14, 63-66, 120 ff., 173-175; Samuel Bannister Harding, *George R. Smith: Founder of Sedalia, MO*, 1-13, for Smith; "The First One Hundred Years," for Sedalia and Smith.
4. *National Standard Atlas of the World*, 101; Berlin, *King*, 13-23; Susan Curtis, *Dancing to a Black Man's Tune: A Life of Scott Joplin*, 71-73.
5. These were "Please Say You Will" and "A Picture of Her Face."
6. James W. Haskins, with Kathleen Benson, *Scott Joplin*, 64-76; Vera Brodsky Lawrence, "Scott Joplin," 369.
7. Berlin, *King*, 20-25; Curtis, 73-81; Rudi Blesh and Harriet Janis, *They All Played Ragtime*, 14-24.
8. Berlin, *King*, 81; Curtis, 18-19, 33-34; Blesh and Janis, 19, 24; Addison Walker Reed, "The Life and Works of Scott Joplin," 23-24, claims that at George R. Smith College, Joplin learned more of musical notation, studied piano under Mrs. Minnie Jackson, and took theory and composition from Professor Murray.
9. From Hasse, Ed., *Ragtime*, 10.

14.2 Texas Interlude: A Ragtime Stunt[1]

Joplin surfaces again (1896) in Temple, Texas, publishing his first three instrumental pieces, a waltz and two marches.[2] He may have been drawn there by a staged spectacular, the high-speed crash of two steam locomotives. This singular event occurred 50 miles north of Temple in a shallow grass valley just above Waco.

Looking back a century, we can appreciate the notion of such a horrendous proceeding. Our newsmedia give a large amount of daily play to atrocities and catastrophes, and filmmakers enhance such events with "special effects." What is difficult to grasp is the novelty of such fare; today very few people would board train or plane to witness such a thing. In 1896 George Crush, a passenger agent of the Missouri-Kansas-Texas Railroad, the MKT or "Katy," inspired by the crowds that turned up to gawk at train wrecks, decided to stage one for the cause of public relations. He picked a site on the open plains near the main line south of Dallas-Fort Worth and planned to run in ticket holders on Katy excursion trains.

First he went to the Katy repair and maintenance shops at Denison, Texas, a few miles south of the Red River crossing from Oklahoma Territory into Texas, where he selected two obsolete but still viable locomotives, Engines 999 and 1001. He had the former painted green with red trim and the later done in the reverse, red with green trim. Each was to pull a train of six stock cars with canvas hanging down the sides, the logos of advertisers painted thereon. These included the Texas State Fair and the Ringling Brothers Circus, which furnished one of its Big Tops for use as a restaurant. Crush sent out notices advertising the "Monster Head-end Collision" to all Texas papers and to every metropolitan daily in the nation. Plus posters bearing a lithograph of smashing trains; plus bulletins and circulars to be tacked onto every fence post, wall, and tree in the state. Ticket orders poured in to be handled by a crew of specially hired stenographers. Newsmen reciprocated with stories about the locomotives, which were making appearances in the towns along the Katy line, and about Charley Crain and Charley Stanton, the brave engineers who would throttle the trains toward their doom, leaping free just in time.

Part of the hoopla was secrecy about the site. Crush tantalized the world about the crash location until the track-laying crew, a small army of 500 workmen turned up just a week before the event. The site consisted of a shallow valley north of Waco just off the main line. Gentle hills rose to the west, the north, and the south, still green during the second week of September. Four miles of tracks were laid, north to south, hilltop-valley-hilltop, allowing each train a momentous downhill run to the center crash-point.

Then construction crews erected a covered grandstand for dignitaries, three speaker's stands, a stand for the press, a bandstand, a nine-foot-high camera platform, two telegraph offices, and a depot. The platform onto which spectators detrained was almost four miles long, 21,000 feet! The Katy superintendent of dining car services came in to dish up enough victuals for the anticipated crowd of 20,000. This was a virtual town; the sign on the depot proclaimed "Crush, Texas."

The synthetic catastrophe was set for 5:00 PM, September 15, 1896, and by 10:00 AM over 10,000 expectant people milled around the site. To amuse these early birds, there was a large carnival midway with medicine shows and game booths. Many folks also rode in on buggies, wagons, horses, and afoot, but most came on thirty-three Katy excursion trains. The cost of a round-trip from any place in Texas was a mere two dollars; this included the price of admission. Some trains huffed in with passengers sitting on top of jammed-full cars.

By 1:00 PM the crowd had increased to more than 25,000, with another 15,000 to come in (doubling expectations). People spread out over the level area, eating and picnicking, listening to the brass bands, attending to the orations of politicians, taking in the midway, and having their pockets picked. Crush had taken some precautions for crowd control. Chiefly he had hired 200 sheriffs' deputies and built a wooden jail to detain lawbreakers. A danger zone of 50 yards on either side of the tracks was marked off with railroad-tie posts holding up a heavy cable. Only photographers could get inside that limit to set up on their raised platform thirty yards from the expected point of impact. The crowd was to be held back 200 yards from this point. But the man who knew how to attract a crowd had given too little consideration to its control. 40,000 souls, collectively excited, became oblivious to 200 deputies and rope lines. At 3:00 PM Engines 999 and 1001 steamed slowly past the crowd, which roared back its readiness and surged to within ten yards of the track. Lacking a public-address system to reach all ears at once, Crush and his pathetic force of deputies had to struggle inch-by-inch, their yells heard only by those nearest, to drive excited thousands back to the fifty-yard danger-zone.

They could do no more. It was now 5:00 PM, and the crowd, tense and expectant, settled down for the coming thrill. First the locomotives met, cowcatcher to cowcatcher, at the mid-point, then backed off, chugging in reverse two miles uphill to their starting positions above the valley. At 5:20 Crush rode in on a prancing white horse, straddling the track where the engineers could see him from their distant positions. He raised his white stetson and began to count back from 120. At zero his hat went down sharply, and a telegrapher clicked "Go!" to fellow operators at the start points who relayed the command to Charley Stanton in 999 and Charley Crain in 1001. The crowd cheered again and pushed against the restraining cables along the line of the danger zone. Small "torpedoes," the fireworks that explode when dashed to the ground, had been set on the tracks every few feet, so that, as the trains came nearer, a sound like the rapid fire of muskets grew louder: "Pop, pop, pop, pop, pop, pop...." The engineers had been instructed to leap clear when reaching the speed of 15 mph; however Charley Crain stayed with No. 1001 until it had run half a mile, which greatly increased the excitement.

Now driverless, the trains hurtled down opposite hillsides, the sounds of driving pistons and cracking torpedoes growing much louder. The crash came thunderous and grinding as the locomotives rose against each other like rams in combat. The front cars of each train telescoped into the wreck. Steam and smoke hid the spectacle. Then, as train noises died down, came violent explosions; both engines' boilers blew up simultaneously. From out of the holocaust flew large and small pieces of metal, sending the crowd back in sudden panic. A young man went down, dead from a piece of flying metal, and a length of large chain killed a boy in a tree seeking a better view. Six others survived hits from flying metal, and J.C. Dean the official photographer up on the high platform took a bolt in his right eye. After recovering, he put a notice in Waco newspapers: "Having gotten all the loose screws and other hardware out of my head, am now ready for all photographic business. Dean, Waco's high-priced photographer." Two trucks, or wheel assemblies, were blown a hundred feet. Part of a smokestack flew 500 feet and landed next to a terrified group. A woman half a mile away was injured by a piece of wood.

Fun had become terror, but when the fright diminished, many came back for souvenirs of what was now perceived as a greater occasion, both thrilling and tragic. They carried off all portable debris. A day later, the Katy wrecker trains got the rest, leaving the site clean. A much troubled George Crush told a reporter: "I begged, entreated, threatened and commanded them to seek places of safety, and they paid no more attention to me or to the orders of the constables...than if we had nothing to do with the affair. I regret that any body should have been injured as a result of the prearranged collision...[but] no one could have foreseen that the explosion of the boilers would occur." To that one asks, why not? Wouldn't such a crash have forced an explosion? Hadn't this occurred in past train wrecks? Someone at the Katy might have had the same perception because the railroad notified Crush that night that he was no longer an employee. However, the next day, a higher authority in the company rescinded the firing and reinstated him. Taking the initiative in that less litigious time, the railroad quickly settled all damage claims. Dean the one-eyed photographer accepted $10,000 and a lifetime pass.

Lacking celebrity casualties, the episode became soon forgotten. But it has survived as a footnote because a probable witness rendered it into music. Exactly one month later (October 15, 1896), in Temple, Texas, Scott Joplin registered for copyright *The Great Crush Collision March*. It carried a dedication to the "M. K. & T. Ry." Written into the printed score are descriptive phrases:

>   The noise of the trains while running at the rate of sixty miles per hour
>   Whistling for the crossing
>   Noise of the trains
>   Whistle before the collision
>   The collision

In this descriptive march, a type of composition popular at this time [3], the dramatic event occurs in a short passage following the march themes. Although the strains of the march are delightful, the attempt to portray the horrendous quality of the crash falls short. [4] Susan Curtis, Joplin's other recent biographer, points out that railroads, which provided the mobility that allowed African Americans to escape their rural isolation, also deeply influenced their musical culture. They wrote railroad songs and instrumental pieces (like *Crush Collision*), but more, the "…steady rhythm of trains and industrial work became embedded in African-American musical forms such as ragtime and later jazz and stride piano." [5]

Notes: Chapter 14.2

1. Most of the details were taken from Allen Lee Hamilton, "Train Crash at Crush: Publicity and tragedy—as big as Texas," *American West*, Vol. XX, No. 4 (July-August 1983): 62-65.
2. *The Great Crush Collision March, Combination March, Harmony Club Waltz.*
3. See *Charge of the Light Brigade* and other compositions of E.T. Paull, who specialized in such programmatic music.
4. See Edward A. Berlin, *King of Ragtime: Scott Joplin and his Era,* 27-29, for a description.
5. Susan Curtis, *Dancing to a Black Man's Tune: A Life of Scott Joplin*, 41-42.

14.3 The Maple Leaf Rag

> He wasn't a very large man, but he had a wonderful personality. He was kind to all of us musicians that would…flock around him, 'cause he was an inspiration to us all. We always treated him as daddy to the bunch of piano players here in Sedalia. [1]

Before it appeared as sheet music bearing the new designation "rag time," the syncopated style of the perfessors was called "jig piano." This new music reminded people of fast dance music heard in saloons and honky-tonks or on festive occasions, the most familiar being the Irish jig. But soon the catchy, flowing syncopation became perceived as an uneven, or "ragged time," in which players were taking a familiar or popular tune and "ragging" it. These racy, syncopated strains lifted the moods of customers with money to spend. From one tune, the perfessor easily segued into another, keeping up the mood, making eye contact with potential tippers. This tendency of combining tunes in sequences quite naturally developed as an art form in which interesting and pleasing effects were created by mixing the quicker strains with the more lyrical. These resulting medleys—"rag music"—were soon called simply "rags."

"Rags" and "ragtime," however, are not synonymous. As Dick Zimmerman puts it: "A 'rag' was a multi-themed syncopated composition, generally for piano. Where 'ragtime' was a syncopated style of playing any music, a 'rag' was a work conceived in syncopation." [2] Most rags consisted of three or four themes but the form was elastic, lacking rules. The march form supplied a model of sorts in that rags used march rhythms, and most strains ran to 16 bars or measures. Perfessors either composed from scratch or searched their memories for lesser-known tunes to blend into a rag sequence uniquely theirs. They also individualized their performance styles, using little "tricks" of tempo, octaves, harmony, and other clever variations, plus embellishments such as repeats, bridge passages, snappy introductions, and conclusions. [3]

Every player or "tickler" played his material, his own personal ragtime, gradually over the years working up a body of music. Although he did this to earn a living, he was denied the rewards granted to musical peers: respect for his art or craft. Ragtime was illegitimate—bastard music—poisoned by its racial and social origins. For respect perfessors had to turn to their fellows, which made ragtime a brotherhood. When one ragtimer turned up to hear another, the performance became sharper, more focused, the one at the piano exerting to demonstrate in order to secure the greater quality of appreciation. Few others could sense in the heightened atmosphere the gesture of musical dialog. But if players craved and needed such communication, they encountered it with very mixed emotions. As with comedians and their routines, so with ticklers and their tricks. Some players jealously feared the loss of musical materials. Their music constituted the artistic property that conferred whatever little fame and reputation they possessed. Obviously this was an irrational fear: imitation flatters much more than it steals. There is no magical means of robbing someone's essence. And this fear conflicted with the motive to compete. The need to demonstrate musical powers far exceeds the desire to protect them. From the start, there were "cutting contests," competitions staged to find out the musical truth, to deflate false reputations and discover true claims to distinction. Blesh and Janis describe this diffusional activity:

> Drifting from one town to the next, following the fairs, the races, and the excursions, these men formed a real folk academy. After the tonks and houses closed, they would meet in some hospitable back-room rendezvous to play on into the morning. Ideas were freely exchanged, and rags, true to the meaning of the name, were patched together from the bits of melody and scraps of harmony that all contributed. [4]

Scott Joplin moved easily in this ragtime culture. Always reticent, he never articulated his goals in ragtime (in any form that was recorded), but every page of his carefully scored rags manifests his artistic vision. Subjectively, beauty exists in the eye (or ear) of its beholder (or listener); however, there is also a comparative level, where we perceive a scale and degrees of esthetic qualities. Joplin aimed to reach high on such a scale, to secure the appreciation of his music by future generations. He sought to take the rag beyond pleasure and delight, to raise it to joy and exaltation. Blesh and Janis, in the first book on ragtime a half century ago, put it thusly: "He was the first to shape folk inspiration into the clear picture of a finished musical form with an indisputable right to be accepted in all quarters as serious music." [5] Joplin certainly envisioned ragtime as an American music artistically worthy; his ambition was to create the art of rag.

By 1898 his first ragtime compositions were on paper. Ragtime sheet music had appeared in music stores the previous year, the jig piano of the underworld having materialized for the piano as the rag, and for dancing as the two-step. In December 1897, Tom Turpin, his close friend in St.Louis, had published *Harlem Rag*, the first by an African American. Thus encouraged, Joplin sought a publisher, going first to A.W. Perry & Son in Sedalia (at 306 Broadway) with two or three compositions (*Original Rags, Maple Leaf Rag,* and perhaps *Sunflower Slow Drag*), but he was turned down. This was not because of any presumed poor musical quality or craftsmanship; Joplin had become a sophisticated and refined musician. The problem lay in ragtime itself: anything labeled ragtime was denied artistic status and approval by the cultural establishment, made up of academics, critics, and certain clergy. They did not perceive this music as "high minded," a favorite term of the period's uplifters, but rather as the opposite, something from out of the "gutter," injurious to society's moral fabric.

Perry later published ragtime, including one of Joplin's (*The Favorite*, 1904), but in 1898 the music's dubious moral reputation may have been too off-putting for a small-town publisher. Equally forbidding may have been the complexity and difficulty of Joplin's scores. Published ragtime was not performance ragtime, as the sheet music was necessarily simplified for home consumption. After this rebuff, Joplin seems not to have approached any publishers until December when he offered his works to the Carl Hoffman firm in Kansas City. Curiously Hoffman bought *Original Rags*, one of Joplin's few rags in the medley form (five successive strains) and probably the first he composed. Thus they passed over the great *Maple Leaf Rag*, destined for both continuous and large sales and major musical influence on the qualities of rag. *Original Rags* reached the music stores in March 1899. This was probably an unhappy publishing experience because he was prevailed upon to sell outright for a paltry sum—he was a black man offering his first work—a work that remained in print and was later reissued by two other publishers. After this he demanded greater considerations. [6]

Blesh and Janis tell us that, "Occasionally in a strange town a pianist needing a few quick dollars would sell a tune for publication." [7] For most African-American musicians, those few dollars were the only reward for publishing. Publishers bought their music outright for $10 or $25, and all cash from hits went to them. To publish was to be cheated; only the tippers in houses paid "good money." Needing a quick cash fix, a black musician would sell any tune he knew to be unpublished. Integrity just didn't pay. The smart thing was to wangle money from white publishers. Undoubtedly after the Carl Hoffman firm exploited him in the sale of *Original Rags*, Joplin meant to get better treatment. As a serious composer, he knew that he had to publish his music for it to become known and available. He realized that the *Maple Leaf Rag* could be important and influential, and he told Arthur Marshall, "Arthur, the *Maple Leaf* will make me King of the Ragtime Composers." [8] This can be seen as the most consequential act of his life; it promised not only some amounts of "fame and fortune," but the achievement of a major contribution to the development of ragtime plus recognition for it.

But what publisher? The small-town publisher (Perry of Sedalia) had refused him, and the nearest big-city publisher (Carl Hoffman of Kansas City) had cheated him. We do not know why Joplin next entrusted his most valuable property to another Sedalian, John Stark, a rival of Perry in the retail music business who had even less interest in publishing. Nor have any of the several accounts of their meeting been verified. In some versions, Stark is amazed at hearing Joplin perform his great rag, and in others Joplin comes to John Stark & Son to demonstrate the composition. Probably we will never know who made the initial gesture. [9]

As for Stark, he was a typical small-town entrepreneur, but he aspired to much more than a full cash box when he locked up at night. John Stillwell Stark started out in Shelby County, Kentucky, in 1841, the eleventh of a farmer's twelve children. The twelfth proved fatal for his mother, and, a few years later, at six, the family sent him to live with his older brother Etilmon near Gosport, Indiana (about 65 miles southwest of Indianapolis). There he received a minimal rural education combined with maximum exposure to rough farm work. Like that other Kentuckian George R. Smith, Stark took the Union side in the Civil War, becoming a bugler in the First Regiment of the Indiana Heavy Artillery Volunteers. Entering the regiment on New Year's Day 1864, he pulled army of occupation duty in New Orleans. What he did there was to find a bride, Sarah Ann Casey, who was only 13 or 14. After marrying her, he sent her up to live with his brother in Indiana, where she continued her schooling until his demobilization in January 1866. They began married life on one of Etilmon's several farms (he possessed 2200 acres by 1866) where their first son Etilmon was born in 1868, namesake of a venerated brother. In 1869 the young Stark family drove west in a covered wagon to northwest Missouri to homestead near Maysville. Here two other children, William in 1870 and Eleanor in 1872, were born.

By 1880 John Stark evidently desired more than to subsist on a quarter section of homestead acreage. As he followed his slow-moving oxen, he probably came to realize that only in a town could he reach the potential that he sensed within himself. He sold the farm and moved to nearby Cameron to reinvent himself as a businessman. Ice cream had recently become a commercial item, and Stark, a man of pioneer spirit in a pioneer century, seized the opportunity to manufacture and market this new product. He loaded his old farm wagon with ice to drive out to sell his chilled produce to erstwhile neighbors. A good start was made in Cameron, but a business must grow, which sent them twenty miles east to the larger community of Chillicothe. There Stark, a musical soul who liked to sing folk songs and strum his guitar, saw the sales possibilities in the new reed organs manufactured by Mason and Hamlin. Having known the dullness and monotony of farm life, he realized that the enjoyment of hymns and songs could be a treasured way of passing a farmer's few hours of leisure. He carted the instrument around, demonstrating it until he convinced a farmer to give it a trial. Then he would start out again with the next one. Later he added pianos; music brought in more than ice cream. When the Chillicothe area became saturated with parlor instruments, he relocated 70 miles south to the fast-growing railroad center of Sedalia where he opened a full-line music store in 1885, John Stark & Son, which included fifteen-year-old William Stark. [10]

The Starks flourished in Sedalia. While young Will learned the music business, both Etilmon and Eleanor studied music, eventually becoming professionals. As for the father, with farming behind him and the music store increasingly in the hands of a capable son, there was finally the opportunity (at 45) to acquire learning. He read widely, finding his greatest interests in history, philosophy, and European classical music. Blesh and Janis characterize him as "…two men in one: the pioneer and the man of new cities, the farmer with folk music in his veins and the new man of culture with opera in his head." [11] By the mid-1890's the Starks were staging recitals and musicales at the store at 514 Ohio Street. Piano solos and duos, vocal solos, and chamber music occurred on mixed programs, performed by leading musicians of the Queen City, including the two young

Starks. Etilmon became music director at a private school in 1893, and Eleanor or "Nellie," a great local favorite on the piano, departed in 1895 to study under two masters in Berlin. By 1899 John Stark was a cultural leader as well as a businessman; in choosing him as a publisher, Joplin may have been acting on a shrewd insight. [12] Wherever he may have first heard it, John Stark (or son Will) must have liked the *Maple Leaf Rag*, and Joplin must have glimpsed this liking. Stark wasn't much of a publisher; he had acquired a few songs when he bought out the stock of a competitor in 1885. As Curtis points out, Stark at 58 owned a profitable retail store and risked very little in venturing the MLR. [13] It couldn't have been a big deal to him. Since the risk was nearly all on the composer's side, Joplin must have sensed some worthy qualities in the aging Ohio Street merchant to entrust a stranger (and a white man) with his major composition. What happened next was the transformation of an agreement into a written contract. This contract, dated August 10, 1899, and typewritten, states in amateur legalese what parties of the first and second parts will undertake: Stark & Son agrees to copyright and publish the rag and possesses the "exclusive right" to market and sell it. Joplin's name was to "appear in print" on every copy; he was to receive ten free copies and be able to purchase additional copies for five cents; and most important: "…the composer of said music shall have and receive a royalty of one cent per copy…." In a clause added in longhand, the Starks agree not to sell it for less than twenty-five cents per copy. [14]

Joplin must have returned home that night well satisfied. Publishers usually drove a hard bargain, offering $25 to $50 for outright purchase; they sometimes threw down only $10 to a black man. The experience of dealing with such dishonorable people generally left a composer feeling degraded. Royalty contracts went to successful white men for whom publishers competed to add to their rosters of hit makers. Joplin's contract struck a blow for human dignity and social justice in giving an African-American artist a share in all sales of his work. We have no direct evidence of any later contracts between Stark and other composers. [15] Because Stark published difficult-to-play rags of high quality, his sales, except for the ever popular MLR, were modest at best. He could not always offer royalty contracts, having to base any offer on an estimate of potential sales, which could be very low. But he dealt honorably in offering as much as he felt he could afford. In Marshall's recollection, "He was pretty fair with us people that he bought rags from." [16]

The *Maple Leaf Rag* did indeed prove Scott Joplin to be "King of the Ragtime Writers." It sold well and steadily into the 1920's; however, despite claims of a million or more copies sold, few rags ever hit this golden number. Songs did; they were far more popular than instrumental pieces, easier to play and all could sing them. Berlin and others have investigated MLR sales, and, putting the known with extrapolations from the less known, it seems that sales exceeded 500,000 copies. Will Stark claimed 500,000 in 1909, and it still sold 5000 per month in the early 1920's. Undoubtedly sales of this work carried both Stark & Son and Joplin through difficult periods and covered basic expenses during prosperous ones. Berlin concludes that Joplin's royalties "averaged about $600 annually." This was the pay of an industrial worker in a time when most houses rented from $100 to $200 per year. The *Maple Leaf Rag* brought to its composer the security necessary for more composing. [17]

As for John Stark, publishing the MLR pushed him out of his retail store onto an unknown path in his sixties. He published music for the next 25 years until his death in 1927 at 86. It is a cliché to call him a convert on a mission, but the metaphor fits. Stark published Joplin rags because he loved them, because the esthetic and spiritual satisfactions inspired him to offer this music to the public; the convert always carries his enthusiasm to others. More than just a publisher and seller of music, he saw himself as a bringer of high culture. And on this quite lofty plane, his spirit and Joplin's met and joined. His Stark Music Company of St.Louis (from 1900) [18] styled itself "The House of Classic Rags." He may or may not have invented "classic" to characterize a rag, but it became the keystone of his marketing strategy. The cultural establishment officially despised ragtime, perceiving it as a degenerate refugee from the underworld. Critics described it as diseased and barbarous; merely listening to it spread the cultural infection. Stark understood that he had to hit that wall of negativism very hard, that a casual battering would fail to open any minds.

So he took off running, offering classic rags by "The King of Ragtime Writers." "Stark Rags" were presented as elite music, American works, yes, but equal to European classics. The composer of such music could only be a star and a celebrity, a "King." Stark's advertisements hit the reader like a strong wind, blowing away the negative associations: "We are the storm center of high-class instrumental rags.... They have lifted ragtime from its low estate and lined it up with Beethoven and Bach." And, "'Maple Leaf Rag'…has throttled and silenced those who oppose syncopations. It is played by the cultured of all nations and is welcomed in the drawing rooms and boudoirs of good taste." Again, "We mean just what we say when we call these instrumental pieces classics. They are the perfection of type." Windy, yes, but also vigorous, forceful, and attention-grabbing; and Stark fulfilled his boasts in two ways: 1) He published most of those who composed after the Joplin model; and 2) He published the full scores as written, without simplification for home consumption, which was the Tin Pan Alley way. Stark never came up with another major seller like *Maple Leaf* or had any influence on trends in popular music, but he preserved some of America's finest music.[19]

RAGTIME ALMANAC

JOPLIN RAGS PUBLISHED BY JOHN STARK & SON

1899 Maple Leaf Rag
1901 Peacherine Rag
1902 A Breeze From Alabama
1902 Elite Syncopations
1902 The Entertainer
1902 The Strenuous Life

1904 The Cascades
1906 The Ragtime Dance
1907 Nonpareil
1908 Fig Leaf Rag
1917 Reflection Rag*

*Posthumously published

CO-COMPOSED RAGS PUBLISHED BY JOHN STARK & SON

<u>Co-composer</u>
1900   Swipesy—Arthur Marshall
1901   Sunflower Slow Drag—Scott Hayden
1902   Something Doing—Scott Hayden
1907   Heliotrope Bouquet—Louis Chauvin
1911   Felicity Rag—Scott Hayden
1912   Kismet Rag—Scott Hayden (20)

Notes: Chapter 14.3

1. "An Interview With Arthur Marshall," *Rag Times*, XXI (September 1987): 3.
2. Richard Zimmerman, "Scott Joplin: His Music," Liner Notes for *Scott Joplin: His Complete Works*, Murray Hill Records #931079, Unpaged.
3. Edward A. Berlin, *King of Ragtime: Scott Joplin and His Era*, 46-47.
4. Rudi Blesh and Harriet Janis, *They All Played Ragtime*, 17.
5. *Ibid.*, 24.
6. Berlin, *King*, 47-51; Blesh and Janis, 25.
7. *Ibid.*, 17.
8. Berlin, *King*, 52.
9. *Ibid.*, 52-54; Susan Curtis, *Dancing to a Black Man's Tune: A Life of Scott Joplin*, 88-89; Blesh and Janis, 31-33, for various versions.
10. *Ibid.*, 36, 45-50, for the fullest version; See also Addison Reed, "The Life and Works of Scott Joplin," 29. Stark's move to Sedalia is usually dated "around 1885," but Berlin, *King*, 72, telescopes Cameron and Chillicothe into two years, bringing Stark to Sedalia "around 1882."
11. *Blesh and Janis,* 48-49.
12. Curtis, 91-93; Blesh and Janis, 49; Berlin, *King*, 72-75.
13. Curtis, 89.
14. Reproduced in Berlin, *King*, 55, and in David A. Jasen and Trebor Jay Tichenor, *Rags and Ragtime: A Musical History*, facing p. 77.
15. Berlin, *King*, 72, quotes Arthur Marshall's testimony that Stark paid royalties on three of his rags and that James Scott also received royalties.
16. *Idem.*
17. *Ibid.*, 57-58; Jasen and Tichenor, 78-79.
18. From 1905 to 1910 Stark lived in New York, after which he returned to St.Louis.
19. See Curtis's discussion, 110-128; also Berlin, *King*, 70-71; and Edward A. Berlin, *Ragtime: A Musical and Cultural History*, 186-187.
20. From Jasen and Tichenor, 86-107. Twenty-one Joplin Rags were published by others.

Part II

Living the Ragtime Life, 1900-1904

15. TR: The New Presidency

> I want to get rid of the bastard, I don't want him raising hell in my state any longer. I want to bury him.
>
> Boss Thomas Platt [1]

> I did not usurp power, but I did greatly broaden the use of executive power.
>
> Theodore Roosevelt [2]

The Rough Riders came home from Cuba on August 15, 1898, disembarking at Montauk on the eastern end of Long Island, where they were quarantined for five days. Theodore Roosevelt, elevated by the press to be the war's chief hero, walked down the gang plank to fame and political opportunity. Republican Boss Thomas Platt needed a candidate for governor; he hated Theodore, but his incumbent had to be replaced: too many frauds and scandals. Although Platt feared that a governorship might lead to the presidency, he sent emissaries to TR's tent at Montauk. He wanted assurances that TR wouldn't attack him or his organization. TR promised party loyalty and to work for harmony, but stated that he would always have to follow his conscience and judgment. Unhappily Platt agreed, saving face by announcing that Roosevelt had promised to "consult" with him on appointments and legislation. [3]

Theodore led a very colorful campaign against corrupt Tammany Hall and its NYC Democratic boss Richard Croker. With him on the campaign trail came a squad of uniformed Rough Riders. As they theatrically lined up, a bugler sounded the charge, and Theodore stepped up to the rostrum. Following a pause for the effect to take hold, Theodore would commence, telling of the victory over Spain, and then explain the new role that the U.S. had undertaken as a world power. This had come about because Spain's defeat had forced us to occupy the Philippines plus other islands in the Pacific and the Caribbean. Very good crowds turned up at each train station on his whistle-stop tour. This campaign supplied two revelations: an unusual popularity—in fact, celebrity—and an ability to affect large numbers of people; he had star quality. [4] Although they were irrelevant, the crowds cheered the Rough Riders, and listened carefully whenever one of these manly figures stepped forward to present a testimonial on their leader. Nor was this either a nostalgic farewell or a one-time thing. Rough Riders would always turn up on major occasions and at reunions. They never left him; they became a perpetual honor guard. [5]

The new Governor was forty and effective. He allowed Platt to chose appointees from lists he submitted, thus fulfilling the commitment to consult. They always met over breakfast at the Fifth Avenue Hotel where Platt lived. Working with the legislature achieved laws to improve working conditions, education, the environment, the civil service, and public health, although he failed in getting the legislature to act on the regulation of trusts. (This had to wait for his ascension to the presidency.) Theodore amazed newsmen with his energy and work habits. He talked to everyone: visitors, politicians, expert consultants, labor leaders, social workers, college professors. During the legislative session, he held two press conferences daily. The sheer openness of his administration astonished everyone (most officeholders operated more or less covertly, offering explanations and information only when they had to). He either vetoed or returned to the legislature 500 bills during his two-year term.

His major conflict, with Platt, the machine, and the corporations, which paid the first two, was over a tax on franchises. Street railways and gas and electric companies operated under franchises, exclusive rights to supply the consuming public with goods and services. To date they had never paid for these privileges. Theodore and others believed that corporations owed something to the public for enfranchising them; expert studies revealed that they secured their positions with bribes and were undertaxed, paying very little for the rights that guaranteed their profits. Platt, heavily pressured by the corporations, threatened political death, but Theodore defied him and prodded the Assembly to pass the franchise bill (by a vote of 109 to 35). This constituted a giant step toward economic justice—and a personal triumph. So much public support and approval rendered Theodore untouchable. [6]

He had accomplished the nearly impossible as governor: maintained his integrity and stuck to his principles while keeping up a civil relationship—at least on the surface—with a boss who smoldered at the thought of him. But Platt, who believed in "the right of a man to run his own business in his own way, with due respect for the Ten Commandments and the Penal Code," simply had to rid himself of this rigidly principled, terribly energetic, and troublesome character. [7] He hated TR (epigraph), and TR, war hero and successful reform governor, probably could not be denied renomination. This meant that the corporations, furious because of attempts to tax and regulate them, might withhold the cash that they funneled to approved candidates through Platt, and Platt's power would shrivel if he had no campaign funds to distribute.

The answer to this threat materialized when Vice-President Garret Hobart died at the end of 1899. Platt exerted all of his political force—as boss of the most populous and wealthy state, he could be very forceful—to control the vice-presidential nomination. But President McKinley and his political backer Mark Hanna disliked the maverick New Yorker only a little less than did Platt. They had been shot up by this "loose cannon" because of his hard-hitting criticisms of the Government's inept conduct of the war with Spain (for failures in transport, supplies, medicine, and food). As for Theodore, he perceived the vice-presidency as political death; he meant to run for President in 1904 and knew vice-presidents almost never succeeded. Platt eventually "won" at the convention, however, because nearly all the western delegates, chanting, "We want Teddy!" helped the eastern Republicans put it through. McKinley had passively left the matter in the hands of Hanna, and Hanna, who screamed, "Don't you realize that there's only one life between that madman and the White House?" failed to muster enough delegates behind someone else. [8]

Willy-nilly, despite his campaign against the vice-presidential nomination, TR found himself McKinley's running mate. He probably sensed that there would be something perverse in the rejection of popularity, that he might have no political future if he took a haughty stance and opted out of the enthusiastic procession. It is almost impossible to get around mass expectations: the chief supplier of campaign souvenirs had already laid in a large stock of "McKinley and Roosevelt" buttons before the convention opened. [9] While McKinley once again greeted supporters from his front porch in Canton, Ohio, Theodore took out after Bryan once more (again the Democratic nominee), vigorously defending the imperial gains of the Spanish-American War. The appeal to American pride, in the victory over Spain and our takeover of former Spanish possessions, succeeded. Voters turned away from Bryan's and the Democrats' demands for troop withdrawals and for hauling down the flag in the Philippines and Puerto Rico. The voters ratified imperialism, and the Republican ticket carried all before it except the "solid" South and four silver-mining states. [10]

Which left Theodore idle after the March 4, 1901, inauguration (back then, Congress seldom met during the warmer months). He went home to Sagamore Hill to spend the summer happily with the family and to take some very preliminary (and very circumspect) steps toward the 1904 presidential nomination. At summer's end both he and President McKinley took off on speaking tours around the country. On September 6, while TR was addressing the Vermont Fish and Game League on Lake Champlain, the President, standing next to a potted palm in the Temple of Music, was greeting people at an open reception at the Pan American Exposition in Buffalo, NY. The President had refused security measures (to the dismay of his Secretary), having no fear of the hundreds of unscreened admirers eagerly waiting for a handshake. Suddenly the next man in line raised a hand wrapped in a handkerchief to the President's vest and got off two shots. McKinley took eight days to die, seeming to improve during the middle of the period. After an initial visit, Theodore felt that, with the crisis possibly past, it would be all right to take the family camping in the Adirondacks (reasonably close to Buffalo). He was soon recalled when the President began to die, arriving twelve hours after McKinley was gone to find himself the 26th President. At 42, he was the youngest. [11]

TR realized that he had to take over very carefully—no wild shots out of loose cannons—if he was going to build party support for the 1904 election. His early utterances promised fidelity to McKinley's policies and retention of his appointees. But after these reassurances to conservatives, he carefully framed a new point on business reform in his first annual message to Congress on December 5, 1901:

> There is a wide-spread conviction in the minds of the American people that the great corporations known as trusts are in certain of their features and tendencies hurtful to the general welfare.... It does not rest upon the lack of intelligent appreciation of the necessity of meeting changing...conditions of trade with new methods.... It is based upon the sincere conviction that combination and concentration should be, not prohibited, but supervised and within reasonable limits controlled. [12]

Spoken softly and carefully, here was the policy conviction that had been developing since election to the New York State Assembly in 1882: regulation. Big did not have to be bad, but it needed regulation to remain good.

Theodore spoke sensitively for the majority. Since the return of prosperity in 1897, the nation had grown increasingly apprehensive while observing the growth and evolution of Big Business into the fewer and larger corporations generically called "Trusts." Trusts like J.P. Morgan's U.S. Steel (1901) controlled prices of commodities and products and determined the wages of workers while seeking maximum profits. The trend pointed to fewer people possessing more of the wealth. Where this might end inspired a growing fear in the collective awareness. A law to control this extreme growth had been passed in 1890: the Sherman Anti-Trust Act, which specified that any business combination "in restraint of trade" was illegal. But it hadn't worked; to date no court had determined that any business combination was doing anything that restrained trade. Judges, along with legislators and elected leaders, believed (as Calvin Coolidge put it in the 1920's) that "the business of America is business." [13] It had become clear to TR that he had to lead where no one else would. Besides getting elected in 1904, he intended to pursue two other goals: to give the presidency the dominant role in government—superseding the Congress, which had driven policy-making since 1865—and to make the Federal Government the leading force in public affairs. The fate that had placed him in the White House also provided a constituency for reform. Just at this time occurred the coalescence of forces known as the Progressive Movement: muckraking journalists, prohibitionists, social workers, reform-minded clergymen, and insurgent, anti-machine politicians. They sought a national leader to support their efforts to make government, local, state, and national, respond to their campaigns of reform. These Progressives did not mutually agree on all measures, but they were united against political corruption, the close relationship between business and government (which fostered the corruption), the trusts, the exploitation of workers, and the social and economic conditions which caused poverty. They also agreed that there was an insufficiency of democracy, that a more "direct democracy" was needed, i.e., more citizen participation. To make democracy more direct, Progressives advocated replacing party caucuses with direct primaries, the direct election of U.S. Senators, the use of initiatives whereby the people could legislate, and the recall vote to remove unsatisfactory elected officials. [14]

They soon called at the White House to talk, and Theodore listened to and encouraged these Progressives, but he continued his honeymoon with the established powers of the nation's capital, biding his time, and attempted nothing significant until February 18, 1902. On this date, the Attorney General broke cover and filed an anti-trust suit against the Northern Securities Company. This was a bombshell that shook J. P. Morgan and the other great lords of finance. Northern Securities was a "holding company," a newer variety of trust, a corporation formed to control an entire group of corporations by "holding" the voting shares of stock. In this case ruinous competition among railroads serving the Northwest had resulted when James J. Hill who controlled both his own Great Northern and the Northern Pacific Railroads had acquired the Chicago, Burlington, and Quincy which owned the best routes into Chicago. This move threatened E. H. Harriman's Union Pacific which also had a line into the Northwest. To mediate this problem, Morgan created the Northern Securities Company to hold the stock of the three competing railroads, give each a share of assets, and stop harmful competition. Harriman, who had been fighting Hill by acquiring stock in the Northern Pacific, was placated with a seat on the board of the NSC.

Very neat and orderly, but it placed monopolistic power over the railroad traffic of a large area in too few hands. Since Harriman's Union Pacific also ran into the Southwest, would the next monopolistic step be to consolidate the railroads of that area, e.g., the Santa Fe and the Rock Island, under the Morgan-Hill-Harriman dominion? An 1895 Decision (the "Knight Case") had found holding companies to be legal (not in restraint of trade) because they did not directly engage in commerce. That decision had stopped anti-trust suits (except those against labor unions for being "in restraint of trade"), causing the belief that the holding-company type of trust was immune to prosecution. However research indicated that the Knight Case had been poorly argued. TR didn't know, at this point, whether the Government had any power to regulate business. The case became very significant because at this time the Government appeared to be in danger of becoming a satellite of Big Business. The President, in filing the case, asserted the Government's authority—both moral and political in his view—which reaffirmed the people's right to govern through their elected officials. This suit became the great test case to discover which was supreme, government or corporation. [15]

The suit had been kept a secret until filed, and the fall-out was considerable. Morgan came as an injured party to the White House demanding, as one gentleman to another, to know why the dispute couldn't have been fixed in a behind-the-scenes meeting of their respective lawyers (the Attorney General and his corporation counsel). But there was real public outrage (and fear) over what Morgan and his allies were up to, and much of the press reflected back strong public support. Theodore took the issue to the public on a speaking tour. This became his strategy: take action, then go to the voters for support. He carefully crafted his speeches, rationally outlining issues and problems, carefully arguing pros and cons. He put it thusly in Cincinnati (9-20-02):

> …Wherever a substantial monopoly can be shown to exist, we should try our utmost to devise an expedient by which it can be controlled. Doubtless some of the evils existing in…great corporations cannot be cured by any legislation…. But there will remain a certain number which can be cured if we decide that by the government they are to be cured…. We do not wish to destroy corporations,

but we do wish to make them subserve the public good. All individuals, rich or poor, private or corporate, must be subject to the law of the land; and the Government will hold them to a rigid obedience thereof. The biggest corporation, like the humblest private citizen, must be held to strict compliance with the will of the people as expressed in the fundamental law. [16]

This was sincere, idealistic, and moral; people understood that he was fighting their fight. It took two years, one to win in the District Court (St.Paul, MN, 4-9-03), and another to win in the appeal to the Supreme Court (3-14-04). For the first time, the Courts upheld "free competition." Government demonstrated its power over great forces in the economy. People now expected the President to lead them in struggles for the greater good. [17]

As Theodore later rejoiced: "The success of the Northern Security's case definitely established the power of the government to deal with all great corporations. We had gained the power." Joseph Pulitzer's Democratic *New York World* not only gave the President credit as the first to enforce the Sherman Act, but also straightforwardly stated that (in Pulitzer's opinion) the nation was close to social revolution when he took office, and therefore he was "…entitled to the greatest credit for the greatest service to the nation." Such unstinting praise from a political opponent is rare. [18] All of which bore upon the New York *Sun's* belated—and ironic—endorsement of the candidate on August 11, 1904. The pro-business, ultraconservative *Sun* could never bring itself to approve of the maverick who riled the Grand Old Party with Progressivism. But, after all, he was the Republican candidate, which produced the shortest editorial in history:

Theodore! with all thy faults—[19]

II

Something more immediate and threatening began to envelop the presidency during the summer of 1902. On May 12, 147,000 miners of anthracite coal in the Scranton and Wilkes-Barre region of Pennsylvania went out on strike. The coal operators refused to negotiate because they would not recognize the United Mine Workers (UMW) or any other union. There was no prospect of a settlement. As the days dragged on, stocks of coal diminished while prices rose steeply. Anthracite, "hard coal," which burned hotter and cleaner than the "soft coal" (bituminous) used in industrial processes, was the chief source of central heating in homes, schools, work places, stores, and public buildings. All anthracite was mined in northeast Pennsylvania; without it, the nation would freeze. By summer's end, a national crisis was near. The Federal Government had never before intervened in a labor dispute, and no laws directed government, by reason of the public interest, to step in to settle or in any way to influence problems in the sphere of economics. Theodore never doubted that he had to do something to avert a catastrophe, but he could not find a handle on the situation.

Desperation ruled the coal towns. The miners suffered low wages, unsafe working conditions (441 fatal accidents in 1901), no compensation to families for the death or loss of a wage earner, debt at the company store, rotten housing, too long a work day (72 hrs/wk), and dishonest weighing practices (pay based upon the weight of coal a miner brought up). More than indifferent, the operators were arrogant and vindictive, determined to eradicate the Union. They strongly resented the 10% raise they had been pressured to grant (by Mark Hanna) in the election year 1900 (to prevent Bryan from carrying Pennsylvania). They lacked any degree of awareness of an obligation to the public, being concerned only with their property rights. They expected a coal shortage, along with violence and sabotage, which would force the President to intervene—on their side—to end the strike. But the immediate pressure came from politicians worried about the November 1902 off-year election and governors and mayors. Abruptly, after keeping a silence on the matter, TR summoned the coal operators and John Mitchell, President of the United Mine Workers, to the White House on October 3. The operators appeared but refused to negotiate or arbitrate. Their leader was George F. Baer, President of the Reading Railroad (the mines were owned by coal-carrying railroads), whose arrogance was exceeded by his insolence. In his refusal to negotiate, he ranted that, "We object to being called here to meet a criminal [i.e., John Mitchell], even by the President of the United States." So insensitive was he that he had previously said of the miners: "They don't suffer. Why, they can't even speak English." He had also proclaimed: "The rights and interests of the laboring man will be protected and cared for—not by the labor agitators—but by the Christian men to whom God in his infinite wisdom has given the control of the property interests of this country...." [20] (Mitchell was called a "criminal" because Baer demanded that unions be prosecuted for being in restraint of trade under the Sherman Act of 1890.)

Such intransigence carried with it the possibility of a civil uprising, a war if it exceeded a few weeks. TR secretly developed a back-up plan to meet such a dire situation. He arranged for the Governor of Pennsylvania to request Federal forces in putting down violence whenever he signaled the necessity. Next he found a competent general who would take the U.S. Army into the state to restore order and to take over operation of the mines. Fortunately no emergency arose because his emissary to J. P. Morgan got the settlement process restarted. Morgan, the actual owner of the Reading Railroad and its coal assets, who better understood the possible consequences of a mass uprising, decreed that Baer and his fellow operators accept arbitration. To save face, these operators refused to deal with an arbitration commission that included a labor leader. Mitchell of the UMW then fought back with a refusal to accept a commission lacking labor representation. Increasingly frustrated and furious, TR finally broke through this impasse when he realized that the operators were refusing to accept a labor representative on the commission—as such. One of the commission's stipulated positions was to be held by an "eminent sociologist," and when the President appointed E.E. Clark, head of the Brotherhood of Railway Conductors, to the sociological slot, not a single objection was raised. The miners quickly agreed and returned to work, averting a coal crisis. [21]

The Arbitration Commission reported a settlement package on March 22, 1903. The miners had to take half a loaf: 1) A 10% wage increase (instead of the 20% they needed); 2) A nine-hour day (instead of eight); 3) The presence of their own checkers at the weighing of coal; 4) A three-year contract. However, union recognition was denied, and the price of coal went up 10% immediately. Still, a new Board of Conciliation was established to settle grievances, and its composition included union representation, a big first step toward union recognition. [22] Beyond the relief of miners and the coal crisis, TR emerged as the pathfinder into new executive territory. In his *Autobiography* he referred to this as the "Jackson-Lincoln theory of the Presidency":

> ...occasionally great national crises arise which call for immediate and vigorous executive action, and...it is the duty of the President to act upon the theory that he is the steward of the people.... that he is bound to assume that he has the legal right to do whatever the needs of the people demand, unless the Constitution or the laws explicitly forbid him to do it. [23]

Seldom has a President faced an apparently hopeless situation in which he had no role to play—except the negative one of harshly applying martial law and military force—but managed to bring about both a positive settlement and a greatly strengthened presidency. Here was a whole new precedent: government could intervene when the general welfare was endangered by forces in conflict. "Govern" now meant more than just enforcing laws and disbursing funds. [24]

III

The other major concern of his first term was the question of an interoceanic canal across the Central American isthmus. Theodore entered office believing that a canal was his first priority. He had long been the principal U.S. champion of the strategic ideas of Navy Captain Alfred Thayer Mahan, whose *The Influence of Sea Power Upon History* (1890) had advocated two doctrines:

1) Great power status required control of the seas by strong naval power.
2) U.S. sea power depended upon an interoceanic canal.

All of his foreign policy plans and moves—before as well as after he became President—were generated by a fundamental, deep conviction of the global destiny of the United States of America. Although 50 years would pass before "superpower" would become current, Theodore Roosevelt believed that it was his role and destiny to prepare the nation for what he foresaw as (and we now call) the "American Century." He perceived that an industrial nation of continental size would eventually tower over the smaller nations of western Europe that dominated the globe in 1900. In his eyes the recent war with Spain had demonstrated the truths of Mahan's doctrines: victory in the Philippines and in Cuba had been achieved by our naval power. The only possible hindrance to victory had come from the need to move our newest and most powerful battleship, the *Oregon*, from the Pacific to the Atlantic. To get from San Francisco to Florida, the *Oregon* had to race around the bottom of South America for 67 days—over two months! While the nation cheered a run (from March 19 to May 24) that was triumphantly in time to help win the Battle of Santiago Bay, it brought the sober perception that a canal somewhere in Middle America would have reduced the race from 12,000 to 4000 miles. "The Race of the Oregon" (the title of a heroic poem) made the canal a certainty. [25]

The original intention, of both McKinley and Roosevelt, had been to construct a canal through Nicaragua. This would be almost 800 miles closer to the U.S., and southern Democratic Senators strongly supported this route because of its nearness to the Gulf ports of New Orleans, Mobile, and Galveston. They believed that a Nicaraguan canal would bring prosperity to the still impoverished South. Technical studies tended to support this political view: Nicaragua offered

1) The lowest mountain pass
2) A river navigable for 60 miles
3) A huge lake at the summit to supply water
4) A country free of tropical disease
5) A politically stable country

But there was another route, across Panama, much shorter (only about 1/3 as long), with a railroad across it. Here a French corporation, led by Ferdinand De Lesseps, of Suez Canal fame, had attempted to construct a canal during the 1880's. This effort had turned into a fiasco, wrecked by yellow fever and malaria, corruption in its finances, and a technology unequal to the task. To most people, Panama had come to suggest death and failure, a place of contamination to avoid, whereas thousands of pages of reports and technical studies by committees, engineers, explorers, and mariners backed up the positive perceptions of Nicaragua. [26]

The decision awaited a final report by the Isthmian Canal Commission (ICC), a group of nine very eminent civilian and military engineers. Submitted in November 1901, the report favored Nicaragua, but it also made a strong case for the Panama route, rejecting it mainly because of the high price demanded by the new French canal company which had been created only to sell the assets of the original company (now bankrupt). The French were asking $109,000,000. To the influential few who scrutinized the report, the favorable evidence on the Panama route came as a revelation. Then in January 1902, a "Panama Lobby" swung into action with a much more reasonable offer of $40,000,000 for the French Concession and its physical assets (buildings, equipment, the Panama Railroad, previous excavations). TR had kept neutral about the canal site until now, leaving the choice to Congress, but this development provoked his intervention. He called in the ICC Members, one at a time, to hear their personal views, then convened them as a group in a secret meeting in his office. What followed was a second report that reversed the earlier one and recommended Panama as the canal site. This caused high political controversy.

Ultimately in Congress, after months of hearings and speeches, intriguing and politicking, the Panama-French interests won. Interestingly, at the end, the vote in Panama's favor was honestly based upon technical and financial considerations. The Panama route was only one-third as long as the Nicaragua route (well over 100 miles shorter); it ran straighter with fewer curves; transit time would be much less (12 hours vs. 33 hours); fewer locks would have to be constructed; Panama had better harbors; the terrain had been mapped, explored, and traveled over; the Panama Railroad had been in place since 1855; a Panama canal would be cheaper to operate. However, besides technical realities, the final vote of June 26, 1902, may have been driven also by the question of volcanoes. Nicaragua contained at least 14 volcanoes, 8 of them considered to be potentially active. The Panama lobby at one point sent all 90 Senators a Nicaraguan One Centavo postage stamp that pictured a volcanic eruption in Lake Nicaragua (Mt. Momotombo).

This was timely because in April-May, Mt. Pelée on Martinique in the Caribbean had suddenly become active. On May 2, 1902, it covered the capital city of St. Pierre with dust and littered the sea with dead birds. Then on May 8, it abruptly exploded, killing 30,000 in St. Pierre within two minutes (there was one survivor, a prisoner in an underground cell) in one of history's greatest disasters. Eruptions continued and Pelée exploded a second time on May 20; there was no one left to kill. Shocked and horrified by these disasters, it was troubling to receive a dispatch from Nicaragua on May 14 describing an eruption of Mt. Momotombo itself. Although this was denied—falsely as it turned out—by the Minister of Nicaragua, Panama's lack of volcanoes probably influenced the congressional vote. The final vote in the Senate on June 19 tallied 42 to 34, an eight-vote victory for Panama, and a week later the House of Representatives passed the canal measure 259 to 8. TR signed it (the Spooner Act) into law on June 28. It was an amazing turnaround, the overthrow of an interest group (the South) that had long expected to reach its goal of an American canal across Nicaragua. [27]

The final stage was simply to negotiate a treaty with Colombia, the nation of which Panama constituted a province. Colombia had been very eager and encouraging as long as the canal site was uncertain. However the selection of Panama turned the relationship suddenly adversarial. The issues were sovereignty and money. To the Colombians, the Isthmus of Panama was their primary natural resource; they anticipated that the construction of a canal would contribute substantially to the income of their poor country. Their treaty with the French corporation had stipulated that, while the canal franchise could be sold to a private corporate entity, it could not be sold to a sovereign country without Colombia's prior agreement. Thus it would be illegal in Colombia for the French to sell the concession and assets of their company to the United States. In the Colombian view, at least $20,000,000, half the sale price, rightfully belonged to them. Why not? Whose franchise was it, anyway? The concession was due to run out in 1904, at which time it would revert back to Colombia.

As for the Americans, they viewed the sale as a simple commercial transaction, with total proceeds going to the seller. Colombian claims were invalid, a corrupt attempt of politicians to skim off the top what did not belong to them. The Americans also intended to control a "canal zone," the area of canal operations. Colombia had a history of civil war and sudden outbreaks of violence, so Americans did not believe that Colombians could keep order; they planned to do their own policing and defending. And the Americans expected that a poor country would go along with a cheap deal. The proposed treaty recognized the sovereignty of Colombia over this canal zone, but the U.S. demanded its own courts and legal system. For what was practically a cession of territory—six miles wide, extending from ocean to ocean—the U.S. offered only $10,000,000 and an annual rent of $250,000. Finally, the concession was to run 100 years, with an option to renew. No mutuality or empathy arose between the negotiators and the talks dragged along until January 1903. The Colombians (three different diplomats exhausted themselves over the course) resisted the smooth words and not-very-negotiable demands of Secretary of State John Hay. Then Hay (at TR's orders) threatened to start dealing with Nicaragua (the Spooner Act prescribed such if we failed to agree with Colombia), at which point the Colombian envoy caved in and signed. But this did not go down in Bogotá. There $10,000,000 appeared a ridiculous sum for ceding such a valuable piece of national territory, and they were already receiving a rental of $250,000 from the railroad! Surely an interoceanic canal should pay much more. Colombia, weak and unstable from decades of civil wars, had accepted a dictator, Jose Manuel Marroquín, but tolerated him chiefly for the stability he provided. Had he accepted the treaty (Hay-Herran Treaty), a wrathful nation might have arisen and overthrown him, plunging that nation into chaos once more.

The Americans understood nothing of Colombia's dilemma. They saw a backward and corrupt country standing in the way of global progress. The Panama Canal would be a noble enterprise that transcended the selfish interests of particular nations in order to benefit all. There was no empathy for (what we now call) "Third World" conditions. Peoples were to blame for their "backwardness" because they had chosen wrongly, decadence over progress, laziness over diligence, immorality over moral uprightness. For world commerce and universal prosperity, the canal was imperative, and Colombian greed should be refused. With these rationalizations, we could glibly reject claims viewed by Colombia as legitimate national aspirations.

What happened next was complicated and has not been fully explained a century later. Simply stated, the agents of the French canal company, with tacit and secret support from the United States, i. e., the Roosevelt Administration, undertook a Panamanian revolution. This was very agreeable to the people of Panama, who had been frequently but unsuccessfully rebelling since voluntarily joining the Colombians three-quarters of a century earlier. Not much was required to bring about a modest little revolution: some secrecy, enough bribe money to obtain support from the small Colombian garrison, good timing, and enough naval force to prevent the landing of Colombian troops.

Despite being physically joined, Panama was an isolated province because of the impassible and mostly unexplored Darien rain forest; no land route existed to connect the slender Isthmus to the large country at the top of South America (an area equal to the states of California, Oregon, Washington, and Arizona). The 300,000 Panamanians had over time developed their own culture and ethnicity. Following the Colombian rejection of the Hay-Herran Treaty on August 12, the revolutionary plot progressed from the talk to the action stage. There were mistakes, misunderstandings, confusion, a betrayal, and scenes of fear and desperation (chiefly among the Panamanian leaders, the Junta, worrying about firing squads), but plans were made and followed, concluding with Panama's announcement of her independence on November 3, 1903. This action was supported by the presence of an American gunboat (*U.S.S. Nashville*) while other U.S. naval vessels (10) were steaming toward both Colon and Panama City.

Once again, it was treaty time. As with the revolution, a French agent—his name is Philippe Bunau-Varilla—manipulated the process. No Panamanian participated in the treaty negotiations. Threatening to withhold the money ($100,000) that he furnished to make good on bribes to Colombian officials and soldiers, Bunau-Varilla pressured the Panamanian Junta to appoint him "Envoy Extraordinary" to the U.S. Government. Working in haste with Secretary Hay before a Panamanian Commission, which was having second thoughts about having given in on this appointment, could reach the U.S., he negotiated a treaty (Hay-Bunau-Varilla Treaty) very favorable to the U.S. The chief reason for so one-sided a treaty was to assure a fast Senate ratification, which would achieve a fast payment of the $40,000,000 to the French interests. (Bunau-Varilla was a major investor in the Company.) He simply altered the provisions of the rejected Hay-Herran Treaty to give to the U.S.: 1) A ten-mile-wide zone across the Isthmus (instead of six); 2) Powers of police and sanitation in the two terminal cities, along with judicial powers in the Canal Zone; 3) Expropriation rights over any additional land or water areas necessary to construct, operate, or defend the canal; 4) The right to exercise all rights of sovereignty in the Canal Zone (Panama got only a nominal sovereignty); 5) A lease "in perpetuity" (instead of a one-hundred-year lease). The Panamanian Commission of three arrived just after Hay and Bunau-Varilla had ceremoniously signed the treaty documents. They were furious and full of objections to what was extremely unfavorable to their country (even by the standards and views of that imperialistic time). But their protests weren't taken seriously because they lacked either power or choices. Bunau-Varilla countered the feeble threats of non-ratification by Panama with counter-threats of U.S. withdrawal and the return of Colombia. This was untrue and unlikely—TR had fully committed to a canal in Panama—but the wily Frenchman had them buffaloed. Meekly they set sail for home, and the new, but reluctant, nation ratified this disadvantageous agreement on November 26, 1903. The U.S. Senate followed on February 23, 1904.

In his *Autobiography*, Theodore Roosevelt stated that, "By far the most important action I took in foreign affairs…related to the Panama Canal." He goes on to say that if he hadn't acted that the decision-making process on the canal could have dragged on for another fifty years. [28] Next he does an unusual thing: he enumerates "a partial list of the revolutions, rebellions, insurrections, riots and other outbreaks" that had occurred in Panama since 1850. This list covers almost two pages and contains 53 items covering a 53-year period. From these entries he derives two major assertions: 1) that the people of Panama desired independence, the recent uprising being only the latest in a series; and 2) that "the experience of over half a century had shown Colombia to be utterly incapable of keeping order on the Isthmus." [29] Thus he justifies, somewhat defensively, the U.S. role of providing the naval support needed by Panama to achieve independence and prevent a reconquest by Colombia. Therefore Colombia could blame only herself for the loss of Panama, and the U.S. had acted "in absolute accord with the highest standards of international morality" in freeing Panama and in going ahead with the canal, which was vital to world commerce and our national defense. [30] Was this self-righteous stance troubled by a few furtive doubts?

We see this differently today. Or do we? The United States has become the superpower that TR foresaw, and the U.S. now appreciates the necessity of intervention in places of instability. If a superpower fails to keep order in the world, who will? Although sometimes it acts under the aegis of an international organization, this is not always possible. TR boasted in a 1911 speech that he "took" Panama, but he did no such thing. [31] The Panamanian rebellion was attempted because the U.S. promised to support it, but the U.S. role only required that the U.S. Navy "visit" there at the requested time. TR may have been complicit, but he wasn't a puppeteer. [32] Still he is assailable: 1) because of the damage to our relations with Latin American countries. This was not apparent at the time, as most of those nations wanted the canal built and just as quickly recognized the new Republic of Panama. But over time, this action greatly contributed to distrust of the "Colossus of the North." 2.) Because of the harm done to Colombia. He—and nearly all of his fellow Americans—failed completely to understand the Colombian position. McCullough (the Canal's chief historian) faults this "inability" and calls it "tragically mistaken and inexcusable." [33] And why was he guaranteeing the payment of $40,000,000 to the French company? There could have been nothing "moral" or correct according to international law in the U.S. upholding the interests of a private corporation against the claims of a sovereign nation. [34] Probably patience, further talk, and a share of the sale price could have brought the Colombians around to ratifying the Hay-Herran Treaty.

There is no simple verdict on either side in the Panama affair. Colombia was harmed, but the independence of Panama and the achievement of the canal were good results. We helped the Panamanian people achieve their cherished ideal of nationhood, but we forced them to accept a treaty degrading to sovereignty. Until the revisions of 1936 (Roosevelt-Arias Treaty), Panama was our imperial protectorate; we even collected her garbage until the 1950's. But in 1903, imperialism was accepted and applauded, challenged by only a few ethical types. The U.S. had become a world power, and world powers had to use their power, not only to further their interests, but also to keep the world in order. TR, in doing what he did, could foresee what the nation would become during the next 100 years. He prophesied well, but unfortunately he also added to what another historian has called "a heritage of ill-will." [35]

RAGTIME ALMANAC

Payments For Territorial Acquisitions

Year	Paid To	For	Amount
1803	France	Louisiana Purchase	$15,000,000
1848	Mexico	Mexican Cession	$15,000,000
1853	Mexico	Gadsden Purchase	$10,000,000
1867	Russia	Alaska Purchase	$ 7,200,000
1898	Spain	Philippine Islands	$20,000,000
1903	*	Panama Canal Zone	$50,000,000

*($40,000,000 to the New French Canal Co. and $10,000,000 to the Republic of Panama)

from Litany of the Heroes

These were the spacious days of Roosevelt,
Would that among you chiefs like him arose
To win the wrath of our united foes,
To chain King Mammon in the donjon-keep,
To rouse our godly citizens that sleep
Till, as one soul, we shout up to the sun
The battle-yell of freedom and the right—
"Lord, let good men unite."

Vachel Lindsay [36]

Notes: Chapter 15

1. Quoted in Nathan Miller, *Theodore Roosevelt: A Life*, 335.
2. *Theodore Roosevelt: An Autobiography*, 372.
3. N. Miller, 314-315; *TR: Auto*, 280-282.
4. William Henry Harbaugh, *Power and Responsibility: The Life and Times of Theodore Roosevelt*, 113-114; N. Miller, 318-321.
5. Peter Collier, with David Horowitz, *The Roosevelts: An American Saga*, 100.
6. Harbaugh, 115-127; N. Miller, 322-329; *TR: Auto*, 296-299, 307-313.
7. N. Miller, 335.
8. *Ibid.*, 334-343; TR, *Auto.*, 317-319; Edmond Morris, *The Rise of Theodore Roosevelt*, 717-729.
9. N. Miller, 340.
10. *Ibid.*, 343-344.
11. *Ibid.*, 346-352; Michael Medved, *The Shadow Presidents: The Secret History of the Chief Executives and Their Top Aides*, 102-103.
12. Mario R. DiNunzio, Ed., *Theodore Roosevelt, An American Mind: A Selection from His Writings*, 129-130.
13. Mark Sullivan, *Our Times*, II, 392-411.
14. N. Miller, 353-359.
15. Sullivan, *OT*, II, 412-419; Henry F. Pringle, *Theodore Roosevelt: A Biography*, 176-180; Harbaugh, 164; N. Miller, 364-369.
16. *Addresses and Presidential Messages 0f Theodore Roosevelt, 1902-1904*, 64-65.
17. N. Miller, 365, 368-369; Pringle, 180-181, 184; Sullivan, *OT*, II, 412-419.
18. Quoted in Sullivan, *OT*, II, 465.
19. *Ibid.*, 459.
20. Quoted in N. Miler, 371-374. TR's account in *TR: Auto*, 481, is cursory and muted. See also Pringle, 190-191.
21. *TR: Auto*, 479-491; N. Miller, 370-377; Pringle, 186-195; Sullivan, *OT*, II, 420-446.
22. *Idem*, Harbaugh, 178; Pringle, 195; N. Miller, 176.
23. *TR: Auto*, 479.
24. Page Smith, *America Enters the World; A People's History of the Progressive Era and World War I*, 19-20; Harbaugh, 179; N. Miller, 377.
25. David McCullough, *The Path Between the Seas: The Creation of the Panama Canal, 1870-1914*, 249-255; see note p. 254 for verses of *Oregon* poem. N. Miller asserts, 234, that TR promoted Mahan's ideas because they agreed with his own, as stated in his *Naval War of 1812*.
26. McCullough, *Path*, 259-263.
27. *Ibid.*, 270-328.
28. *TR: Auto*, 526.
29. *Ibid.*, 528-531.
30. *Ibid.*, 539.
31. McCullough, *Path*, 383-384.
32. *Ibid.*, 384-385.
33. *Ibid.*, 385.
34. *Idem*, and *Ibid.*, 338.
35. Harbaugh, 205.
36. Vachel Lindsay, *Collected Poems*, 193.

16. Progressives (I): The March King

The Roosevelt presidency coincided with an upsurge of progressive activity, activity directed toward changes and reforms in the areas of government, the economy, and society. Theodore Roosevelt easily became the time's central figure because his energy and movement primed the pump of positive action. This must have been contagious because the progressive spirit broke out in other spheres, such as the arts, civic improvements, morals and manners, even nutrition. Communications experts now picture such psychic flows in terms of "interaction," "feedback," "ripple effects," and "synergies." Whatever it was, the national mood became livelier, more optimistic and hopeful, exchanging resignation for belief in improvement. The new popular ragtime exactly mirrored and reflected back these changes in the collective temper. One who sensed this broad appeal of ragtime was the celebrated master of bands John Philip Sousa (1854-1932). Nearing its peak of popularity during the 1900's, Sousa's Band programmed several of the first ragtime instrumental hits, chiefly the cakewalks of Tin Pan Alley professionals Kerry Mills and Abe Holzmann (see Ragtime Almanac, Chapter 11). Traveling abroad, Sousa treated other continents to their first hearings of ragtime.

He may have done more than anyone to increase the ragtime audience. During the 1890's and 1900's, bands and their music grew incredibly popular. When vaudeville took its annual vacation from hot weather in those pre-ventilation times, bands took its place. One estimate indicates that ca. 1900 there were in the U.S. some 10,000 bands made up by 500,000 bandsmen.[1] Towns required bands for all public occasions and celebrations, as well as for scheduled concerts. They ranged from 12 to 15 members to as many as 60 or 70. When people turned out for parades or oratory (popular then), they expected a band to liven up the event. Communities took great pride in their bands and enjoyed hearing them outplay their rivals. Standing at the peak of this phenomenon, John Philip Sousa contemplated his role:

> My theory was, by sensible degrees, first to reach every heart by simple, stirring music; secondly, to lift the unmusical mind to a still higher form of musical art. This was my mission….I wanted to make a music for the people, a music to be grasped at once.[2]

Here was the progressive spirit, transmuting an idealism into music. If quizzed on what Sousa projects in his *Stars and Stripes Forever* (1897), most hearers, influenced by the title with its image of waving colors, might answer "patriotism." But the high-flying mood of this march soars above any ideology in its celebration of human potential. The glory of the nation is part of this, but the thrill of the piece emanates from a sense of great things to come. The music rejoices over anticipations of the future, a progressive essence. Just what Sousa meant above in the reaching of hearts and the minds.

His power over audiences emerges from the following anecdote. The Sousa Band was performing in the capital of the President's home state, Columbus, Ohio, when word reached the concert hall that McKinley had breathed his last. At intermission, Sousa handed out an arrangement of "Nearer My God to Thee." Reassembled onstage, the hymn was played without announcements or impromptu eulogies. The *Columbus Dispatch* of September 21, 1901, described the reaction:

> …the audience hardly breathed, for with one wave of the master-hand they were suddenly lifted from the midst of the grandest band concert ever given in the Ohio capital and set down

beside the catafalque of the dead President. Tears welled in nearly every eye…. It seemed as if its matchless beauty had never been realized before. And midst the solemn, breathing sound, faint as the distant echo from some sacred shrine, there came the tolling of the funeral bell….

It was a song without words, but the words were never so eloquent as the heavenly music of that incomparable band. [3]

More than hype and razzmatazz, these bands touched something fundamental and reflected the aspirations of that aspiring time. The master of this musical activity embodied a curious amalgam of cultural influences. His heritage was mixed, mixed European as well as European-American. His mother Elizabeth (Trinkaus), German and Lutheran, had met his father Antonio Sousa on a visit to Brooklyn, NY. Antonio Sousa had been born in Spain of Portuguese parents, driven out of their homeland during the revolution of 1822. Although there were ten children, young John Philip's musical aptitude received early attention with conservatory studies and violin lessons from age six. Father Antonio, a man of culture, knowledgeable in languages and music, who had played the trombone in the Marine Band, also provided instruction in band instruments. So precocious was John Philip, that he formed and led a small dance orchestra before he turned thirteen. At that point when a circus band offered him a job, his father stepped in and arranged for his enlistment in the Marine Band where he served his apprenticeship for the next five years. From 1872 (age 18), he took leave to perform in and conduct theatre orchestras. His gigs included playing the violin in Jacques Offenbach's orchestra when that famous French composer conducted his operas at the 1876 Centennial Exhibition in Philadelphia. Also during the 1870's, he began composing, not only for band and orchestra, but also his first comic opera *The Smugglers* (1880). Through this last work, he met and married Jane Bellis of Philadelphia in 1880. [4]

That year he received an appointment as conductor of the U.S. Marine Band ("the President's Own"), succeeding one of his mentors, Patrick Sarsfield Gilmore (d. 1892). Gilmore had been an innovator whose experiments had developed the wind band into a symphonic ensemble. Sousa carried on this development, and the symphonic or concert band has become an American art form. [5] A century later, it has accumulated a body of music composed for the sonorities and qualities of wind instruments rather than the strings. Additionally, band arrangements have been made of many orchestral works. Sousa led the Marine Band for twelve years until 1892, by which time it was reputed the best. He then left it to form his own touring or "business band," which traveled annually over the country. Eventually this band toured Europe four times and went around the world during 1911-1912. Sousa's Band thrilled the crowds at all the world's fairs, starting with the World's Columbian Exposition in Chicago in 1893. He interrupted this work to lead an army band in 1898 and navy bands in 1917-1918. Altogether he composed 15 operettas, 70 songs, 12 suites, six waltzes, two overtures, numerous miscellaneous pieces including 322 arrangements of other works for band, and 136 marches. [6]

The marches brought fame and wealth. *The Gladiator* (1886) became his first million-seller, and *Washington Post* (1889) elevated him to the rarefied sphere of celebrity, in part because dancers found it to be just right for the new—and very popular—two-step [7] But Sousa's concerts programmed marches sparingly. The band generally opened with a classical orchestral piece of the melodic variety, often overtures by Rossini (*William Tell*) or Von Suppé (*Poet and Peasant, Light Cavalry),* followed by a female singer doing operatic selections. Then might come an accompanied instrumental solo, perhaps the great trombonist Arthur Pryor or Herbert L. Clarke on cornet or E. A. Lefebre on saxophone. The marches, craved by audiences, usually appeared last in the set, interpolated as encores. People refused to go home without their marches. [8]

Trombone soloist Arthur Pryor hived off in 1903 to form his own band. From St.Joseph, Missouri, Pryor knew his ragtime and had arranged it for Sousa. He not only performed more of it subsequently, but composed it as well. He was also the actual conductor of the first recordings made by "Sousa's Band," and with his own band, he made more records than Sousa (for Victor). Many of the most popular commercial bands were Italian imports. Italian conductors on the podium played their roles with flamboyant and fiery gestures. They offered programming that tended toward the theatrical and schmaltzy. All of which set off the emotions of women. They apparently brought over the percussional extremes that inspired standing ovations, such as the firing of cannons during Tchaikowsky's *1812 Overture*. H. L. Mencken found their "tricks" and histrionics amusing. He tells how many Italian conductors would announce a "new" march, giving it the name of the local newspaper, a ploy to wangle a favorable review from the paper's critic. He describes a frequent program selection, the familiar "Anvil Chorus" from Verdi's *Il Trovatore:* "…using a row of real anvils…and a series of electric wires so arranged that big blue sparks were struck off as gentlemen of the percussion section clouted the anvils with real hammers. For this last effect…the lights were always turned out." [9]

Ragtime was another crowd-pleaser for Sousa's Band. Always sensitive to popular tastes, Sousa included cakewalks in the band's repertory in response to the cakewalk and two-step dance craze of the late 1890's. Less densely syncopated than rags, cakewalks came off very well in a rich arrangement for band. More than a musical fad, this cakewalking set off a brass band tradition that has continued in the literature of circus bands. [10] Curiously, Sousa never liked ragtime and never expected its popularity to hang on very long. He "programmed ragtime sparingly," according to his biographer. [11] However, along with his perceived mission to raise public tastes, he also subscribed to the very practical dictum that he was an entertainer. He always remembered that the first year of Sousa's Band had ended with a deficit. Such tunes as *Whistling Rufus* and *Smoky Mokes* thrilled audiences. Paris in 1900 couldn't get enough of ragtime; it impressed and influenced both Debussy and Stravinsky. [12]

Sousa greatly influenced the development of bands worldwide, the model for instrumentation, style, and musical literature. He was probably the best known musician of the time. His concert band played for millions who never heard a symphony orchestra. When his band train pulled into the station, towns took a holiday and celebrated. [13] What they loved most was his marches. It is a commonplace that he was to the march as J. Strauss, Jr. was to the waltz. [14] People called him the "March King" from the outset of the 1890's because there were simply no rivals. Others composed good marches, but in the general mindset, no numbers two or three existed. Arthur Fiedler points to another distinction: "Sousa probably did more to diminish musical snobbery than any other conductor of his time." [15] As Sousa saw it himself: "…such music [i.e., marches] was closely allied in nature and effect to folk songs and dance tunes;…the universal heart responded easily and always to the simple in art." [16] Two more distinctions: He was the only composer to tour with his own musical organization. He was one of three nineteenth-century composers of American music "whose music sounds as vital today as it ever did…" And all three—the others are Stephen Foster and Louis Moreau Gottschalk—"were content to be considered as popular entertainers." As to the progressive impulse intrinsic in Sousa's marches, Mellers captures this in an ironic suspension:

> They are a necessary part of the experience of all common men…, for they fulfill our most primitive instincts at the same time as they cage them in conformity. They are at once revolutionary and established. [17]

Notes: Chapter 16

1. Reid Badger, *A Life in Ragtime: A Biography of James Reese Europe*, 19-20.
2. Paul E. Bierley, *John Philip Sousa: American Phenomenon*, 119.
3. Quoted in Bierley, 138-139.
4. " John Phillip Sousa," *Dictionary of American Biography*, IX, 407; Gilbert Chase, *America's Music: From the Pilgrims to the Present*, 324.
5.
6. *Ibid.*, 8-9; "Sousa," *DAB,* IX, 407-408; Chase, 323-331.
7. Edward A. Berlin, *Ragtime: A Musical and Cultural History*, 100, states that Sousa used march and two-step "synonymously."
8. Chase, 326, 328.
9. Henry Louis Mencken, *The Days of H. L. Mencken: Heathen Days*, 78-79. *American Art*, 113-114.
10. William J. Schafer and Johannes Riedel, *The Art of Ragtime: Form and Meaning of an Original Black Bierley,* 120.
11. Bierley, 18-19, 142.
12. *Idem;* Marshall W. Stearns, *The Story of Jazz*, 146; Chase, 326.
13. Bierley, 9, 14-15.
14. Wilfrid Mellers, *Music in a New Found Land: Themes and Developments in the History of American Music*, 257.
15. Quoted in Bierley, xii.
16. *Ibid.*, 119-120.
17. Mellers, 244, 260.

17. Mindset

> If there must be a condensed characterization, let us say that the time was marked by a prodigious energy, that much of the energy was ferment, and that the whole was infused by an altruism which, taking on the common characteristic, became a dynamic humanitarianism.
>
> Mark Sullivan [1]

Besides health, wealth, and relationships, what concerns weighed on American minds a century ago? We refer here to the ethnic majority: white in race, British or German in stock, and protestant in religion. The U.S. population had reached 76,000,000 in 1900. This included about 10,000,000 African Americans and another 10,000,000 foreign born. Thus an overwhelming two-thirds majority dominated the culture, and the majority of the majority were "W.A.S.P.'s," white/Anglo-Saxon/protestants. The rapid growth of the cities since the Civil War (35 years) had stimulated a new cultural diversity, but waspish mores and folkways still determined manners and behavior. Rural folk remained the majority with 47,000,000, but urbanites now numbered 30,000,000, a gap destined to close during the twenty years of the ragtime era. About 54,000,000 would be living in cities by 1920. [2]

The mindset of these WASP's, rural and urban, was absolutist, black vs. white, right vs. wrong. They stood on the bedrock conviction of the necessity of hard work; all failure came of insufficient effort. Only a "go-getter," one who went all-out, earned success. They appreciated such maxims as "God helps those who help themselves," and they regularly attended church for both reenforcement and further wisdom. They always sought the "lesson" in any event, and the wisdom it could bestow. Two granite plaques on the facade of a Connecticut elementary school manifest this cherishing of wisdom:

| Happy Is He That | Wisdom Is The |
| Findeth Wisdom | Principal Thing [3] |

Americans had come through the 19C by the sweat of their brows, in pioneer clearings, on long trade and whaling voyages, sodbusting out on prairie claims, laying tracks across the country, and tending the machines that did more and more of the work. Average life expectancy was only 47 years in 1900. [4] Most worked as long as they could, then died. The retirement concept lay in the future. There was work enough for everyone, unemployment being only 5 percent. Only half the school-age population attended school, proof of widespread child labor. Women also worked. Statistically only 21 percent held jobs, but farm women daily performed extra-domestic "chores." As for the fortunate minority of housewives, their days were also arduous, hand-laundering clothes, cleaning with caustic compounds and "elbow grease," and processing raw foods into an edible state. A mere 6 percent of Americans had graduated from a secondary or "high" school, and 11 percent were illiterate. [5]

For most people life seemed thus both serious and arduous, difficult but straight-forward and simple enough. Modern psychology, the work of Freud, Pavlov, and others, was in the formative stage, not yet in the intellectual mainstream. Psychology had yet to moderate, mitigate—or complicate—moral viewpoints. No one analyzed behavior to distinguish the "normal" from the pathological. People "chose" the "right" or the "wrong." Desirable and rational behavior resulted from right choices. Thus Theodore Roosevelt, Sr., on the occasion of his older son's matriculation at Harvard, counseled him to "Take care of your morals first, your health next, and—finally your studies," [6] There are no uncertainties here, no interest in the "why" of it, no awarenesses of compulsions, conditioning, flawed genes, or any other variety of physiological or emotional affects on behavior. Poor choices brought punishment, in this world and the next. A very few, obviously and visibly "out of their minds," were classified as "insane." All others were held responsible for leading a "respectable," i.e., moral life. This absolutist mindset conferred a significant advantage: an untroubled certitude. Hesitation and uncertainty—existential anguish (angst)—troubled fewer people less often. Most believed they knew where they stood.

II

> Later, in a westward-moving nation, when public schools did not have libraries and few teachers were well read, remote communities were brought together by the *McGuffey Readers*, which sold more than 120 million copies. Along with *Webster's Spelling Book* and the Bible, it gave an expanding nation a stable social starting point and a common set of ideals and values.
>
> Daniel J. Boorstin [7]

The American mind of 1890-1920 had been formed between 1865 and 1895 in the one-room common schools and on the nation's farms and in its villages. Outside of school, the major discipline consisted of the drudgeries of farm and home chores. Wood had to be cut, split, and carried, and animals fed and tended everyday. For failing to carry out assigned tasks or any other disobedience, corporal punishment was the universal remedy; all offenses called for strap, ruler, or switch. Whether he or she turned out "good" or "bad," the American child matured tough, tempered by pain and discomfort. [8]

Besides physical hardening, adults of the ragtime era had experienced a moral hardening. Although national and state constitutions both prescribed a separation of church and state, no one had ever applied this principle to education. Education had begun in colonial times with a religious rather than a secular intent, the need to read the Bible, which was indispensable if the individual was to become spiritually responsible. Most other Protestant churches, Lutherans, Baptists, sectarians, generally accepted this tenet of the Calvinist religions (Congregationalists, Presbyterians, Dutch Reformed, Huguenot). When the states took over the provision of education in the 19C, no one thought of changing to conform to the Constitution. Prayers continued to open the school day, Bible texts were memorized and declaimed, and all textbooks instilled morality and piety.

The chief textbooks were readers and spellers. Spelling was a major subject in that time of rote learning, with Noah Webster's "Blue-Back Speller" used in all schools. It was ubiquitous from 1783 to well after 1900, with 35 million copies in print. Teachers constantly drove their "scholars" to master its word lists. The Speller prompted them with the mnemonic device of the sentence in which the combined first letters of each word indicated a given spelling word. Thus "A rat in the house may eat the ice cream" encoded "arithmetic." Reenforcement of this learning came every Friday afternoon when a "bee" or spelling competition occurred in classrooms across the nation. In these weekly spelling bees, students practiced not only to master the week's list and those of weeks past, but also to prepare and later to compete against other classrooms and schools. Spelling bees, in that time before the sports craze took hold, became the principal form of interscholastic competition. Spelling prizes, usually medals, became the chief and coveted awards at promotional and graduation exercises. [9]

Geography like spelling had to be memorized. Lists of counties, states, capital cities, boundaries, rivers, mountains, and countries had to be regurgitated in recitations. Here also mnemonic devices such as songs and chants supported this factual overload. Wall maps were not yet published, and rural taxpayers resisted the adoption of any texts beyond readers, spellers, and perhaps mathematics and history texts. Beyond the physical, geography taught that the English-speaking and West-European peoples led the world in culture and progress, while the remainders lagged far behind in positive development. The laggards, including Moslems, Africans, Asians, and Native Americans, were bluntly characterized as hostile and backward. The U.S. was quite simply "God's Country," and history textbooks, which appeared about 1850, portrayed the Revolutionary War as the greatest event in human history. Students recited its events, legends, hero stories, and "lessons" of liberty, freedom, and independence. They also learned from their literature texts, the *Readers*, the famous utterances of patriots and statesmen such as Patrick Henry, George Washington, Daniel Webster, and Abraham Lincoln. Post-Civil War textbooks added the events of that struggle to the canon of national glories. Those used up North exalted the sectional conflict as the war to end slavery and depicted the south as perfidious and traitorous. Down South the history books asserted the nobility and patriotism of the Confederacy and the tragedy of the Lost Cause. Such conditioning instilled strong patriotic feelings, easily aroused by parades and speeches. [10]

Curriculum in these 19C schools centered on reading. For most pupils, *McGuffey's Eclectic Readers* became standard after 1840. These popular and respected books were created by William Holmes McGuffey (1800-1873) of Ohio. He came of that sturdy Scotch-Irish stock that had pioneered the way west into the Trans-Appalachian region, and he impregnated his creations with the strong, evangelical flavor of his Presbyterian Faith. Six levels of the Readers were in print by 1851, followed by five revisions, reaching a total of 122,000,000 between 1836 and 1900. Morally and ideologically, the McGuffey books supplemented the Bible. They contained fables, stories, mottoes, proverbs, aphorisms, and speeches, with exhortations to hard work, frugality, piety, truthfulness, humility and the avoidance of vanity, the habit of early rising, and the acceptance of death.

Of the six levels, one through four stressed moral precepts, while in five and six, students experienced literature in selections taken from "great" writers. Although the literary segments also presented moral ideas, these selections provided, for most Americans, their only opportunity to grasp the heights of culture (other than the Bible). The *Sixth Eclectic Reader* contained 138 selections from 111 authors. Selection "XLVII" presented "The Character of Columbus" by Washington Irving, taken from his biography. In just three pages, numerous virtues are ascribed to the Great Admiral: "inventive genius"; "ambition…lofty and noble"; an "irascible and impetuous" disposition; a "piety…genuine and fervent"…that kept the Sabbath "a day of sacred rest"; "a poetical temperament," and a "visionary fervor" combined with a "magnanimous spirit." The selection opened with a brief biography of Irving the author and concluded with a summary of Columbus's achievements, adding information and moral reenforcement. [11] Selection 58, "The Landing of the Pilgrim Fathers" by Felicia Dorothea Hemans and number 125, "A Psalm of Life" by Henry Wadsworth Longfellow typify the sententious and earnest qualities of the poetry selections:

> Ay, call it holy ground.
> The soil where first they trod:
> They have left unstained what there they found,
> Freedom to worship God. (Hemans)
>
> *   *   *
>
> Life is real! Life is earnest!
> And the grave is not its goal;

>   Dust thou art, to dust returnest,
>   Was not spoken of the soul. (Longfellow) [12]

A two-page essay by Horace Greeley, number 114, on "Labor," recommends that there be "a universal training in Productive Labor," that everyone have some trade to fall back on in a time of need or even catastrophe. Greeley, Editor of the *New York Tribune*—he who first said "Go West, young man"—clearly had in mind the survival skills useful for a frontiersman. [13]

Besides all of this fulsome guidance, the *McGuffeys* also fostered the nation's great oral traditions. Even though few Americans in that time attended the theatre or a university, they listened far more than they read—to sermons, political speeches, Chautauqua presentations, courtroom forensics, summer revivals, and school programs. Listening to speakers was in fact the chief amusement outside the home. Everyone in the 19C understood from school participation the tradition of elocution, the practice of declaiming texts with appropriate gestures. At most school programs, pupils presented famous speeches, poems, and narrative selections that they had painstakingly memorized, not only words but also the prescribed formulaic gestures that conveyed emotions. Each presenter waited with anticipatory anxiety for his turn when the master of ceremonies would catch his eye and tell him to "Speak your piece." Favorite pieces included Patrick Henry's "Give me Liberty or give me Death" speech; the poem "Casabianca" ("The boy stood on the burning deck"); Shakespeare's "Friends, Romans, Countrymen" (*Julius Caesar*); Tennyson's "Charge of the Light Brigade"; Whittier's "Barbara Frietchie" ("Shoot if you must this old gray head"); the "Gettysburg Address"; Whitman's "Ship of State"; plus well known selections from Kipling, Mark Twain, Dickens, Longfellow, Bret Harte, Poe, James Whitcomb Riley, and, at this time, pieces in support of "temperance" or prohibition.

The remarkable element in this is the extent to which students experienced literature as a spoken thing, recited in class and declaimed in programs. Ragtimer and bluesman W. C. Handy recalls a favorite "declamation" from *McGuffey's Fifth Reader*: "No Excellence Without Great Labor" by William Wirt (a former Attorney General Of the U.S.). Handy states, "I recited this so often and with such great emphasis that it became a governing factor in all my subsequent undertakings." He testifies to being tremendously influenced by its final sentence: "This is the prowess, and these the hardy achievements which will enroll your name among the great men of the earth." [14] Undoubtedly the prime exemplar of oral-moral McGuffey tradition was William Jennings Bryan. From elementary school, he went eagerly on to the debate club and the literary society of his high school, which prepared him for the courtroom and, later, the stump. As we have seen (Chapter 7), it was the power of his oratory, a skill taught everywhere in the common schools, that procured for him the Democratic presidential nomination in 1896. [15]

Without any kindergarten or programs in "reading readiness," these pre-1920 schools achieved a fair standard of universal literacy—in just six grades! When schooling ended, work began, followed a few years later by marriage and family. School's purpose was to prepare for a life as worker, parent, and citizen. To carry out these functions, one had to be able to read, write, figure—and to be a worthy person. Good people received moral instruction in church, at home, and in school. Society knew what kind of people it wanted and how to mold them in its institutions. These institutions met the needs of a simple society, a society in which higher mathematics, science, and a knowledge of lands beyond our borders were irrelevant for most. Unfortunately these backward-looking schools failed to prepare people for either urban life or for the technological and cultural changes that lay ahead in the new century. [16]

III

> Our ancestors had unwittingly to invent [Demon Rum] so they could bring to bear on the matter of alcohol vs.-man their habitual ways of feeling and thinking: black/white right/wrong…. Their alarm at what distilled spirits were certainly doing to people's welfare in this world and probably to their souls in the next was understandable.
>
> J.C. Furnas [17]

Another significant element in the period's outlook was prohibition. A large and growing segment of public opinion advocated the outlawing of alcoholic drinks, their manufacture and sale. It had been a long trend, first surfacing in the 1830's along with abolition and the religious awakening of the first half of the19C. Both abolition and prohibition took a jump start from that "Great Awakening." The movement went through several phases before arriving at the consensus that "rum," i.e. any and all alcoholic beverages, was a demon to be exorcised by prohibiting it nationally. There had been a "temperance" faction in the beginning that advocated moderation as the solution to the problem of excess: drinking was not essentially immoral, and the drinker could be taught to control his intake. But the more fervent folk, touched by the recent spiritual awakening, reacted to such a notion with horror, demonizing its advocates as spreaders of the alcohol contagion. According to their naive viewpoint, the lucky few who could cork the bottle after ingesting two or three would lead to ruin the many who lacked such control. The moderate drinker owed it to society to give up drinking for the greater good of others. [18]

While rejecting moderation, the movement appropriated "temperance" as its logo, but there never was anything temperate about the anti-alcohol movement. The label of temperance really meant prohibition. As late as 1874, the female anti-alcohol organization founded that year to mobilize women against the Demon took the name Women's Christian Temperance Union (WCTU). However the political party set up in 1869 to combat booze bore the more correct name of National Prohibition Party, and increasingly, as the 19C ended, the cause wrote "Prohibition" on its standards. The Party achieved little more than the propagation of its name. It suffered the waning destiny of all third parties. Its one hope was that eventually the Republicans, who had risen on the wave of Abolition, would fold prohibition into their platform. To maintain some continuing appeal, the Prohibitionists regularly stood up for "good" causes such as the direct election of senators, elimination of the middleman electoral college in presidential elections, holding to the "gold standard" for currency, the abolition of prostitution, Bible-reading in the schools, and laws regulating sabbath observance. Later they also espoused women's rights, railroad regulation, and the referendum. The result lacked focus in its mixture of conventional piety and radicalism. Their main accomplishment consisted of the flow of propaganda that kept the cause before the public. [19]

From the 1830's to 1900 the prohibition cause waxed and waned. Laws would be passed on upswings, making dry entire states or permitting counties to expel the Demon ("Local Option"). On the downswings liquor reasserted itself, bribing its way back in with either lax enforcement or repeals of laws. Somehow people always found liquor and places in which to consume it. In one ingenious (and eponymous) dodge, the seller carried a bottle in his boot top, from which he would dispense drinks up an alley, thus the word "bootlegger." On days of fairs and celebrations, barkers outside tents sold tickets to see such wonders as stuffed animals or creatures with stripes painted on them. Inside the tent the ticket procured a drink, which led to illicit drinking places being called "blind tiger" or "blind pig." There were also doctors who prescribed the "medicine," "express companies" shipping the "goods," and private clubs where the drinker indulged secretly. [20]

Thus despite perennial popularity, prohibition just inched along, continually thwarted by the cash power of the liquor and saloon interests and by the thirsts of consumers, ever a fertile source of strategems to defy custom and law. This changed in 1894, when the Anti-Saloon League took the movement in new directions. The Anti-Saloon League was a coming-together of protestant churches which had lost patience with the ineffectual political arm of the movement. It included Methodists, Presbyterians, and Baptists; Episcopalians and Lutherans stayed out. It rejected all extraneous good causes to focus on an agenda of one item, and it worked ruthlessly to achieve its goal of national prohibition. The League also rejected the democratic way, controlling its chapters from the top down. Local chapters collected the funds, and headquarters furnished the propaganda to distribute and gave instructions for actions. Members received instructions on all issues related to saloons and alcohol consumption and on how to vote in elections. The League grappled for every advantage in the fight: legal restrictions, harsher penalties for violations, prohibition by state or by local option, candidates who favored prohibition, and candidates who, whatever their stands on the issue, the League could control or bully. The League even threw its votes to "wet" candidates who would support dry measures. Since members voted as the League commanded, the League's block of votes could decide a close election. In 1904 the incumbent Governor of Ohio, Myron T. Herrick, had proven unreliable on a local option bill. First they offered a petition with 100,000 signatures opposing his renomination, but wet support renominated him. Failing there, the League campaigned among the Democrats and procured a dry candidate. In the close election Herrick lost by 43,000 votes; he had won previously by 100,000 votes. [21]

The League called such tactics "Nonpartisanship": any candidate, either party, as long as the expedient achieved the League agenda of weakening the wets. Along with issues and candidates, the League carefully diffused its ideology to capture and hold the high ground. More than dry-righteous vs. wet-evil, they diagrammed the struggle as a conflict of city vs. country. The better folks lived in the country, on farms and in small towns and villages; they were old-stock Americans of protestant faiths, landowners who made their acres productive and paid their taxes. This did not include any African Americans. The city offered a negative contrast: immigrants recently arrived, most of them Catholic, working low paid jobs in factories. The rural folk perceived themselves as church-going, virtuous, and uncorrupted by liquor; urbanites lived unclean lives as frequenters of saloons, gambling places, dance halls, and brothels. City folk were sabbath-breaking foreigners. This blunt and divisive thrust at ethnic insecurities proved effective at influencing opinion and winning elections, and it brought in the support of Big Money. The Rockefellers, the Wanamakers, Andrew Carnegie, and other plutocrats contributed because sober employees would bring economies of operation. Sobriety on the job meant fewer costly accidents, higher quality and quantity of output, less need for laws on workmen's compensation and employer liability (a demand stoutly resisted), and fewer demands for wage increases—with no liquor habit to support, all of the pay envelope went home. This Big Business support paid for the campaigns and lobbying that eventually put national prohibition over the top in 1918 after most states had been lobbied into dryness. [22]

Prohibition strongly influenced attitudes about drinking. The simple gesture of pouring a drink and raising a glass underwent a transformation from a lighthearted act to an anti-social deed. Small-town drinkers looked over their shoulders afraid to be seen by church members. Even in the city, some forsook the neighborhood saloon for one in another part of town. A bottle in the house indicated to the sharp eyes of visitors that you were a "drinker," if not a "drunkard." Nosey neighbors gossiped if you came home late at night and asked if you had been at a lodge meeting. Where already prohibited, the unhappy drinker had to locate some clandestine spot and put up with some doubtful companions and surroundings. These included the blind pigs and tigers and what the 1920's called "speakeasys." Increasingly the mundane act of enjoying beer, wine, or spirits became an activity fraught with difficulty and inconvenience. The "drinker" endured disapproval and risked criminality. People who still drank did their best to ignore this controversy, but it dogged and troubled their days.

IV

Compared to the Big Business problem, prohibition was a sideshow. Post-Civil War growth had driven businesses and industries toward larger and larger combinations, concentrating greater economic power into fewer hands. In such industries as sugar, petroleum, coal, steel, and railroads, growth, combined with fiercer competition, had led to mergers and agreements among competitors as to supplies, financing, pricing, distributing, marketing, and other things that increased profits and lessened competition. The generic term for these large corporate combinations is "trust." Trusts either destroyed or gobbled up competitors, which resulted in unified control of the wages paid their workers and of the prices charged to their customers. Public concern over the dangers to American life posed by such powers had prodded Congress to pass the Sherman Anti-Trust Act in 1890.

The Sherman Act outlawed any combination that was "in restraint of trade or commerce among the several states, or with foreign nations…," declaring such acts to be "misdemeanors." But this law was vague and unclear; it failed to define such terms as "trust" and "monopoly." The first suits under this law, against the whiskey and sugar trusts, were thrown out of court. In the one against sugar, the E. C. Knight Company case, the court ruled that the American Sugar Refining Company had not monopolized the sugar trade because it was primarily a manufacturer, a producer, and only incidentally engaged in trade. Hence no violation had taken place since the law applied to commerce only. This momentous decision of the Supreme Court opened the door to a new wave of greater mergers, climaxing in the creation of U.S. Steel in 1901. A year later Theodore Roosevelt started the counterattack with the Northern Securities Case (Chapter 15), but the public, looking back at Big Business's triumphs over labor and government opposition in the old century, and peering uncertainly ahead into the new century, feared for the security of themselves and the nation. [23]

Curiously, what jolted public opinion into a sharper perception of the trust problem was a poem, "The Man With the Hoe," published by William Randolph Hearst's *San Francisco Examiner* on January 15, 1899. The poet, Edwin Markham (1852-1940), a California high school teacher, had taken his inspiration from a French painting by Jean Millet (1814-1875) that depicted a bent and brutalized peasant. Like the painter, the poet portrays the subject with heavy strokes to lay bare the effects of cruel exploitation:

> Bowed by the weight of centuries he leans
> Upon his hoe and gazes on the ground,
> The emptiness of ages in his face,
> And on his back the burden of the world.
> Who made him dead to rapture and despair,
> A thing that grieves not and that never hopes,
> Stolid and stunned, a brother to the ox?
> Who loosened and let down this brutal jaw?
> Whose was the hand that slanted back this brow?
> Whose breath blew out the light within this brain?

Line five commences the powerful, accusatory questions through which Markham expresses his outrage at social inequalities. This goes on for four more stanzas, concluding with an address that confronts the master class at the top of the social pyramid in the two final stanzas:

> O masters, lords and rulers in all lands
> . . . .
> How will you ever straighten up this shape;
> Touch it again with immortality;
> Give back the inward looking and the light;
> Rebuild in it the music and the dream
> . . . .

and

> O masters, lords and rulers in all lands,
> How will the future reckon with this man?
> How answer his brute question in that hour
> When whirlwinds of rebellion shake all shores?
> How will it be with kingdoms and with kings—
> With those who shaped him to the thing he is—
> When this dumb terror shall rise to judge the world,
> After the silence of the centuries.

The poem landed a direct hit on the emerging issues of the exploitation of labor and the question of social justice. It brought instant fame to the poet in his own country, and it reverberated worldwide, being reprinted around the globe. It soon progressed from the poetry columns to the editorial pages. There arguments ran pro and con, as apologists for capitalism counterattacked, disparaging it as an insult to labor and a disbelief in progress. Which in turn aroused William Jennings Bryan to its defense. He quoted the poem in speeches against child labor and for the income tax. [24] "The Man With the Hoe" awakened and crystallized a growing concern for the lives of workers. Previously most citizens had perceived criminal intent underlying labor unrest and violence. Now with new awarenesses of social injustice and needs for reform, public opinion began to shift away from blaming violence on various troublemakers and malcontents to an indictment of corporate evils. The journalist William L. Shirer recalls in his memoir that there

> …was the feeling among many people that
> something had gone wrong at home.
> The gulf between the rich and the poor was widening.
> Vast fortunes were being quickly amassed by the
> monopolists and the manipulators, sometimes by fraud,
> chicanery, and corruption, and often with the aid and connivance
> of the democratic government.… [25]

V

From the abovementioned constituents of the end-of-century outlook, we might conclude that American life was, for most, short (a 47-year span) and characterized by drudgery, brutality, and a rural conservatism, petty and unprogressive. But if "The Man With the Hoe" revealed social injustice and implied America's dark side, it also presented a rousing call to reform. And American workers (the white ones) were after all far from being the brute peasants of the Old World. The implications of (a) potential degradation and (b) resulting revolution à la France mandated constructive changes in the system. The brilliant investigative journalist—one of those termed a "muckraker" (Chapter 32)—Ray Stannard Baker evaluated the period thusly:

> Looking back, in later years, I have thought of the period in America, including the last few years of the nineteenth century and the early years of the twentieth as the American Renascence, even the Great American Renascence. [26]

Scattered across the nation, singly and in small associations, having varying reform goals, there existed a faction or party, bound somewhat in a spirit of cooperation, that intended to change human conditions. Collectively we call them "Progressives," and they did unify as a party led by Theodore Roosevelt in 1912. They were a very miscellaneous lot: constitutional reformers, anti-poverty crusaders, seekers of government regulation of the economy, anti-vice types, suffragettes, and prohibitionists.

Generally progressives came from strong protestant backgrounds. Their parents were products of the Great Awakening of the 1830's and 1840's. This intense period of evangelical religion—we seem to experience one in every century—had profound effects. Many progressives were the children of clergy, and most were reared in fervent Christian homes. But when grown, they rejected the religious vocation. They retained the religious impulse and the desire to serve by doing good works, but the clergy no longer appeared to offer the models of leadership they sought. By mid-century, revealed religion had been challenged by the intellectual powers of rationalism in philosophy, history, and the sciences, particularly evolutionary science. The ministry seemed to have lost the battle. These progressives-to-be discerned that they would have to find their life-missions in the secular arena. [27]

Still, these children of religious tradition, motivated by a residue of reformational fervor, injected spiritual and moral attitudes into their programs, their missionary spirit like a cross borne in a procession. One historian defines progressivism as "a climate of creativity within which writers, artists, politicians, and thinkers functioned." [28] With a "climate of creativity" rooted in missionary protestantism and a political heritage coming out of abolition, the understandable choice of hero and model was Abraham Lincoln. Jane Addams, whose mission was to raise up the urban poor by living among slum dwellers and reaching out to them from a communal "settlement house" (Hull House, Chicago, established in 1889), put the case for Lincoln:

> Is it not Abraham Lincoln who has cleared the title to our democracy? He made plain, once for all, that democratic government, associated as it is with all the mistakes and shortcomings of the common people, still remains the most valuable contribution America has made to the moral life of the world. [29]

Progressives have been called preachers without pulpits. They went into social work, education, law, journalism, the arts, and politics. They include such famous figures as Jane Addams the social worker; John Dewey the philosopher; historians Frederick Jackson Turner and Charles A. Beard; Frank Lloyd Wright the architect; Charles Ives the composer; poets Edgar Lee Masters, Carl Sandburg, and Vachel Lindsay; the

"Muckrakers," a group of writers who exposed corruption and social evils; and political leaders Theodore Roosevelt, Robert LaFollette, and Woodrow Wilson. [30]

During the ragtime era, progressives developed significant reform programs in the areas of health and safety; labor and working conditions; government, politics, and suffrage; and government regulation of interstate corporations. All of which was summed up in the Progressive Party Platform of 1912 and evangelically called "The Covenant With the People" Were the progressives "ragging it"? In the sense of being driven by the power of past religious authority, perhaps not. They appear overly genteel, too straight-laced to syncopate. But as dynamic reformers focused on a better future, progressively seeking changes real and beneficial, they partook of the ragtime spirit. They seem unprogressive in the pursuit of such negative ends as the outlawing of liquor, colonies, and vice, but their idealistic legacy enriches our heritage. For them democracy was more than a form of government, rather democracy was social interaction evolving toward the ideal state that would meet citizen needs and foster healthy growth. This accords well with ragtime. [31]

VI

Is it ironic that ragtime provided the soundtrack for the Progressive Era? Ragtime celebrated life's pleasures. The folks who tackled the problems of child labor, alcohol, working conditions, wages, patent medicines, impure food, prostitution, and corruption in government cannot be described as pleasure-loving. But this was more than a heroic age of reform and progressive strivings. It was also, because of urbanization and electricity, an entertainment revolution. In 1869 the playhouses and music theatres of New York City admitted about 25,000 a day; by 1910 the seating capacity of theatres and the new cinemas had reached almost 2,000,000. If we total in the crowds at world's fairs, ballparks, and amusement parks, a picture of a new kind of life materializes. Large populations now enjoyed themselves outside the home regularly and frequently. During the summer of 1909, 20,000,000 adults and children came to the amusement parks at Coney Island, NY. [32]

A ragtime song of 1899, "Living A Ragtime Life," puts it this way:

>Got more troubles than I can stand
>Ever since ragtime has struck the land,
>Never saw the like in all my days
>>Everybody's got the ragtime craze,
>>I stood it just as long as I could,
>At last I got it and I've got it good...
>
>(Chorus)
>
>I got a ragtime dog and a ragtime cat
>A ragtime piano in a ragtime flat,
>>I'm wearing ragtime clothes from hat to shoes
>>I read a paper called the ragtime news,
>I got ragtime habits and I talk that way
>I sleep in ragtime and I rag all day.
>>Got ragtime troubles with my ragtime wife
>>I'm certainly leading a ragtime life.

> I got ragtime buddies and ragtime pals
>   I go to ragtime parties with ragtime gals,
> Ragtime's everywhere, ragtime's right
> And I'm certainly living a ragtime life.
>
> Jefferson and Roberts

As the song indicates, a "craze" had "struck the land," perhaps not the first (big league baseball came in the 1880's), but this one appealed to all ages and both sexes. The critical combining of large populations, mass transit, music and vaudeville, recorded music, moving pictures, and popular periodicals generated mass enthusiasms, something never known before in history. In the past human culture bifurcated into high and low varieties, one the culture of state religions and ruling classes, the other the culture of the commoners or folk. Now the old bi-culture receded as a new uniculture grew rapidly. Popular culture, dynamically flowing and always changing in a sequence of crazes (or rages), mass enthusiasms for the new or rediscovered, transcended—and overwhelmed—much of the high and low cultures. Much of folk culture ended up as artifacts in the collections of fanciers and museums. High culture with its European forms, cultivated and patronized by the wealthy and the educated, continued to exist in the institutional hothouses of universities, museums, legitimate theatres, and concert halls and opera houses. In the new perspective, the high culture would be nicknamed "high brow," and the popular culture would be called, patronizingly and in opposition, "low brow." People sensed the implied value judgments but either ignored the distinction or set their reactions aside. Popular culture offered options, not compulsions, so why indulge in controversy?

Only certain critics chose to "make something of it." Figuratively, they shut the gates of respectability in an attempt to prevent "rag-time" from entering the genteel precincts of polite society. Coming out of slave cabins, coon songs, cakewalks, and rags spread the foul odor of a depravity out of Africa. Extremists, battening on the universal racism of the time, condemned the music as innately immoral and culturally inferior. Those less extreme rebuffed ragtime as vulgar and in poor taste. They pointed out the lowlife elements in coon song lyrics: thievery (chickens and watermelons), gambling, greed, aversion to honest work, sexual promiscuity (adultery, couples not legally married), and violence (razor fights). But, without challenging this negative consensus, people listened anyway. The music radiated energy, a light spirit, infectious tunes, and a novel, appealing syncopation. In darkened vaudeville houses, no one walked out or yelled protests when the "artists" rendered "The Bully Song," "All Coons Look Alike To Me," or "Mr. Johnson, Turn Me Loose." (Chapter 11)

Ragtime had a few defenders, but neither they nor its enemies very much affected the general mindset. Its condemners stirred up race hatred; tried to get laws and resolutions passed (the American Federation of Musicians in 1901 actually resolved not to play the stuff); denigrated it as a passing fad; labeled it morally poisonous and addictive; and otherwise ridiculed it. Its friends pointed out that it was as popular among the rich, famous, and titled (European royalty no less) as among the hoi polloi. They also praised ragtime because some serious composers stood up for it (Igor Stravinsky, Ernest Bloch, Percy Grainger) and the great Sousa programmed it; because of its innovative syncopation and polyrhythms, and because it was a native American music expressive of American life rather than a mere imitation of European music. A few critics also managed to find in ragtime the potential basis of future art music.[33] But who heeds the critics? Relatively few people seek proof or validation of likes or dislikes from self-appointed inspectors of public taste; Americans have always understood the democracy of culture. An exception to this was Edward W. Bok, editor of the *Ladies Home Journal*. In a long and respected career, Bok shaped his magazine into an influence and a force in the expanding American middle class. He published articles and fiction designed to broaden the interests of women, to improve their homemaking skills, and to better marital relationships. Very close to his heart was "good taste," the level of which he constantly endeavored to raise. In May 1912, he felt outraged upon discovering that his young female office workers indulged in ragtime dancing during their lunch hours. Fifteen women were abruptly terminated by the Curtis Publishing Company for doing the turkey-trot.

Another exception to the cultural democracy was the judge in Paterson, NJ, who determined that a young woman had, in dancing the turkey-trot, behaved lewdly. He fined her $25, and, when she proved short of funds, sentenced her to 50 days in jail. In a similar but happier episode, a judge in Millwood, NY, put a woman on trial (disturbing the peace?) because she sang Irving Berlin's "Everybody's Doin' It Now" and capered past his house stepping the turkey-trot. But this time the lady faced a jury and had representation. In his presentation for the defense, her lawyer sang a chorus of the song. When the courtroom spectators came in on the chorus, the jury asked for an encore. Next (according to the source), the lawyer "taking out his tuning fork to pitch the key,…sang the second stanza with more feeling and expression, and as he sang, he gave a mild imitation of the turkey trot." A delighted jury concluded that the defendant was not guilty of a misdemeanor. [34]

The last incident could be apocryphal; certainly it reads like a script for a musical sketch. All three episodes exemplify the terms "craze" and "rage." Previously in history only religion and hunger had generated mass movements. Now with large urban populations, cheap periodicals, mass transit, photography, and electricity, people became joined by their enthusiasms. This caused a new companionship of large groups characterized by like minds and hearts. The ultimate product of mass enthusiasm was the celebrity or "star." Such became the principal objects of the mass enthusiasm or craze. From the initial craze for music, songs, and dances, the "fans" soon refocused on the individual performers. The salaries furnish the proof: In vaudeville, for the first time, the public eagerly grasped for information and gossip about the weekly earnings of headliners. Throughout this period, headliner salaries rose, and top stars topped those. The big Big-Time paid $1000 and more per week, and a superstar like Scotland's Sir Harry Lauder crossed the Atlantic for $4000/week.

Notes: Chapter 17

1. Mark Sullivan, *Our Times*, IV, 41.
2. *Historical Statistics of the United States, Part I, Colonial Times to 1970*, 8, 12, 14.
3. Elm Hill School, Newington, CT. See Bible, Proverbs, 4:7.
4. *Historical Statistics*, 55.
5. Ibid., 126, 133, 370, 379, 382.
6. Noel F. Busch, *TR: The Story of Theodore Roosevelt and His Influence on Our Times*, 26.
7. Daniel J. Boorstin, *Parade Magazine* (July 12, 1998): 11-12.
8. Sullivan, *OT*, II, 135-142.
9. Ibid., 121-133.
10. Ibid., 49-63.
11. *McGuffey's Sixth Eclectic Reader, Revised Edition (1921)*, 192-195.
12. Ibid., 228, 429.
13. Ibid., 398-400.
14. W.C. Handy, *Father of the Blues*, 273.
15. Daniel J. Boorstin, *The Americans: The Democratic Experience*, 462-466; Sullivan, *OT*, II, 94-119.
16. Ibid., 188-212.
17. J.C. Furnas, *The Life and Times of the Late Demon Rum*, 342-343.
18. Ibid., 80-81.
19. Ibid., 270-273.
20. Ibid., 170-171.
21. Ibid., 301-338.
22. Idem.
23. Robert M. Crunden, "Anti-trust Movement," *The Reader's Companion to American History*, 42; H.W. Brands, *TR: The Last Romantic*, 435.
24. Sullivan, *OT*, II 236-253.
25. William L. Shirer, *Twentieth-Century Journey, the Start: 1904-1930*, 69.
26. Ray Stannard Baker, *American Chronicle*, 83.
27. Robert M. Crunden, *Ministers of Reform: The Progressives' Achievement in American Civilization, 1889-1920*, 3-15, 16-38.
28. Ibid., ix.
29. Jane Addams, *Twenty Years at Hull House*, 42.
30. Crunden, *Ministers*, 52-199.
31. Ibid., 200-224.
32. David Nasaw, *Going Out: The Rise and Fall of Public Amusements*, 3.
33. Edward A. Berlin, *Ragtime: A Musical and Cultural History*, 32-60, offers the fullest discussion of the controversy.
34. Sullivan, *OT*, II, 256-268, for these incidents.

18. Vaudeville: Headliners (I)

Vaudeville was America in motley, the national relaxation. To the Palace, the Colonial, the Alhambra, the Orpheum, the Keith circuit and chain variety houses, N.Y, to L.A., we flocked, vicariously to don the false face, let down our back hair, and forget. Vaudeville was the theatre of the people, its brassy assurance a dig in the nation's ribs, its simplicity as naive as a circus.Douglas Gilbert [1]

As the 20C opened, entertainment had become an organized industry. The gamut of stage shows consisted of

Variety, i.e., vaudeville	Cabaret
Legitimate theatre (plays)	Showboat
Musical comedy	Fair
Opera	Wild west show
Burlesque	Medicine Show
Minstrelsy	Circus

Some of these venues, circus, fair, legitimate theatre, opera, were hardy perennials, destined to continue and develop. Others, the wild west show, medicine show, showboat, and minstrelsy, had peaked and gone into decline (or soon would). American musical comedy (Chapter 26) had toddled onto the stage after the Civil War, very loose and unintegrated, very low-grade music drama. Its sketchy narratives permitted frequent interpolations, songs and dances that made the stars to shine, but interrupted the story. It probably owed as much to the variety olios of minstrelsy as to the European comic operas of Gilbert and Sullivan, Offenbach, and J. Strauss. All of this entertainment, along with the new vaudeville, now made up an industry, destined, some decades down the road, to evolve into a huge international business as it would grow and shape itself around the armatures of future technologies: silent film, radio, sound film, color film, television, electronic music, and cybernetics.

Variety, in its new, booming vaudeville phase, controlled by the United Booking Office (UBO), absorbed the nation's variety houses into a monolithic, systematic industry. The term "vaudeville," a pretentious import from France, meant a new, cleaned-up, family-worthy variety entertainment, wholesomely different from the dirty, immoral stuff put on in the men-only concert-saloons. As we have seen (Chapter 5), Tony Pastor was the innovator in 1881, and Keith and Albee, with their theatre chain, the industrializers. It was they (not Pastor who disliked the word) who standardized vaudeville and impregnated it with its connotations of moral correctness.

In the legitimate theatre Klaw and Erlanger had systematized bookings four years earlier in 1896. Along with other magnates, they set up a syndicate to process and market drama. Drama was a product sold to theatre managers in package deals: in order to book a prime attraction, the manager had to take several less desirable shows, including an outright clinker or two. With so much of the market thus controlled, producers had little choice but to distribute through Klaw and Erlanger. To hold out meant difficult one-night stands in isolated independent houses. Outside the larger cities, there were few managers brave enough to flout the syndicate. The few independent companies and stars such as Sarah Bernhardt, Minnie Maddern Fiske, Richard Mansfield, and Maurice Barrymore who struggled against the combine failed abysmally to bring about any changes. [2]

Certain types of shows, circus, fair, wild west, showboat, and medicine show, failed to attract the interest of the corporate powers, for various reasons: insufficient numbers, lack of profit potential, and a want of integrity in the operators. Such show folk lived on the margins of society, and they flew by night, to reappear elsewhere with a change of identity. They did not work under contract and followed impromptu itineraries, trying to avoid difficult sheriffs and locales with too much—or too little—law. The larger circuses and wild west shows (Barnum & Bailey, Buffalo Bill) were the exceptions outside the half-world of cons and shabby showmanship.

The medicine show enlivened the nation's villages from colonial times down to the time of regulated medical science. They flourished because of a shortage of entertainment and because people suffered chronically from illness and sudden death by unknown maladies. Folk listened attentively when pitchmen held up bottles of liniment, oil, or "bitters," and proclaimed the likelihood of "cures." The father of Standard Oil magnate John D. Rockefeller, William Avery Rockefeller, spent his life on the road before the Civil War performing as a marksman, ventriloquist, and hypnotist while touting his herbal remedies. The show seen most often after the War was the Indian show, of which the Kickapoo Indian Medicine Company was the grandest. Three clever pitchmen, John E. Healy of Connecticut, Charley Bigelow of Texas, and "Nevada Ned" Oliver, took the medicine show to the heights of enterprise. During the 1880's about 75 of their shows crisscrossed the landscape, retailing Kickapoo Indian "Sagwa." The Kickapoo show opened with half a dozen Indians seated crosslegged in a semi-circle in front of a painted Indian scene, all very impressive by torchlight. Enter Nevada Ned or some other "scout" in impressive buckskins who would introduce each Native American with a description of his warrior exploits. The first five replied with nods or grunts, but the sixth would launch into a powerful-sounding speech in his own language ("translated" by the scout) about the medicine, its origin, efficacy and benefits, and how much the Indians had sacrificed to make it available to whites. After which, the Indians would beat tom-toms while white company members moved among the spectators exchanging medicine for money.

The vaunted Sagwa contained little more than herbs and alcohol. John Austen Hamlin also sent out many troupes, in this case to promote Hamlin's Wizard Oil, a liniment. Before turning to the more profitable medicine business, Hamlin had done magic shows. Now he served up music, and his magic resided in the name Wizard Oil, from which he conjured fabulous profits. Each troupe consisted of a lecturer, driver, and a male quartet with a parlor organ on the back end of a wagon. All in high urban style: top hats, frock coats, and pin-striped trousers. Between songs the pseudo-professional lecturer pitched the oily product as a sure cure for asthma and neuralgia. Numerous small operators also competed for the dollars of the sickly and the gullible. Dr. C.M. Townsend wintered in Lima, Ohio, where he concocted his "Magic Oil" (these entrepreneurs of cure-alls never bothered to litigate over copyright infringements), King of Coughs, and Cholera Balm. Entering a town, the troupe blew on their horn and handed out advertising fliers. Then they paraded up and down the principal streets tootling on their band instruments. Following afternoon and evening concerts, the Doctor gave his "lectures" while his troupe toted the products around to the listeners. Many other "doctors" did far worse things. Remedies often contained too much alcohol and ingredients of dubious quality: axle grease salve, colored water, bad alcohol, and opium and cocaine. Pitchmen insulted intelligence by claiming that they were giving away the medicine, for either a "small" contribution to cover expenses or a low "introductory" price. The sales pitch would follow a "lecture" full of frightening anecdotes about kidney trouble, worms, rotten organs, and "consumption," i.e., tuberculosis. Shills came up from the audience to achieve on-the-spot "miraculous" cures. [3]

After peaking in the 1880's, the medicine show declined because it would have been laughed out of the city where the much superior vaudeville took over the stages. It was a giant step from the back of a wagon to the proscenium of one of E.F. Albee's theatres. Opulent theatres with beautiful lobbies showcased the talent. Keith-Albee in the East and the Orpheum Circuit west of Chicago created virtual cathedrals in the larger cities, with gold and crimson draperies, expensive carpets, damasked and gilded walls, frescoed ceilings, even huge oil paintings. In New York City Martin Beck of the Orpheum Circuit built the greatest of the houses of vaude, the Palace, challenging K-A in the heart of their kingdom. To "play the Palace" became the summit of ambition for vaudevillians.

Vaudeville mirrored the ragtime era in both content and characteristics. In traits, it was optimistic, fast-paced, humorous, out-going, slangy, and exuberant. Its content was universal, its varied "acts" a spectrum of the greatest talent to the hottest topic. Musicians, dancers, and comedians made up the bulk of the bills, but showtime always included some other specialties: acrobats, animals, magicians, mind readers, sharpshooters (ladies especially), athletes, storytellers, one-act plays (many originally written for vaude), pantomimists, puppeteers, whistlers, celebrities, newsmakers, even a "worst" act. Virtually anyone who excited curiosity was a candidate for the big-time. Celebrities usually meant non-vaudevillians briefly appearing for large sums, actors like Sarah Bernhardt and the Barrymores and classical musicians like the violinist Eduard Kemenyi. Newsmakers included murderers, boxers, suffragettes, anyone notorious at the moment, though seemingly no politicians. There were two chorus girls, billed as the "Shooting Stars," who had shot, in the leg, a wealthy society type. An ex-forger named George Schroder came on as "Convict 6630-The Man Who Sang Himself Out of the Penitentiary." In California people paid to see Ed Morrell, youngest member of a famous gang, just released after sixteen years in prison. Another was the bogus polar explorer Dr. Cook who claimed to have reached the North Pole before Robert Peary (see Chapter 34). Perhaps the ultimate celebrity-newsmaker was ex-showgirl Evelyn Nesbit, the femme in a notorious love triangle, the trophy figure of the biggest celebrity murder of the two decades. Her husband, Harry K. Thaw, an unstable heir to a great Pittsburgh fortune, had, in 1906, in a public place, murdered her lover, Stanford White, NYC's leading citizen and the nation's most renowned architect. From 1913-1919, initially partnered by Jack Clifford, she took the stage and popularized the new "ragtime dances," the one-step and fox-trot.

Even greater oddities reached the bills. At Hammerstein's Victoria in NYC, where the late Oscar Hammerstein I had featured more of the notorious and the celebrated than any other impresario of his time, his less capable successors (in 1915) resorted to sensational acts that went beyond what the public cared to tolerate. Besides Dr. Cook (who was booed), they promoted the "farewell" appearance of the famous dancer Carmencita. The excitement leaked out of this sensation when the news broke that she had been deceased for six years! Other similarly sensational acts were hangings and electrocutions, which went over poorly because they were (1) gruesome and (2) phony pretenses. One "stunt" act that did thrill audiences was billed at the Palace as "12 Speed Mechanics." Excitement swelled as 12 men rapidly assembled a Model "T" Ford onstage in two minutes.

Probably vaude's strangest act, out of Cedar Rapids, Iowa, was the Cherry Sisters, by name, Addie, Jessie, and Effie, and actually billed as "The Cherry Sisters—America's Worst Act!" They began performing their songs and recitations locally in 1893. Right off, the home folks had been horrified, expressing their displeasure noisily and emphatically. The Sisters seemingly mistook disapprobation to be complimentary. No one ever was certain whether they were simply "out of it," i.e., unconnected to reality, or perhaps slyly indifferent. As it turned out, their off-key singing and weird cavortings lured in curious folks ready to be amazed at how utterly abominable they were. As their fame spread, managers eagerly booked them. Soon they were performing behind a net, because hurling missiles at them became an integral part of experiencing the Cherry Sisters. The act triumphed over novelty and went on for years. Audiences loved to scream at them and hurl the rotten veggies and other detritus. Besides patriotic songs and elocutionary recitations, they enriched their act with two skits: "The Wanderer's Return" and

"The Gypsy's Warning." The latter narrated the perils facing innocent young women in big cities. Eventually they headlined the New York big-time for $1000/week. They lasted until WW I, after which they retired to Cedar Rapids to open a bakery. They did good business here because their baking was as good as their performing was bad. Dressed in elaborate 1890's costumes, standing together behind the counter, they were the town's major—and most picturesque—celebrities. [4]

There has been debate over the essence of vaudeville. Was it essentially a medium of comedy, or was it centered on song and dance? E. F. Albee spoke a curious verdict: When the act of Annette Kellerman the aquatic star flopped initially, Albee rescued it with mirrors, saying, "…what we are selling here is backsides, and that a hundred backsides are better than one." [5] Unusual candor from a magnate whose theatre managers posted a sign warning performers that "…your act must be free from all vulgarity and suggestiveness in words, action, and costume…." [6] Albee was wrong, because there was a greater abundance of "backsides" in burlesque and other music halls. The vaudeville audience appreciated its measure of the skin game, but it came weekly to laugh and listen as well as to look. The essence was, after all, variety.

Many of vaude's first stars debuted at Tony Pastor's. Irish-comic singer Maggie Cline scored a hit in 1890 with the prize fight ballad "Throw Him Down McCloskey":

Chorus:
    Throw him down McCloskey was to be the battle cry—
    Throw him down McCloskey you can lick him if you try,
    And future generations, with wonder and delight,
    Will read on history's pages of the great McCloskey fight.

J. W. Kelly [7]

By the 47th round, the fight between McCloskey and McCracken is a draw, the latter losing his upper lip and the former an eye. Douglas Gilbert describes Maggie as "…a large plain-faced woman with a huge toss of auburn hair and a voice that would blast out the walls of a theatre." [8] Another favorite at Pastor's was Lottie Gilson who introduced "Sidewalks of New York" and comic hits such as "You're Not the Only Pebble on the Beach." Best remembered of Tony's finds was Lillian Russell, who soon forsook vaude for musical comedy. She sang competently, clowned professionally, and her very beautiful face and zaftig figure kept them coming back for decades. Perhaps the finest performer to gain fame on Tony's stage was May Irwin, a Canadian. Her career began at 14 in Buffalo in 1876, and Tony caught her a year later teamed with sister Flora as The Irwin Sisters and signed them. They stayed with him for six years, after which they split, and May, like Lillian Russell a few years later, went into musical comedy. She became a ragtimer in the 1890's as the foremost singer, or "shouter," of coon songs. Her greatest hit, "The Bully Song" is another fisticuff number, this one telling of fighting among African Americans. May also did very well with Ben Harney's "Mr. Johnson, Turn Me Loose." She invested in New York real estate and was one of the few "artists" to die rich.

II

Ragtime and vaudeville soon developed a symbiotic relationship. Each new season demanded new songs. Big-timers and headliners needed songs of their own to stay on top. Dancers, jugglers, comedians, and acrobats could devise their own new materials—or "adapt" a few routines from colleagues. But singers needed composers. When they came off the road in hot weather, singers (plus others wanting music) visited the "professional departments" of the song factories to find the right scores for the upcoming season. Staff composers and pluggers demonstrated what they had in stock, often having composed in advance songs tailored for particular performers. They stood ready to create on the spot if nothing in the inventory satisfied, and what one artist rejected, another might jump at. Careers depended on getting the right songs, the ones to lift you into the big-time—and to keep you from falling back into the small-time.

Publishers shared these aspirations because when a song went over onstage, it produced big-time sales of sheet music. Singers wanted cameo pictures of themselves on sheet music covers ("Introduced by ____" or "As sung by ____"); they wanted to be identified with their songs. When it had all begun in the 1880s, they had had to pay for songs and orchestral arrangements, but with the proliferation of the music industry ("Tin Pan Alley"), music became free in the 1890s. In the 1900s, there came, first, Christmas hand-outs of money, which soon led to regular payments, salaries no less, to the few top performers, in some cases more than the UBO paid them, from publishers for presenting and popularizing their tunes. This escalated into a costly, destructive competition: too many publishers, too few big headliners. In NY City such leading publishers as the brothers Witmark, Charles K. Harris, Ed Marks, Joe Stern, Tom Harms, Leo Feist, Pat Howley, and Fred Haviland visited backstage nightly to give out copies of their latest songs and to buy beer, champagne, and cigars. They also recommended their tailors. They pursued all musical acts, soloists, groups, instrumentalists, and singers. If the music had a successful trial, followed by sales, they would make money. Audiences bought what they heard in the theatre. For the big headliners, it came down to bids; when they decided upon a song, they chose a paymaster. Publishers hated the practice. It could, and often did, backfire when the music failed the performers, or vice-versa. Eventually publishers formed the Music Publishers Protective Association (MPPA) to stamp out the vicious practice. The regular payments to acts stopped, but "payola," secret, under-the-counter pay-offs to artists has continued. [9]

The songs that "went over" with audiences, that successfully showcased a singer, appealed with either sentiment or humor. Comic songs tended to go over more easily than the more serious types. The humor in most cases was ethnic: coon songs (Chapter 11) and other dialect songs that made people laugh at Jews, Germans, the Dutch, the Irish, and the Italians. Composer/lyricist Herbert Ingraham in 1909 turned out for Emma Carus "Heinie Waltzed 'Round on his Hickory Limb." In the opening verse, Heinie, "who was a great waltzer," loses his leg to "a disease of the knee." Unable to waltz, he risks losing his Lena, so he learns on his prosthesis. In the chorus,

> Heinie waltzed 'round on his hickory limb—
> Hick, sh, sh, hick, sh, sh, hickory limb;
> Ach my, said Lena, "You waltz with your peg
> Just as good as you did with your leg."

Except that "The crowd all got sore" because "he made "nicks on the floor," Heinie triumphs on his "hick, sh, sh, hick, sh, sh, hickory limb." In "Under the Anheuser Bush" (1903) Harry Von Tilzer and lyricist Andrew B. Sterling nicely combine the Germanic with the sentimental:

> Come, come, come and make eyes with me
> Under the Anheuser bush;
> Come, come drink some Budweis with me
> Under the Anheuser bush;

Hear the old German band—just let me hold your hand—
Ya, du, du, come and have a stein or two
Under the Anheuser bush.

Until Pastor and Keith-Albee cleaned up vaudeville, Jewish songs had a degrading, very anti-semitic edge, as in the 1880s "Let Us Go to the Sheeny Wedding" ("Won't we have a jolly time/Eating motzers [sic] and drinking wine/All the high-tone Hebrews will/Be at the Sheeney wedding.") [10] In 1915, for Belle Baker, Irving Berlin composed a friendlier comic Jewish song, "Cohen Owes Me $97." Here Old Man Rosenthal is dying and commands his son to collect all the monies owed to him so that he "can die with a smile on my face." The son does as bidden, but instead of passing on, the old man pulls through and regains an excellent health. He replies to amazed friends:

Cohen owed me $97,
So my son went out
And made poor Cohen pay;

And he concludes:

Now what would my son do with all that money,
If I should give it up and say good-bye?
It's all right to pass away
But when people start to say,
That's no way for a businessman to die!

For a non-ethnic humorous song Nat D. Ayer's "If You Talk in Your Sleep, Don't Mention My Name" (1911) furnishes a racy example. (Ayer also gave us "Oh, You Beautiful Doll.") A. Seymour Brown's witty lyrics skate dangerously close to the edge of propriety, but it contributed to a successful vaudeville season for Alma Youlin. The verse tells of "a young married lady, who was very much inclined to be just a little indiscreet," who accepts a luncheon invitation from a man casually met. During the course of the meal "in a private dining room," he notices her ring and gently warns in the chorus:

I can see that you are married,
And you know I'm married too,
And nobody knows that you know me,
And nobody knows that I know you;
And if you care to, we'll have luncheon
Every day here just the same,
But sweetheart, if you talk in your sleep,
Don't mention my name.

In the second verse, this indiscreet lady gets her comeuppance, when, one night, <u>her</u> husband starts talking in <u>his</u> sleep, and "she knew every word that he said by heart," followed by an exact repeat of the chorus. [11]

III

> I don't care, I don't care
> What they think of me,
> I'm happy go lucky
> > Men say I am plucky,
> > So jolly and carefree,
> I don't care, I don't care,
> > If I do get that mean and stony stare,
> > If I'm never successful,
> It won't be distressful,
> 'Cos I don't care.

Harry O. Sutton

Such is the chorus of the signature song of vaude's greatest box office attraction, Eva Tanguay. Eva had incredible talent and personality. An authority states: "The terrific Tanguay was an electrified hoyden, a temperamental terror to the managers, a riotous joy to her audiences. A singing and dancing comedienne, it is easy to analyze her act: it was assault and battery."[12] Her only restraints were her limitations; she always threw in all of her talents; she was, in a word, energy. While singing "I Don't Care," or "It's All Been Done Before but Not the Way I Do It" or "I Want Someone To Go Wild With Me," she thrust herself wildly, randomly, across the stage, wriggling hips, waggling breasts, kicking wildly, shaking her backside. Audiences loved her orgiastic gyrations; it was hypnotic. She wore startling costumes. One dress consisted of 1, 5, 10, and 50-dollar bills; another was all coins and weighed 45 pounds; one of coral weighed 65 pounds. Once she wore a pedometer and claimed to have covered four miles at performances. Her press agent ground out a sensational series of headlines:

> The Girl Who Made Vaudeville Famous
> Mother Eve's Merriest Daughter
> Miss Tabasco
> Cyclonic Eva Tanguay
> The Girl the World Loves
> The Evangelist of Joy

She seems more pathological than joyful. Born in 1878 in a rural Quebec wilderness of a French-Canadian mother and a French doctor, she lost her father at age seven after the family moved to Massachusetts. She endured poverty and hunger until the owner of a touring troupe, seeing her golden-haired beauty on the street, employed her for $8/week. She grew up in variety as a chorus girl and acrobat. She developed an unusual degree of upper body strength and used it on those who angered her. She got into brawls, and she hurt people. Sometimes she paid off the injured with a bill of large denomination. Witnesses say she always carried five to fifteen $1000 bills. In Louisville she threw a stagehand down a flight of stairs because "he was in my way" at a curtain call. She settled that civil suit for $1000. In 1910 she attacked a chorus girl, pulling her hair and throwing her against the wall for saying negative things. Once a stagehand in the Mid-west asked what she would do if approached by a masher. Saying "watch," she picked him up and threw him against the wall. He fell unconscious. Once she cut an asbestos fire curtain to shreds to protest a $100 fine for missing a performance (she had been asleep). When managers asked her to share top billing, she walked out. She told off audiences that displeased her. Which strangely only increased her fascination: they always returned.

Critics loved or hated Eva Tanguay. Detractors denounced her morals and lack of talent. She of course "didn't care" what they thought of her behavior, and she was candid about her talents, saying on one occasion, "As a matter of fact, I am not beautiful, I can't sing, I do not know how to dance. I am not even graceful." [13] Percy Williams, soft-spoken owner of a major theatre chain (including the Colonial in NY City) who named a theatre for her, always required a $5000 cash bond from her for keeping both her engagements and the peace. And other critics adored her. One in Chicago said:

> Then the incomparable white silk legs smiting the boards like drumsticks and a wild voice crying an aristocratic ballad that must have made Dear Old Mother whirl in her tomb. In a series of recalls she recited bits of verse. I love her. For nine years she has been my dementia. Long may she rave.
> Ashton Stevens [14]

Keith and the UBO attempted to discipline Eva on occasion, when local theatre managers complained, but she either ignored them or pulled off a more incorrigible gambit. Nor did they dock her $3000/week salary. Her naughtiest turn came in 1908 when she electrified audiences with her version of the "Dance of the Seven Veils" (based upon the sequence in the 1905 opera *Salome* by Richard Strauss). For this she wore only the veils and jewelry. As she dropped the veils, in what was actually a striptease in a "respectable" theatre, she did her dance and sang her songs. And she got away with it: no blue uniform carted her off for indecent exposure. Probably no one else could have done it.

She married briefly, twice, at ages 36 and 49 (1914 and 1926), to minor performers. Alas, she couldn't maintain the frenzy; in the 1920's it was burn-out, not the blacklist, that removed her from the stage. In vaudeville's last days, managers, fed up with her antics and perceiving her diminution, wouldn't book her. Having earned about $2,000,000 in vaude, she was wealthy, but she lost most of it in the 1929 Crash, after which, she made a bare living (like so many others) selling real estate in Los Angeles. The final point about the lost soul Eva Tanguay is this: her high energy smashed the mold of Victorian restraints, making her the forerunner of the twentieth-century culture of personality and individualism. [15]

IV

Perhaps Nora Bayes (b. Leonora Goldberg in 1880), "The Singing Comedienne," was vaude's star singer. She possessed all the technique Tanguay lacked. She lived surrounded by friends where Tanguay was a loner. But her life was equally tragic and unhappy. She could be devious. People learned variously that her birthplace was Los Angeles, Chicago, or Joliet, Illinois, but it was probably Milwaukee, a location where she always refused to appear. At 18 she ran off to Chicago, banking on the talent she had already displayed on amateur nights. She broke into small-time at $25/week and married the first of five husbands, Otto Gressing, an undertaker. She soon moved up into the two-a-day after scoring her first hit with Harry Von Tilzer's "Down Where the Wurzburger Flows." Next she went to Paris to upgrade herself professionally, learning how to dramatize her songs and use her contralto more effectively. Critics raved about her voice control, diction, and enunciation (as they would do decades later about Frank Sinatra).

She traded Gressing for Jack Norworth in 1908. The love of her life, Norworth had it all: looks, charm, talent, creativity. When they teamed up, the marquee proclaimed:

NORA BAYES
Assisted and Admired by Jack Norworth

Ziegfeld put them into the 1909 *Follies*, where they went over big, but this was not enough. He earned half of her $450/week. She became rabidly jealous whenever he flirted with Ziegfeld's glamorous girls. He composed their big hit, "Shine On, Harvest Moon," and she grabbed half the composing credit. She bossed him around in front of others; he walked out of the *Follies*; she followed. They fled to England and scored a major success. Ziegfeld sued and blacklisted them (Tanguay replaced Nora), and all the publicity boosted them further. Their salaries as a two-act rose from $1000 to $2500. They went on in vaudeville as "the stage's happiest couple." Jack finally walked out in 1913 and headed back to Britain where he was once more a big hit. Nora came crying after and begged to reconcile; he refused. Neither seems to have known much happiness after that. Jack had more successes with "Honey Boy" and "Come Along, My Mandy" and achieved cultural immortality with his greatest hit, "Take Me Out To the Ball Game." Nora then flopped in London and became ill. She went to Germany, apparently for treatment of the cancer that troubled her for the rest of her life. Then World War I broke out, and she fled home, arriving to find that the press had headlined her death. Her return and escape from death or war caused a burst of popularity, and she headlined the Palace for a fabulous run.

Her salary soared during the late Teens and early 20's, from $1000 to $1750 to $2000 to $2250 to $2500, and by 1928 she was receiving $5000 (when a manager had a big enough budget). Every few years she remarried briefly, as profligate with husbands as with money. She passed her time in extravagance, traveling with a large entourage of servants, friends, and children (she had adopted three). She traveled in private rail cars and took entire floors in deluxe hotels. Occasionally she rented whole trains! She saved nothing when her annual income reached $100,000; there were always new clothes, jewels, and expensive gifts for favorites. Was she driven by heartbreak over Jack Norworth, who continued not to reconcile, or was it the secret cancer gnawing away inside her? There was regular turmoil, with Albee and the UBO, with theatre managers, with husbands, and with colleagues in vaude. Near the end, at the Palace, she got into a squalid argument with Sophie Tucker over who should go on first. When she refused all offers of compromise, the manager pushed her through the stage door and closed it. Within a year (March 1928), the cancer ended her life. She died insolvent. [16]

Notes: Chapter 18

1. Douglas Gilbert, *American Vaudeville: Its Life and Times*, 3.
2. J. Anthony Lukas, *Big Trouble*, 577-578.
3. For more details, see James Harvey Young, *The Toadstool Millionaires: A Social History of Patent Medicines in America Before Federal Regulation*, 190-202.
4. William L. Shirer, *Twentieth-Century Journey, the Start: 1904-1930*, 143.
5. Quoted in Charles and Louise Samuels, *Once Upon a Stage: The Merry World of Vaudeville*, 40.
6. David Nasaw, *Going Out: The Rise and fall of Public Amusements*, 25; Simon Louvish, *The Man on the Flying Trapeze: The Life and Times of W.C. Fields*, 2.
7. Quoted in Douglas Gilbert, *Lost Chords: The Diverting Story of American Popular Songs*, 202.
8. *Ibid.*, 202-203.
9. Edward B. Marks, *They All Sang: From Tony Pastor to Rudy Vallee*, 133-135; Russell Sanjek, *American Popular Music and Its Business: The First Four hundred Years*, II, 339.
10. Gilbert, *Lost Chords*, 81; composed by Henry Thompson.
11. These songs are taken from a group collected and performed by Annie Lebeaux on her CD *Rare and Ridiculous Vaudeville Songs (1903-1926)*. (2001) Ms. Lebeaux performs this material on the *Delta Queen* steamboat.
12. Gilbert, *Am.Vaude.*, 327.
13. Quoted *Ibid.*, 329.
14. Quoted in Marks, 179.
15. Samuels, 54-67, 149-152; Gilbert, *Am.Vaude.*, 327-331; Marks, 178-180; Robert W. Snyder, *The Voice of the City: Vaudeville and Popular Culture in New York*, 149-151; David A. Jasen, *Tin Pan Alley: The Composers, the Songs, the Performers*, 26-27, 63.
16. Samuels, 80-89; Gilbert, *Am.Vaude.*, 333-342; Jasen, TPA, 62-63.

19. The Art of Rag (III): St. Louis

…By 1900,…the music was clearly winning over the American public, or at least the youthful portion of that public. The music had vigor and excitement, its syncopated rhythms were marvelous to dance to, and its lyrics were a welcome relief from the sentiments of the prevailing "tear-jerker" ballad. From that point on, the music's racial associations were weakened, and by 1905 or 1906 ragtime was the music not just of black Americans, but of all Americans. And unlike so much music whose models were clearly European, ragtime was distinctively American.

Edward A. Berlin [1]

…One thing cannot be denied; it is music which possesses at least one strong element of greatness: it appeals universally; not only the American, but the English, the French, and even the German people find delight in it….Anyone who doubts that there is a peculiar heel-clicking, smile-provoking, joy-awakening charm in rag-time needs only to hear a skillful performer play the genuine article to be convinced.

James Weldon Johnson [2]

RAGTIME ALMANAC

1900 Population, Ten Largest U.S. Cities [3]

New York 3,437,202
Chicago 1,698,575
Philadelphia 1,293,697
St.Louis 575,238
Boston 560,892
Baltimore 508,957
Cleveland 381,768
Buffalo 352,387
San Francisco 342,782
Cincinnati 325,902

The *Maple Leaf Rag* removed John Stark and Scott Joplin from Sedalia to St.Louis. Ragtime became a national enterprise for both publisher and composer. Leaving son William to tend the Sedalia store, Stark, wife Sarah, and daughter Eleanor ("Nellie"), had already relocated in March 1899, several months before the signing of the "Maple Leaf" contract in August. Nellie had completed her European music education, and her next step, a career debut, required a major cultural center. For an itinerant like Joplin, who inhabited a series of sleeping rooms, it wasn't a case of "moving," but of shifting his base of operations. He possessed an identity in both cities, a familiar figure on Main and Market Streets.

As noted previously (Chapter 14.1), St.Louis, at the confluence of the Missouri and Mississippi Rivers, had grown and flourished as the "Gateway City" for the Louisiana Purchase. It had dominated the Midwest and supplied the West until eastern rails reached Chicago in the 1850's. Chicago, closer to the financial and industrial Northeast, situated at a key location on the Great Lakes, and better aligned for a rail route through the Rocky Mountains, rapidly outstripped St.Louis as the regional economic center. The Gateway City, while keeping up a proud front as the hub of steamboat traffic, languished until the completion of James Buchanan Eads' great bridge in 1874, which belatedly put the city on rails, but could not restore her to former greatness. The balloon of St.Louis vanity had deflated rather slowly. As late as 1870, one Logan U. Reavis had published

St.Louis, The Future Great City of the World, convincing proud locals of her destined greatness. By the 1880's visitors remarked on the city's dirt, filth, smoke—and on its large number of brothels. Rather than a world center, St.Louis in 1900 had a reputation for squalor, corruption, and violence. In his muckraking *Shame of the Cities* (1904), Lincoln Steffens revealed it as our worst governed city. Nor did such judgments of outside reformers lead to any solution of deterioration. Not until the "smoke crisis" of 1939 did one of the nation's sickest cities begin to change its collective attitude. [4]

But in that era of coal and municipal corruption, it was a question of degree: few cities could boast of clear air or clean streets. St.Louis grew steadily, from 350,522 in 1880, to 451,770 in 1890, to 575,238 in 1900 and fourth place in the roster of U.S. cities. An atlas of 1900 praises its public and commercial buildings, schools and university, numerous and large parks, and "its wealth, the culture of its inhabitants, its fine society, and the beauty of its women." [5] The difference for Scott Joplin and his black friends lay in the racial situation. When the train rolled away from the Sedalia station, it departed an oasis of relative racial harmony to reenter a region of southern attitudes. Missouri had come in as a slave state in 1821, and most of its whites felt more of hostility than benevolence toward the darker race. In St.Louis black folk were forced into a few crowded city wards, ghettos of crime, vice, and ill health. So terrible were living conditions, rural as well as urban, that from 1880 to 1910, while the statewide census of whites increased by 55%, African Americans increased by a mere 8%, actually decreasing 2.3% between 1900 and 1910. Missouri had no legal segregation on trains or in public accommodations, but only because such a law failed to pass in 1903. Later, in 1916, St.Louis voters did approve a segregation ordinance—by a margin of 3:1—but the Supreme Court nullified it (unconstitutional). Despite the consolation of such moral victories, which manifested some proof of citizenship and place in the human species, nothing changed or ameliorated the reality of de facto segregation in housing, hotels, and eating places. As for school segregation, that had become legal with the Supreme Court's Plessey-Ferguson decision of 1896. And whites never took any notice of police or other brutalities, including occasional lynchings out in the country, where 51 African Americans experienced sudden violent deaths from 1889 to 1918. [6]

From this perspective we can understand why Scott Joplin lingered in Sedalia through 1900. Perhaps he found it something of a safe haven. Sedalia had given him recognition, some respect, warm friendships, and personal security. His biographer Susan Curtis believes that in big cities Joplin was just another "colored" man, faceless and looked through, and characterizes this condition as "lost in urban America": "…the King of Ragtime faded from public chronicles of the urban communities in which he lived." [7] However as noted above, Joplin, by now a renowned ragtimer, could hardly become "lost" in St.Louis. He remained in Sedalia until early 1901, any summons from St.Louis easily handled via the mail or a few hours on the train. Ragtime preoccupied him; he was exploring its potential for an extended work. The resulting *Ragtime Dance* runs nine pages instead of three or four. A narrator-caller describes and calls the steps for eight dances popular with African Americans a century ago, including the cakewalk, slow drag, "World's Fair" dance, and the rag two-step. Brother Will Joplin took this role, and brother Robert, headed for success in vaudeville, may also have participated. This twenty-minute ballet in ragtime, part of an evening of variety entertainment, quite likely received its premier on November 24, 1899, at Woods Opera House, which had been rented by the composer. [8] (Berlin adds that eight years later Robert Joplin directed and narrated another performance of this work.) During this time Belle Jones Hayden, widow of Scott Hayden's brother, had been boarding in the same house on Washington Street as Joplin. At the end of 1900 or early in 1901, they married and subsequently moved from the Sedalia rooming house to their own home at

2658-A Morgan, on the edge of the St.Louis "district." Married at 32, Scott Joplin sought to live a different life. He intended to support a household by selling his music to publishers and by taking pupils. John Stark paid him a royalty of only one cent on the *Maple Leaf Rag*, which had come to a mere four dollars the first year, but sales took off after that, until about 500,000 copies had sold by 1909. This averages 60,000 per year over an eight-year period and comes to $600 annually. [9] On this modest amount, the average industrial worker maintained a family; therefore it constituted a basic income to be supplemented by composing and teaching. The *Maple Leaf Rag* liberated its composer from the "sporting life" of whorehouses and honky-tonks.

Soon after his relocation, he received a very significant notice in the "public chronicles." An article in the *St.Louis Globe-Democrat* of February 28, 1901, headlined—above a full-body photograph—that Joplin was "To Play Ragtime In Europe." In a laudatory tone, the article stated that Director Alfred Ernst of the St.Louis Choral Symphony had "discovered, in Scott Joplin of Sedalia, a negro, an extraordinary genius as a composer of ragtime music." A century later, the combining of ragtime with "genius" still seems strange, ringing not quite true. But there it was: Ernst wished to introduce the *Maple Leaf* composer and his music to the exalted musical figures of Europe "with a view to educating the dignified disciples of Wagner, Liszt, Mendelssohn, and other European masters of music into an appreciation of the real American ragtime melodies." Ernst declared further that he was "deeply interested in this man," and that he (Ernst) had opened "a new world to him" when he played passages of Wagner's *Tannhaüser* ("I believe he felt as Keats felt when he first read Chapman's Homer"). Ernst also promised to "take Mr. Joplin under his care and instruct him in the theory and harmony of music." And

> "…With proper cultivation, I believe, his talent will develop into positive genius. Being of African blood himself, Joplin has a keener insight into that peculiar branch of melody than white composers. His ear is particularly acute." He goes on to compliment Joplin for the "original" and "melodious" qualities of his ragtime, concluding that "I am led to believe he can do something fine in composition of a higher class when he shall have been instructed in theory and harmony. Joplin's work, as yet, has a creative crudeness, due to his lack of musical education." [10]

Some of this comes off as patronizing, but this was, after all, 1901, when people prided themselves on "good taste," and cultural snobbery was a customary affectation of social superiority. What counts here is the accolade; out of crude ragtime had materialized a potential genius—and of the black race! Figuratively this experience must have lodged an arrow deep in the spirit of Scott Joplin: from then on he aspired to classical forms, chiefly opera. How did this meeting of the music masters come about? Stark's daughter Eleanor, who had completed her musical studies in Germany, could certainly have arranged such a meeting. As for Ernst, he seems not to have descended again into the ghetto of ragtime. No evidence exists that he took either Joplin or his rags to Germany. The strong enthusiasm projected by the article leads us to the question of why it cooled. Ernst's endorsement of Joplin's ragtime on its musical merits could have been socially naive. Following the article, a member of the symphony's governing board might have set him straight about where ragtime was, and was not, heard.

Social respect was another of Scott Joplin's aspirations. He wanted to free himself of the night-world and his past associations with it. He conducted himself with modesty and reticence and spoke a careful, precise English. He lived absorbed in music; he approached the rag as an artform, and his musical vision saw beyond that. The *Ragtime Dance* of 1899 evidenced this ambition. He abandoned the ragtime life, including even the "cutting contests" in which players sought the prize for playing hottest and fastest. Fellow "ticklers" admired his music, never his dignified playing of it. A story in the black *Sedalia Times* in April 1902 confirms the serious direction of Joplin's life. Editor W. H. Carter, friend and onetime fellow bandsman in the Queen City group, visited St.Louis and reported to the homefolks that the "Rag Time King" was composing, publishing, and enhancing his reputation nationally. He states that *Maple Leaf, Easy Winners, Peacherine Rag*, and "Rag Time Dances" were "in demand" and being heard in "St.Louis, Chicago, New York, and a number of other cities." [11] (Biographer Berlin, 104, suspects that Joplin's pianistic ability had begun to deteriorate as a result of syphilis contracted earlier. Since there is anecdotal evidence of its effects on his playing [and temperament] six or eight years later, his abilities could have been in decline as early as 1901-02.)

By the end of 1902, he had published twelve pieces of music, of which seven were rags, two were marches, two were songs, and one was a waltz. One of the rags *The Strenuous Life* was a tribute to Theodore Roosevelt, who had first used the phrase in an 1899 speech when he was Governor of New York ("I wish to preach, not the doctrine of ignoble ease, but the doctrine of the strenuous life...") Reprinting had made the phrase a byword, evoking a dynamic president. Six other composers followed Joplin in using this title. [12]

Sometime during 1902, the Joplins purchased a thirteen-room house a few blocks away at 2117 Lucas Street, where they augmented their income with boarders. These included former Sedalia pupils Arthur Marshall and Scott Hayden. June 7, 1903, brought further acclaim in the public prints with another feature story in the *Globe-Democrat*, this one by raffish Tin Pan Alleyman Monroe Rosenfeld (Chapter 3). Rosenfeld begins with a salute to "The King of Ragtime Writers," "who, despite the ebony hue of this (sic) features and a retired disposition, has written more instrumental successes in the line of popular music than any other local composer." The article praises Joplin for his modesty, musical skill, and "the refinement of his speech and demeanor." Rosenfeld continues with the success story of the *Maple Leaf Rag* ("this quaint creation became a byword with musicians"), then mentions later compositions, singling out *The Entertainer* for special praise ("the best and most euphonious of his latter-day compositions"). He concludes: "Joplin's ambition is to shine in other spheres," adding that,

...To this end he is assiduously toiling upon an opera, nearly a score of the numbers of which he has already composed and which he hopes to give an early production in this city. [13]

Like other serious African-American composers (Chapter 26), Joplin sought to create a theatre piece, a narrative or "book show" rather than a form of variety such as characterized minstrel, medicine, or vaudeville shows. These composers were reaching toward musical comedy, but that was still in an evolutionary state. The book shows of that day lacked integrity. Plotting and characterization were not carefully worked out or developed. Songs and comedy routines were "interpolated" into shows to liven up a dull spot or to allow a star turn. But even with these interpolated variety elements, a show with a book could call itself theatre. The term "opera" also conferred some aura of legitimacy. Vaudeville theatres across America took the name "opera house." Thus Joplin staked a claim to be taken seriously by calling his theatre piece a "ragtime opera."

In February 1903 Scott Joplin applied for a copyright (the letter is the only one of his extant) for *A Guest of Honor*. He assembled a company of thirty-two ("The Scott Joplin Ragtime Opera Company"), then rehearsed and staged a trial performance in a dancehall, probably in August. The show opened and played in East St.Louis, Illinois, on August 30, the first of eleven shows in a planned eleven-stop tour, 8/30 to 10/12. Advertisements were published for Springfield and Galesburg, Illinois, dates two and three in the itinerary, but the tour seems to have crashed in Springfield (9/02/03). Evidence is sketchy, but the outcome was catastrophic. Joplin lost his investment, probably all he had been able to accumulate, mostly out of *Maple Leaf* royalties.

A Guest of Honor, its text and music, simply disappeared, and the requisite two copies had not accompanied the copyright application. In an earlier notice to the *Freeman* (Indianapolis), Joplin had described the work as "a ragtime opera" in two parts "on the order of grand opera" and mentioned two of the "big numbers": "the Dudes Parade" and "Patriotic Patrol." That is all we have. Biographer Edward Berlin speculates that the title refers to the African-American leader Booker T. Washington. Soon after taking office in 1901, TR invited Washington to dinner at the White House. When this innocuous-seeming item appeared in the official list of White House activities, the press tore at it like red meat, treating the episode as a lurid and bizarre happening: a colored man was invited to sit at the same table as the President and his family! (Chapter 27) This enraged the South, its press erupted in screaming headlines. But it thrilled the black population that their leader had received such an honor. This event may well have inspired the lost *Guest of Honor*. The creative catastrophe of 1903 was doubled by a marital break-up. An unhealthy girl child born to the Joplins died after a few months, a trauma that a strained marriage could not overcome. Belle Jones Joplin apparently cared little for music and must have greatly resented the financial sacrifices and losses from the opera venture. The drudgery of keeping a boarding house, a failed venture in music, a lost child, were too much to cope with. She abandoned Scott to join her son in Chicago. [14]

II

Undoubtedly during this time of troubles at the end of 1903, Scott Joplin found some diversion and refuge at Tom Turpin's recently opened Rosebud Cafe. Friendship with the Turpins possibly went back to the late 1880's when Joplin was starting out as an entertainer (Chapter 14.1). Turpin, the first African American to publish a rag (*Harlem Rag*, 1897), is a significant figure in ragtime history. He and his family occupied, serendipitously, the central point for the diffusion of midwestern ragtime: the drinking places in St.Louis's "Chestnut Valley." Not far from the river piers, adjacent to the Union Station, here the ragtimers gathered, to find friends and jobs, to learn news and gossip, to listen and to compete in contests. Music came with these players, up river from New Orleans and Memphis, along the rails from Kansas City, Nashville, and Chicago. What people heard in the Turpin bars was folk ragtime, much of it made up of common themes or folk strains that existed in the public domain of folk culture.

A curious "horrible example" is Theron C. Bennett's rag *St.Louis Tickle*, published in 1904. A first hearing usually stopped worldly souls in their tracks. Suddenly there it was, in the second or "B" section, the tune of a very dirty song. They called it "Funky Butt" in Missouri, and if your mother caught you even whistling it, a bar of soap soon reached your mouth. Bennett, who published seven or eight good folk rags, craftily kept his name off the rag, crediting it pseudonymously to "Barney and Seymour." According to Jasen and Tichenor, this rag was published "in commemoration of the St.Louis World's Fair of 1904," and that it "was a hit at the fair and became one of the most beloved rags of all time." [15] (They do not reproduce what they call "the original bawdy lyrics.")

Besides Turpin and Bennett, other folk ragtimers with St.Louis and Missouri associations include Charles Hunter, Charles L. Johnson, Joe Jordan, Calvin Lee Woolsey, E. Harry Kelly, and Euday L. Bowman. Hunter (1876-1906) was white, blind, and from Tennessee. He learned piano tuning in Nashville and taught himself to play. Influenced by white folk music, his rags have been described as having a "southern fried" quality. Moving to St.Louis from Nashville, he spent the final years of a short life composing and playing in the District. Much played are his *Tickled to Death* (1901), *Possum and Taters, A Ragtime Feast* (1900), and *A Tennessee Tantalizer* (1900). Jordan (1882-1971) grew up in St.Louis and passed through on his way to success in both Chicago and New York. He published *Double Fudge* in St.Louis in 1902. Fanny Brice reached fame with his song "Lovie Joe." Woolsey

(1884-1946), a country doctor in northwest Missouri, whimsically entitled his rags *Funny Bones* (1909), *Medic Rag* (1910), *Poison Rag* (1910), and *Peroxide Rag* (1910). Another one was *Mashed Potatoes* (1911). Euday Bowman (1887-1949) of Fort Worth, Texas, was a familiar figure in Kansas City, where his *Twelfth Street Rag* (1914) and *Petticoat Lane* (1915) recall the "district" of that city. Both Charles L. Johnson (1876-1950) and E. Harry Kelly (1879-1955) lived in Kansas City. Kelly is known for *Peaceful Henry* (1901), while Johnson prolifically published thirty-two rags! His *Dill Pickles Rag* (1906) was one of the few rags to sell in the millions. [16]

The Turpin family had originated in Savannah, Georgia, where older brother Charles was born in 1867 and Tom in 1873 (there were also two daughters). By the mid-1880's, father "Honest John" Turpin, who claimed he had never worked for anyone since Emancipation, had become the proprietor of a livery stable and a saloon called the "Silver Dollar" at 425 South 12th Street. There, in the "Chestnut Valley" sin district, whose principal streets Chestnut and Market ran parallel a block apart, the Turpin brothers matured in a tough, crowded, dangerous neighborhood. John Turpin exemplified the survival of the tough: he held the bizarre distinction of being the head-butting champion of the state of Missouri. When danger threatened, he grabbed a man's wrist and butted, either stunning him or rendering him unconscious in one fast movement. The boys turned out like father, enterprising, strong, and able. At 18 Tom had gone west with Charles to prospect and mine for gold at Searchlight, Nevada (south of Las Vegas). When that failed, each knocked around separately for a few years, returning home in 1894. Besides physical strength and intelligence, Tom was born a "natural" in music. He surfaces next tickling the piano for the sports at the Castle, the renowned bordello of Madam Babe Connors at 210 South Sixth Street (Chapter 43). Toward the Nineties' end, he opened his first bar at 9 Targee Street. Legend recalls Targee Street as the site of the deadly lover's quarrel between Allen Britt and Frances Baker, the characters of the ballad *Frankie and Johnny*.

During this time, he published *Harlem Rag* (1897), *Bowery Buck* (1899), and *Ragtime Nightmare* (1900), half of his small published output. He was a huge man, standing six feet or more and weighing ultimately 350 pounds. His belly got in the way sitting down, so he stood his upright piano on blocks and played standing up. His photograph shows a handsome, solid, stiff-necked man, perhaps friendly, but not to be taken advantage of. Saloon operators faced daily challenges to their courage and physical capabilities. On one occasion, according to an item in the *St.Louis Post-Dispatch* (February 1898) entitled "A Duel to the Death," he faced genuine danger. The tone of the piece comes off as insulting and smirky, because of white scorn and because black vs. black furnished amusement: This wasn't serious violence, just some colored folks behaving naturally. The piece alleges that Tom and one Abe Keeler drew guns over a disagreement about "the relative merits of negro women." It informs the reader that Tom carried a Smith & Wesson and Keeler a Colt. Numerous shots are fired (implying poor marksmanship by blacks?), and then occurs "a battle to the death" in which "both of the black men exhibited nerve and bulldog tenacity" (note the last adjective). Finally the bullets hit someone: Turpin receives a graze on the head as he gutshots Keeler, who fires again ineffectively, and is finished off by a final bullet in the left side. Then "Turpin gazed upon the scene a moment and walked to a hydrant to wash his hands...." Next police arrive and arrest Tom and his father. Finally Keeler dies at the hospital. [17]

After this nothing happened: no charges presented, no judicial action or subsequent trial. Clearly the vice district lay outside the municipal jurisdiction, in a de facto sense. The community seemed not to care about the security and safety of the district's inhabitants. When one killed another, it rated only a short, rather detached account, if any, in the press. Whoever desired justice had to pay for it. Quite likely, the Turpins paid an extra assessment to ensure that the episode went officially unrecorded. They manipulated this venal system adroitly, and as they prospered, their political influence increased. In 1910 Charles Turpin won election as constable, the first African American elected to public office in the state. He was reelected in 1914 and served later as Justice of the Peace. He appointed brother Tom as Deputy. The Turpins dominated the district and ran gambling houses, dance halls, and houses of prostitution. When Charles Turpin died in 1935,he left a trust fund of $105,000. [18]

In 1903 Tom Turpin opened the Rosebud Bar, "Headquarters for Colored Professionals and Sports," at 2220-2222 Chestnut Street. The Rosebud has been much mentioned and celebrated as the place where the all the ragtimers had to touch base, where they gathered to listen and critique their peers, where rivalries were settled in cutting contests. Here the black "perfessors" received a welcome and a refuge from the hostile white world they always had to pass through. Here Turpin composed his rags, and here also he showed ragtime performance "tricks" to younger men like Sam Patterson, Louis Chauvin, and Charley Thompson. Although it couldn't have been open more than three or four years—Turpin closed it 1906—much of the above is undoubtedly true because it was so well remembered. Blesh and Janis call him the "Father of St.Louis Ragtime." [19] He always turns up as a chief sponsor or participant at ragtime events from the late 1890's to 1917.

The Rosebud itself filled up most of a city block, with two barrooms, a large gambling room, an upstairs "hotel," probably for short-time use like the "Raines Law" hotels in New York (Chapter 4), and a "wine room" in the rear where Tom's piano sat up on its blocks. For more intimate gatherings, Tom took his friends outside in back to his "Hunting and Shooting Club." Inside this shack he had put up gun racks, fishing pictures, and the antlered heads of his hunting trophies. Here friends conversed (no piano), and Tom occupied his throne-like Morris chair in the corner with spittoon adjacent. When he needed a place quieter than the wine room to listen to someone newly arrived or one of his proteges, Tom moved across the street to the parlor at Mother Johnson's resort where he had use of the piano for half a dollar. On February 22, 1904, in anticipation of the upcoming Louisiana Purchase Exposition, the "Rosebud Club" sponsored its third annual ball and piano contest, which pitted Tom against Louis Chauvin. The amazingly talented Chauvin—who became a ragtime legend—won the gold medal, and two others of great promise, Joe Jordan and Charley Warfield, tied for second place. When Tom lost, it was to the talent he had helped along. [20]

III

Like the World's Columbian Exposition in 1893, the Louisiana Purchase Exposition opened a year late because of the immensity of the project. It marked the centennial of Jefferson's fortunate and wonderful bargain with Napoleon, whereby France received $15,000,000, and the nation doubled in size with the addition of the western half of the Mississippi watershed, including the Missouri River. This year of 1904 was intended to be— and probably was—the glory year in the history of St.Louis. Not only a World's Fair (opened April 30), but the National Convention of the Democratic Party injected more excitement into the summer calendar, and the Third Olympic Games of the modern era ran from August 29 to September 3. The buildings and "pavilions" for the various arts, crafts, and industries—for 43 nations and 45 states and territories—spread out over the 1,275 acre site in what is now Forest Park, a few miles west of Chestnut Valley. A significant innovation was the inclusion of its amusement area, called "The Pike," within the precincts of the fair itself for the first time. In Chicago and at subsequent fairs, the entertainment site had been an adjunct appendage outside the gates.

Scott Joplin's sometime friend in the cultural establishment, Alfred Ernst, conducted the fair's orchestra and chorus. Since Chicago's Expo in 1893, European classical music had drawn poor audiences at American fairs, and this time the "Director of Programmes," Ernest R. Kroeger, promised "music for all," including "brass bands and ragtime for the many." [21] As far as we know, Ernst made no effort to program the music of the King of

Ragtime Writers, a bona fide resident of St.Louis, with whom he had been personally acquainted. People heard the music of John Philip Sousa, Victor Herbert, and Stephen Foster, but not the ragtime of Joplin, Turpin, or any other Missouri composer. Three compositions had been commissioned from prominent American composers (Frank Van der Stucken, Henry K. Hadley, John Knowles Paine) but none by a ragtimer. In 1901, when drumming up community support, planners had promised to include African Americans and to showcase their contributions to the development of the lands of the Louisiana Purchase. Pleased by such recognition, the National Afro-American Council decided to hold its annual meeting in St.Louis during the fair. Black organizations and school children enthusiastically worked on exhibits. Black folk also put in time and money to set up facilities for eating; recreation, including bowling, billiards, and theatre; and for comfort, including a barbershop and baths—St Louis was segregated. Morale rose further with the announcement that black and white could mingle and visit exhibits at the same times (Chicago had set aside separate days for non-whites).

However, despite open attendance, treatment turned out to be very unequal. The hopefully submitted black exhibits had been refused; blacks couldn't get into cafes, and other concessionaires denied them entrance. Management announced disapproval of discrimination, but it did nothing to implement the intended policy of open admissions. The black newspaper the *St.Louis Palladium* advised readers to stay away. But they were allowed to entertain on the Pike and play ragtime. Arthur Marshall, Sam Patterson, and Louis Chauvin did find temporary employment in two of the bars. And the most popular music that summer was Kerry Mills' song "Meet Me In St.Louis" and Joplin's *The Cascades*, a rag impression of the water falls and lagoons in front of the Tower of Knowledge, all of which comprised the fair's theme or icon. Also much played were Tom Turpin's *St.Louis Rag*, James Scott's *On the Pike*, and *St.Louis Tickle* by "Barney and Seymour" a.k.a. Theron C. Bennett. Today this ragtime music furnishes the principal recollection of the Exposition. [22]

Some of the expo's wonders: the world's largest pipe organ (in the Festival Hall); the "Art Palace" (now the St.Louis Art Museum); the many aquariums of the U.S. Fisheries exhibit; a large model of Jerusalem; a reenactment of a battle of the Boer War by real Boers and Englishmen; the giant wheel, 250 feet in diameter and standing 264 feet tall, that engineer George W. Ferris had constructed for the Chicago fair, had been reassembled in Forest Park (it was scrapped two years later); people enjoyed the first ice cream cones (hot dogs were also available); and several Filipino villages: Moros, Visayans, Igorots, and Negritos. As we have seen (Chapter 6), all world's fairs imported "villages" of Africans, Filipinos, or Native Americans, and fair visitors loved them, for their exotic qualities and because such "primitives" reassured Americans of their cultural superiority.

The customs of the Igorots left a permanent impression behind. They exhibited colorful tatoos, and were reputed to be "headhunters," but they attracted much attention because one of their dietary staples was roasted dog. It became apparent after the first few weeks that most of the dogs had vanished from the fair's neighborhood. Later the neighborhood of these tribal encampments acquired the nickname of "Dogtown," thereby causing much heartburn to local property owners. The fair closed on December 1, having been enjoyed by twenty million attendees who paid $32,000,000. On the bottom line, the City actually profited by $600,000. Tom Turpin threw a large party at the Rosebud on Christmas Day and offered a wonder of his own: an "electric Christmas tree," one of the first with colored lights seen in St.Louis. All of his guests received as gifts bottles of his house brand "Rosebud Whiskey." [23]

IV

As usual Joplin screened his reactions to the events of 1904 with restraint and reticence. Probably he was neither surprised nor much hurt by Director Ernst's overlooking him in the musical programming. But he and fellow ragtimers must have keenly felt this rejection of their music. They always anticipated white hostility and indifference; still, this one time, when promises were out there that the contributions of blacks in general and ragtime in particular would receive the deserved honors of some modest presentations, this one time they had dared to hope.

Joplin soldiered on, absorbed in music. A few years later, a journalist meeting him was impressed with his seriousness. This critic (from the *American Musician and Art Journal*) told his readers that Joplin always carried a music pad to record any ideas that came to him at any hour. Others observed that when pupils and others brought him their manuscripts, he could always come up with stylistic suggestions to smooth out or improve a piece. Berlin points out: "It was part of Joplin's musical nature to perceive alternatives and make changes. He did this even with his own music." [24] Music, the art to which he gave nearly all that was in him, sustained and compensated him. Beyond the lost, failed *Guest of Honor*, he published three more rags in 1903: *Something Doing* (with Scott Hayden), *Weeping Willow*, and *Palm Leaf Rag*, plus two songs ("Little Black Baby" and the "Maple Leaf Rag" song). He probably had ready for publication in 1904, or was working on, four more rags: *The Favorite*, *The Sycamore*, *The Chrysanthemum*, and *The Cascades*.

At the start of 1904, Scott Joplin entrained for a visit to the homefolks in Texarkana and Hot Springs, Arkansas. From there he went to Little Rock where he met Freddie Alexander, a girl of nineteen. She apparently inspired *The Chrysanthemum*, as the legend across the top of the title page states: "Respectfully Dedicated to Miss Freddie Alexander, Little Rock, Arkansas." He went from there in early April to Sedalia where he rented a room (from Solomon Dixon, 124 West Cooper), inserted a listing in the 1904 Sedalia directory, and took some gigs. He made it to the opening of the fair on April 30 where he may have introduced *The Cascades*. According to Arthur Marshall's daughter (who would have heard it from her father), *The Cascades* was much played during the fair. [25] In his advertising, John Stark wrote: "Hear it, and you can fairly feel the earth move under your feet. It is as high class as Chopin and is creating a great sensation among musicians." Although this is hype—Stark must have been hopeful for another Joplin hit—there is grace in it; we can imagine Joplin letting go a brief smile of pleasure upon seeing these fulsome words in print.

After playing at or near the fair, Joplin returned to Little Rock, where on June 14, in the home of the Alexanders, he and Freddie were married. At 36 he was almost twice her age. For the reader unfamiliar with the few known facts of the composer's life, this is biographer Edward Berlin's bombshell discovery. No previous biographer or ragtime historian had come upon this second marriage. All believed that Joplin had been maritally single in the years between Belle Jones Hayden and Lottie Stokes. Berlin has unearthed many things to enrich our understanding of Joplin, but Freddie, as will be seen in a later chapter (31), counts for much more than an amazing vital statistic.

From Little Rock, performing (and honeymooning) along the route, they made their way, not to St. Louis and the Fair, but to Sedalia. Scott Joplin chose Sedalia as the place to begin a life with his cherished bride, the community where he knew who his friends were, where he had experienced no terrorism against his race. The arrival was marred by illness, Freddie having to take to her bed with what seemed a bad cold. Joplin nursed her while performing at dances and concerts, which were praised warmly by the press of both races. Alas the professional success of those summer weeks was undermined by Freddie's decline. By August 12, pneumonia had been diagnosed, along with a "relapse." On September 8, her sister Lovie came in from Little Rock, and two days after that, the papers announced the death of "Mrs. Scott Joplin." Two months and it was all over, a false dawn. [26]

V

Afterward Joplin fades from view until early 1905, when he is again in St.Louis, living with the Turpins across from the Rosebud at 2221 Market Street. His next work, his finest waltz *Bethena* has a beautiful unidentified woman on the cover, who could well be Freddie. He also published in 1905 *Binks Waltz*, the song "Sarah Dear," the rag *Leola*, and the *Rose-bud March*, "dedicated to my friend Tom Turpin." His only St.Louis sightings are at a few concerts. He went to Chicago late that year, staying with Arthur Marshall, who now lived there, and moved into his own apartment after three weeks. He sought new publishers and seems to have been well received, but subsequently published only three or four pieces in that city. Joplin also saw Sam Patterson and Louis Chauvin, who, like many others, had discovered that Chicago welcomed new music and musicians. Now he collaborated with the inventive Chauvin. Chauvin seems to have been all music: poorly schooled and unable to score his inspirations, inspiration drove him at the keyboard. When he played, he composed, and awestruck listeners who realized they would never again experience that music, played in just that way, felt their pleasure diluted by a sense of loss. Chauvin gave himself to district life and his musical moments, making no effort to have his music scored and published. On one occasion, the King of Ragtime Writers sat down with the man called the "King of Ragtime Players" to create. *Heliotrope Bouquet* preserves all we have of Chauvin in its first two themes of delicate languor carefully notated by Joplin, who adds a lovely trio and final theme. Stark brought it out in 1907; with another verdict of inspired hype, he proclaimed "the audible poetry of motion." Chauvin died in Chicago the next year of multiple sclerosis. [27]

Joplin sought other publishers chiefly because Stark couldn't handle all of his output. Since the royalty contract of 1899, their relationship had had its problems. After its Sedalia premiere, John Stark had resisted publishing *The Ragtime Dance*, Joplin' first longer work. Success in the music business required a few hits. Most published songs and instrumentals sold indifferently, earning at best enough to break even on expenses. Only hits brought in significant profits. Unlike Tin Pan Alley publishers, who sold simplified sheet music for home consumption, Stark printed all the notes in the manuscripts of Joplin and others. Such integrity performed a great service for art, but the typical home pianist had to struggle more and practice longer to bring off a "Stark rag." Which produced modest or rather poor sales. Whenever Joplin brought him a new score, Stark found himself hoping for that second hit. In 1902 his musician daughter Nellie talked him into publishing the complete *Ragtime Dance*. Prospective customers were underwhelmed, confirming the "better judgment" of businessman Stark. In 1903 he considered adding *Guest of Honor* to his catalog, but length and perhaps narrative weaknesses (true for most operas) caused him to reject it. This refusal probably troubled their relationship.

Stark struggled with his own conflict: survival in business vs. his desire to publish quality music. He incorporated the business in 1904, and then, to widen distribution and compete more effectively with Tin Pan Alley, he relocated to New York in 1905, opening an office and store at 127 East 23rd Street. Son William remained in St.Louis to continue operations there, including the printing plant (210 Olive). By the next year, growth had pushed them into a larger printing plant at 1516 Locust. The Joplin connection, strained or not, continued with *Ragtime Dance* (single piece, 1906), *Antoinette March* (1906), The *Non-Pareil* (rag, 1907), and *Heliotrope Bouquet* (1907). One day in St.Louis in 1905, Joplin brought nineteen-year-old James Sylvester Scott to Stark's office. Scott had traveled from Carthage in southwest Missouri to meet Joplin. After asking directions at the Rosebud (so the story goes), Scott found him at home and demonstrated his music. Impressed, Joplin took the youth over to meet Stark. Stark also appreciated Scott, bought the rag *Frog Legs*, and published it a year later (1906). This was Stark & Son's next decent seller, never quite a hit, but steady in sales for many years. Scott became a major ragtime composer, supplying Stark with 27 more works through 1922, the second of the ragtime trinity to be published by Stark.

As for Joplin, he worked in both Chicago and St.Louis, still at 2221 Market in 1907. Turpin closed down the Rosebud in the summer of 1906, perhaps because other Turpin ventures required his time. Following the climactic fair, much ragtime talent had been drifting to Chicago, including Joplin himself, where the money was greater and audiences were larger and more friendly to people of color. Joe Jordan became music director of Chicago's New Pekin Theatre, a showplace for black talent and black audiences (a new trend nationwide). He composed, arranged, and conducted there for three years before going on to greater success in New York. In St.Louis the Turpin brothers, starting with a tent show, would create another such theatre, the Booker T. Washington Airdome. Here Tom composed and arranged much of the music, aided from 1908 by the skilled Artie Matthews from Springfield, Illinois (whose ragtime Stark would also publish). They erected the permanent theatre in 1913. Joplin (in early 1907) went back to Texarkana for a last visit and was surprised by celebrity treatment. He played for a dance, and people crowded into a music store one day to listen to his music. People there now recognized him as a national figure in music. That summer he made his last Chicago visit to see Arthur Marshall, and then boarded the train for New York. He never saw the Midwest again, and he had opera on his mind. [28]

Notes: Chapter 19

1. Edward A. Berlin, *King of Ragtime: Scott Joplin and His Era*, 86.
2. James Weldon Johnson, *The Autobiography of an Ex-Colored Man*, 100-101.
3. Thomas Bender, "Urbanization," in *The Readers Companion to American History*, 1102.
4. Paul C. Nagel, *Missouri: A Bicentennial History*, 63-70; Lincoln Steffens, *The Autobiography of Lincoln Steffens*, 368-373.
5. *The National Standard Atlas of the World, 1900*, 100-101.
6. Lorenzo J. Greene, Gary R. Kremer, and Antonio F. Holland, *Missouri's Black Heritage*, 107-117.
7. Susan Curtis, *Dancing to a Black Man's Tune: A Life of Scott Joplin*, 130.
8. Berlin, *King*, 75-78.
9. *Ibid.*, 58.
10. Quoted in *Ibid.*, 94-96.
11. Quoted in *Ibid.*, 102; see also 75, 96-97, 102-103.
12. *Ibid.*, 106.
13. Quoted in *Ibid.*, 120-122.
14. *Ibid.*, 115-132.
15. David A. Jasen and Trebor Jay Tichenor, *Rags and Ragtime: A Musical History*, 47.
16. *Ibid.*, 21-76; also Terry Waldo, *This Is Ragtime*, 35-45.
17. Gene Jones, "The Grandee of Chestnut Valley: Tom Turpin and His Domain," 5-6.
18. Rudi Blesh and Harriet Janis, *They All Played Ragtime*, 110-112; Jones, 2-20; Jasen and Tichenor, 28-29; Greene, et al, 112, for political conditions.
19. Blesh and Janis, 112.
20. Berlin, *King*, 133; Jones, 13-14.
21. Quoted in Curtis, 137.
22. *Ibid.*, 136-141; Berlin, *King*, 134.
23. Jones, 14-15.
24. Berlin, *King*, 81, 161.
25. *Ibid.*, 136.
26. *Ibid.*, 133-144.
27. Jasen and Tichenor, 101-103; Blesh and Janis, 56-62.
28. Berlin, *King*, 145-162; Curtis, 143-144, Blesh and Janis, 79-80; Jones, 17-19.

20. Progressives (II): The Unexpected Miracle

Americans nearing the 19 C's end liked to call their time the "Age of Miracles." For decades a stream of inventions had come along to raise the quality of material life: steamship, railroad, photography, telegraphy, textile machines, sewing machines, agricultural machines, steel, rubber, petroleum, and electricity. This material progression reenforced the hopes for social progression that came in with the new century. In this milieu of rising expectations appeared an unexpected miracle reflective of the mood: flight. But at first nobody grasped it. People understood balloons and the new airships based upon the lighter-than-air principle, but even these were fraught with failure and fatalities. There were also stories about heavier-than-air craft which conveyed impressions of cranks and monomaniacs. But if birds could do it, people could not, and oddballs who jumped off cliffs wearing outsize wings simply proved the point. Flight was one of the human limits; either we couldn't or we weren't meant to.

On December 17, 1903, Wilbur and Orville Wright flew in a powered aircraft for the first time and replicated this experiment continuously during the next two years. Always ready to pounce on the next day's scoop, the press reported what the brothers Wright were up to, but the stories failed to register in the collective imagination for the first two years. This satisfied the two Wrights who preferred to work in privacy without the complications spawned by notoriety. They were very focused, an inward pair with no need for the attention of outsiders—until the time came to spread the gospel of aviation.

The cliché tells it that a couple of "bicycle mechanics" invented the first airplane that stayed up. Where Edison has been dubbed a "wizard" and Henry Ford praised as a genius of the mechanical, the Wrights get much less respect, having been characterized as lowly mechanics, fixers of bicycles. We get the implication that any handyman with the time to throw paper airplanes could eventually build and fly one large enough to carry people. They were only high-school educated, at best gifted amateurs. But only results count. Samuel Langley (1834-1906), a highly respected scientist and head of the Smithsonian Institution, spent a government appropriation of $75,000 on an aircraft that crashed ignominiously into the Potomac River just before the Wrights flew theirs successfully (it cost only $1000). Langley had years of aeronautical experiments and published results behind him. Octave Chanute (1832-1910), a successful construction engineer (bridges, the Chicago Stockyards) from Chicago, who became a friend and supporter of the Wrights, likewise failed to produce a successful aircraft.

It was the uneminent Wrights who first became airborne. It wasn't a lucky design but a planned effort, trial and error, results noted, records kept. They did have some superior advantages. They were mentally gifted; according to their biographer Fred Howard, they were "among the blessed few who combine mechanical ability with intelligence in about equal amounts." [1] Plus there were two of them. Thus the synergies, the multiplier effects needed to solve the complex aerodynamic problems of flight. They followed a rigorously rational process: 1) They read the literature on flight to find out what was and wasn't known. 2) They brainstormed, discussing what they knew, observing flight in nature, speculating on possibilities, concluding with hypotheses. 3) They experimented, for three years with unpowered flight, gliders. They understood that it would be foolish to mount a motor on an aircraft of unproven flying capacity, a point Langley seems to have ignored. 4) With a viable airframe, they progressed into powered flight experiments.

Wilbur Wright (1867-1912) and Orville Wright (1871-1948) may have achieved their potential in part because of the family that produced them. Their father, Bishop Milton Wright of the Church of the United Brethren in Christ, always encouraged them to develop their potential. Although a deeply religious pastor and denominational leader, he was not a bigot or a fanatic. Family came first, without patriarchal tyranny, with respect for individuality, kindness, discipline when necessary, encouragement to read in the home library. They observed the Sabbath, but reading and letter writing were encouraged, customs never given up by the brothers. Later, without conflict, Bishop Wright accepted the brothers' decisions not to join the church. He also accepted their decisions not to attend college, a thing he much desired. Wilbur lost those years caring for his invalid mother until her death in 1889. The two older brothers (Reuchlin and Lorin) had gone to work and married, and Orville and sister Katharine the youngest were in school. Bishop Wright had to travel in support of his congregations, which left Wilbur to care for his mother. He used his spare moments to do the reading that completed his education. The Wrights took care of themselves and always seemed happiest with one another.

The brothers entered the world of work in 1889 as job printers and editors of short-lived local newspapers, but the bicycle soon captured their interest. The earlier high wheelers went out in 1890 and were replaced by the modern "safety bicycle," so called because its two equal wheels were lower, resulting in a shorter fall in an accident. They opened their first repair and sales shop in 1892. By 1896 following several relocations, they had branched out into manufacturing, something not too difficult at the time. In that age of the small entrepreneur, about 200 manufacturers supplied parts to more than 1000 fabricators of bicycles. The Wright Cycle Company offered two models, the "Wright Special" and the "Van Cleve" (after an ancestor who founded Dayton). This required ordering parts, assembling them, and then painting and enameling the distinctive finished product. They became as expert at these last functions as they were at repairing. Bicycling had become a popular craze, and the business flourished modestly. The profits accumulating in their joint account may have suggested an attempt in a new direction.

With their newly achieved success, Wilbur and Orville could have married, bought their first homes, and started families. But they did none of these things and never seemed to have rued their absence. We only know that shared interests combined with an unusual closeness. Wilbur was taciturn and shy with outsiders. His critical mind perceived the humor in situations. He was paternal with a tender streak. Orville, natty in dress where Wilbur was indifferent, was social and outgoing. Wilbur led but Orville expressed his own views, and their dialog was continuous. In 1896 when the challenge phase of developing a small business had given way to routine work, they sought new goals. With a secure home that included father Milton Wright (often away on church business), and sister Katharine (now an Oberlin graduate and a high school teacher of classics), and an adequate income, these brothers of 29 and 25 years began to look into flight. News stories of aerial failures aroused interest, which stimulated intellectual curiosity. They sent away for and looked up in the local library available literature on the subject. They found no interest in lighter-than-air flight—how it worked was clear enough. In the heavier-than-air field, most experiments had been with gliders or unpowered flight. Only Samuel Langley in 1896 had flown propeller-driven aircraft. These were thirty-pound miniature airplanes and had been driven by small steam engines. There were two flights, one rising 80 or 90 feet and another that had lasted 90 seconds before their small boilers ran out of steam. None of this information pointed toward a practical future.

The Wright's first conclusion from these early attempts was that nothing had yet been done to achieve adequate control. An aircraft could move in three ways, on three axes: up and down, side to side, and left and right. In performing these movements, the craft had to maintain equilibrium. Equilibrium required that the center of gravity coincide with the center of pressure. The brothers began with the understanding that they had to solve the problem of control based upon equilibrium. This meant that they had to start with gliders. To mount an engine on a craft without control would only repeat the crashes that had ended all previous experiments. They commenced during the summer of 1899 by constructing a small glider with a five-foot wingspan, a biplane, to be flown as a kite. With a tail moved by cords, the glider-kite pointed itself up or down. Turning was achieved by the invention of what they called "wingwarping." By twisting the leading surfaces of the upper wing—using a separate set of cords—forcing one wing surface up and the other down, the plane would turn. By altering part of the surface of the wing—cut-out parts of wings that could be moved separately, ailerons, would later replace this warping of surfaces—Wilbur and Orville had solved a major part of the control problem.

From unmanned kite they progressed to manned glider in 1900. An inquiry to the U.S. Weather Bureau indicated that winds of steadiness and strength enough to support a glider—at least 16 or 17 miles per hour—blew around Kitty Hawk on the upper end of North Carolina's barrier islands known as the Outer Banks. Since the bicycle business slacked off in autumn, they decided to experiment then. Getting there proved to be an expedition. The railroad ended at Elizabeth City on the mainland, and no scheduled shipping reached the Outer Banks. Kitty Hawk was an isolated fishing village. Today sturdy bridges carry the highways over the vast inner bays and sounds that separate the barrier islands from the mainland. Then there were only the occasional coastal ships and the three-times-a-week mail boat. Besides prefabricated glider parts, Wilbur and Orville had to crate and ship all of their needs: scientific instruments, tools, construction materials, tents, bedding, cooking utensils, stove (to heat as well as cook), dried and canned foods, clothing, and other personal effects. They did this for the next three years and soon found it necessary, for both health and comfort, to replace tents with permanent buildings (which required annual repairs of weather damage).

They commenced with one brother lying on the lower wing practicing with the controls while the other flew the contraption as a kite in stiff winds of 25 to 30 miles per hour. Failures and crashes followed over three years, but for the first time, a man was carried prone through the air on wide, white wings. In 1890 Octave Chanute had written in *McClure's Magazine* that the achievement of flight would require the skills of a mathematician, an inventor, a mechanical engineer, a mechanic, and an investing capitalist. [2] Wilbur and Orville possessed exactly these capabilities: the mathematics to calculate stresses and strains on materials, practical mechanical ability combined with a tactile feel for materials, both imagination and inventiveness, and a thriving small business to absorb costs. Plus the literacy to publish their results, in British and German aeronautical journals during the winter of 1900-01. In September 1900 Wilbur spoke to the Western society of Engineers in Chicago, and the printed version, *Some Aeronautical Experiments* was widely reprinted to become what Fred Howard has called "the Book of Genesis of the twentieth-century Bible of Aeronautics." [3]

Later versions of the document describe wind tunnel experiments carried out in Dayton following that year's flights on the Outer Banks. These were undertaken after the Chicago speech in a gaslit workroom behind the bicycle shop. The Brothers didn't invent the wind tunnel, but theirs was the first to yield results on the size and angle of wings for an airplane that flew successfully. Their little six-foot-long by sixteen-inch-square tunnel in which they observed—and ingeniously measured—the flow of air around miniature wings (less than six inches long) accurately indicated the lifting properties and air resistance. All of the materials and tools used were present in the bicycle shop on West Third Street in Dayton. They learned what shapes, curvatures, and angles of wings would fly. The next summer of 1902, they applied this new knowledge in practice flights, which then led them to their final discovery of the system for controlling an aircraft: the integration and combining of rudder control with wing control. In a turn, an airplane "banks," the outside wing goes up while the inside wing points downward. Then the plane comes up level again when steered straight-forward. Everyone who has ever flown as a passenger knows how the craft slants on a turn. If it didn't, and tried to turn on the flat, it would "stall," i.e., go out of control. The Wright system of control, wings-tail-rudder, remains the only known flight system.

Work on a powered airplane, called "The Flyer," began in February 1903. The added weight of an engine required a sturdier airplane, trussed with multi-strand wire (instead of bicycle spoke wire) and tightly fitted upright braces securing the wings. The wingspan was 40 feet, 4 inches. No manufacturer could supply a motor lighter than 180 pounds, so they designed and built their own, the aluminum crankcase cast by a local foundry, and the other parts fabricated and machined by Charlie Taylor, the expert machinist who carried on the bicycle shop during the Wrights' absences. Considerable research went into propellers. The "experts" of that day believed that an aircraft's propulsion would be similar to a ship's. The Wright's experiments proved such theories wrong, forcing them to develop their own theory.

In September they shipped 650 pounds of the parts of the first *Flyer*, along with all the other necessities, including scientific instruments, tools, materials, food, and personal items. Intermittent storms and assembly problems delayed the first powered flight until December 14, 1903, after the onset of winter. This first effort went down after only 100 feet because of pilot errors, but the system had worked! Three days later, repairs completed, with Orville at the controls—Wilbur had drawn the straw for the first attempt—the *Flyer* took off on a wooden rail down a sandhill. (The Wrights used three large sandhills known as "Kill Devil Hills" to launch their various aircraft.) This time, it flew 120 feet in 12 seconds. The second flight that day covered 175 feet, the third went 200 feet, and the fourth managed that day's record of 852 feet in 59 seconds. The season ended abruptly when, on rolling the *Flyer* back to its shed, a powerful gust of wind lifted the plane from the hands of the Wrights and the group of fishermen helping, causing it to come down in a smash-up. They just made it home for Christmas, filled with success and greeted by a few newstories of their accomplishment.

The next two years, the brothers developed new models of the *Flyer* each year. They tested and flew their planes in the cow pasture of a Dayton banker, "Huffman Prairie," just outside of the city along an interurban trolley line. Besides technical improvements, they were learning to fly, a skill up to then possessed by no one, something virtually unknown because never done before. It took until November 1904 for them to accomplish flights of five minutes, circling the field four times. To avoid notoriety, they stayed down when trolleys were passing. By September 1905 the *Flyer* was staying up for 18 minutes; a month later came a 25 minute flight, followed by the record for 1905, 24 1/5 miles in 38 minutes at an average speed of 38 mph. By then the newspapers had belatedly caught on (alerted by astounded passengers on the interurban), and the Wright Brothers found themselves big news. From then they became major figures, flying in France and Germany as well as elsewhere in the U.S. After fame came corporate status as manufacturers and ultimately wealth, plus the inevitable court battles over infringements of their patents.

Wilbur died of typhoid fever in 1912, and Orville lasted until 1948, full of honors. The Wrights undoubtedly imbibed some of the spirit of that progressive time, but they were too inward, too focused to have been much influenced by external attitudes. What boggles the mind is that two young American men in a provincial Midwestern city, lacking higher education, wealth, and institutional support, decided to tackle a problem in physics that no one had ever come close to solving. To that day there had been no common expectation that human beings would ever take flight in a heavier-than-air machine; all efforts had utterly failed, from the myth of Icarus to the expensive and ridiculous failure of Samuel Langley in 1903—at the end of which the Wrights succeeded. For sure, they stood on no shoulders of giants: their experiments continually revealed that nearly all of the experimental data compiled by predecessors was faulty. Quite simply, they were the giants, superior scientists in the tradition that began with Bacon and Descartes. Rationally and patiently, they untangled and classified the confusions and mysteries of aerodynamics. [4]

Notes: Chapter 20

1. Fred Howard, *Wilbur and Orville: A Biography of the Wright Brothers*, 11.
2. *Ibid.*, 54.
3. *Ibid.*, 71.
4. The chief source for this chapter is Howard's superb account.

21. Boley or Self-Segregation

Say, have you heard the story
Of a little colored town
Way over in the nation
On such lovely sloping ground?

With as pretty little houses
As you ever chanced to meet
With nothing but colored folks
A-standing in the streets.

Oh, tis a pretty country
And the Negroes own it, too,
With not a single white man here
To tell us what to do—
       In Boley;

And I will tell that fellow
Whoever he may be
If you don't think we are colored
Just come here and see

Get on the Fort Smith and Western
The train will bring you here.
Take any of the coaches
You have no cause to fear.

Here a Negro makes your dresses
And a Negro makes your pants
And hands your mail out
If you'll give him half a chance—
       In Boley.

          Uncle Will Jesse [1]

  After the Civil War the freedpeople, as newly constituted citizens, entered the mobile national life. Unlike European immigrants, they did not have to be assimilated; they came pre-Americanized. They knew only their native land. Now they possessed the freedom to live where they chose, but this "freedom" became a snare and a dilemma. Since unskilled labor was all they had to sell, remaining where they were threw them into the snare of servitude, sharecropping or labor for too little pay. To go elsewhere put them into the dilemma of uncertainty. Could a black family with only minimal farming skills survive as strangers among whites unlikely to grant either recognition or credit? Young single men could herd cattle out west, enlist in the army, or find a niche performing in minstrelsy or drinking places. But to take a family away from its home to search for a better life was to put their very lives at risk. No surprise then that relatively few chose to venture out of the snare they called home. Desperation seldom overcame fear of the unknown.

As Reconstruction ended in the 1870's, African Americans realized that the old ruling class of ex-Confederates had regained control of government and the economy. Poverty, servitude, the terrorism of nightriders, and threats of eviction would keep them "in their place," seemingly forever. The prospect of such a desolate future made them vulnerable to promoters of western lands. If promises of cheap land, fertile soil, prosperity, and personal freedom had lured the white folks, so did they rouse aspirations in the poorer race. Most apparently just wanted a better life in a new place, but into the despairing minds of certain others, came another idea: separation. If whites don't want us, perhaps we can find us a place somewhere off by itself where we can live apart. With so much empty land, it began to seem possible that if a large enough number of blacks homesteaded in one place, that they would become the majority there. A majority meant political control, which would bring freedom from white hostility and rejection. On a landscape dotted with black faces, no cloud shadows of terrorism would darken the vista.

From the late 1870's to about 1915, a minority of African Americans looked to the west for deliverance. About 60 independent black communities were founded. [2] For nearly all, evidence is sketchy, chiefly the names of post offices and their dates of existence. These towns were scattered across the map from coast to coast with the greatest concentration in the emerging state of Oklahoma. (See Almanac section, end of chapter) Before Oklahoma opened up, at church gatherings and wherever work grouped them, people talked up the "promised land of Kansas." In March 1879, a first group bolted up the Mississippi to St.Louis, the staging point for the journey west. The steamboat fare from Vicksburg, Mississippi, cost $3 to $4; most of this first wave of about 6000 souls came ashore broke at the Gateway City. When whites refused aid, local blacks organized a Committee of 25 to carry out the relief effort, raising the money in their churches. With the $3000 worth of goods and services collected, most of these first migrants made it to Kansas. These western Kansas settlers of the late 1870's and early 1880's became known as the "Exodusters." [3]

Promoters of these towns marketed them with an ideology of self-help, moral uplift, race pride, political self-determination, and a promise of eventual integration into the American mainstream. The immediate goal was a total community: a service center plus surrounding farms. Main street merchants would retail to local farmers. Unfortunately this prospectus had gone out of date. Rural towns were becoming obsolete, replaced by new cities, large and small, as the centers of economic life and culture. Goods, now massproduced in factories—not by local craftsmen—reached consumers by rails via city distribution centers. For better selection and prices, people boarded the train for the closest city. It required capital to transform a town into a city, and the struggling farmers and fledgling merchants of the new black towns came up short on both capital and credit.

The curious career of Edward Preston McCabe (1850-1920) extends across the black town movement. McCabe, a northern black out of New York State and New England, deserves more than a footnote. A vision of relocating his race in the developing lands of the West drove him—and he intended to lead them. His approach to leadership was political rather than pastoral. He trained himself, first as a lawyer's clerk in New York City, followed by another clerkship in the Cook County Treasurer's Office in Chicago. Someone described him as having "Indian color with straight black hair,…dressy and a good talker." [4] He had also worked as timekeeper for Potter Palmer, the Chicago hotel and restaurant man. In his portrait photograph, eager, friendly eyes gaze over a full mustache. He resembles all of the go-getters, adventurers, and promoters who sought to build something in the West that might also be to their benefit.

In 1878 he followed the Kansas Exodusters to Graham County in the northwestern part of the state where Nicodemus, a black town, was sprouting. Rails had yet to reach Graham County, which meant a slow ride in a cumbersome wagon across the treeless grasslands for the final two days of the journey. A companion recalled later that McCabe, a tenderfoot from the big city, couldn't eat because he was nauseated, either by the smell or by the thought of food cooked over dried cow chips. [5] Nicodemus started out very hard scrabble. The first arrivals had been lured by promotional promises of fertile soil and abundant game. By now the game witnessed by previous travelers had vanished, and even the once prolific buffalo had disappeared into a few small fugitive herds. The never-plowed soil was fertile enough, but to get at it required the laborious turning of the sod that overlay it. Sod also had to be cut and laid to make the walls and roofs of the first houses. McCabe likewise had to put up a "soddy," which he shared with Abram Hall, a fellow adventurer who was a journalist. Neither one chose to subdue the land; instead they found places on the government payroll as surveyors and locators of public lands. More typical was R.B. Scruggs, who survived by working odd jobs in towns behind the line of settlement, harvesting enough cash to feed his family while he also managed to get his new farm up and running. Unlike very many, Scruggs not only held on to his land but eventually owned 720 acres. In his recollection, "no matter how bad it got…we was just so proud of the land." [6]

McCabe surfaces next intriguing to persuade the Governor to designate Nicodemus as the temporary seat of Graham County. Here he hit a wall of prejudice. White towns and settlements, through the medium of editorials in local weeklies, expressed very negative views about any civic aspirations of their African-American neighbors. The Baptist Home Mission Board for northwestern Kansas warned the Governor against appointing any blacks. The canny McCabe backed off on Nicodemus but found a trade-off. Due west and centrally located, Hill City, founded and developed by W.R. Hill, showed the most promise. McCabe threw his support to Hill City, and, in return, received the Governor's appointment as county clerk in 1880. Two years later, he secured the nomination of his Republican Party for state auditor. He rode into office along with the rest of the Republican ticket in the election of 1882. He moved to Topeka with wife Sarah and daughter Edwina; he won reelection to a second term in 1884. [7]

While McCabe carried on his political career in Topeka, Nicodemus struggled to gain the prosperity that never came. Lacking capital, merchants' stocks were limited; they couldn't extend much credit, and they wanted to be paid in cash and not in kind, as had often been the case in rural transactions. After hopes of the courthouse died, Nicodemus sought a railroad station. Voters hopefully offered $16,000 in bonds to the Missouri Pacific, anticipating that it would extend its line west from Stockton, a town just to the east. Also the Union Pacific was laying track up from the southeast toward Hill City, the county seat, and Nicodemus seemed to lie along the likely route. Perhaps both railroads would come in. Railroads brought non-farming jobs, tax money, a means of getting crops to market, and a population increase. During the summer of 1887, it felt like a boom, but hopes vanished during the winter. The Missouri Pacific did not move west of Stockton—it never did—and the Union Pacific bypassed Nicodemus, going through Bogue six miles south. By the end of 1888, people had moved away, to Bogue, Stockton, Hill City, and elsewhere, taking with them frame houses and stores, leaving behind an African-American commonwealth that failed. [8]

Time also ran out for State Auditor E.P. McCabe down in the capital city of Topeka. Some editors of rural weeklies had attacked McCabe, saying black men couldn't be trusted and that having one as auditor put him where he might just go into the treasury and help himself to the state's money. This was vicious and preposterous, but it reinforced the negative feelings present in most whites. The party resolved this minor embarrassment of dumping a faithful member by declaring a "no third term" precedent and thus refusing renomination in 1886. Frustrated at being rejected because of his race, McCabe's analysis concluded that he and his people could prevail only in a black commonwealth. As he pondered another western location, the U..S. opened to settlement certain lands in the sparsely populated Oklahoma and Indian Territories in 1889. He determined to promote the Oklahoma lands, or some segment thereof, as a haven for African Americans. His visionary idea was both radical and revolutionary: a black state. We look back on this with some amazement, wondering if McCabe allowed his frustrations and desires to override his politician's grasp of reality. Was he a fool, or did he, along with many others, simply believe that the West offered a limitless potential? Lining up with the rest of the "Boomers," he crossed the border in the fabled land rush of March 22, 1889, and reached Guthrie, the first tent city, from where he surveyed possibilities. After this, he sought out Republican connections for support in getting the appointment of territorial governor! Perhaps McCabe had a friend in a high enough place in his party who could secure an audience for so singular a proposal. But it seems unlikely that it ever reached frosty and aloof President Benjamin Harrison who would probably have snorted it off his desk. [9]

Next McCabe channeled his energies into founding and promoting a new town in Oklahoma Territory: Langston, named for a Howard University professor who had served in Congress. Langston, ten miles from Guthrie, stood on a hill in Logan County near the Cimarron River, about 40 miles northeast of Oklahoma City. From his Guthrie real estate office, McCabe founded the *Langston City Herald* in 1890. Town lots were priced at from $10 to $50, and the *Herald*, like most blacktown papers, as much an advertising brochure as a newspaper, was widely circulated by sales agents pushing land contracts. A contract sold by the McCabe Townsite Company included a railroad ticket to Guthrie and a choice of lots upon arrival. Early comers found that the wooden shacks and tents did not resemble the masonry buildings and paved streets pictured in the *Herald*. But these arrivals were chiefly sharecroppers out of Texas, Arkansas, and other southern states who came on a one-way ticket with few possessions and little cash. After a few hours of disenchantment, these families had to put up some shelter, plant some vegetables, and prepare soil for a cotton crop. Most found consolation in realizing that a few years of installments would transform them from sharecroppers into landowners.

By 1892 seven Negro towns dotted the map of the Indian and Oklahoma Territories. As packed daycoaches unloaded families at Guthrie and other rail points, the dream of a black state glowed fitfully for a few years. McCabe and his fellow town promoters intended to bring about a black majority by the time a statehood bill reached Congress in Washington. McCabe gave it his all, selling land, editorializing about the future, and organizing politically. He started local Republican clubs, attended large meetings as a delegate, took charge of the Republicans of Guthrie, and served as treasurer of Logan County. Then in 1897 the Governor named him assistant territorial auditor, and the territorial legislature created the Colored Agricultural and Normal University and put it in Langston (since 1941, Langston University). [10]

The best known and most successful of Oklahoma's African-American towns, Boley, was founded seven years later in 1904. It was situated in Okfuskee County, about 60 miles east of Oklahoma City. Like many western towns, it was a product of railroad expansion. As it laid tracks across Indian Territory toward Guthrie in Oklahoma Territory, the Fort Smith and Western Railroad fostered new towns. When Boley's promoters sought its support, the railroad laid a short spur from its line to the townsite and erected a small depot. The sign on the depot honored W.H. Boley, an official of the F.S. and W. and a town promoter. Because of this railroad patronage, town lots and farms sold very well. The town bankers, its chief developers, sent out agents with attractive circulars and special booster editions of the *Boley Progress*. Unimproved land sold for $10 to $15 per acre, and, if that was too much, it could be rented for twenty-five to thirty cents an acre. The Fort Smith and Western offered cheap fares if the destination happened to be Boley. By 1907 about 2000 souls resided in Boley and on the farms lying around it. After three years, there was a bank of brick, a second bank, a drugstore, several other stores, a hotel, restaurants, a cotton gin, a lumberyard, a brickyard, an ice plant, and even a telephone system, plus seven or eight religious denominations, five fraternal lodges, and an elementary school enrolling 150 pupils. [11]

However, as was the case earlier in Kansas, the black towns of Oklahoma failed; for three reasons:

> Changing economic conditions
> Poverty
> White resentment

The inhabitants of black towns expected to flourish in a simple give-and-take economic process: local transactions between merchants and consumers. Townspeople and rural neighbors would come to Main Street for all their needs. But it turned out that people now liked to "shop around." Boleyites could hop a train and spend their money in Paden, Okemah, or Weleetka with white merchants who usually offered a better selection and lower prices. White merchants could also extend more credit over a longer period. The blacktown merchant dealt with his back to the economic wall: too few sales and never enough in the cash box to pay suppliers for the variety and amount of inventory needed to keep local shoppers at home. Railroads and the modernization of industries forced rural towns into the struggle for survival of the economically fittest. Besides nearby towns, distant cities went after the consumer's dollars through "mail order." People pored over the "wish books" or catalogs from Sears Roebuck and Montgomery Ward. They were impressed by the attractive pictures, the reputation for quality, and the mass-market prices. In November 1905, O.H. Bradley, Editor of the *Boley Progress* published "LOCAL MERCHANT VS. U.S. Mail Order Houses." He perceived a terrible threat to small-town prosperity. He blamed women because they craved the thrill of getting a package in the mail. He compared this to getting married through correspondence. He pointed out that mail order houses "never tell you to send them any farm products that you may have, all they want is your cash, and when you send them a dollar you may as well kiss it good-by forever." [12]

Which points to the central problem of poverty. Too little currency flowed through the black towns. For sugar, flour, coffee, thread, sewing needles, or yard goods, customers offered eggs, butter, garden produce, chickens, and other livestock. The extent of this threw the economy back into the stage of barter, the primitive economics of exchanging goods for goods. Transactions were figured in dollars and cents, but these were coins of account rather than actual money. And with suppliers demanding money and limiting credit, the blacktown merchant could not afford too many transactions in commodities or carry large unpaid accounts over long periods. This sent most Boleyites to the white towns where merchants would offer more credit. When, near year's end, farmers received their annual infusions of cash from the sales of crops, it went into the cash drawers of merchants in Okemah, Paden, and Weleetka who had carried them. At this point there might be a little cash remaining to spend, on a better plow, a stove, a coffee mill, a piece of furniture, or something ready-made in clothing. For this, they tiptoed past the stores on Main Street to the Post Office to send off orders to Sears or Montgomery Ward. People felt that they couldn't find what they wanted on the dusty, half-empty shelves of local stores with their too few, shopworn items. It never seemed very long before the doors of blacktown emporiums closed. Then new hopefuls replaced them, taking ads in the weekly paper promising "new stock" and a better selection. It was a repeating cycle. [13]

Any blow severely injured the fragile economies of these towns. Boley boasted of a second bank by 1910, but an embezzlement abruptly closed it. Few settlers brought any capital, most being sharecroppers fleeing economic bondage. Their cycles began with purchases of town lots and farmland, a little down, the balance on credit. They heard talks about how diversified farming could help them to survive, but they stuck with the cotton culture they knew. In that time, no departments of agriculture, state or national, sent out demonstration agents to teach more productive techniques of farming. People started out proud of their land, believing that ownership would be the key to improving their lives. Within a year or two, they found themselves strapped, needing credit, which ended hopes of economic independence. In 1905 the *Boley Progress* had vainly promised that "…when you raise a crop the whole of it is yours to dispose of as you see fit," but few came with enough capital to remain debt-free. Most soon turned to white capitalists to furnish them with seed, farm implements, and other credit items to finance their operations— their very lives—until the next harvest. They found themselves sliding backward into the deep trough of working for others and perpetual debt, eventually losing their interest in the land by defaulting on payments. [14]

From the beginning, McCabe had openly touted his scheme of an African-American Oklahoma. This may have had some propaganda value in encouraging settlement, but it also caused white backlash. Newspaper stories quoted whites predicting violence and assassination if President Harrison appointed McCabe governor. [15] McCabe seriously pushed his scheme for a few years, but he soon pulled out of Langston and returned to his political base in Guthrie. The flow of black settlers, steady though it was, never rose to flood stage. About 28 black settlements ultimately dotted the map of Oklahoma (see Almanac at end of chapter), but few achieved the size of Boley or Langston (1000 plus), and the black population of the territories and subsequent state never exceeded ten percent:

African Americans	%age of Total	Total
1890 - 21,609	0.089	241,704
1900 - 55,684	0.070	797,076
1910 - 137,612	0.097	1,414,177*

*Taken 1907 at time of statehood. [16]

The Oklahoma and Indian territories lay in southern latitudes, drawing most settlers, black and white, from the nearest states. Their racial attitudes accompanied them. Blacktown blacks, feeling secure within their municipal boundaries, politically active for the first time, seem to have lost touch with southern realities. They were also beguiled into a sense of security because the territorial administrative and legal systems were federally supervised and controlled. Statehood would abruptly end this protective jurisdiction, but few looked ahead to the dire crossing of this bridge to white supremacy. Blacks in biracial towns never developed any illusions about civil rights. As rapid growth pushed these former Indian lands toward statehood, blacks in white-run towns feared the repressive outcomes of statehood when Federal officials would depart and Oklahomans elect their own. These fears were voiced in a memorial to President Theodore Roosevelt from the Western Negro Press Association in 1905 opposing statehood unless there was a guarantee of no Jim Crow laws. [17]

In rapidly growing, newly founded Boley, a false sense of security encouraged hopes of full political rights. The *Boley Progress* envisioned Okfuskee County as predominantly black (April 6, 1905). After enthusiastically electing their first municipal officials a year later (April 1906), Boleyites participated in the first step toward statehood, the election of delegates to a constitutional convention. Before this, to neutralize—and thus disfranchise—Boley, white leaders had gerrymandered Boley into a district containing the larger white towns of Okemah, Henryetta, and

Weleetka. They couldn't prevent the black vote, and then, ironically, the gerrymander tactic misfired. What happened was that the white vote was split between Republican and Democrat, rendering the Boley vote decisive. Boley's Republican majority tipped the victory to the Republican delegates, thus enraging the southern Democrats, who had carefully planned the opposite result. In January 1907, racial violence broke out in Okemah when two homes were dynamited. At a county convention of delegates in August, most white Republican delegates refused to sit with black colleagues and walked out. This left a rump of 24 whites and 58 blacks, which nominated two blacks for county commissioner, which elicited the following response from the *Weleetka American*:

STOP! LOOK! LISTEN! TO A RAILROAD DANGER SIGNAL! THE COUNTY IS IN DANGER OF NEGRO DOMINATION—WHITE VOTERS CRUSH THE INSO LENCE OF THE NEGRO! PROTECT YOUR HOMES WITH YOUR BALLOT [18]

Later this paper headlined that the Republican candidate for county judge (because he had stayed at the hotel in Boley) "SLEEPS WITH NIGGERS." [19] In September the county election board, controlled by Democrats, refused to certify the black and white slate of Republican candidates. After which, in spite of this, the slate appeared on the ballot—and won! Then this county election board threw out the results from Negro precincts, declaring the Democrats victorious. This was final and marked the end of African-American participation in Oklahoma politics. Two months later, the newly admitted state experienced its first lynching at Henryetta. [20]

On February 15, 1908, Oklahoma's Jim Crow law took effect. Also on that day, Edward P. McCabe filed suit in the U.S. Circuit Court in Guthrie for an injunction to stop it, pending a trial to determine constitutionality. The measure, in Oklahoma as elsewhere, mandated segregated railroad coaches. This and all other subsequent legal challenges failed. As for McCabe, the vision of a black state had been lost years before. Then his political career vanished—a second time—with statehood in 1907. Worse, both of his daughters died, the older in 1907 and the younger in 1908. He felt especially bitter toward the Republican Party which failed to stand by him after decades of his faithful service. With his wife he set off for British Columbia to make a new start. Apparently this move never came to much because he died a pauper in Chicago in 1920. His wife buried him in Topeka. [21]

The black towns, segregated from choice, retained their municipal autonomy, but this provided no resources for the economic struggle. In 1913 the boll weevil reached the cotton fields of Oklahoma, and most of these communities died in the ensuing cotton depression. They decayed into rural ghettoes. Their segregated schools never received a fair share of public funds. McCabe's Langston survived because of the meagre $18,000 annual appropriation for the Colored Agricultural and Normal University. The railroad helped keep Boley alive. These towns had begun as the white towns did, with a platted area, lot sales, businesses established, homes and churches built, schools opened, plus farmers settled in the surrounding lands. They democratically elected officials to govern them; attended churches, lodges, and clubs; and worked very hard to make a go of things. These people were fully American in culture and pattern of settlement. Where they differed from whites was in choosing to segregate in the hope of gaining civil rights. The motto of the *Boley Progress* expressed this aspiration: "All men up, not some men down." [22]

Epilog

Disillusioned by the failure of the black town movement, small minorities abandoned the United States in bitterness and in hopes of socio-economic betterment. After statehood in 1907, a few hundred, like McCabe, headed for Canada. When they turned up in Saskatchewan in 1909, Canadians reacted negatively to the (somewhat imaginary) prospect of a black exodus. Canada responded by turning away many at the border for the lack of documentation as to health and character. Thereby they put up a bureaucratic barrier that served as well as an explicit racial barrier, thus sparing Canadian consciences the guilt of betraying any liberal principles.

The more disillusioned of the black town citizens remained vulnerable to separatist appeals and propositions. In August 1913, as the boll weevil attacked the cotton crop, one Alfred Charles Sam arrived in Okfuskee County, Oklahoma, with the latest in the series of "Back-to-Africa" schemes, periodic since the 1820's. Mr. Sam, a short gentleman with a soft voice and a sincere manner, identified himself as a "Chief" of the Akim people living in the (British) Gold Coast colony (now the Republic of Ghana). He offered to lead these unhappy Oklahomans back to a homeland where they would find acceptance as equals and easy support on fertile and available land. He spoke of jumbo stalks of sugar cane, trees which bore fruit that was bread, and of precious stones in the soil. He pitched stock in the "Akim Trading Company, Ltd." for $25 per share. For this, he promised the shareholder a passage to Africa. About 600 residents of the Clearview and Boley areas bought in by selling homes and farm fields for whatever they would bring. By February 1914, these migrants shivered and waited in two camps near Weleetka for Sam to procure a ship and bring it to Galveston, Texas, from where they would depart for West Africa.

By April, reduced to 500, the group had set up a tent city in Galveston. Meanwhile, Alfred Sam, with too few dollars and too many legal problems, sent his agents back to peddle more stock. Finally he purchased a small, dilapidated, iron-hulled ship that he christened *Liberia* and loaded coal and supplies. They eventually departed on August 21, 1914, but the ship's capacity turned out to be only 60 passengers, leaving the majority destitute and hungry in a hostile city. For reasons unclear, the voyage took three months, and the land Journey to their destination another two months (February 13, 1915). Then Sam abandoned the scheme, transferring the *Liberia* to a Canadian company to cover some of his debts. Once there, the group found little promise in a promised land: strange customs and primitive agriculture. Some of them went with Sam to the black republic of Liberia (the result of an earlier back-to-Africa movement), where he went into business as a cocoa buyer. Some may have returned to the U.S., others may have remained in Africa: we don't know what became of the voyagers. We do know that some of the Akim stockholders left behind in Galveston, probably those with families still in the black towns, returned to Oklahoma. They probably had to listen to a great deal of I-told-you-so-ing. [23]

RAGTIME ALMANAC

Oklahoma Black Towns [24]

Arkansas Colored	Gibson Station	Overton
Baily	Grayson	Red Bird
Boley	Langston	Rentiesville
Bookertee	Lewisville	Summit
Canadian Colored	Liberty	Taft
Chase	Lincoln City	Tullahassee
Clearview	Linn	Vernon
Ferguson	Marshalltown	Wellston
Foreman	North Fork Colored	Wybark

Plus two unnamed towns in the Seminole Nation.

Some Other Black Towns

Allensworth, TX	Grambling, LA	Mound Bayou, MS
Blackdom, NM	Hobson City, AL	Nicodemus, KS
Brooklyn, IL	Kinlock, MS	Whitesboro, NJ
Fairmount Heights, MD	Lawnside, NJ	Wyandott, KS

Notes: Chapter 21

1. Quoted in Thomas Knight, *Sunset on Utopian Dreams: An Experiment of Black Separatism on the American Frontier*, 78.
2. Norman L. Crockett, *The Black Towns*, xii.
3. Lorenzo J. Greene, Gary R. Kremer, Antonio P. Holland, *Missouri's Black Heritage*, 104-105.
4. Crockett, 16.
5. *Ibid.*, 17.
6. *Ibid.*, 47.
7. *Ibid .*, 19.
8. *Ibid.*, 86-91, 145-146, 174-175.
9. Knight, 62-70; August Meier, *Negro Thought in America, 1880-1915: Racial Ideologies in the Age of Booker T. Washington,* 147; Crockett, 20.
10. Knight, 70, 143-144; Crockett, 20-26; Meier, 147.
11. Crockett, 36-39, 123-124, 140; Knight, 92, 116; William F. Bittle and Gilbert L. Geis, "Racial Self-Fulfillment and the Rise of an All-Negro Community in Oklahoma," in Meier and Rudwick, *The Making Of Black America*, 111-113.
12. Quoted in Crockett, 138-139.
13. *Ibid.*, 123.
14. Quoted in *Ibid.*, 116. See 115-143 for economics of black towns.
15. *Ibid.*, 24.
16. Knight, 72, for population figures; Crockett, 23-26, for McCabe.
17. Bittle & Geis, 114-116; Crockett, 91.
18. Quoted in *Ibid.*, 92.
19. Quoted in *Ibid.*, 93.
20. Bittle & Geis, 114-117; Crockett, 91-93.
21. *Ibid.*, 106, 167-168; Knight, 63.
22. Crockett, 106-107, 112-113, 123, 164-167, 178-182; Knight 142-144; Bittle & Geis, 117-118.
23. Crockett, 168-174; Bittle & Geis, 117-118.
24. From Knight, 93.1

22. Ragging It in the White House

> It is no easy job to be president. But I am thoroughly enjoying it
> And I think so far I have done pretty well. (TR to son Ted) [1]

In this candid assertion to son and namesake, we glimpse Theodore Roosevelt candidly viewing his presidential image. He believed that he had the qualifications. The presidency had always been his goal. Observing Cleveland, Harrison, and McKinley, he had sized up the job with the growing conviction that he could do better. His predecessors had merely <u>presided</u>, caretakers of an entrenched system that served growing corporate interests. Theodore's agenda meant to place the common good ahead of corporate interests. The new president was eager to pursue his more benevolent and comprehensive agenda, and he intended to put some spirit into his efforts.

President William McKinley had been ignominiously gutshot by a demented assassin while amiably shaking hands at an open reception in the "Temple of Music" at the Pan American Exposition in Buffalo, New York, on September 6, 1901. He lingered eight days, with Theodore Roosevelt becoming the 26th President on September 14th. On September 23rd the new President, just back from his predecessor's funeral in Canton, Ohio, took possession of the White House. Although mourning continued—flags at half-staff, black borders on official stationery—Theodore felt very upbeat. He was batching it for a few days because Edith and the children had returned to Sagamore Hill to pack and organize the move to their new address. Feeling a need for company and desiring to share his satisfaction, he invited his sisters and husbands for dinner that first night. Toward the end of the meal, he asked Bamie and Corinne if they had noted that this day would have been their father's seventieth birthday: "I have realized it as I signed various papers all day long, and I feel that it is a good omen that I begin my duties in this house on this day. I feel my father's hand on my shoulder, as if there were a special blessing on the life I am to lead here." [2]

Not only were the omens good, but thanks to George Cortelyou, Secretary to President McKinley, there had been an almost seamless transition. Cortelyou (1862-1940) understood everything, mastered all details, organized each day, and foresaw problems, always performing with tact and restraint. He examined all the mail, answered most of it himself, and passed on a fraction of it to the President. He assumed the role of the first White House press spokesman. During the eight days of McKinley's passing, he functioned as the (unacknowledged) acting president. This tour de force of management so impressed TR that he retained Cortelyou, even though he relied upon William Loeb who had become his personal secretary in Albany (who had to accept "Assistant Secretary to the President"). With Cortelyou running the White House and Loeb as personal secretary, Theodore could leave details to this superb team and concentrate on policy. Eighteen months later, he raised Cortelyou to cabinet level as the first Secretary of Commerce and Labor (February 1903). This was no reward for faithful service, but the effective utilization of phenomenal executive talents to provide a new department with a well organized and efficient start-up. Later TR would switch Cortelyou to the chairmanship of the Republican National Committee to supervise his reelection in 1904. During the second administration Cortelyou served first as Postmaster General (1905-07) and then as Secretary of the Treasury (1907-09). Afterwards this exemplar of organizational skills became president of Consolidated Gas, the nation's largest utility; during his 28 years there, the company tripled its value, from $243 million to $990 million. [3]

The single White House telephone sat on Loeb's desk. Loeb took all calls, informed the President about them, and called back any presidential responses. TR disliked telephones so much that he deputized Loeb to speak for him even on matters secret and delicate. Loeb (like Cortelyou before him) answered the mail, arranged appointments, took shorthand in situations of secrecy, and organized the relay of stenographers required by a president who dictated ceaselessly. [4] TR reached his desk at 9:30 AM six days a week after a leisurely family breakfast. His office was about 30 feet square (the "Oval Office" was added later by Taft) with southern windows looking toward the Potomac and Virginia beyond. The Cabinet Room adjoined through sliding doors, and the heads of the nine major departments appeared for meetings on Tuesdays and Fridays at 11:00 AM. Opposite a large mahogany desk Lincoln's portrait hung over the fireplace. Except for bookshelves and a sitting area with an art nouveau lamp, the office was plain, without even a flag. The only photograph was of a bear.

Days began with Loeb handing over a list of appointments. Next TR rapidly dictated answers to letters Edith and Loeb had selected for him to read. When the first stenographer had filled a shorthand pad, a second took over as the first batch of letters went to the squad of typists. This proceeded nonstop until all correspondence and other documents had been dictated, typed up, and signed. After this, Theodore perused clippings from periodicals containing comments on his administration. Edith and staff regularly scanned 350 publications to cull out items both favorable and unfavorable. With paperwork done, he opened the Cabinet-room doors and chatted with visitors. Senators and Congressmen needed no appointments, but others had to go through Loeb. One newsman recalled that up to 20 people might be present, and that TR circulated around the room, attending to everyone, listening, then talking eagerly and laughing delightedly. This newsman concluded: "You don't smile with Mr. Roosevelt; you shout with laughter with him…." [5] John Hay, his first Secretary of State, described a foreign policy session:

> It was a curious sight. I have often seen it, and it never ceases to surprise me. He storms up and down the room, dictating in a loud and oratorical tone, often stopping, recasting a sentence, striking out and filling in, hospitable to every suggestion, not in the least disturbed by interruption, holding on stoutly to his purpose, and producing finally, out of these most unpromising conditions, a clear and logical statement. [6]

Following these animated interactive scenes, he met the press at 1:00. "The Press" consisted of a mere six or seven reporters assigned to the White House beat. Presidential Secretary George Cortelyou, while serving McKinley, had organized the first official relations between press and executive branch. Previously newsmen had gathered the news haphazardly by approaching executive personnel and visitors out on the street and asked them to disclose information. Such reportage was often partial, inaccurate, garbled, and late. Cortelyou, constantly driven by his passion for efficiency, simply produced a daily statement of the President's decisions and policy views and distributed it reporters. Plus whenever the President spoke, stenographers recorded and speedily transcribed the speech for the press. This change of official attitude, from hostility and indifference to cooperation, so pleased newsmen that they failed to realize that they were being handed managed news. [7] Cortelyou (and Loeb from 1903) continued these press measures under TR, himself a past master in the uses of the press. An anecdote tells us that on a wet, chilly day in 1902, TR happened to glance out from the second floor to see a miserable cluster of wet newsmen. Feeling pity for their sodden plight, he ordered a small room on the first floor to be allotted to them. Thus casually the press room became a permanent White House fixture. [8]

Theodore met his reporter friends in a small room between his and Secretary Loeb's office. Waiting there also was a barber from the Treasury Department who lathered him up, and then attempted to shave a hyperactive client holding forth answering questions, expostulating, engaging in sudden body language. Often the laughter of the audience fell off to amazement when the razor pulled away from the presidential face just in time, as he lunged forward or raised an arm to make a point. He never held back during these daily sessions, bluntly saying his opinions and answering questions straightly. Reporters delighted in such intimacy and camaraderie, but it came with a price: whatever TR called off-the-record stayed secret. Violators found themselves banished without hope of reprieve. He liked to let go in a small group, but with the understanding that his humorously outrageous remarks would never reach public ears. This price, however, brought the dividend of a fuller understanding of the President, his policies and decisions. When he did place himself on the record, reporters gave a full and fair presentation. Having listened for weeks, they had their stories ready, stories that usually stressed positive over negative. Which was precisely Theodore's intention:

> …there were multitudes of men, in newspaper offices, in magazine offices,…who actively supported the policies for which I stood…. Without the active support of these men I would have been powerless.[9]

After visitors, cabinet members, the press, the President rolled into lunchtime in full interactive mode, doubly ravenous, for both food and more stimulating conversation. This climaxed most days because he was a day person who relegated evenings to family life and reading, a romp with the children, followed by withdrawal into the book he'd had by him that day. The diurnal extrovert transformed into the nocturnal solitary. Just about everything was of interest, whether literary, scientific, artistic, or practical. As a natural speed reader, he consumed a book or two each day. Authors who impressed him soon received telegrams inviting them to lunch. His guests included, besides the usual statesmen and diplomats, scholars, literary figures, scientists, businessmen, athletes, and men of action, Rough Riders being always welcome. His love of boxing brought in John L. Sullivan, and once he satisfied a curiosity by inviting the notorious Bat Masterson. He mixed his guest lists with old friends, writers, a scientist along with a diplomat or a politician. He turned the spotlight on each guest in turn, questioning them and listening to responses. Out of these human mixtures came not only pleasant company but learning experiences. Theodore wished to know the things his guests knew and their points of view. He read <u>them</u>, just as he read their books. His close friend, and fellow writer on western America, Owen Wister (*The Virginian*) enthused that, "For once in our history, we had an American <u>salon</u>." [10]

TR's high spirits and zest flowed via the press out of the White House. By being accessible and on the record with some item, significant or trivial, he achieved celebrity status (one of the first). He turned his actions and decisions into news. His cleverest manipulation was to call in the press on a Sunday. Since Monday tended to be a slow news day, his releases grabbed the headlines. Going directly to the people, he stirred up national debates that held the public interest. This conditioned people; right off they queried his views on any issue. His influence became so pervasive that Congressmen paid close attention, increasingly afraid to flout "the will of the people." TR captured not only headlines, but frequent editorial cartoons. The new process of photoengraving that had developed during the 1890's had made possible the daily cartoon. Editorial cartoonists arose each day aware that they had in the President a strong subject. He was a walking caricature, and his resonant phrases like "strenuous life" and "big stick" translated easily into cartoon ideas.

Because Roosevelt was always caught up in some conflict or struggle, cartoonists drew him as a uniformed Rough Rider. Again, because he regularly hunted, his enemies could be depicted as wild animals.

Throughout the years, cartoonists drew his likeness hundreds of times, which only increased his celebrity and popularity. Perhaps the most interesting cartoon outcome was the creation of the Teddy Bear. Theodore accepted a hunting invitation in Mississippi in November 1902. Unfortunately very few bears showed up to participate, and his hosts, feeling some embarrassment, allowed their beaters to drive in and then rope a small black bear after it had finished off one of the dogs. Then the smallish creature was offered to the guest of honor as a compensatory target. With some annoyance, he refused this unsporting proposition, allowing the bear to survive—perhaps to be hunted again. Clifford K. Berryman humorously cartooned this in the *Washington Post*, and a New York toy shop owner produced a cuddly stuffed bear honoring the gesture that became instantly and universally popular, the classic toy. [11]

II

The presidential family consisted of Alice (b. 1884, the daughter of first wife Alice Hathaway Lee) and Edith's five: Theodore, Jr. (b. 1887), Kermit (b. 1889), Ethel (b.1891), Archibald (b. 1894), and Quentin (b. 1897). When they entered the White House in September 1901, Alice, 17, was nearly grown; young Theodore, Ted, at 14, was attending the Groton school in Massachusetts; and Kermit, 12, would soon follow his brother to Groton. It was the three younger children, Ethel, 10, Archie, 7, and Quentin, 4, who injected an essence of youthful vitality into the starchy protocols and daily rituals of the executive mansion. Now children suddenly popped up, and the staff had to cope with the unexpected. The young Roosevelts possessed numerous pets, which ranged from snakes to ponies. They were also permitted to bring in their playmates. Theodore and Edith refused to compromise on childhood and permitted all normal juvenile activities; they tolerated no attitudes of what-will-the-visitors-think. Whenever the youthful commotion brought on a headache or a touch of the nerves, Edith simply went into her rooms and closed the door. As for Theodore, he loved children, kept a vigilant eye on them, and often took a time-out from being president for a romp.

Ethel soon left childhood for the more demure life of feminine adolescence, but the two boys, who paused only for meals, school, and sleep, carried on rambunctiously and concocted pranks. Occasionally the staff was startled by the rumble of roller-skate races on the upper floor staged by Archie and Quentin. They liked to clump up and down corridors on stilts. Once the mischievous two rigged the White House elevator, stopping it between floors, trapping Alice, on her way down for a parlor tryst with Congressman Nicholas Longworth (her future husband). Archie's friends included "Big Turkey" and "Little Turkey," sons of the Turkish ambassador, and a cousin, Nicholas Roosevelt. One day, he and Nicholas, in frustration at what they felt was neglect, presented TR with the following poem:

> Good morning Mr President
> How are you today
> We have obeyed your orders
> We're very glad to say.
> We went around the White House
> Araising up a row
> And if you want to know about it
> Then we'll tell you how
> We want to have a pillow fight
> With you this very night
> And if you do not play with us
> We'll squeeze you very tight! [12]

Another time, when Archie was recovering from a near fatal bout with diphtheria, Quentin smuggled their pony Algonquin onto the elevator and took him up to Archie's room. [13]

Quentin, who spent his fifth through almost his twelfth year in the White House, became its best-known child. More so than his siblings, he grew to resemble his father in body type, temperament, and range of interests. TR, who had himself been a much-loved child, inherited the same philoprogenitive tendencies: he applied the diminutive "Quenty-Quee" to his youngest son and delighted in the boy's spirited and zesty traits. Edith called him "a <u>fine</u> little bad boy." [14]

Although intended for the elite institutions of Groton and Harvard, the sons of TR received their elementary schooling publicly. Quentin attended the Force School on Massachusetts Avenue where he often demonstrated his prominence by arriving either on roller skates or on his pony. Right off he became a member of a circle of a half-dozen mates, self-constituted as a "Gang," who eventually referred to themselves as the "White House Gang," because the senior Roosevelts sanctioned the play of children on the national premises. The Gang included Charles Taft, son of the Secretary of War, who would be the next occupant of the White House. A few decades later, gang member Earle Looker recorded its exploits in a memoir, *The White House Gang*, a rare picture of children interacting in a public setting with a president who guided them by becoming one of them. [15] Looker terms him "the most active member of the Gang," because he often joined them, either to mediate a problem, take part in an activity, or lead them on an excursion. [16]

A favorite play spot, "the heaven of the White house," was the attic, "crammed full of mysterious stuff," lit with few electric lights, which allowed the Gang to explore its strange artifacts with their flashlights. [17] On one occasion when TR, "growling ferociously," chased the boys around the attic, Looker, hidden behind a post saw another boy about to be caught. To save his friend from falling into the presidential clutches, Looker reached out and pulled open the electric switch, causing an instant blackout. Immediately came the sound of a large body running into a post and crying out, "By George! Lights! Lights! Turn on the lights! This is worse—worse—than anything I've heard of in darkest Africa!" Illumination discovered the President against a post, having barely avoided a nail sticking out at the level of his eyes. He indicated that he was all right but cautioned to "never, n-e-v-e-r, <u>never</u> again turn off a light when anybody is near a post." [18]

After TR's departure "to bathe his face," the Gang turned on Looker, overpowered him in a scuffle, and threw him into a cedar chest, after which they sat on top, drumming their heels against the side to drown out his poundings. This went too far, as little Earle progressed from anger to panic to the start of suffocation. Suddenly the lid flew open, and a weakening, watery-eyed boy looked up at the President reaching down with a handkerchief. This dangerous escapade did not lead to fury or outrage or an imperious order about never doing such a thing again. Instead Theodore calmly handed down a sensible ruling: "Shutting up boys in cedar-chests for more than sixty seconds is strictly forbidden." [19]

He played a different role in the ordeal of the knitting needles. In front of a window seat, Quentin placed a chair; then, using books for support, he propped up four steel knitting needles. Next he stretched himself over these treacherous points, fingers gripping the chair, toes on window seat. "If you slip doing this," he said, "you fill yourself as full of knitting-needles as a porcupine." As the Gang watched awestruck, Looker discovered TR standing behind a screen quietly observing his son with "the utmost concentration." After a timed thirty seconds, Quentin asked for the needles to be removed and collapsed onto the floor. With a triumphant pleasure, he heard each gang member refuse his dare to attempt the same feat. When Looker glanced toward the screen again, TR had vanished, keeping his reaction to himself, perhaps feeling (as Looker states) that the Gang had "to work out, independently, its own problems and salvation." [20]

In Quentin there was as much brat as daredevil. One afternoon when TR had invited the boys for a fall walk through Rock Creek Park, Quentin, because of "hilarious deportment," had been detained and commanded to write a sentence 25 times on the blackboard. Aware of their host's insistence on punctuality, the Gang had left on foot, knowing that Quentin could easily catch up on his pony. However the sentences took longer than anticipated, and Quentin burst impatiently out of school, agitated over tardiness and any explanations he might be called upon to give. Suddenly, the Gang heard police whistles and looked up to see Quentin galloping Algonquin across a grassy park area, denting the turf and kicking clods and plants from flower beds. Yelling for the Gang to hurry—"Don't keep father waiting! He hates nothing worse!"—Quentin pivoted his pony, dodged around a tree, clattered across the tracks of an oncoming, clanging, streetcar, and shot through the White House carriage entrance. As the pursuing park police came up to this point, the White House police turned them back. As Looker followed behind with the Gang, he noticed the passengers on the streetcar "sitting amazed by the sudden infantry charge bursting out of the park, led by its mounted commander...." [21]

In the best known of these anecdotes of the White House Gang, the President intervened dramatically. One afternoon Quentin exhibited more of his "hilarious" behavior when Miss Wallace asked him to characterize President Grant. Taking a partisan stance, Quentin answered that it depended upon whether Grant was a Republican or a Democrat. Rejecting this nonsense, the teacher demanded an answer, refusing to accept party as a judgmental standard. Very smart-alecky, Quentin responded that the former had been "uniformly good," while the latter had been "without exception terrible." Then he carried it over the edge by declaring that if Grant were a Republican, he would call him "fine-looking," but since his face was hidden behind a beard, "if he was a Democrat, I'd say, and I'm sure I'd be right:

> There was an old man with a beard,
> Who said, "It is just as I feared!
> Two owls and a hen, four larks and a wren
> Have all built their nests in my beard!"

This brought the class down and set the scene for the final indignity. A flustered Miss Wallace abruptly took her class into a formal recitation period. As her composure returned, the incorrigible Quentin sought another opportunity to get a rise out of the class. As gang member Walker White stood to recite, Quentin pulled back on a thick rubber band and shot a spitball, which missed White and caught Miss Wallace in the face. She rose in fury, bore down on Quentin, and marched him into the cloakroom, whence came sounds of corporal punishment. Quentin emerged looking angry and unchastised.

After school had commenced the next morning, the President's carriage drew up in front, to a universal amazement. TR alighted and strode into the building. Soon he appeared in the classroom doorway, followed by a "visibly flustered principal." Quentin sat startled and shocked as his father handed over a large bouquet:

> Miss Wallace, I come to offer my apology for Quentin's rude and thoughtless behavior of yesterday.... I understand he did not make an altogether satisfactory apology to you, if he made

one at all…which he most certainly should have done. And so, the least I could do, I thought, would be to come here myself. Of course, even now, it's not satisfactory because—as Quentin must learn—an apology, in order to be really acceptable, should be immediately made.

Overwhelmed, Miss Wallace thanked him in a small voice while the class sat "quite overawed," viewing the man whose picture hung next to that of George Washington. From "little" Walker White came: "Everybody stand up, for the President…" TR then commented that, "One boy at least has his manners with him today," bowed to Miss Wallace and left. Quentin, quietly, and to himself, said, "Golly!" [22]

III

If Theodore Roosevelt laid the foundation for the modern presidency, then Edith institutionalized the position of first lady. [23]

Edith Kermit Carow Roosevelt (1861-1948) balanced easily between the practical and the imaginative. She attended conscientiously to both the life of her family and her mental life. Through extensive reading she had become learned and critical. She fully participated in the "Roosevelt salon." Her cooler mind and quick wit were appreciated, particularly by guests overwhelmed by her husband's ebullience and enthusiasms. At Sagamore Hill, so full of trophies and other artifacts of hunting, war, and politics, her formal sitting room, with its pastel colors and prim, delicate furniture, presents a striking contrast, a feminine oasis within a caravanserai (or a summer camp). [24]

Publicly Edith masked her intellectual light with polite smiles and some aloofness. Nurtured in Victorian times, she cultivated gentility and the tradition of wifely reticence and restraint. But she rejected the sheltered and coddled life that constrained upper class Victorian women. Before marriage, her father's alcoholism and business failure had forced Edith to confront serious family and economic problems, and, after losing Theodore (her main hope for a better future) to Alice Lee, her prospects—teacher, governess, poor relation—seemed bleak (Chapter 4). After her eventual marriage, she had to untangle and organize Theodore's confused and never quite sufficient finances. Theodore lacked money sense, considered money-grubbing beneath him, and always spent whatever he had in hand. As a politician's wife, this privacy-loving woman had to cope with the curiosity of strangers, and later, during the presidential years, with existence under the glaring spotlight of celebrity. Behind the prim façade, she bore and reared five children and did her best to bring up an often-difficult stepdaughter (see below).

Within her domestic underground, Edith not only spent her quiet time with her beloved Shakespeare and other classics, she also oversaw things political. True to her models of feminine restraint, she usually held back her views until Theodore asked for them. Her chief tactic consisted of pointing out negatives, things to avoid, leaving the viable choices to him. As noted above, she operated the White House clipping service, culling out of media sources all items pertaining to the administration. Then she exercised the authoritative function of selecting those items <u>she</u> considered significant to place upon her husband's desk. Her office lay next to his study, and he came in to communicate with her several times a day. She often chatted with visitors before their appointments with the President. Whatever vibrations or intimations she picked up were passed on that evening before she retired at 10:00, leaving him to finish his book of the day. Years later, daughter Ethel commented, "We all knew that the person who had the long head in politics was Mother." [25]

Soon after moving in, TR, by an executive order, replaced the staid "Executive Mansion" with the more popular "White House." Edith supplemented this cosmetic change with a functional transformation. Previously the building had served chiefly as residence of the Chief Executive, wherein on the second floor were located the president's offices adjacent to the living quarters, and on the ground floor the public rooms used for official balls and receptions. Edith commented that it felt like "living over the store." [26] Everything, walls, hangings, furniture, was old, gloomy, and worn. Worse, beneath this gross shabbiness, the structure was falling apart, near to collapse, because of decades of piecemeal repairs and additions of pipes and wiring and because of insect infestations. Edith took charge and brought in the expertise of architect Charles F. McKim (of NYC's leading firm of McKim, Meade, and White) who aided her in restoring the mansion to the classic décor of Adams and Jefferson. The old second floor offices became bedrooms, replaced by a new West Wing containing space for the President and cabinet meetings, plus offices for 38 administrative employees. [27]

Two of Edith's innovations continue to impress visitors. She created the gallery of portraits of first ladies, and after several years of searches, she assembled the collection of presidential china, which previously had been casually disposed of rather than preserved for posterity. She had special display cases built to show the best representative pieces. She also inventoried all of the china, glass, and furniture to aid the retention of White House artifacts. Her preservation work put an end to 19C indifference. One day, as Quentin and his Gang came down the corridor, they paused to gaze at the splendid sequential arrangement of historical china, carefully secured by lock and key. [28] One gang member, a collector of keys, took out of his pocket a large ring of keys and began to try them in the locks on the display cases. After several attempts, a small key opened two of the cases. Quentin, with fingers muddy from outdoor play, reached in and brought out a number of cups. After a cursory examination, he placed them in the other cabinet. Soon all five of the boys were carefully rearranging the displays, mixing one administration's crockery with another's. No breakage occurred, but they left behind some residue of dirt on the disarrangement. Eager to learn of any perplexing effects of their prank, Quentin patrolled past the cases daily. Although they waited for some official—or parental—reaction, none came, and ten days later, Quentin had to report that the displays had been restored. [29]

Another Roosevelt innovation was to give the First Lady her own office, needed for planning and organizing the increasing White House social events. Progressing from wife of a Civil Service Commissioner through that of New York Police Commissioner, Assistant Secretary of the Navy, Governor of New York, and Vice-President, Edith had learned that she needed support in her official role if she was not to neglect her domestic role. She hired the first White House social secretary, Belle Hagner, member of an old Washington family. What started as a part-time job soon became full-time, the core of the eventual staff for future first ladies. [30] Ms. Hagner also shielded her employer from direct contact with the press. Edith realized she couldn't ban photographers from the premises, but she zealously tried to maintain family privacy. Always uncomfortable with celebrity—made more intense by the increase in Roosevelt news items—she occasionally reached out to the press through Belle, delegating her as press secretary to pass out information to a few approved journalists. Her husband fully shared this reticent attitude, once writing the editor of the *New York Sun* that "…I am living here with my wife and children just exactly as you are at your home…." [31]

Close as a couple, intellectually in agreement, the Roosevelts differed temperamentally, he, always spirited, impatient to move ahead, she, cooler, discreet, and careful, always measuring consequences. She woke up to bad days, with neuralgic pains that brought out sharp words. Her family, never certain of her mood, learned to be wary. She could be demanding. But she accepted them without trying to change them. She let them go forth on their various adventures, make their mistakes, and dirty their clothes. Father and children respected her moral authority, and this plus love kept them from becoming a fighting family. Theodore demonstrated his respect in the comment: "Every time I have gone against Edith's judgment, I have gone wrong." [32] Occasionally an element of fear tempered this respect. One day, felling a few trees—one of those strenuous activities in which he delighted—a tree fell the wrong way, taking with it the telephone wires. That evening at dinner with French Ambassador Jules Jusserand, a dear and close friend, Edith cracked a smile during Theodore's telling of the mishap. Seeing which, he curtly told her to drop the subject. When Jusserand pointed out to him that she hadn't spoken, he complained:

> Ah! But you don't know my wife. She has a language all her own. The telephone will never ring now that my wife will not begin to chuckle to herself, and if the cursed thing ever gets out of order…she will tell the servant to see if the wires are still up or if the trees are down…. She has a humor which is more tyrannical than half the tempestuous women of Shakespeare. [33]

IV

> Alice has been at home very little, spending most of her time In Newport and elsewhere, associating with the Four Hundred—Individuals with whom the other members of the family have exceedingly few affiliations. (TR to sister Corinne Robinson) [34]

On January 3, 1902, barely three months after moving in, Theodore and Edith invited 600 guests to Alice's debut, the first such event in White House history. Thus launched into Washington society, Alice remained there until her death at 96 in 1981. Always a fixture, she attained the status of a legend as Alice Roosevelt Longworth, usually labeled "Grande Dame" by the media of the nation's capital. She experienced those 79 years as a celebrity, probably a record run. Following her debut a few weeks later, when Prince Heinrich of Germany, the younger brother of Kaiser Wilhelm II, arrived to take possession of his new yacht, Alice took center stage when she christened it *Meteor*. Edith came along to chaperone and exert some control, but the event became a media feeding frenzy, creating an instant stardom. The Roosevelt-hating segment of the press had been grumbling about "Princess Alice," when suddenly she beamed forth as a reigning figure. At 17, standing a regal 5 feet, 7 inches, with vibrant looks and a lively manner, the public loved her. She became an industry. A certain gray-blue which matched her eyes was her favorite color, and the public immediately adored "Alice blue." The song "Alice Blue Gown" became an instant hit (another composer offered "Alice, Where Art Thou?"). Praised, discussed, and criticized, she was the most photographed person in the world (causing her stepmother frequent heartburn). She inspired other enterprises as well: dresses, hats, and wallpaper. A generation of girl babies was christened Alice. [35]

Alice contained much more of her father than of her birth mother. Alice Hathaway Lee had been a sweet, demure Victorian girl, sheltered and uncomplicated. Her daughter showed none of these biddable traits. The essential point about Alice was conflict, resulting from the loss of a mother and a father's neglect. Something, probably youth, died in Theodore with the death of Alice Lee. It was so painful, so catastrophic for him that he never mentioned her name again. He named their daughter Alice, then handed her over to sister Bamie, and fled to Dakota. He would likely have given her away (to Bamie) if he hadn't remarried. Edith, over Bamie's reluctance, installed Alice in her father's household, but her place in it, stepdaughter, half-sister, would always be somewhat sensitive. Theodore could never let her come in close enough to bestow the unconditional love he gave her half siblings. Edith, who had to handle Alice, found herself in the exhausting middle, attempting both to discipline and mediate. As for Alice, she retaliated by being difficult and contrary.

Alice performed like a wayward version of her vigorous father. Resenting his failure to grant the assurance of positive reenforcement, she contrived endless attention-getting strategies. For pets, she eschewed dogs and cats in favor of a snake and a large gaudy bird. Her green garter snake was called Emily Spinach, an unkind reference to Edith's thin, expatriate sister. On White House social occasions, Alice enjoyed strolling among guests with a blue and gold macaw riding on her forearm, introducing him as Eli Yale. On more than one occasion, Alice enlivened the proceedings by shooting off a cap pistol. Like her father, Alice was home-schooled. A few years earlier, she had rebelled when her parents sought to enroll her in a Manhattan boarding school. She threatened: "If you send me I will humiliate you. I will do something that will shame you." Some quality of desperation or anguish led them to compromise. Alice received assigned books to read, followed by her father's oral quizzes. This informal approach suited her, and, receiving some "quality time" in the process, she proved bright and intelligent. [36] Along with an agile mind, she inherited her father's political awareness and instincts, traits by which she eventually achieved social leadership in the nation's capital.

But more frequently Alice was an exhibitionist and a pain in the neck. She brought an unwelcome notoriety to the First Family when she took up smoking, something not indulged in by genteel, proper young ladies (or women) of that decade. She sneaked puffs in the pantry, blew smoke up fireplace chimneys, and when an aggravated father exclaimed that she was forbidden to smoke under his roof, she gleefully exhaled from the roof of the White House. [37] Family friend Owen Wister saw Alice in action. Theodore and his friend sat chatting one day when Alice interrupted three times, entering the room to get some item. The third time, her father roared, "Alice, the next time you come, I'll throw you out of the window." [38] Wister (and several others) also recalled the occasion when someone advised Theodore that Alice needed corrective attention. His reply: "Listen, I can be President of the United States—or—I can attend to Alice." [39]

When old enough to venture out alone, Alice indulged in a series of escapades. To her father's annoyance, she regularly consorted with the very rich folk, known as the "Four Hundred" (the number of people Mrs. William Astor felt she could accommodate in her ballroom), in their Manhattan brownstone mansions and their Newport, Rhode Island, "cottages." With a reverse snobbery Theodore looked down upon people who dedicated their lives to acquiring great wealth and possessions. He considered them vulgar and a threat to the national wellbeing. Alice later justified this by saying that these people were "tribal friends" and the only people with big houses who gave big dances. [40] Alice particularly enjoyed yachting with Grace Vanderbilt who often entertained royalty on the *Kingfisher*. The press happily chronicled the exploits of "Princess Alice," and she sometimes rivaled her father in newspaper coverage. He may have been shocked one morning by the newsstory telling that his daughter had briefly descended in a U.S. Navy submarine while it paid a call in Newport. [41]

Alice flourished beyond the White House because she had her own money. Her Lee grandparents (she visited them twice a year) indulged her whims and provided a generous allowance, making her the only wealthy member of the family. One journalist on her trail estimated that during a two-year period, she had attended 407 dances, 350 balls, and 680 teas! [42] Alice again disturbed her parents when she went to racetracks and placed bets on horses. On one such occasion, a photographer clicked her as she collected her winnings from a bookmaker. Her scandalized father persuaded two newspapers not to publish the pictures. (This occurred during 1904 while he was laboring valiantly to be elected "in my own right.") [43] Alice eagerly embraced the automobile, at first a hobby of the rich, which, as an heiress, she could afford. She became a frequent sight, tooling around Washington in her little electric runabout with a veil tying down her broad hat. Another notorious escapade was a lengthy drive from

Newport to Boston. She and friend Ella Drexel Paul piloted a big Panhard racer all the way in a record six hours during which they roared across open stretches at a horrendous twenty-five miles per hour. [44]

The climactic social event of the Roosevelt years was the wedding of the White House Princess to Representative Nicholas Longworth of Ohio. Her parents breathed a relief because the groom was neither a European nobleman who would carry Alice off into exile from family and country nor one of the wealthy "400" who would establish her in an unRooseveltian existence of material excess and shallow pleasures. What they disliked about Longworth was his age—he was 34 and Alice 22—and his reputation as a rounder (hard drinking, wenching, all-night poker). However the Longworths (like the Tafts) held place at the apex of Cincinnati society, and Nick had gone to Harvard (and Harvard Law) and been accepted into Theodore's club, Porcellian. He also possessed good cultural habits: he read books, could produce light verse, and he took music seriously, playing classics well on his violin. He looked like a future leader of Republicans—eventually serving as Speaker of the House. His extravagant lifestyle, which was dribbling away the fortune accumulated by ancestors, showed him off as very eligible indeed.

Alice never appreciated the violin—she went for Strauss, Sousa, and Ragtime—but she adored the boxfuls of roses he sent and his aura of elegance. Things turned serious during the summer of 1905 on an official trans-Pacific voyage. Theodore sent his genial Secretary of War, William Howard Taft, on a diplomatic, good-will mission to the Far East. Fellow Cincinnatian Nick Longworth had been included in the delegation, and Alice persuaded her father to let her join the party—which indeed it was—on this slow boat to the Orient, and back. This generated much media attention; Alice's romantic doings took center on the diplomatic stage, with one newspaper calling the junket "Alice in Wonderland." [45] At one point, when Alice and Nick, too often alone together, put a strain on propriety, the three-hundred-pound Secretary of War (who never liked to rock any boats) felt constrained to inquire of Alice if she and Nick were engaged. Her reply: "More or less, Mr. Secretary, More or less." [46] Nick did not formally ask TR's permission to wed Alice until some months after their return. [47]

Five hundred friends and relatives jammed the East Room on February 17, 1906, while thousands stood outside. Princess Alice received a mountain of gifts from family, friends, governments, royalty, businesses, and manufacturers. The anthracite miners of Pennsylvania, grateful for TR's role in settling the coal strike of 1902, sent a carload of top grade coal. The Rough Riders came through with a silver dinner service marked with the regimental emblem. Crowned heads and the wealthy showered her with precious metal items. Alice, full of elation and delight, said, "I'll accept anything but a red-hot stove." [48] Outside, vendors of souvenirs, balloons, and popcorn pitched their wares. Every florist in the District had sold out, and every church bell rang. The train of her wedding dress stretched twelve feet! Because it was her show, Alice had no maid of honor or bridesmaids. She wore a diamond necklace, Nick's special (and ostentatious) gift. The Marine Band furnished the music. Among the guests was distant cousin Franklin Delano Roosevelt, alone because wife (and niece of the President) Eleanor was six months pregnant. He proved useful when he arranged Alice's train for the official photographer. One of the military aides present was handsome Lieutenant Douglas MacArthur, who, when no knife could be found, gallantly offered his sword for the ceremonial cutting of the wedding cake. The happy couple roared off in a sleek French-made racer, as Theodore tossed an old shoe at them and an exhausted Edith sighed with relief. They honeymooned first on a nearby Virginia estate and then in Cuba, where they toured San Juan Hill. [49]

After departing the White House, Alice reversed her pattern and couldn't stay away. Her runabout could be seen parked in the driveway each afternoon. Marriage seemed to have strengthened her attachment to her father and family. Plus political instincts resulting from growing up a Roosevelt inclined her toward the center of power, a predilection she never lost. As Theodore's term wound down, she dreaded continuing in Washington as the mere wife of a congressman. Having been exposed early to the lore of a superstitious Irish nurse, Alice fancied herself a witch; she had always delighted in the game of casting spells on political enemies. She very much disliked the Tafts and was incensed to learn that when they replaced the Roosevelts, that they intended to turn out certain White House employees whom the Roosevelts had come to cherish. In a generous gesture, the departing Roosevelts invited the Tafts to their final White House dinner to provide useful information and an orientation. Alice attended—unhappily, and when the guests of honor had departed following a dinner, during which the mood felt rather downbeat, she took a supernatural revenge. Quietly she stole outside and buried a small voodoo figurine, putting a malevolent spell on it to bring bad fortune to the next occupants of the White House. [50] Only a few months later, Helen Taft, a dominating woman who had pushed her husband's career, became incapacitated by a severe stroke.

V

Few nineteenth-century Americans went to theatres or attended concerts, because of rural isolation, religious prohibitions, or the infrequency of staged attractions. The East Room of the White House did not become a venue for concerts or entertainment until the 1880's, when President Chester A. Arthur (a New Yorker) held the first concerts. Up to this time, the Marine Band had filled the musical needs of the White House, at receptions, occasional dances and balls, and garden parties. For an East Room gathering in 1890, Caroline Harrison, wife of President Benjamin Harrison, offered the first elegant commemorative program, with the concert selections printed on nine-by-four-inch, cream-colored satin ribbons. Before marriage Mrs. Harrison had taught music at girls' schools in Ohio and Kentucky, and herself played competently on the piano, one of her favorite compositions being Louis Moreau Gottschalk's *The Last Hope*. In 1892 the Harrisons invited Sissieretta Jones, usually called the "Black Patti," to perform at a luncheon in the Blue Room. Jones, trained in opera at Providence Academy of Music in her native Rhode Island, delighted the luncheon attendees with "Swanee River," "Home Sweet Home," and a few operatic selections. Caroline Harrison rewarded her with a bouquet of White House orchids. Banned from opera stages by her color, Jones went on to tour as the star of the popular *Black Patti Troubadours* show from 1896 to 1916. Both William McKinley and Theodore Roosevelt invited her back to the White House for return engagements. [51]

As previously noted (Chapter 16), a tremendous national craze for bands had taken hold during the 1890's; during McKinley's term as many as 5000 gathered on the White House Lawn to hear the Marine Band. In 1899 McKinley signed a law that doubled the Band's size and raised salaries. The orchestral unit now performed full concerts as well as providing music for social functions. McKinley was the first president to be announced with the distinctive drum rolls and bugle notes known as "Ruffles and Flourishes" (along with "Hail to the Chief"). Another McKinley first was the state dinner/musicale pattern, beginning with the Supreme Court dinner in 1898. From then till now, guests proceeded from elaborate dinners in the State Dining Room to the East Room to hear music. The McKinleys also introduced ragtime to the White House. At the Gridiron Club dinner on March 27, 1897, vaudeville star George O'Connor sang coon songs for the president, including "My Gal's a Highborn Lady" and "Mammy's Little Alabama Coon." At a Valentine's Day dance in 1901, following a diplomatic dinner, the program featured American dances, including the two-step, and the Marine Band played cakewalks including Kerry Mills' *Whistling Rufus* and Abe Holzmann's *Bunch O' Blackberries*. [52]

Neither of the Roosevelts inclined toward music as much as they did toward verbal and visual arts. Nevertheless musical events, for the first time, became regularly—instead of occasionally—scheduled on the White House calendar. Much of this activity they turned over to New York's Steinway Piano Company which contracted to supply such leading artists as Busoni, Paderewski, Schumann-Heink, and the Vienna Men's Singing Society. In January 1903, Steinway, in celebration of its 50th anniversary, donated to the White House its first concert grand piano, the legendary "Gold Steinway." The case of this piano, ornately carved and decorated with the coats of arms of the original thirteen states, was overlaid with gold leaf. Under the lid, a leading American artist, Thomas Wilmer Dewing, painted nine elegantly gowned ladies representing the Nine Muses.

Printed invitations several pages long contained the programs of the concerts. Printed on heavy paper stock, they pictured the White House, including the new West Wing added in 1902. Adjoining cameo portraits of Theodore and Edith adorned the first page above the titles. The Steinway Company furnished a steady stream of pianists, singers, chamber ensembles, symphony orchestras, and choral groups. [53] Especially memorable was a performance by the 28-year-old cellist Pablo Casals in January 1904, in which he accompanied a baritone as well as perfoming solo. Casals was taken with the President: "He put his arm around my shoulder after the concert and led me around among the guests, introducing me to everyone…. I felt that in a sense he personified the American nation, with all his energy, strength, and confidence." [54] Almost sixty years later, Casals would play in the same room for President Kennedy.

According to one witness, TR preferred ragtime to European art music. [55] The Rough Riders sang "Hot Time in the Old Town Tonight," and Theodore campaigned and became identified with it. At a Christmas party in 1901, he actually did a cakewalk, to this tune and to Kerry Mills' *Whistling Rufus*. The best-known ragtime anecdote from the White House concerns the *Maple Leaf Rag*. At a diplomatic reception ca. 1905, Princess Alice went up to Marine Band Conductor William Santelmann and requested the Joplin rag. Santelmann expressed astonishment and denied familiarity with the piece. Alice saucily gave the lie to this protestation by insisting that the Band had played it for her on previous occasions. Santelmann gave in and Alice enjoyed her rag. Research reveals that instrumental parts for the *Maple Leaf Rag* dated 1904 have turned up in the Marine—Band archives. [56] It remains in the repertoire.

Ragtime and Theodore Roosevelt have other associations. As previously noted, Scott Joplin's lost "ragtime opera" *Guest of Honor* may have been based upon TR's inviting Booker T. Washington to dinner at the White House (Chapters 19 & 27). Joplin also honored the 26th President with his rag *The Strenuous Life* (1902), a phrase that expressed and encapsulated the Roosevelt recipe for living [57]: "I wish to preach, not the doctrine of ignoble ease, but the doctrine of the strenuous life, the life of toil and effort…." (spoken in1899 in Chicago and much reprinted). [58] Several rags received the title "Bully!" after the President's favorite positive expletive (see Ragtime Almanac below). The Rough riders seem to be recalled in the rag title *Teddy's Pardners* (1903), and the post-presidential big game hunt in Africa brought forth the rags *The African Hunter* (1909) and *Teddy in the Jungle* (1910). The African expedition also inspired a major segment of Ziegfeld's *Follies of 1909*. Ballet girls costumed as animals cavorted onstage to the song, "Moving Day in Jungle Town." [59]

RAGTIME ALMANAC

Ragtime Associated with Theodore Roosevelt

"A Hot Time in the Old Town Tonight" (1898)	Theodore Metz (Song)
The Strenuous Life (1902)	Scott Joplin (Rag)
Guest of Honor (1903)	Scott Joplin (Lost Opera)
Teddy's Pardners (1903)	Horace Dowell (Rag)
Teddy Bear Rag (1907)	Hattie Goben (Rag)
The African Hunter (1909)	Edwin F. Kendall (Rag)
"Moving Day in Jungle Town" (1909)	Seymour Brown & Nat D. Ayer
Bully Rag (1910)	J. Fred O'Connor (Rag)
Who Let the Cows Out? A Bully Rag (1910)	Charles Humfield (Rag)
Teddy in the Jungle (1910)	Edward J. Freeburg (Rag)
Bully Rag (1911)	James E. C. Kelly (Rag)
Bull Moose Rag (1912)	K. M. Gilham (Rag)

Notes: Chapter 22

1. Quoted in H.W.Brands, *TR: The Last Romantic*, 433.
2. Quoted in Nathan Miller, *Theodore Roosevelt: A Life*, 353-354.
3. Michael Medved, *The Shadow Presidents: The Secret History of the Chief Executives and Their Top Aides*, 101-106; 110-111.
4. *Ibid.*, 111-113.
5. N. Miller, 419; Sylvia J. Morris, *Edith Kermit Roosevelt: Portrait of a First Lady*, 249.
6. Page Smith, *America Enters the World: A People's History of the Progressive Era and World War I*, 40.
7. Medved, 101-102.
8. N. Miller, 419 n.
9. Theodore Roosevelt, *Theodore Roosevelt: An Autobiography*, 369; N. Miller, 420, for relations with press.
10. Owen Wister, *My Forty Years Friendship with Theodore Roosevelt*, 87-89, *124, 128;* Willard B. Gatewood, Jr., *Theodore Roosevelt and the Art of Controversy; Episodes of the White House Years*, 16, 17; Noel F. Busch, *The Story of Theodore Roosevelt and His Influence on Our Times*, 177-179; N. Miller, 425-426; Frank Sullivan, *Our Times*, III, 82-84.
11. N. Miller, 423; Sullivan, III, 70-80.
12. Peter Collier, with David Horowitz, *The Roosevelts: An American Saga*, 142.
13. *Ibid.* 137, 141-142.
14. *Idem.*
15. Earle Looker, *The White House Gang.*
16. *Ibid.*, 15.
17. *Ibid.* 23.
18. *Ibid.*, 24.
19. *Ibid.*, 26.
20. *Ibid.*, 172-175.
21. *Ibid.*, 84-86.
22. *Ibid.*, 44-47.
23. N. Miller, 427.
24. It still does today. The National Park Service in taking it over retained the furniture and belongings the Roosevelts left behind.
25. N. Miller, 428; S. J. Morris, 4.
26. N. Miller, 359.
27. *Ibid.*, 417-417. Congress appropriated $540,000 for the renovation. Later in 1949-51, during the Truman administration, inspection revealed the White House to be so dilapidated and unsafe that it had to be totally gutted inside and rebuilt from the outside walls. Apparently McKim's work had not fixed the structural problems and been merely a "cosmetic covering-up," leaving the building unstable until the Truman renovation 47 years later. It had continued to be a fire hazard; partitions were overloaded, rendering the second floor unsafe; and beams had been weakened by notches cut for pipes and wiring. This second job cost $5,412,000. The White House is now held up by a frame of structural steel. See David McCullough, *Truman*, 876-880.
28. S.J.Morris, 254; N. Miller, 428.
29. Looker, 97-98.
30. N. Miller, 427-428.

31. *Ibid.,* 304.
32. *Ibid.,* 298; William Henry Harbaugh, *Power and Responsibility: The Life and Times of Theodore Roosevelt,* 72-73.
33. Busch, 211-212.
34. James Brough, *Princess Alice: A Biography of Alice Roosevelt Longworth,* 148.
35. Howard Teichmann, *Alice: The Life and Times of Alice Roosevelt Longworth,* 36-37. Carl Sferrazza Anthony, *First Ladies: The Saga of the Presidents' Wives and Their Power (1789-1961),* 303.
36. Teichmann, 32-33.
37. *Ibid.,* 36; Collier, with Horowitz, 177.
38. Wister, *87.*
39. *Ibid.,* 89.
40. Brough, *148*-149.
41. *Ibid.* 150-151.
42. Collier, with Horowitz, *120.*
43. Brough, 162.
44. *Ibid.* 150-151.
45. N. Miller, 433; Anthony, 311.
46. Collier, with Horowitz, 138.
47. *Idem.*
48. Brough, 184. Her father added, "She'll take that too, if it doesn't take too long to cool off." Quoted in Teichmann, 57.
49. *Ibid.,* 181-195.
50. Teichmann, 23, 69-75.
51. Elise K. Kirk, *Musical Highlights from the White House,* 73-79.
52. *Ibid.,* 79-83, 161.
53. *Ibid.* 89-93.
54. Quoted in *Ibid.* 92.
55. Quoted in *Ibid.,* 89.
56. Edward A. Berlin, *King of Ragtime:Scott Joplin and His Era,* 152-153, and Berlin, "Scott Joplin at the White House," *Rag Times,* Vol.23, No. 5 (January 1990): 6.
57. *Ibid.,* 105-106.
58. Quoted in *Theodore Roosevelt: An American Mind, Selected Writings,* 184.
59. Ian Whitcomb, *Irving Berlin and Ragtime America,* 163.

23. Varieties of the Social Evil

> How did I feel about it all? That's a sensible question. I wish I could give you a straight answer. One thing though, I was never satisfied…. I always had the feeling that there must be something more—more fun, you know…. Of course, they'd drain me off. I'd be depleted and enervated—but I never had the feeling of satisfaction that I was always looking for. (Comment by a Storyville, New Orleans customer.) [1]

Many accounts romanticize pre-World War I prostitution. Such books exude a nostalgia for the good-old-days of sporting houses (e. g. John Steinbeck: *Cannery Row, Sweet Thursday*). They focus on luxurious furnishings of renowned brothels, plush parlors, gilt tables and chairs, and mirrored boudoirs. Plus the beautiful, extravagantly gowned women welcoming their delighted customers. Some authors color the high-toned aura with humorous anecdotes. In *Those Naughty Ladies of the Old Northwest* [2] (note title), we learn that Madame Lou Graham of Seattle operated "a sumptuous multi-level house that was first-class in every respect. Her girls were recruited from among the best houses world-wide…. The plush furnishings and able staff drew compliments from wealthy patrons…." [3] She catered to a colorful, fun-loving clientele:

> Lou ran a clean house and never had a bit of trouble, except for the usual breakage, several heart attacks by over-eager elderly clients, and a favorite police official who accidentally shot a settee while showing off his gun. And there was the time the shipping magnate's son set fire to Lou's place one New Year's Eve. The fire didn't amount to much and the family paid for the drapes, the wallpaper, and Mary Anne's dress. [4]

As will be shown, the inmates in a first-class house received better pay, treatment, and a greater degree of personal security. However the lot of the working girl, like that of the policeman in the contemporary song, could never have been a happy one. Very few went on to respectable employment, marriage, or advanced years.

Sociologist Howard B. Woolston carried out a contemporary study of prostitution in the United States.[5] Data was spotty and statistics few, but by extrapolating from available figures, Woolston concluded that about 100,000 women inhabited brothels, that the ages of most were between 18 and 29, that the average career in prostitution lasted six years, that about two-thirds were native-born, with almost one-third foreign-born. These figures omitted African-American women who made up a concluding five percent. He also deduced (rather shakily from very few studies) that from 65% to 75% suffered from a venereal disease, and that a majority were addicted to liquor or narcotics. [6]

When reformers studied the social evil, seeking causes that would point to reforms, they hit a wall of puzzlement as to why women chose the perilous and destructive existence of the prostitute. The economic reason didn't explain it. Most women preferred the poverty of $6 per week to the whore's affluence that rose from a floor of $30 to a ceiling as high as $200 per week. The few studies undertaken concluded that half or more of these women were mentally deficient. Some exhibited intelligence considered just below average ("subnormal" and "dull"), while a greater number proved difficult to classify, apparently because they responded negatively to interrogators. These, from one-third to one-half, were classified as "feeble-minded." Poor health and disease were described as complicating factors. Nearly all came from backgrounds of poverty, little schooling, lack of skills, and poor family life. One significant correlation shows up as the lack of a father in many cases. All of this suggests that girls who sold themselves had experienced the damage of trauma. Traumatized by combinations parental neglect, cruelty, poverty, and illness, these women lacked the self-respect and emotional strength to keep them from the harm of prostitution. [7] Recent historian Ruth Rosen believes that "feeble-minded" was the label attached to prostitutes who responded negatively to investigators and who failed to conform to middle-class values. When they showed no shame or remorse, contemporary researchers perceived them as too feeble of mind to grasp the essential evil in their lives. [8]

Not all prostitutes worked full-time. Many working women prostituted themselves only occasionally. Here the gamut runs from those supplementing income to girls out for a good time who accepted presents. Some would eventually give up regular jobs for the higher pay of a full-timer. There were also wives who dabbled in prostitution to add to the family income, often during times of hardship. Another curious figure in the "oldest profession" was the kept woman or mistress. These presented a domestic front to the world, pretending to be wives, but taking cash from a man for rent and other expenses. [9] However if the arrangement lasted a long time and children resulted, the mistress seems to have crossed a line, from prostitution into the limbo of the "second wife," unsanctioned by law or religion, but clearly a partner in a domestic relationship.

II

Part-timers worked outside the house system, as did many of the full-timers. These outside women may be further classified as affiliated or unaffiliated. Unaffiliated prostitutes simply picked up men, on the street, in dance halls, gambling places, or drinking places, any spot that would tolerate free-lance operators. Some of these worked for pimps, some kept their earnings; either way, they had no arrangement or connection with bordellos or places of entertainment such as music halls or concert-saloons. Women who sought their clients out-of-doors were called streetwalkers because they regularly patrolled certain streets and locales. When they picked up a customer, they either took him to a room they rented or to a place of assignation where rooms were rented for sexual purposes. Such "assignation houses," as they were called, could be actual houses that appeared to be homes (gardens in front, parlor inside), houses that proclaimed "Furnished Rooms" to let, or houses that masqueraded as hotels. All rented rooms for short terms, periods of hours rather than days. In New York City, the "Raines Law" (Chapter 4) allowed saloons and bars to serve liquor on Sunday if they qualified as hotels by renting a minimum of ten rooms. In 1905, of 1407 hotels in the city, 1150 were of the Raines-Law type. All hotels renting rooms to more than one guest per night were classified as "disorderly." The free-lance prostitute easily floated from one competing location to another. [10]

Women who worked in establishments that enticed men with entertainment were unaffiliated outside of working hours. What they earned after-hours belonged to them. On-premises they received commissions. These premises ranged from the back rooms of saloons, where very crude and obscene shows went on, to multi-story concert-saloons "with a different specialty on each level." [11] The concert-saloon or music hall appeared after the Civil War and is the predecessor of the twentieth-century cabaret or nightclub (which supplanted it after 1910). They varied from cellars measuring only sixty-by-thirty to large establishments of three or four floors. One historian called them "a department store of vice." [12] They flourished in large numbers; Asbury names 47 of them in San Francisco's "Barbary Coast" district, including such famous ones as the Bella Union, the House of All Nations, the Hippodrome, and the Dew Drop Inn. [13] Near the front door, the main bar pressured customers to purchase drinks before seeking out the attractions within. Everywhere waitresses, called "grissettes" or "beer-jerkers," functioning as B-Girls, circulated to lead men on to the purchase of more drinks. Although the drinks were inferior and overpriced, concert-saloons offered security; here customers weren't beaten, robbed, or drugged as was often the case in such dives as barrel houses or illegal "blind pigs."

In secluded places, back rooms and basements, much more pornographic entertainment was presented. New Orleans historian Al Rose recalls the popular "Oyster Dance" performed by the talented Olivia:

> Completely naked, she began by placing a raw oyster on her forehead and then leaned back and "shimmied" the oyster back and forth over her body without dropping it, finally causing it to run down to her instep, from which a quick kick would flip it high in the air, whereupon she would catch it on her forehead whence it started. [14]

Much lewder were the "circuses," wherein the women, and a few men as needed, staged erotic acts. These circuses also included lesbian shows and women copulating with animals. Asbury recalls an act ca. 1900 taking place in a San Francisco establishment called Madame Gabrielle's Lively Flea. For $25 customers took in an exhibition involving a woman and a Shetland pony. Nearby occurred a weekly show in which white women performed with Negro men, which, for that excessively racist time, may have been considered the ultimate in depravity. [15]

The most singular anecdote from this milieu tells of Frank Mulkey of Portland, Oregon, who liked to come to San Francisco to watch the girls and their dances. He purchased the required drinks, which he never touched, sat in his corner, and chatted with the girls who served him. Whenever a girl treated him well and kindly, he brought out a pocket notebook, took their names, and promised to include them in his will. They smiled at his claim to wealth and indulged him, but when he died in 1927, this wealthy lumber and real estate operator left each a large sum of money. [16]

III

The essential condition of the prostitute was vulnerability. Once across the line of respectability, she became subject to forces and powers that degraded her. These included abuse and violence from customers; exploitation by pimps, police, politicians, merchants, property owners, and madams; diseases; poor working conditions (for most); legal inequality; exile from the support structures of church and family; and society's scorn and rejection. Her final days of hunger, exposure, and sickness, went unnoted, and her death was only a statistic. If many prostitutes left the trade after a few years (as noted above, the _average_ term was six years), perhaps some started over with a new identity. But the process of degradation offered few mercies or second chances.

Degradation put its quickest blight on crib girls. Cribs were shacky, barebones structures, usually in rows, but often multi-storied. The prostitute displayed herself at the window of the small receiving room in front. Behind this, she serviced her customer in a room (the "workshop") just big enough to hold a narrow bed, a kerosene stove with a kettle of hot water, and a washstand with a basin. A strip of oilcloth lay across the bottom of the bed to protect the bedding from the customer's shoes. Customers removed only their hats. Chinese and Negro women could be had for "two bits" (a quarter), and whites cost fifty cents to a dollar. The customer opened or dropped his pants at the washstand where the girl washed his member and inspected it for disease. Then came the sex act, usually over in a few minutes. Glassless, with open studding, cribs flourished in warmer locales, the southern states, the southwest, and the west coast. [17]

In New Orleans' Storyville, where the main parlor houses lined one side of Basin Street for three blocks, most of the rest of the properties, extending five blocks by three blocks, contained cribs. Al Rose tells us that a two-family house "could be partitioned into as many as two dozen cribs. These were rented by the night only, at an average of three dollars a night. The girl would report to the corner bartender, "…pay three dollars in advance, and pick up a key, which she would turn in at daybreak." He notes further that each row of cribs brought in "from forty to a hundred dollars per night." [18] Along the two upper streets (Robertson and Villere), farthest from Basin, blacks inhabited—and patronized—the rows of cribs. [19]

Cribs received minimal cleaning, and bedding was changed seldom. Latinas usually put up small altar-shrines with figures of the Virgin Mary, and walls were decorated with calendar pictures and sentimental mottoes. Over the head of the bed was a framed placard with a woman's name printed within a border of flowers. Asbury observes that "the cribs of San Francisco must have been largely populated by girls named Rose, Daisy, Martha, and Leah." [20] Cribs there were grouped ethnically and racially on particular streets, some given over to whites, others to Negroes, Mexicans, Spanish, and French.

However this tidy system could be overruled by erotic imperative. Elsewhere on the Barbary Coast were streets where "these dens were occupied by women of all colors and nationalities;…even a few Chinese and Japanese girls." [21] Asbury describes these as both "the worst cribs" and "the most popular, partly because of the great variety and extraordinary depravity of the women to be found there, and partly because the police seldom entered the street unless compelled to do so by a murder or a serious shooting or stabbing affray. Further:

> Every night…this dismal bedlam of obscenity, lighted only by the red lamps above the doors of the cribs, was thronged by a tumultuous mob of half-drunken men, who stumbled from crib to crib, greedily inspecting the women as if they had been so many wild animals in cages. From the casement-windows leaned the harlots, naked to the waist, adding their shrill cries of invitation to the uproar, while their pimps haggled with the passing men and tried to drag them inside the dens.

On Saturday nights, the pimps lined up the men, hats in one hand and money in the other. Some of these crib women entertained between 80 and 100 men. Prices there (Morton Street) ranged from twenty-five cents for a Mexican to a dollar for an American girl, with Chinese and Japanese getting fifty cents and French women seventy-five cents. [22] One former prostitute, renowned as "Iodoform Kate" managed—by avoiding pimps—to save enough to purchase a dozen of these cribs in 1895, which allowed her to retire a wealthy woman. [23]

The largest of San Francisco's crib complexes, three- and four-story U-shaped buildings, acquired the name "cow-yard cribs." One of these, a four-story structure at 620 Jackson Street, was originally known simply by its address "620, etc." When the trolley reached that point, the conductor (if no women were on board) announced, "All out for the whorehouse!" [24] Later, because everyone knew that nearly all of its profits went to politicians and city officials, the resort was derisively nicknamed "Municipal Crib" and "Municipal Brothel." Rates varied by floor: Mexicans in the basement—25 cents; Americans on the first floor—50 cents; Americans (younger, more attractive) on the second floor—75 cents; French women on the third floor—one dollar; and "Negresses" on the top floor—50 cents. Altogether there were 133 cribs and a saloon in the complex. [25]

Even grander was the cow-yard structure erected in 1899 (by the Twinkling Star Corporation) and named the "Nymphia." Each of its three floors contained 150 cubicles, at a daily rental of five dollars. Grandiose plans called for an annex of 500 more cubicles, but this never came to pass, as no more than 300 of the existing units were ever occupied. Nor did the police permit the owners to christen it "Hotel Nymphomania." Nymphs in the

Nymphia were required to remain naked during work hours, whereas in cribs along city streets, women exposed themselves in partial coverings such as nightgowns. Any woman refusing a customer lost her concession. Each door had a long, narrow vertical window permitting supervisory inspection of the occupants. A popular, quirky feature when the place opened was a coin slot in the door, which, when a dime was deposited, automatically raised the curtain on the window in the door. Prospective clients delighted in walking the corridors and dropping their dimes for voyeuristic thrills. But despite the immense popularity of this unique feature, it was ended after a few months because customers used slugs bought for a few cents from vendors just outside. [26]

Born of the '49 Gold Rush, the Barbary Coast ran wide open for almost 70 years, until the reformers took it down in 1917, as they did elsewhere. Asbury, its first historian, described it as the nation's most vicious, criminal, and depraved red-light district. Lying along the waterfront, centered on Pacific Street, it contained cheap saloons; dance-halls; "melodeons"; concert-saloons (both offering entertainment); "deadfalls," wine and beer dens, very unsafe; plus many "houses" of different price levels. There were hundreds of these various places, many in dank basements, and all with women. An 1890 survey indicated 3117 places with liquor licenses, one for every 96 residents. This did not account for the illicit places, the "blind pigs," estimated to number 2000. Nearby lay Chinatown with about 25 opium dens containing 325 bunks open to the public. Some of these were actually fake, staged to shock tourists led in by members of the Chinatown Guides Association. [27]

What the slumming tourist did not encounter was Chinatown's sexual slavery. Chinese women and girls, usually sold outright by poor parents, were shipped across the Pacific in lots of 50 or 100 and installed in cribs, without any human rights, few privileges, and no wages. This went on from 1850 to 1914; every ship out of China carried a consignment of them. By the late 1870's, they probably numbered between 1500 and 2000. The Chinese Exclusion Act of 1881 forced the trade underground but failed to limit it. Many women were shipped in crates as cargo; others sent to Canada came down on the train. If seized as "illegals," Chinese men would appear and claim to be husbands. Nothing stopped this very lucrative trade.

Supposedly these slaves were indentured for four to five years, but they never achieved release. Each month, when a girl became "sick" because of her menstrual period, a month was added to her term of servitude. Disease usually took them early. Except for a few exercise periods a week, they never left the premises. Originally purchased in China for about $80, selling prices in the U.S. ranged from $2500 down to as little as $200. Men paid 25 or 50 cents for their services, available to all races and colors, including teenage boys who were kept out of parlor houses. [28] Since about 90% of these women were diseased, so was a high proportion of San Francisco's male youth.

For daring to refuse any customer—or if a customer complained—they received torture. Owners lashed with whips and branded with hot irons. Few reached 20, and after five or six years, because disease had made them repulsive, they were allowed to "escape" to religious missions such as the Salvation Army. Earlier, before missionaries appeared to care for them, sick women were placed in back alley rooms called "hospitals," and left to die, abandoned on wooden shelves with a cup of boiled rice, a cup of water, and a small oil lamp. Chinese sex slaves learned nothing of America, spoke few English words, and understood nothing of American law or legal rights. Few tried to help them, but one of the few who did was Donaldina Cameron, a New Zealander who joined the Presbyterian mission in 1895. She devoted her adult life to rescuing Chinese prostitutes. Donaldina quickly learned all facets of the "system." She knew the vice locations and gained the support of the police. With police assistance, she raided the dens and cribs to bring the women out. In time the girls themselves sent messages, smuggled by sympathetic customers, begging for help. These efforts caused publicity and resulting public awareness of these evils. By 1914 most of this sex slavery had been suppressed. Donaldina operated the mission until 1939, and died at 99 in 1968, surrounded by the descendants of those she had liberated. [29]

IV

The sport with a few dollars in his pocket could steer past the squalid cribs (in the South and West) or the grubby fifty-cent tenements (in the North and East). A little more money raised the possibilities: more appealing women, a longer time, security, a quasi-domestic atmosphere. How much better to make oneself "at home" in a parlor house. The more refined madams greeted their "guests," then called up the stairs, "Company girls!" Those extra dollars lying in the pocket of the sport achieved something almost miraculous; they masked, or papered over, the cold truth of "boughten" sex.

Parlor houses ran a gamut of cost and luxury. At the top flourished the "mansions" costing $20 or more, plus a mandatory $5 for overpriced champagne of dubious quality. For this, one could enjoy a young, clean-looking girl in a boudoir. There would be no crude knock on the door at mid-passage to warn a slow guest to hurry-up. Mansions tended toward exclusiveness in their clientele. A guest had to be known or vouched for, and a very few of these luxury resorts actually required an appointment. Any rowdiness or drunken rough stuff brought permanent expulsion; such banishment meant disgrace in high-tone sporting circles. [30]

From there the drop-off was steep, as very few places kept to such standards of conduct and decorum. The five and ten dollar houses also catered to the affluent, but cash was the only requisite for admittance, and it excused most behavioral crudities. These higher-scale places attempted the genteel pretensions of hosting guests a la mansion, but not-so-subtle differences in ambience revealed the wide gap between what $25 and $5 bought. At the lower end, the process moved faster. Instead of conversation, only bits of small talk and pleasantries preceded the action. One smelled cheap perfume instead of a clean body. The champagne came in "splits," a quick glass for him and her to set the timer on precoital small talk. After thirty to forty minutes, the guest found himself out on the street or having a beer in the next-door saloon. The dollar places served the unaffluent middle-class types. These put on no airs; a hello was followed, if there was no line, by payment and a quick trip down the hall. This took only 15 or 20 minutes. It could go better in a three-to-five dollar place on a slow weeknight. Then the girls would sit around, send out for beer, and chat with customers. One of the women reminisced: "The prostitutes sat around in their underwear or wrappers, drank beer, joshed a lot in country talk, felt at home with the simple horny guests that came to them with dusty shoes and derbies." [31]

Asbury states that "the parlor-house girls were the aristocracy of San Francisco's red-light district…who found life easier and more remunerative in the bagnios than in the dives of the Barbary Coast." [32] The number of girls varied, depending upon the size of the premises, from five to about twenty. A girl in a house could earn, before deductions, as much as $200 a week. Most houses had been private residences and were renovated to contain more (and smaller) bedrooms and a larger parlor or lounge. Each small bedroom contained a brass bed, a chair, and a bureau. The parlor was crammed with decorative elements: bright rugs, erotic paintings and photographs, fancy couches, heavily gilded chairs and tables, plus a musical instrument, a piano or something coin-operated. Prostitutes dressed scantily, in nightgowns, thin dresses minus lingerie, or merely lingerie. Madame Bertha Kahn in 1870's San Francisco dressed her thirty girls identically, in red sandals, long, white nightgowns trimmed with lace, and red velvet caps. Madam Bertha maintained decorum; she forbade the prodding or caressing of her girls, served no liquor, allowed no obscene talk, and formally introduced her girls. On Sunday afternoons she closed the place to all but invited guests. These and the girls socialized and sang sentimental songs that Madam Bertha played on her parlor's organ. Tea and cakes were served. In every bedroom and in the parlor, posted signs announced:

No Vulgarity Allowed
In This Establishment [33]

Parlor houses comprised the central institutions of vice districts. All else, saloons, music halls, gambling places, pawn shops, drug stores (where drugs were sold openly), quacks, shooting galleries, notions stores, revolved around them. Woolston cites a 1911-1913 U.S. Department of Justice census that covered 310 cities in 26 states, indicating 72 known vice districts. [34] Bluesman W. C. Handy describes one such in the small city of Clarksdale, Mississippi:

> Across the tracks of the Y&MV railroad in Clarksdale there was a section called the "New World."…the local red-light district. To the New World came lush octoroons and quadroons from Louisiana, soft cream-colored fancy gals from Mississippi towns. Just beyond this section lived some of the oldest and most respectable Negro families. On their way to the Baptist or Methodist churches they were required to pass before the latticed houses of prostitution. Occasionally they caught glimpses of white men lounging with the pretty near-white "imports." [35]

Contrasting with the subdued atmosphere of Clarksdale's New World was Chicago's wide-open "Levee." Following the Fire of 1871, the Levee grew up on the far southern border of Chicago's downtown where the construction of new railroad passenger terminals caused a narrow north-south corridor to become unsuitable for residences. Major streetcar lines ran through this area. Chicagoans were astonished by the rapid growth and expansion of the Levee's brothels and businesses. In 1881, observers counted 11,600 men and 1007 women entering the district. Another survey a year later tallied, "within twenty square blocks," 500 saloons, six "variety theatres," more than 1000 concert-saloons, fifteen gambling places, between 50 and 60 poolrooms, and about 500 parlor and other whorehouses "harboring" over 3000 women. Police patrolled only its borders, going in only when public indignation demanded a raid or a murder had occurred. Much of the land was owned by Chicago's elite citizens and politicians. [36]

One of the Levee's wonders was the "House of All Nations," which had two entrances. Through one door the price was two dollars, through the other the price was five dollars. The same girls serviced both sets of customers, with the five-dollar people having to spring for champagne. Despite the promise of an international flavor, only a few of the ladies were citizens of other countries. Nor is it likely that this bordello fulfilled the universal promise of "a good time" to any greater extent than others did. Another of the Levee's wonders, probably its crown jewel, was the Everleigh Club, which put Chicago on the world map. It became a "must" on the itineraries of visiting celebrities, tourists, and businessmen.

The madams—and proprietors—of this fabled establishment were the eponymous—and pseudonymous—sisters known in Chicago as Ada (b.1876) and Minna (b.1878) Everleigh. According to what they told a biographer almost 25 years later in New York, they haled from an unnamed town in Kentucky, daughters of a well-to-do lawyer. Coming out of finishing school, Minna the younger, at 19, in 1897, married in a society wedding. Soon after, Ada wed the groom's brother. Each sister claimed to have been seriously abused by her brother-husband. Unwilling to accept brutal treatment during a time when a husband's authority was unquestioned, Ada and Minna took counsel, packed clothes and liquid assets of $35,000, and fled. They never returned or remarried.

Initially they tried showbiz, acting in minor road companies offering such melodramas as *East Lynne.* Seeking another vocation, they followed the crowds to Omaha in 1898 to take in the Trans-Mississippi Exposition.

Deciding to tap into the money streaming out of the pockets of tourists, they rented a house, hired some girls, and opened a brothel. The season netted them another $35,000 and inspired them to head for Chicago to obtain a permanent location. Late in 1899 they purchased a large parlor house at 2131-33 South Dearborn for $55,000. The "Everleigh Club" opened February 1, 1900, projecting an ambience of southern gentility and culture. On this gala occasion grocers and salesmen, desirous of the sisters' custom, furnished complimentary food and wine. The full staff of thirty girls, their services not complimentary, took in a gross of $1000, of which they split $700, or $23 each. With expenses of $200, the Everleigh Club profited $100 on its opening night. [37]

Drawing on their cultured backgrounds, Ada and Minna exercised expertise and elevated tastes that enabled them to create an unpretentious upper-class environment. They hired competent servants who actually cleaned and dusted the expensive furnishings. They dressed their girls in evening gowns and drilled them in courtly manners. Clients were introduced to them formally—no vulgar line-up for selection as elsewhere. An evening with a girl cost an extravagant $50! Ada and Minna philosophised that a single $50 client did less damage to their employees than five ten-dollar clients. [38]

They aimed for grandeur, with eleven parlors, each with a different décor: gold, silver, copper, Moorish, red, green, blue, rose, "oriental," Japanese, and Egyptian. There were also a large dining room, a library, a music room, and—an art gallery! Plus thirty rooms for the "boarders" (girls) and boudoirs for Ada and Minna. With such space, halls were quiet, redolent of flowers and perfume. No loud voices "acting out" feelings and experiences disturbed the serene atmosphere. Clients were screened as to financial condition and character through recommendation. Checks were accepted at departure. With champagne costing $12, an arranged party typically ran to $500 and frequently to as much as $1000, again with a check accepted at party's end. Curiously gentlemen of the press, never big earners or spenders, were always admitted because the sisters loved their lively company. In a discreet age before gossip columnists, journalists never told the secrets of the night world. [39]

Notably the sisters cast their recollections in a mold both humane and feminist. They exercised care in not hiring the underaged or paying procurers. With such working conditions, word of mouth assured plenty of candidates for each vacancy. No resident boyfriends, pimps, were allowed on premises. Any criminal act, e.g., robbing a client, caused immediate expulsion. Each girl received warm and dignified treatment. On their regular drives to the bank in their fine carriage, the sisters always invited one of the "boarders" to accompany them. (Which also conveniently displayed an item of their merchandise.) In an age of primitive medicine, they did their best to maintain the health of their girls. No strongarm type or bouncer skulked about the premises to enforce the sisters' will against any opposition. If a customer caused a disturbance, they relied on the kitchen help. In that age of heavy feeding, Ada and Minna ate lightly and encouraged their girls to do likewise. Years later (it is said), some of them attributed good health to eating habits instilled by the sisters. [40] To their biographer, Minna opined (using the present tense):

> A girl in our establishment is not a commodity with a market price....She's much more on the same level with people belonging to the professional classes, who accept fees for services rendered.... As for the moral and esthetic standpoint—who knows! They write books about it but get nowhere. [41]

Here she offered a defense both ahead of its time and classical in its traditional view of the courtesan as a professional.

The famous visit of Prince Heinrich of Germany in 1902, that brought such notoriety to Alice Roosevelt (Chapter 22), also included the Everleigh Club. Upon debarking in New York, the Prince immediately requested a visit to Chicago to see its renowned bordello. The Club threw him a very major party. The girls, dressed in sheer, fawn skirts, performed a dance of the wine god Dionysus with an increasing frenzy that climaxed, mythologically, with the tearing up of a cloth bull representation of the god. Champagne came next, then a tour of the splendors of the house, after which, the return of the girls, now gowned in their best, followed by a royal banquet. Revelry continued with toasts and a solo dance on the table-top. According to the story, a dancing shoe flew off and knocked over a bottle of champagne, which spilled into the slipper. One of the gentlemen then declaimed: "The darling mustn't get her feet wet," and drank off the wine from the slipper. At this point, another guest lifted his partner into his lap, removed her shoe, poured in wine, and drank it down. Then all the other guests performed the gesture, with one proclaiming that round of toasts in honor of Kaiser Wilhelm II. Additional slippery toasts were drunk off to the Prince himself and to the various beautiful women around the table. According to the sisters, this custom originated on that occasion and spread as a fad nationwide. [42]

The Everleigh Club operated eleven years and employed about 600 girls. It made an annual profit of $120,000. As elsewhere, by 1910 reformers were attacking the social evil and believed that victory, its eradication, would result from closure of parlor houses, the most visible manifestation of the evil. Ada and Minna tried to hold on, but their establishment was so well known that for many it symbolized prostitution. Eventually their many powerful friends could no longer hold back the forces of reform, and on October 25, 1911, the police raided and shut down the club. With over a million in the bank, the sisters reacted philosophically. They quietly packed and took off on a six-month European vacation. They relocated in New York City using a new name (or their original one?), and led lives of culture and cultivation. Minna died in 1948, Ada in 1960. No one ever repaid any of $25,000 carried on their books at the time of closure. [43]

Notes: Chapter 23

1. Al Rose, *Storyville, New Orleans: Being an Authentic, Illustrated* Account *of the Notorious Red-Light District,* 162.
2. Gary and Gloria Meier, *Those Naughty Ladies of the Old Northwest.*
3. *Ibid.,* 58.
4. *Idem.*
5. Howard B. Woolston, *Prostitution in the United States: Prior to the Entrance of the United States into the World War.*
6. *Ibid.,* 37-57.
7. *Ibid.,* 58-73; James Lincoln Collier, *The Rise of Selfishness in America,* 56-57; Ruth Rosen, *The Lost Sisterhood: Prostitution in America, 1900-1918,* 22-23.
8. *Idem*; Timothy J. Gilfoyle, *City of Eros: Prostitution and the Commercialization of Sex, 1790-1920,* 66; George J. Kneeland, *Commercialized Prostitution in New York City,* 102-106.
9. Gilfoyle, 288-290.
10. Woolston, 137-144; Gilfoyle, 243-246; Kneeland, 25-45; Perry R. Duis, *The Saloon: Public Drinking in Chicago and Boston, 1880-1920,* 250-251.
11. *Ibid.,* 238.
12. *Idem.*
13. Herbert Asbury, *The Barbary Coast: An Informal History of the San Francisco Underworld,* 288.
14. Rose, *Storyville,* 85.
15. Asbury, *Barbary Coast,* 254. For concert-saloons, see also Asbury, *Barbary Coast,* 125-132, H. Asbury, *The French Quarter,* 236-237; Duis, 238; Collier, 60-61; Gilfoyle, 127-129, 224-225.
16. Asbury, *Barbary Coast,* 296-297.
17. Rosen, 94; Asbury, *Barbary Coast,* 255; Woolston, 104, 136.
18. Rose, *Storyville,* 96.
19. *Idem.*
20. Asbury, *Barbary Coast,* 255.
21. *Ibid.,* 258.
22. *Ibid.,* 258-259.
23. *Ibid.,* 259.
24. *Ibid.,* 269.
25. *Ibid.,* 268-269.
26. *Ibid.,* 262-263.
27. *Ibid.,* 3, 104-132, 166.
28. *Ibid.,* 168-169, 177-181.
29. *Ibid.,* 183; Anne Seagraves, *Soiled Doves: Prostitution in the Early West.*
30. Kneeland, 19-20.
31. Rose, 92-93; also Kneeland, 4, 17-20; Woolston, 132-136.
32. Asbury, *Barbary Coast,* 243.
33. *Ibid.,* 243-249.
34. Woolston, 38, 119-120.
35. W. C. Handy, *Father of the Blues,* 78.
36. Duis, 236-237.
37. Charles Washburn, *Come Into My Parlor: A Biography of the Aristocratic Everleigh Sisters of Chicago,* 120-121, 183-185.
38. *Ibid.,* 11-24.

39. *Ibid.*, 27-32, 71-72.
40. *Ibid.*, 40, 62-63, 66-68, 70, 74, 155-157.
41. *Ibid.*, 104-105.
42. *Ibid.*, 77-81.
43. *Ibid.*, 40, 188-212.

Part III

The Ragtime Nation, 1905-1910 (and a Little Beyond)

24. "Take Me Out to Lakeside"

In [1880] one hundred thousand horses and mules pulled eighteen thousand cars over three thousand miles of city tracks at an average speed of five miles per hour, leaving behind each day one million pounds of manure, which attracted flies until it was pulverized, dried up, and blown about by the wind. [1]

I guess it's a fact that we have got the "trolley habit" badly. In the days of the slow-moving horsecar most of us preferred to walk as much as possible.... If we had a little journey to make—one of a quarter of a mile or so—we never thought of taking a car; now we just hop aboard an electric and are there in a jiffy.

Letter to the Providence Journal, 1901 [2]

Trolleys went into service just when they were needed. By 1850 industrialization, by forcing large numbers of people to concentrate in small areas, was transforming cities. Previously, slow transit, i.e., mainly foot travel, had restricted city size to a radius of about two miles from the city center. For most people two miles was the practical limit for daily commuting to work and markets. To grow, cities needed a more rapid transit. The development of intercity rails in the 1840's and 50's produced an urban spin-off: the horse railway. Urban rails helped, but lumbering along at five miles per hour—when not trapped in congested traffic—did not take people very far in a short time. To ride cost five or ten cents, too much for poor factory workers, who thus had to live in cheap, dirty, crowded tenements erected near factories. Riders complained about crowding—standees and strap hangers far exceeded those lucky enough to find seats—slowness, the bad smells, and the sufferings of horses in bad weather. Yet horsecars added another mile or two to the city's radius, and by the mid-1880's, there were 525 horse railways in 300 cities. [3]

While horses dragged the dead weight of small vehicles along city rails, over this thirty-year period, electrical technology rapidly evolved. By the end of the 1880's, three new miracles had appeared: generators, incandescent illumination, and the electric motor. During the 1880's, a series of inventions created the electrically driven streetcar or "trolley." The actual <u>trolley</u> consisted of a pulley, mounted on top of a pole, that traveled and rotated along an overhead wire, conveying power to the electric motor that drove the wheels. The first successful, permanent electric streetcar line was installed in Richmond, Virginia, in 1887, where the cars hummed smoothly along the rail line, easily negotiating the many hills of that city.

Electrification thereupon spread contagiously; by 1890 streetcar lines were running or under construction in 200 cities. Electric cars carried more people and could be run in tandem by a single operator or motorman. Start-up costs for power generating plants, rolling stock, wiring, and new rails came high, but this was offset by 1) vastly increased passenger traffic and 2) the end of horse costs. Horses wore out in four years; they required stables, stablehands, blacksmiths and veterinarians; they caught diseases; their daily ten pounds of excretions dirtied the streets and threatened the health of the public; and they annually consumed their value in feed. Trolleys tore through snowdrifts, ran up steep hills, could be heated electrically in winter, were well lighted with electricity, and ran at least twice the speed of horsecars. By 1894 the conversion was complete, as streetcar lines went beyond the old horsecar limits, and new lines continued to be added. [4]

This explosive growth synergistically affected demographic changes by enabling cities to grow outward. Thus during the 1890's, the population of New York City's northern borough of the Bronx grew from 89,000 to 201,000. Cities took their pre-automobile configuration of concentric circles. In the center lay the "downtown" of business and shopping areas. Surrounding this was a zone of factories and warehouses. The next ring, closest to the factories, which employed the most people, contained the cheap housing of workers: tenements, small apartments, two- and three-family structures, attached single-family homes, and some unattached places for the foremen and minor supervisors. Beyond these inner rings lay the series of "streetcar suburbs," progressing outward from middle class to wealthy sectors. By 1902 per-capita ridership in cities equaled one daily round-trip per adult. Virtually everyone boarded the trolley regularly and often. The number of trolley trips that year reached 4.8 billion, with another billion transfers. [5] The trolley industry employed 140,000 and operated over 22,000 miles of track. [6]

Trolleys universalized mass transit. Every location along a streetcar line was joined to the network. The "lady of the house" could step outside, board the trolley, and stroll into the downtown shopping area within fifteen or thirty minutes. This new mobility transformed her from a domestic worker to a domestic partner. This change of status brought a bonanza to the streetcar companies because women out on shopping-lunching trips filled seats that were empty just after and before "rush hours." Eagerly, the large retailers invited them into their new "department stores." Each day crowds of shoppers filled these comprehensive mercantile establishments which offered larger selections at lower prices. Department stores could sell for less because high-volume purchases forced wholesale prices down. A visit to Macy's, Marshall Field, Jordan Marsh, or Wanamaker's filled an entire day. Dozens of departments on several floors took up more shopping time, with a welcome break at mid-day for a leisurely lunch in the store's restaurant. [7]

Oliver Wendell Holmes characterized the plain electric cars as a "broomstick train," a reference to the ungainly pole that stretched from roof to overhead wire. [8] People rode them for pleasure too. On hot, humid nights, city dwellers boarded to ride to the rural end-of-the-line, refreshed by the breezes generated by speeds of 20 to 30 miles per hour. These rides were taken on "summer" cars, which were open on the sides. People rented these summer cars for parties. Fraternal, labor, ethnic, and social/church groups rented special cars that took them to picnic groves, beaches, and the new amusement parks. There would be drinks and refreshments, even decorations and Japanese lanterns, as the festive cars carried the celebrants to clambakes and other get-togethers. [9] Rail historian John Stilgoe vividly conveys the sensation of riding a summer trolley:

> Riding the car seemed like riding a dragonfly. For the first time, Americans rode a power vehicle in which they looked straight ahead, over the motorman's shoulder. Ahead they saw only the rails half-hidden in grass and the line of poles carrying the wire through the landscape. At 30 miles an hour, the silent car thrilled its riders not so much with the sense of speed—express trains tripled that speed by the 1890's—but with an almost overpowering intimacy....Passengers delighted in the wind whipping across their faces and rejoiced in smelling wildflowers, new-mown hay, and other summertime fragrances. The car darted from one enchantment to another exactly as a honeybee hummed from one flower to the next. [10]

Soon rails stretched beyond the urban end-of-the-line to reach rural locations, and beyond these to neighboring cities. In venturing outside the built-up areas, streetcars competed with railroads. Ambling along at 30 mph, they couldn't outrun trains, but they stopped at places the trains ran past, and they reached "inland" towns without rail service. Trolley fares were only half the train fares, and they offered much greater convenience because cars ran every twenty to thirty minutes. Running from city to city, they were called "interurbans." They were cheap to build, riding on lighter rails laid on lightly ballasted roadbeds, and cheap to operate, single cars driven by one motorman. They brought the city to the country and vice-versa. Indianapolis achieved statewide domination because of its million-dollar interurban terminal built in 1904. More than 7,000,000 passengers each year boarded interurbans bound for all parts of Indiana.[11] By 1916 about 1000 companies owned 60,580 miles of track and carried eleven billion passengers per year.[12]

Interurbans never threatened the pre-eminence of railroads in the transportation of goods, but they did carry on successful local freight services. Trolleys each day brought milk and other produce from farm to market and returned to the country with daily papers, groceries, and town goods. More important, interurbans also brought electricity to rural areas. From the outset, streetcar lines, by default, had had to generate their own power. About half the streetcar companies covered generating costs by selling to consumers along their lines. This worked well because homes drew most of their power at night when fewer trolleys were running, thus absorbing excess power. This electrification of small towns stimulated their growth. Outlying towns became suburbs as the mass movement outward reached them. Trolleys suburbanized America.[13]

Just as it liberated the city woman, the trolley also freed the rural wife. No longer isolated and dependent upon her men for wagon rides to town and church, she could now board the interurban, to visit friends or head for the nearest city to seek lower prices and a better variety of goods. She could even take a job without living away from home. Occasionally one saw a fisherman boarding with pole and paraphernalia, and exiting near a lake or stream. If the fish didn't bite, he could reboard and ride to another spot. By 1910, the rural half of the U.S. population had been connected to urban markets by the trolley lines.[14]

These light rail networks greatly contributed to cultural changes. They were largely responsible for the nation's movie habit. Nearly everyone boarded the trolley after supper for the ride downtown, at first to go to the storefront nickelodeons, and later on to the exotic palaces where films by degrees replaced vaudeville.[15] Youth especially benefited, widening cultural horizons when they stepped up into the cars, not only because of urban entertainment, but also because they could now attend larger and better central schools. For much lower tax levies, rural school districts could shut down one-room elementary schools, and either amalgamate with a city district or pay a nominal tax to the county for both elementary and secondary schooling. On the extracurricular side, trolleys made interscholastic competitions possible. Students rode to athletic games and other interscholastic events to cheer on their teams.[16] The trolley also introduced the working classes to tourism. Factory workers boarded their families for Sunday trips to amusement, picnic, and hiking areas beyond the city. Newspapers published guides outlining trips everyone could take. The *Providence Journal's Trolley Trips from Providence Out* went through four editions in two years.[17] In 1895 the *Boston Evening Transcript* published *By Broomstick Train: Our Suburbs by Foot and Trolley*. Suddenly during the 1890's, day-trippers flooded the countrysides on weekends. This caused uneasiness among locals, but rural quietude had ended.[18]

Soon the interurbans themselves, to increase the bonanza of weekend and holiday ridership, published their own guides that identified buildings, views, and landmarks along their routes. Eventually trolleying went beyond day-tripping. In 1910 the *Brooklyn Daily Eagle* put out a ten-cent guide that detailed trips to Boston, Philadelphia—and Chicago. By transferring from line to line, one could travel from NY to Chicago in 45 hours, 24 minutes over a distance of 1143 miles. The cumulative fares came to $19.67. From Los Angeles, interurbans ran in three directions: to the mountains, the fruit orchards, and, via ferry, to Santa Catalina Island. Couples honeymooned on trolleys, getting off at hotels, then reboarding the next day for other locations. One couple took a honeymoon ride from Delaware to Maine. The cost of trolley travel was about 1.5 cents per mile, or $7.50 to travel 500 miles. [19]

But it wasn't all smooth, silent running. Traffic snarls happened on busy streets, when the trolley became part of the problem it was trying to solve. Many slow vehicles converging caused monumental tie-ups, and a few traffic cops, almost invisible and unheard in the roar of collective street rage, provided little amelioration. Tight crowding inside the cars paralleled the congestion outside the cars. Although larger cars were built (over 40 feet), standees often outnumbered seated passengers two to one. The woman returning from a shopping trip who loaded the seat beside her with packages provoked anger in newspaper letters columns. Riders, who, after all, paid to get on, resented being stuffed into cars. Protests, vocal and written, filled the air. One frustrated patron versified his complaint:

> We were crowded on the 'lectric,
> Not a soul would care to speak;
> For thirty-three were on the car,
> Besides those in the seats.
>
> 'Tis a common thing in Providence
> To be packed in hard and fast,
> And to hear a big conductor shout:
> "Please let the lady pass."
>
> So we huddled there in silence,
> And the stoutest held his breath,
> Fearing that to do otherwise
> Might cause his neighbor's death.
>
> And as thus we stood in misery,
> Each one looking for his fare,
> "Move up," the big conductor cried,
> But we couldn't budge a hair.
>
> Then spoke a maiden sweet and fair,
> With hair in curly rings:
> "Doesn't God control electric cars
> As well as other things?"
>
> Ah, no we said with heavy heart;
> We fear from what we read
> That Satan with the company
> Has thus far quite a lead. [20]

Along with congestion, accidents constituted another chronic problem on streetcar lines. In the beginning the choice of overhead wires rather than a "third rail" between the tracks prevented electrocution accidents. Also streetcar motors operated on a voltage too low to cause a fatal electrocution. Nearly all accidents were moving accidents, in the great majority of which a single person was hit. This frequently occurred when people used trolley bridges and rights of way as shortcuts, or when children played too close to tracks. Very rare was the spectacular head-on crash of two cars, usually on single-track lines, when a motorman, running late, failed to wait in a turnout, hoping to make it to the next one before an oncoming car reached that point. History's worst accident occurred at Kingsland, Indiana, in 1910, when 41 people died in such a crash. In 1900, in Tacoma, Washington, a crowded trolley derailed on a bridge and plunged 100 feet into a gulch, killing 36 and injuring 60. During 1901-02, nationally, 1217 were killed in trolley accidents, of which 122 were employees. [21]

Other problems and conflicts troubled the trolley experience. In that time of classist attitudes, members of the middle and wealthier classes took offense from the proximity of immigrant and lower class people; they recoiled from ragged appearances, smells, and raucous behavior. As for the poor, they resented the five- and ten-cent fares which they could ill afford. Transit workers suffered from very low wages and long hours without breaks, and their bitterly fought strikes brought (to them) more impoverishment, violence from strikebreakers, and inconvenience to the public. Union rights and recognition were seldom achieved during the Progressive Era. Serious citizens also perceived the traction companies to be predatory because they usually paid nothing (except bribes) for their monopolistic franchises. Since only one set of tracks could be laid along a street, each line possessed a monopoly. The transit companies paid nothing for right of way, charged "what the traffic would bear," and paid the lowest possible wages. An increasingly aroused public viewed themselves as victims. [22]

II

Recreational riding on the trolley, more often than not, terminated at amusement parks. Nationally the vast majority of amusement parks were created and operated by the transit companies in order to attract riders during the off-peak times of weekends, holidays, and evenings. [23] Amusement parks contrasted with public parks, which had just been developed a generation before in 19C Victorian America. Public parks had not been designed for pleasure but rather for uplift. One entered such a place for the soulful enjoyment of natural scenery, meadows, hills, lakes. The experience was intended to stimulate the imagination, perhaps to achieve an elevated mental state of Wordsworthian "wise passiveness"—a condition of reverie beloved by the 19C—or perhaps some moral inspiration. Frederick Law Olmstead, who created New York's Central Park during the 1860's, intended that his park's vistas would sooth people's discontent and improve their conduct. Again, world's fairs, like the 1893 World's Columbian Exposition in Chicago, were created to inspire and uplift. The symmetry, monumentality, and grandeur of its White City were intended raise people's vision above the gross materialism of American culture (Chapter 6). [24]

However this genteel, idealistic attitude toward culture, the outlook of a relatively few high-minded spirits, quite simply dissipated, vanished like morning fog, when fairgoers stepped onto the Midway. The Chicago Midway was father and model to all the midways of the hundreds of amusement parks across the land. A corridor of delights, featuring food, drink, sideshows, games, rides, animal attractions, water activities, photographers, fortune tellers, shooting galleries, kewpie dolls, cotton candy, dance pavilions, theatres, and bandstands—a cornucopia of diversions, an antedote to uplift! This was the new urban model of public recreation, also found at carnivals, circuses, and other shows. Come one, come all, to the end of the rainbow, at the end of the trolley line!

Coney Island, nine miles south of Manhattan on Long Island, received its name in the late 1640's from Dutch immigrants impressed by the hordes of rabbits in the dunes. [25] By the mid-19C, hotels, three very large ones built by 1880, lured people seeking respite from city heat. The steamboat fare cost 50 cents, and the railroad (opened in 1875) cost only 35 cents. By the 1890's, Coney Island had become a complete summer resort, with restaurants, amusements, saloons, an iron pier 1000 feet long, and a 300-foot iron tower (relic of the Philadelphia Centennial Expo of 1876). The usual criminal and sleaze elements, gamblers, con artists, thugs, and whores, also flourished. With the arrival of the trolley in 1895, the nickle fare opened Coney Island to the masses. Before that, the Sunday crowd ran about 50,000; afterward it could reach 200,000. In 1893 and 1895, fires wiped out much of the architectural chaos and confusion of poor construction and lack of planning. [26]

In 1893 Coney Island native George C. Tilyou honeymooned at the World's Columbian Exposition and tried, and failed, to buy the Ferris Wheel. In 1897, following the Chicago model, he opened 15-acre Steeplechase Park, the first enclosed park with an admission fee. Tilyou was the Tony Pastor of amusement parks; enclosing Steeplechase allowed him to offer clean amusements to families, while keeping out the criminal and seamier types. The 25-cent admission bought all of the rides. Tilyou's formula was fun, seasoned with bits of the risque. He called it "The Funny Place," and its emblem was a huge jester with a massive, slightly wicked grin. Visitors entering from the oceanside had to get through the revolving "Barrel of Love" that toppled the unwary, often into physical contact with total strangers. Caught offguard in the turning drum, long skirts flapped upward, giving brief glimpses of legs. Dishevelment, mild embarassment, a touch of intimacy stimulated a few degrees of titillation without threatening innocence. Besides the standard rides of roller coaster, Ferris wheel, carousel, and other revolving devices, Steeplechase's central attraction, and eponymous ride, consisted of eight wooden horses with double saddles. They carried riders on an up-and-down track to a finish line, a mild roller-coaster effect. The appeal was the intimacy on the double saddle wherein the man grasped the woman's waist as the horses raced along the undulating track. By the turn of the century, over a million people had ridden the Steeplechase. Tilyou placed throughout his park plenty of "funhouse" experiences: distortion mirrors, "blowholes" or sudden jets of compressed air that blew skirts, and rides like the Roulette Wheel and the Whirlpool that threw bodies in all directions. [27]

Tilyou also secured the "Trip to the Moon," a ride first offered at the Pan-American Exposition in Buffalo. Created by Frederic Thompson and Elmer "Skip" Dundy, it launched riders in a spaceship—with plenty of convincing motion—to disembark on a "moon" containing caverns, giants, midgets, and moon maidens passing out green cheese. This exemplified the fun formula of sensation, escape, illusion, and fantasy. After the 1902 season, Thompson and Dundy withdrew their attraction and put it in their own park next door, Luna Park, which opened in 1903. Luna covered 22 acres and featured a fantastic architecture of spires, turrets, minarets, large sculpted animals, pinwheels and crescents, all blazing with lights, about 250,000 of them. Luna's midway replicated Chicago's: Eskimo village, canals of Venice, Dutch windmill, Japanese garden. Its most exciting features were the live shows: diving horses; elephants sliding down the "Shoot the Chutes"; burning buildings with people screaming for help, firemen, and rescue squads; natural disasters, including floods and volcanic eruptions. By August Luna had paid off its investment, and the next year, it drew four million visitors (only three or four of today's theme parks do better than this). [28]

More grandiose than Steeplechase or Luna, Coney Island's third park, Dreamland ("Meet Me Tonight in Dreamland"), opened in 1904. Dreamland, with its classically styled white buildings, columns, and statues, resembled Chicago's "White City" of 1893. Its illumination quadrupled Luna's with 1,000,000 lights. The theme structure, the 375-foot Beacon Tower, dwarfed Luna's turrets and was resplendently white with 100,000 lights. A huge, white, nearly nude sculpted female (Eve?) stood at the entrance. Just inside, five times a day, "The Creation" reenacted Genesis One. Everything in Dreamland outdid its rivals in magnitude. There were <u>two</u> Shoot the Chutes, a Venetian Doge's palace with gondola rides, a Fall of Pompeii building, a miniature railroad, simulated submarine and airplane rides, a "Fighting the Flames" show with a cast of 4000, and a "Lilliputian Village," populated by 300 midgets (who lived there). It also presented a full three-ring circus. There was an immense 25,000 square-foot ballroom with a ceiling shaped like a large seashell. But Dreamland, which stressed an ostentatious effect of "beauty" and rejected the simple fun of other parks, never succeeded. Gate receipts failed to recoup investment and operating costs. Dreamland's most spectacular production turned out to be its demise. On May 27, 1911, a fire broke out in one of its rides and spread rapidly, destroying not only Dreamland but other non-park attractions. [29]

Various investors financed the large urban parks, but traction companies built the smaller ones, to increase trolley ridership and to sell excess generating capacity. Where large parks numbered in the dozens (see Ragtime Almanac, end of section), "trolley parks" multiplied into the hundreds. One estimate indicates that there were between 1500 and 2000 amusement parks in the U.S. by 1919. Many had begun as picnic groves in the 19C, often near a body of water. Picnicking and swimming continued as basic park activities. Admission to these parks was included in the basic five-cent trolley fare, which opened them to all. People brought picnic lunches and enjoyed band concerts, fireworks displays, dancing in the pavilion, and other free shows, such as balloon ascensions, without having to spend money budgeted for necessities. [30] Virtually everyone went: In 1910, with the U.S. population at 92,000,000, Coney Island recorded 20,000,000 admissions, about 22% of the national total. [31] City people rode out to the local park for a rural setting; rural people came for the urban amusements. This transformed rural and urban into a single mass audience for pop culture. One historian concludes:

> The streetcar and the institutions it fostered—advertising, the department store, and the amusement park—were all instrumental in transforming the American populace into a mass society. [32]

Amusement parks were another part of the pop culture (big-time sports, popular music, vaudeville, dancing, cinema, the automobile) that threw out the old values of thrift, restraint, order, sobriety, hard work, deferred gratification, and a narrow social circle limited to family and long-time connections. Such 19C conservatism dissipated in a crowd of pleasure seekers. Amusement parks took people's cash in exchange for immediate pleasures and gratification. People eagerly poured through the park gates to throw off restraints and to forget problems. Many went simply to meet new people. Temporarily the realities of social classes and ethnic tensions could be forgotten. For a few hours, the life of the crowd permitted relaxation and a sense of freedom. Plus, there was a vital difference between the amusement park experience and other pop attractions. At boxing matches, baseball games, football contests, vaudeville shows, theatre, cinema, and concerts, people were passive spectators, whereas at amusement parks, people got to participate in the activities. They rode the rides, swam in the lake, consumed the picnic, danced the dances, shot in the shooting galleries, and reacted physically to freaks and funhouses. A day of active leisure sent people home pleasantly tired to sleep soundly. [33]

However amusement parks excluded the darker races. North or South, the parks intentionally segregated. This never required written policies because the society of that time proscribed interracial activities, dancing, dining, and swimming. No one questioned this situation. Some parks admitted blacks on slow days, and some on occasional days. An Atlanta park admitted Africans on one day each year. A few southern locations had parks for "colored patrons." But if black folk were rejected as patrons, they were accepted as part of the entertainment. The Igorot villagers from the Philippines who, as eaters of dogs, had titillated St.Louis fairgoers (Chapter 19), relocated to Cedar Point on Lake Erie in northern Ohio. Cedar Point's publicity warned Ohioans that Igorot raiding parties were out to snatch family pets. Visitors subsequently poured in to peer at the primitive dog-eaters. The White City in Chicago also featured an Igorot village. Many parks offered these exhibits of "aborigines" in their "native villages." 34

Worse than such racist freak shows were the brutal game attractions, such as "Hit the Nigger—Three Balls for Five," where prizes were earned if the thrower could hit the "Coon" in the head. Also ubiquitous was the "Coontown Plunge," also known as the "African Dip" or "African Dodgers" in which hitting the target dropped the victim into water. This drew derisive crowds as the black man on his precarious perch shouted insults at passers-by. Which pulled in the suckers eager to toss three balls and teach the "uppity" black man a painful lesson. But this game was as rigged as any other, the target (which tripped a lever) being small and resistant to all but the most powerful throws. Similarly, in "Hit the Nigger," the "victim" knew how to dodge artfully and easily eluded most balls. Contestants threw away more and more cash as they progressed from complacency to anger to stubborn fury. These African Americans were paid performers, but the reality was that the "suckers" won in end. 35

RAGTIME ALMANAC

Some Metropolitan Amusement Parks 36

Boston
Paragon Park
Revere Beach
Worcester
White City
Providence
Crescent Park
New York
Coney Island (3)
Steeplechase Park
Luna Park
Dreamland
Palisades Park, NJ
Newark, NJ
Olympic Park
New Haven, CT
Savin Rock
White City
Philadelphia
Willow Grove Park
New Jersey
Atlantic City
Atlanta
Ponce De Leon Park

Louisville
White City
Cleveland
Euclid Beach
White City
Northern Ohio
Cedar Point
Cincinnati
Coney Island
Chicago
Cheltenham Beach
Riverview Park
White City
St.Louis
Forest Park Highlands
Kansas City
Electric Park
Forest Park
Denver
Manhattan Beach Park
New Orleans
West End
San Francisco
The Chutes

Lakewood Park	Portland, OR
<u>Pittsburgh</u>	White City
Luna Park	The Oaks
Kenneywood Park	

III

Situated in a tri-state area (Missouri-Kansas-Oklahoma), Lakeside Park near Webb City, Missouri, served a diverse population, farmers and miners, rural and townsfolk. Lakeside was a "trolley park," on the line connecting Joplin with Carthage in Jasper County, southwest Missouri, on the edge of the northwest Ozarks. A boom in lead and zinc mining had gripped the area. Joplin, with over 10,000, was "wide open," with 55 saloons to catch the miners' earnings. The more sedate Carthage, just under 10,000, with a marble quarry nearby, had only 3 saloons. In 1895 the Southwest Missouri (Electric) Railroad Company built a dam on Center Creek to provide hydroelectric power for its interurban service. On the shores of the small lake that rose behind the dam, the company built Lakeside Amusement Park to serve the two principal cities and surrounding region. Lakeside lasted as long as the trolley, until 1935, when operations ceased along the line.

Like most rural parks, Lakeside kept out liquor and saloons, but it boasted most of the attractions found in urban parks. A suspension bridge crossed the lake to the large bath-house where people could change into swimming costumes. Canoes could be rented and a steam launch took passengers on "cruises." Families could picnic on a hilltop that caught the breezes, purchase food at concession stands, or dine in the park's restaurant. There were the usual rides, including ferris wheel, roller coaster, and carousel, plus such midway attractions as a shooting gallery, "Japanese" bowling alley, kewpie doll displays, food and drink stands. However what distinguished Lakeside as a first-class location was the amount of entertainment. During weekend and holiday afternoons, people filled the grandstand to watch scheduled baseball games of the Trolley Baseball League. Carthage, Joplin, Webb City, Carterville, Alba, Oronogo, and Galena, Kansas, all fielded teams. Also staged on this field were firemen's drill tournaments and brass band competitions. At night, people danced in the large open-air dance pavilion, or, they attended the Lakeside Theatre, which featured vaudeville, bands, barbershop quartets, and a few years later, films. Admission was free to both of these attractions. Special weekend and holiday entertainment included balloon ascensions, parachute drops, pole-climbing contests, greased pig chases, tennis matches, horse and mule dragging contests, and fireworks. There was a hotel, the Lakeside Inn, to accommodate those who wished to vacation at Lakeside. [37]

Something was always doing at Lakeside, but what sets it apart is its ragtime associations. Three important composer/performers grew up near the park, which helped school their talents. Percy Wenrich (1880-1952), son of a Joplin postmaster, became the most famous. Percy learned his syncopation from the "colored players" in Joplin's sporting district as well as out at the Lakeside venues. He began to compose at 17 while working as what he later called "a typical hick-town pianist." He took off for Chicago in 1901 and ended up a major talent on Tin Pan Alley. He is remembered for his superb, songs—"When You Wore a Tulip," "Put On Your Old Gray Bonnet," "Moonlight Bay"—but he loved rags and composed 21 of them, including *Crab Apples, Peaches and Cream, Ragtime Chimes,* and *Persian Lamb*. Throughout his life, he was known as the "Joplin Kid." [38]

Clarence Woods (1888-1956) and James Sylvester Scott (1885-1938) received their schooling and music education in the more restrained atmosphere of Carthage. Both studied with Miss Emma Johns of the Calhoun School of Music. Scott, who was black, received private tutoring. The other center of musical life in Carthage was the Dumars Music Company. Proprietor Charles Dumars, an accomplished musician, led the Carthage Light Guard Band, an outstanding ensemble that played regular concerts during the Lakeside summer season and concertized in other cities as well. Clarence, who loved marches, found early inspiration in the Light Guard Band. When he was 16, Dumars published his first composition *The Meteor*, a march dedicated to the "Frisco" Railroad. That summer, he played piano for the melodramas of The Bleeding Hearts Stock Company, and when it departed, Clarence went along. Later, he toured for ten years in Texas as bandleader and pianist, billed as "The Ragtime Wonder of the South." He published during this period two excellent rags, *Slippery Elm* (1912) and *Sleepy Hollow* (1918). During the 1920's, he played the organ in Tulsa, Oklahoma, movie houses, and later the Barnum and Bailey Circus utilized the talents of this brilliant and creative musician as organist/arranger/composer (1949-53). [39]

"Jimmy" Scott, called the "Little Perfessor" (he only grew to five/four), spent his childhood years in Neosho, Missouri, 25 miles south of Carthage in the same region.

His parents, James Sylvester Scott, Sr. and Molly Thomas Scott, had been slaves, born in North Carolina and Texas. They had come to Missouri in 1878 from North Carolina, part of the "Exoduster" migration (Chapter 21) to escape the white repression that followed Reconstruction. But instead of relocating to the African-American settlements in Kansas (Nicodemus, Wyandott), they had settled in the tri-state mining district where Missouri, Kansas, and Oklahoma borders meet. [40] James was the second oldest of six children (4 boys, 2 girls) in the family of a poor laborer. The Scotts were musical (brother Douglas played saloon/whorehouse piano and died at 26), but James was a "natural," with perfect pitch; rapidly, all of his life, he assimilated everything musical, from keyboard technique through style, theory and harmony, and repertoire. Like Scott Joplin he learned on other people's instruments until his father managed to afford an old upright.

In 1901 when James was 16, following a two-year hiatus in Ottawa, Kansas, the family settled in Carthage. He was ready for the greater opportunities at the center of the mining district. He completed his education at the segregated Lincoln School, received some final music instruction from the accomplished Emma Johns—who perceived his potential—started work as a shine boy in a barber shop, and entered Carthage's musical life, already a competent performer. He soon showed his stuff at Lakeside, where he "sat in" during breaks at the dance pavilion and soon mastered the park's large, splendid calliope. Since none of these guest slots paid, he went to Charlie Dumars for a better opportunity. Dumars started him on janitor work, intending to train him in picture framing, but after listening to Jimmy try out the pianos in the back room, promoted him to the front of the store as salesman/demonstrator/song plugger. Only five feet, four inches, Jimmy would wrap his left leg around the piano bench to anchor himself, as he tore into a tune, almost bouncing as his body went up and down. People passing by would come into the store to listen and watch his fast fingers. He had found a niche in Carthage: day job in a music store, playing nights at the Delphus Theatre and weekends at Lakeside, where he was paid for his superb playing of the calliope. He contributed to the black community by giving church and school performances, and he organized choruses and instrumental groups. He didn't have to play in saloons or red-light districts. He received admiration and respect in the African-American community, and whites treated him well, looked out for him, and liked him. [41]

Ragtime had come to James Scott (rather than the reverse); probably he picked up the developing style from his first teacher in Neosho, John Coleman, a saloon player who gave him lessons. There would have been a string of itinerant ragtimers hitting the main towns along the rail routes, friends of Scott Joplin, such as Otis Saunders, Arthur Marshall, Scott Hayden, Louis Chauvin, possibly even Tom Turpin and Scott Joplin himself. Jimmy had begun to compose by 1903, and his early rags are modeled on Joplin's. Since he played his rags in piano demonstrations, they became familiar to regulars at the Dumars Company, who pronounced them good and asked for the sheet music. This demand led Charlie Dumars into music publishing; Dumars issued Scott's first rag in March 1903, *A Summer Breeze: March and Two-Step*. Six months later came *The Fascinator: March and Two-Step*, and in 1904, *On the Pike*, published jointly with Clarence Woods' *The Meteor*. *On the Pike* celebrated the Louisiana Purchase Expo in St.Louis, and Dumars also published a band arrangement and included it in the repertoire of his Light Guard Band, which presented it to larger audiences at Lakeside. Blind Boone came to town a month later to perform at a Chautauqua event (Missouri State Negro Improvement Association), and the two played a notable duet at the music store. To a recording of "Souza's Band," they improvised a four-hand accompaniment. In the local press's report of this "original stunt," after which, they played "a number of selections both rag time and classical," Scott was termed "Our Local Mozart." [42]

As indicated previously (Chapter 19), Scott realized his dream and ambition by traveling to St.Louis to meet his idol Joplin, who recommended his music to John Stark, who published *Frog Legs*, which became, after *Maple Leaf Rag*, Stark's second best-seller. From then on, Scott mailed all but one or two of his rags to the Stark Music Company in St.Louis and New York. Stark issued 29 of Scott's 38 published scores, 25 rags, 3 waltzes, and one song. (Allen Music Company [Boone's publisher] of Columbia, Missouri, published *Great Scott Rag* in 1909.) Scott never entitled his rags; he simply wrote out a composition, mailed it to Stark, and left the rest—title, cover design, number of copies, advertising, date of publication—to the publisher. This went on from *Frog Legs* in 1906 to *Broadway Rag* in 1922, which was also Stark's final publication. Scott seems to have been absorbed in music; it flowed out of him, joyous strains of "leaping, skipping syncopations." [43] His rags demand more technical skill than most, and many performers learn only a few of his difficult scores—or avoid them altogether. Several people remembered Jimmy Scott as walking along briskly, head down, lost in thought or reverie, presenting an introverted aspect. Interrupted, he always looked up, pleased and a little surprised. He saved his extroversion for the piano where he channeled his upbeat moods into his music. Perhaps he extruded music as much as he composed it.

Also in 1906, Scott (he was now 21) bought a small house for $425, and three months later he married Nora Johnson of Springfield, Missouri. Apparently they had met in church when he directed her as a soloist in sacred concerts. The next eight years were prolific and successful. He played gigs in the region, including Kansas City, Sedalia, and St.Louis, while continuing with the Dumars Music Company. It turned out to be his most prolific composing period, with Stark issuing ten rags, from *Kansas City Rag* (1907) through *Climax Rag* (1914), including three in 1909: *The Ragtime Betty*, *Sunburst Rag*, and what is considered his finest work, *Grace and Beauty*. Another three were published in 1911: *Quality Rag*, *Princess Rag*, and *Ragtime Oriole*, the first birdcall rag, which would inspire Joseph Lamb's *Ragtime Nightingale* (1915) and several others. During these years, he formed and directed both the Carthage Jubilee Singers, a twenty-five voice male chorus, and a marching band for African Americans that paralleled the white Light Guard Band. With segregation a hard reality, mixed ensembles were forbidden, forcing blacks to perform in their own groups. Racial violence occurred often. In 1903, a mob battered down the wall of Joplin's jail and lynched a black man accused of killing a police officer. Three years later in Carthage, a man was almost lynched for hitting a jailer. From 1889 to 1918, Missouri saw 81 lynchings. [44]

Years of after-hours playing at the Delphus and Lakeside Theatres honed Scott's skills as a performer for silent films. In 1914 he published one of his six waltzes, a song called "Take Me Out to Lakeside," a promotional number with lyrics by Ida B. Miller, whose husband owned tourist cabins near the park. This was a simple romantic song, which was locally published. At some point after this, James and Nora said farewell to their

Carthage home and all the associations of a rooted life and moved to Kansas City. [45] No explanation for this radical decision has reached us. Like Scott Joplin, James Scott left no written or recorded testimony about his life and how he felt about it. Sensible black folk did their verbalizing among themselves, out of public hearing and not on paper. Undoubtedly, with cinema attendance in cities growing rapidly, skilled theatre organists found themselves in high demand and very well paid. The Scotts were childless, and perhaps Jimmy felt that his wife needed more of his time. Working three or more jobs seven days a week in Carthage may have pushed him to the limits of his strength. For the next twelve or fifteen years in Kansas City, Jimmy gave lessons at home, performed his nightly film gigs in a succession of theatres, and played in dance orchestras. Then in 1930, Nora and silent films both died, leaving him alone and unemployed. In declining health, he played occasionally in dance orchestras during his last eight years. The final year, he moved in with his cousin Ruth Callahan in Kansas City, Kansas, taking his dog and beloved grand piano. He died of kidney failure in 1938: he was only 53. [46]

Epilog: Calliope Rag

In the third edition of *They All Played Ragtime* by Rudi Blesh and Harriet Janis—one of the major forces in the Ragtime Revival—published in 1966, appeared the music of *Calliope Rag*, attributed to James Scott. Martin Vangilder in both of his articles in the *Rag Times* ("Ragtime Was the Rage at Lakeside" and "James Scott: A Biography") tells us that Scott composed it around 1910 and played it on Lakeside Park's steam calliope. He states that the piece was "discovered years later and restored by Robert 'Ragtime Bob' Darch." Apparently Darch received the incomplete manuscript from Scott's sister who supplied the information about its use at Lakeside. It was subsequently edited for publication by Donald Ashwander.

Undoubtedly, as much because of its tuneful, appealing qualities as because of its attribution, *Calliope Rag* has proven popular. It has been frequently performed and recorded, both by soloists and ensembles. However, it is suspect for two reasons: its un-Scott-like simplicity and its uncertain provenance. The first reason doesn't hold up because, supposedly, it was written for the calliope, a ponderous instrument intended for simple, harmonious music. The chief problem thus is Darch's failure to adequately document his find; we have only his word as to attribution and source. However, *Calliope Rag* continues to delight hearers, and it remains plausible that it was first played on Lakeside's calliope. If not true, it would add distinction to Mr. Darch's reputation as a composer. [47]

Notes: Chapter 24

1. David E. Nye, *Electrifying America: Social Meanings of a New Technology*, 86.
2. Scott Molloy, *Trolley Wars: Streetcar Workers on the Line*, 83.
3. Nye, 86, 93; Molloy, 12-13.
4. *Ibid.*, 87-91.
5. *Ibid.*, 93-96.
6. Molloy, 115.
7. Nye, 112-113; Molloy, 83-84.
8. *Ibid.*, 62.
9. Nye, 120; Molloy, 84.
10. John R. Stilgoe, *Metropolitan Corridor: Railroads and the American Scene*, 297-298.
11. J.C. Furnas, *The Americans: A Social History of the United States*, 802-803; Stilgoe, 289-293.
12. *Ibid.*, 293.
13. Nye, *118*-119; Stilgoe, 308; Molloy, 86-87, 90.
14. Nye, *119;* Molloy, 87.
15. Stilgoe, 293*;* Nye, 119-120.
16. *Idem.*
17. Molloy, 82; Stilgoe, 304.
18. Nye, 120.
19. *Ibid.*, 117-121; Stilgoe, 300.
20. Quoted in Molloy, 101-102; for traffic problems, see also Otto Bettmann, *The Good Old Days—They Were Terrible*, 30-31; Nye, 97-98; Stilgoe, 301.
21. Nye, 102-103; Molloy, 102-103.
22. Nye, 104-105; Molloy, 80-81.
23. Nye, 123.
24. John F. Kasson, *Amusing the Million: Coney Island at the Turn of the Century*, 11-15, 17-18.
25. Judith A. Adams, *The American Amusement Park Industry: A History of Technology and Thrills*, 42.
26. Kasson, 32-38; Adams, 42.
27. *Ibid.*, 43-45; Nye, 82-83.
28. David Nasaw, *Going Out: The Rise and Fall of Public Amusements*, 82-85; Adams, 48-49.
29. Nasaw, 85, 89; Adams, 52-53.
30. *Ibid.*, 57-59; Nye, 126.
31. Nasaw, 95.
32. Nye, 132.
33. Kasson, 8; Nye, 129.
34. Nasaw, 91-92.
35. *Ibid.*, 93-94; Adams, 65.
36. Many amusement parks survived the automobile, the Great Depression, and World War II; many have been kept up and, in some cases, restored. At the start of the new century, there are 600 amusement parks in the U.S. The oldest, which opened in 1846, is Lake Compounce in Bristol, Connecticut, which still flourishes in the Hartford metropolitan area.
37. Marvin L. Vangilder, "Ragtime Was the Rage at Lakeside," *Rag Times,*XI (January 1978): 6-7.
38. David A. Jasen and Gene Jones, *That American Rag: The Story of Ragtime from Coast to Coast*, 11-13.

39. *Ibid.*, 6-7; Marvin L. Vangilder, "The Work of Clarence Woods,' *Rag Times*, XI (January 1978): 1-2; M. L. Vangilder, "The Childhood of Clarence Woods," *Rag Times*, XI (March 1978): 6. For more on Woods, Dick Zimmerman, "Clarence Woods: The Untold Story," in two parts, *Rag Times*, XVIII (May 1984 and July 1984): 1-2 and 6-9.
40. Marvin L. Vangilder, "James Scott," in Hasse, Ed., *Ragtime: Its History, Composers, and Music*, 142.
41. Marvin L. Vangilder, "James Scott: A Biography," *Rag Times*, XI (May 1977): 14-16.
42. William Howland Kenney, "James Scott: An Introduction," in Scott DeVeaux and William Howland Kenney, Ed's., *The Music of James Scott*, 6-7; Jasen and Jones, *American Rag*, 15.
43. Kenney, 20.
44. Lynching statistics from NAACP, *Thirty Years of Lynching in the United States*, 34; also Kenney, 12, 15-16.
45. There is some confusion as to the date of Scott's move to Kansas City, some indicating 1914 and others 1918.
46. Kenney, 7, 9-10, 15, 17, 23-29; Vangilder, "James Scott: A Biography," 17-18; Vangilder, "James Scott," 137-145.
47. Recently at the 2003 Scott Joplin Festival in Sedalia ("Kick-off Concert," 6/4/03), the author heard Sue Keller testify that Darch told her that the original *Calliope* manuscript that he received from a Scott family member contained only 2 strains of the rag, and that he composed the trio after adding to these two strains. If this is true, then the composition should be attributed to Scott-Darch.

25. Progressives (III): "A Man, A Plan, A Canal, Panama!"

> Yet we must reflect that at best, even with the backing and sentiment and finances of the most powerful nation on earth, that we are contending with nature's forces, and that while our wishes and ambitions are of great assistance in a work of this magnitude, neither the inspiration of genius nor our optimism will build this canal. Nothing but dogged determination and steady, persistent, intelligent work will ever accomplish the result, and when we speak of a hundred million yards of a single cut not to exceed nine miles in length, we are facing a proposition greater than was ever undertaken in the engineering history of the world.
>
> John F. Stevens [1]

> …Each man must have in him the feeling that, besides getting what he is rightfully entitled to for his work, that aside and above that must come the feeling of triumph at being associated in the work itself, must come the appreciation of what a tremendous work it is, of what a splendid opportunity is offered to any man who takes part in it.
>
> Theodore Roosevelt [2]

The Panama Canal has fallen out of our historical memory. The beauty of its setting and the excellence of its engineering come as a surprise to the passengers on every cruise ship that makes the transit. Everyone knows that the Canal takes ships from ocean to ocean, but few—mainly those who have made the transit—appreciate the Canal as a human accomplishment on a par with moon rockets. Those who condemn President Carter because he "gave it away" do so chiefly from feelings of a dent in the national pride. Along with the loss of recollection of the titanic effort of its construction, we have also forgotten the names of the epic figures who inspired and drove the enterprise: DeLesseps, Roosevelt, Gorgas, Stevens, and Goethals.

The well-known palindrome of the chapter title declares that cutting a ship canal across the Isthmus of Panama required a man and a plan. Actually the construction of the Panama Canal consumed the talents of several men and required two plans, not one. The plans proved more elusive than the men. The French, who commenced their canal effort in 1880, proclaimed in favor of a sea-level canal. Their leader and promoter, Count Ferdinand DeLesseps, had succeeded triumphantly at Suez, joining the Mediterranean Sea to the Indian Ocean via the Red Sea. His company ultimately shoveled enough sand at the Isthmus of Suez to connect the Mediterranean to the Red Sea in 1869. Afterward DeLesseps and his investors extrapolated a sea-level canal across the Isthmus of Panama based upon the Suez outcome. In their analysis of the job as the simple removal of an estimated number of cubic yards of earth, they ignored the geological and climatic differences of desert vs. tropics and sandy flats vs. mountains. They also failed to base their analysis upon the problems posed by Panama's Chagres River; two-thirds of the route of the proposed canal ran through its valley. Each year, almost

100 inches of rain came down to inundate the Chagres watershed, often flooding its valley at levels 20 to 30 feet above flood stage. With a rainy season of nine months (April to December), no canal was possible without a plan to control the river.

The second plan, necessary for a successful outcome, was a health plan. Tropics were unhealthy, teeming with yellow fever, malaria, dysentery, undulent fever, fungal diseases, typhoid, and others. The French canal effort failed in six years, in part because of corrupt management and inadequate technology, but mostly because yellow fever and malaria killed or incapacitated nearly all of the work force. Those who did not fall ill lost nerve and morale because of fear. The French, despite the brilliance of their engineers and their great pride and courage, could not succeed because their plan for a sea-level canal did not deal with either the wild and unruly river or the health hazards of the Isthmus of Panama.

Unfortunately, at the time the French effort began in 1880, no one understood tropical diseases. The prevalent idea blamed them on filth. Filth contaminated either through touch or it could be borne by "bad air" or a miasma. The word "malaria" simply means bad air. Clean up an area, remove rotting matter, eliminate decay, and the environment would become healthy. This was the prescription for public health in 1880. Not until 1900 was the role played by mosquitos in spreading yellow fever and malaria understood. This came out of the work of an Army medical team in Cuba led by Dr. Walter Reed. Following the discoveries, done experimentally in the field and in the laboratory, that proved yellow fever to be transmitted by a particular mosquito from one human to another, Reed assigned to Major-Dr. William C. Gorgas the job of eradicating this insect from Havana, Cuba. The yellow fever mosquito, *stegomiya fasciata* (later renamed *aedes aegypti*), which required human blood to breed and thus lived near homes, laid its eggs in water. So Gorgas and his sanitation team either covered stagnant water or they poured oil or kerosene on it to kill the larvae. Within the year, Havana had no more cases of yellow fever, and malaria—a bonus—had decreased by one-half.

Two years later in 1904, Lt.Colonel William Crawford Gorgas, U.S.A., (1854-1920) was picked as leader of the health and sanitation team for the U.S. attempt to succeed in Panama where the French had failed. He knew how to eradicate yellow fever, and enough about the malarial mosquito, *anopheles*, to bring that disease under control. His problem was that no one took him seriously. The first Chief Engineer, John Findlay Wallace, and the practical engineering types on the Isthmian Canal Commission (ICC) knew little of biology or medicine. These hard-headed—and complacent—souls simply blinked away what Gorgas tried to tell them about yellow fever and malaria. They refused, then ignored, his continual requests for chemical supplies, metal screening, and a large labor force. They expected Gorgas to tend his dispensary, look after the sick, and work some medical magic to keep off disease, as, they'd heard, he'd done over in Havana (whatever that was). Disciplined soldier that he was (hardened by frontier soldiering in the Indian Wars), what he did was to hold his temper, study the terrain and climate, bide his time, and wait for mosquitos to start biting Americans as they poured in by the boatload to "make the dirt fly."

Chief Engineer Wallace and the ICC blamed the French failure on mismanagement and corruption. It seemed ridiculous to them that mere mosquitos had wrecked a grand enterprise. What these men feared, drawing lessons from past failure, was waste and loss because of boondogles. If they gave in to this fellow Gorgas with his plans to screen all the windows, they might be exposed as incompetent. All this science that Gorgas went about expounding was just theory, fanciful stuff, too unsubstantial to waste the taxpayers' money entrusted to them. The seven members of the Isthmian Canal Commission sat in their Washington offices and carefully, slowly, scrutinized every single requisition, taking pains to weed out whatever they deemed superfluous to the construction of an interoceanic canal. As they understood it, American know-how, along with careful fiscal supervision, would get the job done; they felt certain they were on the cutting edge of that.

John F. Wallace, the man intending to carry out the plan, held all the proper credentials: construction of railroads and terminals, management of the Illinois Central RR, and presidencies of engineering associations. But in Panama, he never quite took charge enough to get things moving on a broad front. He continued and increased somewhat the excavations that the caretaker French company (the "New Panama Canal Company") had carried on (to prevent the concession from reverting to the Colombian government). He salvaged and put back into service excavation and railroad equipment abandoned by the French. He also renovated a sizeable number of decaying French buildings and machine shops. But he never got beyond these minimal efforts. The steamshovels dug, but there weren't enough railroad cars, trains, and tracks to carry away what the shovels, working at capacity, could dig. He provided little in the way of food or housing for new employees now coming off the boats by the hundreds. These had to bunk five or six in small rooms, and the food purchased from Panamanian merchants was inflated in price, poor in quality, and monotonous. Much of this problem derived from the diligent, conscientious ICC up in Washington, processing requisitions at a snail's pace, denying too many items, arbitrarily sending only parts of requests, and actually losing others.

Wallace was as large a part of the problem as the distant bureaucrats. He lacked control, and, as the months dragged by, there grew in him an attitude of fear and loathing toward Panama. When he returned from a Washington consultation with the ICC and Secretary of War Taft, with his wife in tow, he unloaded two expensive metal coffins. The news of this singular gesture very negatively affected isthmian morale. Wallace just concentrated on a minimal amount of digging—presumably in response to TR's "make the dirt fly" imperative—and made no effort to develop a comprehensive, logistical plan for enough equipment, facilities to adequately house and feed the work force, improvements to the antiquated railroad, and measures to deal with tropical diseases and maintain good health. Yellow fever struck at the end of 1904, one case in November, six in December. None of these were fatal, but of eight in January, two died, which set off the panic. Actually this was a small-scale epidemic, killing less than a hundred, but during this "Great Scare" of 1905, three-quarters of the Americans in Panama fled back to the United States. Whenever a ship docked in Colon, a crowd pushed its way onboard as soon as the passengers debarked. And many new arrivals, when they perceived the situation, tried to return on the same ship.

By June 1905, the canal venture had become a shambles, and it seemed the Americans would fade faster than the French. Abruptly Chief Engineer Wallace and his wife packed and sailed for New York, ostensibly for yet another consultation. Soon after in July the panic ratcheted up another notch with the news of a man's death from bubonic plague. On June 25 in New York, Wallace told Secretary of War Taft (TR had placed the Canal under the War Department) that he was resigning to take a higher-paying job! Wallace offered to continue as a consultant and to remain in charge until a replacement could be found. A furious Taft accepted his resignation as immediate and dismissed him. Recently the ICC had been reorganized to eliminate the bureaucratic problems noted above, handing total control to the Chief Engineer (Wallace) and to a Chairman in Washington (Theodore Shonts) to provide back-up and support. Wallace had professed to be satisfied with this excellent revision, and now he went back upon his word and quit. Taft dressed Wallace down for half an hour (in front of a witness), angrily calling him a deserter who cared only for his own advantage. This unhappy business disposed of, Taft just happened to have a replacement handy in John F. Stevens, a leading railroad construction engineer whom he had recently recruited to solve railroad problems in the recently acquired Philippines (before taking on the War Dept.,

Taft had been the U.S. Commissioner in the Philippines). In a hurried consultation with the President, Taft recommended that Stevens be diverted to Panama. TR immediately agreed and offered the assignment to Stevens, who accepted despite some doubts that he kept to himself.

II

He is always in the right place at the right time and does the right thing without thinking about it.

James J. Hill on John F. Stevens [3]

While Wallace was losing his nerve, Gorgas, acquiring more resources as months went by, organized and put into operation a public health plan to fight yellow fever and malaria. He divided the inhabited area into districts, and his workers inventoried every location of standing water, in barrels, tanks, cisterns, even the pottery jars inside homes (called *ollas*). Work went slowly, his inspectors having to be taught what to look for. Anyone taken ill was rushed to the hospital and put in isolation, whatever the illness, the reason being that the mosquitos picked up yellow fever from infected people and carried it to the uninfected. Gorgas had found *stegomiya* mosquitos breeding everywhere, even in offices where glass receptacles held water. In the hospital, to discourage ants, the French had set the legs of beds in small vessels of water, and outside on the grounds, small ceramic rings containing water protected plants. This resulted during the French era (1880's) in death for everyone admitted to Ancon Hospital—and in a universal fear of being hospitalized.

As he analyzed and came to understand these conditions, Gorgas systematically worked to eliminate every mosquito-breeding area. The yellow fever mosquito was a deadly companion to humanity, living and breeding inside and just outside of homes. Water sources had to be covered, drained, or oiled. Shrubs and other foliage were removed to put open spaces between buildings and eliminate the shadowy places where the little mosquito flourished. Every window had to be screened. A familiar sight in Canal Zone towns was the man with a tank on his back spraying oil or kerosene on puddles. In November Gorgas pointed to a man in a hospital bed and pronounced him to be the last yellow fever case, which it was.

Like TR, John F. Stevens (1853-1943) comes across as legendary and more than life-size. Physically he was a big, tough westerner (though born in rural Maine), lacking in formal education, who acquired his learning in the proverbial "college of hard knocks" and from on-the-job training. Surveying came first as he went with the advance crews that mapped the routes of railroads. Then he picked up mechanical engineering from the experiences of putting down roadbeds, laying track, and building bridges and tunnels. As Stevens gained from hands-on experiences, he read and mastered the technical books that explained everything, enabling him to become a great engineer. He also became a serious reader; wherever he went, books were his best companions, including his favorite *Huckleberry Finn*. At 33, he built a 400-mile line across the wilderness of the Upper Peninsula of Michigan, from Duluth, Minnesota, to Sault Ste.Marie. James J. Hill hired him in 1889 to locate a route for his projected Great Northern across the Northern Rocky Mountains in Montana. Alone and on snowshoes that winter, he found for Hill the Marias Pass, which, being only a mile high, turned out to be the lowest and easiest railroad route over the Continental Divide. He also found another good pass (Stevens Pass) over the Cascades in Washington. For Hill he built bridges, tunnels, including the 2 1/2-mile Cascade Tunnel, and a thousand miles of track. As explorer, surveyor, and engineer, he became a legend in the Northwest. But he was a loner, a restless, temperamental man who liked frequent change and new challenges.

Stevens arrived on the Isthmus in late July 1905, said little, settled in, and appeared each day somewhere on the line, hiking alone and smoking large, black cigars. He asked a lot of questions, and the men found him easy to talk to; they liked the way he listened. After a few weeks, he told the men: "There are three diseases in Panama. They are yellow fever, malaria, and cold feet; and the greatest of these is cold feet." [4] What he saw was failure: trains derailed, steamshovels idle. After observing ineffectual operations, he gave two commands. First he ordered a complete stoppage of all work except sanitation. Colonel Gorgas was to get whatever supplies and workers he needed and to carry out his health plan. This included not only the measures noted above, but the paving and clean-up of the terminal cities of Panama and Colon. Second he put everyone else to work on the needed infrastructure, building for the work force entire towns, including houses, barracks, dining halls, clubhouses, churches, warehouses, cold storage facilities, schools, laundries, more hospitals, sewers, reservoirs, and even a hotel (the Tivoli in Ancon) for visitors.

During this time (of the "Great Scare"), from May 1 to August 31, 1905, yellow fever took 47 lives, malaria over 90, pneumonia 49, and diarrhea and dysentery 103. Black workers, most of whom lived away from the towns in jungle shanties, caught most of the pneumonia and malaria. Ultimately 4000 men were working for Gorgas, fumigating houses, spraying, cleaning, and pouring kerosene on wet breeding places. Running water was piped to all locations, ending the need for open pots of water in houses. Stevens didn't understand Gorgas's science any more than Wallace had, but he put his faith in Gorgas because he believed in and respected the man. Over these difficult months—it took a year and a half to sanitize the Isthmus—Gorgas and his men eradicated yellow fever completely and almost ended other threats to health for those living in built-up areas. This health plan made possible the canal plan, which was chiefly the work of Stevens.

Panama lay 2000 miles from its source of supply, the Port of New York. Everything needed for constructing a canal and a large overseas base had to be carried to the Isthmus. Not only personnel and equipment, but also food and all materials and supplies. All such had to be accumulated in back-up and surplus quantities and stored in huge warehouses and bunkers, everything form coal to ketchup. During Wallace's year (1904-05), 336 old French buildings had been renovated and 150 new ones erected. Stevens, during his first year, renovated 1200 structures and built 1250 new ones. By the end of 1906, he had 24,000 men working, of whom 12,000 were renovating and erecting buildings. [5] In effect Stevens had put the territorial entity known as the "Canal Zone" on the map.

The other task that preceded the canal plan was the rebuilding of the Panama Railroad (PRR). Stevens found the railroad to be in appalling condition: a poorly maintained single-track line with equipment (locomotives, cars) inadequate in quality and quantity. The railroad had to carry everything: food, people, supplies, and dirt out of the "Big Ditch." Compared to U.S. railroads like the Great Northern, the PRR was a joke. Equipment moving on the Great Northern was four times the size of the small and obsolete trains creeping through the rain forest of Panama on a shaky roadbed. Immediately Stevens ordered freight cars, dump cars, refrigerator cars, and over a hundred locomotives! He saw to the hiring of hundreds of experienced railroaders, including yard masters, engineers, mechanics, firemen, conductors, and switchmen. He ordered also shiploads of heavier rails, and, within a year, the line was not only completely overhauled but doubletracked as well. No train would stand idle while traffic proceeded in the opposite direction.

Now the men had good rooms to sleep in, dining halls, perishable foods such as eggs, lettuce, and meat in their diets, ice for drinks, and fresh-baked bread—40,000 loaves—daily. Off-duty, they could go to the clubhouses, YMCA-run, to socialize, obtain books, write letters, and shoot pool or play cards. A workforce band formed and provided the weekly concerts popular in all American towns stateside. On Saturday nights came the big dances in the ballroom of the Hotel Tivoli in Ancon just below the old hospital on the Pacificside next to Panama City. Every community along the line fielded a baseball team for the "Canal Zone League"; Stevens had personally stipulated a baseball program. When a clerk told him that no money had been budgeted for baseball fields, he took the money out of sanitation funds. In the principal locations along the railroad line, Stevens built a series of family subdivisions. As quarters became available (cottages, duplexes, 4-plexes), married men were assigned housing on the basis of a simple standard: one square foot per dollar of monthly pay. This measurement limited bachelors to shared sleeping rooms in barracks. Wives also were entitled to a square foot per dollar of a husband's monthly salary. In addition, children and other dependents were rated, on a sliding scale, from five percent (for small children) to 75 percent (other adults) of the pay of the household's breadwinner. Promotions automatically resulted in a move to larger quarters. These homes consisted of bare boards merely painted, but with high ceilings and open, screened porches (which functioned as additional rooms) that ventilated well in the tropics. They came with minimal furnishings, good plumbing, and free rent and electricity. Maintenance, grounds, and garbage services were included in the sanitation program. Bachelors took their meals in dining halls (called "hotels") where a full meal cost only thirty cents, and wives bought food—and all other items—at cost in commissary stores, the prototype of retail operations on later military bases.

With all of this infrastructure in place and the territorial community come to life, Stevens resumed canal excavations in January 1906. Now he began to activate the plan that had undergone gestation in his head during the past five months. There had been no external signs; Stevens was a "clean desk" man, never observed wrestling a pile of paperwork. During working hours, he put in his time out on various locations along the line. The plan consisted of 1) the basis of the project: sea-level or locks, and 2) the system of excavation. At the start of 1906, TR and the Congress had not reached the crucial decision on the type of canal. Which meant that any plan was only tentative, and that Stevens, who desired only to solve engineering problems, had to enlist in the political struggle to reach this decision.

Other than sanitation, the fundamental difficulty in Panama was to tame the unruly Chagres River, prone to violent, destructive flooding during the nine-month wet season. Stevens had come in expecting to undertake a sea-level project, probably because, since the time of the French, a consensus had favored it. DeLesseps had consistently thrown the weight of his, monumental, authority toward the sea-level concept and denigrated the idea of a lock canal. Since then the idea of locks had gained no respect because of the assumption that "experts" would settle for nothing less than a sea-level waterway. This was just something that "everyone" "knew."

Congress, as the appropriator, had to decide on the type of canal, informed by an international panel of experts appointed by the President. The eight Americans and five Europeans began meeting in September 1905, working through reports and data. They visited Panama at the end of the month, toured the line, and interviewed personnel on the Isthmus. At their 25th meeting on November 18, they voted eight to five in favor of a sea-level canal, with all of the Europeans and three of the Americans taking this stand. The White House received the weighty *Report of the Consulting Engineers for the Panama Canal* in January 1906. Dissenting members also turned in their report recommending a lock canal, with locks at either end and a lake in the middle. Five miles inland, there would be a long earthen dam on the Chagres joined to the Atlantic Locks at Gatun. The Gatun Locks would lift ships 85 feet in three stages. Next, ships would cross Gatun Lake for 23 miles, proceed through the "Cut" for another nine miles, and enter a single set of locks at Pedro Miguel, where they would be lowered 31 feet to a small intermediate lake. After crossing this lake, they would be lowered 54 more feet in two stages by the Pacific Locks to sea level.

Strangely—and ironically—this plan was identical to one presented by Godin De Lepinay, a distinguished French engineer, at the Paris Congress of 1879, which, meeting 27 years earlier, had been called to make the identical decision as to canal type. Lepinay's plan had been resoundingly rejected—and derided—but the idea, to tame a river by converting it into a lake, had never died; it had developed a life of its own in the minds of reflective people. Stevens, experiencing the high rainy season in late 1905, and finally catching the Chagres in flood, abruptly grasped the reality that the lock plan was the only one feasible—and affordable. He realized that for a sea-level waterway, no could predict the end of the digging. Whenever rains saturated it, the Isthmian ground became mobile. Reaching the consistency of Jello, it would start to move in obedience to the law of gravity. This land was an inherently unstable mixture of layers of earth and rocks. Either type of canal would require periodic and constant dredging. Stevens saw that there was much more to it than digging a deeper trench. A sea-level canal would require an exponentially greater amount of digging and subsequent dredging, especially because of the destructive effects of the Chagres's annual violent flooding into the channel of the canal. Then, the increased time requirement, estimated at 18 years, double the time for a lock canal's estimated nine years, raised the costs far beyond any realistic consensus.

Stevens now spoke up for the lock plan, and the President, who had carefully stayed neutral until this point, decided to back the man he had put in charge. TR threw in his full support for the plan. All this took several months of political wrangling, and Stevens, who detested every passage he had to make by sea because of extreme seasickness, had to make a special trip to Washington to testify before Congress. Eventually after lengthy committee hearings and speechifying in front of the entire body, the Senate voted 36 to 31 for a lock canal on June 19, 1906. Three less votes and the U.S. would have entered upon an ill-fated attempt to dig a canal at sea-level. George Goethals, Stevens' successor, later stated that there wasn't enough money in the world to pay for a sea-level canal in Panama. [6]

As a railroader, Stevens conceived the actual digging of the canal as railroad plan, in three phases. In phase one, a blasting crew drilled holes, inserted dynamite, and loosened the ground by blowing it up. In phase two, huge 95-ton Bucyrus steamshovels rolled in on newly laid track and lifted the "spoil"—the mixture of earth and rocks—into the dump cars of a train just rolled in on another track laid alongside the rails of the steamshovel. In phase three, locomotives pulled the dump car trains out of the Cut to the dumping sites, emptied their loads, and returned for more spoil. These trains functioned as a perpetual conveyor belt, carrying the spoil to reclamation areas where it was needed: the growing causeway out to the islands at the Pacific entrance (Naos, Flamenco, Perico); the great earthen dam at Gatun; or new townsites like Balboa on the Pacificside being built on wetlands (thus also eliminating major mosquito-breeding spots). Tracks were moved and relaid constantly to blast sites and dump sites, with dozens of trains continually moving, directed to wherever shovels lifted spoil, then to a location for unloading, and eventually back to receive another load. Tracks were laid so that trains chugged upgrade to be loaded and rolled out full on a downgrade. Empty trains were always lined up to receive a load, but they were carefully dispatched to wherever the wait would be short. This plan achieved maximum efficiency because no steamshovel ever sat idle to await a spoil train. At all times along the nine miles of Culebra Cut (later renamed Gaillard Cut after Lt.Colonel David Gaillard, its chief excavator), trains rolled in and chugged out, empty and full, from first light to dusk.

III

President Roosevelt cruised down for a visit in November 1906, saw everything he could in three vigorous days, understood that Stevens had laid the foundations of this monumental project, and returned assuming the right man would carry out the recently determined plan. Again he reorganized the Isthmian Canal Commission to satisfy its chief engineer, this time conferring autocratic power, Stevens now communicating directly with Secretary of War Taft (instead of through a Washington-based Chairman of the ICC). At last Panama prospects seemed sunny. Everything was set, and TR had scored a public relations triumph. Posing in the driver's seat of a great Bucyrus shovel, he had tweaked the nation's fancy and propagated feelings of great pride in the Panama operations. But what followed was some confusion and disturbance, for two months later, TR received an unhappy letter from Stevens. Not exactly a resignation, but he complained—of weariness, of people obstructing him, of separation from family, of not really caring for the job ("The 'honor'...appeals to me but slightly. To me the canal is only a big ditch.... The work itself...on the whole, I do not like...") [7] This odd burst of negativism amazed the President; he couldn't understand it. Here all had seemed nearly triumphant, and now, this surprising revelation of strain and discontent. What could have gone wrong? There never would be an answer, and Theodore Roosevelt wasted no time on the mystery. He knew that when a commander rejected his command that a replacement had to be found. Quickly consulting with Taft, the "resignation" was accepted, and Major George W. Goethals, an engineering officer well regarded by Taft was appointed to take over.

The President heartily concurred because a commissioned officer had to go where he was ordered, remain for the entire tour of duty, and carry out his assignment. As David McCullough, the canal's historian put it: "To Roosevelt, Stevens was a commander abandoning his army." [8] Stevens, the "clean desk" man who wore a mask of certitude in public, was an intense individual who labored in private, a loner who had disliked the public nature of the job. He liked change, and, with his railroad plan working, he no longer felt challenged. Looking ahead, he probably did not desire the responsibility of constructing the locks, a vast project in concrete not in his line and specialty. Stevens was overworked and lonely; it didn't suit him to be out front commanding an army. He probably missed trekking on snowshoes with a railroad laying tracks behind him. The men had loved this figure, known as "Big Smoke" because of the big cigars he puffed endlessly. He always walked right up to them, talking their language about the work, letting them know he understood and appreciated their efforts. For such "vibes" they forgot to take sick days and worked their hearts out.

Goethals arrived to find efficient operations and high morale, but, with the earthslides that came with the deepening of the Cut, and with locks, ports, and the relocation of the railroad to higher ground, there would be no end of fresh challenges. Goethals also knew the loneliness of command, but he was a disciplined soldier. He never flinched from the public side of his job, though, like Stevens, he preferred to concentrate on engineering. He also regularly toured the line of canal work, but in a self-propelled railroad car christened by the men the "Yellow Peril." He was tall, fit, calm in aspect, serious, a chain-smoker, and absolutely in control. Although the construction of the canal was, and remained, a civilian undertaking, it was now commanded by officers of the U.S. Army Corps of Engineers. Goethals received $15,000, where Stevens had been paid $30,000, and a promotion to Colonel. He had extensive experience on river, canal, and harbor projects, having built locks, docks, and coastal defenses. The men, who loved Stevens, didn't welcome Goethals, but they soon learned to respect him because he was fair, never petty, and always accurate about what he wanted. An important innovation was the *Canal Record*, a weekly newspaper that explained things to the men, reported activities on and off the job, and did much to unify sentiment and elevate morale. Publishing excavation statistics drove the men into competition to increase them. Another significant innovation occurred every Sunday morning when Goethals opened his office door to anyone who wanted to speak. Sometimes he listened to as many as a hundred people, hearing everything from petty complaints to valuable ideas for improving the work. He listened patiently and gave his judgment, which was final. Most came away satisfied, but there is the story of the man who said, "If you decide against me, Colonel, I shall appeal." "To whom?" Goethals asked. [9] Such human treatment eventually led the men into his camp.

Goethals saw the job through. Important modifications included increasing the bottom width of Culebra Cut from 200 to 300 feet; widening the lock chambers from 95 to 110 feet; building a three-mile breakwater along the Pacific entrance out to Naos Island (the causeway noted above) to block the currents that carried silt into the channel; relocating the Pacific locks and dam a few miles inland to Miraflores for a more secure placement; and reorganizing the work into three geographical divisions: Atlantic, Central, and Pacific, each run by a single chief. All of these projects, plus the construction of port and terminal facilities and the relocation of the railroad to higher ground above the level of the future Gatun Lake, took seven years, from 1907 to 1914. The job used 61,000,000 pounds of dynamite, which arrived at the port of Colon in shiploads of 1,000,000 pounds; 20,000 fifty-pound boxes had to be unloaded carefully by hand and put aboard special trains which carried the explosive cargo to concrete magazines set back in the jungle. Half the labor force handled dynamite at some phase of the work: loading and unloading it, carrying the boxes to a work site, loading the sticks into drill holes, and setting off the blasts. Several fatal accidents occurred because of faulty or mishandled dynamite, lightening strikes, being too close to explosions, and unexplained causes. The worst disaster came in 1908, when twenty-two tons exploded prematurely, killing twenty-three and seriously injuring another forty. [10]

The excavation record was reached in March 1909, when 68 huge Bucyrus steamshovels removed more than 2,000,000 cubic yards of spoil (ten times the record month for the French). Ultimately 96,000,000 cubic yards came out of the nine-mile Cut.[11] About 160 trains a day ran in and out of the Cut over 76 miles of construction track—which were being relocated constantly (a thousand miles a year). Every piece of equipment, shovels and trains, was located each day with pins on a large map, necessary to create work schedules for all units. Train traffic was regulated by yardmasters and a central dispatcher who directed the movements of each train from loading to dumpsites and back. Everything was organized and coordinated, from dynamite drill to dump car.

The great project wouldn't have taken seven more years if the slides hadn't occurred. As the Cut deepened, rains soaked in and destabilized the walls, which collapsed downward in great movements of earth to fill the bottom of the trench. At the highest point, where the Cut went through the low mountain range, Gold Hill, the worst slides occurred. This recurring phenomenon was called Cucaracha Slide; it began Goethals' first year, and it let go again at intervals. Engineers vainly sought the "angle of repose," or the degree of slant at which the walls would hold. The avalanche of mud and rock came down again in 1910—twice—burying shovels, trains, equipment and closing the south (Pacific) end for months. As the Cut grew deeper, other slides occurred during the rainiest months. Slide removal usually took up one-third of a year. Cucaracha never stopped moving. Thus it went from 1910 to 1913: a soft, porous layer of material, turned to Jello by feet of rain, would slide, like snow off a roof, off the harder, rockier layer beneath it. There was nothing to do for it, but to dig it all out again. Underlying rock formations were unstable and broke easily, not only from rain and the loss of lateral support, but also from the concussive effects of all the blasting. Geologically, this Panamanian terrain was totally unsuited to this vast project in ditching.

IV
RAGTIME ALMANAC

Workforce on Panama Canal Construction [12]

Date	Number Employed
Nov. 1904	3,500
Nov. 1905	17,000
Dec. 1906	23,901
Oct. 1907	31,967
Apr. 1908	33,170
Mar. 1910	38,670
Jun. 1912	38,174
Aug. 1913	39,962
Jun. 1914	33,270

The Panama Canal construction workforce was divided into Americans and non-Americans. The former were paid in gold and the latter in silver, resulting in the classification of employees according to whether they were on the "Gold-Roll" or the "Silver-Roll." Americans were hired for all the skilled and higher-paid jobs. They all were white and most were male. In 1913, these Gold-Roll employees numbered 5,362 out of a workforce of about 40,000. Average pay ran $150/month. Teachers and clerks started as low as $60, engineers at $250. A steamshovel operator received $310, compared to a doctor's pay of $150. There were never more than 300 women working (nurses, clerks), and no woman received over $125. However rent came free, a dining hall meal cost 30 cents, groceries were cheap (sold at cost), and clothing needs in the tropics were minimal. Benefits included six weeks' vacation with pay and thirty days of sick leave with pay. Servants worked for $10/month. [13]

However very little of the actual labor was performed by white Americans on the Gold-Roll, who constituted only about one-seventh of the employees. As McCullough the Canal's historian puts it: "Official visitors [and others]…could not help but be amazed, even astounded, at the degree to which the entire system, not simply the construction, depended on black labor." [14] Non-U.S. workers, mostly black men, were recruited from the West Indies for both heavy and menial labor. Altogether more than 31,000 were thus transported to Panama, the majority from Barbados, with another 7,500 from the French West Indies (Martinique and Guadeloupe). Another 10,000 came from Europe, about 8,400 of whom were from Spain. [15] Less than 400 Panamanians served in this mass of, mainly, unskilled workers. The common word on this was that Panamanians were too lazy to work with picks and shovels. But Panama was an underpopulated country of just over 300,000, of whom only about 50,000 lived in the terminal cities of Panama and Colon. The rest were spread out on subsistence farms, so probably Panama lacked any great number desperate enough to give up their land to grab another subsistence opportunity. Wages, after all, were minimal, about $6/week, paid at the rate of 10 cents/hour for six, ten-hour days. On the islands of Barbados, Trinidad, Martinique, and Guadeloupe, most of the labor force was employed only seasonally in the sugar cane fields and mills, living most of the time in a chronic state of underemployment, ill-fed and ill-housed. To them, a steady six dollars was relative affluence.

Canal Zone Americans rigidly followed the color line: "gold" and "silver" lines at the pay car, the post office, and the commissary; black hospital wards; black schools; and segregated housing. The Tivoli Hotel, YMCA

Clubhouses, and white churches were off-limits to black folk. Although black school children outnumbered whites two to one, there were only half as many black as white teachers. Housing for black families was either overcrowded or non-existent. Most black families lived apart in jungle villages in packing crate houses, unscreened and lacking sanitary facilities. Such conditions were unhealthy. Where whites seldom knew sick days (they sometimes used them to enjoy a day off from work), sickness was common, even chronic, among laborers. They suffered especially from lung diseases: pneumonia and tuberculosis; typhoid, from poor water; and malaria—Col. Gorgas's sanitary squads did not penetrate the rainforest. Of the 4800 deaths during the construction period, all but a few hundred were black. Besides diseases, many were killed on the job by explosions, avalanches, and other violent happenings. These men spent their days working in mud, rain, and terrible heat (temperatures usually rose well over 100 degrees F, with humidity at 90 or 100 percent on the floor of the Cut). Although death rates from disease dropped each year, proof of health hazards is revealed in the statistic for 1913-14 that, during the final year of construction, 24,723 employees were treated for illness and accidents. Another statistic indicates that, where the death rate for U.S. (white) employees was 2.06 per thousand, it was exactly <u>four</u> times greater for non-U.S. employees, 8.23 per thousand.[16]

When the job concluded, these West Indian people were entitled to repatriation to their home islands. Since return meant going back to worse poverty, many (if not most) chose to stay. Many had brought wives to Panama, and these families remained to form a new class of black English-speaking Panamanians, a distinctly unwelcome minority in a Spanish-speaking country. They stayed on in their, already traditional, roles of furnishing labor to the Panama Canal enterprise and domestic service to the Americans, who likewise stayed on in supervisory, skilled, and higher-paid jobs that carried many of the perks and benefits they had become used to. Thus blacks of West Indian origin and ancestry settled in to form the lower part of the Canal Zone's two-class society. As such, they fell into the ambiguous status of a client people, supported and protected by Americans, who furnished them with housing, schools, retail stores, and other facilities, unequal to be sure, but superior to anything possessed by the other poor people of Panama. These other poor never ceased to resent a somewhat privileged status, created by a foreign power dominant in their land, and conferred on a minority that made too little effort to speak the national language and assimilate into the culture.[17]

V

The construction of the Panama Canal was a Progressive-Era triumph. Its motto has been: "The Land divided; the World United." The engineers who designed and built it achieved something close to perfection; later engineers improved its capacity but never had to change anything. Everyone ever employed on the Zone felt pride in its flawless operations. Anyone who has ever ridden a ship across its 50-mile extent has experienced amazement at its rapid, efficient, and very quiet operation during the transit time of seven to eight hours; gates open and close, waters rise and fall; towing locomotives hum along, ringing a bell at intervals; canal pilots give and take orders over two-way radios; ships sound the horn when the transit is completed and then get underway. After working there decades, employees remain in awe of the thing, and no one expresses boredom or nonchalance.

The price of this mechanical excellence, however, is high, a dedicated—devoted—stringent <u>periodic maintenance</u>. Metal parts and mechanisms deteriorate in the tropics. Failure to adhere to maintenance schedules will lead to disaster for the Canal. Not only the canal, but its channel requires maintenance, that is, dredging, to remove silt that flows into the salt-water approaches, and earth that continues to slide into Gaillard Cut. The new owners and operators, the Republic of Panama, must never cut corners or fudge on the maintenance imperatives.

The combined costs of French and American efforts came to $639,000,000 ($352,000,000 for the U.S., including $40,000,000 to the French company and $10,000,000 to Panama). Interestingly, the Canal came in at $23,000,000 less than the estimate of 1907. The nine miles of Culebra (now Gaillard) Cut cost $10,000,000 for each mile. Despite later slides, the Canal opened for business six months ahead of schedule. More remarkable than any other superlative, no evidence of corruption has ever surfaced, either in the construction or in later operations. The entire project was carried out with total honesty, with no graft, payroll padding, or kickbacks. From then till now (the year 2000), there has never been a Panama Canal scandal.

But we must consider the blemish that discolors this proud achievement and diminishes the triumphalism in its recognition. The entire project was erected on the backs of exploited and abused labor. So probably were the Pyramids, the Taj Mahal, and China's Great Wall, and little good comes of wallowing in retrospective guilt, but we should fully recognize and honor the difficult work done by that force of (mostly) black workers from the Antilles. And this should take some concrete or substantive form, a monument, an educational institution, a charitable foundation, a history of their role. They gave much. [18]

Notes: Chapter 25

1. Quoted in David McCullough, *The Path Between the Seas: The Creation of the Panama Canal, 1870-1914*, (1977), 480. McCullough's very full account furnishes the principal source for this chapter. Also useful was the compendious contemporary work, Willis J. Abbot, *Panama and the Canal* (1913). Information found on the Internet came from the Panama Canal Website of 1999.
2. Quoted in McCullough, 508.
3. *Ibid.*, 462
4. *Ibid.*, 464.
5. *Ibid.*, 471, 478.
6. *Ibid.*, 483-487.
7. *Ibid.*, 504.
8. *Ibid..* 508.
9. *Ibid.*, 538.
10. *Ibid.*, 546.
11. *Ibid.*, 546-547.
12. Source: Panama Canal Commission Website, 1999.
13. McCullough, 559-562.
14. *Ibid.*, 575.
15. Source: Panama Canal Commission website, 1999. Total recruitment of non-U.S. workers reached 45,000.
16. McCullough, 582.
17. Cultural assimilation of the descendants of West Indians who immigrated to Panama has taken several generations. The principal reason was their geographical isolation in the U.S. Canal Zone outside of Panamanian jurisdiction, where they did not have to accommodate to the mores and folkways of their adopted country. This allowed them to speak English instead of Spanish, which in turn gave them a hiring preference over Spanish speakers for Canal Zone employment. Since residence and work in the Canal Zone provided a steady wage, housing, retail purchase privileges, medical benefits (including hospitalization), recreation facilities, and security, there were no rewards for learning Spanish and becoming culturally Panamanian: the rewards came from learning English. Some of these privileges and benefits were lost after 1950 because of later treaties, and the end of the Canal Zone completed their immersion. Some of this population after retirement relocated in the United States. Author's Note: I lived and worked "on the Zone" from 1956 to 1981. I witnessed much of what I say above in notes and text. I picked up information through listening as well as through reading.
18. McCullough, 611.

26. There's No Business Like Race Business (III): From Coontown to Jungletown

> I wants to be a actor lady,
> Playin' ya know, star in the show,
> Spotlight for me, no back-row shady,
> I'm the real thing,
> I dance and sing!
>
> *In Dahomey* (1903)

The part it plays in American life and its acceptance by the world at large cannot be ignored. It is to this music that America in general gives itself over in its leisure hours…. At these times, the Negro drags his captors captive.

James Weldon Johnson [1]

Coontown was the worst neighborhood in Tin Pan Alley, and most blacks couldn't wait to move out.

David A. Jasen and Gene Jones [2]

By 1900 African-American artists had, first, proven themselves in minstrelsy, and, then, led by Williams and Walker, cakewalked into vaudeville's big-time (Chapter 11). Yet (figuratively) they remained caught in the mean jaws of the trap of racism. White audiences applauded enthusiastically only when degraded stereotypes of ex-slaves pranced across a stage. When Irish, Germans, and Jews protested the caricatures laughed <u>at</u> by the public, their constituencies arose to demand some respect and more sympathetic portraits. Such public reactions implied fellow feelings and an awareness that these "foreigners" were, after all, human, with a potential to succeed in their new country. But blacks never got any respect because audiences believed the stereotype (see end of Chapter 11). They were not perceived as "greenhorn" immigrants "learning the ropes," but as inferiors who could never grasp them.

But in upbeat ragtime America, these black artists kept up their determination: What they wanted could be termed showbiz parity, to create and perform in shows which would gain them respect and recognition, shows that would take them away from coonery and minstrelsy. Minstrelsy began a decades-long slow fade during the 1890's, as musical comedy, imported as light opera and operetta from Europe, experienced a leisurely evolution toward its American forms. Among the first African Americans to depart minstrelsy was Bob Cole, who has been called "the most versatile theatrical talent of his day (except for George M. Cohan)." [3] Robert Allen Cole (1868-1911) left his name on 120 published songs, the most prolific of the black composers. Besides composing, he worked as actor, dancer, singer, lyricist, librettist, director, and producer.

Growing up in Athens, Georgia (son of ex-slaves), and Atlanta, Cole briefly attended Atlanta University, and, still in his teens, headed north to show business, eventually reaching Chicago where he joined the innovative *Creole Show* in 1890. As previously noted (Chapter 6), the *Creole Show*, produced by white manager Sam T. Jack, was something new under the limelight, the first all-black burlesque company and the first to feature women in leading roles, lavishly costumed. Its three ingredients were low comedy, vaudeville acts, and beautiful women. The *Creole Show* flourished for years and proved a hit at the Columbian Expo in 1893. [4] In it, Cole proved his versatility: he sang, danced, did monologs, stage managed, and composed his first songs (published in 1893). He also found a wife, singer and dancer Stella Wiley. They toured as a song-and-dance act whenever the *Creole Show* took a vacation. Ambitious to create and produce his creations, Bob and Stella relocated to New York in 1894.

In New York Bob Cole put together a creative performance group, the "All-Star Stock Company," consisting of about a dozen talented African Americans. Although they never got beyond small-time vaudeville, and the venture soon folded, its members comprised a core group that would contribute to future projects. Cole and Wiley next returned for brief runs in the *Creole Show*, then moved on to other shows until they landed in the first edition of *Black Patti's Troubadours* in 1896. As noted earlier (Chapter 22), M(atilda) Sissieretta (Joyner) Jones (1869-1933) was a greatly talented African-American soprano who sang for presidents and European royalty but was prohibited from the American concert stage and the Metropolitan Opera. [5] Critics acknowledged her talent when they labeled her the "Black Patti," favorably comparing her with the much admired Italian diva Adelina Patti. Unable to tour in the U.S. as a "serious" artist, she found in all-black shows (post-minstrel) her only opportunity for regular employment. She came onstage in *Oriental America* in 1893, the first such show, and Bob Cole's first such effort. In 1896, when she formed her permanent company (the *Troubadours*), which lasted until 1914, Bob Cole was chosen as both writer-composer and lead performer. The *Black Patti Troubadours* show was a mixed bag in three parts aimed at commercial success: a short musical comedy, variety acts, and the concluding "Operatic Kaleidoscope" in which Jones took the stage with songs and opera selections backed by a chorus. Later she staged entire scenes from operas. Altogether this was a compromise which paid her way and enabled her to pursue an operatic vocation to at least a limited acclaim. She deserves credit for opening up the stage for her race and for demonstrating a major talent before uncaring whites. [6]

Partnered by Billy Johnson, one of the 1894 "All Star" group, Cole wrote, directed, and performed in the one-act "Merry Musical Skit" entitled *At Jolly "Coony"—ey Island*, with a cast of thirteen and a chorus of forty. Forty minutes in length, this was the lowbrow opener of the *Troubadours* show, designed as the sugar-coating to pull in the masses for the highbrow finale. In this elaborate sketch, Johnson and Cole played a pair of shady types, Jim Flimflammer, a small-time con man (Johnson) and Willy Wayside, a seedy tramp (Cole). Their broad comedy and such songs as "The Black Four Hundred's Ball" and "Red Hots" pleased the packed houses that crowded in for the company's initial tour of 1896-97, and later they parlayed these characters into a vaudeville twosome. Fortified by this success, which had propelled the Black Patti company to stardom—and by a growing reputation as composer and librettist—Cole approached the company's white managers for a raise. Refused, he quit, taking Billy Johnson, determined to create and produce his own all-black musical comedy. (Ernest Hogan {"All Coons Look Alike to Me"} replaced Cole.)

A Trip to Coontown opened on September 27, 1897, in a small theatre in South Amboy, NJ. With a cast of eighteen, it was the first full-length musical comedy created and performed by African Americans. Like many 1890's shows, it was a revue-type musical that conveyed its audience on a tour of various "sights," e.g., New York, Chinatown, or Paris. As the title implies, Cole and Billy Johnson stayed with the coonery they had depicted on *"Coony"—ey Island*. Cole came on again as the tramp Willie Wayside, and Billy Johnson retained the persona of the "Confidence Man" (now nameless). What distinguished *Coontown*, besides its humor and energy, was its "book"; as a two-act musical comedy taking up the entire evening, it could claim status as a "book show." Without a Broadway opening, it drifted through third-rate out-of-town houses for six months. In 1898 it reached better houses out in the provinces and a brief run in New York's Third Avenue Theatre. Here the *Times* critic (4-16-98) praised its humor and songs, including "All Chinks Look Alike to Me," a parody of Ernest Hogan's 1896 coonsong hit. This critic concluded: "'A Trip to Coontown' is a great big success." [7] Cole and Johnson proved this assertion by keeping this show on the road until the end of 1900. It returned to New York in 1899, finally getting to "Broadway" when it played the Casino Roof Garden and the Grand Opera House. [8] Now obscure and forgotten, *A Trip to Coontown* was the vehicle that first raised African Americans above degrading minstrelsy and beyond the vaudeville that accepted too few of them, to the edge of book-show respectability. It did so during an upward three-year run to better theatres.

Better remembered is its much shorter successor of 1898, *Clorindy, or the Origin of the Cakewalk*, created by the team of poet Paul Lawrence Dunbar (1872-1906) (*Lyrics of the Lowly Life*, 1896) and composer Will Marion Cook (1869-1944). Opening on the Casino Roof Garden in July 1898, *Clorindy* was the first black show on Broadway (a year ahead of *Coontown*). Billed as "operetta," it lasted only an hour and consisted of a blackface revue ending with a twenty-minute cakewalk. *Clorindy* is remembered for its hit songs: "Darktown Is Out Tonight," "Hottest Coon In Dixie," and "Who Dat Say Chicken In Dis Crowd." It started out with Ernest Hogan, the black vaudeville star of the late Nineties, and closed with Williams and Walker, the black musical comedy stars of the 00's. Where *Coontown* grew and flourished out on the road, *Clorindy's* run was brief, probably because of a lack of content.

II

Like Bert Williams (see below), Will Marion Cook was a casualty of racism. Both were sheltered from it in youth, Williams on the island of New Providence in the Bahamas, Cook in the genteel environment of the campus of Howard University in the District of Columbia, where his father taught and practiced law. Although poverty threatened when Will's father died (of tuberculosis) in 1878, somehow Will continued his musical education and got himself into Oberlin College where his parents had gone. He came out of Oberlin having demonstrated great promise as a violinist and musician. With the aid of family friend Frederick Douglass, money was raised to send Will to Berlin's <u>Hochschule fur Musik</u> to complete his studies with renowned violinist Josef Joachim. Two years later (1890), Will returned, prepared for the concert stage and naively hoping for acceptance into the white cultural establishment. During the next three or four years, Cook countered rejection by performing and associating with the relatively few other African-American classical musicians. His passage through this meagre milieu led to the New York Conservatory, where, during the mid-Nineties, the Czech composer Antonin Dvorak (1841-1904) was attempting to foster an American art music based upon folk sources. Dvorak, who had found his own inspiration in the folk music of his native land, believed that a nation's art music should be rooted in the culture of its common people, i.e., the <u>folk</u>. In America, he had concluded that the music of the Negro offered the most promising foundation on which to construct a genuinely American classical or art music. Dvorak had demonstrated to American composers how to bring this about in his *New World Symphony* (1893), which conveys the essence of a "spiritual" in its second part.

By this time Cook's outlook had become clouded with bitterness. He felt an aversion to Dvorak's influence because Dvorak had not recognized his (Cook's) great potential and accredited him as chief disciple. According to an anecdote, this emotional ferment erupted in 1895 after Cook's solo debut at Carnegie Hall when some critic or listener hailed him as "the greatest *colored* [italics added] violinist in the world." Crushed and outraged, he turned away from classical music, vowing never again to pick up a violin in public. [9] Instead he perversely immersed himself in popular black syncopated music, coonsongs and cakewalks, a rejection of his genteel cultural background. It drove him inward, made him a loner who rejected his rejectors. Whoever dared to reject him fell short of his standards. With so monumental a chip on his shoulder, Will Marion Cook soured into a prickly, antagonistic personality, always on-guard to the world that tormented him.

A year later after a positive encounter with Bert Williams and George Walker (who had discerned his talent), he proposed a musical play about the origin of their vaudeville specialty, the cakewalk. With such encouragement, Cook enlisted Paul Lawrence Dunbar, and they quickly produced a working script with music. With luck and energy, Cook succeeded in presenting *Clorindy* at the Casino Theatre's Roof Garden on July 5, 1898. This wasn't the main auditorium downstairs, but the location was "Broadway," the first black show to get there—and it was a solid hit, as well as the first entirely syncopated show, ever. Other shows had interpolated the occasional coonsong, but this show really took off into syncopation; its cast of twenty-six also danced while they sang, a thing previously unknown on the stage where choruses had merely sung and dancers had only danced. *Clorindy* packed them in all summer. Williams and Walker had been unavailable, yielding this star turn to Ernest Hogan, but in the fall they took it on the road as part of their larger variety show, *Senegambian Carnival*, where, as noted above, it crashed in a short run.

They—Cook, Dunbar, Hogan—tried it again next summer, on top of the New York Theatre, with *Jes' Lak White Folks* (1899). The success of *Clorindy* did not repeat, but after the show's brief run, other companies took it on the road. Several of its Cook-Dunbar songs found their way into later shows. At this point, Dunbar, fed up with the domineering Cook, and frustrated with having his carefully crafted scripts cut and altered for the "good" of the production, severed his relationship with the theatre and returned to literature (he would die in 1906, unhappy with a readership that preferred caricatures and dialect poems). Cook continued with Hogan, composing some of the music for his variety or "vaudeville musicals," which were not true musical comedies following a story line, but a series of variety acts slightly unified by themes. Late in 1901, after the second of these, *The Cannibal King*, was produced, Cook rewrote it as a musical comedy for Williams and Walker.

In Dahomey: A Negro Musical Comedy opened at the New York Theatre (59th Street and Broadway) shortly after Easter in 1903. It was the first full-length all-black musical comedy to reach the fabled theatrical street. All of it, book, lyrics (some by Dunbar), songs, instrumental pieces, staging, direction, and cast, was an African-American accomplishment. It brought the popular vaudeville team of Bert Williams and George Walker to stardom in the theatre. Its book, a slight story developed by Will Marion Cook and completed by Jesse Shipp, concerned a fraudulent back-to-Africa colonization scheme, which set part of the story in an African jungletown (much of the rest takes place in Boston) rather than in a downsouth coontown. Like nearly all early musical comedy, *In Dahomey* lacked integration: the action paused frequently for interpolated songs unrelated to the story line. Artists would interject such songs hoping for hits that would bring them fame as well as to create memorable performances. In the midst of exotic settings: royal palaces, sultan's harems, southsea islands, Chinatowns, or jungletowns, lead singers would take the spotlight and launch into any song that might enhance their careers and sell sheet music fronted by their pictures.

More of *In Dahomey* survives because ragtime historians and performers Richard Zimmerman and Ian Whitcomb recently retrieved the show's score form a London warehouse shortly before it was demolished. In most cases all we possess of early musical comedies are the few songs ventured by publishers, plus the reviews, some advertisements, and miscellaneous information such as memoirs. Scripts of musical comedies (unlike straight plays) weren't published because dialog did not stand alone but functioned as one element in a total production along with music, dance, and spectacle. Also a musical comedy script was never a set thing; it never ceased to be a work-in-progress, altered constantly to satisfy cast and production changes. Curiously this breakthrough show had an initial Broadway run (following the usual pre-opening tour) of only 53 performances (about two months), but it then took off for London, opening at the Shaftesbury Theatre on May 16, 1903. For this second premiere, Cook composed the opening chorus "Swing Along," which achieved a lasting popularity, becoming a kind of signature piece. The show became a "smash hit" when in June, King Edward VII summoned it to Buckingham Palace for a Command Performance in honor of the birthday of the Prince of Wales (later King George V). So popular did *In Dahomey* become that it ran in Britain for a year. Back in New York in August 1904, it ran several months, then toured for forty weeks! After this, a second company headed out to tour both the U.S. and Europe. Ultimately the show's backers (Hurtig and Seamon) realized 400 % on their $15,000 investment.

In Dahomey reached across the footlights because of the high quality of both music and performances. Cook as principal composer provided most of the choral and ensemble numbers, but other talents contributed. These included J. Leubrie Hill, Cecil Mack, Alex Rogers, and star Bert Williams, who always contributed to his own shows (he is credited with a dance number for this show, "Jig"). Jasen and Jones characterize Cook's role in the Williams and Walker shows as the "composer-in-chief" who supplied "the operetta glue that held the vaudeville together." [10] Of the best tunes in the show, he could claim "Brown-Skin Baby Mine," "Swing Along," "Leader of the Colored Aristocracy" (lyrics by James Weldon Johnson), and the infectious march-finale "On Emancipation Day" (lyrics by Dunbar). Cook also composed the "Overture," the "Caboceers Entrance" ensemble number, and the songs "Society" and "The Czar." Cast and production members contributed other excellent songs: "My Dahomian Queen" (J. Leubrie Hill), "That's How the Cakewalk's Done" (Hill), the droll and charming "On Broadway In Dahomey Bye and Bye" (Alex Rogers and Al Johns), Bert Williams' signature specialty "I'm a Jonah Man" (Alex Rogers), and "Rag-time Drummer" (Hill). Curiously the appealing "I Wants To Be a Actor Lady," was supplied by white publisher Harry VonTilzer. The recovered score contains nineteen songs, but other sources indicate that perhaps twenty other songs were interpolated during the show's three-year existence. Beyond the musical highlights, the excitement of its syncopation, and the brightness of its ensembles, it was the comic excellence of Williams and Walker that put it over. Sylvester Russell of the black *Freeman* (Indianapolis) enthused that, "Judging from the serious observations of the people in all parts of the house [a reference to segregated seating], I should venture to say that few comedy teams of any race shine more brightly in the eyes of New Yorkers than Williams and Walker." He praised George Walker for both costume and brilliance of dialog and Bert Williams for the woebegone humor of the hapless, unlucky "Jonah Man" and for "his quaint dancing, full of originality and fun." [11]

For African Americans, *In Dahomey* established their show business on the higher level of musical comedy. Although it retained the negritudinous tinge and such minstrel elements as the cakewalk, it was no minstrel show. Bert Williams unlucky "Jonah Man" was a universal, the schlemiel who turns up in all cultures. Some of its raggy songs were sung in dialect, but none were coonsongs. Coontown to jungletown may have been only a half-step out of minstrelsy, but it was a step away from the degrading to the edge of respectabilty. From opening night, large numbers of black folk manifested their pride and support by filling their segregated seats. Another critic wrote in the *Freeman*:

>...The color line has been drawn during this engagement, a certain part of the house being set aside for colored people; nevertheless, they are there at each performance, arriving in automobiles, coaches, coupes, and on foot [this was 1903];attired in evening gowns, tuxedos, and swallow tails, just the same as the "white 400." At the opening performance there were over 1000 colored people in the house. [12]

On opening night, blacks had festively lined up with cash in hand, expecting box seats, only to be shown to the side entrance to the stairs for the upper gallery (the traditional "n—heaven"). Angry, forceful protests followed, which gained a compromise: blacks were allowed into designated upper boxes, the balcony, and their gallery, but lower boxes and the orchestra were restricted to whites. [13]

Segregation was a symptom of the endemic hostility endured by black performers in northern cities. White audiences expected coonsongs and cakewalks, which dragged out the death of minstrelsy for about thirty years (1890-1920). Although one black act had become the accepted limit on any vaudeville bill, it was continually resented by most white artists. In 1905 at Hammerstein's Victoria Theatre in New York, W. C. Kelly refused to perform on the bill with Williams and Walker. He declared to William Hammerstein that, as a southerner, he could never appear on any stage with Negroes. Hammerstein simply replaced Kelly, and George Walker passed off the incident casually with such comments as "The day is past for that sort of thing," plus a touch of bravado: "…and as we are paid more money in a week for our work than he gets in three months for his." Later it came out that Kelly may have been enraged because Williams and Walker occupied the star dressing room. [14]

Such rage, constantly simmering below the surface of the city, flared up in the New York Race Riot of August 15,!900. Three days before, Arthur Harris, a black pimp, had knifed to death a vice-squad patrolman. This time, an enraged police force churned up the riot, which broke out around 11:00 P.M. in the area between 28th and 42nd Streets, just west of Broadway. Here white hostility had been increasing because of blacks moving onto the west side. Police had spread the word to "clean the niggers out" on the night before the funeral of their brother officer. The mobs simply grabbed and beat every black caught in their advance. Those not clubbed to death were dragged to the nearest police station and beaten more. Out in front, Inspector Thompson roared, "Club every damned nigger you see—kill them—shoot them—be brave—same as I was!" Police themselves stopped all Eighth Avenue streetcars and threw all blacks into the mobs, including women and children. [15] Frequently heard were cries of "Get Ernest Hogan and Williams and Walker! And Cole and Johnson!" Walker, heading out on the town, intending to meet his friend Hogan, after a performance, was caught on a Sixth Avenue streetcar and dragged off at 34th Street. Pursued by screaming hundreds, he somehow tore himself loose and ran fast enough, escaping, much the worse for wear, into a cellar, where he hid until daylight. Hogan, on the way to meet Walker, fared much worse. Recognized at 44th Street and 8th Avenue by a mob of about 500 yelling, "Get the nigger," Hogan ran down Broadway, but was caught and badly beaten, saved only by the compassionate intervention of a police detective who pointed his gun at the mob. [16] Bert Williams, who kept away from the sporting life, had saved himself by going home. But his biographer indicates that he came out of this episode an emotional casualty, becoming withdrawn and no longer affable with strangers. Except to perform, he seldom left his Harlem neighborhood, increasingly a solitary drinker. Bert did most of his drinking in his neighborhood at Matheny's Café (135th Street and Seventh Avenue). If Bert was in his corner at 1:00 AM closing time, Matheny would hand him the keys to lock up when he was ready to go home. Often the day crew would find him still in place when they came in at 5:00.[17]

III

> The one hope of the colored performer must be in making a radical departure from the old "darky" style of singing and dancing....There is an artistic side to the black race, and if it could be properly developed on the stage, I believe the theatre going public would profit much by it.
>
> George Walker [18]

At century's end Bob Cole turned a creative corner by changing partners. He formally ended his arrangement with Billy Johnson at the end of July 1901 when he handed over his share of *A Trip to Coontown*. [19] Whatever other causes there were (excessive drinking is also cited), Cole had outgrown his first collaborator and realized it when he encountered two brothers, also named Johnson, from Jacksonville, Florida. James Weldon Johnson (1871-1938) was a writer: a poet and lyricist; younger brother J(ohn) Rosamond Johnson (1873-1954) was a musician: a composer, a pianist, and a singer. Both were educated, James Weldon at Atlanta University and J. Rosamond at the Boston Conservatory. Both were educators and teachers, the former, principal at Jacksonville's segregated black school, the latter, Supervisor of Music in the Jacksonville Schools. Additionally, James Weldon had "read law" locally and passed the bar exam, becoming the first African American admitted to the Florida bar. The brothers took the train to New York during their 1899 summer vacation to have a look at the big-time and ascertain whether they had any prospects. They discovered a small circle of elite showbiz blacks, including Ernest Hogan, Bert Williams, George Walker, Will Marion Cook, Jesse Shipp, Alex Rogers, J. Leubrie Hill, Harry Burleigh, Paul Lawrence Dunbar, and of course, Bob Cole. These all regularly came and mingled at the Marshall Hotel on West 53rd Street, an old four-story brownstone converted into a fine establishment to serve the black professionals excluded from all of the other hotels in the entertainment district. The brothers Johnson hit it off best with Bob Cole, who had done it all and proved it with *A Trip to Coontown*. Before heading back to Florida, the three tried songwriting together. The result, a love song, "Louisiana Lize" ("Composed by Bob Cole, Words and Music Edited by J.W. and Rosamond Johnson"), was bought by May Irwin for $50 (performing rights).

That winter in Jacksonville, for a combined school chorus at the Lincoln's Birthday celebration, the brothers wrote "Lift Every Voice and Sing," a march of hymn-like exhaltation. The piece impressed music teachers, and it spread, passed in handwritten copies, all over the South. Eventually it became the anthem for NAACP meetings and graduation ceremonies. By the time it reached a publisher twenty years later, it was known as the "Negro National Anthem." These extraordinary brothers returned the next summer (1900) to compose with Bob Cole songs which found buyers right away. The trio's chief accomplishment was to get four songs interpolated into May Irwin's *Belle of Bridgeport*. That following winter, Paul Lawrence Dunbar came down to Jacksonville and unburdened to the Johnsons. Coonery onstage had sickened his soul, and he no longer felt up to writing dialect poems demanded by the public about the delights of watermelon, chicken, and possum. The Johnsons understood—they never wrote coonsongs—but inwardly they disagreed, believing black culture and dialect to be legitimate subjects. Their songs expressed the humor in black life, but with more sympathy than ridicule. They made their break the next summer (1901), moved into the Marshall Hotel, resumed their partnership with the energetic Cole, and immediately placed their songs all over town. Cole and Rosamond took over from Dunbar and completed the book and lyrics for Cook's *Cannibal King*, the short-lived Ernest Hogan show that later evolved into *In Dahomey*. Several shows interpolated their songs (Dockstadter's Minstrels, *Champagne Charlie*, *The Supper Club*). Bert Williams recorded their "My Castle on the Nile."

Next they contracted with publisher Joseph Stern, turning over their initial output of fifteen songs. Stern gave them an exclusive three-year contract with a monthly guarantee (deducted from royalties). Quite an amazing situation for songwriters, white or black: Broadway wanted their songs for interpolations, and a leading publisher bought first rights on all of their output. Right off they succeeded with "The Maiden With the Dreamy Eyes," one of four songs placed in a Florenz Ziegfeld production *The Little Duchess* (October 1901). *Duchess* starred Ziegfeld's glamorous wife Anna Held; "The Maiden With the Dreamy Eyes" became her theme song and sold well for years. Their biggest hit "Under the Bamboo Tree" ("If you lak-a-me, like I lak-a-you") was interpolated by Marie Cahill into *Sally In Our Alley* (August 1902). This song spawned a cycle of "jungle" songs (like "Abba Daba Honeymoon"), and people recognize it a century later. Jasen and Jones assert: "It is one of those rare pop songs that manages to be funny and sexy at the same time." [20] Edward Marks in *They All Sang*, his memoir of the pop music business, relates an anecdote of the song's composition. Marks credits the Johnson Brothers with eliminating the racist crudities of the coon song, quoting Rosamond Johnson: "We wanted to clean up the caricature." One night, walking uptown after performing at the Winter Garden, the three partners were discussing prospects when Rosamond began humming the spiritual "Nobody Knows the Trouble I See." Bob Cole cut him off with, "Wait a minute. That's the song we need for our act." Reacting with mock gravity, Rosamond pointed out that this was a "sacred song…not to be desecrated on the vaudeville stage." Then Cole took the tune, changed it a bit, and it became the chorus of "Under the Bamboo Tree." At first they called it "If You Lak-a-Me," and Stern and his partner Marks held the song back because it seemed nonsensical. But after a hearing, Marie Cahill demanded it for an interpolation, and, retitled, it emerged as a giant hit. [21]

By shifting the scene from the mean streets of coontown to the tropical paradise of jungletown, Cole and the Johnsons reset black culture in a kinder, positive light. Marie Cahill sang "Bamboo Tree" again next year in *Nancy Brown* (February 1903, the month of *In Dahomey's* New York opening) and performed another Cole and Johnson hit, "Congo Love Song," in the same show. She encored the song for 104 performances! In 1902, Stern also published their "Oh, Didn't He Ramble," the roughneck tune that would later become a favorite of jazz bands. By 1903 the trio led Broadway with songs in seven shows, sung by such stars as Eddie Foy, Marie Cahill, Lillian Russell, and *Black Patti's Troubadours*. At the end of 1903, they turned out a set of six songs for a production number in *Mother Goose*. This segment of the show was called "The Evolution of Ragtime," and it ran a gamut from a pseudo "African" song ("Voice of the Savage"), through plantation numbers, ending with a lively dance tune. The ragtime here was the popular syncopation of lively songs rather than the complex syncopation of the instrumental rags of Joplin and Scott, which was unknown to most people.

Bob Cole and Rosamond Johnson were also entertainers, and during this intense compositional period, they created and performed a successful twosome in the New York big-time. It was a "class act," no coonery or buffoonery, no tramp get-ups, or comic songs with punch lines. Instead they came on with elegance in evening clothes, Rosamond sitting at the grand piano; the act was made up of stylish, appealing renditions of their own songs. Occasionally Bob Cole leaned away from the piano to execute a soft-shoe dance as Rosamond rippled the keys. It all looked so casual and effortless, and it delighted the audience. [22] In 1904 Broadway's dominant impresarios, Klaw and Erlanger, rewarded the Cole-Johnson achievement with an offer to score an entire musical comedy. With 250 in the cast, the lavish spectacle of *Humpty-Dumpty* (an English import) opened in November 1904. No hits emerged, but their pleasant music enhanced a richly adorned, colorful show that ran for four months.

IV

Will Marion Cook and wife Abbie Mitchell Cook left the British tour of *In Dahomey* in August 1903, returning to New York to carry out a new project in musical comedy. He composed the score for *The Southerners*, a musical play labeled "a study in black and white." Opening in May 1904, its scene, a plantation in the 1830's, came right out of minstrelsy. It departed from that model in that it was framed by a story concerning the white owners. However it resembled minstrelsy because the story served as the setting for a sequence of variety acts. Songs like "Darktown Barbecue" and "It's Allus de Same in Dixie" presented the traditional matter of the Old South. [23] *The Southerners* stood out because it contained a black chorus in addition to a company of white characters and chorus. Thus Cook could claim the first integrated musical comedy to reach Broadway, the third of his history-making "firsts," the previous two being *Clorindy*, Broadway's first all-black show, and *In Dahomey*, the first such all-black, full length show. *The Southerners* posted a modest success, thirty-six performances, followed by a short tour.

Cook often visited the Johnson brothers at the Marshall Hotel (127-29 W 43rd Street), where, in their rooms, they worked with Bob Cole on songs. There the few African Americans working on Broadway often gathered for informal sessions on projects and problems. James Weldon Johnson tells us in *Along This Way* that "the main question…[was] always that of the manner and means of raising the status of the Negro…in the New York theatre and world of music." He further states that "the only really bitter clashes were those occurring between Cole and Cook." Cook had been briefly a member of Cole's "All-Star Stock Company" in 1894, from which he had departed in anger (as he did most other projects). Cook, the highly trained academic, condescended to Cole the showbiz "pro." Cook perceived himself as a creative artist and Cole as a lowbrow performer on the minstrel level. Although sparks flew whenever Cook walked in, the Johnsons—and Cole as well—perhaps empathizing with Cook's perpetually wounded pride, managed to tolerate him. [24]

Cook turned away from the Broadway stage in 1905 to direct and compose for the "Memphis Students," a large vaudeville group (about 25) of talented black performers assembled by Ernest Hogan. Cook's wife Abbie Mitchell Cook co-starred with Hogan. Vibrant in execution, the Memphis Students put Cook's songs over in an extended run at Hammerstein's Victoria Theatre. Buoyed by this success, Cook later toured the group—renamed "Tennessee Students" (because Cook believed Europeans less likely to know the name of a city than a state), in London, Paris, and Berlin. These multi-talented "students" (none were) sang, danced, and played instruments. Rather than the orchestral tradition of strings, they picked and strummed mandolins, guitars, and banjos, conveying a quality of folk art. The discordant note clashing with this lively presentation was a battle for control between Cook the director and Hogan the originator. When Cook determined to lead fifteen of the group on a European tour, Hogan resorted to legal process to prevent it. Apparently, Hogan yielded only when Cook paid him off. [25]

Cook rejoined the Williams and Walker company in 1906 as chief composer and music director of their next all-black Broadway extravaganza *Abyssinia*. As with *In Dahomey*, Cook composed the basic score: overture, incidental sequences, dance music, some of the songs and arranged the orchestrations. Bert Williams this time received equal billing as composer, all of the six published songs being his, and Alex Rogers (1879-1930), composer of Williams' hits in *In Dahomey* ("I'm a Jonah Man" and "I May Be Crazy But I Ain't No Fool,") contributed the lyrics. Jesse Shipp (1869-1934), the fifth regular on the W&W team, wrote the book. For Williams in *Abyssinia*, Rogers wrote "Let It Alone" and "Nobody," the latter an interpolated vaudeville hit, which became Bert's masterpiece (and the title of his biography by Ann Charters). Rogers had created "Nobody" in 1905, and it perfectly encapsulated the hard-luck stage character ("Who says, 'here's two bits, go and eat?' Nobody!") For the rest of his life, audiences refused to go home until he sang "Nobody."

George Walker, who had developed the show's concept, specified a very large company of about 125, and an elaborate African setting that would contain live animals, a waterfall, and a mountain. He also hoped to stage *Abyssinia* in a large and major theatre. Unfortunately the theatre "Syndicate," the cartel of ruling producers, dominated by Marc Klaw and Abraham Erlanger, did not sympathize with black aspirations. Instead they forced the show into a second-class theatre, the Majestic, poorly located up on Columbus Circle. This meant from the outset that *Abyssinia* could not be profitable: too few patrons in a smallish house. There the W&W team had to settle for a smaller scale: a company of one hundred, fewer animals, and less spectacular scenery; however one hundred was far from a small cast, lighting effects were excellent, and they managed to achieve the waterfall. The story told of Rastus Johnson (Williams) winning $15,000 in a lottery and going with his friend Jasmine Jenkins (Walker) on a visit to their ancestral Africa. Comic misadventures bring them to trial before a stern king, after which came the usual happy ending. But it was not a happy ending for the show; it closed after only thirty-one performances and took off on tour, probably to earn back its high costs of staging. [26] In Indianapolis the *Freeman* (10-22-06) praised the overall show, lauding scenery, singing (both soloists and choruses), comedy (the leads), and the ensemble. The comment that "The opening chorus…would have delighted Wagner himself…" seems fulsome, but the comments on Williams ("…does much of his better work by gestures, glances, sighs and incidental expressions…. He is a man of parts and intellect.") shrewdly observed his comic talents. [27]

Abyssinia led to *Bandanna Land* (February 1907), the third, and final, collaboration of the W&W team of Williams, Walker, Alex Rogers, Jesse Shipp, and Will Marion Cook. For this show Cook composed three of his best songs, including "Bon, Bon Buddy," (lyrics by Alex Rogers), which became George Walker's signature hit, "Rain Song," and "Exhortation, A Negro Sermon" (also with lyrics by Rogers). Bert Williams again interpolated "Nobody" (which audiences loved best), and he also pleased the crowd with his own hit "Late Hours." In another of his songs "Fas', Fas', World," Bert sang of too fast-paced a life (this was 1907!). But his show-stopper turned out to be a pantomime of a poker game, in which he played all four hands, vividly acting out each player's hopes, bluffs, triumphs, and failures. From then, on whatever stage, musical or vaudeville, audiences demanded the "Poker Game." The plot of *Bandanna Land*, set in the U.S.A. but not in Coontown, narrated a get-rich-quick scheme to sell farmland to a street railway company in which the Williams and Walker characters outsmart a would-be victimizer and reap the reward of the land sale. For the Act Two finale, the duo stopped the show with a revival of their vaudeville cakewalk act (Chapter 11). Two of the wives of the creative team, Aida Overton Walker and Abbie Mitchell Cook, played lead roles. The show, despite being consigned to the inferior Majestic Theatre, drew in sizeable crowds of white (as well as black) customers, and received positive reviews. The *Dramatic Mirror* praised its "wholesome merriment," "genuine humor," and "singing of great volume and sweetness." [28] This show ran a successful eleven weeks in New York before taking off on a long tour which lasted through April 1909. [29]

Bob Cole and the Johnsons, by mid-decade New York's top songwriting team, followed their modest success in *Humpty-Dumpty* with *In Newport* (December 1904), another show for white folk. When *In Newport* flopped, Cole and Rosamond recovered by reviving their suave vaudeville act for the West Coast, and then taking it for a long engagement to London, Paris, and The Netherlands. During this extended period, they reset themselves on a new (for them) trajectory, to create their own black musical comedy. Except for interpolations, they had always composed for white shows. In 1906, the team lost brother James Weldon Johnson to the U.S. Foreign Service, appointed by Theodore Roosevelt to be U.S. Consul in Venezuela as a reward for supporting Republican causes. This was seen as a great honor for African Americans, a matter of race pride, too important to refuse. By the time James Weldon had set off on his new course, the team had completed their first all-black show. Set in 1898, *The Shoo-Fly Regiment* relates the adventures and misadventures of a group of students and teachers at the "Lincolnville," Alabama industrial school (suggested by B.T. Washington's Tuskegee Institute?), who enlist in a regiment bound for the Philippines during the Spanish-American War. Over his fiancee's objections, a young teacher enlists, and in Act II leads the regiment to victory, followed by a triumphant return in Act III. Several of the songs became hits: "There's Always Something Wrong" (a "Jonah Man" tribute to Williams), the raggy "De Bo'd of Education," "On the Gay Luneta" (music by James Reese Europe, soon to be a major figure), "Floating Down the Nile," and "Lit'l Gal," composed earlier but held back. Copyrighted in 1902, Paul Lawrence Dunbar had written the dialect lyrics of this lullaby. After the songs, the most interesting element of *The Shoo-Fly Regiment* was its treatment of the love interest. For the first time in a black show, lovers were seriously portrayed, as human beings instead of darktown caricatures. The show's narrative of going-fighting-returning from war achieved a greater degree of integration that had previous black shows.

Bob Cole as janitor at Lincolnville stood out as "the principal purveyor of comedy," according to the New York *Age* (8-23-06), and the critic of the Indianapolis *Freeman* (3-23-07) states, "The audience could have stood more of Bob Cole." Rosamond in the supporting role of Ned Jackson the teacher received praise for both "a worthy piece of acting" and for being an "all-around musician." [30] Despite all of these excellences, the show floundered, from its pre-opening tour through its pitifully short two-week run on Broadway to its second road tour where it did somewhat better. The all-powerful syndicate subjected the show to long journeys with short bookings in lesser theatres. When Cole and Johnson—whose music had contributed greatly to the success of white shows—produced their own show, the syndicate refused to cut them a deal for better theatres. At one point Bob Cole commented:

> Yes we had a pretty rough time of it....we were left in darkest Texas, with an indebtedness of some $12,000, which included printing, railroad transportation, back salaries, etc., all of which we assumed....although we made no money for ourselves, we paid off all obligations....Our route has not been one of the best, but we have made good wherever we went. [31]

The momentum of this can-do attitude carried over into *The Red Moon* (1908), their greatest collaboration, which has been characterized as "American operetta at its best." [32] Like its predecessor, this show attempted to locate somewhere beyond jungletown. Its full title is *The Red Moon: An American Musical in Red and Black*. In it Cole and Johnson combined folk elements of both African-American and Native-American cultures. The story relates the adventures of Minnehaha, a young woman of mixed (Indian-Black) parentage, who is kidnapped from her Virginia home by her estranged father (Chief Lowdog) and taken west to Indian country. There she is desired by a young warrior, Red Feather. Meanwhile her home boyfriend, Plunk Green (Rosamond Johnson) and his sidekick Slim Brown (Bob Cole) go after them. After a series of (predictable) encounters and misadventures with potential hostiles, Red Feather is outwitted, the heroine rescued, and even the parents become reconciled. The delightful score more than made up for the book's lack of plausibility. The *Freeman's* critic singled out "On the Road to Monterey," "Big, Red Shawl," "Pathway to Love," and "I Ain't Had No Lovin' in a Long Time." [33] This last song, mildly naughty and not at all indirect in its point, expresses a young woman's impatience with a too proper boyfriend:

> Chorus:
> ...You must call me by some sweet and tender name,
> It takes a lot of fire to start my flame,
> I ain't had no lovin' in a long time
> An' lovin' is a thing I need. [34]

The music director for *Red Moon*, James Reese Europe (1880-1919), would in a few years become a leading figure in ragtime, composer-conductor for the amazingly popular dance team of Vernon and Irene Castles, organizer-leader of a union of black musicians (Clef Club), and leader of a regimental band in World War I that thrilled France and Britain with its syncopated music. He had already conducted for *Shoo-Fly Regiment* and contributed one of its songs (noted above). In *Red Moon*, he composed "I Ain't Had No Lovin'," "Sambo," and "Ada, My Sweet Potater" (composed jointly with Cole). Cole and Rosamond created the rest of the music, and almost every song was published. [35] The show played successfully to both black and mixed audiences. But despite good reviews and popularity, it endured the same unhappy conditions on pre- and post-New York tours (1908-09 and 1909-10): short runs, long distances, small and low-price theatres, which resulted in receipts insufficient to meet expenses. When the show reached Broadway in May 1909, the syndicate booked it into the same second-class, poorly located theatre, the Majestic, where the Williams and Walker shows had faltered. Reviews were good, but the run ended in three weeks, forcing the company back out on the road. When *The Red Moon* closed in the spring of 1910, Cole and Johnson simply gave up; they announced a return to vaudeville. [36]

Black musical comedies disappeared from Broadway after 1910 (not to return until 1921). Those who carried on the tradition—including Will Marion Cook, J. Leubrie Hill, J. Tim Brymn, and the Black Patti company—did so mainly for black audiences at Harlem's Lafayette Theatre. Broadway audiences had loved these shows, from the bright opening chorus to the grand production number of the finale. They couldn't get enough of superb comics like Ernest Hogan and Williams and Walker. They were delighted by the excellent songs of Cole, the Johnsons, Cook, Williams, Rogers, Europe, and others. The librettos were no better or worse than white shows; jungletown had as much appeal as "Old New York," Chinatown, or "Gay Paree." Only in black musical comedy did lively choruses sing while dancing, and the ragtime syncopation injected the musical stimulant that heightened reactions. It has been argued that whites became bored with the conventions of black shows, their African stories and vestiges of coonery and minstrelsy. The counter-argument, however, points out that these shows never reached their audience potential. Except for *In Dahomey*, their Broadway runs were brief. On the road, the syndicate booked them into low-priced theatres, usually smaller than first-class houses. With films grabbing greater audiences after 1910, small-city theatres tended to book fewer and fewer live shows. Statistically the number of small-city theatres declined, from 1549 in 1910 to 674 in 1925, resulting in fewer touring companies. [37]

Far more damaging and detrimental to African-American musical comedy was the ubiquitous and insidious prejudice against the race. This prejudice dogged black shows unrelentingly from the outset. Marc Klaw and Abraham Erlanger, New York's chief producers and controllers of the syndicate, usually booked black shows into marginal theatres, which kept people away and led either to failure or merely breaking even. Racial tensions were increasing during the period, and whites in the theatre never let down their hostility. In the end these circumstances forced black theatre into Harlem and into black-only theatres around the country (many of which were built during this decade). Since these black houses offered mostly vaudeville, such became the only viable career for most black show people. Not until Eubie Blake and Noble Sissle wowed theatre-goers in 1921 with *Shuffle Along*, did all-black shows return to Broadway.

Another cause for this unhappy effect was the phenomenon of *The Merry Widow*. *The Merry Widow*, an operetta by Franz Lehar, opened in Vienna in 1905. Subsequently, wherever it appeared, it delighted all audiences, becoming the most loved and performed show of the decade. After capturing Europe, it opened in New York at the New Amsterdam Theatre on October 21, 1907. It transformed the collective view of the musical stage, completely changing audience expectations. Gerald Bordman, the historian of the Broadway musical stage, states that: "The older, more stolid comic opera and the new, struggling native musical comedy were stifled." And it "…radically changed the whole direction of the musical theatre…for years to come." [38] A lengthy series of Austrian and German operettas migrated to Broadway during the next seven years. Ironically, the expected next smash hit failed to materialize; there never would be a second *Merry Widow*. But it set a dramatic standard, presenting onstage characters of some interest caught up in a story that audiences cared about. After such an experience, audiences became less tolerant of shows in which situations or locations served mainly as loose structures to admit interpolated songs and vaudeville routines.

A final point in this analysis of black musical comedy's decline is its loss of leadership. Ernest Hogan, George Walker, and Bob Cole provided most of the motivation, organizational skills, financial capability, and much of the movement's creative force and inspiration. All three died during 1909 to 1911. Hogan, whose comedy rivaled Bert Williams, had gone from his Memphis Students vaudeville act into *Rufus Rastus* in 1906 where he had given his finest performance in a musical comedy, which had a successful run in a non-Broadway theatre, followed by an equally successful tour. *Rufus Rastus* spawned a sequel in *The Oyster Man* which opened in 1908. Sadly, his success on the musical stage ended abruptly after the opening when Hogan fell seriously ill. He died of tuberculosis in May 1909. Walker and Cole both succumbed to syphilis. Walker began to fail in *Bandanna Land*, suffering memory loss, slurred speech, and seizures; he left the touring company in February 1909. He died in a sanitarium on Long Island in January 1911. Bert Williams soldiered on alone in one more show. With the collaboration of Rosamond Johnson, Bert wrote the score for *Mr. Lode of Koal*, which opened in September 1909. Although the critics praised Bert's comedy, they were negative otherwise. *Mr. Lode of Koal* ended its run in March 1910 after a six-month tour. Two months later Bert Williams abandoned black showbusiness for a career in the annual *Follies* of Florenz Ziegfeld. [39] Bob Cole fell apart at the end of the final run of *The Red Moon* at Keith's Fifth Avenue Theatre in October 1910. Diagnosed with paresis of the third stage of the disease, he spent months in hospitals and clinics seeking relief. Finally in August 1911, he drowned in a lake in the Catskills at a vacation spot, a probable suicide. They simply had no equal successors. [40]

RAGTIME ALMANAC

Black Musical Comedies In Broadway Theatres, 1898-1910

Broadway Opening	Title	Company	Theatre
1898	*Clorindy*	Will Marion Cook	Casino Roof
1899	*A Trip to Coontown*	Bob Cole/B. Johnson	Casino Roof
1903	*In Dahomey*	Cook & Williams/Walker	New York
1906	*Abyssinia*	Cook & Williams/Walker	Majestic
1907	*The Shoo-Fly Regiment*	Cole & Johnson Bros.	Grand Opera House Bijou
1908	*Bandanna Land*	Cook & Williams/Walker	Majestic
1909	*The Red Moon*	Cole & J.R. Johnson	Majestic
1909	*Mr. Lode of Koal*	Williams & J.R. Johnson	Majestic

Notes: Chapter 26

1. James Weldon Johnson, *Along This Way*, 328.
2. David A. Jasen and Gene Jones, *Spreadin' Rhythm Around*, 26.
3. *Ibid.*, 95.
4. For a detailed account, Henry T. Sampson, *The Ghost Walks: A Chronological History of Blacks in Showbusiness, 1865-1910*, 70-71, 78-79.
5. No African Americans sang at the Metropolitan until 1955 when Marian Anderson debuted late in her career.
6. Rayford W. Logan, "Jones, [Mathilda] Sissieretta [Joyner] [called Black Patti]," in *Dictionary of American Negro Biography*, 367-368.
7. Sampson, 149, 151.
8. Jasen and Jones, *Spreadin' Rhythm*, 98-99; Thomas L. Riis, *Just Before Jazz: Black Musical Theatre in New York, 1890-1915*, 75-79. Riis quotes a source (pp. 75-76) telling that Cole had been blacklisted for quitting Black Patti to create his own show. *Coontown* was in effect, an outlawed show, kept out of syndicate-controlled theatres.and forced to survive in third-rate houses. Finally, success in Canada caused the show's acceptance in better U.S. theatres and its eventual New York runs.
9. Jasen and Jones, *Spreadin' Rhythm*, 81-82; *Dictionary of American Negro Biography*, 127.
10. Jasen and Jones, *Spreadin' Rhythm*, 87. See Gerald Bordman, *American Musical Theatre, A Chronicle*, 190-191, for the show's history.
11. Sampson, 290.
12. *Ibid.*, 288.
13. Edward Berlin, *King of Ragtime: Scott Joplin and His Era*, 226, 228.
14. Sampson, 353-354; see also comments, 140-141.
15. Ann Charters, *Nobody: The Story of Bert Williams*, 54-55.
16. Sampson, 221-222; Charters, 54-55.
17. *Idem.* Tom Fletcher, *One Hundred Years of the Negro in Show Business*, 242.
18. Quoted in Douglas Gilbert, *American Vaudeville: Its Life and Times*, 284.
19. Sampson, 233.
20. Jasen and Jones, *Spreadin' Rhythm*, 105.
21. Edward B. Marks, *They All Sang: From Tony Pastor to Rudy Vallee*, 96-98.
22. Riis, 35; Jasen and Jones, *Spreadin' Rhythm*, 106-107.
23. *Ibid.*, 105-107.
24. *Ibid*, 81; J. W. Johnson, *Along*, 172-173.
25. Jasen and Jones, *Spreadin' Rhythm*, 88-89.
26. *Ibid.*, 53-58, 89; Riis, 113-117; Bordman, 218-219.
27. Sampson, 376-377.
28. Riis, 121.
29. Jasen and Jones, *Spreadin' Rhythm*, 58-60, 89; Riis, 117-122; Bordman, 239-240.
30. Sampson, 368, 393.
31. *Ibid.*, 406-407. For the show's troubles: Jasen and Jones, *Spreadin' Rhythm*, 110-112; Riis, 129-133.
32. Jasen and Jones, *Spreadin' Rhythm*, 113.
33. Sampson, 442-443; Riis, 135-141.
34. Quoted in *Ibid.*, 138.
35. Reid Badger, *A Life in Ragtime: A Biography of James Reese Europe*, 38-40.

36. asen and Jones, *Spreadin' Rhythm*, 112-114; Riis, 141.
37. *Ibid.*, 161.
38. Bordman, 236.
39. Riis, 122-124.
40. Jasen and Jones, *Spreadin' Rhythm*, 39-41, 59-60, 64, 114-115; Riis, 161.

27. "The Brownsville Affray"

...With rare exception, noted anthropologists located Negroes somewhere on the frontier between the great apes and hominids. Biologists found their average brain weight less than Caucasians—considerably less than English-speaking Protestants. Psychologists identified a primal sexuality and irrationality in Negroes that were invariably supposed to erupt in situations of intimacy or stress. Physicians predicted their extinction from disease and depravity, while criminologists and eugenicists warned of the menace of Negro brutality and fecundity. The national white consensus emerging at the turn of the century was that Afro-Americans were inferior human beings....

David Levering Lewis [1]

When Professor Booker T. Washington, Principal of an industrial school for colored people in Tuskegee, Ala., stood on the platform of the Auditorium, with the sun shining over the heads of his auditors into his eyes, and with his whole face lit up with the fire of prophecy, Clark Howell, the successor of Henry Grady, said to me, "That man's speech is the beginning of a moral revolution in America"

New York World (1895) [2]

Theodore Roosevelt came into office with an agenda to weaken the Democratic Party's vise-grip hold on the South. As the son of Georgia-bred Martha Bulloch—and the admirer of his Bulloch relatives who had served with distinction in the Confederate Navy—Theodore fancied himself half-southern. He privately hoped somehow to parlay this positive attitude into some political strategy to win a degree of southern support for his administration, and ultimately perhaps, to bring a significant number of southern whites into the Republican Party. Restoring the two-party system to the South might have been a major addition to the legacy he dreamed of achieving. [3]

Unfortunately, good intentions, good will, and good hope weren't enough to get past the South's rabid obsession with race. Every time Theodore confronted the race issue, it bit him. The first instance came out of a meeting with Booker T. Washington. Washington (1856?-1915) by 1901 had achieved recognition (by whites) as principal leader and spokesman of African Americans. Born into slavery on a Virginia tobacco plantation, he later fled the poverty of a West Virginia coal mine to enter Virginia's Hampton Institute; there he became the star pupil and protegee of Hampton's founder, General Samuel Armstrong. Armstrong's answer to the problem of improving the miserable conditions of ex-slaves was to teach them a vocation. At the Hampton Institute, Washington was indoctrinated with a practical gospel of skill in a trade, diligence, and personal cleanliness. After graduation, followed by a few years' teaching experience, Washington was tapped to answer a call from Tuskegee, Alabama, to create a sister institution. Starting in 1881 with a meagre state appropriation of $2000, thirty students, himself as sole faculty, and a leaky shanty for a classroom, Washington built the Tuskegee Industrial and Normal Institute into a formidable, much respected institution.

The Tuskegee Institute grew phenomenally; Washington combined a great amount of perseverance with strong capabilities in organizing and fundraising. Within three months, he was buying land and planning the first of many buildings. The enterprise rapidly gained more faculty, students, and physical plant. What made it all unique and exciting was that the students did the work. Everything became part of the dynamic curriculum: masonry, carpentry, farming, stock raising, food preparation, dining hall operations, building maintenance, accounting, management. From the outset Washington reached out to the town; carefully he stroked Tuskegee, inviting people to school events, asking for advice (and contributions), always striving for good relations to develop good will and even local pride in the school. Then he moved out in ever-wider circles, making valuable connections and extracting contributions. Eventually he was able to divert large contributions from northern philanthropists away from operations and into an endowment fund. By 1900 the Tuskegee campus contained forty buildings and a resident student body of 1100.

Students, nearly all disadvantaged by poverty, began with life's basics, how to eat properly (seated at a table with crockery, flatware, and napery) and they were immediately instructed in what Washington called the "gospel of the toothbrush." From such basics, it was on to literacy, simple mathematics, and the skills of a trade, learned on campus projects. With these activities came indoctrination. Former slaves came in motivated by the belief that education would lift them out of the working classes, or, as one put it: "to be educated, and not to work." [4] During his initial tour of the locale, Washington had come across "…a young man, who had attended some high school, sitting down in a one-room cabin, with grease on his clothing, filth all around him, and weeds in the yard and garden, engaged in studying a French grammar."[5] Washington concluded that "a few hours of mere book education, I felt would be almost a waste of time." [6] Thus along with the skills of work, Washington inculcated an ethic of work, and the idea of work as the true path to salvation. He put it this way: "The individual who can do something that the world wants done, will, in the end, make his way regardless of his race." [7]

Essentially this was the big idea that drove Booker and shaped his Tuskegee Institute: Whoever possessed the skills and knowledge sought by society would (one day) achieve equality and acceptance. To meet a real need could ultimately transcend race. On September 18, 1895, having been selected as one of the speakers (an unusual honor for a black man) at the opening ceremonies of the Atlanta Cotton States and International Exposition, Washington presented his big idea to the South in the form of a compact. He had a deal for the white folks. He made his points using two figures of speech. First came "Cast down your bucket where you are," an anecdote of sailors off the mouth of the Amazon River who were perishing of thirst. Signaling a passing ship of their dire need of water, that ship signaled back to cast down their bucket because the Amazon's powerful current pushed fresh water out to sea for hundreds of miles. The point was that his people could succeed only by developing their own talents and by mobilizing their own resources at home. His deal was a trade-off: social equality for economic opportunity. Believing that material-economic success would eventuate in social equality, he offered to suspend demands for social equality until his people reached material equality: "In all things that are purely social we can be as separate as the fingers, yet one as the hand in all things essential to mutual progress." [8] There it was! A promise to be docile, to respectfully lower the eyes before the white man boss. And for emphasis, Washington concluded: "The wisest among my race understand that the agitation of questions of social equality is the extremest folly…." [9]

Like Bryan and his "Cross of Gold" speech a year later in Chicago, this was one of those electric moments, the apogee of a career. The Governor of Georgia "rushed across the platform and took me by the hand." People became excited, overwhelming him with congratulations; newspapers rhapsodized editorially; President Cleveland thanked him by letter; lecture bureaus sought to capitalize on the sensation by offering large fees ($200/night). [10] This program of deferential gradualism has been labeled "Accommodation," and its proponent called the Great Accommodator. It went down triumphantly with the old-southern Redeemers and Bourbons, traditional rulers of the South—and with the philanthropists and liberals of the North. By 1900 Booker T. Washington occupied the niche of Mr. Negro; he distributed most of the northern grant money and he controlled the Republican patronage. In the "solid" white Democratic South, most Republicans were black; they elected nobody to anything, but they sent delegates to national nominating conventions that could determine the outcome of a close contest. Thereby, pursuant to the political axiom of *quid pro quo*, favored members of the race received entitlement to a series of assistantships, collectorships, and minor postmasterships. Washington directed the traffic in these appointments.

Two groups opposed BTW's Accommodation. The poor whites (or rednecks) had heard local demagogs rant against "nigger education" as a threat to their security. If any economic opportunity materialized, they intended to grab it for themselves. The political reality was that the rising members of this poor white class, such as James K. Vardaman of Mississippi, "Pitchfork" Ben Tillman of South Carolina, and Tom Watson of Georgia, were taking power away from the declining old-line Bourbon class. These rejected any kind of a deal with an "uppity" black man which would give any advantage to his race. The other negative group consisted of the better-educated African Americans, who refused to bargain away political or civil rights belonging to them as citizens of a democracy. These were college men, many out of such new African-American liberal arts colleges in the South as Fisk, Howard, and Atlanta, and others who had gone to Harvard, Yale, Princeton, or Oberlin in the North. They had entered business and the professions and perceived no role for themselves in BTW's program of racial uplift. They increasingly resented Washington's dominance and control over matters from which they felt excluded. After 1900, their opposition would grow and unify until, eventually, their leadership superseded his after 1910.

Washington's autobiography *Up From Slavery* appeared in February 1901. Although it honestly stated Booker's philosophy of accommodation, it was a highly selective account, cunningly crafted—actually ghostwritten. [11] *Up From Slavery* sold well and propagandized successfully, telling how hard work bolstered by religious faith overcame all obstacles. Prominent people, author William Dean Howells, industrialist George Eastman (Kodak), and Harvard Professor Barrett Wendell, praised it highly. [12] Thus when newly elevated Theodore Roosevelt sought candidates to fill Federal jobs in the South, he naturally summoned Booker T. Washington to the White House for a meeting. On the race question, TR had aligned himself with the northern liberal acceptance of accommodation, viewed in the light of southern attitudes, as probably the only feasible approach to the race problem. Following a preliminary meeting on October 1st, the President invited Washington to dinner on the 16th for a concluding discussion of patronage matters. Booker discreetly came and went, dining with the Roosevelts and conferring after dinner. Later a reporter found BTW's name on the published list of White House guests and inserted it in his paper as a routine item. [13]

When the item reached southern editors, the South exploded in fury at what all saw as a gross violation of the racial code. Bad enough if the two men had taken a bite of lunch together—the horror was that Mrs. Roosevelt had sat at the same table, serving a Negro! This nearly constituted miscegenation: a columnist speculated that one of the President's sons might be on the verge of marrying BTW's daughter Portia, then a student at Wellesley. [14]

The acrimony generated reached a poisonous concentration. From all over the South came anonymous letters threatening the Roosevelt family with violence. The southern press was beside itself:

> Booker Washington holds the boards—
>   The President dines a nigger.

> Precedents are cast aside—
>   Put aside with vigor;
> Black and white sit side by side
>   As Roosevelt dines a nigger.
>
> <div align="right">Raleigh, NC, <i>Post</i></div>
>
> …the most damnable outrage ever perpetrated by any citizen of the U.S. when he invited a nigger to dine with him at the White House.
>
> <div align="right">Memphis, TN, <i>Scimitar</i></div>
>
> White men of the South, how do you like it?
> White women of the South, how do YOU like it?
>
> <div align="right">New Orleans, LA, <i>Times-Democrat</i> [15]</div>

Governor Candler of Georgia proclaimed that : "No self-respecting white man can ally himself with the President after what has occurred." Senator "Pitchfork Ben" Tillman of South Carolina opined that : "a thousand niggers would have to be killed to relearn the lesson of 'place.'" Yet another editor stated that; "Rooseveltism means nigger supremacy as surely as Grantism did." [16] Nor did the South permit the incident to die. During the following years, ranting orators blamed this incident for causing race riots, lynchings, and black discontents. In 1904 an Episcopal clergyman declared that TR "could never atone to the southern people for the act of eating with a Negro." That negrophobe Vardaman of Mississippi blared in 1903 that the White House had become "so saturated with the odor of the nigger that the rats have taken refuge in the stable." In a Washington, D.C., high school in 1905, a student, asked to use the word "debase" in a sentence, wrote on the blackboard: "Roosevelt debased himself by eating with a nigger." The episode even reached showbusiness in 1904 when Democrats paid minstrel impresario Lew Dockstadter to film a skit about the incident on the steps of the Capitol, presumably for use in the presidential campaign (Was this the first political "commercial"?). Hearing of it, TR set the Secret Service and police on Dockstadter, who was searched in several cities. He denied political intent, but the film was summarily confiscated and destroyed. [17]

II

Theodore Roosevelt hunkered down and let the angry, rhetorical fusillades pass overhead. An astute politician, he did not indulge in apologetics or rebuttals that might prolong the episode. He told friends that he had done nothing wrong, but privately he was upset and somewhat baffled by southern intransigence. He believed that the South, having instituted slavery in the first place, then gone to war against the Union to preserve it in the second place, followed by the inhumane treatment of blacks since the war, had caused its own troubles. [18] Proof of how much this thing had galled him shows in the outcome: never again did he break bread with Washington or any other person of color (although he did invite them to White House receptions).

Much has been written about Theodore Roosevelt's attitudes and actions re the race problem. As an intellectual he accepted the "scientific" views of Negro inferiority (epigraph). He had encountered Native Americans during his ranching days and had accepted the prevailing white man's view that they were an inferior race of nomads whose historical destiny was to yield the land to a higher culture, and whose only salvation was to become assimilated. He rejected the "noble savage" sentiment because he perceived Indians as prone to cruelty and drunkenness. He denied the validity of their claims to the land, because, being nomads, they had never <u>settled</u> it. However, on later western visits, he found a new interest in such cultures as the Hopi and the Navajo, and he saw them in a better light as peoples evolving toward civilization. Because of this, he backed off on extreme assimilationism and came to favor the preservation of tribal cultures on reservations. But he never modified his view that Native Americans were, deterministically, the necessary victims of white racial destiny. [19]

Certain ideas about race were strongly held during TR's lifetime. As a child, Theodore's southern mother filled him with many stories and facts of antebellum black life, nearly all showing black inferiority. Until after Harvard, he knew African Americans only as servants. At Harvard, in literature, history, philosophy, and science courses, he learned that English and German cultures were superior; he also absorbed the Social Darwinian notion that Europe's domination of the globe proved Europeans to be fitter than others. Further, as the beneficiaries of Europe who had become refined even more by their conquest of a great continent, Americans, of Anglo-Saxon-Teutonic stock, were indeed the world's superior race. Nor did anyone at the time present any serious opposition to these ideas. Such was the intellectual "dirty secret" of that time (pre- and post-1900), a cheap and facile application of the evolutionary idea, lifted from the context of biological science, to bolster nativist prejudices. Out of such thought was public policy derived. Generally U.S. laws and customs tended to deny from full participation in American life, not only African and Native Americans, but also "orientals," Latin Americans, and immigrants from southern and eastern Europe. [20]

Inheriting such an intellectual and cultural perspective, Theodore Roosevelt believed in the WASP (White-Anglo-Saxon-Protestant) superiority of old-stock Americans, and he viewed increases in minority populations as challenges—ultimately threats—to the rightful domination and leadership of his ethnic class. Perhaps worse, he extrapolated from the declining birthrate of old-stock Americans and north Europeans the threat of <u>race suicide</u>. He fretted that his race, declining in numbers, would fail in its tasks of assimilating other races and passing on the superior traits that had created a high civilization. He actually brooded over the prospect of race suicide, at times wallowing in a pessimism that tended to pull down his normal high spirits and ebullience. Driven by his faith in the nation's destiny of world leadership, his fears for the survival of his race disturbed his grand vision of the coming greatness of America. [21]

At other moments, the evolutionary idea projected a bright ray down through the clouds of TR's pessimism. With improved environments, blacks and other minorities would reach a higher cultural level. Given that some African Americans like Booker T. Washington were much superior to many whites, the entire race could be improved. [22] Yet they numbered ten million and reproduced so rapidly, making assimilation rather doubtful, at best a distant outcome. Two things made TR relatively moderate on race: 1) he stood out against violence, and 2) he believed in equal opportunity, that capable black people should not be denied opportunity. Following the logic of these exceptions, he did not accept the conclusion that an entire race was inferior. Here he had reached a plane of understanding attained by few Americans at the time (North or South): he realized that black people <u>were</u> human, and he supported their rights to the franchise and to hold political office.

Unfortunately his presidency coincided with eight of the most violent years of U.S. racial history. The South never relaxed its demands for the exclusion of blacks from office and for acquiescence in the ongoing terror and oppression. Because of TR's relative moderation, both sides kept up their pressures, and controversies thus happened, including the Booker T. Washington White House dinner and the three considered below. [23] Politically, socially, and culturally, the race situation produced a monumental—and incurable—headache. He felt unable to wholly support either side. Believing that most African Americans weren't ready for equality, he still felt that their small, albeit weak, constituency required a few, appointments to lesser Federal offices. However, up to 1904 (election year), he appointed fewer than had his predecessors, and after 1904, fewer yet. And even a proclaimer of righteousness found himself caught in the grip of political realities. TR understood that it would be fully justified under the Constitution (14th Amendment) to deny representation in Congress to southern states in proportion to the amount of the disfranchised population. But it would be a futile effort without positive majorities of voters and congressmen. [24]

Lynching furnished the one aspect of the race problem where Theodore felt he could take a stand. Once in Little Rock, Arkansas, the Governor, as he introduced the President, added that, "We have an unwritten law in the Southland that when a vile black wretch commits an unmentionable crime, we hang him without judge or jury." Rising, Theodore replied to the Governor: "Before I make my address to the people, I want to say to you that when any man or set of men take the law into their own hands and inflict summary punishment on the 'vile black wretch' of whom you speak they place themselves on the same base level as that same 'vile black wretch.'"[25] In a letter of 1903, he denounced the rule of mobs, stating that torture brutalized people, and that it was a small step to progress from torturing for large offenses to torturing for small offenses. He also noted that three-fourths of lynchings didn't involve rape, the crime usually claimed as a justification. [26]

The President again supported the citizen rights of African Americans in the imbroglio over the postmastership in Indianola, Mississippi. Mrs. Minnie Cox, black and college-educated, had served as Postmistress in Indianola (population 1000 and market center in the Yazoo Delta area) for over a decade (since 1889), having been appointed by Harrison and continued under Cleveland, McKinley, and Roosevelt. In 1902, the demagogic James Vardaman, running for Governor, attacked the veteran Mrs. Cox as unfit; he called her a "menace to white civilization" and demanded her resignation. He attacked her simply because he lacked an issue to defeat his opposition, and because local poor whites resented the Coxes' prosperity. Mrs. Cox had done an outstanding job of operating a Third Class Post Office with 3000 patrons. She had installed a telephone (advanced technology then) at her own expense for patrons to inquire about mail, and she often covered the box rents of poor people temporarily unable to pay. Her college-educated husband worked in the railway mail service, and they owned property and bank stock.

This exemplary performance brought race-baiting James Vardaman to Indianola to rant about the threat of "nigger domination" and the evils of "nigger education." He also went after the President for "social equality policies." This stirring of the pot produced a petition for Mrs. Cox's resignation and frightened a black doctor into leaving town. Under such pressure, Mrs. Cox agreed to give up her place by not seeking reappointment in 1905. Whites angrily refused, threatened her life, and the Mayor and Sheriff refused protection. On December 4, 1902, she resigned, and Vardaman congratulated the town for throwing out the "negro wench." An editorial in his Greenwood, Mississippi, *Commonwealth* (11-28-02) proclaimed that the town had endured the affront of "receiving mail from the hands of a coon" for too long. [27]

Theodore did not hear of this until December 30, at which point, after conferring with the Cabinet, the Postmaster General, and the local Postal Inspector, he ordered the Indianola Post Office closed (1-2-03). Although he could have kept it open with troops, his judgment call rejected such an inflammatory measure. He refused Mrs. Cox's resignation and kept her on the payroll. Townsfolk continued intransigent (expecting influential Senators to get it reopened), and their destructive anger caused the Sheriff to put 20 Deputies on patrol. Fearful, Mrs. Cox fled on January 5th. The Senate did debate the situation, and southern senators denounced TR. The southern press erupted and preached race hatred, spreading such myths as that white women and children entering the Post Office had to step over "crapshooting darkies." Vardaman in his newspaper called the president a "human coyote" and a "political boll weevil pregnant with evil"; in another editorial he stated that "old lady Roosevelt" had been frightened by a dog during pregnancy (Greenwood *Commonwealth*, 1-31-03) For Vardaman the result was victory in the state election of 1903. The President did not reopen the Indianola Post Office until 1904, reducing it from Third to Fourth Class. [28]

Next came a controversy in South Carolina over the appointment of black Dr. William Crum to the Collectorship of the Port of Charleston. The selection of Crum, a highly respected physician, set off a conflict that dragged on for six years. [29] The excessive animosity caused by the appointment is traceable to Crum's having run as the Republican candidate for the Senate against Ben Tillman in 1894. So strong and virulent were the attacks on Crum that the Senate refused confirmation in February 1903. When TR's friend and fellow western writer Owen Wister (*The Virginian*) defended the attitudes of Charleston, Theodore ripped into him:

> I know of no people in the North so slavishly conventional, so slavishly afraid of expressing any opinion hostile or different from that held by their neighbors as is true of the Southerners, and most especially of the Charleston aristocrats on all vital questions.

While he was on the subject, he unloaded his anger about sexual exploitation of black women by white men: "They shriek in public about miscegenation, but they leer as they talk to me privately of the colored mistresses and colored children of the white men they know." [30]

Furious at Crum's rejection and angry at Tillman and South Carolina's "Lily Whites," he resubmitted the nomination, which put Crum into office but without pay until the next session of Congress. This was war against Tillman, a personal struggle; as each session went by without senatorial action on the matter, he granted another recess appointment. Not until January 1905 (following TR's election triumph in 1904), did the Senate cave in and confirm Crum. As Collector, Crum justified the presidential stubbornness by doing a superlative job. He improved the Port's facilities, increased the efficiency of its operations, and receipts more than doubled during his tenure. Improvements included a longer pier, a deeper channel, and a motor launch for boarding vessels. Crum pried money out of Washington for renovations, and inspectors wrote up his facilities for their immaculate appearance. Yet despite such visible and other excellences, local politicians attacked Dr. Crum in 1908, and neither TR nor Taft his successor felt equal to Tillman's threat to filibuster the reappointment. Booker T. Washington was chosen as the emissary to seek Crum's resignation, which was graciously given, Crum saying publicly that he wished to retire when TR did. Two years later (1910), Taft rewarded Crum with the Liberian embassy, where, unhappily, Crum caught the fever that killed him two years later. [31]

These conflicts rewarded Theodore Roosevelt with black convention delegates and black votes in 1904. With Crum's eventual confirmation in 1905, he handed Tillman a significant defeat. Whenever he sensed a useful occasion, he denounced lynching, or he affirmed the rights of black people. In 1908 he threatened legal action against a southern railroad for not providing black passengers with terminal facilities. In his Annual Message of 1906, he spoke up for better public education for African Americans:

> It is out of the question for our people as a whole permanently to rise by treading down any of their own number. The free public school, the chance for each boy or girl to get a good elementary education, lies at the foundation of our whole political situation....It is as true for the Negro as for the white man. [32]

Alas, the fight against the cruelties and injustices of the race system brought no positive results or solutions. Race was like Joel Chandler Harris's "Tar Baby" in *Uncle Remus*: it stuck to you and left you dirty, the only gain being the meagre rewards of the moral variety (payable in heaven). Was it worthwhile to go "all out" in the fight for the rights of a backward people unable to exercise those rights? He preached that, "The only safe principle upon which all Americans can act is that of 'all men up,' not that of 'some men down,'" but preachments had no effect upon unhappy realities. In the end, he was the man of his time, and however much he may have tossed and turned about it in the night, he couldn't get over the barriers of his own prejudices and blind spots to plot a comprehensive policy toward a resolution of the problem. [33]

III

> ...The colored man who fails to condemn crime in another colored man, who fails to cooperate in all lawful ways in bringing colored criminals to justice, is the worst enemy of his own people....Law abiding black men should, for the sake of their race, be foremost in relentless and unceasing warfare against lawbreaking black men.
>
> Theodore Roosevelt [34]

It all came apart—TR's moral house of cards on the race issue—in Brownsville, Texas, in 1906. Some bonehead (or malevolent soul) in the War Department issued orders for Companies B, C, and D of the First Battalion of the 25th Infantry Regiment (Colored) to depart their duty station at Fort Niobrara in the northern Sandhills of Nebraska to take up garrison duty at Fort Brown on the Mexican border near the mouth of the Rio Grande. With Major Charles W. Penrose commanding and four other white officers, the three companies (Company A was in Wyoming) arrived by train on July 28th. Brownsville, population 6000, had very few black residents, and ethnic Mexicans made up two-thirds of the population. Except for a few owners of large ranch and orchard properties and the better-off merchants, Brownsville consisted of poor people. Only recently had the railroad come in to end its isolation. When townsfolk heard that 170 black soldiers were to arrive shortly, they reacted with anger and agitation. The Mayor spoke for everyone: "These people will not stand for colored troops; they do not like them. These Mexican people do not want them here."[35] There was talk of killing, also of getting up a posse to prevent their coming off the train. These threats did not materialize, but a silent, glum crowd observed the soldiers on that Saturday as they stepped down onto local soil, formed up in their units, and marched off to the Fort. [36]

Anti-climactically, the soldiers disappeared into their fort to occupy themselves with garrison tasks that went on from Reveille to Taps. But after a few days inside, off-duty time came along, and the troops poured out to find the nearest recreation. Brownsville had decided that the unwelcome soldiers would be restricted to the few Jim Crow bars; they were to be denied sex and socializing. As the black troops in two's and three's filtered into town, they encountered stares and refusals of service in the stores. Everyone kept good discipline and maintained calm in this negative atmosphere, even when people in the street hissed that they were "black S.O.B.'s." When one of them was pistol whipped on the street a few days later, no one fought back. They patronized the six

Mexican beer-mescal bars—where they felt unwelcome—and the Jim Crow bar at the rear of John Tillman's Ruby Saloon. After a couple of weeks, on Friday, August 10th, two enterprising Privates (one was the group's money-lender) opened a bar for the soldiers across from the Fort. Saturday, August 11, was payday, and the men drank there instead of in the Brownsville joints. All passed very orderly, without fights or drunken incidents. The mayor publically commented, obviously in some surprise, on the quiet state of things on a payday. [37]

On Monday, August 13, a rumor raced through town that one of the soldiers had seized a Mrs. Lon Evans by the hair and thrown her to the ground. Mrs. Evans was apparently a person of dubious respectability who lived with her husband in a tenderloin-area boarding house, and no one claimed she was raped. But the *Daily Herald* instantly headlined the alleged incident as an "Infamous Outrage," in which a Negro soldier invaded a rooming house in an attempt "to seize a White Lady." Her husband gave Major Penrose a third version, that a soldier had grabbed his wife as she rode home from the railroad station on a pony. As she landed on the ground, she screamed and the uniformed miscreant ran away. Strangely, the tellers of these tales indicated that the event had occurred on Sunday, the day before, twenty-four hours having elapsed before this "outrage" became a public matter. Also curious was that Mrs. Evans indicated that she could not indentify her assailant. To Major Penrose, this all came across as dubious; however, realizing the plight of his men, he chose discretion; he cancelled all passes and ordered everyone to remain on post. All were accounted for by 8:00 PM. The mail orderly returned to report a crowd around the Post Office talking up the incident. On his rounds, the Officer of the Day (OD) Captain Macklin found all in a state of calm and order.

In for the night, the troops in their barracks had little awareness of the turmoil rising outside their closed gates. Later, a Corporal told Captain Macklin that the incident may have consisted of a soldier walking past a woman leaning over a fence at a time when some other passerby patted her on the head. Just before midnight, the sound of gunshots woke Major Penrose and roused him from his bed. Dressing hurriedly and apprehending that his fort was being fired upon, he ordered the bugler to blow the Call to Arms. The three companies lined up, rifles at the ready, and each man answered the roll call. Over a ten-minute period, many more shots fired in the town were heard on the dark parade ground. The troops (all small-arms experts) recognized the shots as coming from revolvers and Winchester rifles (they were standing with government-issue!903 Springfield rifles). A soldier on guard at the wall heard voices yelling, "Come out, all you black nigger sons of bitches and we will kill everyone of you." [38]

In Brownsville people tumbled out of their homes with guns, running into others similarly armed. As the confusion grew less, an instant consensus developed that some soldiers from the fort had "shot up the town," killing the bartender at Ruby's and wounding a Mexican policeman (the casualties). Many now spoke up to claim they had seen black troops firing down the streets at random, though the streets were poorly lit and the night moonless. The Mayor talked the hotheads down from attacking the fort, and then he went there and accused the men to their commanding officer. The Major refuted this with the claim that all had been on post in quarters. At a dawn inspection of the men's Springfields, the Major peered down every barrel. Rags were run through a random few of them for telltale specks of burned powder. None had been fired. Later some spent shells and clips from Springfields were found just outside the fort, but the previous garrison had sold or given them to children. As the sun came up on Tuesday, August 14th, fort and town had reached an impasse. [39]

As armed men patrolled the streets of Brownsville, Texas, in a lynching mood, an *ad hoc* Citizens Committee telegraphed its accusations of the soldiers' attack on their community to the President, begging for a replacement garrison to relieve their perilous situation (August 15th). To this singular communication, the President and the

War Department reacted without any skepticism or suspicion of bias. In the absence of Secretary Taft (on vacation), the President ordered the Army's Inspector General to investigate, and Major August P. Blocksom was sent immediately, arriving on August 18th and departing August 29th. Almost without question, Major Blocksom accepted the town's version and telegraphed his conclusion as to the soldiers' guilt to Washington. On August 25, the three companies entrained for Fort Reno, Oklahoma, where they were placed in barracks at hard labor, pending further investigation. Having concluded the men's guilt, Major Blocksom admitted that the Citizens Committee—whose cursory and biased investigation he had adopted as his own—had failed to produce any evidence to indict. The next month, a Cameron County Grand Jury, <u>after three weeks of testimony</u>, failed to indict. In his August 29 report, Major Blocksom recommended a mass punishment and discharge. He gratuitously concluded by saying that the "colored soldier is much more aggressive in his attitude on the social equality question than he used to be." [40]

Further evidence of TR's concurrence with Blocksom's IG report is shown by the course taken by the Inspector General himself. General Ernest A. Garlington now went south and demanded confessions. He threatened a mass discharge "without honor," if the particular culprits did not step forward. Garlington, a South Carolinian who prided himself on his expertise in all things Negro, first interviewed twelve of the Battalion being held at Fort Sam Houston (San Antonio, Texas), who had been accused and arrested, quite arbitrarily, in Brownsville, and kept apart from the others. No additional evidence or testimony had been presented against these twelve. There and subsequently at Fort Reno, the men consistently denied the crime. Finally came the showdown; with the men formed up in their lines on the Fort Reno Parade Ground, General Garlington uttered his final, official threat, demanding the guilty step forward, as the men faced forward in silence. He submitted his report on October 4th; he did not include the mens' sworn, written statements of innocence. Garlington recommended, as per the official threat, that all three companies be discharged "without honor," and gave his personal view that this would teach the Army a good lesson. [41]

On November 5th, the President signed the order of dismissal and directed Secretary Taft to carry it out. From this point, the "affray" (as some newspapers termed it) or incident at Brownsville, slowly at first, grew legs and became a major issue in national politics. Intermittently it ran on for more than three years, causing turmoil, partisan battles, and ruined careers; it shocked the outlook of African Americans into a realization that they had no friends in high places. Political considerations intervened at the outset with the presidential decision to withhold the order for a day. With off-year elections for Congress the next day (November 6), the news was held back until that afternoon, presumably to avoid alienating black Republican voters. [42] Booker T. Washington, working intensely behind the scenes, begged the President not to carry out the sentence. With no indictments or court-martials, the justice was blatantly summary; it brought cries of outrage from the black press. The New York *Age* declared that, "…[the Negro people's] alienation from the President, once their idol, has been spontaneous, bitter, and universal." [43] The Reverend Adam Clayton Powell, Sr., from the Harlem pulpit of the Abyssinian Baptist Church, thundered that the President, "Once enshrined in our hearts as Moses [was] now enshrouded in our scorn as Judas." [44]

The conflict unfolded, TR claiming that race had played no role in the case. At the same time, he unwittingly dragged race into it by implication when he insisted that, "The respectable colored people must learn not to harbor their criminals, but to assist the officers in bringing them to justice." From November 8 to 27, with the President off on his triumphant junket to the Panama Canal, Taft, left in charge, tested the atmosphere and found it very conflicted. He had released documents of the case, which led to comments of surprise in the press that evidence of guilt was lacking, and that Garlington had performed only thirty interviews. Somewhat troubled, he cabled the President to reconsider and, at least temporarily, withhold the order (Taft thought several states might be lost in the 1908 election). Pending an answer, he held up the execution of the "sentence." TR responded testily to carry it out unless new evidence had arisen. On November 12, ringed by white soldiers, the men of Companies B, C, and D, First Battalion, 25th Infantry Regiment (Colored) had to endure the ceremony of being disgraced by having their arms taken away on the Parade Ground at Fort Reno. These troops had fought and served with honor in the Indian Wars, Cuba (1898), and the Philippines (1899-1901). Six of them had received the Medal of Honor. Their discharges "Without Honor" were ordained by an administrative order instead of by a due process, because without evidence, the men could not be tried in a court. A "Dishonorable" discharge required judicial proof. As they handed over their weapons, the men's only reaction was tears. [45]

IV

It is carrying into the Federal Government the demand of the Southern white devils that innocent and law abiding black men shall help the legal authorities spy out and deliver practically, to the mob black men alleged to have committed some sort of crime. The spirit invoked is not only vicious and contrary to the spirit of our Constitution, but it is an outrage upon the rights of citizens who are entitled in civil life to trial by jury and in military life to court martial.

T. Thomas Fortune
in the New York *Age* [46]

When the Fifty-ninth Congress convened its Second Session on December 3, 1906, Senator Joseph Benson Foraker (R-Ohio) offered a resolution calling for an investigation of the Brownsville incident. Foraker was probably going after the Republican nomination in 1908 (over the opposition of TR who intended to choose his successor) and was seeking a wedge issue to split off some of TR's adherents. In Foraker's lawyerly analysis, Brownsville reeked of injustice, cruel and unusual punishment unsupported by either due process or true verdict. He found in it the U.S. equivalent of France's Dreyfus Case. Foraker had recently clashed with the President on the regulation of business and was primed for another go. [47]

Privately the President felt resentful and threatened; there could be political damage. He sent to the Senate a self-justifying message on December 19 in which he insisted that the particular discharges ("Without Honor") were administrative actions rather than punishments based upon verdicts, merely dismissals. Perhaps this sounded like sophistry even to him, because he turned to his best legal advisors, Secretary of War Taft, a leading constitutional lawyer (eventually Chief Justice of the Supreme Court) and Secretary of State Elihu Root, a corporate lawyer second to none. On their advice, he launched another investigation, sending a professional investigator, Milton D. Purdy, members of the Secret Service, and (again) Major Blocksom to Texas to search for some hard evidence needed to bolster what all now perceived as a very weak case. Theodore was furious and determined to bring down his opposition. He started to plot against Foraker in Ohio, asking Booker T. Washington for a list of Cincinnati Negroes to appoint to Federal jobs on the Senator's home turf to gain support against him. Next the War Department announced the court-martials of Major Penrose and Captain Macklin, presumably for not having prevented the soldiers' dastardly deeds against Brownsville. No explanation was offered as to why the other three officers went unaccused. Thus the Government could now claim fairness in laying some of the blame on whites. [48]

On January 14, 1907, the Senate received the "Purdy/Blocksom" report, accompanied by 63 affidavits from Brownsvillians, all affirming the soldier's guilt, plus artifacts which included a bandoleer, 33 shell cases, 4 clips, and 7 ball cartridges, all claimed to have been picked up right after the shooting. The report proclaimed these materials to be conclusive evidence. The next day, Senator John C. Spooner spoke for the President, asserting that the discharges were legal, being simply disciplinary actions for the good of the service. Further, the perpetrators not having confessed made the mass discharge the only correct choice. Acrimonious debate followed, with southern Senators strongly in support of the president's actions. [49] On February 4, Major Penrose went on trial, accused of neglect of duties and failure to prevent the (alleged) attack on the town. The problem of visibility on that night came up in all testimony: a moonless night, streets poorly lit. Penrose's witnesses contradicted Brownsville witnesses' claims to have actually seen the soldiers firing at the town. This testimony of unusual feats of night vision prompted an experiment on a clear, moonless night at Fort McIntosh, Texas (the court-martial venue). Under simulated conditions, it proved impossible to distinguish black from white troops or to distinguish military uniforms, thus discrediting the witnesses' claims. Penrose was able to demonstrate that his dawn firearms inspection proved that none had been fired. Penrose was found not guilty and exonerated (though the court still assumed the soldiers to be guilty). Captain Macklin, the duty officer, had actually slept through the incident. He too was acquitted. [50]

Senate hearings also commenced on February 4 and dragged out over a thirteen-month period (2-4-07 to 6-14-07 and 11-18-07 to 3-10-08). All of the witnesses repeated their previous testimonies, the most substantive being the ballistics evidence that led to certain conclusions: 1) The Springfield rifles (those of the accused) had not been fired on the night of August 13-14; and 2) All of the empty Springfield shells found had been picked up by children at the fort. This seemingly vital evidence did not influence the majority conclusions in which four Republicans loyal to TR joined five (southern) Democrats in affirming guilt. Four other Republicans, the Minority, concluded the opposite, that there was no proof to sustain the charge (and that the men should be reinstated). This being an election year, unity came first for Republicans. Senator Foraker's concluding speech on April 14 gave a lawyer's precise summation, proving, point by point, that eighteen months of relentless probing had not convicted a single soldier. He built a very strong case that the shooters had been townsfolk. Finally he asserted that there was no legal precedent that required the soldiers to prove their innocence; the government had to furnish the proof. Therefore the soldiers had been treated "worse than common criminals." His probing eloquence accomplished nothing. [51]

A journalist probing Booker T. Washington's reaction to Brownsville said to him, "If [TR] stands pat, his name will be an anathema to Negroes from now on." [52] Washington found himself embattled, finding no alternative to loyalty to the Republicans and the President. There being no other port in this terrible storm, he counseled patience—and angered nearly everyone. The rest of black America reacted with outrage, shocked at the incredible injustice inflicted on them by the one white leader believed to have been the friend of the race. If TR was their enemy, who could they call a friend? Many reports and letters describing the African-American revulsion landed on BTW's desk, begging for explanations and insight into a situation they could not understand. They wanted some answers from the white man's black man, who had assured everyone of his direct line and entrée to the offices of powerful whites. His failure and inability to secure positive results drove black people to fill the Senate gallery in support of Senator Foraker. Probably Brownsville can be judged the "nadir," or lowest point in the African-American struggle for the rights that belonged to all citizens. It seemed that something worse had happened, beyond segregation, Jim Crow cars, abuse, and terror: the Government had betrayed the sworn wearers of its uniform, a sacrilege to many. From this time, black people looked for new leaders. [53]

For a generation, Washington had ministered to a despised, poor, and ignorant people with his programs and policies to improve their conditions and motivate them to self-help. Working through three presidents, he secured government jobs and influence; he extracted hundreds of thousands of dollars from northern philanthropists and foundations; he continually fought prejudice and discrimination from behind the scenes; he taught his people cleanliness, morality, and a work ethic; he encouraged them to start businesses (by founding the National Negro Business League); he developed and propagated vocational education, even influencing white educators. But by 1906, people were losing faith in Accommodation. When would inferiority wither away in favor of equality? Black graduates of liberal arts colleges sought the opportunities open to other educated people. By 1900, a small segment of college graduates and professionals had coalesced as a minority within a minority, labeled the "talented tenth" by the man who would become their most articulate leader, W.E.B. DuBois.

William Edward Burghardt DuBois (1868-1963) haled from Great Barrington, Massachusetts, of mixed African-American, French, Netherlands, and Native-American ancestry ("Thank God, no Anglo-Saxon," he once said.). His intellectual brilliance took him from Fisk University (Nashville, TN) to three Harvard degrees and post-graduate study at the University of Berlin. He became the first of his race to receive a Ph.D. from Harvard in 1895. He began as a historian but produced the first sociological studies of black life ever undertaken. Initially he and Washington tested one another in dialogs and negotiations, but by 1903, he had rejected Accommodation because inferiority required him to deny his own superiority. Academically DuBois was a "star," a leader among intellectuals, denied university professorships because of race. Accommodation offered no program for the talented tenth to break down this barrier. In 1903 DuBois published *The Souls of Black Folk*, a beautifully written, at times poetic, series of essays that evoked the conditions and aspirations of his race. Here DuBois conceded the practical good accomplished by the BTW program of vocational training and the accommodation of whites, including the logic of a temporary acceptance of legal discrimination. But he concluded that, with the increase of abuses and terror, conciliation did not stop a lynch mob. With the talented tenth to lead, the race would raise its cultural level; this might take time: "…the biases and prejudices of years [would not] disappear at the blast of a trumpet." But he felt certain that "the way for a people to gain their reasonable rights is not by voluntarily throwing them away and insisting they do not want them." 54

In 1905 twenty-nine of the talented tenth met at Niagara Falls, Canada (after hotels on the American side had refused them), to form a more militant organization. Without attacking Booker T. Washington, they drew up a declaration of their goals: free speech, an end to discrimination based on race and color, and acceptance as equals. They intended to protest until their goals were reached. Under DuBois's leadership, they came together during subsequent summers at locations identified with freedom: Harpers Ferry, West Virginia (1906), Faneuil Hall, Boston (1907), and Oberlin, Ohio (1908). By 1908, not much had been achieved by this "Niagara Movement." Its membership of college-bred intellectuals failed to reach a mass following, because Washington effectively opposed its thirty local branches, and because internal factional disagreements tore it apart. In addition, as the gatekeeper to northern philanthropic funds, Washington denied the Niagara Movement the financial capability necessary to propagate itself.

As the Niagara Movement faded, certain northern philanthropists and progressive reformers had also grown dissatisfied with Accommodation and the leadership of the man who had come to be called the "Wizard" of Tuskegee. They had become increasingly aware of the brilliant professor at black Atlanta University who had written *The Souls of Black Folk*. Dubois always came across as precise, straight-forward, eloquent, and substantive in what he advocated. He contrasted with the Wizard who fronted with preachments of humility, restraint, and idealism, while he maintained behind the scenes the autocratic control of funds and the political influence derived from corporate and Republican connections. Accommodation had made no inroads against segregation, lynching, or race riots. In Atlanta, where BTW had triumphed at the 1895 Exposition, on the evening of September 22, 1906, ten thousand whites attacked every black person on the streets, the atrocities not ending until a dispersal by a combination of militia and heavy rainfall at dawn on the 23rd. Previously the newspapers had carried several stories of alleged attacks by blacks upon white women. Later DuBois declared in an essay that this eruption had followed "two years of vituperation and traduction of the Negro race by the most prominent candidates for governorship, together with a bad police system."[55]

Washington decided not to speak out against the Atlanta Race Riot, saying instead that both black rapists and white rioters were to blame. Then another race riot tore apart Springfield, Illinois, in 1908. Although African Americans numbered only 10% of Springfield's population, many were new arrivals and the poorer whites resented the competion for jobs. Allegedly (again) a black man had raped a white woman. The Sheriff had sent the accused to safety out of town, but the mob, frustrated of its prey, injured 80 people, shot six fatally, and lynched two. They caused $200,000 in property damage, and 2000 African Americans fled the city. The mob in the home city of the Great Emancipator had yelled, "Curse the day that Lincoln freed the niggers!"[56]

This occurrence of a major race riot in the North proved the deciding stimulous for a group of northern progressive reformers to organize the National Association for the Advancement of Colored People (NAACP). During 1909-1910, Oswald Garrison Villard, grandson of the leader of antebellum Abolition William Lloyd Garrison, brought together an influential segment of white liberals and creative black leaders. The stated intentions of the NAACP were "to make 11,000,000 Americans physically free from peonage, mentally free from ignorance, politically free from disfranchisement, and socially free from insult."[57] Whites dominated and led the organization during its early years, but DuBois was selected to be Director of Publicity and Research. He created and edited its monthly publication *The Crisis*, which he launched in 1910. The NAACP soon developed a system of state and local branches, and by 1914 *The Crisis* had a circulation of 31,450.[58] The NAACP fought racial persecution, with publications and in the courts, vigorously, organized from its national office down through state federations to grass-roots chapters enrolling the rank-and-file. Within a few years, most African Americans had turned away from the Uncle Tomism of Accommodation with its acceptance of inferiority. To most whites, Booker T. Washington spoke for his people, and they sent their donations to Tuskegee. But the Wizard was carried off by a sudden heart attack in 1915, and the NAACP at once filled the vacuum.

V

>Theodore Roosevelt does not like black folk. I don't think he ever really knew a colored man intimately as a friend. What after all have we to thank Roosevelt for? [Three things:] for asking a man to dine with him, for supporting another man, quite worthy of the position, as Collector of the Port of Charleston, and for saying publicly, that the door of opportunity ought to be held open to colored men? The door once declared open, Mr. Roosevelt by his word and deed since has slammed most emphatically in the black man's face.
>
> W.E.B. DuBois [59]

Joseph Benson Foraker became a "marked man." During the Senate hearings, he and his family found themselves to be under surveillance. His Senate colleagues were pressured not to support any of his measures.

He never again received a White House invitation. He was offered a high government post if he would call off his investigation of Brownsville. TR publicly attacked him, saying that he was anti-reform (some truth here), and claiming the Brownsville agitation to be a corporate plot against the administration (probably no truth). Then came a Hearst attack on Foraker (not solicited by the Hearst-hating Republicans), the publication of certain letters revealing that Foraker had been receiving payments from Standard Oil for years, at least $50,000. This revelation pounded the ultimate nail into Foraker's political coffin, ruining his 1908 candidacy for the Republican nomination and causing the Ohio Legislature to replace him in the Senate. [60]

The Roosevelt-Foraker vendetta reached the flash point at a Gridiron Club Dinner on January 26, 1907. Annually the press held a banquet to which were invited the nation's leaders for a carnival evening of spoof and satire (a tradition that continues to the present). At these events the humor tends to be rather pointed and intended to draw some reaction from its subject, the results of such gambits becoming the evening's principal entertainment. After taking his seat at head table, Theodore Roosevelt sat turning the pages of the program until he came to a cartoon of Senator Foraker wooing the black vote. Accompanying the cartoon was a parody verse of Ernest Hogan's song:

> All coons look alike to me,
> J. B. Foraker, says he, says he,
> Even if they is black as kin be,
> An' is dressed in blue or yaller khaki.
> All coons look alike to me,
> Since 'mancipation set 'em free,
> Nigger vote hold de balance,
> All coons look alike to me. [61]

Dinner was coming out of the kitchen, but the President rose abruptly and asked to speak at once. The waiters were turned around and sent back. Furiously TR threw the program on the table and asserted angrily, "All coons do <u>not</u> look alike to me!" He took off, going after Foraker for his opposition to the reform of railroad rates (Hepburn Act) and for the Senate investigation of Brownsville. He argued that the legislative branch lacked the constitutional authority to review or reverse actions of the executive branch. Foraker, attending as a spectator, was not on the roster of speakers, but custom dictated a right of rebuttal. He opened saying, "When legal and human rights are involved, all <u>persons</u> look alike to me." [62] He stoutly defended himself, giving blow for blow in defense of the black troops. He ended with an assertion of his independence and integrity. Loud applause broke out—the President's had been sparse and dutiful—and many stepped up to congratulate him. Then, to the company's amazement, TR took the rostrum a second time to argue again that the Brownsville soldiers "were bloody butchers" and "ought to be hung." Ten minutes later, he strode out of the hall, leaving on the field a victorious Foraker and a spoiled evening. It was a costly moral victory. [63]

Before departing the Senate in 1909, Foraker succeeded in getting an Army Court of Inquiry to investigate the incident one last time, which would grant the accused some due process in the form of a trial. Unfortunately the Administration appointed the judging officers and packed it with prejudiced types. In Brownsville the court heard the same testimony given in previous investigations, all of it hostile to the accused. Only 82 of the ex-soldiers were called up to testify; 70 others who asked to testify were refused. On April 6, 1910, the five retired generals who made up the court gave a unanimous verdict that the men of the First Battalion had indeed shot up the town. Then, for no apparent reason, three of the generals ruled that 14 of the men might reenlist. No explanation for this capricious gesture has ever been found. [64]

Theodore Roosevelt never mentioned Brownsville or his other clashes on race in his *Autobiography*. These episodes engendered no sense of accomplishment or pride; he was unable to demonstrate a problem which he had worked to solve. One thing here begs to be noticed: From that first hysterical telegram, he never doubted that black soldiers had turned their guns on a town that had shown them hostility. He <u>knew</u> that they must have done it. The more judicious Taft, a lawyer and judge, might have asked for some proof more substantive, but Theodore, who had once read legal texts in his Uncle's office and then rejected law as a career, attacked things out in the open, not inclined to allow evidence (or the lack therof) to inhibit his strong convictions, once he had made up his mind. Public opinion tended to agree with his (summary) judgment; white soldiers, amenable to discipline, would never shoot up a town, but emotionally immature blacks, with guns in their hands, were very capable of such a thing. Only a few "bleeding hearts" (among white folk) heard the soldiers' vain protestations of innocence. Call it a blind spot or call it race hatred, it was endemic. Very few possessed the insightful combination of compassion and imagination to recognize and admit such a malevolence, a malevolence that blamed an entire garrison, perceiving all as guilty.

[Untitled]

Yes, sir, I am a victim of that Brownsville episode,
Where Herod was outdistanced by a civil unjust code.
And this is the bit of paper that says I was not true
Against my unsullied army life, the years I wore the blue.

Why, sir, I fought the redskins in the Garden of the Gods,
When we gambled with eternity and death had heavy odds.
I climbed old San Juan Hill when the "Riders" cheeks were pale,
When the world was shown that color could face leaden bail.

I campaigned in the Islands where nature vied with man
To murder U.S. soldiers with alapathic plan;
See here my service striped with a record without flaw,
My life was an edition of the regulation law.

But what of that and what of this and all that I had done,
They ordered me one night to stand on guard Post No. One,
In a Texas town of my own land, in the nation of the free,
With men created equal by the code of liberty.

And on that night, it was supposed, a few revengeful blacks
From among the guards off duty, with guns outside the racks,
Stole out the barracks unbeknown, save those within the plot,
And made the streets of Brownsville somehow, extremely hot.

I fired my gun and roused the camp, not knowing what it meant,
And stayed there at my station, until relief was sent.
I did my faithful duty until the row was past,
I did not know a thing about the firing, first to last.

And because I did that duty, fearless of friend or foe,
And would not swear out falsely to things I could not know,
I was kicked out of the army "without honor" in disgrace,
A by word of derision to the service and my race.

Yes, sir, I am a victim of that Brownsville episode,
Where Herod was outdistanced by a civil unjust code,
But the honor of a soldier can not be brushed away
By some Sivaltic order within this age and day.

Sherman D. Richardson [65]

Notes: Chapter 27

1. David Levering Lewis, *W.E.B. DuBois: Biography of a Race, 1868-1919*, 276.
2. James Creelman, *New York World* (9-18-1895), quoted in Booker T. Washington, *Up From Slavery: An Autobiography*, 154-155.
3. Mark Sullivan, *Our Times*, IV, 128-130.
4. Washington, 94.
5. *Ibid.*, 81.
6. *Ibid.* 78.
7. *Ibid.*, 102.
8. *Ibid.*, 145.
9. *Ibid.* 146.
10. *Ibid.*, 146-149.
11. Lewis, 262. The ghostwriter was a Vermont journalist, Max Bennett Thrasher.
12. *Ibid.*, 263.
13. Willard B. Gatewood, Jr., *Theodore Roosevelt and the Art of Controversy: Episodes of the White House Years*, 35-36.
14. Sullivan, OT, III, 130-135.
15. *Idem.*
16. *Ibid.*, 136-138. Also J.C. Furnas, *The Americans*, 854.
17. Gatewood, 36-37, 47.
18. *Ibid.*, 38-39. Also Noel F. Busch, *The Story of Theodore Roosevelt and His Influence on Our Times*, 180.
19. Thomas G. Dyer, *Theodore Roosevelt and the Idea of Race*, 69-88.
20. *Ibid.*, 1-31.
21. *Ibid.*, 148-149, 168-169.
22. Nathan Miller, *Theodore Roosevelt: A Life*, 363.
23. Dyer, 89-102; N. Miller, 362-363.
24. *Ibid.*, 106-109; Page Smith, *America Enters the World: A People's History of the Progressive Era and World War I*, 161; Lewis, 324.
25. Corinne Robinson, *My Brother Theodore Roosevelt*, 297.
26. P. Smith, 160-161.
27. Gatewood, 63-74; Dyer, 102-103.
28. Gatewood, 75-88.
29. In 1892, Harrison had appointed Crum postmaster of Charleston, but had withdrawn the appointment because of opposition. See *Ibid.*, 90-126.
30. Dyer, 107. Wister's account of this after Theodore's death skipped over the anger and displayed a plaintive TR saying, "…why you must see that I can't close the door of hope on a whole race!" Owen Wister, *My Forty-Years Friendship with Theodore Roosevelt*, 114-119.
31. Gatewood, 90-126, 129-133.
32. Quoted in William Henry Harbaugh, *Power and Responsibility: The Life and Times of Theodore Roosevelt*, 293.
33. Author's views: If any problem cost TR some sleep, it was perhaps this one. See also Dyer, 109-114.
34. Theodore Roosevelt, 1905 Lincoln Day Talk to the Republican Club of New York City; in *Theodore Roosevelt: An American Mind, Selected Writings*, 333.
35. Quoted in John D. Weaver, *The Brownsville Raid*, 21.
36. Weaver, 18-23; Ann J. Lane, *The Brownsville Affair: National Crisis and Black Reaction*, 5, 8-10.

37. Weaver, 23-28; Lane 15.
38. Weaver, 29-37.
39. *Ibid.*, 44-63.
40. Lane, 20-21; Weaver, 64-92.
41. Lane, 21—23; Weaver, 93-95.
42. One candidate who needed black votes was Rep. Nicholas Longworth, Roosevelt's son-in-law. *Ibid.,* 97.
43. *Ibid.*, 98.
44. Lewis, 332-333.
45. Weaver, 103-109.
46. Quoted in P. Smith, 166.
47. Harbaugh, 292; Weaver, 110-114.
48. *Ibid.*, 115-122.
49. *Ibid.*, 125-137.
50. *Ibid.*, 145-156,160-164, 166-169.
51. *Ibid.*, 169-189.; Lane, 34-38.
52. P. Smith, 166.
53. Lane, 70-93; Lewis, 332; Harbaugh, 294.
54. Quoted in Robert M. Crunden, *A Brief History of American Culture*, 175-176; see also Benjamin Quarles, *The Negro in the Making of America*, 166-173; Lewis, Chapters 8-12, for a fuller account.
55. *Ibid.*, 334.
56. *Ibid.*, 388.
57. Quoted in Quarles, 175.
58. *Ibid.*, 174-175.
59. Lewis, 339.
60. Weaver, 207-213; N. Miller, 467-468.
61. Quoted in Weaver, 139.
62. *Ibid.* 140.
63. *Ibid.*, 138-143; N. Miller, 467-468.
64. Weaver, 227-248.
65. Quoted in Lane, 53-54.

28. Progressives (IV): SRP

> ...this is but the beginning of an expansion that will continue until a time beyond which we...are not concerned. But for those who have lived and struggled for a quarter of a century...[in] a paradise lacking only water;...those who have toiled, and prayed and cursed, have bought water and stolen water that others had bought...this glad news is the fulfillment of a prophecy, a reward for past industry and faithfulness in overcoming what seemed to be insurmountable obstacles.
>
> *Arizona Republican* (9-4-'08) [1]

Arizona Territory started out in 1863 as an obscure and dangerous region, a lethal obstacle to cross-country travelers encountering its hostile deserts and Indians. The first white settlers hardly improved it. During the 1860's and 1870's, prospectors found enough gold and silver to attract a class of undesirables: gamblers, gunmen, drifters, addicts, and remittance men. [2] Towns rose with the mines and died as these played out. Peering westward, the nation perceived Arizona as unstable and disreputable. Indian wars kept breaking out until Geronimo's final surrender in 1886, and the feuds of white men produced lurid episodes like the 1881 "Gunfight at the OK Corral" in Tombstone and the Pleasant Valley ranchers' war of 1887-1892. Arizona lumped along as a territory for 49 years, from 1863 to 1912.

The miners and soldiers who first inhabited the Arizona frontier discovered economics to be a problem greater than Indians or terrain or climate. Everything that was needed to function and survive, including food, had to be freighted in. Whether from New Mexico or the port of Yuma on the Colorado River, goods had to travel in great "Murphy" wagons, each driven by a teamster and pulled by a six-mule team. Sixteen feet long, four feet wide and six high, rear wheels seven feet in diameter, these mammoth vehicles hauled up to 12,500 pounds. They supplied the forts and mining towns until 1880, when the railroads finally appeared. Such high living costs stimulated demands for local production of food and forage. [3] Ranching grew rapidly during the 1870's out on the various grasslands that flourished to the south around water sources in the Sonoran Desert (with 7 to 12 inches of rainfall), also up north on the Colorado Plateau. By 1882, 21,000 acres (with or near water) had been claimed by ranchers, who turned their animals loose on the open range. Because the coming of the railroads opened U.S. markets to the surplus, cattle numbered 652,500 in an 1885 head count. By 1890 there were over 1,000,000 cattle and perhaps 650,000 sheep on Arizona's ranges, a fatal overstocking that brought on an ecological disaster when drouth struck in the 1890's.[4]

Grass yes (with less cattle and more rain), but crops required irrigation, which restricted large-scale farming to fields along major rivers that flowed year-round. Arizona possesses only one such interior river system, the Gila and its main tributary, the Salt. The prehistoric Hohokam people had farmed the lower valleys of these rivers before 1400 and left behind the somewhat eroded ditches that carried water from the river to their nearby fields. The alluvial valley of the Salt River extends about 50 miles from where it is joined by the Verde River to several miles beyond its meeting with the Gila to the west. American settlement began there in 1865 when, following the Civil War, the U.S. Army began to respond to the white man's Indian problems. Five companies of troops established Camp McDowell where Sycamore Creek met the Verde just north of the Salt. In this isolated spot, 473 men and their horses subsisted on expensively freighted food and feed, eased only by the cutting of wild hay.

Hundreds of hungry soldiers on the rich alluvial plain of a flowing river signaled opportunity to frontier misfit Jack Swilling. Fleeing the drudgery of the mines in nearby Wickenburg, he persuaded a crew to venture along the Salt. Swilling, an ex-Confederate who had deserted, was "a morphine addict and a violent drunk" who would eventually die in 1878 in the Territorial Prison in Yuma while serving time for a stage robbery he may not have committed. In 1867 he and his group of twelve Wickenburg miners dug out an ancient Hohokam canal on the north bank of the Salt River in what is now central Phoenix. The first farmers took up land along the "Swilling Ditch" in 1868, and by 1871 this canal (later renamed the "Salt River Valley Canal") carried 200 feet of water per second to irrigate 4000 acres. [5] Another of those "colorful" characters of the "Old West," Darrell Duppa, English adventurer and alcoholic, the classically educated (University of Paris) son of a diplomat, named the new community "Phoenix" after the mythical bird that was reborn every 500 years out of the ashes of its fiery nest. [6]

Growth followed with about ten different canals on both banks, eventually irrigating over 125,000 acres of corn, wheat, alfalfa, and fruit trees. From a population of less than 300 in 1870, the Phoenix area grew, to 11,000 in 1890 and 21,000 by 1900. The city was laid out and incorporated in 1875. It became connected to the outside world in 1887 when a branch of the Southern Pacific chugged in on July 4th. Its economic dominance became manifest in 1889 when the dynamic little city snatched the territorial capital from Prescott and Tucson, which had wrangled for decades over the distinction. [7] In less than a quarter century, the Salt River Valley had become a great riverine oasis, not only the breadbasket of the territory but a national food supplier as well.

Unhappily, as went livestock, so also went irrigated farming: growth outstripped water resources in the 1890's. In wet years, disastrous floods came roaring down the Salt to wreck the dams, gates, and canals of the irrigation works. In dry years no one got enough water. Angry farmers downstream attacked those upstream for taking needed water. Lawsuits over water filled the courts. Judges and legislators attempted to settle conflicts by ruling on water rights. Earlier settlers pressed claims of seniority ("Doctrine of Prior Appropriation"). Owners of stock in canal companies turned water into a currency; a share of stock, called a "water certificate," was acceptable as collateral by bankers and other moneylenders, based upon water's current scarcity or abundance. Those possessing only land fought this speculation with the legal claim that water belonged to the land. These problems accrued into an insoluble muddle. By 1890 claims to water exceeded 6,600,000 acre-feet, about 5.5 times the average annual flow of the river. [8] On February 21, 1890, the Salt River suddenly rose 17 feet, taking out the railroad bridge and telegraph line connecting Phoenix with Tempe and other upstream locations in the east valley. Exactly a year later (February 18), a greater flood washed away large portions of the squat adobe towns along the Salt, plus again the railroad bridge. Next came an intermittent drouth lasting until 1905. This and the national depression of 1893-1897 brought the Salt River Valley to its knees. From 1896 until 1905, acreage under cultivation declined 24 percent, and the canal companies went through insolvencies and bankruptcies. [9]

From 1895, farmers, representatives of canals, and community leaders inaugurated a series of meetings and press dialogs to seek solutions to their water problems. With a growing season of at least ten months, endless days of sun, generally calm weather, and fertile soil, the Salt River Valley lacked only water. By the mid-1880's, settlers were talking up the idea of a dam to capture the floods of wet years to store for dry years, as well as to prevent flood damages, particularly to the diversion dams, headgates, and ditches. A survey authorized by Maricopa County in 1889 found an ideal site 400 yards below the confluence of Tonto Creek with the Salt River, about 60 miles upstream from the east valley town of Mesa. At this point the river narrowed to 200 feet between canyon walls that rose 800 feet high, with the river bottom close to bedrock. Behind the dam would stretch a two-horned lake, sixteen miles up the Salt and ten miles up Tonto Creek. Even better, the cliffs contained sandstone for blocks of masonry, with deposits of limestone nearby, the chief ingredient of cement. The slopes of the Sierra Ancha Mountains just north could furnish the needed timber. [10]

The committees authorized by mass meetings either came to nothing or broke apart in conflict. What they could not get past or over was finance. Borrowers in the 19C went to banks for loans, whether for currency or to borrow by "floating" an issue of stocks or bonds. Eastern bankers and brokers had no faith in, and felt no concern for, Arizona's prospects and rejected all solicitations to invest. As for the national government, it had never previously lent money for purely local projects. Washington had aided interstate railroads with generous land grants, based upon the theory that rails, necessary for national development, required the income from land sales and the resulting development along the rail lines. Arizonans next turned to a scheme to finance the project with bonds issued by Maricopa County. This measure came to nothing because Congress, which legally had to authorize a territorial bond issue, refused even to consider it. However a rebirth of Arizona's hopes resulted from the efforts of two influential visionaries; these advocated that the Federal Government intervene, directly and with federal aid. Frederick Newell, Chief Hydrographer for the U.S. Geological Survey (USGS), and George Maxwell, President of the National Irrigation Congress, had made the arid lands problem their life's work, and both, having concluded that private capital was insufficient, pushed for a national reclamation act to finance and carry out water projects. After years of campaigning and lobbying, they finally managed to get such a bill before Congress in 1901, only to see it voted down, but the sudden accession of Theodore Roosevelt, friend of the west and of the conservation of resources, gave reclamation the boost it needed; Congress duly passed the Reclamation Act on June 17, 1902. [11]

In his first message to Congress on December 3, 1901, TR enlisted in the cause of "making the desert bloom":

> Great storage works are necessary to equalize the flow of streams and to save the floodwaters. Their construction has been conclusively shown to be an undertaking too vast for private effort. Nor can it be accomplished by by the individual states acting alone....It is properly a national function.... [12]

TR viewed this as no different than other federal water projects, such as levees or canal locks. But politically and philosophically, national reclamation went further. A levee to hold back the Mississippi or an interoceanic canal in Panama was a national, an interstate project, which benefited (in theory) the entire nation. Such projects also benefited big business, large combinations owned by many shareholders, spread nationally. Plus, what was good for business was felt to be in the national interest because the resulting jobs and income made the nation more secure. On the other hand, a project within a state or territory chiefly of benefit to local people was viewed as an improper commitment of federal resources. If approved, where would it end? (Why, every town and village across the land might demand funding from the national treasury for some civic improvements!) National reclamation was new thinking that conflicted with the classical 19C concept of *laissez-faire*, the economic doctrine that governments should not intervene in economic life because disaster might result from tampering with the natural laws that regulated economic activity. So some theorists claimed, but only when this archaic idea served their purposes did late 19C and early 20C entrepreneurs cite it. By this time, the U.S. Government had aided economic activity with enough outright land grants and rivers and harbors projects to such an extent, that progressives like Frederick Newell, George Maxwell, and the President could not be intimidated by an old theory such as *laissez-faire*. However, without fully realizing it, they were enunciating a new doctrine: government concern for the welfare of the people.

Here at the start of the Progressive decade, reclamation became the lead-off program of national social and economic reforms. Government intervened for the "common good" of enabling the greatest number of people to settle upon arid lands. And doing so would both conserve resources and put them to efficient use. For Theodore Roosevelt, Frederick Newell, and their close friend Gifford Pinchot, the nation's Chief Forester, conservation meant both careful management and wise use of natural resources. Their vision combined centralized management with scientific planning. Altogether this constituted a 180-degree turn away from the 19C's rugged individualism wherein each man looked to his own interests, and private hands controlled resources. Beyond these goals of efficiently reclaiming and conserving, these leaders sought another positive outcome: programs aimed at the common good that improved many lives would bring about a higher degree of democracy.[13]

The Arizona leader who grasped and followed this new vision was Benjamin Fowler, a Chicago book publisher who had moved to the territory in 1889 for his health. He bought land and became a gentleman farmer, preferring to spend his wide knowledge and considerable ability on public affairs. His talents soon recognized, he became an elected leader in civic enterprises. Classically educated at Yale and conversant with matters "back east," he was selected to lobby in Washington for the bill to permit Maricopa County to issue bonds to finance the dam on the Salt River at the site below Tonto Creek (1900-1901), There he met Newell and Maxwell and became a convert to their progressive vision of reclamation. When he came back, he was elected to the Territorial Legislature where he further promoted the idea of federal reclamation. On August 3, 1902, Fowler was elected by a mass meeting the Chairman of the ad hoc Water Storage Conference Committee. This committee was delegated to find the ways and means of reconciling and joining federal with local interests. Arizona farmers feared a distant government that might tell them when to irrigate and how much to pay for the water. Fowler thus undertook the task of mediating between local interests and the developing plans for federal reclamation, which, however well intentioned, would inevitably conflict at certain points and times.

Newell and Maxwell in creating their national program, envisioned a Jeffersonian panorama of yeomen farmers, a republic of smallholders as embodied in the series of federal land acts. These began with Jefferson's own Land Act of 1785, which had divided the nation into square-mile sections (640 acres) and 36-square-mile townships, and climaxed with the Homestead Act of 1862, which allotted free quarter-sections (160 acres) to farmers settling on them. Following precedents, the Reclamation Act of 1902 also restricted ownership of acreage under irrigation to 160-acre quarter sections. This was unacceptable to agribusinessmen who cultivated thousands of acres. Equally objectionable was a government take-over of the privately owned canal companies, some of which were corporate (northside) and some communally owned by users of their water (southside). Did the water belong to the land, as determined by Judge Joseph Kibbey in his 1892 *Wormser* decision in the Territorial Supreme Court, or did it belong to the owners and stockholders of the canals? Finally, what institution or organization possessed the legal mandate to negotiate and sign, on behalf of the constituency of the Salt River Valley, a contract with the national government to build a reclamation project? Not only would such an entity act as a "party" in the contract, it would also take responsibility for repaying the costs of the project back into the Reclamation Fund.[14]

Baffled by these problems, Benjamin Fowler turned to the chief booster of reclamation, George Maxwell, President of the advocacy group National Irrigation Congress. Initially the chief tasks were to organize and then apply for government aid. Frederick Newell, now promoted from the USGS to Director of the new Reclamation Service (Department of Interior), put out a set of requirements: economic stability, all water rights settled, approved locations, and viable technology. Maxwell advised the formation of a cooperative water-users association that excluded non-farmers. Maxwell also told Arizonans to follow the leadership of Fowler who had the ear and the respect of government. The ad hoc committee then turned to Judge Joseph Kibbey to serve as counsel to the group and to develop the articles of incorporation for the Salt River Valley Water Users Association (SRVWUA). These articles: (1) restricted membership to farmers (actual water users); (2) determined that each 160 acres would pay the same amount of the costs; (3) designated the SRV Water Users Association as administrator of the project; and (4) offered the land as security for the loan. [15]

Despite the objections and pressures from large landowners (who could ignore the 160-acre limitation until the project reached official completion), the Water Users Association functioned exactly as envisioned by Newell, Maxwell, Fowler, and Kibbey. Political support came straight from the White House in the 1902 appointment of ex-Major of Rough Riders Alexander Brodie as Governor of the Territory of Arizona. Three years later (1905), Brodie's replacement would be Judge Kibbey, who would continue to serve as attorney for the water users. The articles of incorporation were completed by January 1903, and the association became incorporated the next month. Frederick Newell praised the result as the model for all future projects, and on March 6, 1903, he presented the first reclamation proposals to Secretary of the Interior Ethan Allen Hitchcock, who approved, on March 12, the plan for the construction of the "Tonto Basin Dam"—pending the enrollment of sufficient acreage to serve as collateral for the loan. The project was originally estimated at $2,800,000. [16]

Next came the drive to sign up landowners for "subscriptions," pledges of land as collateral. After the first rush of enthusiasm which enrolled 50,000 acres (March 1903), many, including large landowners, held back because of continuing uncertainties about water rights, costs, and the future of the privately owned canal systems. However, as the weeks rolled by, desire for the project overcame doubt, and most farmers had signed up by 1904, when the first bids, for the cement mill onsite and the telephone line to Phoenix, had been opened. On August 24, 1903, supervising engineer Louis C. Hill arrived to commence operations. Hill, 38, held degrees in civil and electrical engineering from the University of Michigan; he had recently been Professor at the Colorado School of Mines (Golden); he had managed a railroad division (Great Northern), but never an irrigation project. He also had the supervision on the other western reclamation projects. When the first contracts were issued on October 14, 1903, celebration broke out in Phoenix with fireworks, a parade led by the Pioneer Band, and speeches in front of the Adams Hotel by Governor Brodie (believed by many to have secured the President's support) and by Benjamin Fowler, the first President of SRVWUA. 200 men were already working at the damsite digging tunnels, stringing wires, and erecting buildings at the newly named town of "Roosevelt." [17]

The explanation of Hill's inexperience is that the Salt River project was the first large irrigation system ever undertaken. With no model, Hill and his engineers, particularly Chester W. Smith, in-charge at Roosevelt, had to create designs, rigorously plan everything, and do battle with nature, contractors, and workers to adhere to timetables. With a site in wilderness country, a sixty-mile trek through desert and over mountains, expensive roads had to be engineered and constructed, from both the Valley and from the mining town of Globe to the east, the closest railhead, needed most at the outset to bring in the heaviest machinery. Timber had to be dragged out of the Sierra Anchas, north of the site; a canal to carry water to the generators in the powerhouse below the dam had to be excavated; a temporary electrical plant had to be built before the hydropower system was in place; the town called Roosevelt—furnished with electricity, a cold storage plant, and a hospital—was required for housing and logistical support; tunnels to divert the river had to be bored through rock; cofferdams were necessary to keep the riverbed dry while the dam's foundation and first courses of masonry were laid; the powerhouse below the dam had to be built; the quarry for the dam's blocks of sandstone (weighing tons) had to be set up by the cliffs; limestone had to be dug at nearby deposits and conveyed to the cement plant that had to be erected; and there had to be machine shops and large pieces of machinery such as derricks, cableways, and steamshovels. Altogether this was an enterprise of multi-complexities and daunting difficulties, something never before attempted at such a location on such a scale. The actual dam construction could not get underway until late1905, when enough of the infrastructure of roads, communications, power generation, cement plant, shops, and town had been accomplished. [18]

To construct what was first called the "Tonto Dam," twenty bids came in on February 23, 1905. The low bid of $1,147,600 was submitted by John M. O'Rourke of Denver. Before he could begin work, however, he had to assemble machinery, put up housing for his employees, build the temporary steam plant to generate electricity, begin construction of the miles-long power canal to convey water to the permanent powerhouse below the dam (completed 4-1-'06), and drain the riverbed with the cofferdams he had to build. O'Rourke believed—and promised—he could finish the dam in two years (1905-07), but the job required four years beyond that, and nothing went as planned. Tension became constant between O'Rourke and engineer-in-charge Chester Smith over the quality of the work. There were shortages and problems with workers because of the isolation and low wages, the latter being O'Rourke's main strategy to keep costs down, but nature dealt O'Rourke and the project the heaviest blows. Floods in November 1905 washed out the expensive cofferdams and carried away costly machinery. O'Rourke's rebuilding went slowly, and no masonry was laid on bedrock until September 1906, the first permanent work. [19]

The town of Roosevelt could boast a population of over 500 by the end of 1906. It contained several stores (three general stores, a drugstore, a meat market, a shoe shop), a number of restaurants, two lodging houses, a livery stable, a water supply, a Post Office, a Town Hall where Saturday dances were held, and an ice plant. There were a dozen wood-frame buildings and over 60 tents. The first brick building (bricks made on-site) housed the steam plant that produced the first electricity, and the Reclamation Service built its own offices. Hill decreed Roosevelt and the vicinity of the dam to be a "dry" community; no saloons were opened and no liquor to was be consumed in the area. This early experience with prohibition succeeded no better than the constitutional amendment imposed fifteen years later. Despite occasional arrests and seizures of the outlawed commodities, liquor was smuggled in constantly, hidden in supply shipments, secreted in the bottoms of grocery bags, carried in on stagecoaches and in private automobiles. Drinking may have been held down, but the controls were merely superficial. The "Roosevelt Road" (now Arizona 88), though far from complete, had opened in November 1904, bringing in mail and stagecoach services from Mesa, a trip of 11-1/2 hours. In a few years automobiles would be running the road and setting records for speed and time, which angered the teamsters carefully controlling their nervous animals on the steep and dangerous grades. The Roosevelt School opened in in 1905 with 100 pupils, and the first theatrical company in town performed *Miss Hursey from New Jersey* on November 23, 1905. On January 20, 1906, the "Roosevelt Peerless Orchestra" and the "Mormon Trio" gave a first concert. A school of the dance opened on February 1st. A new church was dedicated on March 1st, previous services having been held in the Town Hall. Also in March 1906, the *Roosevelt Tattler* first went to press. [20]

Progress on the dam itself merely inched along during these early years. From conception to conclusion, troubles seemed the norm; the project was beset with disastrous floods, labor shortages, machinery breakdowns, controversies, and the frequent wrangling of Smith and O'Rourke. Yet the work inexorably moved forward, evolving upward into a graceful structure spreading across its deep canyon. From bedrock, running continuously along the river bottom, and later up the canyon's sides, the designers cut a deep notch into the bedrock to secure the masonry structure against quakes and floods. Thickness at the base was 164 feet, tapering to 16 feet at the top, 245 feet above the bed of the river. In shape the dam rose vertically on its upstream side (facing the water), then descended in a series of giant steps arcing outward on the downstream side. Across the top, it bridged 400 feet from the north cliff to the south cliff, but this surface stretched a thousand feet in a convex curve upstream, which made it all but impervious to whatever pressures of water built up behind it. Twin spillways were inserted at the top at extremes of north and south. [21]

Two floods during the winter of 1907-08 slowed the work, but now the floodwaters only ran over the dam's northside; the southern side, having risen to 40 feet, was well above floodwater levels. From then on, floods couldn't interrupt the work. On June 28, 1908, two-thirds of the dam toward the south side stood 75 feet high, the low north point having reached 22 feet. On May 27 the downriver Granite Reef Diversion Dam (about 40 miles to the southwest) reached completion at the Valley's east end. This low dam stood only 15 feet above the bed of the river and ran 1100 feet across the stream. Main canals, the Arizona and the Southern, commenced the distribution of water from either end, carrying the water to the branch canals. Below Granite Reef, the river ran dry except when floods caused by rain below the "Tonto" dam poured over it. Progress on the big dam now moved along at a faster rate. By the end of 1909, the dam's high (south) and low (north) points had reached 228 and 150 feet, able to contain any possible floods. Behind it stretched a lake than ran about five miles in one direction (Salt) and four miles in the other (Tonto), containing about 140,000 acre-feet of water. Such was the "good news"; the "bad news" was that the project was two or three years behind schedule, and that delays, losses, and additional costs, such as the Granite Reef Diversion Dam (which had been added after the project purchased the northside canal system—another added cost), had driven the price up to $8,000,000! [22]

By April 1910, the dam, now officially the "Roosevelt Dam," neared completion. "Roosevelt Lake" behind the dam, because of heavy water demands during a drought, held steady with only a slight increase to 145,760 acre-feet by January 1911. However, the Reclamation Service's report on the crops of 1910 indicated that 490 miles of canals had conveyed water to 131,364 SR Valley acres, a triumph for the still unfinished project. Rains returned in 1911 as the finishing touches were added to the top of the dam, and the Lake rose rapidly to over 500,000 acre-feet, about half of capacity, by the time of its March dedication. [23] In the end the dam came in four years later than originally scheduled, and the add-ons, a higher structure, hydroelectric capacity, the downstream diversion dam, plus losses of time and equipment because of floods, pushed the final project cost to $10,500,000. This revelation caused protests and discontent among the 3,048 members of the SRVWUA, but unanticipated receipts for the sale of electric power eventually covered much of this debt. Since repayment could not begin until the "official" opening, delaying it for several years provided some relief to the farmers. Their complaints prompted Congress to pass the 1914 Reclamation Extension Act, which doubled the repayment period from ten to twenty years. Then in 1917, Interior Secretary Franklin Lane deeded the project over to its water users association, which took the name it still bears: "Salt River Project." The SRP has continued to supply water to the lands pledged to repay its original debt, and to sell electricity to purchasers, but it has flourished more as a corporate entity than as the egalitarian cooperative envisioned by Newell, Maxwell, Fowler, and Kibbey. There would never be a Jeffersonian aggregation of small farmers, each thriving on his 160-acre holding. Its 3000 enrolled members included smallholders, but many of these were only rent-paying tenants. The large agribusinessmen simply ignored this provision of the law, and no public-spirited group took them into court. They could pay their large water bills when due, and these receipts were necessary for operating expenses and for servicing the debt. In the end, the SRP proved a viable compromise, somewhat democratic, between national and local interests. The government lent the money and built the project; local interests operated it, determining membership, distributing water, and selling and generating electric power. [24]

If Phoenix was a rebirth of organized society on the plain of the Salt River, the State of Arizona required the aid of the Salt River Project to get its forty-eighth star up on the flag (February 14, 1912). In 1909 newly inaugurated President William Howard Taft came out to survey the progress of the reclamation program. Impressed and satisfied by the SRP, he returned convinced that Arizona had at last earned statehood. Phoenix is the only state capital surrounded by a reclamation project; it required only water to secure its future. Civic leadership understood this from the beginning and gave full support to reclamation. The SRP changed everything, bringing statehood, growth, and prosperity. Phoenix has known an amazing transformation, from a dusty, obscure town at the end of a branch line to a dynamic metropolis. [25]

The day of joy eventually arrived on March 18, 1911, when ex-President Theodore Roosevelt rode in on the Santa Fe to dedicate the dam and project he had fostered. Phoenix had devoted weeks to preparations: new paint on houses, streets cleaned up, all trash disposed of—in case he pulled any random inspections. Downtown sparkled with festive flags, strings of lights, and patriotic bunting on the speakers' stand in City Hall Plaza, where the city celebration would occur after the dedication at the damsite. On that morning, the *Arizona Republican* displayed his picture over the caption: "The World's First Citizen." The train rolled in at 9:20 AM, and a large crowd cheered his appearance on the rear platform of the private rail car. The caravan of 24 automobiles to carry him up to Roosevelt lined up with former Rough Rider Wesley A. Hill of Tempe at the wheel of the lead car. TR took the front seat by his driver, and Louis C. Hill, Supervising Engineer, and John Orme, who had replaced Benjamin Fowler as Association President, sat in the rear seat. The automobile was a shiny new, 60-horsepower "Kissel Kar." Proceeding north for a few miles on Central Avenue, the caravan paused at the Phoenix Indian School. Here the former President spoke briefly to the uniformed students after the presentation of arms and the band's performance of "Hail to the Chief." After which, the vehicular procession turned right and headed out of town on Indian School Road. In case of breakdowns, car 13 carried two mechanics. At Granite Reef, Hill demonstrated the diversion of water into the two main canals for distribution. Out of town, the cars kept a distance of 300 feet to minimize dust. The only other stop was at peaceful Fish Creek after the slow and tortuous descent of Fish Creek Hill's 10% grade.

At 4:15 PM the lead car rounded a bend and TR could gaze up at the great dam named for him. On top, he received an eleven-gun salute and was greeted by the 1000 who had previously arrived. Louis Hill, following Bishop Atwood's invocation, opened with the observation that Roosevelt Lake, only half-full at present, contained a two-year supply. Then the man who had striven the hardest, Benjamin Fowler, now President of the National Irrigation Congress, said: "To a great and growing community in an arid region, it is guarantee for all time of prosperity and happiness, comfort and peace." Coming last and speaking extempore, Theodore Roosevelt, after saying how proud he felt about the honor, stated that he had begun work on reclamation one week after taking office. He had realized that only the government could bring about reclamation. He asserted that his two proudest achievements were "this reclamation work in the West and the Panama Canal." At 5:48 PM, he pressed a button that released the water. [26]

Notes: Chapter 28

1. Quoted in Earl Zarbin, *Roosevelt Dam: A History to 1911*, 185.
2. Remittance men received money to stay away from home.
3. Thomas E. Sheridan, *Arizona: A History*, 105, 107.
4. *Ibid.*, 130-136, 140-141.
5. *Ibid.*, 199.
6. Dean Smith, *Tempe: Arizona Crossroads*, 20, 20. Duppa also renamed Hayden's Ferry, just east of Phoenix, "Tempe," after the idyllic valley in Thessaly inhabited by some of the Olympian gods. He may also have named the farming area south of Tempe "Kyrene."
7. Sheridan, 200-202.
8. Zarbin, 19.
9. Sheridan, 200-202; Zarbin, 20-22, 25; Karen Smith, *The Magnificent Experiment: Building the Salt River Reclamation Project, 1890-1917*, 2-6.
10. Zarbin, 19, 24-25; Sheridan, 206.
11. K. Smith, 12-23; Sheridan, 206-208; Zarbin, 27, 30-32.
12. *Ibid.*, 35.
13. K.Smith, 155-156.
14. *Ibid.* 16-23, 29; Sheridan, 208-209; Zarbin, 44-46.
15. K. Smith, 29-30, 32-33, 34; Zarbin, 44-47; Sheridan, 209.
16. K. Smith, 35-39; Sheridan, 209; Zarbin, 48-58. Four other reclamation projects were also submitted: Milk River, Montana; Gunnison, Colorado; Sweetwater, Wyoming; Truckee, Nevada.
17. *Ibid.*, 62-78; K. Smith, 40-66, 76.
18. *Ibid.*, 70-76; Zarbin, 81-96.
19. K. Smith, 78-85; Zarbin, 97-115.
20. *Ibid.*, 81, 90, 94, 96, 106, 115-116, 121-129. By mid-1907, automobiles could run the Roosevelt Road in 5 or 6 hours; see, 156-157.
21. K. Smith, 85-88; Sheridan, 209.
22. Zarbin, 134-135, 178, 181, 215-217; K. Smith, 89-90, 92-93.
23. Zarbin, 236, 238-239, 241.
24. K. Smith, 92-93, 122, 141-146, 156; Sheridan, 212; Zarbin, 219, 223.
25. *Ibid.*, 157.
26. *Ibid.*, 242-245.

29. THE ART OF RAG (IV): NEW YORK (I)

As previously told (Chapter 11), Ben Harney startled New York with its first dose of ragtime in 1896. His syncopated songs ("You've Been A Good Old Wagon, etc." and "Mr. Johnson, Turn Me Loose") created a sensation and left New Yorkers with a perception of ragtime as songs rendered with energy and animation. May Irwin reinforced this impression by "shouting" the coon songs of Harney and others in vaudeville and on the musical stage. This exciting new style hit Mike Bernard (1881-1936) with the force of revelation. Right after his triumphal run at Keith's, Harney was booked into Tony Pastor's 14th Street Theatre where 19-year-old Mike Bernard directed music in the pit. As he supplied the bass oompahs to Ben's treble in the stick dance, Mike studied all the moves of Ben's rapid right hand. A child prodigy, classically trained at the Berlin conservatory, Mike saw he could do it all on the piano, minus the stick, the funny straw hat, and the quirky supporting players. Just take a pop song and play the hell out of it! Soon he was showcasing his ragtime virtuosity on Pastor's weekly bill, on his way to becoming a New York legend.

By 1900 his numberless fans, led by the racy, sporting *Police Gazette*, had acclaimed him "King" of ragtimers. On January 23, 1900, at Pastor's in the AM, Richard K. Fox, owner of the *Police Gazette*, staged a piano-playing contest (called a "cutting contest" in St.Louis) to determine who might be the genuine article, the "Ragtime King of the World." The *Gazette* frequently staged contests in boxing, wrestling, and even such frivolous things as opening oysters or eating quail. It openly boomed Bernard as the favorite to win the diamond-studded prize medal. What became the legendary New York contest was actually a big thud. If there were any excellent players skulking in the honky-tonks and brothels of the Tenderloin, they must have stayed away in the belief that a contest staged by Mike Bernard's most vociferous fan had to be fixed. None of the five or six competitors came close to Mike's technical powers. He walked away from that pianistic late show with title and medal, New York's Mr. Ragtime, a "legend in his own time." [1]

The Bernard effect, fast tempi and tricky stuff on the vaudeville stage, ruled NY ragtime until 1907. Coincidentally with Joplin's arrival that year, publishers began to offer the rags of other Midwestern composers, such as Percy Wenrich, Charles L. Johnson, and George Botsford. In 1905 the two chief publishers of rags, Jerome H. Remick & Company of Detroit and the Stark Music Company of St.Louis, opened New York offices. Percy Wenrich (1880-1952), better known for his songs (Chapter 24), had published in Chicago {rags: *Ashy Africa* (1903), *Noodles* (1906), *Made in Germany* (1906), *The Smiler (1907)*}, and played in its concert-saloons and bordellos until 1908, when he moved to New York as a staff writer for Remick, which put out his *Peaches and Cream* (1905) and *Ragtime Chimes* (1911). Like Percy Wenrich, George Botsford (1874-1949) of South Dakota produced hit songs, "The Dance of the Grizzly Bear" (1910) and "Sailing Down the Chesapeake Bay" (1913), and worked for Jerome Remick. Botsford published about seventeen rags, many of them excellent and revealing (like Wenrich) the folk-melodic qualities of Midwestern rag writing. Two of these became enormous hits; *Black and White Rag* (1908) sold over 1,000,000 copies, was the first to be recorded on solo piano, and remained popular into the 1920's and '30's. The *Grizzly Bear Rag* (1910) equaled its song form, also running up a magic 1,000,000 in sales. [2]

Charles Leslie Johnson (1876-1950) succeeded in Tin Pan Alley without leaving Kansas City (born on the Kansas side, died on the Missouri side). He may have been ragtime's most successful composer, certainly its most prolific: over 200 publications, including 32 rags. He published them in Kansas City (13), New York (1),

Chicago (11), Detroit (3), Cleveland (1), Denver (1), Williamsport, PA (2), and Louisville (1). Because he published so many, he used pseudonyms as a marketing strategy, issuing seven rags by "Raymond Birch," and one each by "Ethel Earnist" and "Fannie B. Woods." Four of his rags sold over 1,000,000 copies: *Dill Pickles* (1906), *Powder Rag* (1908), *Porcupine Rag* (1909), and *Crazy Bone Rag* (1913). Doing almost as well in 1916 were *Teasing the Cat* and *Blue Goose Rag*. All of his rags are zesty, blithe, lyrical, and light-hearted. He kept them simple and seldom deviated from the three-theme structure (AA-BB-A-CC), usually ending with a repeat of "A" or "B". Three of his other pieces, the Indian intermezzoo "Iola," the waltz "Dream Days," and the song "Sweet and Low" also sold over 1,000,000 copies. Johnson was the compleat musician, a piano pro also competent on the violin, banjo, guitar, and mandolin, an arranger who rendered other folks music into published forms, a composer who furnished music on demand for any occasion, and the publisher of much of his own work. Even when the money rolled in, he put in full days, working at whatever musical task or inspiration lay on his desk. From 1906 until now, *Dill Pickles* has been played regularly, its only rival being Euday Bowman's *Twelfth Street Rag* (1914), which also recalls Kansas City. [3]

The most important Tin Pan Alley ragtimer from the east was Henry Lodge (1884-1933) of Providence, Rhode Island. Lodge was the first of a second generation of rag composers, born from the mid-1880's, which include James Scott (Chapter 24), Joseph Lamb (below), Eubie Blake (Chapter 35), Luckey Roberts, Jelly Roll Morton (Chapter 35), Paul Pratt (Chapter 30), and May Aufderheide (Chapter 30). Until 1908 and Botsford's *Black and White Rag*, no rag hits had been first published in New York. Remick had purchased Johnson's *Dill Pickles* and issued it in Detroit and New York in 1907, but St.Louis had been the site of its first publication the year before. Thus Lodge's *Temptation Rag* of 1909 became the first rag hit to originate in New York. Like Charles Johnson, Henry Lodge was a thorough professional, a superb pianist, conductor, arranger, composer. Again like Johnson, he had started out demonstrating in a music store, published a few early works locally, kept at it until he had a hit (in *Temptation*), and followed that up with three more in 1910, *Sneaky Shuffles*, *Sure Fire Rag*, and *Red Pepper Rag*. *Temptation Rag*, with its exciting "A" section in a minor key and thrusting movement, became immediately popular with pianists and vaudeville orchestras, which used it to accompany dance and acrobatic acts. Words were added to turn it into a hit song, and dance orchestras played it long after the ragtime era closed. *Red Pepper Rag* gave Lodge a follow-up hit the next year. In 1912 he gave up teaching in Providence to move to New York for work as a pianist in vaudeville and dance orchestras. In 1914 he accompanied Vernon and Irene Castle at their Castle House on East 46th Street where they offered dance lessons and tea dances (for the affluent). From 1909 to 1918, he published 14 fine rags; his *Black Diamond Rag* of 1914 also sold very well. At least fifty different records of his rags were issued. [4]

II

...After a three-year dry spell, [Joplin] was thinking in ragtime again. He was coming into a productive period, and he knew it. He could not set the precedent of selling good rags to John Stark for peanuts. [5]

He [Stark] made only one mistake, and that was fatal. He brought with him music instead of merchandise. [6]

John Stark set up the Stark Music Company in New York at 127 East 23rd Street in August 1905, five blocks south of Tin Pan Alley, which was located on West Twenty-eighth but now migrating north to the Forties. With a location so far south and a few blocks east of Fifth Avenue, Stark had placed himself off to the side of the music and entertainment businesses. Which symbolized his stubborn attitude; he refused to play the selling games of pushing "professional" copies out to cabaret and vaudeville performers, and cruising around to music stores and departments to place his product. He never hired or bribed anyone to plug his rags or songs. Except for Joseph Lamb (see below), he did not recruit any eastern composers. His catalog continued to feature Missouri ragtime, chiefly Joplin and James Scott. For the most part, his business stagnated, consisting mainly of filling wholesale orders to jobbers for the *Maple Leaf Rag* and for Scott's *Frog Legs*. Occasional retail sales added little to his gross. Without *Maple Leaf*'s steady sales of 3000 per month, he couldn't have eaten or paid his rent. Since it cost more to live in New York City, he was worse off financially than if he had remained in St.Louis. The sole advantage gained from this relocation was being near his daughter Eleanor who was pursuing her career there.

The remarkable thing about John Stillwell Stark is not his inadequacies in confronting the crude giants of music publishing, but the Quixote-like idealism that overcame his hardheaded, small-businessman viewpoint. Something he called "classic ragtime" possessed him. As he grew old in the music business—he was 64 in 1905 when he took on the challenges of New York—his enthusiasm grew for the ragtime he championed. Supporting this contention is his publication, ca. 1909, of *Fifteen Standard High-Class Rags*, a folio (eleven by Joplin) of rags arranged for eleven instruments; this became the only published folio of rag orchestrations from that period. [7] After his return to St.Louis (following the death of wife Sarah Ann), he published more rags by more composers than in New York previously. Whereas he had published six of Scott's rags and four of Lamb's in New York, he went on in St.Louis to publish nineteen more by Scott and eight by Lamb. Also in St.Louis he added several new composers of quality to his catalog, including Paul Pratt and J. Russel Robinson of Indianapolis and Artie Matthews, Rob Hampton, and Charlie Thompson of St.Louis, plus his musician son E.J. Stark and daughter-in-law Carrie Stark (wife of other son William). In a 1915 advertisement in the *Rag Time Review* (a Chicago publication), Stark affirmed his product:

> We have advertised these as classic rags and we mean just what we say. They are the perfection of a type. They have lifted ragtime from its low estate and lined it up with Beethoven and Bach. [8]

There it was, the essential point that the ragtime he published was of a special, <u>classic</u>, kind. Eventually (decades later) this led to controversy: what about the works of others? Was the Tin Pan Alley product mere musical rubbish, ephemeral pop, briefly enjoyed novelties soon forgotten? What about Botsford's *Black and White Rag*, or Lodge's *Temptation Rag*, or the rags of Charles Johnson, Percy Wenrich, Ford Dabney, or Harry Austin Tierney? Purists answered (adhering to the views of Blesh and Janis) that only the trinity of Joplin-Scott-Lamb produced rags of high enough quality to be ranked "classic." Over time, this purist view has faded, but many, if not most, ragtimers believe that the rags of Joplin and his followers do indeed possess high qualities of inspiration and style that set them apart. Ragtime historians David Jasen and Trebor Tichenor prefer the term "Joplin Tradition," which certainly applies, and elicits few objections. But Stark called them classic, and Edward Berlin, Joplin's biographer, says, why not: classic means the best of kind; Joplin consciously aimed at classicism; and Stark, who deeply cared, loved the term. So apparently have most ragtimers felt since the start of the "Ragtime Revival" (from the 1950s).

Scott Joplin stepped off the train in New York during the summer of 1907 sufficiently recovered from his loss to attempt new dimensions in ragtime. We may surmise that he was thinking about combining ragtime styles with operatic styles. He had probably brought with him several new piano rags in various stages of completion. He settled into a small boardinghouse, the Rosalline, at 128 West 29th Street, one block west of Broadway, one block north of Tin Pan Alley, close to theatres, and near the clubs and saloons of Black Bohemia.

Black Bohemia consisted of the nightspots patronized by African Americans in New York's very much segregated Tenderloin. Joplin continued to publish with Stark who brought out *Heliotrope Bouquet* and *Nonpareil* in 1907, and *Fig Leaf Rag* in early 1908. However this relationship had apparently been cooling, and Joplin sought better terms elsewhere. Soon after his arrival, Joplin called on Joseph W. Stern & Company (102-104 West 38th Street). As the composer of *Maple Leaf Rag*, he had professional standing, and Edward B. Marks, the headman at Stern's, purchased *Search Light Rag* and *Gladiolus Rag* for immediate publication, bringing out the former in August and the latter in September. Was Stark troubled or surprised at how quickly Joplin launched himself with a major New York publisher? At the same time, he also found a publisher in Boston, the Joseph M. Daly Music Publishing Company, that brought out his *Rose Leaf Rag* in November.

The break between Joplin and Stark came in 1908. Except for *Felicity Rag* (1911), *Kismet Rag* (1913)—both co-composed with Scott Hayden, and *Reflection Rag* (1917), all obtained earlier, Stark published no more Joplin rags after *Fig Leaf* in February 1908. Stark's conviction, that he could only afford to purchase outright for flat fees instead of royalties, seems to have precipitated the break and hard feelings thereafter. For both, dignity was lost, Stark because the offer was paltry and beneath his generous standards, Joplin because it degraded him back to the condition of other poorly compensated black composers. Beginners like Lamb and J. Russel Robinson received $25 plus another $25 after 1000 copies were sold. Operating in high-cost New York, Stark felt too squeezed to offer more. Stark may have offered Joplin more than $25 or $50, but the "King of the Ragtime Writers" could never accept such a devaluation. He felt unable to allow even Stark, who had given him quality publication—no Tin Pan Alley simplified scores for easy home performance—and the dignity of royalties, to take back the status he believed that he had attained. [9] For Joplin as a black man, these few shreds of dignity were worth far more than whites of that time could imagine. Another likely reason for the break was Stark's negative view of publishing longer works. He had published the *Ragtime Dance* ballet, when daughter Eleanor had overcome his better judgment, and Joplin certainly realized Stark's fear of getting burned a second time.

At this time Joplin, creatively, was "on a roll," and looking for a publisher who would pay more, who would reward his artistic growth. After trying Stern, he went to the Seminary Music Company, 112 West 38th Street, just east of Broadway. Seminary was one of several firms owned and operated by Henry Waterson, a businessman, and Ted Snyder, a composer. Later, after publishing such hits of Irving Berlin as "Alexander's Ragtime Band," they would recombine to form Waterson, Berlin, and Snyder. In these years around 1910, perhaps Joplin and Berlin knew one another at least slightly. Jasen and Tichenor divide Joplin's creative span into three periods. First, the early Sedalia-St.Louis phase, characterized initially by the bright, upbeat quality of the *Maple Leaf Rag* (1899) and *Peacherine Rag* (1901), after which Joplin eased into the more flowing style of *Easy Winners* (1901) and *The Entertainer* (1902). The second phase begins in 1904 and continues on through such rags as *The Cascades*, *The Sycamore* (both 1904), *Leola* (1905), *Eugenia* (1906), *Gladiolus Rag*, *Rose Leaf Rag* (both 1907), and concludes with *Fig Leaf Rag*, *Sugar Cane*, and *Pine Apple Rag* (all 1908). In these mature works, Joplin expressed deeper emotions and different moods within single rags. Jasen and Tichenor comment that, "In this he was unique. For all other writers one emotion per rag was sufficient." [10] From 1909 with *Wall Street Rag*, he entered a third period which was experimental. This covers his last seven or eight rags in which he ventured further emotionally and harmonically. These rags project authority and power. [11] They include *Country Club*, *Euphonic Sounds*, *Paragon Rag* (all 1909), *Stoptime Rag* (1910), *Scott Joplin's New Rag* (1912), and *Magnetic Rag* (1914)—and perhaps they grant Joplin another title: King of American Composers. [12]

In the later years, Joplin had at least a small success with *Pine Apple Rag*. In New York he had run across one of his oldest fellow ragtimers, Sam Patterson. Sam Patterson had gone into vaudeville (as had Joplin himself whenever opportunities arose) with William Spiller and formed a musical group, variously known, depending on the current number, as the Spiller Musical Trio or the Five Musical Spillers. They were extremely versatile, playing whatever instruments a selection called for and often performed as a brass quintet. Joplin dedicated *Pine Apple Rag* "to the Five Musical Spillers," who had done quite well in the big-time. The rag went into their repertory and utterly delighted audiences. Spiller's wife Isabele recalled *Pine Apple* being played on massed xylophones and marimba with orchestral accompaniment. She remarked that, "*Pineapple Rag* [sic] was such a favorite that every time we [left] it out we had to put it back." [13] This rag was a rouser and was published with lyrics in 1910. Jasen and Tichenor call it "among the finest rags ever written." [14] Recently classical pianist Roy Eaton ranked Joplin with the European composers thusly:

> [Joplin] said, "OK, I will take this form, these black American rhythms, and I will elevate them to classical status, just as Chopin had taken a peasant dance, the mazurka, and elevated it to levels of expression that cover a range of human experience that few composers have ever achieved.…Bach did the same thing with the gigues and sarabands, which he used as the model for his suites. They were originally folk dances, and he transformed them. That's the operative word, transformation. [15]

III

> …Lamb did not conceive of a dichotomy between musical concepts and their notation; improvisation seemed baffling, awkward, redundant. In this respect Lamb realized Scott Joplin's vision of ragtime as a notated art form more thoroughly than did Joplin himself. [16]

The casual first encounter of Scott Joplin and Joseph F. Lamb at Stark's place on East 23rd Street in late 1907 led to significant consequences for ragtime. Lamb, a youth of twenty and already a three-year veteran of the work force, had composed his first music as a schoolboy of thirteen (songs) and had been attempting rags for three years. After hearing the *Maple Leaf Rag* in 1904, he knew he wanted to turn out rags on the Joplin model. Having entered Stark's to browse, as he chatted with Mrs. Sarah Ann Stark about why he admired his favorite composer, she pointed to a black man sitting nearby with a bandaged foot and a crutch and indicated, "Well, here's your man." She added that Joe Lamb had recently submitted "a couple of rags" which had been rejected. Joplin asked Lamb about his compositions and invited him over to his boardinghouse to play them. A few nights later, he sat at the piano in the parlor of the Rosalline where, "A lot of colored people were sitting around talking. I played my *Sensation* first and they began to crowd around and watch me. When I finished, Joplin said, 'That's a good rag—a regular Negro rag.' That was what I wanted to hear." He played two more, *Dynamite Rag* and *Old Home Rag*, and Joplin offered to intercede with Stark to get *Sensation Rag* published. To get buyer attention, Joplin suggested that "Arranged by Scott Joplin" be put below the name of the composer. Stark approved this touch and bought the rag for $50, an initial $25 and another $25 after 1000 copies had sold. [17]

Joseph Francis Lamb (1887-1960) was born in Montclair, New Jersey, to Irish immigrant parents, the youngest of four children (one brother, two sisters). From his contractor-carpenter father, he learned the practical skills that he enjoyed pursuing at home, but he picked up his love of music from older sisters Katherine and Anastasia. These two had progressed from the genteel piano lessons typical of the time to professional competence, one a church organist and the other a music scholarship student. At eight Joe begged them to teach him how to read music as well as to play. A "natural," he never stopped learning. After his father's death in 1900, his mother sent her obstreperous thirteen-year-old to a strict preparatory school in Canada, St.Jerome's College in Berlin, Ontario. While completing a pre-engineering course (he was accepted at Stevens Institute of Technology in Hoboken, but never attended), he wrote and actually published songs, waltzes, and intermezzos (Harry H. Sparks Publishing Company, Toronto). In 1903 he composed his first rag, *Walper House Rag*, named for the hotel in Berlin, Ontario (renamed Kitchener during World War I). He took his first job with a dry goods company in 1904, then went to join his brother in San Franciso during 1905-1906, working odd jobs and returning to Montclair two weeks before the terrible earthquake hit California. [18]

When he met Joplin, Lamb was working in New York for a clothing company, playing nights in a dance orchestra, and composing in spare time. The convergence of Joplin and Lamb may have caused a synergy. Lamb's next two submissions to Stark, *Ethiopia Rag* and *Excelsior Rag* were two of the finest classic rags ever composed. Stark called *Excelsior* a "heavy weight" (Lamb: "because it was written in five and six flats..."). [19] Lamb and Joplin kept up their friendship until "at least 1914" (according to a recent account). [20] They actually collaborated on a rag, *Scott Joplin's Dream*, Joplin contributing the A and B strains and Lamb the C (trio) and D strains. Joplin and Stark had parted bitterly, and when Lamb submitted their joint effort, Stark refused anything with Joplin's name on it. Later Lamb lost the manuscript. During this 1907-14 period, Lamb composed prolifically, fourteen or fifteen rags, and developed the style of what are called his "heavy" rags, romantic and lyrical works that contrast with his "light," humorous rags. [21] Jasen and Tichenor state that Lamb "synthesized" Joplin's flowing melodic style (legato) with Scott's exuberant rhythms and keyboard complexities to create works of "great originality." [22]

Lamb befriended both Joplin and Stark and may have kept each informed about the other. Stark issued one more Lamb rag before returning to St.Louis with his dying wife. This was the lighter and happier *Champagne Rag*. The year before, 1909, he gave *Contentment Rag* to the Starks for a Fiftieth Anniversary present, in celebration of what he perceived as an exemplary marriage. *Contentment*, like *Champagne*, was on the lighter side, but more subdued and tender. Grieving, Stark held it back for five years, until 1915; it was one of the eight Lamb rags that he published in St.Louis through 1919. The full dozen published by Stark also included *American Beauty Rag* (1913), *Ragtime Nightingale* (1915), *Top Liner Rag* (1916), *Patricia Rag* (1916), and *Bohemia Rag* (1919). These plus *Excelsior* and *Ethiopia* constitute Lamb's most loved works and most (not all) of his major works. Of them, *Bohemia Rag* may be the masterpiece of the lighter rags, hitting a stupendous stride in the inexorable movement of its repeated trio (C section).

As for Joplin, he gained not only a friend who shared similar musical aspirations, but also the satisfaction and thrill of Lamb's flowering as a composer. It may have renewed his faith in himself and his work as well as relieved his professional loneliness. The synergy may have been less for the mature Joplin, but the major publications of 1908-1910, the seven rags and the habanera *Solace* are certainly an inspired body of work. Figuratively speaking, for Joplin, to look behind and see such brilliant followers as Scott and Lamb creating so well, may have been justification enough for the hard road of his vision.

As for Lamb, he married, reared a family, and worked at the business of importing textiles, spending forty-three years with a single employer. He worked at his piano in the evenings, composing into the 1920's. One anecdote describes him rocking a cradle with one foot while busy at the keyboard. His first wife died in 1920, one of the last victims of the great World War I influenza epidemic. He remarried a few years later (1922), adding a girl and three more boys to the first son. So supportive were Joe and second wife Amelia to the local elementary school, that Brooklyn's P.S. 206 was eventually (1976) renamed the Joseph F. Lamb School. His coworkers at the L.F. Dommerich Company remembered him with great affection as a competent boss who looked after his employees and created a family-like work atmosphere. [23] When ragtime began to revive during the 1940's, no one knew anything about the composer of the twelve Stark rags except his name. Rudy Blesh, resorting to New York telephone directories, finally located and informed him (1949) of his importance in ragtime history. Stimulated by this belated recognition, Joseph Lamb returned to composition and produced more than twenty works. When he died suddenly in 1960, he was no longer obscure and forgotten. His biographer tells us that Lamb was proudest of *Alaskan Rag* (in honor of statehood) written after his rediscovery and the final masterpiece of his "heavy" romantic rags. [24]

RAGTIME ALMANAC

The Biggest Rag Hits [25]

<u>Title</u>	<u>Composer</u>	<u>Published In:</u>	<u>Date</u>
Black and White Rag	George Botsford	New York	1908
Carbarlic Acid	Clarence Wiley	Iowa/Detroit	1901
Cannon Ball	Jos. C. Northrup	Chicago	1905
Canadian Capers	(Various)	Chicago	1915
Chicken Chowder	Irene Giblin	Detroit	1905
Dill Pickles	Charles L. Johnso	Kansas City	1906
Down Home Rag	Wilbur Sweatman	Chicago	1911
Dusty Rag	May Aufderheide	Indianapolis	1908
The Entertainer's Rag	Jay Roberts	Oakland, CA	1910
Everybody Two Step	Wally Herzer	New York	1911
Frog Legs Rag	James Scott	St.Louis	1906
Grizzly Bear Rag	George Botsford	New York	1910
Hungarian Rag	Julius Lenzberg	New York	1913
Kitten On The Keys	Zez Confrey	New York	1921
Lassus Trombone	Henry Fillmore	Cincinnati	1915
Maple Leaf Rag	Scott Joplin	Sedalia, MO	1899
Memphis Blues	W.C. Handy	Memphis	1912
Peaceful Henry	E. Harry Kelly	Kansas City	1901
Pickles and Peppers	Adaline Sheperd	Milwaukee	1906
Powder Rag	"Raymond Birch"	Kansas City	1908
Raggin' the Scale	Ed Claypoole	New York	1915
Red Pepper Rag	Henry Lodge	New York	1910
Russian Rag	George Cobb	Chicago	1918
St.Louis Blues	W.C. Handy	Memphis	1914
The Smiler	Percy Wenrich	Chicago	1907
Temptation Rag	Henry Lodge	New York	1909
Tickled to Death	Charles Hunter	Nashville	1901
Tiger Rag	JR Morton & Various	New York	1917
Tres Moutarde	Cecil Macklin	London	1911

12th Street Rag	Euday Bowman	Ft. Worth	1914
Wild Cherries	Ted Snyder	New York	1908

"It proves that ragtime was truly a national music."—Dick Zimmerman

Chapter 29: Notes

1. David Jasen and Gene Jones, *That American Rag: The Story of Ragtime from Coast to Coast*, 260-261; Rudy Blesh and Harriet Janis, *They All Played Ragtime*, 214-218.
2. Jasen & Jones, *Am. Rag*, 266-269; Blesh & Janis, 122-123. For Wenrich, *Ibid.*, 123-127; Jasen & Jones, *Am. Rag*, 11-13, 132-133, 287.
3. *Ibid.*, 56, 60-64; David A. Jasen and Trebor Jay Tichenor, *Rags and Ragtime: A Musical History*, 38-46; Blesh & Janis, 119-120.
4. Jasen & Jones, *Am. Rag*, 262-266; Jasen & Tichenor, 143-147; Dick Zimmerman, "The Henry Lodge Story," *Rag Times*, 9 (January 1976): 1-3. At least fifty records of Lodge's rags were issued.
5. Jasen & Jones, *Am. Rag*, 40-41.
6. Blesh & Janis, 219.
7. Vera Brodsky Lawrence, Liner Notes to "Scott Joplin: The Red Back Book," Angel Records, S-36060, 1973. The folio became known as the "Red Back Book" from the color of its cover; Edward A. Berlin, *King of Ragtime: Scott Joplin and His Era*, 250, indicates the date of publication as "around n & Tichenor, 84.
8. Quoted in Blesh & Janis, 253.
9. Jasen & Jones, *Am. Rag*, 39-40.
10. Jasen & Tichenor, 84.
11. *Ibid.*, 84-85.
12. Author's note: My opinion.
13. Edward A. Berlin, *King*, 180.
14. Jasen & Tichenor, 96.
15. David Reffkin, "An Interview With Roy Eaton," *Mississippi Rag*, (January 2000): 25.
16. Joseph R. Scotti, "The Musical Legacy of Joe Lamb," in John Edward Hasse, Ed., *Ragtime: Its History, Composers, and Music*, 243.
17. Blesh & Janis, 236-237.
18. George A. Borgman, "Joseph F. Lamb, Classic Ragtimer," *Mississippi Rag* (August 2001): 2.
19. Russ Cassidy, "Centennial Recollections With Joseph Lamb," *Rag Times* XXI (November 1987):4.
20. Borgman, 4.
21. *Idem*.
22. Jasen & Tichenor, *123*-124.
23. Joseph R. Scotti, "Joe Lamb: A Study of Ragtime's Paradox," Ph.D. Dissertation, University of Cincinnati, 121-122.
24. Scotti, in *Ragtime*, 253.
25. Source: Dick Zimmerman, "Tin Pan Alley: Birthplace of Rag Hits? Wrong!" *Rag Times*, XXVII (March 1994): 8.

30. The Art of Rag (V): Indianapolis Excursion and the Ragtime Women

Ragtime's everywhere, ragtime's right.

"Living a Ragtime Life" [1]

Of the list of 31 of "The Biggest Ragtime Hits," only ten were published in New York and five in Chicago, the rest in medium- and small-sized cities, giving Tin Pan Alley a claim on only half. [2] A "claim" only, because, of the Tin Pan Alley 15, just eight were actually composed in New York or Chicago. [3] The first three, Carbarlic Acid, Peaceful Henry, and Tickled to Death, appeared in 1901 in Oskaloosa, Iowa, Kansas City, Missouri, and Nashville, Tennessee, respectively. Ragtime diffused rapidly and became the chief national music. Although whites believed it to be the music of "colored people" and thought of it as originating in "bad" locations, e.g., honky-tonks or brothels, the reality was that all but three or four of the composers on this list were whites, and very few had played in the fleshpots. These "piano rags" largely appealed to the piano-owning middle class. They achieved some universality when virtuosos like Mike Bernard rendered them for vaudeville audiences, but they were more often heard in middle class homes where mothers and daughters, accomplished on the piano, played them for their menfolk.

Indianapolis exemplifies well the ragtime activity of a small city. In a survey sample of 1,327 piano rag publications (1897-1921), Indianapolis ranked seventh, with 49, compared with 264 in New York, 208 in Chicago, and 142 in St. Louis (ranked 1-2-3). [4] Rapid economic growth and rich musical traditions probably account for this city's important contributions to ragtime. From 1890, the city grew, from 105,436 to 169,164 in 1900, to 233,650 in 1910, more than doubling its population in 20 years. [5] In 1907 Indianapolis ranked fourth in automobile manufacturing—this would increase to second by 1914—producing such brands (64 in all) as Duesenberg, Marmon, Stutz, Premier, and the Waverly Electric. The Indianapolis Speedway racetrack, built in 1909 (the first "Indy 500" ran in 1911), recalls this industrial concentration. Radiating outward were fourteen railroads, plus interurban lines to every part of the state (Chapter 24). These convergences produced such labels as "Crossroads of America," "Railroad City," and "Pivot City." Everything met downtown where Market and Meridian Streets intersected at Monument Circle, containing the massive Indiana Soldiers and Sailors Monument, dedicated in 1902 after 14 years of construction and expenditures of $600,000. [6]

Indianapolis's ethnic minorities consisted chiefly of German-Americans and African Americans, making up about 30% and 10% of the population. Before the southern migration that took off in 1915, most local African Americans claimed Indiana or Kentucky origins. Germans had flowed in after the failed revolutions of 1848 that had rocked Europe and left it more conservative. Although blacks occupied the lowest socio-economic level of laboring jobs and ghetto housing, they had developed a full set of institutions: churches, businesses, social organizations, musical groups, and three weekly newspapers. The Indianapolis *Freeman* circulated nationally and carried advertising for music and theatre and reviews of entertainment. Along with the Chicago *Defender* and the New York *Age*, it was read everywhere. The industrious Germans had flourished greatly, and nearly all had gained success as businessmen, professionals, or skilled tradesmen. They published two German-language daily papers and several weeklies.

What both had in common was music. The Germans carried on European art-music traditions with numerous ensembles, vocal and instrumental; these included superb choirs and a 60-piece orchestra. In popular music, their brass bands performed on all festive and official occasions. Likewise, blacks also fielded bands for parades, popular occasions, and dances. They produced local minstrel shows and held barbershop quartet contests. Music could be heard all over the city, in hotel dining rooms, at conventions, political events, fairs, summer park concerts, circuses, and in vaudeville theatres, saloons, and sporting houses. The directory of the musicians' union in 1905 listed about 30 categories of occasions for which they furnished music, including nearly all of the abovementioned, plus balls, commencements, picnics, sports, rollerskating, weddings, dedications of monuments, "escorts," and "serenades." Both ethnic communities produced national figures in music/entertainment. Successful blacks included Dora Dean, Billy McClain, and Noble Sissle. Whites in the big-time included J. Russel Robinson, Abe Olman, Paul Pratt, and Hoagy Carmichael. [7]

All of the above four white men started off in ragtime. About 25 denizens of the "Circle City" (another of the city's nicknames) composed and published at least one ragtime piano solo. Of these, about fourteen were German-Americans and six were women. [8] During this period music publishing was ubiquitous; not only did proprietors of music stores (like Missourians John Stark and Austin Perry in Sedalia and Charley Dumars in Carthage) publish local composers, but people also self-published, sending songs and instrumentals to music printers who would run off a few hundred copies for a reasonable cost. Will B. Morrison (1874-1937) and Cecil Duane Crabb (1890-1953) both acquired the title of publisher. Will Morrison who clerked in a music store published the works of others first: Crabb's *Fluffy Ruffles* in 1907 and *Honeymoon Rag* by Abe Olman in 1908. Olman (1888-1984), who was a professional, managed and demonstrated in the music department at the L.S. Ayres department store from 1908 to 1912, when he left for Tin Pan Alley in New York and Chicago for a successful career in song-writing ("Down Among the Sheltering Palms" {1915} and "Oh, Johnny, Oh, Johnny, Oh!" {1917}). His rags numbered eight and included *Seaweeds Rag* (1910), *Halloween Rag* (1911), and his best known, *Red Onion Rag* (1912), all with other publishers. He eventually published over 100 songs. As for Morrison, he composed *Trouble Rag* (1908), jointly with Crabb, and remained in publishing a few more years (Will B. Morrison Publishing Company). His *Scarecrow Rag* and *Sour Grapes Rag* both appeared in 1912. [9]

Cecil Duane Crabb, b. rural Centerville, came to Indianapolis as a homeless boy who was taken in by F.D. Staley, Sr. after being injured in a rollerskating accident. Immediately the Staleys discovered in "Cece" gifts for playing the piano and for graphic design. Staley set him up in a sign business that offered both outdoor display signs and elegant gold lettering on office doors. Then, strangely, this 18-year-old waif and sign painter from the "wrong" side of the tracks became associated with a well-to-do debutante about to graduate from an eastern finishing school. Her name was May Aufderheide, and what Cece Crabb did was to publish her *Dusty Rag*. First he gave it to a third 18-year-old, Paul Pratt, to arrange, and then he drew the cartoon for the cover (a darky minstrelman), after which, he sent it off to a printer. Thus into its brief existence came the "Duane Crabb Publishing Company"; *Dusty* was its sole publication, and May's father soon bought out the rights. Crabb went on painting signs and playing ragtime for friends. He let May's father publish his last two rags. [10]

Like Crabb and Pratt, May Frances Aufderheide (1890-1972) had reached 18 years and landed abruptly on the threshold of adulthood in 1908. Born to affluence and privilege, she (and her brother Rudolph, b.1891) was the only Indianapolis ragtimer of high socio-economic status. Her father John Henry Aufderheide (1865-1941) had studied violin and played competently in amateur orchestras, but he had chosen a financial career instead. Following a humble start as a bank teller and another term in real estate, he found an opportunity in a new area, the "personal loan." Banks then (and for decades afterward) operated locally and conservatively. A banker regarded himself principally as the custodian of other people's money, which he invested carefully only in "safe" securities, to bring modest profits to himself and his depositors. Loans also had to be safe investments; the security of the funds under his care demanded solid collateral, usually land. Few bankers would speculate on people of worthy character who might be considered good risks (if they lacked the collateral). Folk wisdom proclaimed that banks only lent money to people who "didn't need it." Thus John Aufderheide, along with a few shrewd contemporaries, prospered by lending money (at rates well above banks) to those whom banks did not regard as credit-worthy. Doing well from the outset, over time he carefully built up what became incorporated in 1922 as the Commonwealth Loan Company, which at his death had become huge, with 81 branches in eleven states. [11]

John Aufderheide lavished all of the advantages and benefits his money could provide on his daughter. May received much of her musical training and piano lessons from her aunt (and namesake) May Kolmer, who taught at the Metropolitan School of Music and had been piano soloist with the Indianapolis Symphony Orchestra. Young May completed her education at an eastern finishing school, Pelham Manor in New York. Upon graduating, her parents conveyed her to Europe for the cultural tour that, presumably, put the final, high sheen on a debutante. May was already betrothed to a neophyte architect, Thomas M. Kaufman, of Richmond, Indiana, and upon her return from Europe, she became caught up in the parties and preparations for her nuptials. The year 1908, with graduation, betrothal, and a fairly grand tour, capped by marriage, turned out to be a crowded year for a young lady just emerging from a sheltered and protected childhood. How was it that she also found the time to focus on ragtime? *Dusty Rag* had gone through the printer's even before she left Pelham Manor.

Shortly afterward came the intervention of a loving father. Seeing a copy of *Dusty Rag* evoked an empathetic response in a man who had probably once set aside his own musical aspirations. John Aufderheide, doing very well in the loan business, wasn't seeking opportunity outside his current sphere; however, with his grasp of music, he sensed the quality of his daughter's talents, plus, as a canny businessman, he knew how to market a commodity. With obvious pride in his daughter, he launched the J.H. Aufderheide & Company, Music Publishers, to bring out her music late in 1908. He made a real business out of it, renting office space in the downtown Lemcke Building, and hiring young Paul Pratt to manage and do the arranging, with Cece Crabb on call for graphic design. After reissuing *Dusty*, the new company brought out May's *Richmond Rag* in December 1908. *Richmond Rag* pulsates with happiness, a certain celebration of May's move to Richmond, Indiana, where she and Thomas were beginning married life.

More new works followed in 1909: Crabb's delightful *Orinoco: Jungle Rag, Two-Step*, Pratt's first, *Vanity Rag*, and two by May in September, *Buzzer Rag* and *The Thriller*. *Dusty* and *Richmond* had been selling well, which received notice in a piece on May in the New York *American Musician and Art Journal*. [12] It carries a photo of May, chin erect, her rich, dark hair piled high, exemplar of the Gibson Girl, a pretty girl verging on mature beauty, what men of that decade called a "peach." The article praises the first two rags and predicts the next ones to be "winners." *The Thriller* also became a good seller, eventually becoming, along with *Dusty,* her most popular works. Both rags came out several times on piano roll, and both were later popular with jazzmen. In January 1910, J.H. Aufderheide published manager Paul Pratt's *Colonial Glide* (a dance rag) and *Walhalla*. Abe Olman's *Candlestick Rag* appeared a few months later, followed by May's next two, *A Totally Different Rag* and *Blue Ribbon Rag* in October 1910. Next, to extend the market, Aufderheide sent Paul Pratt to Chicago in 1911 to open a branch office.

The Aufderheide company quickened its pace in 1911 with Crabb's *Klassicle Rag*, Will Morrison's *Scarecrow Rag*, and two by women: *Piffle Rag* by Gladys Yelvington and *Horseshoe Rag* by Julia Lee Niebergall. Gladys Yelvington was a musical girl friend of May's, and *Piffle Rag* was her only published work. Following Paul Pratt's move to Chicago, Niebergall had joined the firm to do the musical arrangements. Married and divorced early, Julia Lee Niebergall (1886-1968) worked as a pianist all of her life in Indianapolis, supporting herself with music. She published only three works, *Hoosier Rag* in 1907 (with Remick) and *Horseshoe Rag* (1911) and *Red Rambler* (1912), both with Aufderheide. May herself published *Novelty Rag* in April 1911, her final piano composition.

Just after the appearance of *Red Rambler*, John Aufderheide abruptly shut down what had become a viable music-publishing business and sold its catalog to a firm in Cincinnati. For May the happy music had stopped flowing. What we know is that she and Thomas Kaufman abandoned Richmond for the spacious Aufderheide residence in Indianapolis, after an apparently unsuccessful try at architecture. Subsequently, another effort to make it on his own in Indianapolis seems also to have foundered, because in 1916, his father-in-law put him to work in the personal loan business. We know also that even though Thomas rose to head the Commonwealth Loan Company (after JHA's death in 1941), that he fell into alcoholism and never got out. What about him? He must have seemed a promising specimen in 1908, upbeat with talent and potential, when he gained the heart of a smart, lovely girl who saw in him a good future. She cannot have anticipated her descent into a life of stress and conflict, having to care for a depressive (was he also manic?). In 1948 they retreated to a custom-built home ("Rose Villa," designed by Thomas Kaufman himself) on the beautifully landscaped grounds of the Huntington-Sheraton in Pasadena, California. Thomas died there in 1959, and May, crippled by arthritis and in a wheelchair, lasted until 1972. [13]

From 1908-1912, Paul Charles Pratt (1890-1948) had run a business that published 43 pieces, rags-songs-waltzes, of which 21 were rags (one-third of them by May Aufderheide). Besides sheet music, the Aufderheide company made additional money from selling the rights to piano rolls, which JHA had shrewdly retained. [14] The dissolution of the firm stranded Paul Pratt in the major cultural and business center of Chicago, where he found numerous doors of opportunity on which to knock. During the next six or seven years, he worked for other publishers, arranged piano rolls (U.S. Music Company), and kept up his composing. His lyrical and moody *Teasing Rag* appeared in Chicago in 1912 (recently rediscovered and not to be confused with Joe Jordan's better known work *That Teasing Rag*), after which he mailed his rags to John Stark in St. Louis, who brought out *Hot House Rag* (1914), *Spring-Time Rag* (1916), and *On the Rural Route* (1917). Besides these, Pratt brought out four unpublished rags on piano rolls; four more were never put on a roll or published. The original qualities and complexities of his rags point to him as the most important of the Indianapolis ragtimers. This judgment gains support from the many songs he composed, upwards of one hundred, in collaboration with lyricist and close friend Will Callahan. From 1919 to 1923 Paul Pratt traveled in vaudeville, after which, from 1924 on into the 1930's he conducted in musical comedies, both on Broadway and on tour. He led orchestras for such New York hits as *Wildflower* in 1923, the Ziegfeld *Follies* of 1926, and Rodgers and Hart's *Connecticut Yankee* in 1927 (it ran three years). The Depression, and perhaps a desire to return to home and roots, brought Paul and his wife back to Indianapolis. For a time he led a dance orchestra (Paul Parnell and His Sycamores), but after a few years of night gigs, he reverted to an old interest and opened a portrait photography studio in 1934. He worked at this, with music for an avocation, until his untimely death in 1948 (from a coronary attack). [15]

J.H. Aufderheide published three women: daughter May, Julia Lee Niebergall, and Gladys Yelvington, who provided just over one-half of his list of rags, an unusual percentage. Except for decidedly unrespectable showgirls, few women supported themselves in performing or creative arts. About twenty years ago, ragtimers Max Morath and John Edward Hasse assembled a list of women who had published at least one rag or ragtime song (before 1930), reaching a total of 220. [16] Recently Nan Bostick and Nora Hulse have added to and updated this list to a total of 315. [17] But other than the names on copyrights or sheet music, we know very little about nearly all of them. From Jennie Aaron who composed *Old Carpet Rag* (1911), published in Denver, Colorado, to Carrie E. Zeman who published *Kinky, A Ragtime Two Step* in 1906 with the Andreas Publishing Company of Davenport, Iowa, the women of ragtime dwelled everywhere. Few had any connection with Tin Pan Alley. Of the few we know, four, May Aufderheide, Gladys Yelvington, Irene Giblin of St.Louis, and Adaline Shepherd of Milwaukee, forfeited musical careers to marry, undoubtedly the typical pattern. From 1905 to 1913 Irene Giblin (1888-1974) published ten ragtime compositions, marking her as the most prolific of the ragtime women. She worked as a pianist-demonstrator in the music section of St.Louis's Stix, Baer, and Fuller department store. Her first rag *Chicken Chowder* (1905) was issued by Jerome Remick (Detroit-New York), the leading rag publisher and eventually sold enough copies to earn a place on the "hits" list of top sellers. She was one of only three to earn this distinction. She married and gave up her job when her second child was born. She continued composing for a few more years, and Remick later brought out several more of her rags: *Sleepy Lou*, *Soap Suds* (both 1906), *Columbia*, *Ketchup Rag*, and *The Aviator Rag* (all 1910). She also published in Chicago, Boston, and Cleveland. [18]

The third woman (after May Aufderheide and Irene Giblin) to attain the "hits" list was Adaline Shepherd (1883-1950), whose *Pickles and Peppers* (1906) was a top seller and considered (by two leading ragtime historians) to be "one of the most beloved rags." [19] Later she published *Live Wires Rag* and *Wireless Rag* in 1909, but she gave up music after marrying Fred Olson, a prosperous Milwaukee insurance man, in 1910. *Pickles and Peppers* brought additional fame and fortune in 1908, when William Jennings Bryan used it in his last presidential campaign. Bryan loved the piece, and his patronage did much to increase its sales in 1908 to 200,000 copies, making it the top seller for a woman. [20] Among the ragtime women with more than two or three publications—about whom we know little—were Charlotte Blake of Detroit (11); Grace M. Bolen (4) of Kansas City; Louise V. Gustin (7), also of Detroit; Marcella A. Henry (8) of Peru, Illinois; Lora M. Hudson of Chicago (5); Effie Kamman, another Detroiter (6); Verdi Karns of Bluffton, Indiana (4); Florence McPherran, Chicago (7); Bess E. Rudisill (7), who published in Chicago and St.Louis; Nellie M. Stokes (5), yet another Detroiter; Mamie E. Williams (7) of Kansas City; Carlotta Williamson (7) of Boston; Florence M. Wood, Toledo, Ohio (4). [21]

Besides Julia Lee Niebergall (of Indianapolis) who supported herself as a movie theatre pianist and as an accompanist at a dance academy, the only other lifelong female professional in music was Muriel Pollock (1895-1971). Born of Russian immigrant parents in Kingsbridge, New York, Muriel Pollock was a superbly trained classical musician, a pianist, an organist, and a composer. She started out in ragtime with *The Carnival: Trot and One-Step* in 1914, but is better known for her delightful *Rooster Rag* of 1917. During the Twenties she composed songs and musical comedy scores, including *Jack and Jill* (1923) and *Pleasure Bound* (1929). She worked for the NBC radio network during the 1930's as staff organist and composer (*Piano Notions* suite, 1935). She earned a reputation as a thorough musician with a grasp of the classics, jazz, and popular music. She married songwriter Will Donaldson in 1938 and moved to Hollywood, where both worked in films. "Molly" Pollock was one of very few women in music to have a full, equal career. [22]

RAGTIME ALMANAC

SELECTIONS FROM THE RAGTIME WOMEN

COMPOSER	TITLE	PUBLISHED IN:
May Aufderheide	The Thriller (1909)	Indianapolis
Charlotte Blake	Poker Rag (1909)	New York-Detroit
Grace L. Bolen	The Smoky Topaz (1909)	Kansas City
Irene Cozad	Affinity Rag (1910)	Kansas City
Ella Hudson Day	Fried Chicken Rag (1912)	Galveston, Texas
Geraldine Dobyns	Bull Dog Rag (1908)	Memphis
Irene Giblin	Ketchup Rag (1910)	New York-Detroit
Imogene Giles	Red Peppers: Two-Step (1907)	Quincy, Illinois
Louise V. Gustin	X-N-Tric: Two-Step Characteristic (1900)	Detroit
Laverne Hanshaw	Niagara Rag (1914)	Dallas
Sadie Koninsky	Eli Green's Cakewalk (1898)	New York
Grace LeBoy	Pass the Pickles (1913)	New York-Detroit
Elma Ney McClure	The Cutter (1909)	Memphis
Frances Willard Neal	Nothin' Doin' (1914)	Dallas
Julia Lee Niebergall	Red Rambler Rag (1912)	Indianapolis
Mueiel Pollock	Rooster Rag (1917)	New York
Adaline Shepherd	Pickles and Peppers: A Ragtime Oddity (1906)	Milwaukee
Mabel Tilton	That Sentimental Rag (1913)	New York
Nell Wright Watson	That Texas Rag (1913)	Dallas
Susie Wells	The Rattler (1912)	Henrietta, Texas
Margaret Agnew White	Ragged Terry (1913)	Dallas
Gladys Yelvington	Piffle Rag (1911)	Indianapolis

Notes: Chapter 30

1. See quoted lyrics, Chapter 25.
2. Exactly that, because one, *Tres Moutarde*, was published in London, England.
3. See Note 23, Chapter 37: Zimmerman also includes the places of composition.
4. John Edward Hasse, "The Creation and Dissemination of Indianapolis Ragtime, 1897-1930, Ph.D. Dissertation, Indiana University, 265-266.
5. *Ibid.*, 105.
6. *Ibid.*, 89, 91, 93.
7. *Ibid.*, 102, 107-113. Harry and Albert Von Tilzer, Paul Dresser, and Cole Porter also came from Indiana.
8. *Ibid.*, 203.
9. *Ibid.*, 141, 145-147, 203.
10. Dick Zimmerman, "Cecil Duane Crabb: Ragtime Pianist, Composer, Artist, Florist, and Fisherman," *Rag Times* XXIX (September 1995):1-2; David Jasen and Gene Jones, *That American Rag: The Story of Ragtime from Coast to Coast*, 154; Hasse, Diss., 166, 171-172.
11. Max Morath, "May Aufderheide and the Ragtime Women," in *Ragtime: Its History, Composers, and Music*, John Edward Hasse, Ed.:157; Hasse, Diss., 134.
12. Which would grant Joplin's *Treemonisha* a favorable review a few years later.
13. Morath, 157-161; Jasen & Jones, *Am. Rag*, 153-157; Hasse, Diss., 134, 137-140, 177-180. Also *Rag Times*, XV (May 1981):1.
14. Hasse, Diss., 228.
15. Terry Parrish, "The Paul Pratt Story," Part I, *Rag Times*, XVII (January 1984): 2-5 and Part II, *Rag Times*, XVII (March 1984): 3-6; Hasse, Diss., 152-153, 156-157; Jasen & Jones, *Am. Rag*, 157.
16. Max Morath and John Edward Hasse, "Ragtime Compositions by Women," in Hasse, Ed., *Ragtime*, 368-375.
17. Nora Hulse and Nan Bostick, "Ragtime's Women Composers: An Annotated Lexicon," in *The Ragtime Ephemeralist*, No. 3: 106-139.
18. Jean Huling, "Irene Giblin, St.Louis Ragtime Queen," *Rag Times* XVIII (November 1984): 1-2; also Jean Huling, "Let's Remember Irene Giblin!" *Ragtimer* (September/October 1983): 5-8.
19. David Jasen and Trebor Tichenor, *Rags and Ragtime: A Musical History*, 72.
20. *Idem.*
21. Morath, in Hasse, 368-375; Hulse & Bostick, 106-139.
22. Morath, 161-162

31. THE ART OF RAG (VI): NEW YORK (II)

…In his travels, Joplin played in bars and brothels and dreamed of acceptance as a skilled, well-trained artist, imagined himself a famous and respected black composer. One dream, evidently, was to demonstrate that a black man could, only two decades after emancipation, be considered a great artist, creating music which was genuinely black but clearly a form of art comparable to the best white music. [1]

> If the *Green Pastures* was a picture of a God who was a Negro and of a heaven made for the dark of skin, then *Treemonisha* is the legend of a Negro Eden. [2]

We don't know when Scott Joplin started to write his opera *Treemonisha*, but it seems likely that it had been conceived and begun by the time he reached New York in mid-1907. New York, cultural center of the nation, was where you had to go to produce an original music drama. On March 5, 1908, Joplin's opera project received a positive notice from Lester Walton, critic for the New York *Age*, member of black showbiz's inner circles, a leading supporter of African-American music drama, and a devout crusader against darky stereotypes in entertainment (known today as racism). Walton stated, perhaps fancifully, that news of Joplin, "known as the apostle of ragtime" "composing scores for grand opera," had stirred" "music circles." He also noted that, "From ragtime to grand opera is certainly a big jump," and went on to add that, "Critics who have heard part of his new opera are very optimistic as to its future success." Quite likely, this was in response to information received from Joplin, and Walton was responding with encouragement and a friendly pat on the back, merely a puff piece, not to be taken literally. However it points to Joplin's operatic preoccupation as the main piece of baggage that he carried to New York. [3]

There is nothing grandiose about this claim of "grand opera." *Treemonisha* is essentially operatic: it contains recitative and aria passages, an overture and a prelude to Act Three, interactions between soloists and chorus, and ballet passages. The story depicts the post-emancipation struggle of a rural black community to progress from the debased conditions of slavery to the enlightened state of free citizens, i.e., equality. Joplin locates the setting precisely outside of Texarkana (where he grew up) a few miles from the Red River on the Arkansas side. The owners of the plantation have abandoned the big house, evidently preferring town amenities to rural isolation, and the ex-slaves remaining are either tenants or sharecroppers. At the outset, the inhabitants of this isolated setting are oppressed and terrorized by conjuremen, petty criminals averse to labor who are hardselling "bags o' luck." These felons flourish because superstition possesses this ignorant community of former slaves.

In the opening scene, three villains (Zodzedrick, Luddud, and Simon), pushing their bags o' luck at a rural assembly, are turned away by 18-year-old Treemonisha, the enlightened foundling daughter of Monisha and husband Ned, the village headman. Earlier, Monisha and Ned, wanting a better life for their daughter, had traded their services to an educated white woman in exchange for teaching her. Now Treemonisha has matured to stand against these oppressors. After she refutes their magical claims, they later kidnap her with homicidal intentions of throwing her into a giant wasp nest. This dire outcome is prevented when her friend—and protegee in learning—Remus rescues her and captures the culprits. In the conclusion the rescue is celebrated, the evildoers, at the intercession of Treemonisha, forgiven (in ignorance, they knew not what they did) and readmitted to the community, and Treemonisha accepts the people's call to lead them out of ignorance and superstition.

Treemonisha consists of 27 musical numbers, ranging from short bursts of action to full arias. These segments are performed by eleven named characters and the Chorus. Joplin did not adhere to any rigid sequence of recitative-aria. Instead there is an ensemble texture, sequences of interactions of characters with characters and characters with chorus. The Chorus of neighbors resembles that of Greek tragedy in that it functions as a full character, at times dominating the action. In giving the Chorus an active role instead of a passive function as background for the strife of characters, Joplin is portraying the drama of the group, the community. Some have observed that in its series of solo, ensemble, choral, dance, and instrumental numbers that this opera resembles a variety show or minstrel olio. [4] Since *Treemonisha* is clearly an allegory (symbolic representation) of the struggles of emancipated African Americans, others have found resemblances to that most allegorical of operas Mozart's *Magic Flute*. In one elaborate comparison, which discerns "uncanny parallels," the critic sees both works as an "exalted vision" in which truth-seekers are opposed by "comic villainy," "hassled by monsters" (here, wasps & bears), and menaced by three creatures of evil (Mozart's Three Ladies—Joplin's three conjurers). [5]

The opera does not consist of a series of rags and raggy songs stitched together (which may have been true of the lost *Guest of Honor*). The vocal idiom is closer to black folksongs, but there is also much of light opera or operetta. Monisha's songs ("The Sacred Tree," "I Want To See My Child") are certainly operatic, as is Treemonisha's "We Ought To Have a Leader." But Remus's "Wrong Is Never Right" and Ned's "When Villains Ramble Far and Near" mix operatic and folk styles. More folk-like are the delightful "Superstition" sequence with Simon and Chorus and the sententious Parson Alltalk's "Good Advice", and very folk-like are the ring song "We're Goin' Around," the comic barbershop quartet number "We Will Rest Awhile," and the choral selection "Aunt Dinah Has Blowed De Horn." The Overture, Prelude to Act Three, and "Frolic of the Bears" fully engage the orchestra. But ragtime, stylistically, was there all along in the syncopations inherent in black culture. A reward comes in the Finale, "A Real Slow Drag," a sequence of black ragtime dancing, with Treemonisha and Chorus singing the steps, as all perform them. This last may well be Joplin's masterpiece, delightful and glorious, ragtime triumphant!

After several refusals, Joplin self-published the piano-vocal score of *Treemonisha* in May 1911. He offered it at $2.50 and again notified Lester Walton, who duly informed readers of the New York *Age* that the "colored composer" of *Maple Leaf Rag* had completed music, lyrics, and book of a three-act opera set in rural Arkansas. [6] Joplin sent a review copy to the *American Musician and Art Journal,* which had been previously favorable toward him. This small investment paid the major return of a thoughtful and quite laudatory review. The editor-critic hailed the composer for serving his race as teacher and for creating "a thoroughly American opera," which had accomplished "an entirely new phase of musical art" (no less!). In praising Joplin for creating an "indigenous" work (an American story told in American music), the reviewer faulted one of the country's foremost men of music, Professor Horatio Parker of Yale (the teacher of Charles Ives), whose prize-winning opera *Mona* fell short of *Treemonisha's* example as a genuine product of American culture ("sprung from our soil"). [7]

But praise from a white learned publication failed to impress hard-bitten African-American promoters and showmen (who probably didn't read such things), who had other problems and agendas. African-American music dramas, popular half a dozen years ago when *Clorindy* (1898) and *In Dahomey* (1903) had played to full houses on Broadway, had lost appeal to white audiences. The last black shows of Williams and Walker (*Bandana Land*, opened 2-3-08) and Cole and the Johnsons (*Shoo-Fly Regiment*, 8-6-07, and *Red Moon*, 5-3-09) had struggled to keep open and pay expenses. All had disappointing New York runs and difficult tours, booked into small houses for short runs. Black musical comedy's greatest setbacks came from the deaths Ernest Hogan (1909), George Walker (1911), and Bob Cole (1911), who had been its chief creators and leaders (Chapter 26).

Audiences are fickle, and in 1907 two new trends drew them away from black shows. On July 8, 1907—at the very time Scott Joplin arrived with a plan to raise the quality of black music drama—Florenz Ziegfeld presented his *Follies of 1907* as a starring vehicle for his wife Anna Held. The inaugural *Follies* somewhat resembled its predecessor, the famous Paris revue *Follies Bergere*, but with Nora Bayes in the cast and the "Anna Held Girls" to entice the gentlemen in the audience, it was not a copycat show. From the start "Flo" Ziegfeld kept adding and subtracting material in the quest for his unique theatrical recipe. By 1908, he had manipulated his annual *Follies* into the "glorification" of the American girl. Tall, leggy, gorgeously costumed women promenading to elegant music, punctuated by the routines of comics, sold out the houses night after night. [8]

On October 21st Franz Lehar's operetta *The Merry Widow* reached Broadway and eclipsed everything else. Within a few months, as many as six road companies had fanned out to premiere *Merry Widow* across the land. Its eponymous "Waltz" and the songs "Maxim's" and "Vilja" became instant classics. For the next seven years, indigenous productions, other than the *Follies*, stirred little interest. Not until Irving Berlin's *Watch Your Step* tore loose with the bright dancing of Vernon and Irene Castle to its fresh, raggy score in 1914, did American musical comedy revive. Lehar followed up with five more light operatic confections, none of which measured up to the first. But the rage for operetta brought in other European imports, including two by Emmerich Kalman and one each by Oscar Strauss, Heinrich Reinhardt, Rudolph Friml, and even Johann Strauss, whose *Die Fledermaus* (1874) was retreaded as *The Merry Countess* (8-20-12). The most prolific of the operetta men was Ireland-born Victor Herbert (1859-1924) who opened eleven different shows in seven years. Of all the would-be *Merry Widow* clones, the few big hits were Oscar Strauss's *The Chocolate Soldier* (9-13-09), based upon G.B. Shaw's *Arms and the Man*, Heinrich Reinhardt's *The Spring Maid* (12-26-10), Victor Herbert's *Naughty Marietta* (11-7-10), Rudolf Friml's *The Firefly* (12-2-12), and Emmerich Kalman's *Sari* (1-13-14). This seven-year binge of *alt* Vienna and idyllic Ruritania proved to be only an intermission, but it inhibited indigenous music drama, and not until Sissle and Blake's *Shuffle Along* in 1921 did African-American musical comedy return to Broadway. [9]

Which very much diminished the prospects of Scott Joplin, who had no Broadway illusions and aimed lower. In September 1911 he found a prospective producer in Thomas Johnson, who had recently operated Harlem's small Crescent Theatre (36-38 West 135th Street). Johnson proposed to stage *Treemonisha* in Atlantic City, which intention Joplin announced in the *Age* (10-5-11), calling for eleven "colored singers" and forty chorus members. A hectic period followed with Joplin holding rehearsals and arranging orchestrations with the aid of old friend Sam Patterson. Then abruptly, for whatever reason, the project fell apart. Desperate to go on, Joplin rented a hall in Harlem and invited some other prospective backers and friends to a concert performance at which he played and conducted from the piano. The audience of seventeen was underwhelmed, momentum was lost, and nothing came of it. [10] These urban blacks reacted negatively, put off perhaps because *Treemonisha* reminded them of unhappy rural things put behind them. Also the history in it rang falsely: Reconstruction had begun with hopes of betterment, a leg up from white emancipators. But the Reign of Terror after Reconstruction brought instead lynching, race riots, disfranchisement, and all of the anguish of segregation, which had dashed all hopes. Instead of leadership, they had known abandonment, poverty, and cruelty. [11]

Joplin's notion of a female leader also may have rung falsely to the opera's first hearers. The idea of a young girl as agent of deliverance must have seemed an oddity, if not downright ridiculous. To label this as a precursor of feminism would distort what we know of the period, and *Treemonisha*, which deals with rural concerns and achieving a modest enlightenment beyond superstition, depicts a culture not yet ready to take up "votes for women." Recently Joplin's biographer Edward Berlin has come up with an inspired guess. Convincingly he argues for the opera as Joplin's memorial to his too briefly known, beloved second wife Freddie. He conjectures that Freddie may have exerted a consciousness-raising effect upon Joplin's sense of racial heritage. He also notes that the one piece dedicated to Freddie was *Chrysanthemum,* subtitled, *An Afro-American Intermezzo.* And *Treemonisha,* which depicts and celebrates African-American life, tells the story of a young woman, and, curiously, it is set in 1884, the year of Freddie's birth. [12] Finally we have the evidence of Joplin's monomania. In his final years, the opera absorbed him entirely: completing, publishing, orchestrating, and presenting it. He expended all of his resources, creative and material, on getting *Treemonisha* before the public. Had his powers not been undermined and drained away by a destructive illness (Chapter 35), he might have succeeded.

II

Epilog: What Might Have Been

In creating what we call the "classic rag", and in publishing a significant body of these works, Scott Joplin earned a portion of respect and honor among his colleagues in music and in the African-American entertainment milieu. In saying this, we may ask why his work received so little recognition and remembrance? One commentator suggests that part of the difficulty came from being "lost in urban America," the state of being diminished by the crowd and out of step with urban ways. [13] But this is the plight of the stranger, the unintegrated newcomer, for most a temporary condition. Cities are not undifferentiated masses that dissolve human identities. Cities subdivide into neighborhoods, work places, institutions, interest groups, and families. Scott Joplin spent his last ten years in New York, and from day one, he knew where to reside and where to find friends and connections. Besides John Stark, he came to know such music publishers as Ed Marks (Stern Co.), Ted Snyder, and Irving Berlin. [14] Undoubtedly he made the rounds of the watering holes of Black Bohemia, including those of Ike Hines and Barron Wilkins. As a theatre-goer, he must have attended Broadway's current black shows during 1907-1910: *Bandana Land, Shoo-Fly Regiment,* and *Red Moon*. He also made himself known to Lester Walton and the New York *Age,* read by all literate African Americans. Reticent though he may have been, Joplin always put himself forward as the composer of *Maple Leaf* and "King of Ragtime Writers."

Why then was he so little known to such important black musicians as Rosamond Johnson, Bert Williams, Harry Burleigh, or James Reese Europe? Along with other prominent black showmen, Joplin became a charter member of the Colored Vaudeville Benevolent Association (CVBA) at its founding in 1909. He contributed and helped organize some of its benefit performances, including one on January 10, 1910, which featured some of his music, including *Paragon Rag*, which he had previously dedicated to the CVBA, evidence of serious involvement. [15] From 1907 Joplin was visible in New York's black music and entertainment circles. How large a population did this involve? Could all of the African American performers, musicians, composers, business people, and others in vaudeville, musical comedy, the music business, and cabaret have exceeded several hundred in New York City before the 1920's? Joplin belonged to a select few of blacks in showbusiness and art music who <u>composed</u>. He was a successful composer with at least one hit to his credit. The *Maple Leaf Rag* had become a classic, the pattern for ragtime piano solos. The *Cascades* and *Pine Apple Rag* also attained some popularity. Then, in 1910 this small world of black entertainers and music professionals read in the *Age* that Joplin had composed an opera. Good, bad, or indifferent, an opera by a colleague amounted to significant cultural news. Why then didn't someone in the Marshall Hotel group—James Reese Europe, Rosamond Johnson, Will Marion Cook, Will Vodery, or Ford Dabney—call on Scott Joplin and invite him to share his aspirations? His and their interests were mutual.

This disconnection perplexes even more when we consider the role of James Reese Europe (1880-1919) in opening up showbusiness and the musical arts to African Americans. Europe was more fortunate in background than Joplin. His family belonged to the nation's small black middle class, and he grew up in cities instead of culturally deprived rural areas. After childhood in Mobile, Alabama, his family relocated in Washington, D.C. (his father was a civil servant), where he attended the "Preparatory High School for Colored Youth," founded in 1870 and the first such for African Americans (later renamed Dunbar High School for the poet). High standards demanded much from its students, and 80% of its graduates went on to post-secondary institutions, a remarkable accomplishment in that time. Like Joplin, he had musical parents, but unlike him, Europe's parents could afford music instruction, one of his teachers being Enrico Hurlei, an assistant director of Sousa's Marine Band. Also unlike Scott Joplin, Jim Europe was a big boy, outgoing, popular, and an organizer. The family ran into a time of troubles when father Henry Europe died in 1899, as Jim was about to start his career. He had to wait four years before he could go to New York, helping to support his mother and sister Mary. By 1904, older brother John had established himself as a pianist in New York cafes, and Mary had graduated and begun her career in Washington as an art musician and teacher. Jim now took his violin to New York, but found no openings for black violinists (theatre orchestras hired only white musicians), so he switched to mandolin and piano, getting enough gigs to survive on. While getting started, he continued his music studies, on his own and with Harry Burleigh, a singer, composer, and black musician of some renown. Right off, this drew him into the circle at the Marshall Hotel, which recognized his abilities, intelligence, and appealing personal qualities. [16]

At the Marshall Europe found a helpful friend in John W. Love, private secretary to Rodman Wanamaker, who offered him a gig to furnish music for Rodman's birthday in February 1905. Thus began Europe's close connection to the wealthy Wanamakers of Philadelphia (department store) and to white society folk, for whose gala functions he would increasingly supply musicians and orchestras. Already in 1904, he had been hired as music director for *A Trip to Africa*, a musical farce at the black Third Avenue Theatre (Will Vodery replaced him on the show's tour). Then early in 1905, Ernest Hogan put together the innovative "Memphis Students" show, with Europe playing in the twenty-member band. The Memphis Students (who were show people and not students) delivered a thirty-minute vaudeville act that proved the hit of the summer. Subtitled "Songs of the Black Folk," it opened at Proctor's Thirty-second Street Theatre in the early spring, ran for several weeks, and moved to the prestigious Hammerstein's Victoria in June for the rest of the summer. Audiences found a fascination in the novelty of a band whose members sang while playing, sometimes getting up and dancing to their syncopations. There was also the unusual instrumentation of mandolins, banjos, and harp guitars which filled the air with sound effects of plucking and strumming, rather exotic and strange to white audiences accustomed to violin textures. Will Marion Cook had composed most of the music, and its total effect pointed Jim Europe in new directions. [17] James Weldon Johnson who saw this act commented:

> The Memphis Students deserve the credit that should go to pioneers. They were the beginners of several things that still persist as jazz-band features. They introduced the dancing conductor, Will Dixon,…. All through a number he would keep his men together by dancing out the rhythm….Often an easy shuffle would take him across the whole front of the band….Another innovation…was the trick trap drummer. "Buddy" Gilmore…it is doubtful if he has been surpassed as a performer of juggling and acrobatic stunts while manipulating a dozen noise-making devices aside from the drums. [18]

After this stint, the Cole and Johnson team hired Jim Europe as their music director, and from 1906 through 1910, he conducted, arranged, and even composed some of the songs for their two shows (Chapter 26), spending much of this time out on tours.[19] Between these shows, he joined S.H. Dudley's Smart Set Company to direct and conduct *The Black Politician*, a slight musical comedy that never made it to Broadway. After *Red Moon*, he conducted Bert Williams's *Mr. Lode of Koal* (minus the dying George Walker) until it closed in March 1910; this was the final musical comedy for both. By now James Reese Europe had reached the top of his profession, recognized as a gifted conductor, composer, and leader of fellow black artists. Where Hogan, Walker, and Cole had stood in black showbusiness, only he remained. With European operetta now dominant, musical comedy, of whatever race, had lost appeal. Many former theatre musicians now had to find gigs in orchestras and ensembles that played for the balls, parties, and ceremonial occasions of the rich and for the institutions and lodges of the middle class. Local #310 of the American Federation of Musicians (AFM) excluded blacks, and white musicians refused to let blacks play in theatre orchestras. Jobs were scarce going into 1910, and, lacking a union, black musicians had no place to gather, no hiring hall except the Marshall Hotel (used by many as a professional address).

Besides the abilities and qualities noted above, Jim Europe's powers derived much from a large measure of self-confidence. The constant endurance of white folks' rejection and indifference engendered feelings of inferiority and depression in most blacks, tending to erode self-confidence. Apparently unsusceptable to these "blues," Europe perceived a simple solution to this employment problem: organization. Previously he had joined the black Chicago Local # 208 of the AF of M, and now (April 1910) he gathered 135 fellow musicians into the "Clef Club," a combined union and booking agency. Supporting this move were Joe Jordan, Ford Dabney, Clarence Williams, and brother John Europe. Jim, with his Wanamaker connections, and his associates, who brought in other similar connections, had already been supplying the rich and elite with occasional and dance music. Suddenly after 1910, their gigs multiplied as the ragtime dances, e.g., turkey trot, grizzly bear, etc., became the latest "craze," and "respectable" people dared to dance them in public places. With its elite support, the Clef Club zoomed upward on this major trend because of the insatiable demand that materialized for the exciting syncopations of black musicians. Just as suddenly, white orchestras found too many blank dates on their calendars. Within the City, out on Long Island, down in Palm Beach, over in London and Paris, the Clef Club struggled to handle almost more business than it could take care of.

In December 1910, the Clef Club opened its headquarters at 134 West 53rd Street, across from the Marshall, and Europe had not only solved his colleagues' employment problems, he also revolutionized their working conditions. There were abuses to correct. Previously it had been the practice to hire black musicians for menial jobs, dishwashing, bussing tables, cleaning up, and they had received only the small wages specified for such jobs. To supplement their miniscule guarantees, they relied on tips for their musical offerings. Jim Europe ended all that. Now hiring became contractual for a fixed salary or scale; transportation had to be paid to and from the jobsite, plus room and board for overnight assignments. Such enhanced status called for the reciprocity of "good form," and Europe responded with a strictly enforced dress code. For advance bookings, tuxedos, cleaned and pressed, had to be worn, and for gigs on short notice, dark suits, white shirts, bow ties. After reporting to the Clef Club and passing a rigorous inspection, each dance orchestra went out under the rubric "(Someone) and His Clef Club Orchestra." Many customers demanded a "Europe" orchestra for their functions, and he often duplicated himself by sending out "Europe's" orchestras led by assistants. During the evening, he would turn up briefly at each location, become visible on the podium, then, after the set, move on to the next event.[20]

Beyond full and profitable employment, and the dividend of fellowship, the Clef Club had musical aspirations. To pay the office and personnel costs of the CC, Europe decided that its members would display their talents at semi-annual benefits. The first "Musical Melange and Dance Fest" was held at Harlem's Manhattan Casino (155th Street and Eighth Avenue) on May 27, 1910. There were the predictable variety acts followed by dancing, but the remarkable feature of the evening was the inaugural performance of the "Clef Club Symphony Orchestra." Thus had germinated in Jim Europe the seed of his experience with the Memphis Students, a seed from vaudeville that sprouted to symphonic dimensions. He had a different take on ragtime. To him ragtime was a dog with a bad name, a name without cultural respect; for white people, "ragtime" carried a burden of low-minded connotations, of the gutter and loose morals. Where Joplin had embraced the ragtime label and tried to elevate it to respectability, Europe repudiated it:

>...In my opinion there never was any such music as "ragtime." "Ragtime" is merely a nickname, or rather a fun name given to Negro rhythm by our Caucasian brother musicians.

He saw it as a temporary pejorative and noted that

>...so many eminent Anglo-musicians have become innoculated with that serum—Negro rhythm ("ragtime"), and with their knowledge of musical theory embroider the plaintive ragtime theme with a wealth of contrapuntal organization and a marvelous enrichment of tone coloring and complicated instrumentation.... No! "Ragtime" is neither dead nor dying, but is *undergoing a vast development* [italics added] and is more popular now than ten years ago. [21]

This gives a surprising glimpse of the musical vision that drove Europe. Like Joplin, he prospected for cultural gold among the detritus of the popular; both appreciated the falseness of the dichotomy of serious (art) vs. popular (non-art) music. But where Joplin could only follow his inspiration, Europe could convincingly display his vision to others.

Instead of "ragtime," Europe combined the elements of syncopation, instrumentation, and musical arrangement into something symphonic on May 27, 1910, with a company of 100—instrumentalists, singers, dancers—and ten upright pianos, for a thirty-minute concert of previously unheard music. Among the works presented were Joe Jordan's *That Teasing Rag* and Paul Lincke's concert waltz *Spring, Beautiful Spring*. On October 20, at the "Second Grand Musical Melange and Dance Fest," works by Clef Club members William Tyers, Al Johns, Henry Creamer, Tom Lemonier, and Ford Dabney were performed. And Europe introduced what became the CC Symphony's signature work, his *Clef Club March*. [22] By now a semi-annual tradition, the "Monster Melange and Dance Fest" of March 11, 1911, continued the symphony-variety-dance formula with more new compositions by "Eminent Colored Composers," including Will Marion Cook for the first time. The orchestra, principally of strings (violins, mandolins, banjos, guitars, harp guitars, pianos) was augmented this time with an organ, two flutes, and two clarinets, its first woodwinds. The program consisted of "sacred music, waltz, and ragtime compositions" (according to Lester Walton in the NY *Age*). The *Clef Club March* was repeated and Harry Burleigh's arrangements of spirituals comprised the sacred selections. The concert closed with Cook's rousing "Darktown Is Out Tonight" from *Clorindy*. Europe also conducted his *Lorraine Waltzes*, named for his mother. [23]

On May 2, 1912, white philanthropists—who felt Europe's attraction as much as his own race did—raised the Clef Club Symphony Orchestra out of the ghetto to the stage of Carnegie Hall. The original plan had been to stage a benefit concert for the Music Settlement School in Harlem, which Europe supported as a training facility for the next generation of CC members. From this impulse emerged the idea for a "Concert of Negro Music" to attract white support. The few whites who had attended the CC's "Musical Melanges" had been impressed by what they had heard in Harlem and concluded that it should be brought to white audiences (lately out on the town with the new syncopated dance music). Still this was <u>terra incognita;</u> no one could be certain as to how a Carnegie Hall audience would react to the efforts of musicians who played in cabaret and dance orchestras (a majority of whom did not even <u>read</u> music). But those who had experienced the Clef Club music prevailed over the doubters, and this historic "first" took place. It was decided to comprehensively program Negro music: traditional, religious, secular, modern, vocal, instrumental. Besides the orchestra, performers consisted of a choir from St.Philip's Church; the Royal Poinciana Quartette (plantation songs Stephen Foster-style); vocal soloists Harry Burleigh, Rosamond Johnson, and contralto Elizabeth Payne; the "Versatile Entertainers Quintette," a guitar-banjo group out of the CC orchestra; and a piano solo from Rosamond Johnson, who played his *Danse Heroique*. [24]

Because scheduled gigs had to be fulfilled, preparing was hectic: rehearsals were few and the orchestra could get together only in sections. Initial sales were sluggish, but a late publicity push brought an SRO, packed sell-out. The 125-strong orchestra led off with its signature *Clef Club March*; Europe's biographer, Reid Badger, states: "When the chorus joined the orchestra to conclude the rousing piece, the audience—for the first time at any concert in the United States composed equally of the two races—came to its feet and New York 'woke up to the fact that it had something new in music.'"[25] From the "high" of this overture, the concert presented 21 works, including Rosamond Johnson's "Lit'l Gal" (lyrics by Paul Lawrence Dunbar), "Panama—Characteristic Dance" by Will Tyers, and "Swing Along" (*In Dahomey*) and "Rain Song" by Will Marion Cook. Europe also contributed his "Lorraine Waltzes" and a new march "Strength of the Nation." Having never heard anything like it, whites found it amazing, the texture of sound made by banjos, mandolins, guitars, strings, 14 upright pianos (served by New York's best ragtime pianists), and percussion. One spectator put it this way:

> "Barbaric," we exclaimed in astonished admiration. That an orchestra of such power, freshness, vitality, and originality could have remained so long undiscovered in novelty-hunting New York, was a silent and reproachful comment on the isolation of the Negro Quarter. [26]

The evening's hit seems to have been Cook's "Swing Along." The temperamental Cook had been invited to conduct his pieces, had dithered about it, changed his mind several times, and finally taken a place in the string section. "Swing Along" received three encores, and Cook took his bows with tears, too choked up to speak. [27] David Mannes, the white musician who had been instrumental in bringing the Clef Club downtown, described Europe as "an amazingly inspiring conductor. Of a statuesquely powerful build, he moved with simple and modest grace, always dominating this strange assemblage before him with quiet control." [28]

The 1912 Clef Club concert proved a climactic event, probably the apogee of James Reese Europe's tragically short life. [29] Its effects opened whatever doors had remained closed to black musicians. Not only did black musicians have all the jobs they could handle, they found themselves preferred over whites. Nor was this concert a one-time thing; the Clef Club Symphony Orchestra returned to Carnegie Hall in 1913 and 1914 (after this Europe moved on to other work). Eubie Blake, later a close associate and friend, affirmed Europe's historical significance on (at least) two documented occasions, comparing him with Martin Luther King. In one instance: "To colored musicians he was as important—he did as much as Martin Luther King for the rest of the Negro people." And the other: "He was our benefactor and inspiration. Even more, he was the Martin Luther King of music." [30]

But why was Scott Joplin absent from the feast? Had he attended any of these Carnegie Hall Concerts, and what were his reactions? Europe, Dabney, Tyers, and Jordan were creative ragtimers, which raises two questions: What did they know of Joplin's work? Did they know he lived in New York? Ed Marks, one of Joplin's publishers, had this to say in his memoir of the pop music scene (*They All Sang*) about Joplin and Europe in oddly consecutive paragraphs:

> Jim Europe, who was to make a national name as a bandmaster during the war and lead the first jazz invasion of Europe thereafter, teamed up with Ford Dabney, and wrote so many dance hits that we had to spell their names backward on some title pages, "Eporue and Yenbad," to lend an appearance of variety.
>
> Scott Joplin, *another great trick pianist* [italics added], gave us "Scott Joplin's Rag" [sic]. He is better remembered for "Maple Leaf Rag," which, in the words of Chris Smith, "ain't nobody can play it, but lots of folks like to play at it."
>
> Joplin's was a curious story. His compositions became more intricate, until they were almost jazz Bach. "Boy," he used to tell all the other colored song writers, "when I'm dead twenty-five years, people are only going to begin to recognize me." He wrote an opera called *Treemonisha*, and had it printed, music and all, at his own expense. Joplin went mad, and *Treemonisha* remains up in the stately Harlem mansion of his widow, an awesome problem for the colored musicians who frequent the house and "play at it." [31]

Marks' company, Joseph Stern, published four of Joplin's rags, including "Scott Joplin's [New] Rag" noted above. Marks reminisces breezily about ragtime dances and the "colored" composers who helped meet a new demand. In this context, he mentions in passing Charles "Luckey" Roberts and jumps to Jim Europe in the following paragraph. Then, abruptly, in almost a non sequitur, he shifts to Joplin, who did <u>not</u> supply music for the grizzly bear, bunny hug, or fox-trot. Instead he glimpses a "trick pianist," which Joplin wasn't, whose story is modified by "curious." But Marks isn't wandering off into non sequiturs; the context is music for entertainment, dancing, vaudeville. Joplin played in vaudeville, and he composed the *MLR*. Vaudeville featured many "trick" artists, singers who could reach and hold very high or low notes, tap dancers sustaining a set of steps at high speed, drummers banging out a variety of noises at a deafening volume, jugglers who sang while juggling. Audiences loved acts with "trick" sequences. Jay Roberts' *Entertainer's Rag* of 1910 was composed to thrill the rubes out on the vaudeville circuits; with its counterpoint of "Yankee Doodle" and "Dixie," it grabbed attention. It became very familiar and popular, and pianists won contests with it. [32] Thus Marks associates Joplin's masterpiece with hackneyed musical material like the Roberts work: to him both fall into the pigeonhole of "trick" rags, music for the virtuoso pianist to capture an audience. Similarly Marks characterizes Europe as an ordinary pop composer who turned out danceable music. Although he (Marks) published some of their music, he exhibits no awareness of their great contributions to music and to African-American culture. Joplin comes off in Marks' garbled version as some kind of eccentric who turned out very difficult, i.e., unsaleable, music, including (of all things) an opera! Nor is he surprised that a black trick piano player who thought he could write an opera went mad. A decade or so later Joplin has been reduced to a character in an anecdote.

We can only fall back on Joplin's reticence. A reserved black man, conditioned never to interrupt white folks, he let his music speak for him. The public, when they came across a rare copy of the sheet music, found his scores difficult and forgot all but *Maple Leaf Rag*. Marks went the public one or two better (Joplin had been in his catalog) by recalling the complexity of the scores and the name of the opera. (Where did the "stately Harlem mansion" come from?) All we can conclude is that Joplin managed to remain obscure in his own time. What else can explain Europe's omission of his finest ragtime contemporary? It could not have been merely because Europe rejected something with a ragtime label; he devoted much of his life to the music and musicians of his race. Had Europe approached Joplin for something to program for Carnegie Hall, the audience might have heard one or more of his rag masterpieces, *Pine Apple Rag, Heliotrope Bouquet,* or *The Cascades,* or perhaps *Solace* or a selection from *Treemonisha.* Any of these would have enhanced the quality of the evening. [33]

RAGTIME ALMANAC

Ragtime Topics For Future Research [34]

1. Cutting contests and other performance settings
2. The degree of simplification of ragtime scores for publication
3. Contemporary African-American attitudes toward ragtime
4. Extent of improvisation in performance
5. Ragtime outside the U.S.
6. Home consumption of ragtime in the U.S.
7. Contemporary understanding and awareness or ragtime's varieties
8. Differences between styles of black and white ragtime
9. Influences on ragtime of German and other non-U.S. ethnic music

Notes: Chapter 31

1. William Schafer and Johannes Riedell, *The Art of Ragtime: Form and Meaning of an Original Black American Art*, 219-220.
2. Rudy Blesh and Harriet Janis, *They All Played Ragtime*, 248.
3. James Haskins, *Scott Joplin*, 161-162; Edward A. Berlin, *King of Ragtime: Scott Joplin and His Era*, 176-177, identifies Walton as the writer.
4. Schafer & Riedell, 213, 218-219.
5. Hubert Saal, "Joplin's Black Gold," *Newsweek* (September 22, 1975): 62; Schafer & Riedell also find parallels with the *Magic Flute*, 222-223.
6. Berlin, *King*, 198-199.
7. *Ibid.*, 199-202; Haskins, 177-179. Parker's *Mona* had recently won the $10,000 Metropolitan Opera prize.
8. Gerald Bordman, *American Musical Theatre: A Chronicle*, 231.
9. *Ibid.*, 236-237.
10. Berlin, *King*, 214-215.
11. Schafer & Riedell, 221-222; Haskins, 191; also Russell Sanjek, *American Popular Music and Its Business: The First Four Hundred Years*, II, 301.
12. Berlin, *King*, 208.
13. Susan Curtis, *Dancing to a Black Man's Tune: A Life of Scott Joplin*, Chapter 5, 129 ff.
14. Edward B. Marks, *They All Sang: From Tony Pastor to Rudy Vallee*, 158-160.
15. Berlin, *King*, 189, 192-193.
16. Reid Badger, *A Life in Ragtime: A Biography of James Reese Europe*, 10-28.
17. *Ibid.*, 29-31.
18. James Weldon Johnson, *Black Manhattan*, 122.
19. Badger, 31-36, 38-42.
20. *Ibid.*, 52-60.
21. *Ibid.*, 51.
22. *Ibid.*, 57.
23. *Ibid.*, 59-60.
24. *Ibid.*, 62-63.
25. *Ibid.*, 66-67. The internal quote is from Tom Fletcher, *One Hundred Years of the Negro in Show Business*, 259.
26. Quoted in Badger, 67.
27. *Ibid.*, 68.
28. *Idem.*
29. He was killed, bleeding to death before help arrived, from a jacknife stab wound in the neck, in Boston in 1919, by his drummer, while on a triumphal tour with the military band he had led in France during the war.
30. First quotation: Al Rose, *Eubie Blake*, 57; the second: Bob Kimball and Bill Bolcom, *Reminiscing With Sissle and Blake*, 72.
31. Marks, 158-160.
32. David A. Jasen and Trebor Tichenor, *Rags and Ragtime: A Musical History*, 159-160. Roberts' work is not to be confused with Joplin's rag *The Entertainer*.
33. See comments in Curtis, 153.
34. John Edward Hasse, "The Creation and Dissemination of Indianapolis Ragtime, 1897-1930," 31.

32. TR: Regulation, Reform, Conservation

> ...the great development of industrialism means that there must be an increase in the supervision exercised by the government over business-enterprise. Such men as the members of this club should lead in the effort to secure proper supervision. Neither this people nor any other free people will permanently tolerate the use of the vast power conferred by vast wealth without lodging somewhere in the government the still higher power of seeing that this power is used for and not against the interests of the people as a whole.
>
> Theodore Roosevelt, Address to the Union League Club of Philadelphia
> (January 1905) [1]

Theodore Roosevelt went into his second term a popular president, determined to use his power to rally the nation behind his agenda. He had carried every state outside the "Solid South," winning 56.4% of the popular vote and 58% of the electoral vote (the highest electoral figure up to that time). [2] Free now of any party obligations to uphold the conservatism of McKinley, TR wanted to lead toward progressive goals. No radical, he saw himself as a _true_ conservative, preserver of American life and institutions against the revolutionary threats of anarchism and socialism (anarchist assassins were the terrorists of that time). He intended to save the capitalistic system from its own excesses. The great industrial combinations, or "trusts," logically tended toward monopoly, the end of competition. In this theoretical outcome, a few huge mega-corporations—U.S. Steel and Standard Oil presaged such a possibility—would gain absolute control of the nation.

Therefore it was imperative that the people, acting through their elected government, modify the capitalistic system, change it from predator to benefactor. TR had come to realize that there were two very different approaches to pulling corporate fangs. The first was judicial, the course prescribed under the Sherman Anti-trust Act of 1890. Under the Sherman Act combinations "in restraint of trade" that hindered competition were illegal (and had to be broken up). He used this remedy in the Northern Securities Case (1902-04) which broke up a monopoly in western railroads attempted by the Hill-Morgan-Harriman interests. This was a landmark case with major results in defining illegal combinations. (Chapter 15) But the President saw no cure-all in judicial remedies. Such suits were costly, time-consuming, and limited in effects to the entities in the case; they usually did not result in any general applications. And over time they failed to reverse the tendency of corporations to combine into larger entities. He concluded that the only way to transform the bad into the good trusts was, not to flail away judicially at their immensities, but to take the _executive_ (and legislative) approach of regulating them. Let them grow but control their practices and prices, keep them fair and honest. The key word here was "interstate": all things affecting more than one state came under federal jurisdiction and control. [3]

The regulation of interstate commerce cut a wide swath: shipping costs, passenger rates, pure food, pure drugs, child labor, employer liability for work injuries, hours of work, supervision of insurance companies, and protection of natural resources. Railroads were central to the creation of progressive policies: They were the largest entities; they reached everywhere and touched the lives of everyone in more ways than anything else. If railroads could be controlled, the rest of the agenda seemed reachable. Theodore itched to win this battle in 1905, but the first railroad bill, to enable the Interstate Commerce Commission (ICC) to adjust rates, went down in the last session of the "old" Congress elected in 1902. (In that leisurely time Congresses did not assemble until the end of the year following the year in which they were elected; the Congress elected in 1904 did not sit until December 1905.) However, investigations during the summer of 1905 revealed that railroad rates unfairly penalized the small shipper. Disclosures of these and other corporate abuses galvanized the public to demand reforms, and the President stood out front speaking regularly on railroad rate reform, climaxing his campaign in his annual message given to the "new" Congress in December 1905.

His message called for pure food and drug laws, supervision of insurance companies, an investigation of child labor, an employer's liability law for the District of Columbia (for states to copy), and legislation authorizing the ICC to set maximum railroad passenger and freight rates following official complaints. To hard-core conservatives who ran the Senate, this was all political pie-in-the-sky, merely Teddy reaching for headlines, but he showed his teeth on rates when the Department of Justice ordered U.S. Attorneys to charge corporations giving or taking rebates with criminal conspiracy in violating the Elkins Anti-Rebate Act passed in 1903. Conviction meant jail time for corporate executives. Within days grand jury indictments hit Standard Oil, American Tobacco, the big meat packers, and several railroads. [4]

Corporate moguls and senate conservatives deeply resented being shot at by the "loose cannon" in the White House with the resulting media exposure. They believed in the sovereignty of ownership, in absolute rights to set rates and prices; they, not the government, were the true authorities. Government could intervene only to preserve public order or for national defense. Thus they preached *laissez-faire* to the fullest, a nearly total freedom from government restrictions; however they missed the blindspot. Actually government had <u>given</u> them many things, e.g., land grants for railroads, exclusive—and free—franchises for utilities and transportation companies, tax exemptions, dredging of rivers and harbors, geographical and engineering surveys, law enforcement, protection of property and personnel. For Theodore Roosevelt *laissez-faire* was out of date—and out of control. In developmental stages, entrepreneurs had risked much on new enterprises. Huge profits came to those who succeeded. This was fair enough; big risks deserved enormous rewards. But now, successful, secure in their bigness—and furnishing a livelihood to large numbers of employees—the giant corporations had become answerable to the nation. With profits assured, risks now minimal, huge profits were no longer justified. It was a new and different game, and the rules had to be changed for the common good, toward a redistribution of wealth through better wages and taxes to bring social justice. [5]

Essentially what TR wanted was what he called the "Square Deal," a fair shake for all interests, capital, workers, farmers, small businessmen, and he believed the national government's role was to bring this about by mediating conflicts with progressive measures. The term originated in a conversation with reform journalist Lincoln Steffens shortly after taking office, over the political practice of *quid pro quo*. One day Steffens remonstrated that Theodore, his eye on the 1904 nomination, was cutting deals and using patronage to gain power instead of going all-out for reform. To provoke a response, Steffens challenged with, "All you represent is the square deal.' 'That's it!' he shouted, and rising to his feet, he banged the desk with his hands. 'That's my slogan: the square deal. I'll throw that out in my next statement.'"[6] Theodore aimed for progress, but he had to have results. Ideals had to be "realizable." Thus at some point radical challenges resisted by unyielding conservatives had to give way to compromise, half-a-loaf, something for everyone. Declare victory, return home, and regroup for the next battle. And in compromising, bargain for a little more besides.

His proposals for government regulation of transportation costs and the purity of food and drugs were without precedent. Never before had government laid regulating hands on private property. *Laissez-faire* (which most interpreted to mean "hands off") had come "under the gun." The railroad rate bill reached the House of Representatives at the end of January 1906, taking its name from its sponsor Rep. William P. Hepburn (R., Iowa). Because the popularly elected House reflected the strong nationwide support of both the President and the reforms he called for, the "Hepburn Act" received a quick passage on February 8, with a mere seven negative votes. Die-hard opposition lay waiting in the Senate, which was elected, not by the people, but by state legislatures, where business interests tended to dominate. Led by "railroad senators" Nelson Aldrich (R.I.), Chauncey DePew (N.Y.), Joseph Foraker (OH), and Stephen Elkins (W.VA), about 24 of the "Old Guard" Republicans found themselves unable to defeat the bill, either in committee or on the floor, because of its popularity, but they intended to effectively nullify it with amendments before eventual passage. It fell to Elkins, Chairman of the Senate Interstate Commerce Committee, to sponsor the bill and guide it through the legislative process, but he demonstrated his hostility to the bill in a singular fashion by refusing the assignment. This was a measure proposed by his own Republican Party, and this denial of senatorial courtesy (almost unheard of) ripped across the chamber like a cannon ball, its target the White House, where it scored a very palpable hit. Then Elkins followed up this insult with an injury: he designated as the Hepburn Bill's floor leader, not the next ranking Republican, but the ranking Democrat on the committee, Senator "Pitchfork Ben" Tillman of South Carolina.

Tillman and TR cordially detested each other. As a virulent hater of the black race, Tillman had damned the President for having Booker T. Washington to dinner, and TR had banned Tillman from White House functions in 1902 for attacking a fellow senator with his fists. Now the President had to deal with Tillman (through an intermediary), and Tillman had to stand up for the poor farmers of his state victimized by the high costs of shipping their cotton and tobacco. Tillman, instead of enjoying the spectacle of majority Republicans battling one another over the measure, had to get cracking on rallying his fellow Democrats (about one-third of the Senate), many of whom shared his loathing of TR (high political drama for aficionados of politics). He needed a minimum of 26 Democrats to add bipartisan support to the Republican minority of 20 (46 needed for passage). While debate went on for 60 days during March-April of 1906, the two sometime antagonists worked on compromises.

Meanwhile measures for meat inspection and purity of food and drugs followed different courses. Popular demand for these measures had built up because scientists like Dr. Harvey W. Wiley, principal chemist in the Department of Agriculture, had performed studies and presented evidence about adulterated foods, misbranded patent medicines, and filthy conditions in food processing. Drawing on these findings, journalists, both sensational and otherwise, had aroused the public to a disturbed awareness and fear of the products they consumed. The President agreed with these conclusions and supported demands that the government "do something" about these dangers, but he was troubled about irresponsible journalism that distorted the truth by exaggeration and misrepresentation of facts. He saw that conservatives often defeated reform measures by simply refuting sensational claims. He also sought to prevent the Old Guard from pinning on him the radical label. During these months he countered extremists in a speech that became famous when he called them "muckrakers," comparing them to "the man with the muckrake" in *Pilgrim's Progress* who became so fixated on raking up muck, i.e., evil, that he ignored the offer of a heavenly crown. Although the President was gunning for sensationalists, many honest, earnestly disposed writers at first resented the label, feeling that TR had become too thin-skinned and resentful. In time "muckraking" lost its sting and was felt to be a badge of honor, as the term became applied to all who had wielded pens for progressive causes.

The pure food bill reached the Senate first in February 1906, and immediately became blocked in committee. However the American Medical Association reacted by warning Majority Leader Senator Aldrich that it would turn its 135,000 members loose on Congress. This time the Senate pulled off a quick approval (February 21, 63-4) and passed the bill on to the House where a powerful committee chairman could be counted on to thwart it. But coincidentally, Upton Sinclair's novel *The Jungle* unleashed an expose of conditions in meat-packing plants. Sinclair churned up a near hysterical reaction by simply telling it as it was:

> …Most scraps were also found being shoveled into receptacles from dirty floors, where they were left to lie until again shoveled into barrels or into machines for chopping. These floors, it must be noted, were in most cases damp and soggy, in dark, ill-ventilated rooms, and the employees in utter ignorance of cleanliness or danger to health expectorated at will upon them. In a word, we saw meat shoveled from filthy wooden floors, piled on tables rarely washed, pushed from room to room in rotten box carts, in all of which processes it was in the way of gathering dirt, splinters, floor filth, and the expectoration of tuberculous and other diseased workers. [7]

TR quietly sent out his own investigators who simply corroborated the sensational facts that had the nation in an uproar. (He also remembered the rotten meat supplied to the Army in 1898.) But as with the railroad rates bill, the basic issue remained the question of federal authority over business. In opposition was Congressman James W. Wadsworth (R) of New York, Chairman of the House Agriculture Committee and himself a livestock producer. Wadsworth offered an amendment to weaken the bill, bottled it up in his committee, and finally released it in a weakened form in early June, close to the adjournment that would end the struggle. At this point, the president worked out a compromise with enough funding to assure federal inspection of meat. With public clamor demanding action, Wadsworth also had to compromise, and the Meat Inspection Act sailed through the House, carrying along the Pure Food and Drug Act in its wake.

Probably the momentum built up by the food and drug issues helped propel the Hepburn Act through the Senate. In final form, the bill empowered the ICC to set maximum railroad rates when a protest was lodged. It also allowed railroads to counter such rate revisions in the courts. Fearing public outrage if they killed the bill outright, the Old Guard Republicans believed that this judicial review of rate decisions, set forth by their amendment calling for a "broad review," would effectively nullify the Hepburn Act, because this allowed the courts to pass upon all details of the ICC's conduct, not just upon the fairness of the rates in question. Thus the ICC might determine lower rates, but the courts could delay them indefinitely. By May Senator Tillman and a few colleagues were developing another amendment to "narrow" the scope of this judicial review, but it seemed unlikely that Tillman could deliver all of the needed 26 Democratic yea's. Grasping this—and very uneasy about a bipartisanship that threatened the unity of Republicans—TR went behind Tillman and negotiated a compromise on the "broad review" question by backing an amendment by Senator Allison (R, Iowa). Suddenly the Democrats found themselves irrelevant as the Republican majority lined up in favor of the Hepburn Act, approving it on May 18, with only one Republican and two Democrats dissenting.

The President received and signed the bill into law on June 29. The Hepburn Act was a historic measure that covered not only freight rates but passenger fares, pipeline fees, storage costs, refrigeration contracts, express services, and any other costs of moving or switching cars. He was vindicated in these political results because the courts rejected the "broad review" approach in favor of quicker settlements of rate cases. The next day, he ended this round of executive-legislative controversy by signing the Meat Inspection and Pure Food and Drug Acts. Other progressive measures had reached his desk earlier that month of June 1906, including laws establishing the liability of federal agencies for job accidents, for Oklahoma Statehood, prohibiting hydroelectric development at Niagara Falls, granting immunity to witnesses in anti-trust cases, setting stricter standards for alien naturalization, and a measure that determined a lock system for the Panama Canal (Chapter 25). Finally, on June 8, he signed "An Act for the Preservation of American Antiquities." This epochal measure gave authority to the President to determine sites (on Federal land) historic and prehistoric as National Monuments. No congressional approval required. [8]

II

> ...That the President of the United States may, from time to time, set apart and reserve in any state or territory having public lands bearing forests, any part of the public lands, wholly or in part covered with timber or undergrowth, whether of commercial value or not, as public reservations, and the President shall, by public proclamation, declare the establishment of such reservations and the limits thereof.
>
> (Section 24, Forest Reserve Act of 1891) [9]

Theodore Roosevelt stands alone on the environment. No other president has done as much for the cause and necessity of protecting and managing the nation's resources. He used his "bully pulpit" to develop the awareness that trees, water, and minerals existed in finite quantities, and he drove through the policies and measures that regulated the exploitation of resources on Federal lands. He overcame determined opposition from both political parties, from corporations, and from those who worked at cutting, mining, and grazing. Against bitter, implacable resistance, he never compromised or slackened his efforts. He succeeded in turning the nation around to reject the prospect of a wasteland.

Ironically conservation (the first environmentalism) began with sportsmen, those who hunted and fished. Disturbed by the growing scarcity of certain varieties of game during the 1870's—the near extinction of the bison stands out—sportsmen banded together into clubs (nearly 350 were formed) to improve sport by promoting measures to protect species and preserve habitats. Four magazines founded at this time (*American Sportsman, Forest and Stream, Field and Stream, The American Angler*) aroused interest in conservation. Of these *Forest and Stream*, cofounded and coedited by George Bird Grinnell, led the way with articles and editorials on diminishing game and fish and the resulting need to develop habitats through forest management, game laws, reduction of water pollution, and the propagation of fish and animals. Grinnell and other crusading naturalists elicited strong, positive responses from concerned sportsmen, which created a constituency and growing demand to protect and conserve natural resources. [10]

Grinnell's review of Theodore Roosevelt's *Hunting Trips of a Ranchman* brought the two together in 1887 for what became a lengthy series of discussions that explored problems. Grinnell was a scientist (Yale, 1870, Ph.D., 1880) and a naturalist who had hunted and traveled widely through the West. In 1887 they collaborated on organizing the Boone and Crockett Club, a group of experienced big-game hunters (minimum of three species bagged) organized to lobby politicians for conservation laws. Twenty-four wealthy and influential men attended the first meeting in 1888, and membership soon reached a maximum of one hundred. The Boone and Crockett Club constitution listed five objectives: promotion of the sport of rifle-hunting, exploration of unknown areas, the study of natural history, the diffusion of information among members, and

> To work for the preservation of the large game of the country, and so far as possible to further legislation for that purpose, and to assist in enforcing the existing laws. [11]

The Boone and Crockett Club soon set up a Committee on Parks to work for the enlargement and protection of the species in Yellowstone, the nation's sole national park (created by President Grant in 1872). By the late 1880's developers and promoters had invaded Yellowstone, obtaining leases on mineral deposits, timberlands, and tourism sites. B and C Club members, led by Grinnell and Club President Theodore Roosevelt (at this time living in Washington, DC, as Civil Service Commissioner), campaigned and lobbied for six years to secure passage of the Park Protection Act of 1894, which ejected the exploiters and provided law enforcement for national parks. A byproduct of these efforts was a realization of the necessity for forest conservation. Originally forests had overlain half the nation, estimated to have numbered one billion acres. By 1900 half of this was gone, and four-fifths of the remainder were privately owned. [12] Initially concerned about the timberlands on each side of Yellowstone, the B & C Club joined forces with the American Forestry Association, officers of the Division of Forestry, U.S.D.A., and F.H. Newell of the U.S. Geological Survey (Chapter 28) to push for passage of the Forest Reserve Act of 1891, which created our system of National Forests (originally called "reserves"). Then President Benjamin Harrison authorized the first forest reserves around Yellowstone in Wyoming, 1,239,040 acres (see epigraph above). [13] After this, Presidents Harrison, Cleveland, and McKinley, over the decade 1891-1901, established reserves totaling nearly 50,000,000 acres. [14]

TR thus had involved himself with conservation before becoming a national figure. He and his B & C colleagues worked to establish NYC's Bronx Zoo and for passage of game laws prohibiting jacklighting (the sudden blinding of animals at night) and using dogs to drive game into water (1897). He also edited and contributed to three B & C Club books on hunting, and he contributed eleven articles to the two-volume, English *Encyclopedia of Sport* (1897-98). In several of the latter, he discussed the threat to species from overhunting. [15] As Governor of New York (1899-1900), he exposed the incompetence of the Fisheries, Forest, and Game Commission and got it reorganized under capable leaders. In two years he couldn't overcome special interests to enact new state conservation laws, but his spoken words did much to educate and arouse the public to demand (and get) cleaner streams and protection for forests and wildlife. [16]

At some point during the 1890's, Theodore Roosevelt bonded with Gifford Pinchot (1865-1946), the nation's Chief Forester (from 1899) and its only professional in the field. Heir to great wealth in Pennsylvania, Pinchot studied sciences at Yale but had to go to France and Germany to learn forestry (1889-90), becoming the only American with such training. He returned dedicated to the idea that "forestry is the art of using a forest without destroying it." [17] Conservation is predicated on the doctrine of "wise use," rather than simple preservation (which permits only esthetic use of resources). Back in the U.S., Pinchot looked for a demonstration project and found it near Asheville, North Carolina, managing the woodlands of George Washington Vanderbilt (grandson of the "Commodore"). Biltmore House, the huge chateau in the French Renaissance style (and the largest private home in the country), was surrounded by farms and 3000 acres of forest land. Instead of cutting down the small trees to get at the big trees, the usual lumbering process, Pinchot directed his loggers to cut down only the mature trees selected and marked by his foresters. After which, five to ten seedlings were planted in the empty spot. This approach to management preserved the tree density necessary to produce useful timber. The old practice of cutting young growth and planting single trees resulted in wide-spreading shade trees rather than full stands of straight trunks growing their foliage on top. [18]

By 1897 Pinchot had become active in the Boone and Crockett Club and a close friend and associate of the man who became president in 1901. He advised Governor Roosevelt in Albany while serving as chief of the Division of Forestry in the Department of Agriculture; he was monolithic in his field. TR characterized him thusly:

"I have one friend…in whose integrity I believe as I do my own." [19] He fully supported all of Pinchot's initiatives, which validated his belief that the forests belonged to, and should be held in trust for, the American people, not for the timber companies. However the office of Chief Forester lacked real power because it was only advisory. The Forest Service (as it came to be called) had been set up in the Department of Agriculture, while Congress (in its wisdom) had placed the forest reserves in the old General Land Office of the Department of the Interior. It suited the timber companies to keep the foresters out of the forests; they lobbied to retain this status quo. The House of Representatives defeated the first bill to transfer the forests to the Agriculture Department in 1902. Not until 1905 did Pinchot bring all the parties together (at the "American Forest Congress") for the consensus that prompted passage of the Transfer Act. This law placed the Bureau of Forestry under the USDA, giving a new Forest Service control of the nation's forests, by this time increased to 86,000,000 acres. [20]

As previously indicated (Chapter 28), the first measure in Theodore Roosevelt's conservation program was the Reclamation Act of 1902. This program of constructing dams and waterways conserved water for farming dry lands. By 1904 sixteen reclamation projects had gotten underway in the West to irrigate many thousands of acres. As a naturalist and hunter, TR felt a strong personal interest in wildlife conservation. He spoke publicly against the wanton slaughter of game animals and against the killing of birds for feathers. Between 1903 and 1909, he created fifty-one wildlife refuges (there are about 400 today). He also cajoled Congress into creating five national parks, including Crater Lake, Oregon, and Mesa Verde, Colorado, bringing the number to ten. After passage of the Antiquities Act in 1906 authorizing the President to declare prehistoric and historic sites as "National Monuments," he took that bone in his teeth and established the first eighteen of these, including Devil's Tower, Wyoming, Tonto and Montezuma's Castle, Arizona, and Utah's Natural Bridges. When Congress denied national park status to the Grand Canyon, he included that colossal landmark among his group of national monuments. [21]

These victories over corporate interests guaranteed eventual opposition. By 1907 lumber interests, mining companies, cattlemen, power companies, lobbyists, and politicians had united against a lameduck president who had limited their extractions of natural resources and enforced land laws and mining regulations. In 1905 Oregon's Senator Fulton attacked rigorous law enforcement because several prominent Oregon Republicans, including the state's other Senator, were either in prison or being tried for violations of federal laws. Many westerners spoke out against "Pinchotism" and "Gifford the First," fearing that too much land was being withdrawn. Pinchot fought back, traveling extensively to wherever he could get a hearing for his programs. TR unflinchingly backed him, speaking regularly about conservation, stressing the needs, not only to conserve timber, but also the necessity of forests for water and soil conservation. In 1907 came the showdown with Congress, when Senator Fulton attached a "rider" to the Agriculture Appropriations Bill preventing the President from withdrawing any more land in six western states (Oregon, Washington, Idaho, Montana, Wyoming, Colorado) for forests without congressional approval. Its passage revealed the extent of anti-Roosevelt feeling.

Fulton and his western cohorts believed they had driven a stake through the heart of the progressive forest program, but the President and his Chief Forester still had some arrows in their quiver. Knowing Pinchot had on file plans for twenty-one new forests and the expansion of eleven existing forests, TR put the USDA bureaucrats into overdrive on paperwork for thirty-two proclamations. He signed these on March 2, 1907, two days before he had to sign the Appropriations Bill that would limit his powers. Over congressional teeth-gnashing and howls of protest against "midnight" proclamations, 16,000,000 million acres had been added to the nation's forest system. (Such were howls of impotence because any counter-measures would have been vetoed.) At the same time Pinchot exacerbated their pain when he withdrew over 2500 waterpower sites from exploitation by declaring them ranger stations. When Theodore Roosevelt left office in 1909, forest reserves amounted to nearly 200,000,000 acres, of which he (aided by the expertise of Gifford Pinchot) had contributed 150,000,000 acres. [22]

In his last year he staged the National Conservation Congress, a grand finale to disseminate and reenforce the conservation gospel. On May 13-15, 1908, over 500 delegates assembled in the East Room of the White House to consider the disposition of the nation's resources. Invited were the Governors of all 46 states (44 came), the Cabinet, Supreme Court Justices, Congressmen, businessmen, certain foreign dignitaries, plus learned experts and scientists. Even William Jennings Bryan, Andrew Carnegie, and James J. Hill attended (usually critical of TR). TR's fifty-minute opening speech elicited full support for conservation and a "coherent plan" for resource development. His objective was not to lock up resources but to use them in ways to increase the yields for future generations. The Congress ended with an epochal "Declaration of Governors" which asserted public rights over private interests and called for interstate cooperation. Afterward forty-one states set up their own conservation commissions to carry on the work. Scientific bodies organized committees on conservation, and a National Conservation Commission was created (it would operate until 1923). The first task of the N C Commission was to compile an inventory of the nation's resources, which, led by Pinchot, it achieved in less than a year (January 1909). The enthusiasm generated by this 1908 meeting reverberated throughout the country and led to the North American Conference, inclusive of Canada and Mexico, in February 1909. But Congress licked its wounds and refused to fund any of the lameduck president's last conservation initiatives, which included two more commissions, one appointed to study "Country Life" and the other to improve "Inland Waterways." TR's last input into his abundant legacy was thus a comprehensive program of resource management: forests, water supplies, soil, flood control, waterways, and irrigation, but Congress, preferring the hit-or-miss pork-barrel approach—and solidly behind corporate interests—soundly rejected this great progressive agenda. Yet the seeds of environmentalism had been well planted, to be harvested by future generations. [23] Gifford Pinchot put it simply: "…he changed the attitude of the American people toward conserving the natural resources."[24]

III

An assessment of Theodore Roosevelt's presidency must take into account his mistakes. "Mistake" means a decision which negatively affected goals or outcomes. He accomplished many things (see Almanac below), but, as noted just above, he didn't always get everything he wished. There were no ignominious defeats, but many wins were partial, and some goals, e.g., tariff reduction, weren't attempted.

His most avoidable error was to announce on the night of his election triumph in 1904 that "under no circumstances" would he run for reelection. Idealistically he shone in this declaration. He refused to run for a third term on the basis of the technicality that he had not been elected to his first term, only six months short of a full term. He respected Washington's two-term precedent as a defense against tyranny and corruption. His self-image required the upright stance, taken on high moral ground. But he could have kept them guessing by simply avoiding the subject until after the mid-term election of 1906. The grand gesture of the election night converted a winner into a lame duck. He could have tap-danced around this negative inevitability for years. Arguably he might have accomplished more, a stronger Hepburn Act granting more regulating powers to the Interstate Commerce Commission, more funding for inspections of food, meat, and drugs.

The decision to discharge a battalion of black soldiers without due process in the Brownsville case (Chapter 27) came back to bite him. Resurgent conservatives in Congress during 1907-08 found it to be a handy weapon. Senator Foraker (who was gunning for the Republican presidential nomination) and other senatorial foes kept the controversy going for the remainder of his term. Increasingly the impression that TR had acted vindictively and in haste nudged him off the high ground in the view of many. A restive Congress grew more resistant to his progressive agenda. Ultimately this battle left blood on the floor, TR's lost prestige mingled with the wreckage of Foraker's career. He seems to have based this very summary decision on the imperative of maintaining military discipline. The Army lived or died by discipline; any faltering thereof had to be subversive. Not to strike at any breach of discipline constituted a grave neglect of priority number one. For a proud military amateur, anything less than severity was a betrayal, and a failure to drive home a vital lesson.

It is much less clear as to whether Theodore Roosevelt's choice of a successor can be classified as a mistake. True, he tapped William Howard Taft because of a faith that Taft would carry out "my policies," which turned out to be misplaced. Taft was an old friend who dated back to Civil Service days during the Harrison Administration (as Solicitor General, Taft pleaded Justice Department cases before the Supreme Court). He had proved subsequently a very capable administrator and team player. He made his reputation as a troubleshooting Governor-general in the Philippines and went on to the War Department in 1904. There he also made his mark, serving 255 days on special assignments that included overseeing the construction of the Panama Canal (the President gave his complete trust on this pet project) and two special and very delicate missions to Japan. But Taft was essentially a jurist; he had become a judge after leaving the Harrison Administration. Having a fine legal mind, his heart was in the law; he really desired to become Chief Justice. (Eventually, under Harding, he would reach that post in 1921, with the distinction of being the only president to sit on the Supreme bench.) TR offered the Supreme Court at least twice, but wife Nellie (Helen Herron Taft) wanted the White House. Taft loved Theodore (though Nellie hated him) and glowed when he received praise, but he lacked the inner fire of his boss and became the victim of his wife's ambition. He also lacked leadership qualities and had never exhibited the independence of disagreement. The hint of this showed in the Brownsville case where Taft, uneasy about the lack of due process, tried to delay the final decision (Theodore apparently failed to notice). But in 1908, it came down to Taft being the only electable choice. TR would have preferred his Secretary of State Elihu Root. Root was the only cabinet member with a mind that awed him, but Root was a corporation lawyer of conservative aspect with little charisma or popularity. What befell after Taft took over is a later story, but in 1907-08 he stood out as the competent operative of his progressive master. [25]

If at the end, Congress looked forward to Bill Taft, hoping for complaisance from the easy-going big man (he weighed about 350 lbs. and couldn't tie his shoes), the people and the Republican rank-and-file still wanted their "Teddy." At the convention in Chicago on June 17, Chairman Henry Cabot Lodge's mention of the President set off a forty-nine-minute demonstration, which went on ten minutes longer than the acclamation given William Jennings Bryan for his "Cross of Gold" speech (in the same hall) in 1896 (Chapter 7). Twelve thousand delegates and attendees stood roaring for "four more years!" Toy bears were held up to shouts of "We want Teddy!" When Taft's name was heard, Helen Taft said, "I only want it to last more than forty-nine minutes." But it went on for less than thirty. [26] By then, this larger-than-life president had become fixed in the emotions of much of the population. He had always pitched his programs to the mid-to-lower classes whom he characterized as the "ordinary" or "plain" people, clerks, small businessmen, farmers, tradesmen. In 1904 right after his election victory, he told friend (and colleague in western writing) Owen Wister:

It is a peculiar gratification to me to have owed my election not to the politicians primarily…not to the financiers…but above all to Lincoln's "plain people"; to the folks who work hard on farm, in shop, or on the railroads, or who own little stores, little businesses which they manage themselves. I would literally, not figuratively, rather cut off my right hand than forfeit by any improper act of mine the trust and regard of all these people. [27]

This special constituency reciprocated. Before leaving the White House in 1909 for his year-long African hunt, there were 20,000 farewell letters, many stating that they would worry about the state of the nation until his return. [28] A friend tells the story of a train trip through the Mid-west in 1910. Having heard that the ex-president would be coming through in a private car attached to the rear of a scheduled train, crowds turned up at crossings, depots, and by their homes waving flags. It was Sunday, with no stops scheduled, and TR had insisted, no speeches. As the train went through a settled area, a sound abruptly rose and faded, a crescendo and diminuendo of voices. Each time he came out on the rear platform to wave to cheering crowds. Thirty times, he laid aside his book to acknowledge the feelings and regard of the many who had walked and driven over rough country roads for just a glimpse. [29]

He spoke out for his people in his final, December 8th, message to Congress. Having grown more progressive with the years, he articulated a comprehensive program for social justice. By now at an impass with a hostile congress, the message was more directed to the nation—and the future. He grounded his program in the assertion that "…under the interstate clause of the Constitution the United States has the complete and paramount right to control all agencies of interstate commerce…." Besides reforms of corporate practices, he enunciated reforms of labor practices. In the first category he advocated regulatory commissions like the Interstate Commerce Commission (ICC) to oversee and set both corporate rates <u>and</u> corporate financing ("no defrauding of investors"). Such commissioners would regulate not only railroads (the largest group of corporate entities in 1908), but also telecommunications and banks. In that time before the Glass-Steagall Act of 1933 (providing for the Federal Deposit Insurance Corporation), he called for "Postal savings banks" to protect the small depositor. Of particular interest was his advocacy of highway regulations and standards, which points to the coming age of automobile and truck. The remaining standards pertained to the more humane treatment of labor: an end of child labor, limits on female labor, shorter working hours, employers' liability for on-the-job injuries, and "steps toward providing old-age pensions" (quite radical in the US of 1908). [30]

This wasn't a valedictory, so much as a promise of action after a hiatus. But fortune, circumstances, and a too-early death (at 60 in 1919) precluded a return to political power. Taft (always the jurist) would pursue anti-trust cases in the courts as his progressive strategy, and Woodrow Wilson would get a few important progressive laws on the books—the Federal Reserve Act of 1913, Federal Trade Commission Act of 1914, Clayton Anti-Trust Act of 1914—before wars (Mexico, then the Central Powers) snuffed out the progressive impulse. With TR's departure, the national life altered, a falling off, a depletion, a spark missing. As some commentators would note, most of the fun went out of things. No one else had ever executed the presidency with such verve and zest to become the charismatic standard-bearer of the ragtime republic.

RAGTIME ALMANAC
Theodore Roosevelt's Presidential Achievements

Enlargement of the role and power of the presidency
Programs to conserve natural resources
Implementation of the principle of the regulation of economic enterprise
Construction of the Panama Canal
Made the U.S. a world power
Creation of the modern Navy [31]
National security through diplomacy:
    Control of the Caribbean
    Settlement of the Alaska boundary
    Close ties with Great Britain
    Handled problems with Germany and Japan
Negotiated Treaty of Portsmouth (1905) ending Russo-Japanese War (Nobel Peace Prize)
Inspired the nation to support progressivism from his "Bully Pulpit"

Notes: Chapter 32

1. Quoted in Henry F. Pringle, *Theodore Roosevelt: A Biography*, 254.
2. Nathan Miller, *Theodore Roosevelt: A Life*, 441.
3. *Ibid.*, 451-452.
4. George E. Mowry, *The Era of Theodore Roosevelt, 1900-1912*, 200-203; N. Miller, 455; Edmund Morris, *Theodore Rex*, 426-428, 429-430.
5. *Ibid.*, 431.
6. *The Autobiography of Lincoln Steffens*, 506.
7. Quoted in Thomas A. Bailey, Ed., *The American Spirit*, 639.
8. Information sources: E. Morris, *Rex*, 426-440, 442-448; N. Miller, 456-462; Mowry, 203-208; H.W. Brands, *TR: The Last Romantic*, 541-552; William Henry Harbaugh, *Power and Responsibility: The Life and Times of Theodore Roosevelt*, 233-244, 247-251. For contemporary views and background, Mark Sullivan, *Our Times*, III, 192-213, 223-275. For a retrospective view, Arthur M. Schlesinger, Jr., *The Cycles of American History*, 31-34, 232-239.
9. Quoted in Paul Russell Cutright, *Theodore Roosevelt: The Making of a Conservationist*, 177.
10. Grinnell coedited the magazine until 1880 when he became sole owner; for thirty-one years (1880-1911) thereafter, he was sole editor. See Cutright, 167-172.
11. *Ibid.*, 173.
12. *Ibid.*, 215.
13. *Ibid.*, 172-178.
14. *Ibid.*, 216.
15. *Ibid.*, 178-181, 196.
16. *Ibid.*, 199-200, 203-205.
17. *Ibid.*, 201.
18. J. Anthony Lukas, *Big Trouble*, 615-618; Cutright, 200-201.
19. Lukas, 620.
20. *Ibid.*, 620-622; David H. Burton, *Theodore Roosevelt, American Politician: An Assessment*, 73-75.
21. Cutright, 213-214, 222-227; Harbaugh, 308-311; *Theodore Roosevelt: An Autobiography*, 413-414.
22. *Ibid.*, 215-221, 418-420; Lukas, 622-624; Mowry, 214-215; Harbaugh, 311-313; Burton, 75-76.
23. Cutright, 227-231; Harbaugh, 315-318; Mowry, 216; *TR: Auto.*, 424, 427-428, 430-431.
24. Quoted Cutright, 233; see eulogy, 266.
25. For succinct analyses of these problems, see Burton, 69-72, 125-129, 129-133.
26. E. Morris, *Rex*, 525-526.
27. Owen Wister, *My Forty Years Friendship with Theodore Roosevelt*, 188.
28. Corinne Robinson, *My Brother, Theodore Roosevelt*, 254.
29. Lawrence F. Abbott, *Impressions of Theodore Roosevelt*, 88-89.
30. Mario R. DiNunzio, Ed., *Theodore Roosevelt, An American Mind: Selected Writings*, 132-138. See also Schlesinger for commentary, 232-245.
31. See Kenneth Wimmel, *Theodore Roosevelt and the Great White Fleet: American Sea Power Comes of Age*, for his role in the development and modernization of the Navy.

33. Vaudeville: Headliners (II)

> We were in love with show business, the excitement of getting onstage. Nothing else mattered to us. The only politics any of us cared about was why the Orpheum Circuit had booked "Flora D'Aliza's Educated Roosters" instead of "Camilla's Pigeons." The only thing any of us knew about sports was what boxing champion or Olympic medal winner was playing Hammerstein's. The only thing that really mattered to any of us was getting the next booking.
>
> George Burns [1]

Humor may have been vaudeville's most salient feature. Except for serious musicians, a few lecturers, and high-wire acrobats, most performers tried to work a few humorous gambits. The knife-thrower, juggler, contortionist, ventriloquist, music player, nearly all inserted a few tricks or wrinkles into their routines to raise smiles or laughter. Laughter was reassuring; it showed the audience liked you. In his teens William Claude Dukinfield juggled his way into showbusiness, but he masked his skills with a tramp persona and climaxed each routine with a humorous exposure of his trickery or a retrieval of an apparent slip-up. Eventually shortening the name to W.C. Fields (1880-1946), he juggled comically as a silent or "dumb" act for about 20 years, until Florenz Ziegfeld elevated him to the *Follies* in 1915. There he added speech to his tricks with balls and boxes and developed his misanthropic character, the whiny, gravel-voiced sharper and saloon habitue out to swindle the hypocrites with phony schemes and crooked games.

He seems to have left an unhappy home—his father operated a pool room—early, around eleven or twelve, and lived by his wits, learning to juggle, until he became proficient enough to do it for audiences a few years later. From his native Philadelphia, he drifted to Atlantic City, where he advanced from five to ten dollars per week. It had to be a raffish life, outside the pale of respectability, each day a struggle to capture enough to survive on. At the "Fortescue Pavilion," where a customer could take in the show along with his nickel stein of beer, they staged fake rescues. Fields and others in the company took turns going into the surf and yelling for help, pretending to be caught in an undertow:

> We would all be ready, rush in the water, and drag the rescued person into the pavilion. Naturally the crowd followed, and if it was a woman we rescued, the crowd was particularly large. Once inside they bought drinks and we were supposed to be entertaining enough to keep them there. It was a great racket and we got plenty of fun out of it. [2]

Fields debuted in New York in 1899 at Miner's Bowery Theatre in burlesque. Burlesque then (see below, last section) combined humorous, risque sketches or skits with acts of variety (olio). For $25/week Fields juggled and played in several skits, his first spoken words onstage. This was entertainment of the pre-Tony Pastor type with an audience entirely masculine. A rough type of place, but many showbusiness greats started there: Weber and Fields, McIntyre and Heath, the Four Cohans, Gus Williams, Fred Stone, and Eddie Cantor. Miners also originated the "hook" in 1903, when the manager used a cane to drag off bad acts on amateur nights. [3] From Miner's, Fields, billed as "The Eccentric Juggler," rose abruptly to the big-time for $125/week, moving onto Keith-Albee and then to the Orpheum (1900).

He came onstage in old, ragged clothing and fake beard. All he had with him were tennis balls, a balancing stick, a top hat, and some cigar boxes (which kept down expenses). Along the way he picked up a female assistant, Harriet (Hattie) Hughes (whom he soon married) dressed in tuxedo and satin pants. (She would leave the stage in 1904 when only child W.C. Fields, Jr. was born). He juggled six tennis balls with ease, almost but never quite losing one. Surrounded by cigar boxes, he would juggle three, then, bending down, drop one while picking up another from the floor. He did this so fast that many never caught it. He would kick the top hat up to a stick balanced on his forehead. Then, balancing top hat, a whisk broom, and a cigar, he kicked them upward, with the hat landing on his head, the cigar in his mouth, and the whisk broom in his back pocket. Later he added a trick pool table under a mirror with each ball rigged on invisible string. Then with a poke at the cue, all the balls ran into their pockets. [4]

Fields soon reached stardom in the big-time, playing not only the top American houses, but regularly crossing the Atlantic where his mute act boosted him over language barriers in the great music halls of Paris and Berlin. In Britain he became so popular that King George V and Queen Mary summoned him for a Command Performance in 1913, an honor received by no other American performers. By 1906 he was pulling down $375/week, ultimately reaching a weekly $800 by 1914. An English critic in 1902 explained his appeal:

> If you go to the Hippodrome you will see a remarkably clever comic juggler, W.C. Fields, performing all sorts of tricks with an apparent contempt for his own cleverness. Many of the tricks we have seen over a hundred times before, but this American's manner invests them all with a new interest; it is not exactly what he does but the tricky way he does it. [5]

Along the years, something went sour with the marriage. Perhaps long absences and geographical distance estranged them as much as stubborn wills in opposition. Fields never filed for divorce and unfailingly sent checks "home" the rest of his life, but kept his distance from an acrimonious relationship.

His chief professional problem, never alluded to in recollections, seems to have been a rivalry with the magician Harry Houdini. In his prime no one impressed audiences as much. Fields first encountered Houdini on his (Fields) first European tour at the Winter Garden in Berlin in 1900, but usually their intineraries crossed on the big-time circuits on both continents. Born Erich Weiss in Budapest in 1874, Houdini and five siblings came over as a child, and like Fields, entered showbusiness as a teenager. They appeared only once on the same bill, at London's Hippodrome in 1904, but wherever Fields headlined, Houdini had often sensationally preceded him. Houdini had begun with card tricks at dime museums but made his success as an escape artist. What he escaped from was locks: handcuffs, jail cells, chains and padlocks, trunks, anything that required a key to open, plus straitjackets which did not. Besides vaudeville, he staged publicity-grabbing spectaculars by breaking out of prisons or out of shackles underwater. His secret was an encyclopedic knowledge of locks; he had obtained the patent papers of every lock manufactured in the U.S., Great Britain, France, and Germany. He knew how to pick them all, and it was rumored that wife Bess who assisted him would pass him pick or key when she kissed him "for luck." One way or another, it was all a subterfuge, but he beat all challenges except one offered by a Gloucester, Massachusetts, fisherman: tie his thumbs behind his back. That was beyond even Houdini. He rose to No. 1 at the box office, but his draw faded as vaudeville declined in the 1920's. He died of a ruptured appendix in Detroit in 1926. [6]

Fields may have felt diminished by Houdini on occasion, but he remained a favorite and his earning power grew. Nothing changed for him until the fateful summer of 1914. He reached England on his eleventh foreign tour, then went on to Australia, where in August World War I abruptly overtook showbusiness. Patriotic dramas and displays roused more applause than comic juggling. While there he received an invitation to audition for Irving Berlin's new musical *Watch Your Step*, and, welcoming an escape from what had become for him a marginal status, he headed home in November. With vaudeville in subsequent decline, never again did he cross an international border. Unfortunately his juggling routine was dropped from the show just after the opening. Then he returned to the national circuits until Flo Ziegfeld put him into the *Follies of 1915*, where (for $1000/week) he starred for the next six years until 1921. By then he had given up juggling for the verbal comedy that convulsed audiences. In the play *Poppy* (1923) on Broadway, he perfected the misanthrope rebelling against the stifling forces of respectability. From there he took the characterization into about 40 films, silents and talkies, shorts and features, between 1915 and 1944. He continues to be honored, along with Bert Williams, Charlie Chaplin, Stan Laurel and Oliver Hardy, and Buster Keaton, as one of the great comedians. [7]

II

The humorist Will Rogers (1879-1935) shares with the comedian W.C. Fields a curious set of parallels and divergences. Both entered the world in 1879-1880, one the son of a prosperous rancher on the plains of the Indian Territory (eastern Oklahoma), the other the son of a pool room proprietor in urban Philadelphia. Both rejected schooling for showbusiness and both made it early into the big-time. They achieved this as silent acts demonstrating superb physical skills, Fields as juggler, Rogers as roper. Both injected humor into their routines, Fields the tramp who always somehow retrieves the falling object, Rogers suddenly roping someone in the audience and pulling them onstage. Both gave up vaudeville for *Follies* stardom in 1915. Both moved their acts away from the physical toward the verbal. And both went on to major film careers, Rogers making 71 films (of both kinds) before his untimely death in a plane crash in Alaska in 1935.

Very similar careers, very different personality types, Rogers came off positive where Fields' humor resulted from conflicts and misfortunes. However both had difficult beginnings, Fields escaping home misery to develop a talent while struggling to survive, Rogers trying to escape a strong-willed father who insisted that he settle down in ranching. William Penn Adair Rogers claimed one-quarter Cherokee, but he was ethnically more than that, growing up in Oklahoma's Cherokee Nation. The Rogers clan received their name from a British army officer who married a half-Irish/half-Cherokee woman and then himself joined the tribe. Will's father Clement (a grandson of this union) was born in 1839 after the family had chosen to move with the Native Americans to Oklahoma. At 17 Clement Rogers and two slaves set up a ranch along the Verdigris River (about 20 miles NE of modern Tulsa). Indian land was communally owned, and a young man could take up any that was unoccupied. He also established a trading post and married in 1859. As slaveholders Clement and fellow Cherokees allied with the Confederacy (though many other Indians in Oklahoma stood with the Union). After a war of raids and guerilla fighting, Clement mustered out of his cavalry regiment as a Captain and had to restart and relocate his ranching and businesses. He prospered on the cattle boom of the post-Civil War era, acquired thousands of acres, and built an impressive two-story home in 1875. Will arrived in 1879, the eighth child (a brother and three sisters surviving), and the son of a wealthy rancher, businessman, and member of the Cherokee Senate. [8]

Will grew up a cowboy, learning to ride from age five before he was big enough to mount or dismount by himself. An ex-slave Uncle Dan looked after him and taught him skills and tricks with the lariat. He played with a mix of white, black, and Indian children, including some of Uncle Dan's twelve. Preferring an outdoor life of horses, games, and livestock, Will did badly in the several schools tried by his parents. His sporadic schooling never went beyond the tenth grade, and at 18, he worked in one of the last cattle drives on American soil, just before the railroad arrived in his part of the territory. He also tried to enlist in the "Rough Riders" that year of 1898 but was rejected for his youth and inexperience. He played and cowboyed for the next few years, alternating work for his father with running off on trips, and getting himself to every dance in that part of Oklahoma. Will didn't smoke, drink, or gamble, but he liked the girls and loved to dance. He also won a few prizes in the roping and riding contests of early rodeos. Finally rebelling against his father's desire that he learn to manage the family enterprises of wheat, ranching, and banking (his brother had died earlier), Will wandered right out of the country in 1902. First to Argentina whose cattle frontier seemed to offer no opportunities, then on to South Africa working his way on a cattle boat. After a few misfortunes, he signed on with Texas Jack's Wild West Show and found his vocation doing rope tricks as the "Cherokee Kid—the Man Who Can Lasso the Tail Off a Butterfly." [9]

Back in the U.S. Will joined "Colonel" Zack Mulhall's "Wild West" show, where he excelled to become its headliner at the St.Louis World's Fair in 1904. Here he formed a lasting friendship with Tom Mix, who eventually became the top star in "westerns," playing lead roles in over 300 films. In 1905, along with Tom Mix, Will rejoined the Mulhall show in New York's Madison Square Garden. At the end of the run, he experienced a flurry of fame when he successfully lassoed a longhorn steer that had run amuck into the audience. Afterward he haunted the United Booking Office (UBO) for a month before landing a job at Keith's Union Square Theatre as an "extra act" during the off-hour "supper show." Instant success came suddenly as audiences and critics raved over him. This led a few days later to the heights, literal and figurative, a contract to play the Paradise Roof at Hammerstein's Victoria, getting a raise from $75 to $140/week. At this most elite of summer venues, where celebrities and the powerful comprised the audience, Will was an overnight success. In this "dumb" act he rode in on his horse Teddy (named for his hero), who was outfitted with felt-bottom boots to keep a secure footing, jumped off, then patted the horse to send him off to the side. Now came a series of rope tricks as the orchestra softly crooned a cowboy song medley: ropes twirled as he jumped in and out, both vertical and horizontal; he next did the "crinoline" which sent a big rope in a long arc over the audience; now he threw two ropes at once, lassoing both the horse and someone else. They loved it, calling him, "The Lariat King." Will practiced constantly, adding and augmenting tricks. He never had a rival. [10]

He had a problem with endings, usually just walking off after the last trick. Someone then showed him how to take a curtain call, and others suggested that he "say something," and comment on his moves. Will held back, afraid to speak in his southwestern twang. Then one night, he abruptly told the audience what he intended to do next, saying he had a few doubts about it. The audience startled him with its hearty laugh, which lit a new awareness. Which led to more remarks and more laughter, particularly when he highlighted a mistake. His sometimes rueful, half-humorous comments brought greater closeness with audiences. By late 1905 he was everywhere in demand, all over the Keith Circuit, from Boston to Washington and from Philadelphia to Detroit. Bookings now paid $250/week. [11] When he reached a new town, he walked down the main street toward the theatre leading Teddy who carried a sign that proclaimed "Will Rogers, The Lariat King," usually followed by every child in the neighborhood. [12]

Again like Fields Will toured Europe successfully, but in the Germany of Kaiser Wilhelm II, his laid-back democratic ways led to trouble. This time began well enough when, on his morning ride in the park, he was saluted pleasantly by another early rider, well mounted and with an upturned moustache. Later he learned that this singular gentleman was the Emperor himself. Buoyed by such recognition on successive mornings, Will felt secure going on at the premier showplace of Berlin, the Winter Garden. One night he spotted a man glaring at him with apparent disapproval. A little piqued, Will chose to snare this man in the lassoing trick, and dragged him, furiously protesting, to the footlights. What had always gone over in the U.S. with good humor and laughter produced roars of anger and resentment. Afterward rumors of the man's importance and the possibility of a jailable offence unnerved Will enough to leave Berlin. His frayed nerves took another hit at the railroad station when the porter spied part of a shirt extruded from one of the bags. The porter sternly reprimanded him, pointing out that such an untidy bag was unacceptable and could not be checked. He felt much relief in England where his act proved a very big hit at London's Palace, applauded by King Edward VII and other members of the Royal Family. [13]

Rogers and Fields diverge in their marital situations. Where Fields seems to have married in some haste and repented in the leisure of the rest of his life, Rogers approached the wedded state with uncertainties and difficulties. By the time he entered vaude, Will had fallen for home-type girl Betty Blake of Arkansas. Betty, who was sought after, popular, and better educated than her cowboy suitor, possessed a strong personality. It took eight years of a bumbling, sporadic courtship before Will managed to demonstrate enough eligibility by proving that he was more than the shallow, show-off son of a rich man. Betty had standards, and Will, with his sketchy verbal education, had a hard time communicating the solid stuff underneath his grinning, "aw, shucks" persona that served so well onstage. He eventually convinced her, and they settled easily into closeness and companionship, raising a family of three (Will, Jr., Mary, and Jim—a baby Fred died of diphtheria at two).

Beyond vaudeville lay "Broadway," prior to "Hollywood," the prestige goal of the aspiring performer. Will, who came into vaudeville behind Fields, surged ahead by landing a role in Blanche Ring's new musical *The Wall Street Girl* in 1912. During the show's run and subsequent tour, Will raised his billing to number two, listed just below the star who is remembered for introducing her signature song "I Want a Regular Man," plus the perennial hit "In the Good Old Summertime." Will came on initially a bit nervous with the line, "I knew I could do all right at fifty cents, but I was a little afraid at two dollars." He needn't have worried: one critic called him "a poet with the lariat," and the theatre press noted that his act "stopped the show," always ultimate praise. Opening night turned out even more memorable because news of the loss of the *Titanic* reached the theatre halfway through the show. Many prominent—and theatre-going—New Yorkers had been aboard. The producer selected Will to go onstage to announce the tragedy, which he did with a hoarse dignity. A shockwave went through the audience, and many departed displaying genuine anguish. [14]

It was back to vaudeville in 1913, then to London that summer of 1914 for another musical show, *The Merry-Go-Round* with Nora Bayes (Chapter 18). He scored another success, but as with Fields, the distraction of the War's outbreak drove him home, though he was offered $400/week to continue. Will got back on Broadway the summer of 1915 in the Shuberts' production *Hands Up* (music by Sigmund Romberg). His talking and roping near the show's end drew the most applause. [15] Right after an early close, Ziegfeld hired him for the *Midnight Frolic* show on the roof of the Amsterdam Theatre. After catching the *Follies* with Fields, Fanny Brice, and Bert Williams downstairs, patrons could unwind and refresh themselves at a second show in the cooler air of late night. Pay was only $175/week, much less than vaude, and at first Ziegfeld, a man with no sense or fondness of humor, disliked Roger's tart remarks and routines with ropes. He told Gene Buck his director to remove this rustic individual from his smart show. When Buck approached Will, Will hit him first with a demand for a $50 increase. He also promised a renovation of his act: wife Betty, after living with a man who read several newspapers, had persuaded him to offer the comments that he typically made on news items he'd just read. Buck held back on the firing, but he informed Will that Z only tolerated comedians because they filled the times when chorus girls were off changing costumes. Will augmented his performance, and when Z got back from a trip, the laughter Will drew from impressions of current events brought a reprieve—and the $50 increase. More and more Will's act consisted of needling politicians and other big-shots. He explained: "I started reading about Congress in the newspapers, and I discovered they were funnier 365 days a year than anything I ever heard of." [16]

Flo Ziegfeld never laughed at Will's remarks, but he grew to like Will very much and kept him in the *Follies* from 1916 until Will gave up New York for films. For his part Will thought so well of Z that he insisted on working without the protection of a contract. He rose to $600 the first year, with a raise to $750 in 1917. Audiences fell under his charm when he sauntered onstage with the line, "Well, folks, all I know is what I read in the papers." He always performed with houselights on to see who was there and to decide whom to rope that night. [17] He mastered all the media eventually: stage, film, radio, magazines, books, and the newspapers he so loved to comment on. With his books (6 of them) and magazine and daily and weekly newspaper columns, he achieved the singular and unique distinction of becoming the people's philosopher. From semi-literate cowboy, he made himself into a popular author. People took comfort from such sayings as, "Don't worry if a man kicks you from behind, it only proves you're ahead of him." [18] His unexpected death in the crash of Wiley Post's airplane sent a nation already traumatized by economic depression into deep mourning for its most loved and popular figure.

RAGTIME ALMANAC
A Selection of Will's Sayings [19]

- My ancestors didn't come over on the *Mayflower*, but they met 'em at the boat.
- I don't make jokes, I just watch the government and report the facts.
- No matter how much I may exaggerate it, it must have a certain amount of truth…Now rumor travels faster, but it don't stay put as long as truth.
- We are here for just a spell and then pass on…So get a few laughs and do the best you can. Live your life, so that whenever you lose, you are ahead.
- …I maintain that it should cost as much to get married as to get divorced. Make it look like marriage is worth as much as divorce, even if it ain't.
- The short memories of the American voters is what keeps our politicians in office.
- Never blame a legislative body for not doing something. When they do nothing, they don't hurt anybody. When they do something is when they become dangerous.
- We shouldn't elect a president; we should elect a magician.
- Elect 'em for a six-year term; not allow 'em to succeed themselves. That would keep their mind off politics.
- If we got one-tenth of what was promised in the acceptance speeches, there wouldn't be any inducement to go to heaven.
- Even if you're on the right track, you'll get run over if you just sit there.
- Now if there is one thing we do worse than any other nation, it is to try and manage somebody else's affairs.
- Nobody wants to be called common people, especially common people.
- Liberty don't work as good in practice as it does in speeches.
- It's not what you pay a man but what he costs you that counts.
- Everybody is ignorant, only on different subjects.
- Our foreign dealings are an Open Book, generally a Check Book.
- I joked about every prominent man of my time, but I never met a man I didn't like.
- So live that you wouldn't be ashamed to sell the family parrot to the town gossip.

III

Sophie Tucker (1884-1966) was expelled from her mother's womb along the side of a Polish road as the family made its way to America. Her father Charles Kalish, on the run from service in the Czar's army, had gone before them to Boston. As he was hurrying out of southern Russia, one of his traveling companions named Abuza had died; Charles, to escape detection by the Russian police, had taken the man's papers and identity (perhaps an early example of identity theft). Having come in as Abuza, he kept the name, and so was the family called thereafter. After eight years in Boston, they moved down to Hartford and bought a restaurant on Front Street along the Connecticut River. They lived upstairs and rented out some of the rooms. "Abuza's Home Restaurant" mostly prospered because mother Dolly and the children worked hard to put out a good, cheap dinner for 25 cents (appetizer, soup, main course; salad and dessert cost more). Dolly managed to be friendly, outgoing, and charitable, giving away the occasional meal to those in need. She was the strong one who kept things going, helped by children Philip, Sophie, Anna, and Moses. As for Charles, he strutted about as the proprietor and liked to host illicit poker games in the attic, often losing the restaurant's hard-earned receipts. [20]

School, where she excelled, was the first escape for Sophie who hated the drudgeries of the restaurant/rooming house. But she was always the good girl, doing her jobs and with a smile. The good food served with a smile brought tips, and the tips got her into Sylvester Poli's vaudeville theatres on Main Street. Sophie loved the songs, learned them, and when her mouth opened, they came booming out. She started to sing for the customers, which brought in more customers to enjoy the free entertainment that accompanied the cheap, well-prepared food. Sophie was a "natural" who won people over; even her school music teacher praised her "personality." She appeared at the stage doors of Hartford's theatres after matinees; with the promise of "the best meal in town for the least money," she lured the artists to Abuza's. There the show people applauded her singing and gave her their songs. She learned them fast and constantly practiced songs and routines. Even with her chunky figure, 145 pounds by age 13, she won many amateur at contests in Riverside Park. People began to call for the "fat girl," who delighted them with lusty singing and copied comedy routines. [21]

Coming out of the eighth grade at fifteen, Sophie began, like her contemporaries, to go out with a few young men, a process presumed in that time to end in courting. She had dreams of showbusiness, but these faltered when confronted with parental rejection. Escape from kitchen drudgery and waitressing became her first priority. Along came Louis Tuck, a handsome, easy-going drayman for a brewing company who escorted Sophie to her first dance. At graduation the Principal had awarded her diploma, saying, "For Sophie Abuza the girl with the personality." There it came again, another intimation that she belonged onstage. She still pined for showbusiness, but Louis talked her into eloping. Her parents acquiesced in the outcome, but kept them apart until after an orthodox Jewish wedding. Louis could afford only a tiny apartment, where they played house until pregnancy set in. Amiable, laid back, Louis lacked any "push" to lift himself above the drayman's meagre $15/week. What he chiefly enjoyed was to don his best suit and join his male friends on their Saturday night rounds of festive places. Balked in her modest hopes for betterment, Sophie moved back to Abuza's, resigned to another siege of tiresome chores. The birth of their son failed to break the stand-off. Louis went his carefree way, and Sophie added motherhood to her workload.

She held on through her under-21 years, eventually giving in to her obsession and boarding the train for the short 120-mile ride to New York. There she canvassed Tin Pan Alley for jobs, auditioning when they'd listen, asking for advice, help, recommendations. Having once rejected the piano lessons her mother had furnished, she hadn't learned to read, which disqualified her from plugging in stores or in-house in TPA. She finally walked into restaurants and offered to sing for her supper, as she used to do at Abuza's, and got her first temporary jobs. When asked her name the first time, Mrs. Louis Tuck responded, "Sophie Tucker!" She continued her daily rounds along TPA, getting pluggers to teach her songs (she kept up the song-search all her life). Eventually she landed a real job at the uptown "German Village" rathskeller, a huge establishment spread over three floors, employing 15 to 20 singers who performed and led patrons in songs. Set in NY's Tenderloin, the GV was not a place where men brought their wives to dine, and ladies of the evening made themselves available to men without companions. A high, tumultuous noise level greeted Sophie the first night, and an obnoxious drunk grabbed at her as she came in. She just knocked him down, but the commotion brought the police, and the defensive manager sent her home for looking too innocent and out of place. But she returned a few days later having made herself over with a better dress, and they took her on for $15/week (November 1906). They worked her hard, 50 to 100 songs a night, be nice to customers, do all requests, some of which might not be musical. Tips, 50 cents to a dollar, rolled in, and soon money orders reached Hartford for the boy's support. After expenses, the rest went for clothes to sing in. In the daytime that "big girl from the German Village" dropped in daily on TPA, and now the alleymen pressed professional copies on her and came uptown to oversee her work. She could really put a song over. One night the tips added up to $75, and she now cleared $100 to $150/week. [22]

But, this was coasting along a rough edge. The friendly gals of the German Village weren't show people, and the other female tenants where she rented her room brought men upstairs each night. One night the police raided her house and dragged her out of bed to load her in the paddy wagon along with the others for a trip downtown and a court appearance. She crawled free of this dragnet because the others vouched unanimously that she was only a singer. This rude awakening sent her to an amateur contest at one of the Bowery theatres where producers and agents were known to spot talent. Backstage the director forced her to black up and shoved her out to sing. She won and began a career in coonshouting, scoring enthusiastic applause from the outset. She hated the grime of burnt cork, but an agent put her into the small-time for $25/week as a "World Renowned Coon Shouter" and also as "Sophie Tucker, the Ginger Girl, Refined Coon Singer." At the end of the act, off came a glove to show white skin, and to get a final laugh. The small-time grind proved rugged and exhausting, even for someone with her driving energy, one-week and three-day stands on a metropolitan circuit. A room cost $5/week, $5 went to Hartford, $2.50 (10%) went to her agent, and other expenses ate the rest. She darned stockings and did handwashing before bed and ironed the dry clothes in the morning. She kept to herself, asked no favors, and humped her own bags.

As she departed each theatre, she asked for a return date, promised new songs. Gradually it all paid off. Audiences remembered, and when her card went up at the side of the stage, a round of applause came forth. She struggled for success, always available for extra shows or at clubs and conventions. On a small-time circuit Sophie filled the spot of the young girl singer or dancer. She shared the bill of six or seven acts with a male/female dance team, a family of acrobats, a single comedian, a musical "family," a couple of male hoofers, and a comedy sketch of three actors. Most young, single women traveled with their mothers, but Sophie handled all of the arrangements of touring, a big husky girl who projected self-reliance, friendly enough but never outgoing. Preferring loneliness to vulnerability, she could fend off a predator with a few blows and loud words (women alone were considered "fair game" by the masculine fraternity). By now she had two good dresses, a red and a black velvet, plus make-up, a black wig, and a wrapper for the dressing room; for streetwear, two suits, three shirtwaists, and two sets of underwear. A second wrapper was necessary for rooms with baths down the hall. She carried also framed family pictures, a music case, and a hat box with two hats. Each week required six fresh towels to remove the greasepaint make-up that so stubbornly adhered to textiles, virtually invulnerable to the soaps of that era. When she came into the dressing room, she first cleaned her area, then laid a runner along the shelf before setting out her boxes of make-up. People soon sensed her order and cleanliness. [23]

They also appreciated her generosity and consideration. Arriving Monday, upbeat and smiling, she said hello to all backstage, usually handing out to musicians and stagehands a little cash "for smokes." This prevented glitches in her lights and music. At every showplace, she left friends behind. She took down the names and addresses of every manager, news and public relations person, and theatre-goer she'd met. This became her lifelong habit: a week or two before an appearance, she sent postcards to acquaintances, hoping to see them again. She accumulated dozens of address books and thousands of names. Her act evolved along the way, spiced with funnier songs, more movements and stage business, and comic monologs and dialogs. When she'd "perfected" her routines, she tried them out on Tony Pastor, who was pleased to put her on his bill for $40 and a debut in the big-time. By now young Irving Berlin had become a TPA friend, helping her with fresh songs. Instead of the glove, she now doffed the wig for the final laugh. The Monday afternoon audience loved her, and Tony headlined her for the evening show in the number two spot after intermission. He told her, "You've got something, young lady. You're going places. You've got personality!" (That word, always since grade school.) [24]

But instead of Keith's or Hammerstein's Victoria, her next offer, which raised her to $50, was to open in Pittsburgh, not in the big-time, but in burlesque, albeit as the olio headliner. Plus she would play in sketches. For six months she toured the Mid-West in Harry Emerson's *Gay Masqueraders*. The good parts consisted of making a lifelong friend of Fanny Brice and a temporary end of loneliness as part of a company. But she kept some distance by refusing to "double up" on the tour with a male performer, a regular practice among burlesque people to "save money." [25] Burlesque itself constituted the bad part. Burlesque had originally meant a raucous satire of something such as people, politics, or manners, but such literary presumptions had been long abandoned, and though it changed over the years, it remained essentially a sleazy, commercialized sex show. Although stripping did not become its main feature until the 1930's, tights had come in after 1900, and women's bodies, not the songs and dances ballyhooed, were what male audiences came to view. The goal was to present as much raw sex as possible without getting raided. Raw sex meant lewd dancing and "dirty" songs and sketches. Sketch humor was crude:

What's the difference between mashed potatoes and pea soup?

I don't know the difference between m.p. and p.s. What is the difference between m.p. and p.s.? [Note repetition to carry the slower of wit]

The difference between m.s. and p.s. is that you can mash potatoes but you can't..." [Rim shot on the drum] [26]

The only compliment earned by burlesque was that it gave starts to such great talents as Weber and Fields, Eddie Cantor, and Sophie Tucker, but talented people ran away as soon as they got better booking. No people of talent stayed in it, and burlesque just ran on in its tawdry, tacky ways. It had no "golden age," and it existed to enrich those who financed it. The majority of performers, the chorus "girls," working for a meagre $16/week, tended to be past their prime, unattractive, and feeble of talent. Vaudeville developed talent and burlesque did not. [27] Those historians of showbiz, Abel Green and Joe Laurie, tell us that burlesque killed melodrama, that by

1915 the top house of burlesque, Broadway's Columbia, was pulling in $10,000/week (an $11 top ticket), and that burlesque's motto was, "I hope it rains today." [28]

Luck turned in 1909 when impresario Mark Klaw "discovered" Sophie one night in Holyoke, Massachusetts. Klaw and Erlanger produced for Flo Ziegfeld, and Klaw believed the *Follies* needed a coonshouter. Because her trunk came in too late, she had to do it in "whiteface," which went over so well that she never blacked up again. Now she came on as the Junoesque glamor queen in sequins, velvet, and ostrich feathers. At the Atlantic City opening, she just "stole the show." Initially when Klaw handed her over, no one knew exactly how to fit this plump, animated gal into a glamor show. Her only certainty was the agreed-upon $100/week. Then came inspiration from the ex-president's African big game hunt, the song "Moving Day in Jungle Town," a song-and-dance routine with the Ziegfeld Girls cutely costumed as animals. Sophie got to belt out the tune, and they elected her to come on again later to sing three songs of her choosing. She decided on "Cubanola Glide" (Von Tilzer), "The Yiddisha Rag" (Berlin), and "The Right Church But the Wrong Pew." Both Berlin and VonTilzer came down for the show. This opening-night crowd was fussy, and while "Jungle Town" went over all right, it caused no sensation. Then Jack Norworth and wife Nora Bayes wowed them with their "Shine On Harvest Moon" for a successful act-one finale. After that Sophie proved to be no anti-climax. She just sailed in and put her songs over—and drew wild applause and demands for encores. Six minutes ran to twenty-four! After the curtain, Bayes exploded into rage demanding that Sophie be sacked. Z mollified Bayes by cutting the three songs, leaving only "Moving Day." Later after a month in New York, the show terminated Sophie. [29]

But—Sophie had become a star, the *Follies* had "made" her; she now headlined any bill (and Z apologized later). William Morris signed her to a permanent contract and personally guided her career from then on. In Chicago Jack Lait called her the "Mary Garden of Ragtime," and there for the first time she saw her name in lights (always her "lucky town"). On that Chicago bill, she sang "There's Company in the Parlor Girls, Come On Down," her first double entendre song. One night, it drew out all the Everleigh Club girls. From then, her act always closed with a "hot" number. With her friendly charisma and maternal figure, she came off funny, not smutty. And so the money rolled in, and she carried her entire family into fine style. Her son attended a good boarding school, and she put a smart brother through Yale and then NYU Law School. Her parents reveled in a big new home. Sophie's only extravagances were the gowns and jewels that glamorized her performances. More Chicago luck came in 1912 when she bought her signature song "Some of These Days" from black composer Shelton Brooks ("Darktown Strutters Ball"). It lasted her thirty years. [30]

Her ultimate, well deserved triumph was attained during one October week in 1913 when she finally headlined at Poli's Theatre in her hometown of Hartford. Posters all over town proclaimed, "Sophie Tucker, the Pride of Hartford" and "Hartford's Own Sophie Tucker." Her entire family and a large crowd met the train. Sophie's pictures adorned the walls of the new home. Poli's manager framed her contract—$500/week—and hung it in the lobby. Those who had once criticized her for abandoning domestic responsibilities fell all over themselves offering fulsome praise to enjoy a little reflected glory. She played to capacity houses all week. When the Monday evening curtain rose, not only did old friends and neighbors fill the front row seats and her family occupy a main box, but in the next box sat the principal and all of her grade school teachers. [31] For the rest of her life, she would always be welcomed as "Hartford's Own." [32]

Notes: Chapter 33

1. Quoted in Simon Louvish, *The Man on the Flying Trapeze: The Life and Times of W.C. Fields*, 74.
2. W.C. Fields, "From Boy Juggler to Star Comedian," *Theatre Magazine* (October 1928). "Extracts" downloaded from Internet website: www.juggling.org.
3. *Idem*; Louvish, 62-63.
4. Rich Chamberlin, "W.C. Fields, The Crown Prince of Comedy…A Juggler First!" *Jugglers World* (May 1983), 1-2; downloaded from Internet website: www.juggling.org.
5. Louvish, 108, 109, 110-111; Chamberlin, 1-2.
6. Douglas Gilbert, *American Vaudeville: Its Life and Times*, 309-313; Louvish, 95-97, 124.
7. *Ibid.*, 110-111, 167-168, 172-173; Chamberlin, 2.
8. Ray Robinson, *American Original: A Life of Will Rogers*, 7, 14-21.
9. *Ibid.*, 22-25, 34-41, 55-58.
10. *Ibid.*, 76-80.
11. *Ibid.*, 80-81.
12. *Ibid.*, 82.
13. *Ibid,.* 84.
14. *Ibid,.* 85, for courtship; 106-107, for Broadway and *Titanic* anecdote. See Gerald Bordman, *American Musical Theatre: A Chronicle*, 276, for Will in *Wall Street Girl*.
15. *Ibid.*, 308; Robinson, 107-109.
16. *Ibid.*, 112-114.
17. *Ibid.*, 115-120.
18. Louvish, 183.These sayings came from several Will Roger websites on the Internet; most came from ellensplace.net/rogers.html.
19. Sophie Tucker, *Some of These Days: The Autobiography of Sophie Tucker*, 1-3.
20. *Ibid.*, 8-11.
21. *Ibid.*, 12-31.
22. *Ibid.*, 32-40.
23. *Ibid.*, 41-52.
24. *Ibid.*, 52-60.
25. Irving Zeidman, *The American Burlesque Show: A History*, 112, for the quote, 11ff. for other details.
26. *Ibid.*, 35, 43, 45.
27. Abel Green and Joe Laurie, Jr., *Show Biz: From Vaude to Video*, 74, 75, 77.
28. Tucker, 60-76.
29. *Ibid.*, 78-88, 94-95, 100-107, 114.
30. *Ibid.*, 118-119, 121-122.
31. Author's note: This is a personal memory.

34. Progressives (V): Peary and Henson

"...as it [flag] snapped and crackled with the wind, I felt a savage joy and exultation....whenever the world's work was done by a white man, he had been accompanied by a colored man. From the building of the pyramids and the journey to the cross, to the discovery of the new world and the discovery of the North Pole, the Negro had been the faithful and the constant companion of the Caucasian, and I felt all that it was possible for me to feel, that it was I, a lowly member of my race, who had been chosen by fate to represent it, at this, almost the last of the world's great work.

Matthew Henson [1]

By 1900 nearly all of the earth's regions had been explored or at least visited by representatives of the civilization of western Europe/North America. As they observed the quarto-centennial of Columbus's "discoveries" at the World's Columbian Exposition in Chicago in 1893 (Chapter 6), people understood that few areas remained to be explored. The sources of the Nile River had been located, as had other geographical obscurities such as the Australian Outback and the interiors of Alaska and the Sahara Desert. At the Columbian Expo, historian Frederick Jackson Turner read a paper to colleagues in the American Historical Association that pronounced the closure of America's "frontier." No longer on the map of North America could a continuous line of settlement, north to south, be traced. Americans began to realize that they had crossed into a new watershed: their 20C descendents would grow up without the conditioning of life on a frontier. For any who coveted the title and job description of "explorer," opportunities had dwindled to the frigid regions. Those feeling an itch for the unknown and uncharted must travel to the earth's extremes, the Poles, where they would have to survive unrelenting cold and the dangers of ice caps and pack ice.

Most polar exploration was being undertaken by British (Scott, Shackleton) and Norwegian (Nansen, Amundsen, Steffansson) rivals, but an American, Robert Edwin Peary (1856-1920), intended the "stars and stripes" to be first over the North Pole. Although born in Cresson, Pennsylvania, Peary grew up in Maine (of a Maine family) and graduated from Bowdoin College in 1877 as a civil engineer. In this capacity, the Navy commissioned him a Lieutenant in 1881, a billet concerned not with seagoing tasks but constructions on land. But in 1884, he experienced a reprieve from navy yard routines with a posting to Nicaragua as assistant engineer in the ongoing survey of an interoceanic canal route. Having tasted the exotic, Peary sought more travel opportunities. Back in the U.S. in 1885, he read a paper about Greenland that whetted his appetite for the unexplored. He wangled a six-month leave in 1886 to see for himself. From Godhavn he and a companion ascended the escarpment of the Greenland Ice Cap and traveled east for three weeks, covering 100 miles up to an elevation of 7500 feet. He came home fascinated and churning with new ambition. Not for him the bland life expectations of a civil engineer in naval service. It wasn't even a toss-up; the tropics had already been staked out in the numerous canal surveys. With the French holding the Panama concession, there were small prospects for a U.S. canal. Peary desired fame; wherever it might be, he had to get there first. [2]

From the Greenland adventure he had carried back some Arctic furs to recoup travel expenses. At a Washington, D.C., furrier he encountered a young black man ten years junior, Matthew Henson, who reacted enthusiastically to Peary's tales. Since his next assignment was a return to Nicaragua on another survey, Peary hired Henson to go along as personal assistant and valet. Henson (1866-1955) had grown up in Washington, the son of freeborn former sharecroppers. After his parents died he ran off (at twelve) to Baltimore where an elderly and kind sea captain named Childs took him aboard the *Katie Hinds* as cabinboy. For six years Henson sailed with Childs and matured into an able seaman. Childs, lonely and in his sixties, became fond of Henson and tutored him in academic subjects and the Bible. When Childs died suddenly at sea (1883), Henson made his way back to Washington. In Henson Peary had gained a man of practical abilities and survival skills. What made him unique were the intelligence and talents that matched his vital skills.

After Nicargua Peary shifted Henson to the federal payroll as a messenger at Philadelphia's League Island Navy Yard, where Peary attended to naval duties over the next three years (1888-1891). He fought the boredom of navy yard work by planning his next Greenland expedition, intended to reach its northernmost point. He also courted and married Josephine Diebitsch of Washington, D.C. During 1889, F. Nansen of Norway achieved the first crossing of Greenland, a blow which stole some of Peary's intended thunder. Finally after securing 18 month's leave and having raised the funds to charter the *Kite*, a Newfoundland sealer, Peary, along with Josephine and Henson, plus six others, departed for Greenland on June 6, 1891. (One of the six was ship's surgeon Frederick A. Cook, who would later claim to have beaten Peary to the North Pole.) They ran the *Kite* up Greenland's west coast to Wolstenholme Sound where they set up a base camp to spend the winter. Expeditions had to get to the Arctic before winter froze the sea, then wait until March for the return of light. Henson as chief carpenter built the two-room house that became headquarters. Here he first encountered the Inuit people (Eskimos) and began to learn their language, culture, and arctic survival skills. Although a mishap injury forced Henson to return early, Peary did reach the north cape of Greenland and proved it to be an island. With this geographical "discovery" to his credit, the expedition returned to New York in September 1892 to much acclaim, Peary's first taste of success. [3]

The momentum of success aided Peary's return to Greenland the next year (1893), where Mrs. Peary (along for the second, and final, time) gave birth to her first child, a girl. This turned out to be the only noteworthy accomplishment because the party nearly starved to death on the ice cap when they couldn't locate food caches. They ate their dogs. Peary (and Henson) chose to remain, sending the rest of the party home on the *Kite* in August 1894. In the spring of 1895 they did manage to cross the Greenland ice cap and returned to New York in August. Peary had promised to try for the Pole but had not even made a start in that direction. To sustain the interest of his backers, he had brought back a consolation prize: voila! two sizable meteorites, one of 1000 pounds and another of 5500. And he promised a gigantic third one, which he went back for in a summer voyage the next year. Unfortunately their equipment wasn't heavy enough to move this 100 T (200,000 pounds) monster, which required a second try the following summer. [4] Interest in these objects of planetary science ran very high at the time, and Peary coveted them for the $40,000 later paid by the American Museum of Natural History (where one of them can still be seen). These had long served the Inuit as the iron source for spear points; Peary justified the taking, saying that he had traded them enough iron points to cover the loss, a contention that later aroused some disagreement. [5]

Such found money helped but did not much ease the constant and semi-desperate canvassing for funds to send Peary to the Pole. When U.S. sources came up short, he passed his explorer's hat in Britain to raise enough to charter the *Windward* for a run as far poleward as possible (1898-1899). On this journey Henson bonded with the Inuit. He lived with them, became comfortable in their garments, ate their food, learned their skills, and became a friend. Later he said, "I have come to love these people....They are my friends and they regard me as theirs." [6] Donald MacMillen, a member of the final 1908-1909 expedition, corroborates:

> He was the most popular man on board the ship with the Eskimos. He could talk their language like a native. He made all the sledges that went to the Pole with Peary because he was a better man than any of his white assistants. As Peary himself admitted, "I can't get along without Henson." [7]

They called him (in Inuit) "Matthew the Kind One," and they followed Peary because they loved Henson. [8] Henson did the managing, going out with the Inuit to hunt when meat was short, taking care of Peary on dangerous treks over oceanic pack ice. Peary in his books claimed to be the ethnographer, but Henson oversaw the work, and whenever Peary needed something, he directed Henson to convey his demands and solve the problem. [9]

Peary and company spent four years in the Arctic on the *Windward*. He made several attempts to cross the pack ice, but never got above 84 degrees, 17 minutes, over 5 degrees short of the Pole. Disasters occurred, including Peary's loss of eight toes and the deaths of six Inuit. On one attempt they had to turn back because food ran short and because "leads," stretches of open water, held them up or required detours. They came home frustrated in the fall of 1902. Much had been learned, and Peary had become convinced of the necessity for a sturdier ship. With TR in the White House, much more support for Peary's venture materialized in high places, which brought in the large contributions necessary for a new ship capable of withstanding the hazards of the Arctic. Peary called it the *Roosevelt* and had it designed with a reenforced hull shaped so that when the pack ice caught it, the ship would rise, evading the pressures that might crush it. With this stronger hull, it could break its way through the lesser ice to get farther north than before. In 1905-1906, on its maiden voyage, the *Roosevelt* performed as intended, enabling the company to reach 87 degrees, 6 minutes, just 174 miles from the goal. But again too many leads of open water, plus the usual problems with food and dogs forced them to return in failure. [10]

By 1908 Peary had reached 52 and the painful realization that he had already reached his physical limits, that he would soon have to settle down and either declare his triumphs or quietly accept failure. If he didn't get all the way and return with true navigational records, his would be a very notable failure. The *U.S.S. Roosevelt* got underway out of New York on July 6. By September 5 they had finally covered the distance to Cape Sheridan on the Arctic shore of Ellesmere Island at the end of the long, narrow strait between Greenland and Canada. This location lay at latitude 82 degrees, 30 minutes, which no other ship had ever reached. The explorers wintered on the *Roosevelt* until March, when they carried supplies laterally to the west to set up a base camp at Cape Columbia. Their very large party included 19 sledges, 17 Inuit, 6 whites, 133 dogs, plus Peary and Henson. [11] While waiting aboard ship for the light, they had hunted musk-oxen, deer, and rabbits. No information exists about socializing or moments of relaxation during the dark weeks on the ice-bound *Roosevelt*. There was a player piano aboard, but we don't know who pumped the pedals or what rolls were heard. Henson had kept busy building the 19 sledges and training the inexperienced whites in handling dogs. At Cape Columbia they cached supplies and built igloos. On March 1, 1909, Peary sent Henson ahead to break the start of the trail.

This was a dangerous task because pack ice is unstable and constantly in motion as wind and ocean currents keep drifting it. This sea ice often builds up into small mountains, or pressure ridges, as high as 60 feet. Surfaces are never smooth, and the ice frequently breaks open into leads, which either a sledge must detour around or wait and risk crossing newly formed thin ice, both courses equally dangerous. Besides the tormenting cold, there can be sudden storms and white-outs. Peary fell twice into leads and Henson once. They could have frozen in minutes without dry clothes and fire. Dehydration—in a realm composed of moisture—is always one of the greatest problems. Melted snow was the only source of water, and alcohol in a stove the only heat source. According to one vignette, Henson had to solder a leaking tin of alcohol. Impossible with gloves on, he risked freezing and burning if the alcohol ignited. If the alcohol had leaked away, they could have perished, or failed, from thirst. [12]

From Cape Columbia the expedition had to run across 413 nautical miles or almost six degrees of latitude (one degree ='s 69 nautical miles or 110 km.). (A nautical mile is 6076 feet or 16% longer than a land mile of 5280 feet.) Following a new plan, five teams started, but the other four traveled to support Peary's team and boost it to success. Previous failures had been chiefly the result of supply problems; enough supplies had to be placed at reachable points to insure completion in both directions. Previously, because leads, pressure ridges, and storms had delayed progress, there had not been enough supply points or quantities of supplies. On this final trip, leads would be encountered on 14 days. Peary intended a surfeit of supplies, hence the plan for five parties to drive ahead with full loads. Each team was to go a certain distance, cache their supplies, and turn back, leaving a string of caches to sustain Peary, Henson, and their four Inuit on the return leg. When Bob Bartlett, who was also Captain of the *Roosevelt*, turned back, the last to do so, Peary and Henson had 174 miles to go or two and one-half degrees of latitude, still a long way. They drove forward, pushing hard because potential failure lurked ahead at some ultimate lead or pressure ridge. On April 6, 1909, five weeks after Henson first went out to break trail, Peary's sextant indicated 90 degrees north, the point at which the only direction is south. They also cut through ice and dropped a rope to make a depth sounding. The rope ran out at 9000 feet with no bottom reached. This added verification because a deep trench underlies the North Pole. Ironically, with the goal reached, they still had to cover half the distance, which they accomplished, remarkably, in sixteen days, averaging 26 miles per day, just under half of the outward time. [13]

Peary and Henson had been adventuring together since 1887, twenty-two years. After reaching what they had so long striven for, Peary turned very cool and casual toward the man with whom he had shared his most vital times. Author Wally Herbert, himself an Arctic explorer who has reached the Pole, states that when he had determined that the Pole lay only three miles off, that Peary denied Henson a place in the final dash, so that he, Peary, would be not only first but alone at the goal. Afterward he ignored Henson's outstretched hand as he entered his tent to sleep. On the return, Peary spoke only when he gave an order, and the treatment continued on the homeward voyage. Later, in an account of the expedition Peary belittled Henson, saying he did well under close supervision, but that he lacked "daring and initiative" because of racial inheritance. This surprised not only Henson but other members of the expedition, all of whom in their accounts quote Peary, who insisted on partnering with Henson because, "I can't get along without him." [14]

Herbert, who has not only covered Peary's ground, but also spoken with the descendents of Peary's Inuits, asserts that Peary lacked all care for and only used these people. Both Peary and Henson mated with Inuit women and produced families. By teenaged Aleqasina, Peary fathered sons in 1900 and 1906. He had taken up with her when she was 13 and married—Inuit customs permitting a high degree of sexual freedom. Earlier, at first sight, he had called her the "belle of the tribe." Peary boasted of his closeness to the Inuit and claimed to speak their language, but actually relied on Henson for all of his communicating. The Inuit respected Peary because he possessed great amounts of material goods on great ships and because Henson told them that Peary's spirit equaled their gods. Peary barely concealed an indifference. On one occasion he took seven dogs in an unfair exchange, and on another he dismissed several Inuit who had served him for years because of grumbling. In the case of the meteorites, Peary highhandedly helped himself to their vital source of iron, claiming to have replaced the loss with better implements. Yet another incident unmasks his callousness. In 1897 he returned with six Inuit for Dr. Franz Boas the leading anthropologist at New York's American Museum of Natural History. Boas had requested only one such "specimen" and was unprepared to maintain six. He had to house them in the museum basement and soon all contracted pneumonia. By the next year, five had died. Two of these had hunted for Peary. Their remains were dissected, and the bones mounted for display. The young survivor was a son of one of these, and later in 1907, someone unfriendly to Peary broke the story of an Eskimo boy who wanted to return his father's bones to the Arctic. Peary had done nothing about any of this; having delivered the six specimens, he had washed his hands of the matter. [15]

Peary's racism is easy to parse for that time The inferiority of nonwhites was a given, unquestioned by the WASP master class. At every world's fair, from Chicago in 1893 to San Diego in 1915, Americans found some delight watching "native" peoples enacting "daily life" in replicas of villages, including Indians, Eskimos, Filipinos, and Africans (Chapter 6). Such "scientific" displays of nonwhites confirmed white American superiority, and, for the well-meaning and thoughtful, confirmation of what Rudyard Kipling had called the "white man's burden," a responsibility to rule with benevolence these primitive tribal folk (and of course to extract whatever natural resources their lands contained in return for such services). Mark Twain was one of the few to question this "natural order" in the chain of being. In *Huckleberry Finn* (1884) white Huck and black slave Jim run away together on a raft down the Mississippi. This suggests a parallel and a comparison with Peary and Henson alone together out on the pack ice. In the course of their adventures, Huck the ignorant white boy, was cared for and saved from catastrophe because of Jim's intelligent and tender ministrations, and the reader becomes aware of Jim as a fellow human. Twain tells this in a series of comic misadventures, which contemporaries perceived merely as a sequel to its humorous predecessor *Tom Sawyer* (1876). They failed to notice that Jim is not caricatured as a comic darky, but fully depicted as a rare human being of almost saintly goodness.

We may ask what happened between Peary and Henson as they shared, in a similar conditon of intimacy, adventure and adversity? Peary may have been a "stuffed shirt" back in civilization, but in the constantly precarious Arctic, he had to behave informally and let down some of his defenses. He obviously possessed a full appreciation of Henson's very visible virtues, because he relied on them, he wagered his life on them. Normally such relationships produce warm feelings. Did Peary ever experience such? Can we doubt that there were not at certain times exchanges of mutual friendliness (or at least some pretense of it)? But if so, in the end, Peary suppressed such positive feelings. Why? Perhaps out of jealousy? After all, Henson exercised a charismatic control over the Inuit; they would do anything for him, for Peary too, but always to please Henson. Henson built the sledges, taught dog-handling skills, and oversaw the logistics. Did Peary decide that he couldn't go back and tell the real story without diminishing himself? Or was it not so much jealousy as the chronic inability to allow credit to others? Certainly Peary sought fame and the sole credit for accomplishing a great thing. And giving a black man so much credit would have diminished him (Peary) more. Call it meanness of spirit, but such a threat forced Peary into denial. How could he have faced Theodore Roosevelt?

TR had been the savior. By 1902 the Navy had become negative toward Peary's polar aspirations and wanted him back on active duty. At 42 he was no longer young and had had his chances. But the President fancied him; TR saw a brave, determined exponent of the "strenuous life," much like himself (he was only a couple of years younger than Peary). He overruled the Navy Department, smoothing the explorer's way, becoming his unofficial patron. From 1902 the lights all turned green for Peary, as private purses opened to design and construct a vessel sturdy in Arctic ice, appropriately christened the *Roosevelt*. TR took care of Peary's promotion to Commander, and after the 1906 failure, came to the public relations rescue again with a gold medal from the National Geographic Society. Underway in 1908, Peary's first port of call was Oyster Bay, Long Island, for a visit to Sagamore Hill. There TR hosted a bon voyage luncheon and inspected the ship, going over it very thoroughly. He sent the eponymous ship off saying, "I believe in you, Peary." He had made Peary into a national hero. [16]

On the way back, as the explorers began to swell with anticipation, a jolt of the unexpected abruptly quelled the celebratory mood. A century later we take it as comic relief, but they weren't amused. Heading south, at a stop at Etah, Greenland, Peary and company were astounded and troubled to learn that Dr. Frederick A. Cook (1865-1940) had proclaimed himself the first to have reached the Pole, one year earlier (April 21, 1908)! However skepticism superseded shock when two Inuit who had wintered with Cook laughed and said that Cook had advanced no farther than 20 miles out on the pack ice before returning to the stout hut where he had lived snugly through the dark months. In the pack of polar explorers, Cook jumps out as the joker. With two years training at the New York Medical College, Cook, in that time of underdeveloped medical science, had qualified as ship's surgeon on Peary's early 1891 Greenland expedition. He later went to Antarctica in 1897-99 with a Belgian expedition. [17] He parlayed his polar jaunts into a successful career as a travel writer and lecturer. He thrilled listeners with his adventure tales, and to freshen up his repertoire, he began to make sorties to Alaska in 1903. Mt. McKinley aroused grander ambitions in him; he would be the first to gain its summit—and live happily off the proceeds of popular books and larger audiences. He scouted the project craftily, and in 1906 posed himself at a dramatic vista, which he passed off as the 20,000 ft. summit of North America's tallest mountain. When only minor opposition to his claims—easily passed off as jealousy—resulted, Cook chose to leap from the controversial to the preposterous with the allegation that he had reached the Pole before Peary (whom everyone knew was trying very hard to get there). [18]

This bogus claim soiled the triumph of Peary's return. Peary walked down the gangplank into controversy but emerged victorious because his navigational records and depth soundings produced the substantive evidence that demolished Cook's claims. Recently when an uncropped original of Cook's McKinley photo surfaced, scientific analysis demolished that claim too, revealing scenery of the 5000-foot level. After the exposure of his polar fakery, Cook dropped from view, until 1925 when he was convicted of peddling phony oil well stocks to naive rural folk. He received a fourteen-year sentence and was paroled in 1930. Cook imagined greater things than most felons, and his charm and verbal skills earned a comfortable living. Magazines paid well for articles of interest, and lecturers found eager audiences in pre-radio days. But a felon's greed drove him to blowing louder notes on his little horn. [19]

For Peary, a retirement promotion to the two-star rank of Rear Admiral came in 1911. He settled comfortably on an island in Maine's Casco Bay near Portland where he had grown up. He lived only nine more years, dying prematurely at 64, a year after his patron and comtemporary TR, in 1920. Both may have overpaid their dues to the "strenuous life." Peary not only received the full honors of burial in Arlington National Cemetery, but he and his wife lie under a handsome monument of white Maine granite of his design. From a broad platform, the monument recedes upward two levels to support a globe on which the North Pole is marked by a three-inch bronze star. Inscribed on the globe is his chosen motto: "I shall find a way or make one."

For Henson there was no fame but a few belated marks of recognition: honorary membership in the New York Explorers' Club in1937 and a Navy medal in 1946, nine years before his death in 1955. Full recognition came only posthumously in 1988, when his remains were removed from the Bronx to a spot near Peary at

Arlington. But Henson had always been celebrated by African Americans. He belongs in the small, select pantheon of black heroes that includes Joe Louis, Jackie Robinson, Bert Williams, Paul Robeson, Bill Robinson, and Marian Anderson (to which should be added Scott Joplin). These had all achieved greatness on the world stage in times when few of their brothers could aspire. Their examples had brightened and lifted up the spirits of those in poverty and repression; they had cut through the despair lying heavily over black life. The inscription on Henson's monument rectifies the injustice: "Co-Discoverer of the North Pole." [20]

Notes: Chapter 34

1. Matthew Henson, *A Black Explorer at the North Pole*, 136.
2. "Peary, Robert Edwin," *Dictionary of American Biography*, VII, 362-363. This older 1934 account ignores Henson and his vital role in Peary's explorations; nor does Henson have an entry in this volume.
3. *Ibid.*, 363; "Matthew Henson: Arctic Explorer," *Virtual Exploration Society*, 1-3; Wally Herbert, *The Noose Hangs High: Robert E. Peary and the Race to the North Pole*, 27-64, 66-68, 92, 114-115, 122-125, 140-142;
4. "Peary, Robert Edwin," 363-364.
5. Herbert, 106-108.
6. Henson, 6-7.
7. Susan A. Kaplan, "Introduction to the Bison Book Edition," of Henson (above, note 1), xvii-xviii.
8. *Ibid.*, xiv; Henson became an Inuit legend.
9. Herbert, 170-174, 193-194, 219.
10. "Peary, Robert Edwin," 365; Henson, 3.
11. "Peary, Robert Edwin," 366.
12. Henson, 4-5, 54, 80, 105.
13. *Ibid.*, 6-7; "Peary, Robert Edwin," 365-366.
14. Herbert, 230-234, 244, 246-251, 254, 256.
15. *Ibid.*, 106-108, 138, 142, 193-194, 204-206, 219-220, 238-239, 336.
16. *Ibid.*, 152-156, 203-204, 217.
17. "Matthew Henson: Arctic Explorer," 6.
18. John Tierney, "Explorer faked famed photo," *Arizona Republic* (November 29, 1998): A24.
19. "Matthew Henson: Arctic Explorer," 6-7. Currently there exists a "Frederick A. Cook Society," operated by a descendent, which desires to rehabilitate Cook's reputation as a genuine polar explorer, and which can be located at the website www.cookpolar.org. An opposing website, www.drfrederickcook.com carries on a polemic against the "Cook Society."
20. "Peary, Robert Edwin," 367; "Matthew Henson: Arctic Explorer," 7.

35. The Art of Rag (VII): Ragtime and the Social Evil

It is inconceivable the Levee served such a purpose, but the fact remains that scant information exists about the employment opportunities experienced by Joplin, et al, in this place and time. The Levee is a black hole of ragtime lore. The pimps and whores that peopled its streets weren't in the habit of amassing evidence against themselves. Hence there are no cancelled checks stating "Pay to the Order of Scott Joplin" and bearing the signature of Madame Carrie Watson…. [1]

RAGTIME ALMANAC

Some Ragtime Titles Associated With the Social Evil [2]

Title	Composer/Location	Year
Ta-Ra-Ra-Boom-Der-e (Song)	Henry Sayers	1890's
A Hot Time in the Old Town Tonight (Song)	Theodore Metz	1890's
Mandy's Broadway Stroll (Rag)	Thomas Broady	1898
Bowery Buck (Rag)	Tom Turpin	1899
Coon Hollow Capers (Patrol)	Frank R. Gillis	1900
Queen of Love, Two-Step (March)	Charles Hunter	1901
Levee Rag	Charles E. Mullen	1902
Heliotrope Bouquet (Rag)	Louis Chauvin, Scott Joplin	1907
Sponge Rag	Walter C. Simon	1911
Pride of the Smoky Row (Rag)	J. M. Wilcockson	1911
Pretty Baby (Song)	Tony Jackson	1916
Twelfth Street Rag	Euday L. Bowman	1914
Petticoat Lane (Rag)	Euday L. Bowman	1914
The Naked Dance	Jelly Roll Morton, Tony Jackson	?
Chestnut Street in the 90's	"Brun" Campbell	?
Lulu White (Rag)	"Brun" Campbell	?
Key Stone Rag	Willie Anderson	1921

Although ragtime has been called "whorehouse music," the short list above doesn't add up to a celebration of the sporting life. From three latterday ragtimers we have also:

Chestnut Valley Rag (1961)	Trebor Tichenor	
The Storyville Sport (1960's)	Tom Shea	
Stormin' the Castle (1976)	Robert Ault	

But these don't fatten the anemic list. In their compendious, and valuable, list of 2000 rags published up to 1938 (in *That American Rag*), David Jasen and Gene Jones have not found any rags entitled "Tenderloin Rag,"

"Red Light Rag," or "Sporting House Rag." Who, other than a few prurient or daring souls, would have dared to be seen purchasing them? What music or department store would have stocked them? When Theron Bennett inserted a "dirty" folk strain into his *St.Louis Tickle* (Chapter 19), he published it pseudonymously.

For the operator of a brothel, music, unlike linens, servants, and security, was a frill. Liquor—at outrageous prices—provided the other main source of profits. But music did serve as a "come-on" that put patrons in the mood, so it was a useful frill. It speeded up the process of separating customers from their money in the shortest possible time; significant profits depended on turnover, the numbers that inflated the "bottom line." In the cheap fifty-cent houses, affordable to the mass of workers, no consideration had to be given to the mood of customers: they simply came in, got in line, waited their turn, got serviced, and departed, usually to the nearest beer joint. Music might have made the wait more pleasant, but it couldn't possibly have speeded up the process, and such a *lumpen* clientele never tipped.

In the classier resorts, the ambience required music. Music dissolved awkward moments. For a shy male, appearing in a room where six or eight gussied-up females turned abruptly toward him in the silence of their broken-off chatter, there was a potential for embarrassment, even humiliation. Music warmed and opened up the scene. It prompted smiles and quips, a sense of "we're glad you came." Music papered over any rough spots, prompted feelings of well being that later bolstered the recollections of pleasure that assured repeat business. The smart, experienced entrepreneurs of sex learned that music increased their take. Some of the stingier madams, grasping for the quicker return, opted for coin-operated music machines, but this diminished the illusion by raising the awareness that cash trumped pleasure.

Parlor houses didn't advertise their attractions and kept no employment records, so our knowledge of their musical doings comes from a few memoirs and reformers' critiques. Here is a jaundiced account from the back room of a New York saloon where men found available women:

> Efforts are frequently made to enliven the scene by music and singing. In the ordinary rear room, with cheap furniture, flickering lights, bad air, and filled with rough men, a sallow faced youth, with a cigarette hanging out of the corner of his mouth, sits at a piano and indifferently bangs out popular airs in wild discordant notes. This becomes a "concert hall" when the proprietor provides more music and additional singers. [3]

Recent research on Chicago's "Levee" districts [4] turns up similar information: in "evil," "degenerate" bordellos, the "incessant banging and clanging of ragtime" provided the musical accompaniment. [5] None of these hostile accounts names any musicians. If Scott Joplin led a band during the 1893 World's Columbian Expo, or Louis Chauvin delighted listeners ca. 1907 in Levee resorts, local sources don't tell. Our source on the Levee's elite Everleigh Club (Charles Washburn, 1934), which was very untypical (Chapter 23), informs us that the "Professor," a Mr. Vanderpool, was required to play requests and keep modestly in the background. His piano was secondary, subordinate to the small string groups (violin, cello, piano, harp) playing innocuously in the genteel, ornate parlors of the Dearborn Street mansion. Vanderpool's main job was to fill in between sets for the string players. They called him "Van the piano man," and Ada Everleigh once said, "A bagnio pianist learns to play *Poet and Peasant* like a vaudeville xylophonist, without stopping for twelve minutes." [6] Van wore a tuxedo, worked from 10:00 PM to 7:00 AM, and received the relatively generous compensation of $50/week. He was fortunate because elsewhere the pay was tips. Occasionally he over-imbibed, and the Sisters ordered him thrown off the premises, but they always took him back. [7]

A black Denver violinist, George Morrison, corroborates Washburn's account of genteel music in the classier resorts. During 1913-14 he played violin and led a trio of violin, guitar, and piano in the parlor house of Mattie Silks. They played "quiet music," "short" pieces, songs like "Red Wing," "Silver Threads Among the Gold," "Lady Lou," "Call Me Back," and "Just a Dream." Sometimes, when a customer requested a dance, they played livelier stuff like "Darktown Strutters Ball." Never a ragtimer, Morrison later formed "George Morrison and His Jazz Orchestra" to play for dances, and he further states that in 1911, when he married, that he was already playing "…improvised jazz music. I don't mean 'Maple Leaf' or anything like that. Just taking a tune and jazzing it up by improvising." [8] (Does his "jazzing it" really mean ragging, or does "improvised" refer to a jazzier style with syncopation in the bass?)

What does the art of rag owe to tenderloins? From Daniel Kelly's investigation of the polemics of prostitution in Chicago, we learn that only white professors received any notice ("in all these accounts the professors were palefaces"). [9] White witnesses simply failed to see black musicians. Yet we have regularly read that most piano players in whorehouses, dance halls, and saloons were African Americans. Eubie Blake, who got his start in cathouses, reeled off to Al Rose a significant list of early ragtimers with black faces: Jesse Pickett, "Big Head" Wilbur, Jack "the Bear" Wilson, "One-Leg Willy" Joseph, "Old Man Metronome" French (on the banjo), "Big Jimmy" Green, William Turk, Sammy Ewell, "Shout" Blake (no relation to Eubie), "Slew Foot" Nelson, and Willy "Egg Head" Sewell. [10] Like French many ex-slave musicians progressed from banjo to piano to meet a new demand as the piano became mass-produced. They jigged and ragged the tunes they knew and the new ones they heard. But we know very little of the musicianship of these legendary "perfessers."

Which brings us to a significant exception, Tom Turpin, the central figure in St.Louis ragtime. Before setting up his own establishments, Tom played at the "Castle" for Babe Connors in the late 1890's. Like the Everleigh Club in Chicago and the Arlington and Mahogany Hall in New Orleans, the Castle (210 South 6th Street) was an elite house. Customers liked to recall plump, bronze Babe Connors, "dripping with diamonds," descending her grand staircase to welcome them and present her eight or ten "Creole" girls, genuine products of Louisiana, considered refined because of their "French" gowns, accents, and suave deportment. [11] On busy nights these fetching ladies became sylphs as they cavorted, in long dresses but sans innerwear, over a mirrored dance floor. Motivating their performance was the frolicsome "Ta-Ra-Ra-Boom-Der-e" (original wording).

During his time there, Turpin probably played this and other tunes that subsequently, with clean lyrics, found publishers and became popular. What caused the Castle's renown was not so much the high quality of its inmates as the unique quality of its entertainment. Houses of ill repute tolerated some music and dancing, but the intent remained the encouragement of lust; a few drinks, a few tunes, a few touches, followed by the (brief) main event upstairs. But at the Castle there was big Mama Lou, almost a parody of the bandannaed kitchen mammy a la Aunt Jemima, who M.C.'d, "insulted" customers, and belted out vulgar and funny songs. After which she led the girls and audience in the snappy choruses. Beside the infectious "Ta-Ra-Ra-Boom-Der-e," customers roared at "Who Stole the Lock Off the Hen House Door," "Honey on My Lip, God Damn," and "There'll Be a Hot Time in the Old Town Tonight." Theodore Metz heard the "Hot Time" song, about what the singer planned to do to the woman in bed with her man, sanitized it into a hit song, and saw it adopted by the Rough Riders, later to become a campaign song for TR. Most were probably folk songs, but Mama Lou popularized them upward from their subculture of origin. Another of her semi-creations was the "Bully Song," conveyed (one night on a Pullman, it is said) by writer Charles Trevathan to May Irwin. In 1895, "When I walk dat levee round, etc.," jumpstarted the coonsong craze and pushed May to stardom ("I'm lookin' for dat bully an' he must be found"). When, after a satisfying dinner at Tony Faust's renowned restaurant, a fellow diner said, "Let's go storm the Castle!" the intent may have been carnal, but there would be plenty of fun preceding the main event. [12]

James Hubert "Eubie" Blake (1883-1983) testifies further to the connection between ragtime and the social evil. His parents former slaves from Virginia, his father John Sumner Blake knocked down $9/week on the Baltimore docks, while his mother Emily Johnston Blake laundered. Eubie's view of the world was conditioned by the whip scars on his father's back and by his father's first pair of shoes, issued when he enlisted in the Union Army. [13] Eubie was their one child, the eleventh, none of the first ten having survived, and thus very "special." Musically Eubie was a "natural." At age six he strayed from his mother in a department store into the music section, where he was discovered trying to pick out tunes on a Weaver organ. A manipulative manager professed amazement at Eubie's innate talents and conned Emily into a budget-busting $75 purchase, $1 down and 25 cents a week. Mother Emily, very devout, arranged for lessons from a neighbor lady; she envisioned Eubie doing her proud accompanying the hymns at services. But while running errands in his lowdown Baltimore neighborhood, he caught snatches of hot playing coming out of saloons and disreputable resorts. When his mother came on him syncopating a hymn tune, she irately ordered, "Take that ragtime out of my house!" [14]

No rebel, Eubie loved and respected his parents, basked in their devotion, and absorbed their values. His father, who had actually fought for his freedom, impressed on his son the evils of race hatred. Eubie appreciated his mother's severity because: "Life was hard. Not like it is now. You had to come up tough or you wouldn't make it." He credited his mother with his achieving literacy, morality, and the skills to survive. [15] Still, with his keen ear and great ability, Eubie absorbed popular music, increasingly able to play anything he heard. His long fingers gave him the reach for any pianistic challenge. A piquant detail: noticing those long fingers, his mother told him on the streetcar to double them up because he looked like a pickpocket. [16] One day in 1898 a local whorehouse pianist, Basil Chase, having to leave town because of a death in the family, offered the job to Eubie (now 15, he must have already demonstrated his considerable talents in a few saloons). Aggie Shelton, white, ran a fairly genteel five-dollar house and guaranteed $3/night if tips fell below that minimum. This clandestine opportunity called for some tricky logistics (plus deception that must have troubled him). Not only did he have to sneak past his sleeping parents (soon knocked out from their hard day), but he then had to get to the pool room, where he rented long pants from the friendly proprietor. After which this sleep-deprived adolescent had to perform for six or seven hours, usually getting back to bed just prior to first light. [17]

Eubie states that he played no "dirty" songs at Aggie's, and as a black boy playing for whites in a parlor, praise rather than temptation came with the substantial tips that rewarded his superb playing. He recalled playing such tunes as "Hello, Ma Baby," "After the Ball," and "A Bird in a Gilded Cage," as well as piano ragtime. There came the night a neighbor, up late, walked past the place and was alerted by the peculiar wobble-wobble quality of the bass. Eubie's wobbling already had a signature quality, and the neighbor tossed this bombshell to Emily, who handed her boy over to his father for disciplining. In his room, Eubie rolled back the carpet from under his bed to reveal over $100 in earnings. This exceeded by more than ten what a black stevedore took home in a week. Stevedoring, dependent on ship traffic and whims of hiring bosses, was never steady. The insecurity of poverty inspires respect for cash; so much of it awed his father. Emily could never go along with such "wages of sin," but she accepted her husband's decision to permit their only beloved son to delve into the night world's moneypot. [18]

Eubie worked on this level for six or seven years, at Aggie Shelton's until the summer of 1901, then in a series of ventures: an abortive stint with a medicine show (1901), a "plantation revue" in New York in 1902, plus saloon work in Baltimore, followed (from 1903) by steady work at Ann Gilly's low-class dollar house where violence regularly ended in knife and razor fights. Gilly's was a large establishment with many girls, tough ones, no bouncer to keep order, just (in Eubie's phrase) "a big, wild party all night long." Eubie learned never to sit with his back to the door. [19] When the impulsive, inebriated customers pocketed weapons and resumed dancing, the interrupted piano player reaped a multitude of tips for multiple requests. During these salad days in late 1890's Baltimore, he listened and learned from the older, skilled veterans of thirty years of ragging (named above), learning their "tricks" as he perfected his own. In 1899 he composed a fast and complex performance piece to showcase his talent and compete in occasional competitions (cutting contests). Apparently this was the first of nine or ten rags completed during the ragtime era, of which only three were published. Another half dozen or so surfaced later during the post-1950 "Ragtime Revival." [20] This first rag lacked a name until 1906 when Will Marion Cook (Chapter 26), after hearing Eubie do it in Atlantic City, attempted but failed to get it published under his chosen title, "Sounds of Africa." So it was named until Eubie retitled it, after the popular dance of the 1920's, *Charleston Rag*. Jasen and Jones rate it as "...one of the most original compositions in ragtime," and call it "...the first truly urban rag, so sophisticated in its syncopated ideas that it would have been startling had it been written thirty years later." [21]

With *Charleston Rag* in 1899, Eubie, albeit obscurely, joined Joplin, Scott, Lamb, and a very few others in the first rank of ragtime composers. With those pickpockety fingers, he could reach deftly and rapidly all over the keyboard to create dense, exciting music that ran hot and fast, "beyond any other ragtime thinking or writing that was going on in 1899" (the year of *Maple Leaf Rag*). [22] By 1905 a recognized master, he was getting good gigs in the summer resorts of Atlantic City. From 1907 to 1910, he reigned over the piano at Baltimore's new Goldfield Hotel, black-owned by lightweight boxing champion Joe Gans (who constructed it from the purse won in his big fight at Goldfield, Nevada, in 1906). There Eubie's reputation grew as showbiz celebrities came to listen, and he added such works as *Baltimore Todalo* (1910), *Troublesome Ivories* (1911), *Kitchen Tom* (1908), and *Eubie's Boogie* (1904) to his repertory of display pieces. Until 1915 Eubie stuck to local gigs in Baltimore and Atlantic City, but relocated in New York after teaming up with lyricist Noble Sissle. Then he worked a few years as a top musician with the James Reese Europe organization (Chapter 31), playing society gigs. When ragtime played out after WWI, he and Sissle went on together, both as a vaudeville act and as collaborators who brought African-American music back to Broadway, most notably in their long-running 1921 musical comedy *Shuffle Along*. Eubie retired after WWII, but reached stardom again in ragtime's revival, prominent and beloved until his death in 1983 at 100. [23]

Certainly he got his start in houses of prostitution and picked up much from others in that milieu. But, with so much innate talent, Eubie had good prospects for stardom. The whorehouse helped, but he could have found other opportunities. In all of his many interviews—Eubie never refused to talk about his life—he did not sentimentalize the experiences or display nostalgia. He had seen them plain and knew where the life led. Whorehouse playing fed, clothed, and eased the economic desperation of his family. He did not become a Louis Chauvin, addicted to drugs, alcohol, or sex. He chose survival instead, and once beyond that life, never returned. He named no rags for Aggie Shelton or Annie Gilly. His only vice was tobacco, which does not seem to have much affected his longevity.

II

> This urbane New Orleans ragtime, salty with West Indian rhythms, was the inspiration for Morton's best melodies, tunes that recall the days when he tagged the serenade bands along Rochblave and Tonti Streets, gogging at Picou and his Creole cousins.
>
> Alan Lomax [24]

Storyville, New Orleans, carries the double distinction of being the most written-about red light district and of being the most prominent in music history. New Orleans has been dubbed the "Cradle of Jazz," and some of those Storyville folk certainly helped rock the cradle. Yet another distinction: Storyville was the sole "legal" tenderloin or sin district in the country, from January 1, 1898, when the enabling ordinance took effect, until November 12, 1917, when the U.S. Navy shut it down for its presumed threat to the health and morals of servicemen during WWI.

Perhaps more than most, New Orleans, largest city and chief port of the South, had been troubled by vice. Respectable citizens lacked any legal means of keeping saloons, dance palaces, and brothels out of their neighborhoods. As with other cities, since the problem refused to vanish at the issuance of a decree, <u>control</u> of some kind offered at least a partial solution. Alderman Sidney Story during travels in Europe had observed that control could be best achieved by confining vice to an area or district. Fine, but any legal permission for vice constituted public approval, a measure as likely to be anathematized in New Orleans as in any other U.S. community. Therefore to bring about the mutually opposed purposes of outlawing and controlling crime, Alderman Story crafted an ordinance that specified that no prostitution would be permitted <u>outside</u> a prescribed area. The business remained illegal, but its practitioners, the law <u>implied</u>, would not be interfered with if they no longer carried on their business outside the carefully specified boundaries. So there came into existence a district bounded on the west by Canal Street, the north by Claiborne Avenue, the east by St.Louis Street, and the south by Basin Street. Railroad tracks paralleling and running along Basin Street created a boundary separating the district from the French Quarter (Vieux Carre) downtown area. Right off, the press impudently named it "Storyville," which jazz historian Al Rose, who was Story's grandnephew, tells us "mortified" the good alderman. His angry protests only chiseled the name more deeply into the public awareness. [25]

At the time that jazz went through its gestation and infancy in New Orleans, ragtime flourished there as elsewhere. Syncopation had flowed upriver from both Africa and Latin America long before the Civil War. Louis Moreau Gottschalk, b. New Orleans in 1829, whose music reflected both European and Afro-Latin American influences, inserted syncopation into art music ca. 1850, while achieving renown as America's first internationally recognized composer. When cultural historians reach for a metaphor to characterize New Orleans music, they settle on the indigenous "gumbo," a conglomeration that tastes spicy and hot. When ragtime flowed downriver on steamboats and steamed in on the passenger trains of the Illinois Central, it was quickly assimilated by local musicians. The late 19C-early 20C was the era of fraternal organizations; every wage earner in the "Crescent City" belonged to a "lodge," each of which fielded bands for ceremonial, festive, and funereal occasions. These dozens of bands all performed in the upbeat march tempo of ragtime. They ragged everything, including the funeral dirges as they marched back to dispersal point from the cemetery. New Orleans ragtime may have tasted a bit like gumbo, but it wasn't jazz.

Al Rose, jazz historian, biographer of Eubie Blake, and author of *Storyville, New Orleans*, eventually culled 110 rags from his collection of locally published music. These had been acquired incidentally, he tells us, "purely for documentary reasons, never suspecting their high musical value." [26] Which indicates the latterday obscurity of New Orleans ragtime, which skips over the reality that the two finest pianists to come out of New Orleans, Tony Jackson and Jelly Roll Morton, both of whom garnered the munificent tips of Storyville's big spenders, had been grounded in ragtime and constantly played it.

Storyville gave employment only to a small number of the city's musicians. Rose tells us that only fifty played there on most nights, with perhaps another twenty-five taken on as temps during holidays and Mardi Gras. [27] He further states that the earliest forms of jazz predated Storyville, that "[jazz] grew out of the whole way of life in and near the country's most cosmopolitan city…," rather than as some potted syncopations fertilized with the dollars of the patrons of elite brothels along Basin Street. "The facts are that the majority of black musicians of outstanding ability in New Orleans never worked as much as a single night in Storyville…." [28] That said, and getting back to ragtime, only a few of the black professors, the keyboard stars of the five-dollar houses, carried home the big money each night, fifteen dollars or more. The other Storyville musicians played in the bands of dance halls and saloons. After splitting their collective tips, the leader took home fifty to seventy-five dollars each week and his sidemen about thirty. A professor in a mansion in the best weeks reaped as much as a thousand, and never less than ninety in a slow week. [29]

Although his only published artifact is the song "Pretty Baby," considerable testimony has accumulated that Tony Jackson at the piano yielded an unforgettable experience. He flourished in about a half dozen of the higher class resorts along two blocks of Basin Street. Trains coasting into the station across the street afforded passengers a close-up of the panorama of two- and three-story facades, a typical cityscape at night, except for the women at the windows and the men outside gazing up at them. The plusher establishments were operated by Hilma Burt, Lizette Smith (very small but high priced), Josie Arlington (a splendiferous <u>four</u> stories), Lulu White (her Mahogany Hall a rival to the "Arlington"), "Countess" Willie Piazza, Antonia Gonzalez, Gypsy Shafer, and Emma Johnson. Except for Emma Johnson, who specialized in extremely lewd "exhibitions"—during which music would have been superfluous—Tony found regular employment with these madams. No request ever stumped him, pop, opera, ragtime, blues, symphonic strains; he had mastered virtually all the music available to him, plus all of the lyrics, which he sang with a fine voice. Jelly Roll Morton called him "the World's greatest Single-Handed Entertainer." Others, including Johnny St.Cyr, Clarence Williams, Bunk Johnson, and Baby Dodds (all great jazzmen) gave similar testimonials. [30]

Tony Jackson certainly needed his superior talents to survive. Born an epileptic, he lacked physical appeal and was both homosexual and alcoholic, dying in Chicago at 45. Reared and protected by females, he easily absorbed the music around him, playing an original hymn tune at age seven. At thirteen he was permitted to learn and practice on a saloon piano mornings before the noon customers came in. By fifteen he knew the varieties of music and had been recognized as king of the piano in the tenderloin: "Old-timer" Manuel Manetta recalled:

> Tony was in charge from the day he went to work. We <u>all</u> listened to him. Nobody could match him. He played <u>anything</u>! Blues, opera—anything!

Another recalled: "He'd start playin' a cakewalk, then he'd kick over the piano stool and <u>dance</u> a cakewalk—and never stop playin' the piano—and <u>playin'</u> man! Nobody played like him!" From another came: Tony sang "like a bird". [31]

But, alas, Tony's immortality exists only in these spectacular recollections. His creations were piddled away, sold for five or ten dollars or given free. He is identified with "Pretty Baby," "Michigan Water Blues," "I'm Cert'n'y Gonna See About That," and "Some Sweet Day." [32] Jelly Roll recalled for Alan Lomax *The Naked Dance*, an instrumental number played at Gypsy Shafer's. In the recollection, "Tony would dig up one of his fast speed tunes and one of the girls would dance on a little narrow stage, completely nude. Yes they danced absolutely stripped, but in New Orleans the naked dance was a real art." [33] In another version, a nude woman performed a naked dance by balancing a raw oyster, moving it from top to bottom with her muscles until it reached the tip of her foot, then flipping it up to catch it in her mouth. For Lomax, Morton recorded some strains, perhaps his own, that captured the ambience of this salacious and exhibitionistic athleticism. [34] Tony's most appreciative employer may have been Antonia Gonzalez. Etched into her glass entrance was the legend, "Gonzalez, Female Cornetist." Customers remembered that she enjoyed playing duets with him. [35] By 1907 he had relocated to Chicago where he performed in Levee parlor houses, including the Everleigh Club, plus Pony Moore's famous saloon, and cabarets. [36] He died there in 1921, probably from alcohol and nightworld living, a major talent denied mainstream success.

Which brings us to Ferdinand Joseph LaMothe a.k.a. Jelly Roll Morton (1890-1941), the most important musical figure to be associated with the tawdry opulences of Storyville. Thanks to the great folklorist and historian of our culture Alan Lomax, who recorded Jelly Roll verbally and musically in 1938, we see Mr. Jelly Roll close-up and animated. [37] Where Scott Joplin and his black colleagues in ragtime languish in a smudged and obscure limbo of vague recollection and scant documentation, Jelly Roll, driven by his high self-valuation, found the means to insert himself into the historical memory. This brought him victory in his war against the race system.

Two chief influences shaped the personality and spirit of the person who became known as "Jelly Roll." A century later, we would describe him as a neglected child in a troubled (dysfunctional?) family. Although an only child, his mother Louise Monette abandoned his father Edward LaMothe for Willie Mouton when young "Ferd" was four in 1894. Ed LaMothe, a laid back soul, spent more time playing a trombone than at his small-time contracting business. Musical instruments lay around the house, and from the time he toddled, the boy went at them, trying to reproduce what he heard. Other than to enroll him in Catholic school, family and parents ignored his activities; he ended up on the streets with other musically inclined children in little groups called "spasm" bands, playing for pennies and any other hand-outs, like food. Two half-sisters resulted from the marriage to Mouton, who had anglicized the name to "Morton," which Jelly, curiously, took as his own. The only adult to provide emotional support was his godmother Eulalie Echo (from her married surname Hecaud), a woman of vitality and affluence, who was one of the city's leading practitioners of voodoo. Adept at seances, many of New Orleans' wealthy folk handed over large sums to communicate with departed loved ones. Eulalie also retailed many charms and spells. This well-to-do, raffish lady paid for the music lessons that turned a street kid into a musician.

Color was the other shaper of the Morton destiny. Jelly Roll bore the classification "Creole of Color." In New Orleans, as in all French and Spanish culture areas, prosperous men "kept" mistresses who bore them "second families." In the colonial Americas, the shortage of white females led to the taking of slave mistresses, which generated the problem of the uncertain status of the children of such extra-marital unions. To insure the freedom of their illegitimate offspring, these men of substance freed their mistresses. Down through five or six generations during the 18C-19C's, there accumulated a mixed blood population of Creoles of Color that ran a gamut from brown to indistinguishable-from-white. These, the products of genes of mental superiority and physical beauty, numbering about 10,000 by 1860, had become a <u>solid</u> element of the city's middle class. As productive and creative citizens, the majority of them achieved at least a modest prosperity as business, professional, and crafts people. A few became wealthy, many spoke French as a first language, and nearly all wore clothing of finer style and quality than working-class whites. [38] Creoles of Color were better schooled, and because music enriched all of their formal and social occasions, most received music lessons.

Up to the Civil War, these less-than-white people enjoyed a respect that ameliorated their inferior status. Ruling whites tacitly acknowledged the class nearest to them as fellow human beings, both sides behaving with courtesy and civility. But after the Civil War, everything changed. As poor whites moved in to escape rural poverty, their resentment of the superior status of <u>colored</u> people swelled to a political reality. By the 1890's the southern race system (Chapter 2.1) had degraded and infected Creole life. Jelly Roll's grandfather had prospered in the liquor business, his father failed as a small contractor, and, outside music, his best prospects would have been making barrels (cooperage) or laying bricks (masonry), $3/week leading to $2/day on the foreman level. And even this paltry security might prove precarious should whites covet his job. [39]

As he reached the teens, Jelly Roll found his musical metier as a pianist. Ignored and unsupervised, he began to roam the nightworld with a set of neophyte sports, unquestioned by family members as long as he remained visible in their day world. Storyville was so off-limits that those outside it never suspected the fast teen crowd that lurked near the parlor houses, scattering whenever a beat cop approached. There came a Saturday night when word spread that a madam lacked a pianist. His companions put him up to crossing the forbidden threshold for an audition. After an hour, his tips had piled up to an incredible $20, and young Ferd—perhaps only 13, if his claim of 1902 is correct—had taken up his musical vocation. He didn't, like Eubie Blake, have to rent his long pants, just secretly "borrow" them from family members—until he could use his newfound affluence to stylishly outfit himself. In 1906 he was fifteen when his mother died, further weakening the tie to a family that knew him not. He continued using the family residence as a dormitory until the Sunday morning the next year when, as he returned to the neighborhood from his night's work, he ran into his Great-grandmother. In a family where the men were either dead or estranged, this old woman Mimi Peche dominated. She had been to mass, and, encountering her great-grandson, a 16-year-old in a Stetson, a fancy suit, and beautiful footwear, she grasped all. Taking him down with a series of sharp questions about money and where he obtained it, she summarily read him out of the family. He had disgraced them, become a bum, and as a threat to the moral nurture of his younger half-sisters, he could no longer live in their home. [40]

This vindictive rejection traumatized a still vulnerable adolescent. Creole society had been backed against the wall by white supremacy, forced to live and work, at lower wages, alongside ignorant, uncultured darker folk; any fraying of social position and respectability was felt as a threat to survival. For Mimi Peche this downfall of the young male hope of her family was a calamity, a blight on her house. For a man-boy the loss of home and family identity went beyond calamity, a wound that never healed. He reacted by becoming the complete sport, gambler, pool shark, all around "goodfellow," even a pimp running a string of girls when it suited his inclination. One of his nicknames, "Wining Boy," short for "winding boy," implied a reputation for sexual athleticism. As a hot piano player pulling down as much as $100 a night, he gained a prestige that he reveled in. Along with Tony Jackson, he became one of the stars at the bar known as the "Frenchman's," corner of Villere and Bienville. Storyville usually closed down at 4:00 AM, and the music-loving element then repaired to the establishment of one Eugene Tournier for exhibitions not of sex but pianism. As Jelly Roll himself told it:

> Some friends took me to "The Frenchmans"...which was at this time the most famous nightspot after everything was closed. It was only a back room, but it was where all the greatest pianists frequented after they got off from work in the sporting houses....and there would be everything in the line of hilarity there. All the girls that could get out of their houses was there. The millionaires would come to listen to their favorite piano players. There weren't any discrimination of any kind. They all sat at different tables or wherever they felt like Sitting They all mingled together just as they wished to and everyone was just like one big happy family. People came from all over the country and most times you couldn't get in. So this place would go on at a tremendous rate of speed—ty plenty money—drinks of all kinds—from four o'clock in the morning until maybe twelve, one, two or three in the daytime. Then, when the great pianists would leave, the crowd would leave. [41]

Fabulous! Yes, but also "one big happy family." Here during the few years that spanned the middle of the century's first decade, Jelly Roll regained some lost security. At the Frenchman's, among aficionados, he felt the recognition and approval that soothed the outcast and rewarded the artist. Perhaps more than most, he suffered the separation and isolation that are the plight of the artist. An artist exists alone with his visions and intentions. Only when he transfers internal perception to the finished work does communication occur. At the Frenchman's, Jelly could try out his creations before audiences. No extraneous background noise, no indifference or inattention, no distractions of mundane life, nothing intruded upon or diluted the musical experience. He played, they listened, to mutual satisfaction. It never happened, to such an extent, again, elsewhere. He spent much of the rest of his life attempting to reveal and explain his art, only to be put down as an egotist and braggart. In jazz he stubbornly adhered to his ensemble concept, bored by the (to him) simplistic theme-solo-theme progression of the jazz that became the standard. [42]

As a jazzman Jelly Roll understood, and allowed for, improvisation, a soloist out there, reaching—for truth, beauty, enchantment, thrills, glory, his intimations of the ineffable—but improvisation was one trick in the bag and not the centerpiece. Instead, grounded in ragtime, he composed, arranging it all in advance, giving each actor his lines that created the total effect. This allowed room for solo spots and improvising, but the main movements were a coming-together, ensemble with dialogs and choruses. His New Orleans background of ragtime, dance music, marches, European art music (opera, symphony), enriched his output with a variety ranging from spasm bands to grand opera.

From ragtime (and marches, waltzes, etc.) he took the basic form of two to four strains of sixteen bars or longer. To this he added what Gunther Schuller calls "the concept of perpetual variation." [43] Variations, the primary course of musical development, took him beyond the rag form, which repeats more than it develops. Rags develop more simply, with changes of volume and emphases in repeats, augmenting and diminishing the time value of notes, plus modulations, interludes, and thematic contrast. Jelly Roll found new routes to variation. As Jasen and Tichenor put it:

> Of all the ragtime composers, Morton had many more diverse moods in his works than anyone else.... Morton was also the first ragtimer to consider the audience and to insure continued interest...by creating unexpected rhythmic patterns within a performance and by continually improvising the same section over and over. However unlike the later jazzmen, Morton's variations were carefully built upon each section in the rag. [44]

A metaphor comes to mind: his performance pieces are to rags as free verse is to more traditional poetry with a regular beat and rhyme scheme; think of them as free-form rags, the form shaped by the composer's intentions. Works such as *King Porter Stomp, Grandpa's Spells, Shreveport Stomp, The Pearls, The Finger Breaker,* or *Kansas City Stomp* seem to proceed casually, even whimsically, but after hearing them, the listener realizes that he has been conveyed very carefully to destinations of joy and delight.

Like Eubie Blake, young Ferd Morton donned his first long pants to develop his creator/performer talents in tenderloin resorts. This environment certainly nurtured a youth at a very impressionable age, and subsequently affected the attitudes and behavior of a lifetime—far more than it did the unrejected Eubie. But did a youth spent in whorehouses exert a major influence on creative output? The simple answer is no, a genius creates anywhere. More complexly, the environment comprised not only Storyville but also the socio-economic decline of Creoles of Color, a degradation of status that dropped them into the reign of terror afflicting all African Americans. Arguably the effects were more blighting than nurturing. Would he have done better as white? Perhaps not, the tough streets of New Orleans fostered in him a resilience that made him a survivor. Struggle is positive for survivors. But in the realm of the nightworld, he had to endure the buffets of exposure to a very "strenuous life" indeed; he barely made it out of his forties to a premature death. In a less "challenging" environment he might have done more. In 1908 he departed Storyville and his home city, seasoned and toughened, for the underground existence of migrancy and vagrancy: minstrel shows, pool hustling, pimping, grifting, and music when he could get the gigs. Storyville had provided on-the-job training, excellent starting wages, a bolstering of confidence—and those ineffable after-hours moments at the Frenchman's.

III

The Debt

This is the debt I pay
Just for one riotous day,
Years of regret and grief,
Sorrow without relief.

Pay it I will to the end—
Until the grave, my friend,
Gives me a true release—
Gives me the clasp of peace.

Slight was the thing I bought,
Small was the debt I thought,
Poor was the loan at best—
God! But the interest!

Paul Laurence Dunbar [45]

Scott Joplin's final years (1912-1917) compounded disappointments with declining health. By this time Lottie Stokes had thrown in with him, the one steady light in a darkening world. Lottie claimed later that she and Scott had lived together since 1907 and married in 1910, but no record of the marriage exists, and the 1910 census lists Joplin as a widower living at 128 West 29th Street, an address with only male lodgers. Biographer Edward Berlin also discovered that not until a 1913 copyright application (of a separate publication of *A Real Slow Drag*) does another address, 252 West 47th Street, come to light. By this time he and Lottie shared an apartment; in October a document establishing "The Scott Joplin Music Publishing Company" indicates Lottie Stokes as co-owner. [46]

Joplin's biographers have been unable to pin down where, when, or how the couple met. During 1911, as Scott drove himself to complete the score of *Treemonisha* and get it into production, Lottie may have entered his life. If not then, they may have come together as Joplin recovered from disappointment and determined to try again. He continued to teach a few pupils at fifty to seventy-five cents a lesson, but his composing fell off from the pace of 1909-10 to only two new rags, his final works: *Scott Joplin's New Rag* (1912) and *Magnetic Rag* (1914). These do reveal growth and stand with his finest works. During this time John Stark issued two more rags, probably acquired before 1908, both co-composed with Scott Hayden, *Felicity Rag* (1911) and *Kismet Rag* (1913). But Joplin remained focused on *Treemonisha*, revising it after failing to gain support for the production. None of these revisions has been found, leaving us with only the publication of 1911. He made another attempt to get it staged in the spring of 1913, indicated by an announcement in a Bayonne, NJ, paper of a performance of "In a Real Slow Drag" by "Scott Joplin's Merry Makers" on July 14, 15, and 16. This must have been a truncated version, perhaps with some humorous revisions. Since neither that paper or the New York *Age* or the *Indianapolis Freeman* mention or review any performances (Joplin would have written to these), probably the project fell through. After this came further announcements of a performance at Harlem's Lafayette Theatre, planned for late September-October (in the *Freeman*), but again nothing materialized. [47]

From the above it is clear that Joplin's creative powers ran strong at least through 1914. He still taught pupils and advertised his music. At year's end he posted a notice of a new address, 133 West 138th Street, showing that he had joined the African-American migration into Harlem at the top of Manhattan. The notice also declared that he would continue to instruct for piano and violin. Originally intended for whites, Harlem had been built solidly by its developers. African Americans began to move in at a time when whites failed to take up the slack in vacancies. When a few strapped landlords and developers gave way at a strategic time and began to allow in blacks, a domino effect happened, with whites either fleeing neighbors with black faces or, hearing of this, refusing to move there. White flight gave a rare opportunity for decent housing. Scott and Lottie were able to rent an excellent row house, enabling Lottie to create a rental income, enough to support them as Scott's health failed and his income diminished. His only musical accomplishment during 1915 was a student orchestra's performance of *Treemonisha*'s "Frolic of the Bears" at Harlem's Martin-Smith Music School on May 5.

[48] But if he retained his mental powers, he had by this time lost much of his physical strength and abilities. Eubie Blake, in his frequently quoted testimony to Al Rose, paints a wretched picture:

> I only met Scott Joplin one time, in Washington. Some kind of big dinner in a big hotel. I guess I have to say I heard him play, but the poor fellow, they made him play *Maple Leaf*. It was about 1915. So pitiful. He was so far gone with the dog [syphilis] and he sounded like a little child trying to pick out a tune. They shouldn't have made him do it. I hated to see him tryin' so hard.
>
> He was so weak. [49]

The medical consensus points to a diagnosis of tertiary neuro-syphilis. After being sexually transmitted, syphilis goes through three stages: After ten days to three months, but typically about twenty-one days, a lesion called a chancre appears on the genitalia, which subsequently heals. Six weeks to several months later appears the rash that is the second stage. During both of these periods, the victim can infect others. Then ten or even twenty years will pass before the tertiary, fatal, stage strikes. But this is <u>not</u> inevitable because the disease remains latent in two-thirds of all cases; for reasons unknown, the symptoms and agonies of the disease's fatal sequence fail to appear. Also throughout, syphilis varies greatly in the severity and extent of these stages. When Joplin caught the disease, it was both poorly understood and endemic. Some have compared it to AIDS. Both were/are spread by sexual contact, both were/are incurable, and both caused a great fear.

A century ago, the fear of fatal contamination was doubled by the darkness of ignorance. Pasteur's revealed universe of micro-organisms had yet to enter most imaginations, which still perceived misfortunes as coming from Divine Judgment for sins committed—or as the diabolical malevolence of darker powers. The extreme variability of syphilitic symptoms baffled researchers, and Dr. Alfred Fournier of France, who, along with others, commenced his researches in 1875, required thirty years to comprehend the stages and finally to isolate the obscure bacillus *treponema pallidum* in 1905. Just before this in 1901, Fournier gathered fellow researchers to declare syphilis to be, like tuberculosis, a <u>social</u> disease, and hence a public-health matter. [50]

Even more harmful to public health, because of its much greater prevalence, was gonorrhea. Detectable in men by a telltale penile discharge and a degree of pain, the infection had no visibility in women. Men liked to tell themselves that it was "no worse than a bad cold," but there could be dire effects. Infants passing through an infected birth canal came out blind. In 1884 occurred the fortunate discovery that irrigating the eyes of the newborn with a 2% silver nitrate solution prevented this, but in a time of home births, ignorant midwives, and poorly trained doctors, this vital information diffused too slowly. Gonorrhea also caused sterility; a 1901 estimate judged one out of seven marriages to be childless because of sterility. Too many wives a century ago complained of "poor health," a euphemism for inflammations of the pelvic region. In the doctor's office women usually heard that they suffered from "ovaritis." Eva Remington, wife of western artist Frederic Remington, contracted the condition after seven years of marriage (when she was 32, he 30). His social life, typical of that macho era, centered on male drinking companions, with whom he indulged large appetites. She became ill on one of his western painting trips, bedridden with diagnosed "inflammation of the ovary." Remington was observed to be very tender with her during these bouts of illness. For good reason: he and the doctors knew the source of the trouble, but concealed it from female victims. Most doctors upheld the double standard: gentlemen do not reveal one another's secrets, and given the lack of cures, why increase the hurt in a family? [51]

Many case histories commenced with a "night on the town" for an incipient bridegroom, a final fling before the straitened life of husband and father. The high point of the evening followed the jolly alcoholic dinner when the more "experienced" companions of the ignorant and unwary groom led him into a pricey parlor house (no danger, <u>clean</u> girls) and deposited him into the waiting arms of a pre-selected, enticing lady-of-the-evening. Later came domestic tragedy as the infected newlyweds lost both health and peace of mind. In 1910 Katharine Houghton Hepburn of Hartford, CT, (mother of the actor) wrote that, "Seventy-five per cent of all operations peculiar to women are necessary because the husband has infected the wife with…diseases…of the social evil." [52] In 1904 an investigator stated that <u>60%</u> of the male population caught a venereal disease at some point in life, and a 1910 report stated that 60 to 75 percent of men of "marriageable age" had gonorrhea. [53] What aroused Dr. Thomas Hepburn and wife Katharine to involvement was such an afflicted couple. In 1910 the husband-to-be had come in for a check-up examination just prior to the wedding. Six months later, he appeared with a very sick wife, who received a diagnosis of "gonorrheal peritonitis," of which she died shortly after. The husband confessed that his wild stag party had concluded in a whorehouse. Appalled, this tragedy galvanized the Hepburns to start a crusade against prostitution. As reform-minded progressives, they investigated, they organized. They pushed energetically enough to enlist Dr. Charles Eliot, retired President of Harvard, to head the American Social Hygiene Association. The Hepburns found mental asylums full of victims of these diseases, and they learned that many landlords of parlor houses were wealthy, respected fellow citizens. When they opened their campaign against organized prostitution and venereal diseases, Hartford "society," in which they had been a popular, regularly invited couple, coldly shunned them.

But the Hepburns persisted, importing the French expose play *Damaged Goods* (helped by fellow crusaders Mr. and Mrs. George Bernard Shaw, who became their friends), and they went into a house of ill repute in the daytime to photograph squalid conditions, during which they found small children. One photo even made it into an early edition of the *Hartford Courant* before a hostile editor pulled it. Katharine then set up a meeting and caused an uproar with posters depicting a mother and daughter gazing at a sign: "DANGER! Sixty Thousand White Slaves Will Die This Year in the U.S." The *Hartford Times* editorialized angrily against putting up such materials where women could see them. The Mayor attempted to rescind the meeting's license because of indecency. A receptive audience showed up to hear Katharine tell her story and assert that women would have to lead because, "We have been reaping the wild oats the men have sown—from the prostitute, to the girl with the illegal child, to the wife with a hidden disease she dare not mention." This elicited a strong response and commenced Hartford's campaign to close the "houses." [54]

The Hepburns, along with like-minded progressives and scientists, eventually brought venereal diseases out into the open as recognized public health problems, but this required decades. In 1906 Edward Bok in the *Ladies Home Journal*—he who later fired fifteen office girls for ragtime dancing during lunch hour (Chapter 17)—broke ground with a series of articles on the subject. He lost 75,000 subscribers. [55] Instead of syphilis, the death certificates of respectable folk usually indicated the cause of death as a "rare blood disease." Dr. Paul Ehrlich of Germany in 1909 developed an arsenical compound, Salvarsan, that achieved some success in aleviating syphilis. Salvarsan, considered at first to be a "magic bullet" cure, replaced mercury the traditional remedy, but as with mercury, there were often severe side effects (though none as bad as mercury poisoning). Too often, the long, unpleasant course of Salvarsan treatment failed to rout the delicate, tiny corkscrew bacillus *trepanema pallidum*, its toxic effects endured in vain. The addition of bismuth to arsenicals later in 1921 softened the effects and proved more effective, but this "cure" remained difficult to endure and doubtful of success. [56]

This very limited degree of scientific progress arrived too late for Joplin and his contemporaries. He and Ernest Hogan, George Walker, Louis Chauvin, Bob Cole, and other black musicians were too far back along the time line and below the color line. For them the only recourses were quacks, patent medicines, and indifferent doctors who would poison them with mercury. White reformers only desired to close down the nightworld's houses, hotels, and dance halls; get offenders off the streets; and rid themselves of what the Chicago Vice Commission in 1910 called "a leprous plague." [57] Hospitals, lacking facilities for treatment, refused admission to <u>known</u> cases of VD (though of course not to cases termed "rare blood disease"). [58]

Scientific opinion suggests that Scott Joplin contracted syphilis during the 1890's. [59] His physical decline probably began after 1900, as hinted at by comments on his piano-playing, which ran a downhill gamut from very good through mediocre to the pathetic efforts mentioned in Eubie Blake's 1915 testimony. His body failed him first, and his obsessive fixation on *Treemonisha* was probably an effect of neuro-syphilis, which rendered him unable to concentrate on other things. The disease progresses to a final "paresis," or "general paralysis of the insane," a condition of both paralysis and dementia, the result of the infection spreading from the outer cortex into the substance of the brain. What has occurred is "the gross destruction of the central and peripheral nervous systems." [60] By late 1915 Scott Joplin still instructed a pupil or two and worked at his piano—or attempted to. He did cut seven hand-played piano rolls during April, May, and June of 1916, but with poor results. In September he claimed to have written a musical comedy (entitled "If") and to be working on "Symphony No. 1." Such grandiose claims certainly point to increasing dementia. In January 1917, he entered Bellevue Hospital and was transferred later to a mental ward at Manhattan State Hospital, where he died on April 1,1917. [61]

The next day, President Woodrow Wilson sent his war message to Congress, thrusting the nation into WWI. The Progressive Era, manifested in spirit by ragtime, had gone away. For three years the U.S. had been drifting into war, from imbibing Allied propaganda (posters showing Belgian babies impaled on German bayonets), through our intervention in the Mexican Revolution to pursue the renegade Pancho Villa, to our righteous anger at unrestricted German submarine warfare. War kills idealism as it substitutes patriotism. As the collective mood turned sanguine, a much hotter music, jazz, elbowed ragtime out of the way. Ragging it gave way to jazzing it. Joplin's artistic vision didn't die with him; it languished on the shelf until the future found it.

Notes: Chapter 35

1. Daniel Q. Kelly, "Ballum Rancum," *The Ragtime Ephemeralist*, No. 3: 185.
2. "Ta-Ra-Ra-Boom-Der-e" and "Hot Time, etc." have been traced to Mama Lou, singer and entertainer extraordinaire at Babe Connor's, who popularized them in their early, bawdy versions. Coon Hollow was a Chicago location (Kelly above, 187). Chauvin and Joplin may have collaborated on a Chicago whorehouse piano. "Sponge" seems to have been a term for pimp. 'Smoky Row" refers to a line of cribs in Storyville, New Orleans. *Twelfth Street Rag* refers to the Kansas City tenderloin, as does *Petticoat Lane*. Brun Campbell's pieces refer to the St.Louis district and to Storyville's best known madam. *Key Stone Rag* is said to refer to a sleazy hotel popular in the St. Louis Tenderlion.
3. George J. Kneeland, *Commercialized Prostitution in New York*, 56.
4. Kelly, above n 1.
5. *Ibid.*, 193.
6. Charles Washburn, *Come Into My parlor: A Biography of the Aristocratic Everleigh Sisters of Chicago*, 167-168.
7. *Idem*.
8. In Gunther Schuller, *Early Jazz: Its Roots and Musical Development*, 362.
9. Kelly, 197.
10. Al Rose, *Eubie Blake*, 20, 104, 150, 151; Eileen Southern, *The Music of Black Americans: A History*, 327-328.
11. Gene Jones, "The Grandee of Chestnut Valley: Tom Turpin and His Domain," 4.
12. Douglas Gilbert, *Lost Chords: The Diverting Story of American Popular Songs*, 206-210 for Mama Lou, and Jones, 4-5, and David A. Jasen and Gene Jones, *Black Bottom Stomp*, 2, for Turpin.
13. Jasen and Jones, *Stomp*, 31.
14. *Ibid.*, 35; Bob Kimball and Bill Bolcom, *Reminiscing With Sissle and Blake*, 38-39.
15. Rose, *EB*, 10, for the quotation, 4-16, for homelife.
16. Kimball and Bolcom, 42.
17. Jasen and Jones, *Stomp*, 35; Kimball and Bolcom, 42; Rose, *EB*, 19-22.
18. *Ibid.* 21-26; Kimball and Bolcom, 42-43; Jasen and Jones, *Stomp*, 36.
19. Rose, *EB*, 32; Kimball and Bolcom, 43-44.
20. See list *Ibid.*, 245.
21. Jasen and Jones, *Stomp*, 37.
22. *Idem*.
23. *Ibid.*, 39 ff.; Kimball and Bolcom, 45-47; Rose, EB, 40-43, 44-53, 55-68.
24. Lomax, *Mr. Jelly Roll: The Fortunes of Jelly Roll Morton, New Orleans Creole and Inventor of Jazz*, 36-39.
25. Al Rose, *Storyville, New Orleans*, 36-39.
26. Al Rose, Liner Notes to *Creole Rags*, Jazzology Records, JCE 94.
27. Rose, *Storyville*, 123.
28. *Ibid.*, 106.
29. *Ibid.*, 109,124.
30. *Ibid.*, 109-110.
31. *Ibid.*, 110-111.
32. Jasen and Jones, *Stomp*, 124-135.
33. Quoted in Rose, *Storyville*, 90.
34. Jasen and Jones, *Stomp*, 135.

35. Rose, *Storyville*, 92, 111.
36. Marshall W. Stearns, *The Story of Jazz*, 162. Jelly Roll was also in Chicago at that time: 1910.
37. Lomax, *Mr. Jelly Roll* (n. 24).
38. William Ivy Hair, *Carnival of Fury: Robert Charles and the New Orleans Race Riot of 1900*, 71-72.
39. Lomax, 22-23; Hair, 74.
40. Lomax, 22-28; Rose, *Storyville*, 113-114; Jasen and Jones, *Stomp*, 132, 136-137.
41. Quoted in Rose, *Storyville*, 94.
42. Schuller, 151.
43. *Ibid.*, 149.
44. David A. Jasen and Trebor Jay Tichenor, *Rags and Ragtime: A Musical History*, 251.
45. In James Weldon Johnson, Ed., *The Book of American Negro Poetry*, 58.
46. Edward A. Berlin, *King of Ragtime: Scott Joplin and His Era*, 222-224.
47. *Ibid.*, 212-213, 218-222, 225-226.
48. *Ibid.*, 233-235.
49. Rose, EB, 149-150.
50. Claude Quetel, *The History of Syphilis*, 134-138, 140.
51. Allan M. Brandt, *No Magic Bullet: A Social History of Venereal Disease in the United States Since 1880*, 15-18; for Remington, Peggy and Harold Samuels, *Frederic Remington: A Biography*, 161, 181.
52. Mark Thomas Connelly, *The Response to Prostitution in the Progressive Era*, 76.
53. *Ibid.*, 70.
54. Christopher Anderson, *Young Kate: The Remarkable Hepburns and the Childhood That Shaped an American Legend*, 95-99, 108-109, 147-150; Katharine Hepburn, *Me: Stories of My Life*, 20-21.
55. Brandt, 24.
56. Quetel, 140-143; Brandt, 40; Connelly, 68-70.
57. Brandt, 32.
58. *Ibid.*, 44; Connelly, 74-75.
59. Frederick J. Spencer, "Examining Scott Joplin's Fatal Illness," *Mississippi Rag* (May 1998): 32-33; John O'Shea, *Was Mozart Poisoned? Medical Investigations into the Lives of the Great Composers*, 189.
60. Spencer, 32-33; O'Shea, 189.
61. Berlin, *King*, 236-238.

Acknowledgements

Influences: My nurturers during the 1930's and 40's impressed upon me the attitudes and values of their formative years in the preceding decades. Parents, grandparents, family friends, neighbors, teachers had been either children or young adults when "Teddy" Roosevelt led the nation, when the cinema was silent, cars were cranked, and the very rich referred to their summer mansions in Newport, RI, as "cottages." I enjoyed adult talk, their humor and their seriousness. I sometimes "asked too many questions," about the price of food, who was in the movies, how far people drove their cars, why women wore such bulky clothes, and when boys got their first "long pants" (I must have been in the last generation that had to wear "knickers"). They told me that I could accomplish "anything you set your mind to" and that "there is no such word as **can't**." However I was developing in a later time and that ideology of success stuff aroused my first skepticism. But I never lost my curiosity about that era when parents were young and the century was getting started. I thank my predecessors for their role in getting me started on their period.

More seriously, I'm deeply grateful to David Reffkin, distinguished leader, violinist, and Director of the American Ragtime Ensemble; Contributing Editor, columnist and reviewer for the *Mississippi Rag*; and since 1981, the producer and host of *The Ragtime Machine*, a ragtime program on KUSF-FM, San Francisco. As I was doing the final chapters, David appeared providentially to give edits, comments, suggestions, and help with typos. An enterprise like this will always have flaws, but thanks to David's knowledge and discernment, there are many fewer. His encouragement has equaled his assistance.

When I began writing ca. 1992, I felt a need for more published sources on ragtime. Blesh and Janis (who opened up the field in 1950 with *They All Played Ragtime*), Jasen and Tichenor (whose *Rags and Ragtime* is the closest thing we have to a handbook), the works of John Edward Hasse, Edward Berlin, Alan Lomax, Terry Waldo, Joseph Scotti, Schafer and Riedell, Ian Whitcomb, and the decades of materials available in Dick Zimmerman's important journal *Rag Times* presented a fine body of material to draw from, but I would be skating on pretty thin ice in some places. To my good fortune, year by year, superb new works appeared. Most important: Edward Berlin's *King of Ragtime: Scott Joplin and His Era*, a (very readable) master work assembled from years of patient digging of the most difficult kind. Inhabiting the unliterate, underground realm of blacks in those times, Joplin's defensive reticence hid his tracks from the most persistent searchers. For Dr. Berlin's discoveries, validations, and solid analyses, the ragtime community is heavily indebted. Five years earlier (1989) Thomas L. Riis's *Just Before Jazz* gave a comprehensive account of the ragtime stage, an area of vital significance in the music's history. *King of Ragtime* was followed by *A Life in Ragtime*, Reid Badger's excellent, full biography of perhaps the least known major ragtimer James Reese Europe. The same year (1995), Gene Jones (in conjunction with the Turpin Festival in Savannah) published his essay on Tom Turpin "The Grandee of Chestnut Valley." This was the harbinger of a series of brilliant new ragtime works coauthored with David Jasen. In 1998 Jasen and Jones gave us *Spreadin' Rhythm Around* covering 50 years of African-American songwriters. Two years later, they gave us *That American Rag* which surveyed the areas and cities of ragtime publication, and two years after that came *Black Bottom Stomp*, incisive and vital biographies of "Eight Masters of Ragtime and Early Jazz" (Joplin, Eubie Blake, Luckey Roberts, James P. Johnson, Willie the Lion Smith, Fats Waller, Jelly Roll Morton, and Louis Armstrong). Yet another weak spot in the historical edifice was shored up with Jack Batterson's *Blind Boone*, Joplin's slightly older comtemporary who yields some insights into ragtime's earliest, incipient phase. Finally, thanks to Chris Ware and his editorial group for their occasional periodical *The Rag-Time Ephemeralist*, whose three issues thus far enrich our understanding with photos, facsimiles, sheet music, and well researched articles on the period. I am greatly indebted to all these authors both for the enrichment of what is offered here and for the pleasures of reading works of dedication and enthusiasm.

Many thanks also to my old Panama colleague in history Charles R. "Bob" Bowen of Murfreesboro, TN, who read the early chapters on the 1890's, caught some of my bad habits, and pronounced these efforts a beginning. My good Phoenix, Arizona, friend Bob Rockwell kindly listened to some of my aspirations and came back a couple of times with some very usable stuff from his own researches. My fine stepson Dr. Vincent Smith of Wilmington, NC, helped with the chapter on that city (No. 12), both with his comments and by submitting it to a local librarian. Bob Lynn, Rocky Mountain area columnist for the *Mississippi Rag*, Editor-Publisher of our local *Desert Ragtimer*, and main mover of ragtime in Arizona, has read the book and been very generous with support and encouragement. Equally kind and generous, I'll never quite repay my wife Evelyn for going along with my ragtime obsession. She's OK with ragtime, but an obsession calls for great reserves of tolerance. Thanks, Dear.

H. Loring White
Phoenix, AZ
September 2004

BIBLIOGRAPHY

I. Biographies and Memoirs

A. General

- Lawrence F. Abbott. *Impressions of Theodore Roosevelt*. Garden City, NY: Doubleday Page & Company, 1919.
- Jane Addams. *Twenty Years at Hull House*. New York: New American Library, 1961 (orig. pub. 1910).
- Christopher Anderson, *Young Kate: The Remarkable Hepburns and the Childhood That Shaped an American Legend*. New York: Henry Holt and Company, 1988.
- Carl Sferrazza Anthony. *First Ladies: The Saga of Presidents' Wives and Their Power*. New York: William Morrow and Company, 1990.
- Ray Stannard Baker. *American Chronicle: The Autobiography of Ray Stannard Baker [David Grayson]*. New York: Charles Scribner's Sons, 1945.
- Sol Bloom. *The Autobiography of Sol Bloom*. New York: G. P. Putnam's, 1948.
- Kathleen Brady. *Ida Tarbell: Portrait of a Muckraker*. Pittsburgh: University of Pittsburgh Press, 1989.
- H. W. Brands. *TR: The Last Romantic*. New York: Basic Books, 1997.
- James Brough. *Princess Alice: A Biography of Alice Roosevelt Longworth*. Boston—Toronto: Little, Brown and Company, 1975.
- Noel F. Busch. *T. R. The Story of Theodore Roosevelt and His Influence on Our Times*. New York: Reynal & Company, 1963.
- Irene Castle and B.& W. Duncan. *Castles in the Air*. Garden City, NY: Doubleday & Company, 1958.
- Allen Churchill. *The Roosevelts: American Aristocrats*. New York: Harper & Row Publishers, 1965.
- Peter Collier, with David Horowitz. *The Roosevelts: An American Saga*. New York: Simon & Schuster, 1994.
- Paul W. Glad. *The Trumpet Soundeth: William Jennings Bryan and his Democracy, 1896-1912*. Lincoln, NE: University of Nebraska Press (a Bison Book), 1960.
- William Henry Harbaugh. *Power and Responsibility: The Life and Times of Theodore Roosevelt*. New York: Farrar, Straus, 1961.
- Samuel Bannister Harding. *George R. Smith: Founder of Sedalia, MO*, Sedalia, MO: Privately Printed, 1904.
- "Matthew Henson: Arctic Explorer." *Virtual Exploration Society*. Unmuseum.mus.pa.us./henson.htm: 1-7.
- Matthew A. Henson. *A Black Explorer at the North Pole*. Lincoln and London: University of Nebraska Press, 1984 (reprint of 1912 edition).
- Katharine Hepburn. *Me: Stories of My Life*. New York: Alfred A. Knopf, 1991.
- Wally Herbert. *The Noose of Laurels: Robert E. Peary and the Race to the North Pole*. New York: Atheneum, 1989.
- Hamilton Holt, Ed. *The Life Stories of Undistinguished Americans*. New York: Routledge, 1989.
- Ari Hoogenboom. "William McKinley," in *The Reader's Companion to American History*. Eric Foner & John McGarraty, Ed's. Boston: Houghton Mifflin Company, 1991.
- James Weldon Johnson. *Along This Way: The Autobiography of James Weldon Johnson*. New York: Viking Press, 1968.
- Philip B. Kunhardt, Jr., et al. *P. T. Barnum: America's Greatest Showman*. New York: Knopf, 1995.

- Margaret Leech. *In the Days of McKinley*. New York: Harper & Brothers, 1959.
- David Levering Lewis. *W. E. B. DuBois: Biography of a Race*. New York: Henry Holt and Company, 1993.
- Earle Looker. *The White House Gang*. New York: Fleming H. Revell Company, 1929.
- Simon Louvish. *Man on the Flying Trapeze: The Life and Times of W. C. Fields*. New York: W. W. Norton & Company, 1997.
- David McCullough. *Mornings on Horseback*. New York: Simon and Schuster, 1981.
- _____. *Truman*. New York: Simon and Schuster, 1992.
- Henry Louis Mencken. *The Days of H. L. Mencken: Happy Days, Newspaper Days, Heathen Days*. New York: Dorset Press, 1989 (reprints, orig. pub. 1940, 41, 43).
- Nathan Miller. *Theodore Roosevelt: A Life*. New York: William Morrow and Company, 1992.
- Edmund Morris. *The Rise of Theodore Roosevelt*. New York: Ballentine Books, 1980 (reprint, orig. pub. 1979).
- _____. *Theodore Rex*. New York: Random House, 2001.
- Sylvia Jukes Morris. *Edith Kermit Roosevelt: Portrait of a First Lady*. New York: Coward, McCann & Geohegan, Inc., 1980.
- "Peary, Robert Edwin." *Dictionary of American Biography* VII: 362-367. New York: Charles Scribner's Sons, 1934.
- Henry F. Pringle. *Theodore Roosevelt: A Biography*. New York: Harcourt, Brace and Company, 1931 (revision, 1954, reprint, 1984).
- Ben Proctor. *William Randolph Hearst: The Early Years, 1863-1910*. New York & Oxford: Oxford University Press, 1998.
- Edward J. Renehan, Jr. *The Lion's Pride: Theodore Roosevelt and His Family in Peace and War*. New York & Oxford: Oxford University Press, 1998.
- Corinne Roosevelt Robinson. *My Brother Theodore Roosevelt*. New York and London: Charles Scribner's Sons, 1921.
- Ray Robinson, *American Original: A Life of Will Rogers*. New York & Oxford: Oxford University Press, 1996.
- Theodore Roosevelt. *Theodore Roosevelt: An Autobiography*. New York: Da Capo Press, 1985 (reprint).
- Peggy and Harold Samuels. *Frederic Remington: A Biography*. Austin, TX: University of Texas Press, 1985.
- William Wingate Sewall. *Bill Sewall's Story of TR*. New York & London: Harper & Brothers Publishers, 1919.
- William L. Shirer. *20th Century Journey: A Memoir of a Life and Times: The Start, 1904-1930*. Boston: Little Brown and Company, 1976.
- Lincoln Steffens. *The Autobiography of Lincoln Steffens*. New York: Harcourt, Brace, and Company, 1931.
- Jean Strouse. *Morgan: American Financier*. New York: Random House, 1999.
- Mark Sullivan. *The Education of an American*. New York: Doubleday, Doran & Co., Inc., 1938.
- Ida M. Tarbell. *All in a Day's Work: An Autobiography*. Boston: G. K. Hall & Co., 1985 (reprint, orig. pub. 1939).
- Howard Teichmann. *Alice: The Life and Times of Alice Roosevelt Longworth*. Englewood Cliffs, NJ: Prentice-Hall, Inc., 1979.
- John Tierney. "Explorer faked famed photo," *Arizona Republic* (November 29, 1998): A-24 (orig. for *New York Times*).
- Sophie Tucker. *Some of These Days: The Autobiography of Sophie Tucker*. Garden City, NY: Doubleday, Doran and Company, Inc., 1945.

- Booker T. Washington. *Up From Slavery: An Autobiography.* New York: Modern Library, 1999.
- William Allen White. *The Autobiography of William Allen White.* New York: The Macmillan Company, 1946.
- Owen Wister. *My Forty Years Friendship with Theodore Roosevelt.* New York: Macmillan, 1930.

B. Musical Figures

- Reid Badger. *A Life in Ragtime: A Biography of James Reese Europe.* New York, Oxford: Oxford University Press, 1995.
- Jack A. Batterson. *Blind Boone: Missouri's Ragtime Pioneer.* Columbia and London: University of Missouri Press, 1998.
- Paul E. Bierley. *John Philip Sousa: American Phenomenon.* Englewood Cliffs, NJ: Prentice-Hall, 1973.
- Edward A. Berlin. *King of Ragtime: Scott Joplin and his Era.* New York Oxford: Oxford University Press, 1994.
- George A. Borgman. "Joseph Lamb, Classic Ragtimer," *Mississippi Rag* (August 2001): 1-7.
- _____. "Joseph Lamb, Classic Ragtimer: Part II," *Mississippi Rag* (September 2001): 23-27.
- Nan Bostick and Nora Hulse. "Ragtime's Women Composers: An Annotated Lexicon," *The Ragtime Ephemeralist* No. 3 (2002 A. D.): 106-139.
- Lawrence T. Carter. *Eubie Blake: Keys of Memory.* Detroit: Balamp Publishers, 1979.
- Ann Charters. *Nobody: The Story of Bert Williams.* New York: Macmillan Co., 1970.
- Russ Cassidy. "Centennial Recollections with Joseph Lamb," excerpted in *Rag Times* XXI (November 1987): 2-6.
- Susan Curtis. *Dancing to a Black Man's Tune: A Life of Scott Joplin.* Columbia and London: University of Missouri Press, 1994.
- Ken Emerson. *Doo-Dah: Stephen Foster and the Rise of American Popular Culture.* New York: Da Capo Press, 1998.
- W[illiam] C[hristopher] Handy. *Father of the Blues: An Autobiography.* Arna Bontemps, Ed. London: Sidgwick and Jackson, 1957 (orig. pub. NY: Macmillan Co., 1941).
- James Haskins, w/Kathleen Benson. *Scott Joplin.* New York: Doubleday & Company, Inc., 1978.
- Jean Huling. "Irene Giblin, St. Louis Ragtime Queen," *Rag Times* XVIII (November 1984): 1-2.
- _____. "Let's Remember Irene Giblin!" *Ragtimer* (September-October 1983): 5-8.
- William Howland Kenney. "James Scott: An Introduction," in *The Music of James Scott.* Scott De Veaux and William Howland Kenney, Ed's. Washington, D. C.: Smithsonian Institution Press, 1992: 1-29.
- Vera Brodsky Lawrence. "Scott Joplin," *Dictionary of American Negro Biography*: 369-371.
- Rayford W. Logan. "Jones, [Mathilda] Sissieretta [Joyner] [called Black Patti]," *Dictionary of American Negro Biography*: 367-368.
- Alan Lomax. *Mr. Jelly Roll: The Fortunes of Jelly Roll Morton, New Orleans Creole and "Inventor of Jazz".* New York: Duell, Sloane and Pearce, [1950].
- Max Morath. "May Aufderheide and the Ragtime Women," in *Ragtime: Its History, Composers, and Music.* John Edward Hasse, Ed. New York: Schirmer Books, 1985: 154-165.
- Terry Parrish. "The Paul Pratt Story," Part I, *Rag Times* XVII (January 1984): 2-5.
- _____. "The Paul Pratt Story," Part II, *Rag Times* XVII (March 1984): 3-6.
- Al Rose. *Eubie Blake.* New York: Schirmer Books, 1979.

- Joseph R. Scotti. "Joe Lamb: A Study of Ragtime's Paradox," Ph. D. Dissertation, University of Cincinnati, 1977.
- _____. "The Musical Legacy of Joe Lamb," in *Ragtime: Its History, Composers, and Music*. John Edward Hasse, Ed. New York: Schirmer Books, 1985: 243-255.
- "Sousa, John Philip." *Dictionary of American Biography*. Dumas Malone, Ed. New York: Charles Scribner's Sons, 1964: 407-408.
- Marvin L. Vangilder. "The Childhood of Clarence Woods," *Rag Times* XI (March 1978): 6.
- _____. "James Scott," in *Ragtime: Its History, Composers, and Music*. John Edward Hasse, Ed. New York: Schirmer Books, 1985: 136-145.
- _____. "James Scott: A Biography," *Rag Times* XI (May 1977): 14-18.
- _____. "The Work of Clarence Woods," *Rag Times* XI (January 1978): 1-2.
- Dick Zimmerman. "Cecil Duane Crabb: Ragtime Pianist, Composer, Artist, Florist, and Fisherman," *Rag Times* XXIX (September 1995) 1-2.
- _____. "Clarence Woods: The Untold Story," Part I, *Rag Times* XVIII (May 1984): 1-2.
- _____. "Clarence Woods: The Untold Story," Part II, *Rag Times* XVIII (July 1984): 6-9.
- _____. "The Henry Lodge Story," *Rag Times* IX (January 1976): 1-3.

II. African Americans

- Arthur R. Ashe, Jr. *A Hard Road to Glory: A History of the African-American Athlete,* Volume I: 1619-1918. New York: Warner, 1988.
- Ray Stannard Baker. *Following the Color Line: An Account of Negro Citizenship in the American Democracy.* Williamstown, MA: Corner House Publishers, 1973 (reprint of 1908 work).
- William E. Bittle and Gilbert L. Geis. "Racial Self-Fulfillment and the Rise of an All-Negro Community in Oklahoma," in *The Making of Black America: Essays in Negro Life and History*. 2 Vols. August Meier and Elliott Rudwick, Ed's. New York: Atheneum, 1969: II, 106-118. (Orig. pub. in *Phylon*, XVIII [Third Quarter, 1957]: 247-260.)
- Norman L. Crockett. *The Black Towns*. Lawrence, KS: Regents Press of Kansas, 1979.
- Charles Crowe. "Racial Violence and Social Reform—Origins of the Atlanta Race Riot of 1906," *Journal of Negro History* 53 (July 1968): 2334-256.
- Martin Dann. "From Sodom to the Promised Land: E. P. McCabe and the Movement to Oklahoma Colonization," *Kansas Historical Quarterly* 40 (Autumn 1974): 370-378.
- John Hope Franklin. *From Slavery to Freedom: A History of Negro Americans*. 4th Edition. New York: Alfred A. Knopf, 1974.
- Ralph Ginzburg. *One Hundred Years of Lynchings*. New York: Lancer, 1969.
- Dewey W. Grantham, Jr. *Hoke Smith and the Politics of the New South*. Baton Rouge, LA: Louisiana State University Press, 1967 (paper, orig. pub. 1958).
- Lorenzo J. Greene, Gary R. Kremer, Antonio F. Holland. *Missouri's Black Heritage*. Rev. Ed. Columbia and London: University of Missouri Press, 1993.
- William Ivy Hair. *Carnival of Fury: Robert Charles and the New Orleans Race Riot of 1900*. Baton Rouge, LA: Louisiana State University Press, 1976 (paper).
- J. William Harris. "Etiquette, Lynching, and Racial Boundaries in Southern History: A Mississippi Example," *American Historical Review*, Vol. 100, No. 2 (April 1995): 387-410.

- James Weldon Johnson. *The Autobiography of an Ex-Colored Man*. New York: Alfred A. Knopf, 1927 (reprint, orig. pub. 1912).
- Thomas Knight. *Sunset of Utopian Dreams: An Experiment of Black Separation on the American Frontier.* Washington, DC: University Press of America, 1977.
- Ann J. Lane. *The Brownsville Affair: National Crisis and Black Reaction.* Port Washington, NY: Kennikat Press, 1971.
- Craig Lockard. "Integrating African History into the World History Course: Some Transgressional Patterns, *World History Bulletin*, X, No. 29 (Fall-Winter 1993-94): 21.
- August Meier. *Negro Thought in America, 1880-1915: Racial Ideologies in the Age of Booker T. Washington.* Ann Arbor, MI: University of Michigan Press, 1963.
- NAACP. *Thirty Years of Lynching in the United States, 1889-1918*. New York: Negro University Press, 1969 (reprint of 1919 pub.).
- John Edward Philips. "The African Heritage of White America," in *Africanisms in American Culture*. Joseph E. Holloway, Ed. Bloomington, IN: Indiana University Press, 1990: 225-239.
- H. Leon Prather, Sr. *We Have Taken a City: Wilmington Racial Massacre and Coup of 1898*. Rutherford, NJ: Fairleigh Dickinson University Press, 1984.
- Benjamin Quarles. *The Negro in the Making of America*. New York: Collier Books, 1987.
- Theodore Rosengarten. *All God's Dangers: The Life of Nate Shaw*. New York: Avon Books, 1975 (paper, orig. pub. Knopf, 1974).
- Elliott M. Rudwick. *Race Riot at East St. Louis, July 2, 1917*. Carbondale, IL: Southern Illinois University Press, 1964.
- George Sinkler. *The Racial Attitudes of American Presidents: From Abraham Lincoln to Theodore Roosevelt.* Garden City, NY: Doubleday, 1972.
- Sterling Stuckey. "Slavery and the Freeing of American History Instruction," in *Perspectives (American Historical Association Newsletter)*. Vol. 33, No. 4 (April 1995): 12-17.
- Arthur L. Tolson. *The Black Oklahomans: A History, 1841-1972*. New Orleans, LA: Edwards Publishing Co., 1974.
- John D. Weaver. *The Brownsville Raid*. New York: W. W. Norton, 1970.
- C. Vann Woodward. *The Strange Career of Jim Crow*. New York: Oxford University Press, 1974 (Third Rev. Ed.).
- Richard Young. "The Brownsville Affray," *American History Illustrated*, 21 (October 1986): 10-17.
- Robert L. Zangrando. "Lynching," in *The Reader's Companion to American History*, Eric Foner & John A. Garraty, Ed's. Boston: Houghton Mifflin Company, 1991: 684-686.
- _____. *The NAACP Crusade Against Lynching, 1909-1950*. Philadelphia: Temple University Press, 1980.

III. Ideas and Culture

- Frederick Lewis Allen. *The Big Change: America Transforms Itself, 1900-1950*. New York: Harper & Brothers Publishers, 1952.
- Thomas Bender. "Urbanization," *The Reader's Companion to American History*. Eric Foner & John A. Garraty, Ed's. Boston: Houghton Mifflin Company, 1991: 1100-1104.
- Otto Bettmann. *The Good Old days—They Were Terrible*. New York: Random House, 1974.
- W. J. Cash. *The Mind of the South*. New York: Vintage Books, 1961 (orig. pub. Knopf, 1941).

- Sean Dennis Cashman. *America in the Age of the Titans: The Progressive Era and World War I.* New York: New York University Press, 1988.
- James Lincoln Collier. *The Rise of Selfishness in America.* New York: Oxford University Press, 1991.
- Robert M. Crunden. *A Brief History of American Culture.* New York: Paragon House, 1994.
- _____. "Antitrust Movement," *The Reader's Companion to American History.* Eric Foner & John A. Garrraty, Ed's. Boston: Houghton Mifflin Company, 1991: 41-43.
- _____. *Ministers of Reform: The Progressive Achievement in American Civilization, 1889-1920.* New York: Basic Books, Inc. Publishers, 1982.
- John D'Emilio and Estelle B. Freedman. *Intimate matters: A History of Sexuality in America.* New York: Harper & Row Publishers, 1988.
- Mario R. Di Nunzio, Ed. *Theodore Roosevelt, An American Mind: Selected Writings.* New York: Penguin Books, 1994.
- Perry R. Duis. *The Saloon: Public Drinking in Chicago and Boston.* Champaign, IL: University of Illinois Press, 1983.
- Lewis A. Erenberg. *Steppin' Out: New York Night Life and the Transformation of American Culture, 1890-1930.* Chicago: University of Chicago Press, 1981.
- J. C. Furnas. *The Americans: A Social History of the United States, 1587-1914.* New York: Putnam, 1969.
- _____. *The Life and Times of the Late Demon Rum.* New York: Capricorn Books, 1973 (reprint, orig. pub. 1965).
- James Gilbert. *Perfect Cities: Chicago's Utopias of 1893.* Chicago: University of Chicago Press, 1991.
- William Grimes. *Straight Up On the Rocks: A Cultural History of American Drink.* New York: Simon & Schuster, 1993.
- Howard Mumford Jones. *The Age of Energy: Varieties of American Experience, 1865-1915.* New York: The Viking Press, 1970.
- Jon Kingsdale. "The Poor Man's Club: Social Functions of the Urban Working Class Saloon," *American Quarterly* 25 (October 1973): 472-489.
- J. Anthony Lukas. *Big Trouble.* New York: Simon & Schuster, 1997.
- *McGuffey's Sixth Eclectic Reader.* Rev. Ed. New York, Cincinnati, Chicago: American Book Company, 1921.
- Samuel Eliot Morison. *The Oxford History of the American People.* New York: Oxford University Press, 1965.
- Paul C. Nagel. *Missouri: A Bicentennial History.* New York: W. W. Norton & Company, Inc.,1977.
- *The National Standard Atlas of the World.* Chicago: Thompson & Thomas, 1900.
- Kathryn J. Oberdeck. *The Evangelist and the Impresario: Religion, Entertainment and Cultural Politics in America, 1884-1914.* Baltimore; Johns Hopkins University Press, 1999.
- Jacob Riis. *How the Other Half Lives: Studies Among the Tenements of New York.* New York: Dover Publications, 1971 (reprint of orig. pub. 1890).
- Robert W. Rydell. *All the World's a Fair: Visions of Empire at International Expositions, 1876-1916.* Chicago: University of Chicago Press, 1985.
- _____. "World's Fairs," *The Reader's Companion to American History.* Eric Foner & John A. Garraty, Ed's. Boston: Houghton Mifflin Company, 1991: 1168-1170.
- Sedalia Public Library. *The First One Hundred Years: A History of Sedalia, Missouri, 1860-1960.* Centennial History Committee, 1960.
- Thomas E. Sheridan. *Arizona: A History.* Tucson, AZ: The University of Arizona Press, 1995.
- Dean Smith. *Tempe: Arizona Crossroads.* Chatsworth, CA: Windsor Publications, 1990.

- William Strauss and Neil Howe. *Generations: The History of America's Future, 1584-2069*. New York: William Morrow and Company, Inc., 1991.
- Mark Sullivan. *Our Times*. 6 Vols. New York: Scribner's, 1926.
- James Harvey Young. *The Toadstool Millionaires: A Social History of Patent Medicines in America Before Federal Regulation*. Princeton, NJ: Princeton University Press, 1961.

IV. Music

- Edward A. Berlin. *Ragtime: A Musical and Cultural History*. Berkeley: University of California Press, 1980.
- _____. *Reflections and Research on Ragtime*. I.S.A.M. Monographs, No. 24. Brooklyn, NY: Institute for Studies in American Music, Conservatory of Music, Brooklyn College of the City University of New York, 1987.
- Rudy Blesh and Harriet Janis. *They All Played Ragtime*. Fourth Edition. New York: Oak Publications, 1971 (reprint, orig. pub. Knopf, 1950)
- Gilbert Chase. *America's Music: From the Pilgrims to the Present*. Rev. Third Ed. Urbana and Chicago: University of Illinois Press, 1987.
- John Cleophus Cotter. "The Negro Music in St. Louis." Masters Thesis. St. Louis: Washington University, 1959.
- Ronald L. Davis. *A History of Music in American Life*. 3 Vols: I. *The formative years, 1620-1865*; II. *The Gilded Years, 1865-1920*; III. *The Modern Era, 1920-Present*. Melbourne, FL: Krieger Publishing Company, 1980-82.
- Scott De Veaux and William Howland Kenney, Ed's. *The Music of James Scott*. Washington, DC: Smithsonian Institution Press, 1992.
- Peter Gammond. *Scott Joplin and the Ragtime Era*. London: Abacus, 1975.
- Douglas Gilbert. *Lost Chords: The Diverting Story of American Popular Songs*. New York: Doubleday, Doran and Company, 1942.
- Isaac Goldberg. *Tin Pan Alley*. New York: Frederick Ungar, 1961 (orig. pub. 1930).
- John Edward Hasse. "The Creation and Dissemination of Indianapolis Ragtime, 1897-1930," Ph. D. Dissertation, Indiana University. Bloomington, IN, 1981.
- _____ Ed. *Ragtime: Its History, Composition, and Music*. New York: Schirmer Books, 1985.
- _____. "Ragtime: From the Top," in *Ragtime: Its History, Composers, and Music*. Ed. John Edward Hasse. New York: Schirmer Books, 1985.
- David A. Jasen. *Tin Pan Alley: The Composers, the Songs, the Performers*. New York: D. I. Fine, 1988.
- David A. Jasen & Gene Jones. *Black Bottom Stomp: Eight Masters of Ragtime and Early Jazz*. New York & London: Routledge, 2002.
- _____. *Spreadin' Rhythm Around: Black Popular Songwriters, 1880-1930*. New York: Schirmer Books, 1998.
- _____. *That American Rag: The Story of Ragtime from Coast to Coast*. New York: Schirmer Books, 2000.
- Edward B. Marks. *They All Sang: From Tony Pastor to Rudy Vallee*. New York: The Viking Press, 1934. David A. Jasen & Trebor Jay Tichenor. *Rags and Ragtime: A Musical History*. New York: Dover Publications, Inc., 1989 (reprint, orig. pub. 1978).
- Gene Jones. "The Grandee of Chestnut Valley: Tom Turpin and his Domain," in *Tom Turpin: His Life and Music*. A Publication of the Tom Turpin Ragtime Festival, Inc. [n.p., n.d.].
- Bob Kimball & Bill Bolcom. *Reminiscing With Sissle and Blake*. New York: Viking Press, 1973.

- Elise K. Kirk. *Musical Highlights from the White House*. Malabar, FL: Krieger Publishing Company, 1992.
- Ernst Krohn. *Music Publishing in St. Louis*. Completed and Edited by J. Bunker Clark. Warren, MI: Harmonie Park Press, 1988.
- Alain Leroy Locke. *The Negro and his Music*. Washington, DC: Association in Negro Folk Education, 1936.
- Wilfrid Mellers. *Music in a New Found Land: Themes and Developments in the History of American Music*. London, Boston: Faber & Faber, 1987 (reprint, orig. pub. 1964).
- Thomas L. Morgan and William Barlow. *From Cakewalks to Concert Halls; An Illustrated History of African American Popular Music From 1895 to 1930*. Washington, DC: Elliott & Clark Publishing, 1992.
- Burton W. Peretti. *The Creation of Jazz: Music, Race, and Culture in Urban America*. Urbana, IL: University of Illinois Press, 1992.
- Addison W. Reed. "The Life and Works of Scott Joplin." Ph. D. Dissertation. University of North Carolina, 1973.
- Craig H. Roell. *The Piano in America, 1890-1940*. Chapel Hill, NC: University of North Carolina Press, 1989.
- Al Rose. Liner Notes to *Creole Rags*. New Orleans: Jazzology Records, 1987. JCE 94.
- Russell Sanjek. *America's Popular Music and its Business: The First Four Hundred Years*. Vol. I, *The Beginning to 1790*; Vol. II, *1790-1909*; Vol. III, *From 1900-1984*. New York: Oxford University Press, 1988.
- William J. Schafer and Richard B. Allen. *Brass Bands and New Orleans Jazz*. Baton Rouge, LA: Louisiana State University Press, 1977.
- William J. Schafer and Johannes Riedel. *The Art of Ragtime: Form and Meaning of an Original Black American Art*. Baton Rouge, LA: Louisiana State University Press, 1973.
- Gunther Schuller. *Early Jazz: Its Roots and Musical Development*. New York: Oxford University Press, 1968.
- Eileen Southern. *The Music of Black Americans: A History*. New York: W. W. Norton and Co., 1971.
- Marshall W. Stearns. *The Story of Jazz*. New York: Oxford University Press, 1956.
- Marvin L. Vangilder. "Ragtime Was the Rage at Lakeside," *Rag Times* XI (January 1978): 6-7.
- Terry Waldo. *This Is Ragtime*. New York: Da Capo Press, 1991 (reprint, orig. pub. Hawthorn Books, 1976).
- Ian Whitcomb. *After the Ball: Pop Music from Rag to Rock*. 2nd Ed. New York: Limelight Editions, 1994 (reprint, orig. pub. 1972).
- _____. *Irving Berlin & Ragtime America*. New York: Limelight Editions, 1988.
- Isadore Witmark and Isaac Goldberg. *From Ragtime to Swingtime: The Story of the House of Witmark*. New York: Da Capo Press, 1976 (orig. pub. 1939).
- Dick Zimmerman. "Scott Joplin: His Music," in Liner Notes for *Scott Joplin; His Complete Works*. New York: Murray Hill Records, 1974, No. 931079 (unpaged).

V. Politics

- Thomas A. Bailey, Ed. *The American Spirit: United States History as Seen by Contemporaries*. Vol. II. Boston: D. C. Heath and Company, 1963.
- David H. Burton. *Theodore Roosevelt, American Politician: An Assessment*. Cranbury, NJ: Fairleigh Dickinson University Press, 1997.
- John Whiteclay Chambers II. *The Tyranny of Change: America in the Progressive Era, 1900-1917*. New York: St. Martin's Press, 1980.
- Paul Russell Cutright. *Theodore Roosevelt: The Making of a Conservationist*. Urbana and Chicago: University of Illinois Press, 1985.

- Thomas G. Dyer. *Theodore Roosevelt and the Idea of Race*. Baton Rouge and London: Louisiana State University Press, 1980.
- Willard B. Gatewood, Jr. *Theodore Roosevelt and the Art of Controversy: Episodes of the White House Years*. Baton Rouge: Louisiana State University Press, 1970.
- Morton Keller. "The Spanish-American War," in *The Readers Companion to American History*. Eric Foner & John A. Garraty, Ed's. Boston: Houghton Mifflin Company, 1991: 1015-1016.
- Michael Medved. *The Shadow Presidents: The Secret History of the Chief Executives and Their Top Aides*. New York; Times Books, 1979.
- George E. Mowry. *The Era of Theodore Roosevelt, 1900-1912*. New York; Harper & Brothers, 1958.
- Page Smith. *America Enters the World: A People's History of the Progressive Era and World War I*. New York: McGraw-Hill, 1985.
- Kenneth Wimmel. *Theodore Roosevelt and the Great White Fleet: American Seapower Comes of Age*. Washington, London: Brassey's, 1998.

VI. Prostitution & Disease

- Herbert Asbury. *The Barbary Coast; An Informal History of the San Francisco Underworld*. New York: Alfred A. Knopf, 1933.
- _____. *The French Quarter*. New York: Alfred A. Knopf, 1936.
- "Underbelly of a City: Dig Reveals Vice," *Arizona Republic*, September 14, 1989.
- Allan M. Brandt. *No Magic Bullet: A Social History of Venereal Disease in the United States Since 1880*. New York: Oxford University Press, 1985.
- William J. Brown, et al. *Syphilis and Other Venereal Diseases*. Cambridge: MA, Harvard University Press, 1970.
- Mark Thomas Connelly. *The Response to Prostitution in the Progressive Era*. Chapel Hill, NC: University of North Carolina Press, 1980.
- Timothy J. Gilfoyle. *City of Eros: Prostitution and the Commercialization of Sex, 1790-1920*. New York; W. W. Norton & Company, 1992.
- Daniel Q. Kelly. "Ballum Rancum," *The Ragtime Ephemeralist*, No. 3 (2002): 184-1991.
- George J. Kneeland. *Commercialized Prostitution in New York City*. Montclair, NJ: Patterson Smith, 1969 (reprint of 1913 work).
- Gary and Gloria Meier. *Those Naughty Ladies of the Old Northwest*. Bend, OR: Maverick Publishers, 1990.
- John O'Shea. *Was Mozart Poisoned? Medical Investigations into the Lives of the Great Composers*. New York: St. Martin's Press, 1991.
- Claude Quetel. *History of Syphilis*. Trans. Judith Braddock and Brian Pike. Cambridge, UK: Polity Press,1990.
- Al Rose. *Storyville, New Orleans: Being an Authentic Illustrated Account of the Notorious Red-Light District*. University, AL: University of Alabama Press, 1974.
- Ruth Rosen. *The Lost Sisterhood: Prostitution in America, 1900-1918*. Baltimore: Johns Hopkins University Press, 1982.
- Anne Seagraves. *Soiled Doves: Prostitution in the Early West*. Hayden, ID: Weanne, 1994.
- Frederick J. Spencer. "Examining Scott Joplin's Fatal Illness." *The Mississippi Rag* (May 1998): 31-33.
- Charles Washburn. *Come Into My Parlor: A Biography of the Aristocratic Everleigh Sisters of Chicago*. New York: Arno Press, 1974 (reprint of orig. pub.1934).

- Howard B. Woolston. *Prostitution in the United States: Prior to the Entrance of the United States into the World War*. Montclair, NJ: Patterson Smith, 1969 (reprint of orig. pub. 1921).
- James Harvey Young. *The Medical Messiahs: A Social History of Health Quackery in Twentieth-Century America*. Princeton, NJ: Princeton University Press, 1967.

VII. Transportation & Technology

- Willis J. Abbot. *Panama and the Canal: In Picture and Prose*. London: Syndicate Publishing Company, 1913.
- Edwin L. Dunbaugh. *Nightboat to New England, 1815-1900*. New York: Greenwood Press, 1992.
- James J. Flink. *The Automobile Age*. Cambridge, MA: M I T Press, 1988.
- George W. Hilton. *The Night Boat*. Berkeley, CA: Howell-North Books, 1968.
- Fred Howard. *Wilbur and Orville: A Biography of the Wright Brothers*. New York: Alfred A. Knopf, 1987.
- Peter J. Ling. *America and the Automobile: Technology, Reform, and Social Change*. New York: Manchester University Press, 1989.
- Albro Martin. *Railroads Triumphant: The Growth, Rejection, and Rebirth of a Vital American Force*. New York, Oxford: Oxford University Press, 1992.
- David McCullough. *The Path Between the Seas: The Creation of the Panama Canal, 1870-1914*. New York: Simon & Schuster, 1877.
- Scott Molloy. *Trolley Wars: Streetcar Workers on the Line*. Washington, DC: Smithsonian Institution Press, 1996.
- David E. Nye. *Electrifying America: Social Meanings of a New Technology, 1880-1940*. Cambridge, MA: M I T Press, 1992.
- John B. Rae. *The American Automobile: A Brief History*. Chicago: University of Chicago Press, 1965.
- Karen L. Smith. *The Magnificent Experiment: Building the Salt River Reclamation Project, 1890-1917*. Tucson: The University of Arizona Press, 1986.
- John R. Stilgoe. *Metropolitan Corridor: Railroads and the American Scene*. New Haven and London: Yale University Press, 1983.
- John F. Stover. *The Life and Decline of the American Railroad*. New York: Oxford University Press, 1970.
- Earl Zarbin. *Roosevelt Dam: A History to 1911*. Phoenix, AZ: Salt River Project, 1984.

VIII. Vaudeville & Entertainment

- Judith A. Adams. *The American Amusement Park: A History of Technology and Thrills*. Boston: Twayne Publishers, 1991.
- Gerald Bordman. *American Musical Theatre: A Chronicle*. New York: Oxford University Press, 1978.
- Rich Chamberlin. "W. C. Fields, The Crown Prince of Comedy…A Juggler First!" *Jugglers World*, May 1983: 1-2. Taken from Internet Website w.w.w.juggling.org.
- Tom Fletcher. *One Hundred Years of the Negro in Show Business*. New York: Da Capo Press, 1984 (reprint, orig. pub.1954).
- Douglas Gilbert. *American Vaudeville: Its Life and Times*. New York: Dover Publications, 1963 (reprint, orig. pub. 1940).
- Abel Green & Joe Laurie, Jr. *Show Biz: From Vaude to Video*. New York: Henry Holt & Company, 1951.
- Allen Lee Hamilton. "Train Crash at Crush: Publicity and Tragedy—as big as Texas," *American West*, Vol. XX, No. 4 (July-August 1983): 62-65.

- James Weldon Johnson. *Black Manhattan.* New York: Arno Press and the New York Times, 1968 (reprint, orig. pub. Knopf, 1930).
- John F. Kasson. *Amusing the Million: Coney Island at the Turn of the Century.* New York: Hill & Wang, 1978.
- Russell Lynes. *The Lively Audience: A Social History of the Visual and Performing Arts in America, 1890-1950.* New York: Harper & Row Publishers, 1985.
- Ethan Mordden. *Broadway Babies: The People Who Made the American Musical.* New York: Oxford University Press, 1893.
- David Nasaw. *Going Out: The Rise and Fall of Public Amusements.* New York: Basic Books, 1993.
- Thomas L. Riis. *Just Before Jazz: Black Musical Theatre in New York, 1890 to 1915.* Washington, DC: Smithsonian Institution Press, 1989.
- Henry T. Sampson. *The Ghost Walks: A Chronological History of Blacks in Show Business, 1865-1910.* Metuchen, NJ: 1988.
- Charles and Louise Samuels. *Once Upon a Stage: The Merry World of Vaudeville.* New York: Dodd, Mead & Company, 1974.
- Robert W. Snyder. *The Voice of the City: Vaudeville and Popular Culture in New York.* New York: Oxford University Press, 1989.
- Mark Steyn. *Broadway Babies Say Goodnight: Musicals Then and Now.* New York: Routledge, 1999.
- Irving Zeidman. *The American Burlesque Show: A History.* New York: Hawthorne Books, 1967.

IX. Poetry Sources

- Arnold Adoff, Ed. *The Poetry of Black America: Anthology of the Twentieth Century.* New York: Harper & Row, 1973.
- Arna Bontemps, Ed. *American Negro Poetry.* New York: Hill & Wang, 1964.
- James Weldon Johnson. *The Book of American Negro Poetry.* New York: Harcourt, Brace and Company, 1922, 1931.
- David Levering Lewis, Ed. *The Portable Harlem Renaissance Reader.* New York: Viking, 1994.
- N. Vachel Lindsay. *Collected Poems.* New York: Macmillan, 1934.
- Louis Untermeyer, Ed. *Modern American and British Poetry.* 2 Vols. New York: Harcourt, Brace and Company, 1942.
- Oscar Williams, Ed. *A Little treasury of American Poetry.* New York: Charles Scribner's Sons, 1948.

INDEX OF NAMES AND TITLES

A Bird In a Gilded Cage, 51, 364
A Breeze From Alabama, 133
A Bundle of Rags, 123
A Coon Band Contest, 98
A Guest of Honor, 179-180, 184, 185, 217, 320
A Hot Time in the Old Town Tonight, 3, 94, 216, 217, 361, 363
A Real Slow Drag, 320, 372
A Summer Breeze:March and Two-Step, 243
A Tennessee Tantalizer, 180
A Totally Different Rag, 314
A Trip to Africa, 323
A Trip to Coontown, 68, 104, 261-262, 266, 272
Abba Dabba Honeymoon, 267
Abuza, Charles (Kalish), 348
Abuza, Dolly, 348
Abyssinia, 268-269, 272
Act for the Preservation of American Antiquities, 334
Ada, My Sweet Potater, 271
Adams, Henry, 56
Addams, Jane, 161
Affinity Rag, 317
African Hunter, The, 216, 217
After the Ball, 12, 49, 364, 388
Age (New York), 285, 312, 319, 321, 322, 325, 372
Alaskan Rag, 309
Albee, E(dward) F(rancis), 62-63, 87-89, 166, 168, 169, 171, 174
Aldrich, Nelson, 332-333
Alexander's Ragtime Band, 1, 306
Alger, Russell, 95, 112
Alice Blue Gown, 212
All Coons Look Alike to Me, 98-99, 104, 163, 261, 289
Along This Way, 86, 105, 268, 273, 381
American Beauty Rag, 308
American Musician and Art Journal, 184, 314, 320
Anderson, Marian, 359
Anti-Saloon League, 158
Antoinette March, 185

Arlington, Josie, 367
Arms and the Man, 321
Arthur, President Chester A., 215
Asbury, Herbert, 221, 222, 223, 224, 225
Ashwander, Donald, 244
Ashy Africa, 303
At a Georgia Camp Meeting, 98, 123
At Jolly "Coony"—ey Island, 261
Aufderheide, John Henry, 313-315
Aufderheide, May Frances, 304, 309, 313-315, 316, 317
Ault, Robert, 361
Aunt Dinah Has Blowed De Horn, 320
Ayers, Nat, 171
Badger, Reid, 326, 379
Baer, George F., 142
Baker, Belle, 171
Baker, Ray Stannard, 80-82, 161
Baltimore Todalo, *365*
Bandanna Land, 269, 272, 320, 322
Barnum, P. T., 61
Barrymore, Maurice, 166
Bartlett, Bob, 356
Bayes, Nora, 32, 173-174, 321, 346, 351
Beard, Charles A., 161
Beck, Martin, 168
Belle of Bridgeport, 266
Bennett, Theron C., 180, 362
Berlin, Edward A., 132, 176, 180, 184, 305, 322, 372, 379
Berlin, Irving, 1, 88, 171, 306, 321, 322 344, 350, 351
Bernard, Mike, 303, 312
Bernhardt, Sarah, 89, 166, 168
Berryman, Clifford K., 209
Bethena, 185
Bethune, Thomas ("Blind Tom"), 16, 99, 103
Big, Red Shawl, 270
Bigelow, Charley, 167
Bill Bailey, Won't You Please Come Home, 104
Binks Waltz, 185
Black 400 Club, 122
Black and White Rag, 303-305, 309
Black Bohemia, 305-306, 322
Black Diamond Rag, 304

Black Patti Troubadours, The, 261, 267, 271
Black Politician, The, 324
Blaine, James G., 22
Blake, "Shout", 17, 363
Blake, Charlotte, 316, 317
Blake, Emily Johnston, 364
Blake, James Hubert ("Eubie"), 2, 16-17, 271, 304, 321, 326, 363-365, 369, 371-372, 375
Blake, John Sumner, 364
Bland, James, 40
Blesh, Rudi, 1, 129, 130, 182, 244, 305, 309, 379
Blind Boone Concert Company, 8
Blind Boone's Southern Rag Medley #1: Strains From the Alleys, 9
Blind Boone's Southern Rag Medley #2: *Strains From the Flat Branch*, 9
Blocksom, Major August P., 284-286
Bloom, Sol, 67
Blue Goose Rag, 304
Blue Ribbon Rag, 314
Boas, Dr. Franz, 357
Bohemia Rag, 308
Bok, Edward W., 164, 374
Bolen, Grace M., 316, 317
Bon, Bon Buddy, 269
Boone and Crockett Club, 334-335
Boone, Eugenia, 8
Boone, John William ("Blind Boone"), 7-10, 16, 99, 103, 243
Boone, Rachel, 7
Bostic, Nan, 316
Botsford, George, 303
Bowery Buck, 181, 361
Bowman, Euday L., 180-181, 304, 361
Broadway One-Step, 1
Broadway Rag, 243
Broady, Thomas, 361
Brodie, Alexander, 298
Brooks, Shelton, 351
Brown, A. Seymour, 171
Brown-Skin Baby Mine, 264
Bryan, William Jennings, 71-75, 103, 138, 156, 160, 276, 316, 337, 338
Buck, Gene, 346
Bull Dog Rag, 317
Bull Moose Rag, 217
Bully Rag (two of them), 217
Bunau-Varilla, Philippe, 146

Bunch O' Blackberries, 98, 215
Burleigh, Harry, 266, 322, 323, 325, 326
Burt, Hilma, 367
Buzzer Rag, 314
By Broomstick Train: Our Suburbs By Foot and Trolley, 235
By the Light of the Silvery Moon, 52
Caboceers Entrance, 264
Cahill, Marie, 267
Cakewalk in the Sky, 98
Call Me Back, 363
Callahan, Ruth, 244
Calliope Rag, 244
Cameron, Donaldina, 224-225
Campbell, Sanford Brunson ("Brun"), 1,120, 361
Canadian Capers, 309
Candlestick Rag, 314
Cannery Row, 220
Cannibal King, The, 263, 266
Cannon Ball, 309, 332
Cantor, Eddie, 88, 342, 350
Carbarlic Acid, 309, 312
Carl Hoffman, 130-131
Carmichael, Hoagy, 313
Carnegie, Andrew, 158, 337
Carnival: Trot and One-Step, 316
Carter, W. H., 179
Carus, Emma, 62, 170
Casals, Pablo, 216
Cascades, The, 133, 183, 184, 306, 322, 328
Castle, Irene, 13, 271, 304
Castle, Vernon, 13, 271, 304
Cedar Point, 240
Champagne Rag, 308
Chanute, Octave, 188, 190
Chaplin, Charley, 344
Charleston Rag, 365
Charley Thompson, 2, 182
Chase, Basil, 364
Chauvin, Louis, 182, 183, 185, 242, 361, 362, 374
Cherry Sisters, 168
Chestnut Street in the Nineties, 361
Chestnut Valley Rag, 361

Chicken Chowder, 309, 316
Chocolate Soldier, The, 321
Cholera Balm, 167
Christy, Edwin P., 38
Chrysanthemum, The, 184, 322
Clark, E. E., 142
Clarke, Herbert L., 150
Clayton Anti-Trust Act of 1914, 339
Clef Club, 271, 324-326
Clef Club March, 325-326
Clef Club Symphony Orchestra, 325-326
Cleveland, Grover, 12, 22, 55, 56, 67, 71, 72, 117, 204, 276, 280
Clifford, Jack, 168
Climax Rag, 243
Cline, Maggie, 88, 169
Clorindy, or the Origin of the Cakewalk, 268, 320
Cohan, George M., 1, 260
Cole, Robert Allen ("Bob"), 68, 104, 260-272, 329, 324, 374
Collier, James Lincoln, 63
Colonial Glide 314
Come Along, My Mandy, 174
Congo Love Song, 267
Connecticut Yankee, 315
Connors, "Babe", 99, 181, 363
Contentment Rag, 308
Cook, Abbie Mitchell, 268, 269
Cook, Frederick A., 168, 358, 354, 360
Cook, Will Marion, 262-266, 268, 269, 271, 322, 323, 325, 326, 365
Coon Hollow Capers, 361
Coon, Coon, Coon, 98, 104
Coon's Frolic, The, 123
Cortelyou, George, 204, 205
Cotton, Sarah Smith ("Sed"), 121-122
Country Club, 306
Cox, Mrs. Minnie, 280-281
Crab Apples, 241
Crabb, Cecil Duane, 313-314
Crane, Stephen, 91, 95
Crazy Bone Rag, 304
Creamer, Henry, 325
Creole Belles, 98
Creole Show, 68, 260-261

Crisis, The, 288
Croker, Richard, 137
Cross of Gold speech, 72-73, 276, 338
Crum, Dr. William, 281
Crush, George, 125-127
Curtis, Susan, 127-128, 132, 177
Cutter, The, 317
Czar, The, 264
Dabney, Ford, 305, 322, 324, 325, 327
Damaged Goods, 374
Dance of the Grizzly Bear, The, 303
Dance of the Seven Veils, 173
Dancy, John Campbell, 106
Daniels, Josephus, 107
Danse Heroique, 326
Darch, Bob, 2, 244
Darktown Barbecue, 268
Darktown Is Out Tonight, 262, 325
Darktown Strutters Ball, 351, 363
De Bo'd of Education, 270
De Lepinay, Godin , 253
De Lesseps, Count Ferdinand, 143, 247, 252
Dean, Dora, 313
DePew, Chauncey, 332
Dewey, Admiral George, 93
Dewey, John, 161
Die Fledermaus, 321
Dill Pickles Rag, 181, 304, 309
Dirks, Rudolph, 50
Dixie, 9, 28, 38-39, 262, 268, 327
Dixon, George Washington, 38
Dockstadter, Lew, 278
Dodds, Baby, 367
Dogtown, 183
Donaldson, Will, 316
Donley, Enoch, 7
Double Fudge, 180
Down Among the Sheltering Palms, 313
Down Home Rag, 309
Dream Days, 304
Dream Rag, 17, 68
Dreamland, 238-240

DuBois, W(illiam) E(dward) B(urghardt), 287-288
Dumars, Charles, 242-243, 313
Dunbar, Paul Lawrence, 262, 263, 266, 270, 326, 371
Duppa, Darrell, 295, 302
Dusty Rag, 309, 313-314
Dvorak, Antonin, 262
Dynamite Rag, 307
Eads, James Buchanan, 120, 176
Eastman, George, 277
Easy Winners, 179, 306
Eaton, Roy, 307
Echo, Eulalie, 368
Edwin Markham, 159
Ehrlich, Dr. Paul, 374
Eli Green's Cakewalk, 98, 317
Eliot, Dr. Charles, 374
Elite Syncopations, 133
Elkins, Stephen, 332
Emmett, Daniel Decatur, 19, 38, 39
Entertainer, The, 1, 133, 306
Entertainer's Rag, The, 309, 327
Erlanger, Abraham, 166, 267, 268, 271, 351
Ernst, Alfred, 178, 182
E*thiopia Rag*, 308
Eubie's Boogie, 365
Eugenia, 8, 306
Euphonic Sounds, 306
Europe, James Reese, 270, 271, 322-328, 365
Europe, John, 323, 324
Everleigh Club, 226-228, 351, 362-363, 368
Everleigh, Ada, 226-228, 362
Everleigh, Minna, 226-228
Everybody Two-Step, 309
Everybody's Doing It, 2
Evolution of Ragtime, The, 267
Ewell, Sammy, 17, 363
Excelsior Rag, 308
Exhortation, A Negro Sermon, 269
Exodusters, 195-196
Fas', Fas', World, 269
Favorite, The, 130, 184
Federal Deposit Insurance Corporation, 339

Federal Reserve Act of 1913, 339
Federal Trade Commission Act of 1914, 339
Feist, Leo, 170
Felicity Rag, 133, 306, 372
Ferguson, Bob, 95
Ferris, George W. G., 68, 183
Fiedler, Arthur, 151
Fields, Harriet ("Hattie") Hughes, 343
Fields, W(illiam) C(laude) (Dukinfield), 342-344, 346
Fifteen Standard High-Class Rags, 305
Fig Leaf Rag, 133, 306
Finger Breaker, The, 371
Firefly, The, 321
Fisher, Bud, 50
Fiske Jubilee Singers, 16, 42
Fiske, Minnie Maddern, 166
Fletcher, Tom, 100
Floating Down the Nile, 270
Fluffy Ruffles 313
Follies, 174, 216, 272, 315, 321, 342, 344, 346-347, 351
Follies Bergere, 321
Foraker, Senator Joseph Benson, 285-290, 332, 338
Forest & Stream: Polka or Two-Step, 123
Foster, Stephen Collins, 8, 39-40, 151, 183
Four Cohans, 342
Fournier, Dr. Alfred, 373
Fowler, Benjamin, 296-298, 300, 301
Fox, Richard K., 303
Foy, Eddie, 62, 267
Frankie and Johnny, 181
Freeman, The, 180, 264, 270, 312, 372
French, "Old Man" "Metronome", 16, 68, 363
Fried Chicken Rag, 317
Friml, Rudolph, 321
Frog Legs, 185, 243, 305, 309
Frolic of the Bears, 320, 372
Funny Bones, 181
Fusion Party, 106, 109
Gaillard, David, 253
Gans, Joe, 365
Garfield, Pres. James A., 55
Garlington, General Ernest A., 284-285

George R. Smith College for Negroes, 122
Giblin, Irene, 316, 317
Gilbert, Douglas, 166, 169
Gillis, Frank R., 361
Gilly, Ann, 365
Gilmore, Patrick Sarsfield, 150
Gilson, Lottie, 169
Gladiolus Rag, 306
Glass-Steagle Act of 1933, 339
Goethals, George Washington, 247, 253-257
Gonzalez, Antonia, 367, 368
Good Advice, 320
Gorgas, William Crawford, 247-251, 257
Gottschalk, Louis Moreau, 151, 215, 366
Grace and Beauty, 243
Grandpa's Spells, 371
Great Crush Collision March, 127-128
Great Scott Rag, 243
Greeley, Horace, 156
Green, "Big Jimmy", 17, 363
Green, Abel, 350
Grinnell, George Bird, 334-335
Grizzly Bear Rag, The, 303, 309
Gustin, Louise V., 316, 317
Halloween Rag, 313
Hamlin, John Austen, 167
Hamlin's Wizard Oil, 167
Hammerstein, Oscar I, 168
Hampton, Rob, 396
Hands Up, 452
Handy, W(illiam) C(hristopher), 25, 27, 41, 84, 156, 226
Hanna, Marcus Alonzo, 73-74, 138, 141
Hardy, Oliver, 344
Harlem Rag, 123, 130, 180-181
Harms, T. B., 49, 170
Harney, Benjamin Robertson ("Ben"), 99-101, 303
Harney, Jessie Boyce, 100
Harriman, E. H., 140
Harris, Charles K., 12, 49-51, 170
Harris, Joel Chandler, 282
Harrison, Caroline, 215
Harrison, President Benjamin, 55, 56, 204, 215, 280

Harte, Bret, 156
Hasse, John Edward, 316
Haviland, Fred, 170
Hay, John, 56, 94, 145-147, 205
Hay-Bunau-Varilla Treaty, 146
Hayden Scott, 177, 179, 242
Hayden, Belle Jones (Joplin), 177, 180, 184
Hay-Herran Treaty, 145-147
Healy, John E., 167
Hearst, William Randolph, 92, 159
Heinie Waltzed 'Round on His Hickory Limb, 170
Held, Anna, 321
Heliotrope Bouquet, 133, 185, 306, 328, 361
Hello, Ma Baby, 364
Hemans, Felicia Dorothea, 155
Hemingway, Ernest, 91
Hendrix, Harrison, 7, 8
Henry, "Plunk", 68, 363
Henry, Marcella A., 316
Henson, Matthew, 353-359
Hepburn Act, 289, 332-333, 337
Hepburn, Dr. Thomas, 373-374
Hepburn, Katharine Houghton, 373-374
Hepburn, William P., 332
Herbert, Victor, 1, 102, 183, 321
Herrick, Myron T., 158
Hewitt, Abraham, 54
Hicks, Charles B., 39
Hill, J. Leubrie, 264, 266, 271
Hill, James J., 140, 250, 337
Hill, Louis C., 298, 299, 301
Hill, Strap, 100
Hines, Ike, 322
Hirschfeld, Al, 50
Hitchcock, Ethan Allen, 298
Hobart, Garret, 138
Hogan, Ernest, 48, 98, 99-100, 103, 261, 262, 263, 264, 268, 271, 289, 320, 323, 374
Holzmann, Abe, 102, 149
Honey Boy, 174
Honey On My Lip, God Damn, 363
Honeymoon Rag, 313
Hoosier Rag, 315

Horseshoe Rag, 315
Hot House Rag, 315
Houdini, Harry (b. Erich Weiss), 343
Howley, Pat, 170
Huckleberry Finn, 250, 357
Hudson, Lora M., 316
Hulse, Nora, 316
Humpty Dumpty, 269
Hungarian Rag, 309
Hunky Dory, 98
Hunter, Charles, 180, 361
Hunting Trips of a Ranchman, 334
Hyer Sisters, 99, 105
I Ain't Had No Lovin' in a Long Time, 270
I Want a Regular Man, 346
I Want Someone to Go Wild With Me, 172
I Want to See My Child, 320
I Wants To Be a Actor Lady, 260, 264
I'm a Jonah Man, 264, 268
I'm Cert'n'y Gonna See About That, 368
If You Talk in Your Sleep, Don't mention My Name, 88, 171
In Dahomey: A Negro Musical Comedy, 260, 263-265, 266, 268, 271, 272, 320
In Newport, 269
In the Good Old Summertime, 52, 346
Influence of Sea Power Upon History (1660-1783), The, 92, 143
Ingraham, Herbert, 170
Interstate Commerce Commission, 31, 330, 337, 339
Iola, 304
Irving, Washington, 155
Irwin, Flora, 62, 169
Irwin, May, 49, 62, 99, 169, 266, 301, 364
Isthmian Canal Commission (ICC), 31, 144, 248, 249, 254
It's All Been Done Before, But Not the Way I Do It, 172
It's Allus De Same In Dixie, 268
Ives, Charles, 1, 161, 320
J. H. Aufderheide & Company, Music Publishers, 314
Jack and Jill, 316
Jack, Sam T., 68, 260
Jackson, Tony, 361, 367, 369
Janis, Harriet, 1, 129, 130, 182, 244, 305, 379
Jasen, David, 260, 264, 305, 306, 307, 361, 365, 370, 379
Jerome H. Remick & Company, 303

Jes' Lak White Folks, 263
Joachim, Joseph, 262
Johns, Al, 264, 325
Johns, Emma, 241
Johnson, Billy, 261, 264, 266
Johnson, Bunk, 367
Johnson, Charles L., 180-181, 303, 305
Johnson, Emma, 367
Johnson, J. Rosamond, 266-269, 272, 322, 326
Johnson, James Weldon, 99, 176, 260, 266-269, 323
Jones, Gene, 260, 264, 361, 365, 379
Jones, M. Sissieretta ("Black Patti"), 215, 261
Joplin, Florence Givens, 17
Joplin, Freddie Alexander, 184, 185, 322
Joplin, Giles, 17
Joplin, Monroe, 17
Joplin, Robert, 18, 120, 177
Joplin, Scott, 1, 2, 17-18, 68, 120-133, 176-180, 182, 183-186, 242, 267, 304-308, 319-328, 359, 361, 362, 368, 371-375
Joplin, William ("Will"), 120, 177
Jordan, Joe, 180, 186, 324, 327
Joseph, "One-Leg Willy", 17, 363
Jungle, The, 333
Jusserand, Jules, 212
Just A Dream, 363
Kalman, Emmerich, 321
Kamman, Effie, 316
Kansas City Rag, 243
Kansas City Stomp, 371
Karns, Verdi, 316
Kaufman, Thomas M., 314-315
Keaton, Buster, 344
Keith, B(enjamin) F(ranklin), 62-63, 87-89, 166, 168, 171, 173
Kellerman, Annette, 88
Kelly, Daniel, 363
Kelly, E. Harry, 180-181
Kennedy, Joseph P., 88
Ketchup Rag, 316-317
Key Stone Rag, 361, 376
Kibbey, Judge Joseph, 296-298, 300
Kickapoo *Sagwa*, 167
King of Coughs, 167

King Porter Stomp, 371
King. Karl L., 1
Kipling, Rudyard, 56, 156, 357
Kismet Rag, 133, 306, 372
Kitchen Tom, 365
Kitten on the Keys, 309
Klassicle Rag, 315
Klaw, Marc, 166, 267, 268, 271, 351
Ladies Home Journal, 164, 374
Lady Lou, 363
LaFollette, Robert, 162
Lait, Jack, 351
Lakeside Park, 241, 244
Lamb, Amelia, 308
Lamb, Joseph F., 304, 305, 306, 307-309
LaMothe, Edward, 368
Lampe, J. Bodewalt ("Ribe Danmark"), 102
Lane, Franklin, 300
Lange, John, 8
Langley, Samuel, 188, 189, 191
Lassus Trombone, 309
Late Hours, 269
Lauder, Harry, 89, 164
Laurel, Stan, 344
Laurie, Joe, 350
Leader of the Colored Aristocracy, 264
Lee, Alice Hathaway (Roosevelt), 21, 22, 54, 207, 212
Lefebre, E. A., 150
Lemonier, Tom, 325
Leola, 185, 306
Let It Alone, 268
Levee Rag, 361
Lift Every Voice and Sing, 266
Lincke, Paul, 325
Lincoln, Robert Todd, 74
Lindsay, Vachel, 74, 147, 161
Lit'l Gal, 270, 326
Little Black Baby, 184
Little Egypt, 67-68
Live Wires Rag, 316
Living a Ragtime Life, 162-163, 312
Locke, Alain, 40

Lodge, Henry, 304
Lodge, Henry Cabot, 22, 55, 74, 92, 93, 338
Loeb, William, 204, 205, 206
Loew, Marcus, 88
Lomax, Alan, 366, 368, 379
Long Tail Blue, 38
Long, John D., 92-93
Longfellow, Henry Wadsworth, 155, 156
Longworth, Alice Roosevelt, 22, 55, 207, 212-215, 228
Longworth, Rep. Nicholas, 207, 214
Looker, Earle, 208
Lorraine Waltzes, 325-326
Louis, Joe, 359
Louisiana Lize, 266
Louisiana Purchase Exposition, 65, 182-183, 243
Louisiana Rag, 123
Lovie Joe, 180
Lucas, Sam, 41
Lulu White, 361
Luna Park, 238, 240-241
Lyrics of the Lowly Life, 262
MacArthur, Douglas, 214
Mack, Cecil, 264
MacMillen, Donald, 355
Made in Germany, 303
Magnetic Rag, 306, 372
Mahan, Alfred Thayer, 92, 143
Mahogany Hall, 363, 367
Maiden With the Dreamy Eyes, The, 267
Mama Lou, 363, 376
Man With the Hoe, The, 159-160
Mandy's Broadway Stroll, 361
Manetta, Manuel, 367
Manly, Alex, 108, 110, 112
Mannes, David, 326
Mansfield, Richard, 166
Maple Leaf Club, 122
Maple Leaf Rag, 129-130, 132-133, 176, 178-179, 184, 216, 243, 305-307, 309, 320, 322, 327-328, 365
Marks, Edward, 51, 170, 267, 306, 322, 327-328
Marshall, Arthur, 130, 132, 179, 183, 186, 242
Marshfield Tornado, 9
Mashed Potatoes, 181, 350

Masterson, Bat, 206
Matthews, Artie, 186, 305
Maurice Shapiro, 49
Maxim's, 321
Maxwell, George, 296-298, 300
McCabe, Edward Preston, 195-200
McClure's Magazine, 190
McCullough, David, 147, 254, 256
McDowell, Edward, 1
McGuffey, William Holmes, 155
McGuffey's Eclectic Readers, 155
McIntyre and Heath, 342
McKim, Charles F., 211
McKinley, Ida, 74
McKinley, William, 66, 72-75, 91-94, 103, 112, 138-139, 143, 149, 204, 215, 280, 330
McManus, George, 50
McPherran, Florence, 316
Meat Inspection Act, 333
Medic Rag, 181
Meet Me in St. Louis, 183
Mehara's Minstrels, 41
Memphis Blues, 309
Memphis Students, 268, 272, 323, 325
Mencken, H(enry) L(ouis), 25, 83, 151
Merry Countess, The, 321
Merry Widow, The, 271, 272, 321
Merry-Go-Round, The, 346
Meteor, The, 242, 243
Metz, Theodore, 361, 363
Michigan Water Blues, 368
Midway, 31, 44, 49, 67-69, 120, 125-126, 237-238, 241
Mills, Frederick Allen ("Kerry"), 49, 102, 123, 149, 183
Miner's Bowery Theatre, 342
Mississippi Rag, 98, 123, 311, 377, 379-380, 383, 389
Mitchell, John, 142
Mona, 320, 329
Moonlight Bay, 241
Moore, Pony, 368
Morath, Max, 316
Morgan, John Pierpont, 139, 140, 142
Morris, William, 351
Morrison, George, 363

Morrison, Will B., 313
Morton, Jelly Roll (Ferdinand Joseph LaMothe), 43, 304, 361, 367-371
Morton, Louise Monette LaMothe, 368
Mother Goose, 267
Moving Day in Jungle Town, 216-217, 351
Mr, Johnson, Turn Me Loose, 98, 100,163, 169, 303
Mr. Lode of Koal, 272, 324
Muckrakers, 80, 162, 332
Mulhall, "Colonel" Zack, 345
Music Publishers Protective Association (MPPA), 170
My Castle on the Nile, 266
My Coal Black Lady, 98
My Dahomian Queen, 264
My Gal Is a High Born Lady, 98, 215
Naked Dance, The, 361, 368
Nancy Brown, 267
Nansen, F., 353, 354
National Association for the Advancement of Colored People (NAACP), 3, 99, 288
National Conservation Commission, 337
National Conservation Congress, 337
National Prohibition Party, 157
Naughty Marietta, 321
Naval War of 1812, The, 21, 92
Nelson, "Slew Foot", 17, 363
Nesbit, Evelyn, 168
New South, 27, 384
New World Symphony, 262
Newell, Frederick, 296-298, 300
Niagara Movement, 287
Niagara Rag, 317
Niebergall, Julia Lee, 315-317
Night on the Levee, 123
Nobody, 268-269, 273, 277, 327, 347, 383
Non-Pareil, The, 133, 185, 351
Noodles, 303
Northern Securities Company, 140-141, 159, 330
Norworth, Jack, 173-174, 351
Nothin' Doin', 317
Novelty Rag, 315
O'Rourke, John M., 299
Offenbach, Jacques, 150, 166
Oh, Didn't He Ramble?, 267

Oh, Johnny, Oh, Johnny, Oh!, 313
Oh, You Beautiful Doll, 171
Old Home Rag, 307
Oliver, "Nevada Ned", 167
Olman, Abe, 313
Olmstead, Frederick Law, 237
On Broadway in Dahomey Bye and Bye, 264
On Emancipation Day, 274
On the Gay Luneta, 270
On the Pike, 183, 243
On the Road to Monterey, 270
On the Rural Route, 315
Original Georgia Minstrels, The, 40
Original Rags, 130
Orinoco: Jungle Rag, 314
Orme, John, 301
Oyster Man, The, 272
Palm Leaf Rag, 184
Panama—Characteristic Dance, 326
Pan-American Exposition (Buffalo), 139, 204
Paragon Rag, 306, 322
Park Protection Act of 1894, 335
Parker, Professor Horatio, 320
Pass the Pickles, 317
Pasteur, Louis, 373
Pastor, Tony, 12, 61-63, 166, 171, 303, 350
Pathway to Love, 270
Patricia Rag, 308
Patterson, Sam, 182, 183, 185, 307, 321
Payne, Elizabeth, 326
Peaceful Henry, 181, 309, 312
Peacherine Rag, 133, 179, 306
Peaches and Cream, 241, 303
Pearls, The, 371
Peary, Josephine Diebitsch, 354
Peary, Robert Edwin, 353-358
Peche, Mimi, 369
Penrose, Major Charles W., 282-286
Peroxide Rag, 181
Perry & Son, A. W., 130, 313
Persian Lamb, 241
Petticoat Lane, 181, 361, 376

Piano Notions Suite, 316
Piazza, "Countess" Willie, 367
Pickett, Jesse, 17, 68, 363
Pickles and Peppers, 309, 316-317
Piffle Rag, 315, 317
Pike, The, 182, 183
Pinchot, Gifford, 296, 335-337
Pine Apple Rag, 306-307, 322, 328
Plantation Echoes: Rag Two-Step, 123
Platt, Thomas, 137-138
Pleasure Bound, 316
Poison Rag, 181
Poker Rag, 317
Poli, Sylvester, 348, 351
Police Gazette, 303
Pollock, Muriel, 316-317
Populists, 71, 73-74, 106
Porcupine Rag, 304
Possum and Taters: A Ragtime Feast, 180
Powder Rag, 304, 309
Powell, Rev. Adam Clayton, Sr., 284
Pratt, Paul Charles, 304, 305, 313-315
Pretty Baby, 361, 367-368
Pride of Bucktown, 123
Pride of the Smoky Row (Q Rag), 361
Princess Rag, 243
Proctor, Fred F., 88
Progressive Era, 1-2, 83, 119, 148, 162, 218, 237, 292, 375, 377, 386, 388-389
Pryor, Arthur, 150, 151
Pulitzer, Joseph, 91, 141
Pullman, George, 31
Pure Food and Drug Act, 333
Put On Your Old Gray Bonnet, 52, 241
Quality Rag, 243
Queen City Cornet (or Concert) Band, 122
Queen of Love, Two-Step (March), 361
Rag Medley, 123
Rag Time Review, 305
Ragged Terry, 317
Raggin' the Scale, 309
Ragtime Betty, The, 243
Ragtime Chimes, 241, 303

Ragtime Cowboy Joe, 1
Ragtime Dance, The, 133, 177, 185, 306
Ragtime Drummer, 264
Ragtime Nightingale, 243, 308
Ragtime Nightmare, 181
Ragtime Oriole, 243
Ragtime Revival, 2, 244, 305, 365
Ragtime Wonder of the South, 242
Rain Song, 269, 326
Raines Law, 57-58, 182, 221
Rainey, Ma, 41
Rastus on Parade, 98
Rattler, The, 317
Reavis, Logan U., 176-177
Reclamation Act of 1902 (Newlands Act), 296, 336
Reclamation Extension Act of 1914, 300
Reconstruction, 25, 66, 80, 107, 195, 242, 321
Red Moon, The, 270, 272, 320, 322, 324
Red Onion Rag, 313
Red Pepper Rag, 304, 309
Red Rambler, 315, 317
Red Wing, 363
Reed, Walter, 248
Reflection Rag, 133, 306
Reinhardt, Heinrich, 321
Remington, Eva, 373
Remington, Frederic, 373
Rice, Thomas Dartmouth ("Daddy"), 38-39
Richmond Rag, 314
Rifkin, Joshua, 1
Right Church but the Wrong Pew, The, 351
Riis, Jacob, 75
Roberts, "Luckey" (Charles Luckeyth), 304, 327
Robeson, Paul, 359
Robinson J. Russel, 305, 306, 313
Robinson, Bill, 359
Robinson, Jackie, 359
Rockefeller, John D., 158, 167
Rockefeller, William Avery, 167
Rodgers, Robert W., 17
Rogers, Alex, 264, 266, 268, 269, 271
Rogers, Betty Blake, 346

Rogers, Clement, 344
Rogers, Will, 344-347
Romberg, Sigmund, 346
Rooney, Pat, 62
Roosevelt, Anna ("Bamie" or "Bye"), 21, 54, 204, 212
Roosevelt, Archie, 207
Roosevelt, Corinne, 21, 54, 95, 204
Roosevelt, Edith Carow Kermit, 54-55, 92, 95, 204-205, 210-212, 216
Roosevelt, Eleanor, 20, 54, 214
Roosevelt, Elliot, 21
Roosevelt, Ethel, 207
Roosevelt, Franklin Delano, 20, 214
Roosevelt, Kermit, 55, 207
Roosevelt, Martha Bulloch, 21, 275
Roosevelt, Quentin, 207-210, 211
Roosevelt, Robert B., 20, 21
Roosevelt, Theodore (TR), 2, 20-23, 54-58, 73-76, 92-96, 115, 137-147, 149, 153, 161, 162, 179,199, 204-217, 247, 252-254, 269, 275-290, 296-301, 330-340, 355, 357-358
Roosevelt, Theodore, Jr., 55, 96, 207
Roosevelt, Theodore, Sr., 20-21, 153
Roosevelt-Arias Treaty, 147
Rooster Rag, 316-317
Root, Elihu, 285, 338
Rose Leaf Rag, 306
Rose, Al, 222, 363, 366-367, 372
Rose, Wally, 1
Rosebud Bar, 180-182
Rose-bud March, 185
Rosen, Ruth, 221
Rosenfeld, Monroe H., 51, 179
Rough Riders, 3, 94-95, 110-111, 137, 206, 214, 298, 345, 363
Roustabout Rag, 123
Rudisill, Bess E., 316
Rufus Rastus, 51, 272
Russell, Lillian, 62, 169, 267
Russell, Sylvester, 264
Russian Rag, 309
Rydell, Robert W., 69
Sacred Tree, The, 320
Sailing Down the Chesapeake Bay, 303
Sally in Our Alley, 267
Salt River Project (SRP), 294-302

Salvarsan, 374
Sam, Alfred Charles, 201
Sambo, 271
Sandburg, Carl, 161
Santelmann, William, 216
Sarah Dear, 185
Sari, 321
Saunders, Otis, 68, 242
Sayers, Henry, 361
Scarecrow Rag, 313, 315
Scott Joplin's Dream, 308
Scott Joplin's New Rag, 306, 327, 372
Scott, James Sylvester, 185, 241-244, 267, 304, 305
Scott, James Sylvester, Sr., 242
Scott, Molly Thomas, 242
Scott, Nora Johnson, 243
Search Light Rag, 306
Seaweeds Rag, 313
Senegambian Carnival, 263
Sensation Rag, 307
Sewall, Willy "Egg Head", 17, 363
Seymour, Johnny, 68
Shafer, Gypsy, 367
Shafter, General William, 94-95
Shame of the Cities, 177
Shaw, George Bernard, 374
Shea, Tom, 361
Shelton, Aggie, 364
Shepherd, Adaline, 316
Sherman Anti-Trust Act, 139, 141, 159, 330
Shifty Shuffles, 123
Shine On, Harvest Moon, 174, 351
Shipp, Jesse, 263, 266, 268, 269
Shirer, William L., 160
Shoo-Fly Regiment, The, 270-272, 320, 322
Shreveport Stomp, 371
Shubert Brothers, 87
Shuffle Along, 271, 321, 365
Silks, Mattie, 363
Silver Threads Among the Gold, 363
Sinclair, Upton, 333
Sissle, Noble, 271, 321, 365

Sleepy Hollow, 242
Sleepy Lou, 316
Slippery Elm, 242
Smiler, The, 303, 309
Smith, Bessie, 41
Smith, Chester W., 298-299
Smith, George R., 120-122, 131
Smith, Lizette, 367
Smith, Martha, 122
Smokey Mokes, 151
Smoky Topaz, The, 317
Smugglers, The, 150
Sneaky Shuffles, 304
Snyder, Ted, 306, 322
Soap Suds, 316
Solace, 1, 46, 308, 328
Some Aeronautical Experiments, 190
Some of These Days, 64, 351-352, 382
Some Sweet Day, 368
Something Doing, 133, 184
Souls of Black Folk, The, 287
Sounds of Africa, 365
Sour Grapes Rag, 313
Sousa, Antonio, 150
Sousa, Elizabeth Trinkaus, 150
Sousa, Jane Bellis, 1150
Sousa, John Philip, 1, 40, 49, 102, 149-151,183
South Before the War, The, 100
Southerners, The, 268
Sponge Rag, 361
Spooner, Senator John C., 144, 286
Spring Maid, The, 321
Spring, Beautiful Spring, 325
Spring-Time Rag, 315
St. Louis Rag, 183
St. Louis Tickle, 180, 183, 362
St. Louis, The Future Great City of the World, 177
St.Cyr, Johnny, 367
St.Louis Blues, 309
Stark Music Company, 132, 243, 303-306
Stark, Carrie, 305
Stark, Eleanor, 131-132, 176, 178, 185, 305

Stark, Etilmon, 131, 132, 305
Stark, John Stillwell, 131-133, 176, 178, 184, 185, 304-307, 313, 315, 322, 372
Stark, Sarah Ann Casey, 131, 305, 307
Stark, William, 131, 132, 185
Stars and Stripes Forever, 149
Steeplechase Park, 238, 240
Steffens, Lincoln, 177, 331
Steinbeck, John, 220
Sterling, Andrew B., 170
Stern, Joseph, 49, 170, 327
Stevens, John F., 247, 249-254
Sting, The, 1
Stokes, Lottie (Joplin), 184, 371-372
Stokes, Nellie M., 316
Stone, Fred, 342
Stoptime Rag, 306
Stormin' the Castle, 361
Story, Sidney, 366
Storyville Sport, The, 361
Storyville, New Orleans, 47, 115-116, 119, 220, 222, 229, 366-371, 389
Strauss, Johann, 151, 166, 321
Strauss, Oscar, 321
Strength of the Nation, 326
Strenuous Life, The, 133, 179, 216
Sugar Cane, 201, 256, 306
Sullivan, John L., 206
Sunburst Rag, 243
Sunflower Slow Drag, 130, 133
Superstition, 319-320, 322
Sure Fire Rag, 304
Sweet and Low, 304
Sweet Thursday, 220
Swilling, Jack, 295
Swing Along, 264, 326
Swipesy, 133
Sycamore, The, 184, 306
Taft, Helen Herron, 215, 338
Taft, William Howard, 2, 56, 205, 314, 215, 249, 254, 281, 285, 290, 301, 338, 339
Take Me Out to Lakeside, 233, 243
Take Me Out to the Ball Game, 174
Tanguay, Eva, 88, 89, 172-173
Ta-Ra-Ra-Boom-Der-e, 361, 363, 376

Taylor, Charlie, 191
Teasing Rag, 315
Teasing the Cat, 304
Teddy Bear, 207, 217
Teddy Bear Rag, 217
Teddy in the Jungle, 216-217
Teddy's Pardners 216-217
Temptation Rag, 304-305, 309
Texas Medley Quartet, 18
Texas Medley Quartette, 120-121
That Sentimental Rag, 317
That Teasing Rag, 315, 325
That Texas Rag, 317
That's How the Cakewalk's Done, 264
Thaw, Harry K., 168
The Bully Song, 98-99, 163, 169, 364
The Gladiator, 150
The Gold Bug, 102
There's Always Something Wrong, 270
There's Company in the Parlor, Girls, Come On Down, 351
They All Played Ragtime, 1-2, 19, 70, 105, 124, 134, 187, 244, 311, 329, 379, 387
They All Sang, 175, 267, 273, 327, 329, 387
Thomas, Theodore, 68
Thompson, Charley, 2, 182, 305
Those Naughty Ladies of the Old Northwest, 220, 229, 389
Thriller, The, 314, 317
Throw Him Down, McCloskey, 169
Tichenor, Trebor, 305, 306, 307, 361, 370, 379
Tickled to Death, 180, 309, 312
Tiger Rag, 309
Tillman, Benjamin R. ("Pitchfork Ben"), 72, 277, 278, 281, 332, 333
Tilyou, George C., 238
Tin Pan Alley, 1, 12, 14, 42, 49-51, 53, 63, 102, 105, 133, 149, 170, 185, 241, 260, 303-306, 311-313
Tom Sawyer, 357
Top Liner Rag, 308
Tournier, Eugene, 369
Townsend, Dr. C. M., 167
Transfer Act, 336
Treemonisha, 318-322, 327-328, 372, 375
Tres Moutarde, 309, 318
Trolley Trips from Providence Out, 235
Trouble Rag, 313

Troublesome Ivories, 365
Tuck, Louis, 348
Tucker, Sophie, 89, 174, 348-351
Turner, Frederick Jackson, 161, 353
Turk, William, 17, 363
Turpin, "Honest John", 120, 181
Turpin, Charles, 120, 181, 182
Turpin, Thomas ("Tom"), 120, 123, 130, 180-182, 183, 185, 186, 242, 361, 363
Twain, Mark, 156, 357
Twelfth Street Rag, 181, 304, 310, 361
Tyers, William, 123, 325, 326, 327
U. S. S. Roosevelt, 355
Uncle Remus, 282
Under the Bamboo Tree, 68, 267
United Booking Office (UBO), 87, 89, 166, 170, 173, 174, 345
United Mine Workers, 141-142
Up From Slavery, 277, 292, 383
Vangilder, Martin, 244
Vanity Rag, 314
Vardaman, James, 277-278, 280-281
Vilja, 321
Villard, Oswald Garrison, 288
Virginian, The, 206, 281
Vodery, Will, 322, 323
Von Tilzer, Harry, 49, 51, 170, 173, 264, 351
Wadsworth, James W., 333
Walhalla, 314
Walker, George, 41, 102-103, 260, 262, 265, 266, 268, 271, 320, 324, 374
Wall Street Rag, The, 306
Wallace, John Findlay, 248-249, 251
Walper House Rag, 308
Walton, Lester, 319, 322, 325
Waltz (Merry Widow), 321
Wanamaker, John, 55-56, 92, 158
Washburn, Charles, 362, 363
Washington Post, 150, 207
Washington, Booker T. (BTW), 112, 180, 216, 272-288, 332
Watch Your Step, 321, 344
Watson, Tom, 277
We Ought to Have a Leader, 320
We Will Rest Awhile, 320
We're Goin' Around, 320

Weaver, General James B., 71
Weber and Fields, 342, 350
Webster, Noah, 154
Weiss, Julius, 17
Wendell, Barrett, 277
Wenrich, Percy, 241, 303, 305
When Villains Ramble Far and Near, 320
When You Wore a Tulip, 241
Whistling Rufus, 98, 151, 215-216
Whitcomb, Ian, 38, 263, 379
White City, 67, 237-238, 240-241
White, Lulu, 367
White House Gang, The, 208-209
White, Stanford, 168
Who Dat Say Chicken In Dis Crowd, 262
Who Let the Cows Out? A Bully Rag, 217
Who Stole the Lock Off The Hen House Door, 363
Wilbur, "Big Head", 17, 363
Wilcockson, J. M., 361
Wild Cherries, 310
Wildflower, 315
Wiley, Dr. Harvey W., 332
Wiley, Stella, 261
Wilkins, Barron, 322
Williams, Bert, 41, 102-103, 105, 260, 262, 265, 266, 271, 320, 322, 324, 344, 346, 359
Williams, Clarence, 324, 367
Williams, Gus, 342
Williams, Mamie, 316
Williams, Percy, 173
Williamson, Carlotta, 316
Wilson, "Jack the Bear", 17, 363
Wilson, Woodrow, 2, 73, 162, 339
Wireless Rag, 316
Wister, Owen, 206, 213, 281, 338
Witmark, M. & Sons, 12, 49, 170
Women's Christian Temperance Union (WCTU), 157
Wood, Florence M., 316
Wood, General Leonard, 94-95
Woods, Clarence, 241-242
Woolsey, Calvin Lee, 180-181
Woolston, Howard B., 220, 226
World's Columbian Exposition, 65, 67-68, 150, 182, 237-238, 261, 353

Wright Brothers, 3, 188-192
Wright, Bishop Milton, 189
Wright, Frank Lloyd, 161
Wright, Katharine, 189
Wright, Louis, 41
Wright, Orville, 188-192
Wright, Wilbur, 188-192
Wrong Is Never Right, 320
X-N-Tric: Two-Step Characteristic, 317
Yelvington, Gladys, 315, 316
Yiddisha Rag, The, 351
You've Been a Good Old Wagon, But You Done Broke Down, 98, 100-101, 303
Youlin, Alma, 171
Ziegfeld, Florenz, 174, 267, 315, 342, 344, 346, 347, 351
Zimmerman, Richard "Dick", 129, 263, 379

978-0-595-34042-2
0-595-34042-3

LaVergne, TN USA
30 October 2009

162604LV00003B/106/A